AMERICAN
PHILOSOPHIC
NATURALISM
IN THE
TWENTIETH
CENTURY

EDITED BY JOHN RYDER

Prometheus Books
59 John Glenn Drive
Amherst, New York 14228-2197

Published 1994 by Prometheus Books

98 97 96 95 94   5 4 3 2 1

Library of Congress Cataloging-in-Publication Data

American philosophic naturalism in the twentieth century / John Ryder.
    p.   cm.
    Includes bibliographical references.
    ISBN 0-87975-894-5 (alk. paper)
    1. Philosophy, American—20th century. 2. Naturalism. I. Ryder, John (John Joseph).
B944.N3A44   1994
146'.0973'0904—dc20   94-18813
                                             CIP

Contents

Contents

Introduction

As we come ever closer to the third millennium, it is tempting to survey the course of philosophy in America during the past century. One could identify more than a few distinct trends, noteworthy figures, and highlights. One impression emerging from such a survey is that much of American philosophy in the twentieth century, like its European counterpart, has been one or another form of antiphilosophic therapy. Logical positivism, for example, included an attempt to jettison metaphysics and ethical theory, since on positivist principles no genuine knowledge in these areas is possible. In rejecting metaphysics and ethical theory, positivists were abandoning two areas traditionally at the center of philosophic inquiry. In Europe since the ancient Greeks, and in India and China even earlier, philosophically minded people have asked themselves what the world is like in general and in what the good life consists. To argue, as the positivists have, that no meaningful answers can be given to such questions is to urge that we give up philosophy altogether. At the very least such arguments undermine philosophy's traditional content. The ordinary language school of thought, influential in this country primarily during the 1950s and 1960s, also had misgivings about traditional philosophy. Following the work of Ludwig Wittgenstein and others, ordinary language philosophers tended to believe that a careful look at the way we use language will be likely to clear up philosophical problems, or in many cases simply *dissolve* them. In particular, people close to Wittgenstein have felt that many of the difficulties, problems, paradoxes, and conundrums of philosophy are not genuine concerns, but rather result from our misunderstanding of how language works. The goal of this school of thought is to clarify language so that our misunderstandings will disappear, and we will then be freed from the inclination, or worse the compulsion, to ask philosophic questions.

Even pragmatism, probably the most widely known and influential strain of contemporary American philosophy, has the flavor of this kind of antiphilosophic therapy. A good deal of traditional philosophy, William James and John Dewey both might have argued, suffers from an excess of intellectualism, from a tendency to divorce philosophical inquiry from the lived and practical concerns of people. Furthermore, even the criteria of knowledge have been over intellectualized. The proper criterion of truth, James argued, is what works, what gets us somewhere, what moves us along. This anti-intellectualist, in some respects anti-philosophic, tendency in American pragmatism has been adopted by the contemporary school of thought generally called antifoundational-ism and associated with the work of Richard Rorty. On this view philosophy, ancient and modern, has been mistaken in its attempt to describe the general nature of things and in its search for the structure and foundations of knowledge. These kinds of inquiry, Rorty and his colleagues argue, are impossible to complete successfully, and we are best served by giving them up entirely and turning our attention to other cultural concerns.

These schools of thought, and others one might identify, no doubt have their virtues, and they are all probably right in any number of respects. They do not, however, exhaust the landscape of twentieth-century American philosophy. American naturalism is a distinct school of thought, one that, despite its connections with other movements and ideas, has an identifiable history and its own special concerns. Like the other prominent strains of twentieth-century American thought, naturalism has tried to overcome the inadequacies of early philosophy. Unlike many of the others, however, it has continued to ask traditional philosophical questions and to regard them as capable of resolution. In the naturalist tradition, nature is available to philosophic inquiry, which in turn is capable of providing knowledge. Just what nature, inquiry, and knowledge *are* remain philosophic questions themselves, but naturalists have not, for the most part, shied away from them or, in the words of John Herman Randall, Jr., from the attempt to "approach nature directly."

American naturalism, as it developed in the twentieth century, has several roots. It is in many ways an expression of characteristics that for centuries have played a central role in American culture. For example, despite the fact that religion and a religious worldview have been a part of American culture, it is also true that our society has always had another, far less speculative and abstract side. It is commonly argued that America is and always has been decidedly practical, interested less in the hereafter and more in the material and pragmatic concerns of daily life. In the culture as a whole this trait is often associated with a kind of anti-intellectualism, but even in the more intellectual circles in American cultural history one can find traces of a similar turn away from the supernatural and toward natural and material matters. Consider the influence of philosophic materialism, natural science, humanism, and "free thinking" in the period of the American Enlightenment and the Revolution. Among the most influential figures on the intellectual scene in colonial America many were overtly materialistic—Cadwallader Colden, Thomas Jefferson, and Thomas Cooper—and others were very close—Benjamin Franklin, Ethan Allen, Benjamin Rush, and Joseph Buchanan. All were humanists in the sense that they rejected religious intuitions and biblical or church authority as sources of knowledge, insisting rather that it is through reason and experience that knowledge develops. This humanism was adopted later by the more influential figures in nineteenth-century transcendentalism, and one might argue that twentieth-century naturalism is the heir to much of what is distinct and valuable in Enlightenment and even in transcendentalist thought.

While naturalism in the present century is continuous with American cultural and intellectual history, it also has roots in the history of Western philosophy as early as the classical Greeks, especially Aristotle. The Greeks were interested in what makes something what it is, in what causes events to happen as they do and objects to be as they are. Plato gave one possible answer: the causes of things are ideal Forms, or universals, which in Plato's view exist independently of any events or objects and resided in their own "realm." Aristotle agreed with Plato that there are ideal Forms that serve as causes of particulars, but he disagreed with Plato about their independence. Universals, Aristotle thought, do not exist independently of particulars, or, to put it another way, there is no "realm" of Forms outside or independent of nature. Aristotle further contributed to a naturalist perspective by arguing, unlike Plato, that Forms are not the only causes of things. In order to understand what causes an event or object one must also look to its relations with other natural events and objects, specifically to the material of which it is constituted and to what Aristotle called the efficient cause, the mediate or immediate agent of change. In Aristotle, not only were Forms brought into nature, but natural processes were accorded much more importance.

In the modern period, that is, in the seventeenth and eighteenth centuries, the most influential source for twentieth-century American naturalism was Baruch Spinoza. His importance derives primarily from his rejection of René Descartes's rigid distinction between material and mental substance, and from his alternative view that there is in fact only one substance, which he interchangeably called "nature" or "God." This position expresses two distinctive traits of philosophic naturalism. First, by referring to substance as God or nature, Spinoza rejected the distinction between nature and anything outside of nature, between the natural and the supernatural. Whatever exists is no more or less an aspect of nature than anything else, or in Spinoza's own technical vocabulary, substance has infinite attributes. Second, in treating matter and mind as natural, as attributes of substance, Spinoza asserted the continuity of the mental and the physical, that both are available to the methods we have for inquiry into nature.

Finally, American naturalism, and a good deal of the rest of twentieth-century culture, has its roots in the work of Charles Darwin. Darwin's theory had two general relevant implications. First, it undercut the view, which had prevailed from antiquity into the middle of the nineteenth century, that behind the changes in nature there had to be something fixed and finished, essences which themselves did not change. Second, and no less important, Darwin demonstrated by example that reliable knowledge of changing, developing nature is possible without recourse to eternal forms, without anything fixed and final. Aristotle had brought Plato's Forms down to earth; Darwin eliminated them altogether.

From this brief account of its background in Western philosophy, in American thought and culture, and in Darwin, we can begin to see some of the defining characteristics of American naturalism. While looking at them, however, we need to bear in mind that though naturalistic philosophy has traits distinct from other philosophic traditions, it also has extraordinary variety, as the readings in this volume will show. To understand and appreciate American naturalism it is necessary to take account of both its distinctive traits and its internal disagreements. Among its distinguishing traits is its central philosophic category, or concept, of "nature." Naturalists have held that to one degree or another nature is objective, which means that it has characteristics the content of which is not determined by our opinions of them, by our perspectives on them, or by our knowledge of them, and nature, as we have already said, may be studied and known. We have also already made the point that nature, following Spinoza, consists of whatever there is. Nothing, in other words, is "outside" nature; that is, there is no supernatural realm, there are no supernatural beings, and nothing is "other than" natural, which is to say that nothing is literally unnatural. There may be and indeed are many objects, ideas, events, or processes that in one way or another are unusual, irregular, undesirable, or even perverse, but all of them are fully natural in the sense that they are aspects of some natural processes; they are continuous with other natural objects and events. One of the implications most significant for understanding human life and activity of the view that there is nothing "outside" or "other than" nature is that naturalists do not endorse the traditional dichotomy between nature and human being. Human life, including its purposes, goals, meaning, value, and ideals, is wholly natural. The ramifications of this position are immense, not least because it means that the meaning and value of our lives, and the ethical ideals on which we choose to act, have their source in nature, not in the supernatural. As we will see, it becomes an important project for many naturalists to ask how meaning and ideals might arise from human life instead of descending from the heavens.

Naturalism, then, holds that whatever there might be is entirely an aspect of nature. Beyond this, however, there is extensive disagreement among naturalists as to how nature might be understood, or about what nature is. On this question there have been three great traditions in the history of Western philosophy. The first, and traditionally the most influential, has been the view that nature is secondary to an independent supernatural realm. This is the position first given detailed articulation by Plato, and it is the perspective that permeates mainstream European monotheistic theology. The second tradition is that nature is wholly material, in the sense that whatever might exist is reducible to or explainable in terms of matter and material processes. This view was found among the ancient Greek materialists, reappeared in Thomas Hobbes and during the Enlightenment, and has had its proponents in the twentieth century, primarily in the English-speaking world. The third traditional conception is that nature includes more than simply matter in motion, and whatever such nonmaterial aspects of nature are, they are neither reducible to matter nor explainable in material terms alone. This is the tradition that stems from Spinoza, and in some respects from Aristotle.

The first, Platonic, approach to nature is not naturalist at all, while the second and third are, at least in the sense that it is possible for them to refuse to acknowledge anything beyond nature itself. On these grounds, naturalism could be said to include traditional, reductive materialism. Twentieth-century American naturalism, however, has tended not to take this approach; it has for the most part fallen into the third category. Even here, though, two major strains of thought emerge. One is a form of materialism holding that while nature consists of material and nonmaterial phenomena, matter is the more fundamental in the sense that anything nonmaterial emerges from the material. This view is represented in section 2 of this volume in the article by Roy Wood Sellars and to an extent in the article jointly written by John Dewey, Ernest Nagel, and Sidney Hook. The other strain of thought might be called a metaphysical pluralism holding that there is more to be found in nature than simply matter, but it refuses to acknowledge any ultimate or fundamental primacy to any aspect of nature. This view is the more direct descendent of Aristotle and Spinoza, and it is represented here in section 2 by John Herman Randall, Jr., and by Justus Buchler.

With respect to its conception of nature, then, naturalism distinguishes itself in two crucial respects. The first, as we have already emphasized, is the rejection of anything other than nature. The other is that in both its "reformed" materialist (using Sellars's terminology) and its pluralist forms, American naturalism pursues a conception of nature that avoids reductionism and rejects one of the traditional components of mechanical materialism: strict determinism. American naturalists, whether materialist or pluralist, are likely to regard nature as malleable, because while natural processes are in some respects determined, they are in other respects open; nature can be described by both law and chance.

Despite the centrality of the question of the "nature of nature," American naturalists have not all been, and are not all now, proponents of this sort of metaphysical inquiry. There is disagreement among naturalists concerning the nature of knowledge, the forms inquiry might usefully take, and more generally about the character of human interaction with the rest of nature, and with experience. Part II is concerned with all these questions. To reject Cartesian dualism, as naturalists are likely to do, is to take seriously a continuity between human being and nature with respect to the full range of experience. How to understand experience in light of its natural status, and what implications experience has for our understanding of nature, are fundamental issues for naturalism, issues about which naturalists disagree. The centrality of experience for naturalists suggests a connection to empiricism, the other traditional school of thought for which experience is crucial. Perhaps the best way to describe naturalist approaches to experience is to consider some of the similarities and differences between naturalism and empiricism.

Like empiricism, naturalism takes seriously empirical observation and evidence in the process of inquiry, philosophical and otherwise. It avoids the extreme rationalism of speculative idealist traditions, and it tends to be oriented toward the scientific method as the most valuable avenue for acquiring knowledge. There are, however, important differences. Empiricism has been prone to something John Dewey has pointed to, namely, the temptation to interpret experience solely in terms of the acquisition of knowledge. In attempts to overcome this approach naturalists have developed broader conceptions of experience offering the hope of encompassing a fuller range of human processes. The way knowledge is acquired, in other words, is not the paradigm or model for an understanding of experience; instead it is treated as one of the many forms experience takes—active manipulation, creative expression, emotional experience, etc.

Another aspect of both eighteenth- and twentieth-century empiricism that naturalism has often tried to avoid is its approach to the distinction between fact and value. Empiricism has traditionally taken the view that nature consists of facts, while the valuation of the facts is a human addition. Nature, on this view, is a collection of value-free facts. From the point of view of some naturalists, however, if human beings and human activity are fully aspects of nature, no less than anything else that exists, then the value of natural phenomena for us and the process of valuation itself are both also fully aspects of nature. Nature, in other words, cannot adequately be understood as "value free." Dewey is the figure who most explicitly develops this approach in his treatment of experience and nature, though in doing so he associates himself with contemporaries such as Alfred North Whitehead who, while usually not considered naturalists, develop a similar experiential conception of nature. Some naturalists, however, have been wary of the kind of idea Dewey and Whitehead endorse. Buchler, for example, is equally convinced that an adequate approach to experience and its relation to nature requires a conception of experience broader than empiricism allows, and one which includes valuation. But Buchler is concerned, and on this point an earlier naturalist, Morris R. Cohen, agrees, that philosophers like Dewey and Whitehead might go too far in reading nature as a whole in terms of the categories of experience. In pursuing an alternative to traditional empiricism, then, naturalists disagree about precisely how to understand valuation and experience, and how to relate both to the rest of nature.

There is still another aspect of the naturalist approach to experience and knowledge that distinguishes it from both empiricism and modern rationalism. When Descartes said, "I think, I am," he did more than assert the basis of a metaphysical dualism. He also described the point of departure for a good deal of philosophy ever since—the self! The self, mental substance, and its essential attribute, to think, is for Descartes the starting point for a constructive philosophy. For empiricists, too, the foundation of knowledge, and of their own philosophic point of view, is experience understood as the private perceptions of individuals. To give the self, or self-consciousness, center stage has been common in philosophy since the origins of modern rationalism and empiricism. In our century the empiricist focus on private sensations or perceptions has been evident in positivism and related schools of thought. But the emphasis on the self and on self-consciousness has been most notable in the phenomenological, existential, and vitalist traditions that began in Europe but have been influential in Asia and in the Americas. Naturalists, by contrast, tend to disapprove of this focus on self-consciousness. Their concern is not primarily the self, nor is it to describe the world as it appears to consciousness; their concern, rather, is to reach an understanding of nature in general that is beyond simply the human. Having said that, however, it is important to realize that naturalists are not uninterested in human affairs. On the contrary, they are inclined to think that an understanding of nature's general traits, and of human experience as an aspect of nature, is valuable for the resolution of human problems and for insight into the oldest of philosophic issues—the question "What is the good life?" Despite a reluctance to privilege self-consciousness, however, naturalists tend not to be simply dismissive of other philosophies, and there may well be room for some version of subjective reflection under the naturalist umbrella, as Marvin Farber urges in section 3.

If self-consciousness is not a methodological point of departure for naturalism, science tends to be, though here, too, there is extensive disagreement among naturalists. In the 1930s and 1940s naturalism tended to be more attached (than before or since) to the method of science as appropriate for philosophy. An exception to this generalization is a version of naturalism, currently popular among some philosophers, in which it is thought that anything real is describable in the language of the natural sciences. The forms of naturalism more related to the traditions, however, are likely to be less "scientistic." Earlier in the century there had been more of an emphasis on rational metaphysics, for example in F. J. E. Woodbridge's Aristotelianism. There had also been the view that a wide range of activities provides access to and knowledge of nature—literature, poetry, and art no less than science. In the early years of the century this approach was advocated by George Santayana, and in recent years it reappears in no uncertain terms in Buchler's theory of judgment. Despite these alternative positions, however, science continues to recommend itself to naturalists if for no other reason than its success. Dewey insisted on the importance of the method of science, as does Cohen in section 4. And in a well-known essay from the 1960s W. V. O. Quine, objecting to traditional empiricist epistemology, argues that the sciences, specifically psychology, may be best situated to understand knowledge and the process of its acquisition, so that "to naturalize epistemology" is to turn it over to psychology.

Naturalism's inclination to value science as a model for all inquiry, and its related insistence that nature has objective traits, that is, characteristics independent of an experiencer or a knower, both give naturalism a very traditional flavor. The fact that naturalism has such a traditional air about it raises the question of the effect on naturalists of recent criticisms of modernism, or to put it a different way, of the relation between naturalism and what is referred to generally as postmodernism.

I mentioned early on that some philosophy in the twentieth century has been antiphilosophic. It would be more precise to say that it has been opposed to the central project of *modern* philosophy. Modern philosophy inherited from ancient thought the idea that there is a reality wholly independent of mind, an objective and absolute reality. It also inherited the view that it is the function of inquiry to discover that reality, to learn what is truly the case, as opposed to what merely appears to be the case. This aspiration raises the central problem of modern philosophy: How can this be done, or how is knowledge of the objective and absolute reality possible? With respect to the study of material nature, the modern answer has been the methods of the natural sciences. With respect to more philosophic matters, philosophers thought that they needed to uncover the foundations of knowledge, from which arose the two great traditions of the modern period: the foundation of knowledge is in reason or the foundation of knowledge is in simple sense perceptions. In one way or another, either as extensions of one or the other tradition or as attempted syntheses, technical philosophy ever since has developed from these seventeenth- and eighteenth-century approaches.

Contemporary antiphilosophy, or, to use the more common though admittedly vague term "postmodern" philosophy, calls *all* of this into question. To put it simply, modernity supposed a truth independent of the inquirer and unaffected by the process of inquiry, but developments in science and in recent philosophy of science challenge these suppositions. There is evidence that at least in some cases the process of study affects the objects being studied, and in general the view of modern science that it progressively approaches the truth is questionable at least. For example, when he argued that the changes in scientific ideas are not examples of continual progress but of "paradigm" shifts, Thomas S. Kuhn was calling into question a fundamental assumption of modern science, and by implication of modern philosophy. Kuhn's point about scientific theories is a specific example of a position common to post-modernist thought. The project of modern philosophy, which was to find the foundation of knowledge and construct an accurate picture of reality, assumes the possibility of a pure, "God's eye" point of view. But this, it has been argued, is impossible because it would be equivalent to a perspective that is not a perspective. The postmodernist insight is that inquiry is always conducted from some point of view, from some perspective. We invariably bring with us some set of ideas, some concepts, and, to push the point further, we always operate with some interests and for some purposes. This, in one way or another, is the theme that runs through the antimodern or postmodern philosophers, from Nietzsche to Foucault and the poststructuralists, from Wittgenstein and from the pragmatists to Rorty's antifoundationalism. The implication of all this for a conception of inquiry is that objective inquiry, and by implication objective knowledge, is impossible. With respect to a conception of nature, the upshot of the postmodernist position is either that nature is con-tinuously constructed by human activity (a view with which Dewey flirts and for which he has been criticized by Buchler and Cohen), or that there may well be an objectively determined reality, but since all inquiry is perspectival it is impossible to know it, and therefore pointless to concern oneself with it.

The relevant question for us is where naturalism stands in this regard.

Does it have responses to the postmodernist arguments, does it in some way accommodate them, or is it little more than a modernist holdover? To be more specific, we need to ask whether naturalism's commitment to an objectively determinate nature and the possibility of knowledge of it somehow addresses the often powerful criticism from post- or anti-modernist philosophers. As in many other cases, these are issues about which naturalists in the past have disagreed, and about which they may continue to disagree today. We should begin with the point, though it may seem a bit ironic, that in naturalist writings from the early years of the century to the present one will find many of the same criticisms of the modernist project. Santayana, for example, insists on the biological contextuality, or perspective, of human activity, including inquiry. He calls this perspective and its impact on the individual "animal faith," a concept that plays an important role for a conception of knowledge in which he explicitly rejects the metaphor of mind as a mirror faithfully reflecting a wholly independent reality. Along similar lines, Dewey's insistence on the constructive, creative role of human activity, and consequently his entire "reconstruction in philosophy," imbues one strain of naturalist thought with a decidedly postmodernist flavor. To give one last example, much of postmodernism has a functionalist flavor, by which I mean it urges that natural objects and processes be understood in terms of their functions and purposes rather than as fixed and finished realities. One finds a similar theme in Nagel's approach to logic, to be found in section 4, and in Randall's pluralistic metaphysics.

It is safe to say, then, that naturalism has not ignored or been devoid of compelling criticisms of the modernist project. At the same time, however, it has not necessarily abandoned the modernist ideas that there is a reality to be discovered and that inquiry, including philosophic inquiry, is capable of knowledge. Santayana's perspectivalism and his rejection of the mirror metaphor does not preclude his defense of a kind of materialism, and Randall's functionalism does not prevent his desire to "approach nature directly." Naturalism, in other words, has developed as a synthesis, retaining much of the project of modern philosophy while embodying many of the insights of postmodernism. The degree to which naturalism has succeeded is open to debate, of course, and in any case this attempted synthesis is an ongoing project in naturalist philosophy. Each of the essays in section 9 may be read with all this in mind, because in some respects each is an attempt to interweave the two grand trends of modernist and postmodernist thought. In the end, of course, the reader must judge whether the attempt is successful, or for that matter whether the synthesis is even possible.

However that may turn out, this unique character of naturalism— its continued pursuit of knowledge while acknowledging human con- textuality—has its influence when naturalists turn their attention from the consideration of reality and knowledge to the study of matters of somewhat greater concern to a wider range of people. Specifically, naturalists have written extensively on ethical theory, social philosophy, aesthetics, and religion. One of the reasons naturalists have been con- cerned with these areas has to do with their own theory of experience. Once experience is no longer understood as the accumulation of sense data, once it is understood as encompassing the broad range of what people do and undergo, it becomes necessary to address the most pervasive and influential aspects of experience. Naturalism, in other words, is not eliminative. Other traditions (one thinks first of logical positivism) have tended to argue away central constituents of human life such as ethics or religion. Naturalism, by contrast, looks to include them and to understand them no less than one would look to understand any other aspect of nature.

Each area presents its own difficulties, however, which stem in part from the fact that decidedly nonnaturalist traditions have been dominant in all of them. This may be most clear in the study of ethics. Often more influential approaches in the history of ethics have been non- naturalist in that they tend to seek ethical principles that are held to be valid or true regardless of time or place. Ethical theories, in other words, have usually asserted timeless truth or an eternal good. Even consequentialist theories can have this trait, since the principles that define them, for example act or rule utilitarianism, are themselves taken to be timeless. There is, nevertheless, a naturalist tradition in ethical theory, as Abraham Edel points out in his article found in section 5. One of the distinctly naturalist traits of Edel's own ethical theory is that he very consciously takes account of the relations between ethics and other disciplines and of the corresponding relations between morality and other aspects of human lives. A characteristic trait of many strains of naturalist thought is that they avoid treating their subject matter, whatever it might be, as if it were an atom, or as if it could be isolated from other factors and studied and understood purely on its own terms. It is not surprising, then, that we find Edel's ethical theory to be sensitive to the complexity of human life, to the relations between moral and other human issues. And it should not be surprising to find a similar relational approach in Evelyn Shirk's attempt to reconcile the individual and the general good.

As the theme of Shirk's essay suggests, ethical theory and social philosophy are closely related. Social thought, after all, asks a normative question: how *ought* society to be organized, or what *should* be the principles of social structure, or most simply, what is the good society? The question of the relation between the individual and the general good is in Shirk's treatment an ethical problem, but it is also one way of casting the basic issue of naturalist social philosophy. As in other areas, naturalists have differed widely in their social theory, and they continue to disagree today. There have been two prominent strains in naturalist social thought. The first is a libertarianism, which derives from the individualistic and materialist naturalism so influential in the American Enlightenment. The second influential trend has been a kind of democratic socialism, which is closer to a Marxist materialism and which regards communal and relational social structures to be necessary in order to protect the individual and to foster many of the social values of the American revolutionary tradition. In section 6 the more individualist position is expressed by Paul Kurtz, while Corliss Lamont develops the socialist line of thought. It is important to notice that despite their differences, the two traditions have in common a philosophic humanism, which is to say that both take the view that social cohesion and progress do not require a supernatural element, and that human reason and intelligence, not authority and tradition, are capable of discerning and resolving social problems. Humanism in this sense has deep roots in philosophic naturalism, and it here receives an instrumentalist expression in the essay in section 6 by Sidney Hook.

A word is in order at this point about the relation between naturalism and Marxism, one that has been ambiguous at best. On the face of it there are many points of agreement between the two. Both deny the supernatural, and both take science very seriously as a model of inquiry. Furthermore, materialism plays an important role in both traditions, and Marxism no less than naturalism is humanist in the sense just described. These points of contact have in fact led many naturalists either wholly into the Marxist camp or very close to it. Earlier in his career Sidney Hook was one of the most articulate supporters of Marxism among American academics, developing an original approach to Marx under the influence of Dewey's pragmatic naturalism. In his ontology, epistemology, and social thought Roy Wood Sellars was very close to dialectical and historical materialism, as was Marvin Farber, and Abraham Edel takes Marxian materialism seriously in his ethical theory. Meyer Schapiro, as we will see, remains a leading figure in Marxist art history, and among a younger generation of naturalist thinkers there are those such as Peter Manicas who are clearly influenced by Marxist theory. One needs to realize, however, that there has also been a good deal of hostility to Marxism within the naturalist camp. Dewey was always suspicious of Marxism, regarding it as relying too heavily on Hegelianism in theory and in practice too ready to sacrifice the method of intelligence for violence in the resolution of social problems. Hook became a staunch enemy of Marxism as it developed in the Soviet Union, Eastern Europe, China, and elsewhere, and, as we have seen, Paul Kurtz would regard the collectivism inherent in socialism as inimical to individual freedom. To the extent that Marxism and naturalism continue to develop as philosophic traditions, we can expect the strains that push them together and pull them apart to continue also. They are not likely to marry, nor are they likely to separate, though their continued interaction could well be a source of mutual enrichment.

Like ethical and social theory, aesthetics and religion have been central concerns for American naturalists, though they remain immensely difficult areas, and they are at times regarded as the traits of human experience most resistant to a naturalist rendering. With respect to aesthetics, for instance, traditional conceptions of art and aesthetic experience seem to be called into question by naturalist perspectives. Until relatively recently it was common to regard art's function as primarily ideological, which is to say that its role was to express a culture's commitments and values. A naturalist aesthetics, however, cannot take this view, at least not in this simple a fashion, if for no other reason than that as a result of its general aversion to reductionism and eliminative materialism it will not regard individual experience as reducible to cultural and social influences. It will not, however, go to the other extreme either. In place of treating art as having an ideological role it has become more common to regard it largely as a matter of self-expression. But for naturalism art cannot simply be about self-expression either, because though individual experience is not reducible to society or culture, neither can it be divorced from social and material relations. Here the naturalist's inclination to avoid dualism and subjectivism is the relevant philosophic influence. The richness and complexity of aesthetic experience cannot be exhausted either by art's ideological functions or the degree to which it embodies the artist's intentions. For the same reasons, a naturalist is unlikely to endorse a strict formalism in aesthetic theory. Formalism, the view that art is primarily a matter of the manipulation of the formal elements of the artistic product, also unjustifiably privileges one aspect of esthetic experience over the rest.

These remarks not only indicate what a naturalist aesthetics is not, but they also suggest the sorts of issues that a positive conception of aesthetic experience must address. How precisely is art related to other aspects of experience? What is the connection of the process of artistic creation, or of the product of that process, to the many social factors that influence the artist, her work, and its results? And what role or roles do art and aesthetic experience play in human life? Are they primarily expressions of internal, subjective conditions, or are they judgments of a kind, ways we may interact with the rest of nature? The readings in section 7 provide a sense of the ways these and other related questions might be addressed.

If naturalism appears to call into question traditional conceptions of art, it seems to rule out of court anything that might reasonably be called religion. Traditional religion is almost invariably associated in some way or another with the idea that beyond the world of our experience, beyond nature, there is something else (God, as a rule), and that this "supernatural" reality is responsible for nature and for us. God is the creator and sustainer of nature, and God is the redeemer of human beings. Naturalistic metaphysics, of course, denies such a supernatural reality by definition, and so is in that respect at odds with religion. On the other hand, by regarding all of human experience as fully natural, and worthy of study and understanding, naturalism cannot simply dismiss the religious impulse, as some other philosophic schools of thought have done. Naturalism must take seriously the inclination toward religious experience, and it must address the same issues with which traditional religion has dealt. It appears that no matter what else may change, the human condition is such that we continue to consider many questions: What is the human "place" in the world? What is the human relation to the rest of nature? How is the meaning and significance of life provided? What sense, if any, can be made of the inevitability of death?

Naturalist treatment of questions like these has varied. Many have wished to "reclaim" religious experience from its supernatural associations and have tried to identify a naturalist religious sentiment. In section 8 the essays by Santayana and Dewey represent this approach. Others, and John McDermott is an example, are less comfortable with appropriating religion and religious language, but they agree nonetheless that many of the issues associated with religion continue to require thought. Naturalists, perhaps not surprisingly, take the view that no philosophy worthy of the name is entitled to divorce itself from an understanding of any aspect of nature, least of all from natural processes and predicaments so central to a meaningful and valuable human life.

Part I

Conceptions of Nature

Section 1

Nature Discerned

Our glimpse into American philosophic naturalism begins with selections from two of the most influential members of what we might call the first generation of twentieth-century American naturalists, a generation which includes John Dewey, George Santayana, Frederick J. E. Woodbridge, Roy Wood Sellars, and Morris Raphael Cohen. It may be interesting to note that of all these figures, John Dewey is the only one who was born in the Uni d States. Woodbridge and Sellars were born in Canada, Santayana in Spain, and Cohen in Minsk, the capital of what is now Belarus. Their place in the history of American philosophy is secured, then, not by their being native Americans, but by the richness of their thought and by the immense impact their work has had on the development of philosophy in the United States.

George Santayana, the author of the first two selections in this section, was born in 1863 in Madrid, Spain. He moved with his family to Boston in 1872, entered Harvard years later, and in 1889 received a Ph.D. in philosophy and an appointment at Harvard as instructor of philosophy. He taught at Harvard until 1912, when he retired to devote more time to writing. In 1941 he moved to Rome, where he died in 1952. One of Santayana's earliest philosophic works was the five-volume *Life of Reason,* and the two readings here are from volume 1, *Reason in Common Sense,* first published in 1905. In them one already finds some of the distinctive traits of American naturalism: whatever there is is fully natural; nature is indeed the human home; mind or consciousness is a product of natural processes; and reason is a natural, not transcendental, activity. One also finds in these selections the roots of ideas Santayana would develop later in the four volumes of his *Realms of Being,* that one finds in nature distinct kinds or "realms" of being which he would call matter, essence, spirit, and truth. Even in these early pieces, though, Santayana asserts the naturalist view that nature, whatever it may consist of, is unified in the sense that nothing is discontinuous from the rest of nature. Though for specific purposes Santayana will distinguish nature, spirit, and sense, for example, he will also argue that they are continuous: sense is not a veil between nature and mind, spirit is not a realm cut off from nature, and nature is more than a spiritless machine.

A similar vision is to be found in the selection from F. J. E. Woodbridge, which is taken from his book *An Essay on Nature,* first published in 1940. Woodbridge was born in Windsor, Ontario, in 1867, though within a year his family moved to Kalamazoo, Michigan. He began his career teaching at the University of Minnesota, and in 1902 he was appointed professor of philosophy at Columbia University in New York. It was at Columbia that his influence was most strongly felt. Woodbridge was a cofounder of what became the *Journal of Philosophy.* From 1912 to 1929 he was the dean of graduate faculties at Columbia, and through his teaching he had an impact on the next generation of philosophic naturalists, some of whom are included in this volume. Woodbridge died in 1940. In the chapter from *An Essay on Nature* excerpted here Woodbridge, like Santayana, identifies "nature" as a name for whatever there is. In what may be the most relevant pages, though, he explicitly rejects the existence of anything which might be considered a criterion (and by implication a foundation) of knowledge, while continuing to argue that knowledge of nature is possible.

1

The Discovery of Natural Objects*

George Santayana

At first sight it might seem an idle observation that the first task of intelligence is to represent the environing reality, a reality actually represented in the notion, universally prevalent among men, of a cosmos in space and time, an animated material engine called nature. In trying to conceive nature the mind lisps its first lesson; natural phenomena are the mother tongue of imagination no less than of science and practical life. Men and gods are not conceivable otherwise than as inhabitants of nature. Early experience knows no mystery which is not somehow rooted in transformations of the natural world, and fancy can build no hope which would not be expressible there. But we are grown so accustomed to this ancient apparition that we may be no longer aware how difficult was the task of conjuring it up. We may even have forgotten the possibility that such a vision should never have arisen at all. A brief excursion into that much abused subject, the psychology of perception, may here serve to remind us of the great work which the budding intellect must long ago have accomplished unawares.

Consider how the shocks out of which the notion of material things

*Originally published in George Santayana, *Reason in Common Sense,* vol. 1 of *The Life of Reason* (New York: Charles Scribner's Sons, 1905; Dover, 1980), chapter 3.

is to be built first strike home into the soul. Eye and hand, if we may neglect the other senses, transmit their successive impressions, all varying with the position of outer objects and with the other material conditions. A chaos of multitudinous impressions rains in from all sides at all hours. Nor have the external or cognitive senses an original primacy. The taste, the smell, the alarming sounds of things are continually distracting attention. There are infinite reverberations in memory of all former impressions, together with fresh fancies created in the brain, things at first in no wise subordinated to external objects. All these incongruous elements are mingled like a witches' brew. And more: there are indications that inner sensations, such as those of digestion, have an overpowering influence on the primitive mind, which has not learned to articulate or distinguish permanent needs. So that to the whirl of outer sensations we must add, to reach some notion of what consciousness may contain before the advent of reason, interruptions and lethargies caused by wholly blind internal feelings; trances such as fall even on comparatively articulate minds in rage, lust, or madness. Against all these bewildering forces the new-born reason has to struggle; and we need not wonder that the costly experiments and disillusions of the past have not yet produced a complete enlightenment.

The onslaught made in the last century by the transcendental philosophy upon empirical traditions is familiar to everybody: it seemed a pertinent attack, yet in the end proved quite trifling and unavailing. Thought, we are told rightly enough, cannot be accounted for by enumerating its conditions. A number of detached sensations, being each its own little world, cannot add themselves together nor conjoin themselves in the void. Again, experiences having an alleged common cause would not have, merely for that reason, a common object. Nor would a series of successive perceptions, no matter how quick, logically involve a sense of time nor a notion of succession. Yet, in point of fact, when such a succession occurs and a living brain is there to acquire some structural modification by virtue of its own passing states, a memory of that succession and its terms may often supervene. It is quite true also that the simultaneous presence or association of images belonging to different senses does not carry with it by intrinsic necessity any fusion of such images nor any notion of an object having them for its qualities.

Yet, in point of fact, such a group of sensations does often merge into a complex image; instead of the elements originally perceptible in isolation, there arises a familiar term, a sort of personal presence. To this felt presence, certain instinctive reactions are attached, and the sensations that may be involved in that apparition, when each for any reason becomes emphatic, are referred to it as its qualities or its effects.

Such complications of course involve the gift of memory, with capacity to survey at once vestiges of many perceptions, to feel their implication and absorption in the present object, and to be carried, by this sense of relation, to the thought that those perceptions have a representative function. And this is a great step. It manifests the mind's powers. It illustrates those transformations of consciousness the principle of which, when abstracted, we call intelligence. We must accordingly proceed with caution, for we are digging at the very roots of reason.

The chief perplexity, however, which besets this subject and makes discussions of it so often end in a cloud, is quite artificial. Thought is not a mechanical calculus, where the elements and the method exhaust the fact. Thought is a form of life, and should be conceived on the analogy of nutrition, generation, and art. Reason, as Hume said with profound truth, is an unintelligible instinct. It could not be otherwise if reason is to remain something transitive and existential; for transition is unintelligible, and yet is the deepest characteristic of existence. Philosophers, however, having perceived that the function of thought is to fix static terms and reveal eternal relations, have inadvertently transferred to the living act what is true only of its ideal object; and they have expected to find in the process, treated psychologically, that luminous deductive clearness which belongs to the ideal world it tends to reveal. The intelligible, however, lies at the periphery of experience, the surd at its core; and intelligence is but one centrifugal ray darting from the slime to the stars. Thought must execute a metamorphosis; and while this is of course mysterious, it is one of those familiar mysteries, like motion and will, which are more natural than dialectical lucidity itself; for dialectic grows cogent by fulfilling intent, but intent or meaning is itself vital and inexplicable.

The process of counting is perhaps as simple an instance as can be found of a mental operation on sensible data. The clock, let us say, strikes two: if the sensorium were perfectly elastic and after receiving the first blow reverted exactly to its previous state, retaining absolutely no trace of that momentary oscillation and no altered habit, then it is certain that a sense for number or a faculty of counting could never arise. The second stroke would be responded to with the same reaction which had met the first. There would be no summation of effects, no complication. However numerous the successive impressions might come to be, each would remain fresh and pure, the last being identical in character with the first. One, one, one, would be the monotonous response forever. Just so generations of ephemeral insects that succeeded one another without transmitting experiences might repeat the same round of impressions—an everlasting progression without a shadow of progress. Such, too, is the idiot's life: his liquid brain transmits every impulse without resistance and retains the record of no impression.

Intelligence is accordingly conditioned by a modification of both structure and consciousness by dint of past events. To be aware that a second stroke is not itself the first, I must retain something of the old sensation. The first must reverberate still in my ears when the second arrives, so that this second, coming into a consciousness still filled by the first, is a different experience from the first, which fell into a mind perfectly empty and unprepared. Now the newcomer finds in the subsisting One a sponsor to christen it by the name of Two. The first stroke was a simple 1. The second is not simply another 1, a mere iteration of the first. It is 1^1, where the coefficient represents the reverberating first stroke, still persisting in the mind, and forming a background and perspective against which the new stroke may be distinguished. The meaning of "two," then, is "this after that" or "this again," where we have a simultaneous sense of two things which have been separately perceived but are identified as similar in their nature. Repetition must cease to be pure repetition and become cumulative before it can give rise to the consciousness of repetition.

The first condition of counting, then, is that the sensorium should retain something of the first impression while it receives the second, or (to state the corresponding mental fact) that the second sensation should be felt together with a survival of the first from which it is distinguished in point of existence and with which it is identified in point of character.

Now, to secure this, it is not enough that the sensorium should be materially continuous, or that a "spiritual substance" or a "transcendental ego" should persist in time to receive the second sensation after having received and registered the first. A perfectly elastic sensorium, a wholly unchanging soul, or a quite absolute ego might remain perfectly identical with itself through various experiences without collating them. It would then remain, in fact, more truly and literally identical than if it were modified somewhat by those successive shocks. Yet a sensorium or a spirit thus unchanged would be incapable of memory, unfit to connect a past perception with one present or to become aware of their relation. It is not identity in the substance impressed, but growing complication in the phenomenon presented, that makes possible a sense of diversity and relation between things. The identity of substance or spirit, if it were absolute, would indeed prevent comparison, because it would exclude modifications, and it is the survival of past modifications within the present that makes comparisons possible. We may impress any number of forms successively on the same water, and the identity of the substance will not help those forms to survive and accumulate their effects. But if we have a surface that retains our successive stampings we may change the substance from wax to plaster and from plaster to bronze, and the effects of our labor will survive and be superimposed upon one another. It is the actual plastic form in both mind and body, not any unchanging substance or agent, that is efficacious in perpetuating thought and gathering experience.

Were not nature and all her parts such models of patience and pertinacity, they never would have succeeded in impressing their existence on something so volatile and irresponsible as thought is. A sensation needs to be violent, like the sun's blinding light, to arrest attention, and keep it taut, as it were, long enough for the system to acquire a respectful attitude, and grow predisposed to resume it. A repetition of that sensation will thereafter meet with a prepared response which we call recognition; the concomitants of the old experience will form themselves afresh about the new one and by their convergence give it a sort of welcome and interpretation. The movement, for instance, by which the face was raised toward the heavens was perhaps one element which added to the first sensation, brightness, a concomitant sensation, height; the brightness was not bright merely, but high. Now when the brightness reappears the face will more quickly be lifted up; the place where the brightness shone will be looked for; the brightness will have acquired a claim to be placed somewhere. The heat which at the same moment may have burned the forehead will also be expected and, when felt, projected into the brightness, which will now be hot as well as high. So with whatever other sensations time may associate with this group. They will all adhere to the original impression, enriching it with an individuality which will render it before long a familiar complex in experience, and one easy to recognize and to complete in idea.

In the case of so vivid a thing as the sun's brightness many other sensations beside those out of which science draws the qualities attributed to that heavenly body adhere in the primitive mind to the phenomenon. Before he is a substance the sun is a god. He is beneficent and necessary no less than bright and high; he rises upon all happy opportunities and sets upon all terrors. He is divine, since all life and fruitfulness hang upon his miraculous revolutions. His coming and going are life and death to the world. As the sensations of light and heat are projected upward together to become attributes of his body, so the feelings of pleasure, safety, and hope which he brings into the soul are projected in this spirit; and to this spirit, more than to anything else, energy, independence, and substantiality are originally attributed. The emotions felt in his presence being the ultimate issue and term of his effect in us, the counterpart or shadow of those emotions is regarded as the first and deepest factor in his causality. It is his divine life, more than aught else, that underlies his apparitions and explains the influences which he propagates. The substance or independent existence attributed to objects is therefore by no means only or primarily a physical notion. What is conceived to support the physical qualities is a pseudo-psychic or vital force. It is a moral and living object that we construct, building it up out of all the materials, emotional, intellectual, and sensuous, which lie at hand in our consciousness to be synthesized into the hybrid reality which we are to fancy confronting us. To discriminate and redistribute those miscellaneous physical and psychical elements, and to divorce the god from the material sun, is a much later problem, arising at a different and more reflective stage in the Life of Reason.

When reflection, turning to the comprehension of a chaotic experience, busies itself about recurrences, when it seeks to normalize in some way things coming and going, and to straighten out the causes of events, that reflection is inevitably turned toward something dynamic and independent, and can have no successful issue except in mechanical science. When on the other hand reflection stops to challenge and question the fleeting object, not so much to prepare for its possible return as to conceive its present nature, this reflection is turned no less unmistakably in the direction of ideas, and will terminate in logic or the morphology of being. We attribute such independence to things in order to normalize their recurrence. We attribute essences to them in order to normalize their manifestations or constitution. Independence will ultimately turn out to be an assumed constancy in material processes, essence an assumed constancy in ideal meanings or points of reference in discourse. The one marks the systematic distribution of objects, the other their settled character.

We talk of recurrent perceptions, but materially considered no perception recurs. Each recurrence is one of a finite series and holds forever its place and number in that series. Yet human attention, while it can survey several simultaneous impressions and find them similar, cannot keep them distinct if they grow too numerous. The mind has a native bias and inveterate preference for form and identification. Water does not run downhill more persistently than attention turns experience into constant terms. The several repetitions of one essence given in consciousness will tend at once to be neglected, and only the essence itself—the character shared by those sundry perceptions—will stand and become a term in mental discourse. After a few strokes of the clock, the reiterated impressions merge and cover one another; we lose count and perceive the quality and rhythm but not the number of the sounds. If this is true of so abstract and mathematical a perception as is counting, how emphatically true must it be of continuous and infinitely varied perceptions flowing in from the whole spatial world. Glimpses of the environment follow one another in quick succession, like a regiment of soldiers in uniform; only now and then does the stream take a new turn, catch a new ray of sunlight, or arrest our attention at some break.

The senses in their natural play revert constantly to familiar objects, gaining impressions which differ but slightly from one another. These slight differences are submerged in apperception, so that sensation comes to be not so much an addition of new items to consciousness as a reburnishing there of some imbedded device. Its character and relations are only slightly modified at each fresh rejuvenation. To catch the passing phenomenon in all its novelty and idiosyncrasy is a work of artifice and curiosity. Such an exercise does violence to intellectual instinct and involves an aesthetic power of diving bodily into the stream of sensation, having thrown overboard all rational ballast and escaped at once the inertia and the momentum of practical life. Normally every datum of sense is at once devoured by a hungry intellect and digested for the sake of its vital juices. The result is that what ordinarily remains in memory is no representative of particular moments or shocks—though sensation, as in dreams, may be incidentally recreated from within— but rather a logical possession, a sense of acquaintance with a certain field of reality, in a word, a consciousness of *knowledge*.

But what, we may ask, is this reality, which we boast to know? May not the skeptic justly contend that nothing is so unknown and indeed unknowable as this pretended object of knowledge? The sensations which reason treats so cavalierly were at least something actual while they lasted and made good their momentary claim to our interest; but what is this new ideal figment, unseizable yet ever present, invisible but indispensable, unknowable yet alone interesting or important? Strange that the only possible object or theme of our knowledge should be something we cannot know.

An answer to these doubts will perhaps appear if we ask ourselves what sort of contact with reality would satisfy us, and in what terms we expect or desire to possess the subject matter of our thoughts. Is it simply corroboration that we look for? Is it a verification of truth in sense? It would be unreasonable, in that case, after all the evidence we demand has been gathered, to complain that the ideal term thus concurrently suggested, the supersensible substance, reality, or independent object, does not itself descend into the arena of immediate sensuous presentation. Knowledge is not eating, and we cannot expect to devour and possess *what we mean*. Knowledge is recognition of something absent; it is a salutation, not an embrace. It is an advance on sensation precisely because it is representative. The terms or goals of thought have for their function to subtend long tracts of sensuous experience, to be ideal links between fact and fact, invisible wires behind the scenes, threads along which inference may run in making phenomena intelligible and controllable. An idea that should become an image would cease to be ideal; a principle that is to remain a principle can never become a fact. A God that you could see with the eyes of the body, a heaven you might climb into by a ladder planted at Bethel, would be parts of this created and interpretable world, not terms in its interpretation nor objects in a spiritual sphere. Now external objects are thought to be principles and sources of experience; they are accordingly conceived realities on an ideal plane. We may look for all the evidence we choose before we declare our inference to be warranted; but we must not ask for something more than evidence, nor expect to know realities without inferring them anew. They are revealed only to understanding. We cannot cease to think and still continue to know.

It may be said, however, that principles and external objects are interesting only because they symbolize further sensations, that thought is an expedient of finite minds, and that representation is a ghostly process which we crave to materialize into bodily possession. We may grow sick of inferring truth and long rather to become reality. Intelligence is after all no compulsory possession; and while some of us would gladly have more of it, others find that they already have too much. The tension of thought distresses them and to represent what they cannot and would not be is not a natural function of their spirit. To such minds experience that should merely corroborate ideas would prolong dissatisfaction. The ideas must be realized; they must pass into immediacy. If reality (a word employed generally in a eulogistic sense) is to mean this desired immediacy, no ideal of thought can be real. All intelligible objects and the whole universe of mental discourse would then be an unreal and conventional structure, impinging ultimately on sense from which it would derive its sole validity.

There would be no need of quarreling with such a philosophy, were not its use of words rather misleading. Call experience in its existential and immediate aspect, if you will, the sole reality; that will not prevent reality from having an ideal dimension. The intellectual world will continue to give beauty, meaning, and scope to those bubbles of consciousness on which it is painted. Reality would not be, in that case, what thought aspires to reach. Consciousness is the least ideal of things when reason is taken out of it. Reality would then need thought to give it all those human values of which, in its substance, it would have been wholly deprived; and the ideal would still be what lent music to throbs and significance to being.

The equivocation favored by such language at once begins to appear. Is not thought with all its products a part of experience? Must not sense, if it be the only reality, be sentient sometimes of the ideal? What the site is to a city that is immediate experience to the universe of discourse. The latter is all held materially within the limits defined by the former; but if immediate experience be the seat of the moral world, the moral world is the only interesting possession of immediate experience. When a waste is built on, however, it is a violent paradox to call it still a waste; and an immediate experience that represents the rest of sentience, with all manner of ideal harmonies read into the whole in the act of representing it, is an immediate experience raised to its highest power: it is the Life of Reason. In vain, then, will a philosophy of intellectual abstention limit so Platonic a term as reality to the immediate aspect of existence, when it is the ideal aspect that endows existence with character and value, together with representative scope and a certain lien upon eternity.

More legitimate, therefore, would be the assertion that knowledge reaches reality when it touches its ideal goal. Reality is known when, as in mathematics, a stable and unequivocal object is developed by thinking. The locus or material embodiment of such a reality is no longer in view; these questions seem to the logician irrelevant. If necessary ideas find no illustration in sense, he deems the fact an argument against the importance and validity of sensation, not in the least a disproof of his ideal knowledge. If no site be found on earth for the Platonic city, its constitution is nonetheless recorded and enshrined in heaven; nor is that the only true ideal that has not where to lay its head. What in the sensualistic or mystical system was called reality will now be termed appearance, and what there figured as an imaginary construction borne by the conscious moment will now appear to be a prototype for all existence and an eternal standard for its estimation.

It is this rationalistic or Platonic system (little as most men may suspect the fact) that finds a first expression in ordinary perception. When you distinguish your sensations from their cause and laugh at the idealist (as this kind of skeptic is called) who says that chairs and tables exist only in your mind, you are treating a figment of reason as a deeper and truer thing than the moments of life whose blind experience that reason has come to illumine. What you call the evidence of sense is pure confidence in reason. You will not be so idiotic as to make no inferences from your sensations; you will not pin your faith so unimaginatively on momentary appearance as to deny that the world exists when you stop thinking about it. You feel that your intellect has wider scope and has discovered many a thing that goes on behind the scenes, many a secret that would escape a stupid and gaping observation. It is the fool that looks to look and stops at the barely visible: you not only look but *see*; for you understand.

Now the practical burden of such understanding, if you take the trouble to analyze it, will turn out to be what the skeptic says it is: assurance of eventual sensations. But as these sensations, in memory and expectation, are numerous and indefinitely variable, you are not able to hold them clearly before the mind; indeed, the realization of all the potentialities which you vaguely feel to lie in the future is a task absolutely beyond imagination. Yet your present impressions, dependent as they are on your chance attitude and disposition and on a thousand trivial accidents, are far from representing adequately all that might be discovered or that is actually known about the subject before you. This object, then, to your apprehension, is not identical with any of the sensations that reveal it, nor is it exhausted by all these sensations when they are added together; yet it contains nothing assignable but what they might conceivably reveal. As it lies in your fancy, then, this object, the reality, is a complex and elusive entity, the sum at once and the residuum of all particular impressions which, underlying the present one, have bequeathed to it their surviving linkage in discourse and consequently endowed it with a large part of its present character. With this hybrid object, sensuous in its materials and ideal in its locus, each particular glimpse is compared, and is recognized to be but a glimpse, an aspect which the object presents to a particular observer. Here are two identifications. In the first place various sensations and felt relations, which cannot be kept distinct in the mind, fall together into one term of discourse, represented by a sign, a word, or a more or less complete sensuous image. In the second place the new perception is referred to that ideal entity of which it is now called a manifestation and effect.

Such are the primary relations of reality and appearance. A reality is a term of discourse based on a psychic complex of memories, associations, and expectations, but constituted in its ideal independence by an assertive energy of thought. An appearence is a passing sensation, recognized as belonging to that group of which the object itself is the ideal representative, and accordingly regarded as a manifestation of that object.

Thus the notion of an independent and permanent world is an ideal term used to mark and as it were to justify the cohesion in space and the recurrence in time of recognizable groups of sensations. This coherence and recurrence force the intellect, if it would master experience at all or understand anything, to frame the idea of such a reality. If we wish to defend the use of such an idea and prove to ourselves its necessity, all we need do is to point to that coherence and recurrence in external phenomena. That brave effort and flight of intelligence which in the beginning raised man to the conception of reality, enabling him to discount and interpret appearance, will, if we retain our trust in reason, raise us continually anew to that same idea, by a no less spontaneous and victorious movement of thought.

2

Nature Unified and Mind Discerned[*]

George Santayana

When the mind has learned to distinguish external objects and to attribute to them a constant size, shape, and potency, in spite of the variety and intermittence ruling in direct experience, there yet remains a great work to do before attaining a clear, even if superficial, view of the world. An animal's customary habitat may have constant features and their relations in space may be learned by continuous exploration; but probably many other landscapes are also within the range of memory and fancy that stand in no visible relation to the place in which we find ourselves at a given moment. It is true that, at this day, we take it for granted that all real places, as we call them, lie in one space, in which they hold definite geometric relations to one another; and if we have glimpses of any region for which no room can be found in the single map of the universe which astronomy has drawn, we unhesitatingly relegate that region to the land of dreams. Since the Elysian Fields and the Coast of Bohemia have no assignable latitude and longitude, we call these places imaginary, even if in some dream we remember to have visited them and dwelt there with no less sense of reality than

*Originally published in George Santayana, *Reason in Common Sense,* vol. 1 of *The Life of Reason* (New York: Charles Scribner's Sons, 1905; Dover, 1980), chapter 5.

in this single and geometric world of commerce. It belongs to sanity and common sense, as men now possess them, to admit no countries unknown to geography and filling part of the conventional space in three dimensions. All our waking experience is understood to go on in some part of this space, and no court of law would admit evidence relating to events in some other sphere.

This principle, axiomatic as it has become, is in no way primitive, since primitive experience is sporadic and introduces us to detached scenes separated by lapses of our senses and attention. These scenes do not hang together in any local contiguity. To construct a chart of the world is a difficult feat of synthetic imagination, not to be performed without speculative boldness and a heroic insensibility to the claims of fancy. Even now most people live without topographical ideas and have no clear conception of the spatial relations that keep together the world in which they move. They feel their daily way about like animals, following a habitual scent, without dominating the range of their instinctive wanderings. Reality is rather a story to them than a system of objects and forces, nor would they think themselves mad if at any time their experience should wander into a fourth dimension. Vague dramatic and moral laws, when they find any casual application, seem to such dreaming minds more notable truths, deeper revelations of efficacious reality, than the mechanical necessities of the case, which they scarcely conceive of; and in this primordial prejudice they are confirmed by superstitious affinities often surviving in their religion and philosophy. In the midst of cities and affairs they are like landsmen at sea, incapable of an intellectual conception of their position: nor have they any complete confidence in their principles of navigation. They know the logarithms by rote merely, and if they reflect are reduced to a stupid wonder and only half believe they are in a known universe or will ever reach an earthly port. It would not require superhuman eloquence in some prophetic passenger to persuade them to throw compass and quadrant overboard and steer enthusiastically for El Dorado. The theory of navigation is essentially as speculative as that of salvation, only it has survived more experiences of the judgment and repeatedly brought those who trust in it to their promised land.

The theory that all real objects and places lie together in one even and homogeneous space, conceived as similar in its constitution to the parts of extension of which we have immediate intuition, is a theory of the greatest practical importance and validity. By its light we carry on all our affairs, and the success of our action while we rely upon it is the best proof of its truth. The imaginative parsimony and discipline which such a theory involves are balanced by the immense extension and certitude it gives to knowledge. It is at once an act of allegiance to nature and a Magna Charta which mind imposes on the tyrannous world, which in turn pledges itself before the assembled faculties of man not to exceed its constitutional privilege and to harbor no magic monsters in unattainable lairs from which they might issue to disturb human labors. Yet that spontaneous intelligence which first enabled men to make this genial discovery and take so fundamental a step toward taming experience should not be laid by after this first victory; it is a weapon needed in many subsequent conflicts. To conceive that all nature makes one system is only a beginning: the articulation of natural life has still to be discovered in detail and, what is more, a similar articulation has to be given to the psychic world which now, by the very act that constitutes Nature and makes her consistent, appears at her side or rather in her bosom.

That the unification of nature is eventual and theoretical is a point useful to remember: else the relation of the natural world to poetry, metaphysics, and religion will never become intelligible. Lalande, or whoever it was, who searched the heavens with his telescope and could find no God, would not have found the human mind if he had searched the brain with a microscope. Yet God existed in man's apprehension long before mathematics or even, perhaps, before the vault of heaven; for the objectification of the whole mind, with its passions and motives, naturally precedes that abstraction by which the idea of a material world is drawn from the chaos of experience, an abstraction which culminates in such atomic and astronomical theories as science is now familiar with. The sense for life in things, be they small or great, is not derived from the abstract idea of their bodies but is an ancient concomitant to that idea, inseparable from it until it became abstract. Truth and materiality, mechanism and ideal interests, are collateral projections from one rolling experience, which shows up one aspect or the other as it develops various functions and dominates itself to various ends. When one ore is abstracted and purified, the residuum subsists in that primeval quarry in which it originally lay. The failure to find God among the stars, or even the attempt to find him there, does not indicate that human experience affords no avenue to the idea of God—for history proves the contrary—but indicates rather the atrophy in this particular man of the imaginative faculty by which his race had attained to that idea. Such an atrophy might indeed become general, and God would in that case disappear from human experience as music would disappear if universal deafness attacked the race. Such an event is made conceivable by the loss of allied imaginative habits, which is observable in historic times. Yet possible variations in human faculty do not involve the illegitimacy of such faculties as actually subsist; and the abstract world known to science, unless it dries up the ancient fountains of ideation by its habitual presence in thought, does not remove those parallel dramatizations or abstractions which experience may have suggested to men.

What enables men to perceive the unity of nature is the unification of their own wills. A man half-asleep, without fixed purposes, without intellectual keenness or joy in recognition, might graze about like an animal, forgetting each satisfaction in the next and banishing from his frivolous mind the memory of every sorrow; what had just failed to kill him would leave him as thoughtless and unconcerned as if it had never crossed his path. Such irrational elasticity and innocent improvidence would never put two and two together. Every morning there would be a new world with the same fool to live in it. But let some sobering passion, some serious interest, lend perspective to the mind, and a point of reference will immediately be given for protracted observation; then the laws of nature will begin to dawn upon thought. Every experiment will become a lesson, every event will be remembered as favorable or unfavorable to the master-passion. At first, indeed, this keen observation will probably be animistic and the laws discovered will be chiefly habits, human or divine, special favors or envious punishments and warnings. But the same constancy of aim which discovers the dramatic conflicts composing society, and tries to read nature in terms of passion, will, if it be long sustained, discover behind this glorious chaos a deeper mechanical order. Men's thoughts, like the weather, are not so arbitrary as they seem and the true master in observation, the man guided by a steadfast and superior purpose, will see them revolving about their centers in obedience to quite calculable instincts, and the principle of all their flutterings will not be hidden from his eyes. Belief in indeterminism is a sign of indetermination. No commanding or steady intellect flirts with so miserable a possibility, which insofar as it actually prevailed would make virtue impotent and experience, in its pregnant sense, impossible.

We have said that those objects which cannot be incorporated into the one space which the understanding envisages are relegated to another sphere called imagination. We reach here a most important corollary. As material objects, making a single system which fills space and evolves in time, are conceived by abstraction from the flux of sensuous experience, so, *pari passu,* the rest of experience, with all its other outgrowths and concretions, falls out with the physical world and forms the sphere of mind, the sphere of memory, fancy, and the passions. We have in this discrimination the *genesis of mind,* not of course in the transcendental sense in which the word mind is extended to mean the sum total and mere fact of existence—for mind, so taken, can have no origin and indeed no specific meaning—but the genesis of mind as a determinate form of being, a distinguishable part of the universe known to experience and discourse, the mind that unravels itself in meditation, inhabits animal bodies, and is studied in psychology.

Mind, in this proper sense of the word, is the residue of existence, the leavings, so to speak, and parings of experience when the material world has been cut out of the whole cloth. Reflection underlines in the chaotic continuum of sense and longing those aspects that have practical significance; it selects the efficacious ingredients in the world. The trustworthy object which is thus retained in thought, the complex of connected events, is nature, and though so intelligible an object is not soon nor vulgarly recognized, because human reflection is perturbed and halting, yet every forward step in scientific and practical knowledge is a step toward its clearer definition. At first much parasitic matter clings to that dynamic skeleton. Nature is drawn like a sponge heavy and dripping from the waters of sentience. It is soaked with inefficacious passions and overlaid with idle secretions. Nature, in a word, is at first conceived mythically, dramatically, and retains much of the unintelligible, sporadic habit of animal experience itself. But as attention awakes and discrimination, practically inspired, grows firm and stable, irrelevant qualities are stripped off, and the mechanical process, the efficacious infallible order, is clearly disclosed beneath. Meantime the incidental effects, the "secondary qualities," are relegated to a personal inconsequential region; they constitute the realm of appearance, the realm of mind.

Mind is therefore sometimes identified with the unreal. We oppose, in an antithesis natural to thought and language, the imaginary to the true, fancy to fact, idea to thing. But this thing, fact, or external reality is, as we have seen, a completion and hypostasis of certain portions of experience, packed into such shapes as prove cogent in thought and practice. The stuff of external reality, the matter out of which its idea is made, is therefore continuous with the stuff and matter of our own minds. Their common substance is the immediate flux. This living worm has propagated by fission, and the two halves into which it has divided its life are mind and nature. Mind has kept and clarified the crude appearance, the dream, the ·purpose that seethed in the mass; nature has appropriated the order, the constant conditions, the causal substructure, disclosed in reflection, by which the immediate flux is explained and controlled. The chemistry of thought has precipitated these contrasted terms, each maintaining a recognizable identity and having the function of a point of reference for memory and will. Some of these terms or objects of thought we call things and marshal in all their ideal stability—for there is constancy in their motions and transformations—to make the intelligible external world of practice and science. Whatever stuff has not been absorbed in this construction, whatever facts of sensation, ideation, or will, do not coalesce with the newest conception of reality, we then call the mind.

Raw experience, then, lies at the basis of the idea of nature and approves its reality; while an equal reality belongs to the residue of experience, not taken, as yet, into that idea. But this residual sensuous reality often seems comparatively unreal because what it presents is entirely without practical force apart from its mechanical associates.

This inconsequential character of what remains over follows of itself from the concretion of whatever is constant and efficacious into the external world. If this fact is ever called in question, it is only because the external world is vaguely conceived, and loose wills and ideas are thought to govern it by magic. Yet in many ways falling short of absolute precision people recognize that thought is not dynamic or, as they call it, not real. The idea of the physical world is the first flower or thick cream of practical thinking. Being skimmed off first and proving so nutritious, it leaves the liquid below somewhat thin and unsavory. Especially does this result appear when science is still unpruned and mythical, so that what passes into the idea of material nature is much more than the truly causal network of forces, and includes many spiritual and moral functions.

The material world, as conceived in the first instance, had not that clear abstractness, nor the spiritual world that wealth and interest, which they have acquired for modern minds. The complex reactions of man's soul had been objectified together with those visual and tactile sensations which, reduced to a mathematical baldness, now furnish terms to natural science. Mind then dwelt in the world, not only in the warmth and beauty with which it literally clothed material objects, as it still does in poetic perception, but in a literal animistic way; for human passion and reflection were attributed to every object and made a fairyland of the world. Poetry and religion discerned life in those very places in which sense and understanding perceived body; and when so much of the burden of experience took wing into space, and the soul herself floated almost visibly among the forms of nature, it is no marvel that the poor remnant, a mass of merely personal troubles, an uninteresting distortion of things in individual minds, should have seemed a sad and unsubstantial accident. The inner world was all the more ghostly because the outer world was so much alive.

This movement of thought, which clothed external objects in all the wealth of undeciphered dreams, has long lost its momentum and yielded to a contrary tendency. Just as the hypostasis of some terms in experience is sanctioned by reason, when the objects so fixed and externalized can serve as causes and explanations for the order of events, so the criticism which tends to retract that hypostasis is sanctioned by reason when the hypostasis has exceeded its function and the external object conceived is loaded with useless ornament. The transcendental and functional secret of such hypostases, however, is seldom appreciated by the headlong mind; so that the ebb no less than the flow of objectification goes on blindly and impulsively, and is carried to absurd extremes. An age of mythology yields to an age of subjectivity; reason being equally neglected and exceeded in both. The reaction against imagination has left the external world, as represented in many minds, stark and bare. All the interesting and vital qualities which matter had once been endowed with have been attributed instead to an irresponsible sensibility in man. And as habits of ideation change slowly and yield only piecemeal to criticism or to fresh intuitions, such a revolution has not been carried out consistently, but instead of a thorough renaming of things and a new organization of thought it has produced chiefly distress and confusion. Some phases of this confusion may perhaps repay a moment's attention; they may enable us, when seen in their logical sequence, to understand somewhat better the hypostasizing intellect that is trying to assert itself and come to the light through all these gropings.

What helps in the first place to disclose a permanent object is a permanent sensation. There is a vast and clear difference between a floating and a fixed feeling; the latter, in normal circumstances, is present only when continuous stimulation renews it at every moment. Attention may wander, but the objects in the environment do not cease to radiate their influences on the body, which is thereby not allowed to lose the modification which those influences provoke. The consequent perception is therefore always at hand and in its repetitions substantially identical. Perceptions not renewed in this way by continuous stimulation come and go with cerebral currents; they are rare visitors, instead of being, like external objects, members of the household. Intelligence is most at home in the ultimate, which is the object of intent. Those realities which it can trust and continually recover are its familiar and beloved companions. The mists that may originally have divided it from them, and which psychologists call the mind, are gladly forgotten so soon as intelligence avails to pierce them, and as friendly communication can be established with the real world. Moreover, perceptions not sustained by a constant external stimulus are apt to be greatly changed when they reappear, and to be changed unaccountably, whereas external things show some method and proportion in their variations. Even when not much changed in themselves, mere ideas fall into a new setting, whereas things, unless something else has intervened to move them, reappear in their old places. Finally things are acted upon by other men, but thoughts are hidden from them by divine miracle.

Existence reveals reality when the flux discloses something permanent that dominates it. What is thus dominated, though it is the primary existence itself, is thereby degraded to appearance. Perceptions caused by external objects are, as we have just seen, long sustained in comparison with thoughts and fancies; but the objects are themselves in flux and a man's relation to them may be even more variable; so that very often a memory or a sentiment will recur, almost unchanged in character, long after the perception that first aroused it has become impossible. The brain, though mobile, is subject to habit; its formations, while they lapse instantly, return again and again. These ideal objects may accordingly be in a way more real and enduring than things external. Hence no primitive mind puts all reality, or what is most real in reality, in an abstract material universe. It finds, rather, ideal points of reference by which material mutation itself seems to be controlled. An ideal world is recognized from the beginning and placed, not in the immediate foreground, nearer than material things, but much farther off. It has greater substantiality and independence than material objects are credited with. It is divine.

When agriculture, commerce, or manual crafts have given men some knowledge of nature, the world thus recognized and dominated is far from seeming ultimate. It is thought to lie between two others, both now often called mental, but in their original quality altogether disparate: the world of spiritual forces and that of sensuous appearance. The notions of permanence and independence by which material objects are conceived apply also, of course, to everything spiritual; and while the dominion exercised by spirits may be somewhat precarious, they are as remote as possible from immediacy and sensation. They come and go; they govern nature or, if they neglect to do so, it is from aversion or high indifference; they visit man with obsessions and diseases; they hasten to extricate him from difficulties; and they dwell in him, constituting his powers of conscience and invention. Sense, on the other hand, is a mere effect, either of body or spirit or of both in conjunction. It gives a vitiated personal view of these realities. Its pleasures are dangerous and unintelligent, and it perishes as it goes.

Such are, for primitive apperception, the three great realms of being: nature, sense, and spirit. Their frontiers, however, always remain uncertain. Sense, because it is insignificant when made an object, is long neglected by reflection. No attempt is made to describe its processes or ally them systematically to natural changes. Its illusions, when noticed, are regarded as scandals calculated to foster skepticism. The spiritual world is, on the other hand, a constant theme for poetry and speculation. In the absence of ideal science, it can be conceived only in myths, which are naturally as shifting and self-contradictory as they are persistent. They acquire no fixed character until, in dogmatic religion, they are defined with reference to natural events, foretold or reported. Nature is what first acquires a form and then imparts form to the other spheres. Sense admits definition and distribution only as an effect of nature and spirit only as its principle.

The form nature acquires is, however, itself vague and uncertain and can ill serve, for long ages, to define the other realms which depend on it for definition. Hence it has been common, for instance, to treat the spiritual as a remote or finer form of the natural. Beyond the moon everything seemed permanent; it was therefore called divine and declared to preside over the rest. The breath that escaped from the lips at death, since it took away with it the spiritual control and miraculous life that had quickened the flesh, was itself the spirit. On the other hand, natural processes have been persistently attributed to spiritual causes, for it was not matter that moved itself but intent that moved it. Thus spirit was barbarously taken for a natural substance and a natural force. It was identified with everything in which it was manifested, so long as no natural causes could be assigned for that operation.

If the unification of nature were complete, sense would evidently fall within it, since it is to subtend and sustain the sensible flux that intelligence acknowledges first stray material objects and then their general system. The elements of experience not taken up into the constitution of objects remain attached to them as their life. In the end the dynamic skeleton, without losing its articulation, would be clothed again with its flesh. Suppose my notions of astronomy allowed me to believe that the sun, sinking into the sea, was extinguished every evening, and that what appeared the next morning was his younger brother, hatched in a sun-producing nest to be found in the eastern regions. My theory would have robbed yesterday's sun of its life and brightness; it would have asserted that during the night no sun existed anywhere; but it would have added the sun's qualities afresh to a matter that did not previously possess them, namely, to the imagined egg that would produce a sun for tomorrow. Suppose we substitute for that astronomy the one that now prevails: we have deprived the single sun—which now exists and spreads its influences without interruption—of its humanity and even of its metaphysical unity. It has become a congeries of chemical substances. The facts revealed to perception have partly changed their locus and been differently deployed throughout nature. Some have become attached to operations in the human brain. Nature has not thereby lost any quality she had ever manifested; these have merely been redistributed so as to secure a more systematic connection between them all. They are the materials of the system, which has been conceived by making existences continuous, whenever this extension of their being was needful to render their recurrences intelligible. Sense, which was formerly regarded as a sad distortion of its objects, now becomes an original and congruent part of nature, from which, as from any other part, the rest of nature might be scientifically inferred.

Spirit is not less closely attached to nature, although in a different manner. Taken existentially it is a part of sense; taken ideally it is the form or value which nature acquires when viewed from the vantage-ground of any interest. Individual objects are recognizable for a time not because influx is materially arrested but because it somewhere circulates in a fashion which awakens an interest and brings different parts of the surrounding process into definable and prolonged relations with that interest. Particular objects may perish yet others may continue, like the series of suns imagined by Heraclitus, to perform the same office. The function will outlast the particular organ. That interest in reference to which the function is defined will essentially determine a perfect world of responsive extensions and conditions. These ideals will be a spiritual reality; and they will be expressed in nature insofar as nature supports that regulative interest. Many a perfect and eternal realm, merely potential in existence but definite in constitution, will thus subtend nature and be what a rational philosophy might call the ideal. What is called spirit would be the ideal insofar as it obtained expression in nature; and the power attributed to spirit would be the part of nature's fertility by which such expression was secured.

3

Knowledge of Nature*

F. J. E. Woodbridge

Nature Identified

The word "Nature" is used in this essay as a name for the familiar setting of human history. I like Sir Thomas Browne's picture of it in his *Religio Medici* as "that universal and publick Manuscript that lies expansed unto the eyes of all," because it is something evidently seen and like a book to be read with enjoyment and profit, a book which we are all engaged in reading either superficially or attentively. And I like Santayana's reference to it as "public experience . . . the stars, the seasons, the swarm of animals, the spectacle of birth and death, of cities and wars . . . the facts before every man's eyes."[1] His list of particulars could be much enlarged, but one would grow weary in the enumeration of them and be content to sum them up in "heaven and earth, the sea, and all that in them is." Such is the *familiar* setting of human history. It is also the primary subject matter of all human inquiry. I would not have it displaced by any other, because when I try to displace it or consider what others do when they try, I find that

*Originally published in F. J. E. Woodbridge, *An Essay on Nature* (New York: Columbia University Press, 1940), chapter 1. Reprinted by permission.

a substitute for it cannot be found and that I am seeking ignorance instead of knowledge. In recognizing it as the setting of *human* history, I would not exclude other histories from it—neither that of living creatures other than man nor that of the stars—for I must think of it as expansed not only unto the eyes of all, but unto the eyeless also, for heaven and earth, the sea, and all that in them is make up a sum which seems to leave nothing out. "Nature" is here used as a name for that sum.

In so naming it, I have no intention of conveying information about it. So I spell the name with a capital letter to indicate that it is what we call a "proper" and sometimes "Christian" name. The heathen had in their languages somewhat equivalent words, suggestive of generation and decay, and that suggestion still influences our English use of the Latin word *natura,* as if Nature were once born of dubious parents and might later die, remaining meanwhile like a fertile mother who, in spite of never having had a husband, has had a prodigious offspring. I confess to some sympathy with the heathen in this matter. Personification is difficult for me to resist. I am afflicted with a sense of indecency whenever I refer to Nature as "it." My ancestors are all dead, but I feel like a child of Nature, cradled in her arms until my turn comes to die and to remain somewhere and somehow in her embrace. This sentiment I shall not resist. But I intend to be impersonal, since that which is here named "Nature" is evidently not a woman. Since, however, I am a man, my piety, growing as it does so spontaneously from a deep sense of intimately belonging to what is named, may be forgiven by those who dislike it. Let Nature's proper pronoun be "it" for those who like it better and would avoid all suggestions of personality. I would not have noun or pronoun lead the reader or me astray in what follows. I would not have the name informative.

The sacrifice of the common noun "nature" is, therefore, imperative, for its use could easily be misleading. I shall try to expose what Nature is as I think I have found her out by studying her character as best I could and beset by the limitations of my ignorance. Yet I hesitate to say that I am trying to discover *the* nature of Nature or to determine whether she is really nature or not. I accept her as quite genuine. Heaven and earth, the sea, and all that in them is are very real, so real that it is difficult to think of a reality in competition with them, especially when the all that in them is, is so far from having been discovered. The name "Nature" in this essay is not the noun "nature." The name as here used could be justified by much current usage. Not to poets alone does it call to attention the stars and life, but to farmers also, to toilers thinking of vacation, to explorers, and even to scientists and philosophers when they are off their guard. So I need not apologize for its use. Apology is needed only for what will be said about the named.

The adjective "natural" and the adverb "naturally" I need. They, like the noun "nature," are ambiguous. Let, then, that be "natural" which is characteristic of Nature and leads us naturally to expect this or that as a consequence. The behavior of adjectives and adverbs is, however, unruly and annoying. They will suggest opposites—the unnatural, the artificial, the supernatural—and tend to turn expressions which are ordinarily clear and sensible into a dialectical play of meanings. The context may save us from that. It is doubtless natural enough for a woman to paint and powder in order to make herself more good looking than she naturally is. We are all naturally artificial in many ways, of which the cited illustration is a sample. We are naturally artists, working with and upon Nature in ways that transform the natural into the unnatural. And the behavior of Nature, although all of it must be said to be natural, often exhibits the unusual and the astonishing, leading us to call these exhibitions unnatural and sometimes monstrous when they are not. Even the supernatural and certainly belief in it may be called natural in accordance with the same kind of play of adjectives. Respect for context can save us from letting this play lead to confusion. When we let adjectives generate opposites or, by putting a "the" before them, new nouns, we ought not to forget what we have done. One travels a perilous road by going from finite to infinite, to the infinite, to arrive in infinity. I hope to keep respect for context.

So "Nature," a word with historical associations and redolent of meaning, is here used, not as a noun substantive in need of a definition, but as a name calling only for an identification of what is named such as has already been given. Although historical and current usage give point to its choice, I would keep the name free from unfortunate alliances. Sometimes I shall use the words "world" and "universe" as if they were partially or wholly equivalents of Nature. Of the two, "universe" is the more troublesome. We currently speak of the "visible world," "the social world," "the business world," and so forth without confusion of thought. "The natural world" and "the physical world" follow the same pattern. "Universe," however, has been lately so preempted by astronomers and physicists and sometimes allowed to have a plural, that its use suggests forgetfulness of much that I would wish to have remembered—the swarm of animals, the spectacle of birth and death—even if the universe, like a creature subject to morality, is growing progressively colder, until all its heat is dissipated. Moreover, books about the universe have become increasingly mathematical and require considerable competence in mathematics to understand them properly. Translated into the language of daily use they often contain illustrations which seem more like fairy tales of a mathematical imagination than sober conclusions reached by men who work in laboratories and use instruments of precision. There is, for example, the tale of the remarkable twins, Peter the stay-at-home and Paul the adventurous traveler. When they were young men, Paul started out one day for a year's journey to visit distant parts of the universe. He traveled so fast that when he returned, still in the bloom of young manhood, he found his brother an old man tottering on the edge of the grave. I can take the tale as a myth indicative of a mathematical truth involved in the measurement of velocities, but not as an illustration of a possibly conceivable incident in the lives of a pair of twins; for it is not the requirements of measurement that beget children.[2] We are sometimes told what we would see if we traveled with the speed of light and are also told that only light can travel with that speed. Indeed, the universe seems to be generating a modern mythology surpassing the ancient in extravagance. It gets into the papers and has a credulous acceptance such as the tales of Hesiod once had. But "universe" is a good word when used with caution. It suggests all things unified and whole however they turn and I shall now and then use it when emphasizing the comprehensiveness of Nature.

Knowledge

Having identified that to which the name "Nature" is given, and commented upon the use of cognate words, I would consider knowledge next. The literature on the subject is confusing. That there should be skepticism or doubt about much that we affirm and deny, and, consequently, a search for a criterion which would remove it, is natural. To affirm that knowledge is that criterion is also natural. To demand, however, a criterion for knowledge, although it may seem natural and sensible, may turn out to be the reverse. In Plato's *Meno* a slave is asked by Socrates to double a square and responds by doubling its side. A little knowledge of squares removed the absurdity. But what is the criterion of such knowledge? What would prove a proposition in a geometry like Euclid's to be knowledge? He proved many propositions which were difficult to prove and had criteria for doing so, but I have not found that he had a criterion for proving that the knowledge contained in those propositions was knowledge. It has been often affirmed that Euclid's geometry is knowledge of space. That is very doubtful, but its doubtfulness does not turn that geometry into ignorance. The demand for a criterion which will prove that knowledge is knowledge begins to look ill-advised.

It looks more so the further one pursues the matter. I have deliberately chosen an example from geometry because the search for a criterion for geometry as knowledge turns out to be an exposition of what a geometry is. I could have used other examples. That Napoleon lost the battle of Waterloo is historical knowledge. I can imagine one trying to prove that he did not lose it and succeeding in doing so; but I can imagine no criterion which will prove that historical knowledge is knowledge of history, nor can I imagine one that will prove that natural knowledge is knowledge of Nature. Trying to find criteria for knowledge irrespective of what it is knowledge of appears to me ridiculous. It is trying to identify knowledge without anything to know. The end of such trying is skepticism absolute and complete. We may say so in words, but for my part I can make no sense out of it. I cannot identify skepticism without something to be skeptical about. Descartes lived in vain if subsequent philosophers have still to learn that a man cannot doubt that he doubts when he's doubting. The reason is not that if he did so he would contradict himself; the reason is that he can't do it.

The preceding paragraphs of this section are not exhibitions of acumen. That is their merit. Every child is virtually familiar with Descartes's principle *cogito ergo sum* without giving it expression in Latin, French, or English. Calling attention to it suggests asking why should a criterion for knowledge be ardently desired by anybody? I shall deal with that question later after having exposed what natural knowledge is. It is obviously knowledge of Nature. If what we learn by exploring heaven and earth, the sea, and all that in them is, is not knowledge, something else must be; and I look in vain for that something else. When a chemist tells me that water boils at 212° Fahrenheit, I understand what he says and do not think he is lying. I am quite sure I have at least that much chemical or physical knowledge and am disgusted if asked whether that knowledge is really *knowledge*. If it is not really knowledge, then I must ask for a sample of what real knowledge would be. Failing that I must do precisely what the chemist does, go to Nature, put questions to her, and accept her answers and refrain from trying to imagine what knowledge should be like before any knowledge is acquired.

That vital and intimate connection with Nature which we call our consciousness is not knowledge except in a sense gratuitous or beside the mark unless it involves curiosity satisfied or ignorance dispelled, and even then it may be knowledge only in a gratuitous sense. For not to know the taste of sugar means not to have tasted it or to have forgotten its taste rather than to be ignorant of anything. Tastes assist us to identify and to discriminate, but are hardly knowledge of that which is identified or discriminated. Were consciousness of Nature knowledge, the sight of the stars ought of itself to give us astronomy, and the mere memory of events ought to give us history. Knowledge is acquired, not given: If we ask, then, whence it is acquired, the answer is from Nature, not from our consciousness of her, even if that consciousness is indispensable. To equate it with her is like equating the reading of a book with the book read, like equating that universal and public manuscript expansed unto the eyes of all with seeing it. Even Berkeley, who held that there are no sights unless seen and no sounds unless heard, held also that neither sights nor sounds are knowledge. His basic principle of human knowledge that *esse est percipi* is not so foolish as it sounds, when construed as meaning that the *being* of objects of knowledge *is* what they are *perceived to be,* but that those objects themselves are neither knowledge nor perception. Trees are objects of knowledge but not knowledge of anything. The same is to be said of Nature. Natural knowledge and consciousness of Nature are not equivalent. When we say that we "know" that we are conscious, that we see, hear, taste, smell, and touch, and that we think, we are not laying down the foundations of that knowledge which it has been man's great ambition to acquire. We are giving expression to what our natural status is. To do more we leave that natural status to be just what it is and turn to Nature to explore her ways.

To be sure, our natural status can itself be explored. Both biologists and psychologists spend much time and labor upon it. We owe much to their researches. They do not, however, leave Nature out of the account. They cannot examine our natural status without her help. As for men called "philosophers," they often try, but are driven at last to admit, as Santayana does in the book from which I have already quoted, that Nature is the proof of their philosophy no matter how extravagant that philosophy may be. An appeal to the stars, the seasons, the swarm of animals, and the rest is an appeal to the ultimately supreme court of all knowledge. Setting ourselves apart is like setting anything else apart. It gives us "Nature *and* man" just as it gives us "Nature *and* the sun," "Nature *and* anything else" which can be so distinguished for purposes of study—this frog or this rock. Distinguishing man is not taking him out of Nature in order to secure for him a privileged position wherein he is fitted to receive Nature as a gift from an alien benefactor. Is it not time, I am forced to ask, to stop such nonsense and cease to think, as Hume apparently did, that what is called "human nature" is not only the source of knowledge but also the only thing that we know anything about? Is it not time to stop identifying experience with what we experience and trying to have philosophies of "pure experience"? Our natural status is as inseparably bound up with Nature as is that of the largest star or the smallest microbe.

Being the kind of beings that we are, living in and with Nature in a union intimate and profound, we profit by reading her signs and symbols. The candle may draw us when babies as it does the moth to be burnt by its flame, but it makes us even then cautious about repeating the experience. To be exceptionally teachable belongs to our natural status. The moth does not seem to learn that candles scorch. Its natural status is different from ours, for, even in our cradles we are quick logicians, turning the sight of a flame into an expectation of what may happen to a finger, into knowledge of the way candles behave. Soon we are using candles to lighten our darkness. Nature responds. Later we make candle-power a measure of how much light. Later we try to measure the velocity of light, and look, not to our ability, but to Nature for the answer. Such is the path to knowledge. We go from what Nature suggests in consequence of our intimacy with her and her intimacy with us to what we affirm Nature to be, distinguishing between her vital presence and something in that presence which we can express as knowledge of what she is—from what Nature is to what she is found out to be, guided by suggesting candles. Such is the way of knowledge. We find no other even when we turn around and retrace our steps, calling the forward way induction and the reverse of it deduction.

As we follow the way carefully, trying to avoid erring excursions which lead us off the track of our pursuit, we find ourselves more and more compelled to look upon Nature as a coherent and integrated system, an order, a cosmos, a universe which can find expression in language and, so expressed, be handed on from generation to generation and be from generation to generation improved. Much warfare, illusion, debate, and controversy attend the long tradition. A commonly accepted understanding is not always easy to obtain. But a good understanding is easy to define. Aristotle defined it by an illustration suitable for all purposes when he pointed out that a man without knowledge may be surprised that the diagonal and side of a square are not commensurable, while the geometer would be surprised if they were. Understanding is the elimination of surprise. We do not eliminate it; Nature does that. The man with a crowbar may be surprised at its effectiveness, just as many of us may be in seeing how easily great weights are hoisted by block and tackle. Neither is surprising to one who knows mechanics. We may be surprised that we have tuberculosis; the bacteriologist is not. Aristotle may be cited again in a somewhat cryptic statement to the effect that all knowledge proceeds from what is better known to us to what is naturally better known. It is as if Nature possessed without acquiring it the knowledge we acquire—possessed at any rate something inherent which can be translated into human speech, thereby eliminating surprise from anything that happens. Therein lies the power of knowledge. The airplane and the radio are surprising human inventions; but it would be more surprising, knowing what we do about Nature, if they could not be invented. And what but our ignorance makes it surprising that a spider can spin a web to catch flies in a world where the thing is done? Who would dare set a limit to Nature's symbolic power? From our ignorance we go to her knowledge, not only to Nature familiar but also to a nature understood.

The naturally effective symbolism which is developed by us into knowledge arises from natural events or occurrences or from what may well be called Nature's behavior. Our expectations, even when wayward, follow clues in the natural courses of events, as when changing weather comes with changing wind. But Nature—that universal manuscript, the stars, the seasons, the spectacle of birth and death, of cities and wars, heaven and earth, the sea, and all that in them is, the setting of human history—is not cognitively a symbol of anything. This I would emphasize. I do not mean that we never regard it as a symbol, for that would be to fly in the face of facts. It has often been looked upon as a symbol of God's glory, as the evidence of his creative power, as the justification of his ways to man. Sir Thomas Browne, in addition to calling it a manuscript, called it "God's servant" who can teach us much divinity. This I could readily believe. The spectacle of Nature does not diminish in grandeur the more it is contemplated. Its effect is overwhelming and can humble us to our knees, leaving even the hard-headed of us touched with awe. When face to face with Nature's sublimity and impartial indifference and free from taint of superstition, we must confess ourselves in the presence of our owner, confess no rights or privileges of our own, confess ourselves useless and needless unless we can justify our existence by a dignity it might attain. Otherwise we look pretty cheap, for all our cities and wars. The lilies of the field look a little better. To regard Nature as the symbol of God's glory is not at all strange or unnatural. It is very human. It is, perhaps, the thing we are ultimately led to do when, thoroughly sophisticated, disillusioned and disenchanted, we take ourselves seriously in hand and ask what is our business here? Then we stand confronted by the Ancient of Days.

Yet this cannot be set down as an increment to knowledge even if we are now warranted in saying that we know that there is ultimately necessary existence if contingent existence like ours is to be, that we are dependent on it, not it on us, and that it holds us, as it were, in the hollow of its hand. But this is not knowledge of Nature. It is rather intimacy with Nature peculiarly and powerfully heightened, an experience of the loss of our selves, to find them again made or marred as that experience breeds aspiration or indifference. The experience may be studied. We may acquire knowledge of its power and operation; but we must take it for just what it is, a genuine natural experience from which important consequences flow for the lives and fortunes of men.

Nature's own evident being has sometimes been regarded as symbolic in an indirect and elliptical way which raises the question of a criterion for knowledge to which I have already referred.[3] No one needs to be told that unless we are affected by our surroundings we have no knowledge of them. If, however, we turn so obvious a circumstance into the question whether our surroundings are in their own right what they are to us when we are affected by them, we have a question which has frequently been answered by affirming that what they are to us is symbolic of what they are in their own independence or is a substitute for it. We now have a strange problem of knowledge on our hands which ought to be solved as a problem generally. It is not the problem of advancing natural knowledge, but one of finding an antecedent criterion which will determine how far such knowledge *is* knowledge or how far knowledge of our surroundings is *real* knowledge of what they are. Of course one may stoutly affirm that our surroundings are the same in both cases, that the garage into which we drive our car to let it remain overnight is the identical garage in which it actually remains during that period, but one so affirming will be challenged to demonstrate how that can be *known*. I should like to avoid being embroiled in such controversy.

I have called this way of regarding Nature as symbolic, indirect, and elliptical. That it is indirect should, I think, be clear from the preceding paragraph because it begins, not with an analysis of what our surroundings actually are in our dealings with them, but with a hypothetical question about their status. It is elliptical because it overlooks the fact that the question raised cannot be answered unless it is possible to answer it in one context. In other words, it cannot be intelligibly answered unless our surroundings when we are not affected by them and also when we are, are *both* somehow accessible to the questioner. If they are not, both question and answers are nonsense. That is something which, I hope, this essay will clarify without committing me to an answer. Nature, I find, does not pose the mooted question. She poses questions of a different sort: Since our surroundings are spatial, what is space? Since they are temporal, what is time? Since knowledge of them is expressible in language, what is language? So far as such questions are conceived, they are answerable only by an analysis of how our natural knowledge is actually built up. It is immaterial to me whether the analysis I shall attempt leaves me classified as idealist or realist. I hope it will leave me having told the truth in some measure.

Why is the mooted question asked? As I review the literature, I find that the answer is that the problem of perception is put before the problem of knowledge in such a way that the former becomes one of the validity and possibility of knowledge, not one of examining the mechanism of perception, in spite of the fact that such an examination is admitted to give us knowledge of what that mechanism is. But why is *this* done? The answer is best exhibited by citing illustrations like the following:

> External objects are known not intuitively but through the medium of a substitute. This is proved by the fact that when a distant cannon is fired the flash is seen before the sound is heard. The seen flash and the heard sound are both, in different degrees, *later* than the real event, and, therefore, cannot be identical with it. In looking up at the starry vault, we see simultaneously objects that existed and from which light set out a varying number of centuries ago; these past objects are known by a single substitute which contains them all and is in the present. In double vision *two* substitutes are seen when there is but one thing—a clear proof that they are substitutes.[4]

In other words, peculiarities in what we perceive prove that what we perceive is a substitute for the known objects and events that produce those peculiarities. All this looks to me like relying on the validity of natural knowledge—optics for example—to prove that there are substitutes for its objects in order that we may know what those objects are. The habit of regarding what we perceive as knowledge of something else—as if two moons seen were knowledge of one moon existing, or one star, like Vega, seen, were knowledge of a double star—is a habit I regard as vicious. I shall, however, have occasion to refer to it repeatedly in the course of this essay. Knowledge is of what we perceive, and I have named that "Nature." I can find, however, no convincing reason for turning what we perceive into a substitute for something else. I do not find Nature to be symbolic in that sense. . . .

Objectivity

Since knowledge is in the interest of better living, and since our success in acquiring it is measured by Nature's clarifying responses to our questions, knowledge should be disinterested or objective. A man who looks to Nature, not for truth, but for a confirmation of his own prejudices, is not highly commended. He is not disinterested. His intellectual integrity is under suspicion. We usually forgive mistakes when they are made accidentally and even when a man, sure that he is on the right track, overlooks facts which are evident to a less confident person. Suspicion of one's own conclusions is recommended. Willful distortion of evidence, however, and stubbornness in admitting it when adverse are hard to forgive. Truth is sacred, so much so that calling a man a liar, even when he is, usually causes him to appeal to force in his own justification. He prefers to be told that he may be mistaken. Then he is less irritated, content that a euphemism has avoided the nasty word. All this is a little curious—this obligation to be disinterested in our own interest, to accept truth even when it hurts, to put ourselves out of the way and let Nature alone decide, no matter what the consequences are. Yet we are under that obligation and under it naturally. We need neither schools nor parents to acquaint us with it. An infant's first cry is proof enough. It has lost its familiar world and cries for restoration of familiarity, finding it at its mother's breast. Objectivity has then been recovered, recovered in the baby's interest.

The illustration is not fantastic. We are like babies, content to be at Nature's breast so long as we are not discontented and disturbed. We are born of her and so enfolded that to be enfolded without disturbance is to be at peace. Again I am emphasizing the obvious. I do so because in this instance of it we find what objectivity is. It is far more a state of nature than a state of mind and is the latter only because something happens to us as we search for it. Objectivity is Nature with or without our crying, but as if we did not cry or as if we had never been born. It is Nature undisturbed by our presence, although our disturbances and presence are among her events. Now, dialectically, there is an argument that objectivity is impossible for us to attain. It is well illustrated both by Berkeley and by Kant and in much the same way, although their idiosyncrasies in the presentation of it obscure the likeness. Berkeley argued that what perceiving beings perceive is objective to their minds because not of their creation; he strangely concluded that God also perceives, but that what he perceives he also creates. Kant argued that perceiving beings perceive the experienced world of space and time and that the world is objective to them because experience makes it so; he strangely concluded that experience is not otherwise objective. With Berkeley *real* objectivity was an association of spirits; with Kant, an association of "things-in-themselves." In neither case could the association be delivered. In both cases it was assumed, and assumed to be capable of delivering the circumstances responsible for the search for it. When we search for Nature as if she were without our presence, how can our presence find her?

The dialectical argument does no more than leave us with the problem of creation on our hands, the solution of which is irrelevant to our knowledge. I use the word "creature" frequently and could readily believe nature to be created, for she often does not seem to be wholly self-sustaining. But I do not see how this belief, if justified, could alter human knowledge of a created world or free us from the obligation of disinterestedness. So in considering objectivity I am not impressed by dialectical arguments. I do not have to be reminded that I cannot get myself outside of Nature. I turn, therefore, to an analysis of what happens when I try.

When we ask in our own interest what Nature is as over against oursleves, the sense of individuality is heightened. We are turned into persons each of whose personal histories has an absorbing interest of its own. We do not cease to be residents of Nature, but become residents with the sense of possessing and being possessed acute. There is established a kind of trinity, *Nature* and *you* and *I,* with these three in a dramatic unity in which the fortunes of the *I* are at stake. Nature becomes *my* world, yet you and Nature are there to be taken into account. The consequence is that this very circumstance forces us to take them into account objectively. This is not a matter of our own choosing, as is sufficiently proved by the fact that we commonly wish that all that is objective were amenable to our wishes or our prayers. The story of Aladdin and his lamp is not instructive. The story of Midas is. And a common proverb warns us that we cannot have our cake and eat it too. All this indicates a natural wisdom which is forced upon us despite ourselves, the power of which increases as we proceed. It drives us to consider ourselves and to be so ultimately reflective that the bare fact of being reflective becomes the core of our being and all else goes into Nature as a single integrated system demanding of us that we find out what such an integrated system is. Our bodies have not lost their own integrity. They are as passionate as they were before, but they have become minds, looking as it were through an open door at Nature going on of herself.

That is the only meaning of objectivity I can find that suits the character of our experience of Nature. Too many who talk about Nature, explore her ways, and try to solve the problems she suggests seem to forget that the universe of their discourse is none other than the universe at their door. They talk sometimes as if it were an alien universe which explains their own. They expect to be understood and convincing; but they pay little attention to that expectation, although it is the natural and compulsory admission of the commonly accepted and accessible world, in which the births of minds is as natural as the birth of babies, the coming of seeds to fruitage, or the rolling of a stone downhill. Does the solving of a problem mean anything else than the discovery of its solution? Where then does one go for a solution—to his own mind or to Nature objective? Even those "brain-twisters" with which we socially amuse ourselves illustrate the answer. Given six matches, arrange them so that they will form four equilateral triangles the sides of which equal a match in length. How often have we seen even the acute and agile work at that problem, give it up as unsolvable, and even wager that it is unsolvable. How foolish they feel when they discover that Nature solves it by providing something more than the surface of a table. Going to Nature to discover solutions is something quite different from going to something else to discover Nature. The universe of discourse may change in language when we become scientific, but it does not change in objectivity.

That disinterestedness and objectivity are names for the same natural occurrence needs now no further exposition. The failure to solve that match puzzle on the table's surface is objective in spite of our interest in trying to solve it there. Nature won't let it be solved that way. She is amused at the stupidity of one who tries. Personifying her thus, as if she laughed and cried, is an inversion of our own sense of detachment when objectivity is in force. We are then like onlookers at a play in which we have neither part nor responsibility, while the play goes on exhibiting its actors comically or tragically caught in their destiny in spite of their attempts to escape it. That "theater" and "theory" are verbally akin is more than accident. I often think of Lucretius theorizing about Nature in his poem *De rerum natura,* how, having glorified the spring as the work of Venus, he proceeded to instruct Memmius how all that glory and much besides came originally from tiny first bodies in the void, like motes in sunbeams, and would finally return to them. There they stood watching the vast panorama unroll before their imagination, as calm and aloof as that suave man of the second book of the poem who, safe and undisturbed on shore, watched another's great labor with the great and storm-tossed sea.

Objectivity has that effect upon us, giving us the sense of truth approached or attained, of something in Nature which is inevitable, without which Nature could not be what she is. That philosophical excitement of a few years ago known as "pragmatism" had the great merit of reminding us that Nature, not our wit, controls and evaluates all our definitions and conjectures in the use of them and that the internal logical consistency of a theory is not the ultimate guarantee of its validity or worth. All that was and is salutary. But truth is not "that which works" but something in Nature that is worked with. The facts that we have found little of it and have frequently to revise what we thought we had found are no proof to the contrary; for all inquiry proceeds governed by the principle that there is a way of an eagle in the air, of a serpent on a rock, of a fish in the midst of the sea, of a man with a maid, quite irrespective of our understanding it. Wherever we are lost, there is a way home whether we find it or not. That principle is misread when named a principle of "human nature," as Hume would have it, or a presupposition of all science, as some others affirm. It is a principle of Nature. Who in his senses can sincerely assert that a habit of man or the presupposition of anybody has anything to do with a river finding its way to the sea or our finding it out? We have our habits, and we make presuppositions as we go along, but Nature is the critic of them. Faith in her principles, if one will speak of faith, is not wishful thinking or any hypothesis that governs human understanding. There is an order in Nature which we flout at our peril. The many-times-quoted opening sentence of Bacon's essay "Of Truth" deserves repetition because those who do not jest, but stay for answer, are those who learn.

Objectivity is, moreover, a natural intensification of individuality. I have already suggested this when referring to Lucretius. It is like having the universe lie at one's door without entering one's house, or like a beholding of Nature which is both attentive and passive. The experience is not extraordinary. We have it every time we go sight-seeing. The more attentive we are to the scene, the more the scene isolates us from it as if it were pushing us out and we were passively submitting. In order to be calm, we are advised to relax; the advice is so good that relaxation is often prescribed as the best of medicines and often pushed so far that it is recommended as a remedy for all our ills, on the theory that if we relaxed completely Nature would do the rest and for our good. Striving and crying is what ruins us. We should stop it and let Nature take her course. "Why so hot, little man?" That question of Emerson's was asked, as I remember, to convince us of the Oversoul.

It may be asked just as well to convince us of Nature. It is asking for our individual exclusion, although we are expected to remain in Nature. That is what I mean by an intensification of individuality. It is often regarded as something only psychological.

It is psychological, but I hesitate to add the "only." It looks to me too much like a natural principle which our knowledge does not escape. Why so hot, little atom? What can *you* do when "left to yourself"? Yet I must isolate you and even try to break you up in spite of your name. That is one sort of thing we are doing all the time—dividing atoms and trying to find the smallest. Every individual, whether large or small, is a challenge to divide it. It is an atom in its individuality. That is sufficiently proved by dividing a man in two or a line in two, for after the division that which has been divided is no longer the individual as it was before. *An* individuality has been lost. The new individuals are less *intense*. There is obviously a loss of integrity when a man or a line is divided. An intense effectiveness is lost. One need try no more elaborate experiment than that of retying a package after the string with which it was originally tied has been cut. Multiplying illustrations of trying to find *the* atom by division or breaking up may readily lead to thinking of Nature as a hierarchy of individuals with varying degrees of intensification, which have, for all that, a residence in common— from the atom of modern science, which does not build guns to bombard itself to pieces, to the human atoms that do and that sometimes deliberately commit suicide with a gun. Such a theory of Nature looks quite intelligible and compelling when we divide, but not so much so when we start putting the pieces together again, for then we find ourselves in need of some sort of glue. Yet if man can break up the atom in Nature, atomic theories ought to remove all surprise that we see and hear beyond our bodies or think of places and times remote from them. We ought not to be surprised that Nature seems comprehensible to some individuals in such a way that the universe lies at their door, which opens—opens out into its immensities and minutenesses—while they stay at home trying to see things without any refraction due to their own mode of living. They illustrate the intensity of individuality at a maximum or intimacy with Nature so intense that bodily individuality is lost in the consequent objectivity. "The union of the mind with the whole of Nature"—to borrow Spinoza's words—may sound like a grandiose expression, but it is illustrated, however limitedly, in every act of thought.

Although in objectivity we are passive in the sense I have indicated, the attainment of objectivity leads to the release of power. In objectivity we discover our freedom. I see no merit in trying to solve the "problem" of the "freedom of the will" or in arguing whether we are "fated or free." I always suspect some failure in analyzing what knowledge factually is or some confusing of the discovery of the necessary conditions under which an action can be performed with the performing of the action; as if the binomial theorem actually developed $(x + y)^2$. I dare affirm, quite confident that I am speaking the truth, that neither knowledge nor what is known *does* anything. I am sometimes tempted to wish that they did, trying to delude myself into believing that we should then live happily forever after. But, as I have said, the attainment of objectivity leads to the release of power. Then actions can be performed which were not performed before. Knowledge can be applied. What possible sense is there in discussing whether it can be or not when it actually is? We do not discover our freedom by futilely trying to break endless chains of causation. We discover it in the release of power through objectivity and in applying knowledge. That is why we hold objectivity sacred, insist on disinterestedness and that "teachers" especially should be left free to tell the truth even when it hurts and not be like those "politicians" who tell it only to please, to enrage, or to delude their hearers. That puts a heavy responsibility on teachers, forbidding them to turn "academic freedom" into a shelter for security of tenure, incompetence, ignorance, and political pressure. Objectivity is too sacred for that, and I could wish that the expression "academic freedom" had never been invented. It clouds too many issues. It fosters the habit of going to school to learn and stopping there for a diploma of some sort, instead of going through school to Nature which lies expansed to all and is the only place where truth is eventually found. She is the great teacher, and the proper aim of all human teaching is to get rid of other teachers as soon as possible and to turn children into adults who will not have to be under tutelage their whole life long. That is the road to freedom.

Notes

1. *Scepticism and Animal Faith* (New York: Scribner's, 1924), p. x.

2. For literature on the subject see A. O. Lovejoy's "The Paradox of the Time-retarding Journey," *Philosophical Review* 40 (January, March, 1931): 48–68, 153–67.

3. The literature on the subject is voluminous. The examination of it reveals how philosophers are often classified as empiricists, realists, idealists, monists, dualists, and the like. *The Revolt Against Dualism,* by A. O. Lovejoy (Chicago: Open Court; New York: Norton, 1930), is written in support of "dualism" and contains an expert presentation of the evidence for and against it. C. A. Strong's *Creed for Sceptics* (London: Macmillan, 1936) offers an ingenious solution of the problem in support of "critical realism."

4. C. A. Strong, *Creed for Sceptics,* p. 1. I do not overlook the fact that Strong, who has spent his studious life on the problem involved, has dealt with it in this work with acumen. He impresses me, however, not as having solved it, but as having removed it.

Section 2

The Nature of Nature:
Materialism and Pluralism

In his *Scepticism and Animal Faith,* published in 1923, Santayana referred
to himself as a materialist, "apparently the only one living." Roy Wood
Sellars must have been surprised to read Santayana's self-description,
since Sellars had already been advocating a form of materialism for
several years, and he would continue to do so throughout his life. R. W.
Sellars was born in Ontario in 1880, and like Woodbridge he soon
after moved with his family to Michigan. He studied philosophy at
the University of Michigan, graduating in 1903 and returning as an
instructor in 1905. He received his doctorate there in 1909, taught at
the University of Michigan until his retirement in 1950, and died in
Ann Arbor in 1973. Sellars had been active in the development of philosophic realism early in his career, and he later became interested in
articulating a materialist ontology which would be appropriate to naturalism. In the article reproduced here, which was first published in 1944,
Sellars argues for a materialism which is neither reductionistic nor
atomistic, thereby preserving naturalism's emphasis on the variety of
nature and on the complex relational character of natural entities.

Nineteen forty-four was a significant date in the development of
naturalism in the United States, since it was the year *Naturalism and
the Human Spirit,* edited by Yervant V. Krikorian, was published by

Columbia University Press. The book is a collection of articles by a number of philosophers, most of whom at that time were still early in their careers, and many of them are represented in this volume. The book is important in the history of philosophic naturalism because it represents something of a manifesto of what might be called "Columbia naturalism," and its publication was the occasion for a good deal of critical discussion. One of the responses to the naturalist spirit expressed in the book was W. H. Sheldon's "Critique of Naturalism," which appeared in the *Journal of Philosophy* in 1945. In it Sheldon "accuses" naturalism of being little more than a disguised version of materialism, a philosophic position which he regarded as long since discredited. The article reprinted here by John Dewey, Sidney Hook and Ernest Nagel was written as a response to Sheldon.

Dewey, Hook, and Nagel were all contributors to *Naturalism and the Human Spirit,* with Dewey being the one representative of the older generation. Dewey was born in Burlington, Vermont, in 1859, and received his doctorate from the Johns Hopkins University. He began his teaching career at the University of Michigan, but he moved in 1894 to the University of Chicago, where he continued his work in philosophy and developed his theoretical and practical studies in education through the "Laboratory School," which he founded. Dewey resigned from the University of Chicago in 1904, and the next year joined the Department of Philosophy and Psychology at Columbia, where he worked until the end of his career. Dewey died in 1952. Sidney Hook, born in 1902, attended the City College of New York, where he was a student of Morris R. Cohen, and graduate school at Columbia, where he studied with John Dewey and received a doctorate in 1927. Hook taught philosophy at New York University from 1927 until his retirement in 1968. Ernest Nagel was born in 1901 in Czechoslovakia, and like Hook attended the City College of New York. In 1930 he received a doctorate in philosophy from Columbia, where he taught from 1931 until his retirement.

One of the interesting things about the article by Dewey, Hook, and Nagel is that unlike Sellars, or Santayana, none of them were staunch advocates of materialism. The individual articles they contributed to *Naturalism and the Human Spirit* bear an instrumentalist or pragmatist stamp more than anything else, and Dewey was often an outspoken critic of materialism. Yet in response to Sheldon's criticisms they found themselves prepared to associate naturalism with materialism of a certain kind. Like Sellars, the three authors explicitly avoid the reductionism of traditional materialism, and they argue for a materialist reading of the scientific method, which they advocate as the most reliable method of achieving knowledge, though not as the paradigmatic form of experience.

Notwithstanding the sort of materialism which Dewey, Hook, and Nagel defended, it remains the case that the naturalism which developed out of Columbia, especially in the work of John Herman Randall, Jr., and Justus Buchler, was pluralist rather than materialist in character. Born in 1899 in Grand Rapids, Michigan, Randall received all his higher education at Columbia, where he studied with Woodbridge and Dewey, finishing his doctorate in 1922. He joined the philosophy department as an instructor in 1920, and taught there for his entire career. Buchler was born in 1914 in New York City, graduating from City College in 1934 and receiving his doctorate from Columbia in 1939. He became an instructor at Columbia in 1937, and he remained a member of Columbia's philosophy department until 1971, when he became Distinguished Professor of Philosophy at the State University of New York at Stony Brook. Buchler retired from teaching in 1981, and died in 1991.

One of the reasons neither Randall nor Buchler have been inclined to accept materialism is that for both of them nature is irreducibly plural, and they would argue that there is no way to ascribe a general priority to one aspect of nature, to matter, without distorting or misrepresenting the variety and plurality of nature. Nature, on this sort of view, is not a single, all-inclusive system or unity, which raises two questions—what kinds of unity are there in nature and what is their source? In his essay Randall answers that unification is provided by human relations with and participation in natural processes. Science and knowledge, myth and symbol, logic and theology, discourse and language are what Randall calls "connectives," which provide unity in nature and which are "functionally real." One must be careful not to misunderstand Randall here. He is not saying that these connectives, and therefore unity itself, are human additions to or a subjective filter over an objective reality; on the contrary, connectives are fully natural, and they are themselves aspects of what Randall calls Substance, the natural processes which include human beings.

By locating the source of natural unity where he does, Randall demonstrates an affinity with the tendency, also evident in Dewey, to read nature in terms of human activity. Buchler, though his thought was very much influenced by Randall, is uncomfortable according such a central role to human beings in a metaphysics of nature. On his view natural unity is to be found in the very structure of natural entities and processes, human or otherwise. To clarify and refine that idea Buchler developed a highly original set of philosophic concepts which together convey his sense of nature's irreducible plurality and variety. In the article reprinted here, which appeared in 1978 and was his final published essay, Buchler explores the various meanings of the term "nature," and describes how his own philosophic categories help to provide a positive conception of nature.

1

Reformed Materialism and Intrinsic Endurance*

Roy Wood Sellars

There are optional horizons in philosophy. Thus one can ignore ontology or one can commit oneself to the ontological enterprise and grapple, as best one can, with some rather abstract distinctions and their implications. Pragmatism and positivism have, in the main, made the first choice and within that horizon have done, as all acknowledge, admirable analytic work. Realism, on the other hand, has in its various modes accepted an ontological horizon. Even such opposing positions as materialism and neo-Thomism have at least this much in common, that they take ontological categories seriously.

The drift of my own thought has been in the direction of a reformed materialism less dominated by extreme atomism and strict mechanical notions than has usually been the case in materialism. Recognition is given to internal relations, to integration, to immanent causality, to emergence and local wholeness. At the same time, epistemological reflection

*Originally published in R. W. Sellars, *Philosophical Review* 53 (1944): 359–82. Subsequently published in R. W. Sellars, *Principles of Emergent Realism* (St. Louis, Mo.: Warren H. Green, Inc., 1970), pp. 150–73. Reprinted by permission.

has convinced me that material systems have far more to them than is grasped by abstract scientific knowledge about their composition and properties. Dualistic traditions have been hurtful here. Likewise injurious has been the Humian denial of causal agency. It is my opinion that we must think more along the lines of a reformed notion of *substantive being* fully capable of doing justice to becoming, events, and process.

Now, as I see the ontological situation, materialism reformed along these lines is confronted by ontologies having a theistic dimension. It is, I take it, the very genius of all forms of materialism to postulate the intrinsic endurance and immanent existence of material systems. Theism, on the other hand, looks upon nature and natural things as pointing beyond themselves for their endurance and existence. Neo-Thomism is very frank about this and conceives *esse,* or existence, as something contributed by God to the vast range of essences or quiddities. And such existence is different in different things, since it is received and not absolute. Non-catholic writers, such as Whitehead and Parker, approach the question from different assumptions; and yet I sense in them the postulate of dependent, or contributed, existence.

It is my desire in the present paper to connect naturalism with the principle of intrinsic endurance and to explore the meanings to be given to such terms as matter, being, and existence, within such a context. It is my intention to use neo-Thomism largely as a foil and to contrast its hylomorphism and its conception of substance and existence with those of reformed materialism. But I shall raise questions which, I feel sure, all antinaturalists will want to debate. Not only will I give definitions but I will also indicate cosmological principles dealing with such topics as conservation, intrinsic endurance and becoming, being and nothing, existence and nonexistence of denotables, eternity, quantity of being and quality, generation and corruption. In short, I shall permit myself something of an ontological debauch.

Now it goes without saying that a philosophically respectable materialism must have some epistemological and ontological subtlety. Atomic materialism united with classical mechanics had neither. The only intrinsic endurance it could think of was Eleatic. But in these energistic and evolutionary days the Eleatic types of intrinsic endurance is out of the question. Intrinsic endurance must be linked with activity, relations, and conservation. It cannot be a static permanence, or, as Whitehead calls it, simple endurance. All this sums up to my conviction that the postulates essential to a nonreductive materialism have as yet scarcely been explored.

It is relevant to recall that, during the first two decades of this century, the most persistent philosophical problem outside the epistemological field was that of the conquest of Cartesian dualism. How could mind and matter be brought together? And it is worthy of note that the dependence of these terms upon a God as a more primary substance was largely disregarded. Cartesian dualism, so conceived, found its focus in the mind-body problem. Radical empiricism and neutralism represented one line of approach which is, perhaps, still reflected in the positivist's double-language formula. The critical realist was, as naturally, led to explore the possibilities such as a double knowledge of the organism and the replacement of reductive mechanism by more evolutionary and integrative principles.

In those days the general drift in American philosophy—far more, I take it, than in English—was toward some sort of naturalism. And I do not say that is still the case. But, for various cultural reasons, theism cannot now so easily be left out of the picture. Naturalism is being challenged to state and defend its postulates. Theologically inclined physicists have entered the lists; and, in the realm of technical philosophy, we have such distinguished thinkers as Maritain, Gilson, Whitehead, Montague, Parker, Northrop, and Hartshorne, standing for some form or other of theism.

Now anyone who has an ontological horizon cannot brush this challenge off as easily as can the pragmatist or the positivist. An existential question is at stake and so a mere redefinition of God as an ideal does not meet the issue.

It is my conviction that this theistic challenge to naturalism is both desirable and stimulating. It should force the naturalistic physical realist to explore his most basic assumptions. In my own thinking, at least, it has led to a study of the existential theory implied by materialism. Of course, the type of materialism must first pass other tests. It must be of a philosophical kind responsive to the niceties of theory of knowledge. The name is of less consequence. It can be called the new materialism, reformed materialism, qualitative materialism—all expressions which

I have used.[1] At this philosophical level inert brickbats are left behind and are replaced by categorical analyses. Existence, stuff, activity, relations, space, time, endurance, becoming, all these must be clarified and integrated. All of which means that materialism must be stepped up philosophically.

As I see it, the materialist holds that the cosmos is material in nature *and exists in its own right*. To assert this is to deny the contingency of the world. Another way of putting it is to affirm the *intrinsic endurance* of physical systems in their very becoming.

Now it is this principle that theism denies whether in terms of creation *ex nihilo,* most characteristic of Christian philosophies, or in terms of emanation or Platonic ingredience. The antimaterialist holds either that there is no material world (the idealistic alternative so dear to liberal Protestantism) or that it has a secondary, or derived, sort of existence. There are, of course, all sorts of philosophical complications and combinations. Thus Montague and Northrop seem to hold that the physical world needs supplementation to account for order and evolution. But I am, at present chiefly interested in the question of *aseity* as against contingency.

This question is, of course, a hoary one. Looking up *aseity* in the Oxford Dictionary, I found three interesting quotations: "The natural world for any self stability, aseity, or essential immutability of its own may again cease to be"; "By what mysterious light have you discovered that aseity is entail'd on matter?"; "The obscure and abysmal subject of the divine aseity." To the positivist, no doubt, such quotations reflect obscurantism. To the physical realist they do not. It is important to get clear ideas about the meaning of existence and to connect them up with endurance and becoming. I shall, therefore, be engaged in the present article in looking at such categories from a materialist's point of view. A contrasting position is always of value in such matters; and so I shall employ neo-Thomism . . . , partly because its postulates are so definite and partly because its Aristotelian principles enable me to bring out a contrasting way of handling generation and corruption. For the Thomist there are two modes of existence, the divine and the created; and existence is rather a mysterious *transcendental* along with truth and perfection. I may as well say at once that I shall argue against these transcendentals and change existence into the factual recognition of *existency,* so that to be a denotable entails existence. While I shall not discuss truth as a transcendental, it is obvious that, for the materialist, it cannot be a harmony between essence and the eternal thought of God, while perfection dissolves into properties and triadically founded valuations. All of which indicates that neo-Thomism helps to bring the categories of materialism into relief. Now, while I shall employ Christian Aristotelianism as a contrast, I shall also have in mind Whitehead's union of theism and reformed subjectivism. . . .

Metaphysics has been so much associated with the postulation of a higher reality beyond nature, with a meta-physics, that I have preferred the more neutral term ontology. I note that Marxists have the same preference, as also does Santayana. Materialism, then, is an ontology isomorphic with modern science. Much could be said for the post-Aristotelian division of philosophy into physics, logic, and ethics. But the science of physics, as it increasingly expressed metric knowledge about nature and retreated from natural philosophy (wisely, I think), came to engross the first term of this trinity. But must not the science of physics give us knowledge about physical existence? Materialism holds this belief and is an ontology.

After considerable reflection I have chosen the expression, intrinsic endurance, in place of simple endurance. While intrinsic endurance rejects dependent, derived, or contributed, endurance, it does not entail passivity, Eleatic fixity, or brickbatness. Matter I take to be active, dynamic, relational, and self-organizing. It is an endurance which goes with activity for which I am contending. All composite existents which emerge are generated and corrupted, are maintained by activity. My divergence from *eventism* has other roots than a desire to defend outgrown notions of substance. Rather is it the expression of realism, as against sensation-alism, and reflects the recognition of structure, ontological causality, *and the generation of composite wholes.* Eventism does not seem to me to do justice to unavoidable categories. Thus those who build upon sensations and being, as Russell and Whitehead do, cannot accept sub-stantiveness and force. There is a perpetual perishing of consciousness which, as I pointed out long ago in an article, is not conserved. What, then, can possess intrinsic endurance? Is it creativity? God? the permanent possibility of sensibilia? or material being? *Or can we get along without intrinsic endurance?*

*   *   *

I

Four primary principles of the new materialism may be stated as follows: (1) stuff or material, (2) dynamic connections and organization, (3) intrinsic endurance, and (4) levels of integrative and efficient causality. These principles qualify one another.

Stuff, or material, is a category of a fairly complex sort. It reflects the common notion of thinghood in terms of recoverable constituents. There is danger here since pattern and organization tend to be neglected as they were in traditional mechanical notions. I shall have something to say about this point in the later discussion of quality. Nor is this all. The concept of stuff has a relational moment. Here it ranges from the artist's idea of a medium upon which to work to the scientist's more analytic perspective. The term is realistic, denotative, manipulative, analytic, and synthetic. It does not imply that we need know very much about the intrinsic nature of materials. To the philosopher the concept of stuff, or material, is a challenge to categorical analysis. Plasticity, activity, form-making, recoverableness, intrinsic endurance, all stand out for comprehension.

And this brings us to the consideration of connections and organization. I note that Pepper and many others assume that materialism involves mechanicalism. That, surely, is a prejudice. Why should materialism lag behind science? Classical materialism thought in terms of classical physics, that is, in terms of Eleatic particles having *simple endurance* of the static variety. But there is nothing about materialism as an ontology which limits it to such outworn postulates. From the very beginning of my thinking I rejected Newtonian absolute space and time and made both space and time, ontologically speaking, adjectival and relational. And I have always argued that s and t as metric qualities presuppose space and time as ontological characteristics of matter. Particles must be conceived in terms of connections, causal activities, fields. And this signifies that ontological time is to be correlated with *change of constitution* but not with a perpetual perishing of matter.

I shall, in fact, argue that activity and intrinsic endurance are not contradictory.

From its inception in Greek thought materialism emphasized the positive and independent nature of matter. It did not depend upon the God nor was it under the control of purposes or ends external to itself. Instead, it endured in its own right, was self-sufficient and self-concerned. And it was the possession of these characteristics that made it from the first *the logical correlate of naturalism*. Let us admit at once that intrinsic endurance was conceived too simply and statically in traditional materialism, as it was later in classical physics. Changes were thought of as not involving the atoms themselves and reducible to mere shifts of position. This compromise with Eleaticism satisfied the demands of elementary physics and a philosophy hardly awake to the requirements of biology and psychology.

But I would still hold it true that the genius of materialism, as of naturalism, requires an intrinsic endurance, or self-conservation, on the part of material being. Such endurance must be underived and ultimate. And this, I take it, is a flat rejection of the contingency of nature. We shall have more to say about this as we come to distinguish between the existence of any denotable and the intrinsic endurance of material being. . . .

II

Let it be noted, then, that the overhauling of materialism must needs be a drastic one to make it compatible with evolutionary naturalism. There is no excuse for tying it down to past reductive and mechanical postulates. Simple location must not mean the denial of dynamic connections. At the most it means something of the nature of the law of inverse squares. Even the general relativity theory admits determinable warpings expressive of the localization of matter. In reading Eddington on *The Philosophy of Physical Science* I find that the only kind of realism he is acquainted with is the Joadian type and I have considerable sympathy with his criticism of it. To make sensations distinct from sensings and thoughts independent of thinking does not appeal to the critical realist. Yet Eddington's conception of mind seems to me unempirical. But I have not the space to consider in detail his epistemology. Jeans, on the other hand, has developed a Kantian kid of agnosticism combined with an ontological Platonism. In any case both have developed a recognition of the difference between the form of scientific knowledge-about and *being*. To the philosopher this points to the need of the clarification of categories. Being, stuff, space, time, causality, as ontological, must be distinguished from their cognitive translation.[2] To use Professor Hall's term, categories are *constants*; and we should not expect ontological statements to be verifiable in quite the fashion of predictive, scientific theories.[3]

It is important to bear in mind that traditional materialism not only had no adequate epistemology back of it but was identified with dualistic assumptions which left material being a washed-out abstraction, such as mere extension, with no positive, intrinsic content. I am led to think of this tradition when I am told that mine is an agnostic kind of materialism. Rather is it a protest against these dualistic caricatures.[4] As I see it, science does not reduce material being to a mere quality but merely deciphers the metric quantities obtainable by its technique. It is such *knowledge about* material systems. It is the very import of ontology to deny that being can be reduced to knowledge. Surely it has been one of the weaknesses of idealism to flirt with such a reduction. Materialism and Aristotelian philosophies have been far healthier in this respect. Matter as *being* must have a positive and determinate content. Its actuality cannot be vacuous. But the materialist takes it to be wise not to jump too hastily to the panpsychistic universalization of feeling as a kind of sample. Have we not expected too much from external knowledge resting on sensory disclosures aided by metrical techniques? Ontology puts scientific knowledge in better perspective. Science does an excellent job. Why should we expect it to make nature transparent? Idealism, sensationalism, and positivism have, as I see it, nourished absurd pretensions which materialism must protest against. Knowledge merely makes certain quantitative, structural, and behavioral facts about nature stand out. So far it is a *disclosure*; but reflection on ontology and its categories should swing us over to the implications of causal agency. Post-Humian philosophy has, in my opinion, been vitiated by the *overstress on prediction.* Predictions and *if-thens* have made philosophers too temporalistic, neglectful of constants and constitution.

*   *   *

Let us grant, again, that materialism has, on the whole, been dominated by its approach in terms of the inorganic sciences. What I have called external, or nonparticipative, knowledge called the tune. Now the evolutionary materialist recognizes that the organic self is a material system which has the peculiar property of having knowledge directed at itself. This fact is unique for human beings and must have basic significance for reformed materialism. Here we have what I would call *participative knowledge.* Here, and here alone, are the data of knowledge intrinsically integral to functional activities of the brain-mind. What they disclose is a sustained series of processes resting on habits and capacities. In them we have some slight glimpse into organizational complexities, a glimpse which fits in with external knowledge of the brain.

Now, as I see it, the shifting field of private consciousness must be regarded as a "natural isolate" of the functioning brain. As such, it demonstrates that a unified physical system has a qualitative dimension of this sort coterminous with activities. And, surely, that is what we might expect, once we freed ourselves from the negative notions associated with purely external knowledge. Brickbat notions of matter, when united with the Eleatic and Cartesian traditions mentioned above, fostered a reluctance to conceive physical systems as having a qualitative, ontological dimension or insideness. And, as I have argued, phenomenalistic empiricism worked in the same direction by its rejection of ontology. But the critical materialist is forced to postulate a positive content to being, a content responsive to the relations and activities discernible even to external knowledge.

Participative knowing, not realistically enough interpreted, has been, of course, the *raison d'être* of idealism and panpsychism. But because they never did justice to external, or nonparticipative, knowing, they were easily misled even here. It was the question of the epistemology and ontology of the "self" which offered difficulties. Berkeley proclaims only a vague notion of the self. But the self is not the notion. And Kant is agnostic with respect to the noumenal self. How much simpler and franker is the proposal of the materialist that the self is the organism! Here, however, we have a twofold knowledge, the one participative, the other external, or nonparticipative. It is historically interesting to note that, as C. A. Strong and Durant Drake moved from Kantian agnosticism to critical realism, they at the same time became materialists, only materialists of a still mechanistic type who did not see the importance of organization and functional unity. One reason for Drake's theory of essences, which have no existence, was his belief that the brain is merely an aggregate of moving particles and that its functional unity is merely a sort of statistical resultant. It was upon this ground that he rejected my form of the double-knowledge approach to the brain and left to the brain only the vague intrinsic sentiency of material particles. In a conversation I had with Strong at Fiesoli in 1937 he admitted that he had not done justice in his thought to organization and a *functional togetherness*. I do not hesitate to say that the dividing line between the old and the new materialism lies here. The wise handling of relational and functional togetherness which avoids the atomism of completely external relations, on the one hand, and the mystical rendition of the phrase that the whole is more than the sum of its parts, on the other, is the desideratum. As I see it, Whitehead's Platonic concretion of events is one alternative to an activistic and pattern-forming materialism. I am also inclined to think that the brain is a very specialized organ for the formation of action-patterns and that what holds of it does not apply to liver or stomach.

While, then, experiencing in the concrete is, I believe, intrinsic to the functioning brain, there is no *intuition* of the ontological context of such experiencing.

Now two conclusions seem to me to follow from these principles: we have (1) no intuition of matter, and (2) no acquaintance with an intrinsic endurant.[5] All of which means that a sample of intrinsic endurance cannot be found in consciousness. And that is precisely what we should deductively expect, since consciousness is correlated with functional activity and expresses what I call the qualitative dimension of material systems. *Activity is to me unthinkable without a variable in that which is active.* The antithesis is Eleaticism, inertness. Active intrinsic endurance entails duration, time. But duration applies to existents and their acts. Consciousness is inseparable from cerebral action-patterns. Thoughts are participial events while the organic self is a continuant existent.

It follows that the *mode of being* of consciousness is *participial* rather than substantive. The principle of conservation, or intrinsic endurance, does not apply to it.

The empirical base of the apprehension of the meaning, continuance, is a tantalizing psychological question. And yet the meaning stands out in both external perception and self-awareness and, as I think, by mutual support. That is, I doubt that if we could not develop the apprehension of our numerical self-identity we could develop the meaning of thinghood. At both poles, as I see it, we have the constant working of interpretative, cognitive activity. As regards the self, continuance and numerical sameness stand out cognitively through continuing felt attitudes and rememberings until we rightly comprehend ourselves as agents. Such experiences, heightened by social relations, operate as natural symbols of the self much as sensations are employed as natural symbols of external things. It is participative knowing since feelings and thoughts are in their mode of being participial to the organic self. By such participation we approach an intuition of the attitudes and activities of the self, for I see no reason to deny that these natural symbols have a disclosure-value with respect to the tides of our being. Certainly, the situation is even more intimate than in the use of sensations in perception as natural symbols having disclosure-value for external things. We must, however, be very careful in our use of the term intuition. I am inclined to think that cognition of the self is mediated, that is, symbolic and referential.

If, then, consciousness has only participial being and does not furnish us with a sample of intrinsic endurance, we must turn to the realm of denotables, that is, to self and things. To these, as we are aware, some measure of continuance is assigned, even though composite denotables are generated and corrupted and, consequently, are commonly characterized as having contingent, or historical, *existence*.

But we must be very careful to distinguish between being and existence. It seems to me clear that all physical denotables are forms of being. To deny this would be to consider them phenomenal or of the nature of illusions. They would be like bubbles which could burst and not leave a wrack behind. As I see it, reformed materialism is here confronted with the perennial question of process or becoming. There must be nothing illusory or transcending being about process and becoming. Matter must by its very nature be active and relational; and, to me, the two expressions imply one another. In short, I shall argue for the aseity of matter and maintain its intrinsic endurance.

And here we come upon basic questions which science alone can in the long run answer. Is the *floor* of physical being particulate even though the particles are never in isolation? Eddington holds strongly that there is a determinate number of both electrons and protons. In some fashion these are integrated to form the nucleus of atoms. They are in the nucleus as the eggs are in the omelette. Some kind of a dynamic organization has taken place which must not be pictoralized in billiard-ball terms. At any rate we must, I take it, postulate primary endurants which form what I called secondary endurants.[6] Thereafter, generation and corruption are on a more macroscopic scale; and we enter the realm of the countable and the describable. It is at this level that the term existence most properly comes into play. Such complex denotables are generated and corrupted so that existence is epistemically balanced by nonexistence. If such a denotable is an existent, in a very real sense *it* can cease to exist. Such is the very nature of history, becoming, and process. It is clear that we must so conceive existence that it permits the significance of nonexistence or ceasing to exist. But *being* must be made of sterner stuff. It is conserved and, as we shall argue, never conceivably becomes nothing. Change of existence is, rather, within being, an affair of constitution and process. In this sense there is no conservation of existence even though there is conservation of being. But we shall have more to say about these distinctions when we come to discuss quality and the kind of substantiality which goes with composite individuality. We humans have only this kind of temporary and contingent existence within the domain of physical being.

III

The ontological alternatives are fairly definite. By its very logic materialism must harmonize the intrinsic endurance of its ultimate stuff with the generation and corruption of composite wholes; and the facts indicate that integrative causality gives rise to the emergence of *novel levels of existence within being*. If wholeness applies, then mechanistic atomism must be rejected with its reductionism and its denial of causal agency to composite existents like human beings. On the other hand, theism moves from the contingency of existents to the contingency of matter, from a contributed kind of existence to an existence of a higher order. In this setting creation is supposed to become logically thinkable if not realizable.

There are many subtle variations of the theistic hypothesis. A brilliant recent development of emanation is Parker's Omega System which makes what I call the floor of being higher in quality than the monads which are sustained by it.

The hylomorphism of materialism, as we have noted, makes the unity and organized wholeness of an existent the expression of integrative causality so that the higher arises from the lower. Such a thesis is contrary to the genius of Christian Aristotelianism just as it was contrary to the unrevolutionary outlook of Aristotle. While a composite may have a unity and form, it is, I understand, held that this form must be given an existence commensurate with the potencies of the forms of the parts. The demand is logical and would correspond to the thesis of the evolutionist that the whole is not indifferent to its parts. But where the Thomist says form or quiddity, the materialist says organized wholeness. It is in this fashion that integrative causality makes room for immanent causality.

Lexicographers inform us that the verb "to exist" had a surprisingly late appearance in English and that the primary meaning was "to stand out, to be perceptible." Then came "having being in a specified place, to continue in being, to maintain in existence." Such existence has an epistemic and ontological pole. The gist of the latter is an acknowledgment of a denotable, that is, of something which can be referred to by pointing and description. Being is not blank and undifferentiated but ordered and cut up into denotables. We do not intuit these denotables but select them through natural symbols and descriptions. But what we are seeking is supposed to have the same sort of reality we have. I take it that appreciation of the brute fact of existence is grounded in self-awareness, in doing and suffering. Those who drop this meaning from perception are unrealistic. Denotables are then reducible to "If-then" predictions. There is no appreciation of expendable energies.

Logicians who have been interested in so-called existential propositions have, very naturally, concerned themselves with the epistemic pole and the applicability of concepts. Russell has never been afraid of paradoxes and so defined existence as a property of concepts. Obviously, it cannot be a property of all concepts but only of those which are exemplified. Hence it must be a relational property. The final test comes in perceptual verification. Is there a denotable describable by the concept? It seems to me clear that it is the denotable which we acknowledge to be an existent, to be out there; and yet the epistemic and relational element in the acknowledgment must not be forgotten. Were we able simply to intuit denotables there would not be this complication. And, as we have noted, the nearest approach to this is in self-awareness.

The Russellian view has something in common with the scholastic tradition with respect to essences or forms. Existence was conceived as a plus except with respect to that essence which necessarily existed or entailed its own existence. It is obvious that the realistic empiricism is skeptical of finding any concept which implies its own exemplifications. But even St. Thomas rejected the ontological proof. It is the contingency of the existence of denotables which is emphasized. But what if denotables are but organizations *within being* whose contingency is that of their composite wholeness and unity? Then being is something ultimate which contingent denotables themselves are regarded as being expressions of. Now, as I see it, that has always been the theory of materialism and finds formulation in the concept of recoverable stuff and intrinsic endurance. Contingency and variability are then assigned to relations, organization, to the process side of being. On the other hand, the more theistic and creationalistic theory denies this notion of being.

One of the reasons why the secular realist is accustomed to emphasize the categories of existence and being is his long controversy with idealism and positivism. Idealistic systems, as A. K. Rogers never tired of pointing out, neglected the question of existence and tried to remain within the context of merely logical coherence. The realist, in opposition, asserted that thought, from perception to judgment, always referred to something beyond itself. I have argued that the pragmatist in his rejection of the correspondence-theory of truth[7] still remained with the idealist, though ambiguously and equivocally. But the naturalistic realist is thereupon confronted with the choice between materialism and theism with various forms of panpsychism hovering between.

But must we not have a *sample of being* if the concept is to have empirical meaning? Now I have argued that we have only a sample of participial being as in sensations and feelings; and yet that both external and participative knowing operate in terms of meanings and references involving such categories as endurance, activity, capacity, constitution. All of which signifies that cognition is not the same as sensing and rests upon interpretation and intellection. I once remarked to Russell that perceiving should be distinguished from sensing; but he refused to consider the distinction, and that was that.[8] But without such a distinction eventism follows logically. The whole concept of substantive being arises in cognition. As I see it, then, we should not expect an intuition of substantive being either in self-awareness or in external perception. And, as a matter of fact, consciousness is to be correlated with becoming and functioning, with patterns and shifts of relations.

IV

We are brought, then, to the question of the proper conception of the relation between being and intrinsic endurance or conservation in activity.

It is fairly evident that composite denotables, such as chemical substances and organisms, are contingent existents, entities which come and go in the tides of being. What I have called qualitative substances, the highest emergent level of which, so far as we know, are human beings, are of this sort. They are generated, live their span, and vanish. They are continuants and have duration. Self-awareness ceases at death but the bodies remain for others to study and science informs us that the stuff of which they are composed is conserved. The kind of self Hume looked for, and could not find, has no existence. There is no inert, and changeless, soul-substance. And so we have consciousness, as a natural isolate and a case of experienced participial being, the organic self as a denotable, known externally and participatively and adjudged a continuant, or contingent substance, sustained by processes. Is this all? The materialistic says there is more. There must be a stuff, active and rational but self-conserving and having intrinsic endurance.

I take it that fact and reflection push the human mind on to the postulation of intrinsic endurance and the eternal. And the reasoning is not difficult to uncover. For instance, generation and corruption are seen to be supplementary. Already in Heraclitus this note is struck. Empedocles has his recurrent cycles driven by love and hate while the later atomism of Epicurus has much the same *dramatis personae*. Naturalism, in short, has been unable to conceive absolute beginnings and endings. And it should be recognized that orthodox theism has its own eternity of intrinsic endurance. It is to creation that there is assigned a secondary kind of being and endurance.

Now, as I see it, the generation of being from nonbeing is unthinkable for the simple reason that it is meaningless. The nonexistence of a continuant or contingent substance is thinkable since it merely signifies that no denotable is currently symbolized by A since it has ceased to exist. But being is that which is presupposed by all denotables, for it is that within which they arise and cease to be. That A exists and that A does not exist are contradictories. But *being* cannot in the same logical fashion be set over against *not-being*. So far as I can see, not-being is only a verbalism. Such seems to me the philosophy of the aseity of matter. Out of nothing arises nothing because the term can have no application.

I judge that it was thoughts such as these that led the Greeks to postulate the eternity of the universe and its self-maintenance through change. Aristotle but agreed with the Ionians; and the materialists only emphasized the same postulate. Christian thought merely transferred it to a supernatural realm, while emanation doctrines sought a *via media*.

And so we come to the alternatives: either the intrinsic endurance of materialistic naturalism or the contributed endurance of supernaturalism in all its sophisticated forms. It seems to me evident that physical realism implies the first alternative. Existence signifies an acknowledgement of specified being; and, while we cannot intuit the intrinsic endurance of matter, we equally cannot intuit its dependent endurance. The burden of proof rests, therefore, upon anyone who postulates another kind of being to be granted intrinsic endurance.

Reformed materialism reverses Aristotelianism or, to use Marxism phraseology, stands it on its head. There must be a lowest limit of material texture and an open series of integrative emergence. It is, of course, the task of science to determine the most elementary level of stuff. But, since I do not believe in a linear evolution for the universe, as Lloyd Morgan and Alexander apparently did, I would hold that all levels of material organization are, or can be, contemporaneous. About this I shall have more to say in the next section. It may well be that the universe has always been much as it is at present, that is, has always had a variegated and spatially dispersed cosmography; and this without an eternal recurrence or great year. This would mean that ontological time has no direction since it is always local and is but a name for what is involved in all activity. We must avoid reading the distinctions of our temporal knowledge with its linear implications into nature. Real time is only an actual activity; and activity is local, relational, and spatial.

As I follow the argument of Gilson, it rests upon two bases: (1) the rejection of emergence, and (2) the unempirical, or metaphysical, postulation of an act of existing. And these are closely connected in this form of natural theology.[9]

It is, apparently, Gilson's thesis that philosophers have shut themselves up into essences and have, therefore, never got to existence. A hit, if you will, at Plato, Spinoza, and Santayana. But not a hit at Berkeley or Hume or at the outlook of the more empirical form of critical realism. In ourselves we have participative cognition and, in sensation and feeling, *being* is given participially and denoted both practically and theoretically *through* what is given. Thus being is factual and is both given and acknowledged.

But the materialist, while he does not believe in the metaphysical, recognizes and acknowledges what the pragmatist or the positivist is wont to call the *transexperiental,* but *not,* of course, the undenotable and the unknowable. External being cannot be intuited and internal being can be intuited only participially. The intriguing consequence is that what the neo-Thomist calls *esse* and assigns to God is by the materialist assigned to dynamic and pattern-forming matter. While the former asserts the contingency of the material world and postulates two modes of being, the materialist denies the contingency of the material world and finds no evidence for two modes of being. And with the denial of the contingency of the material world goes the affirmation of its intrinsic endurance.

It would lead us too far to consider Gilson's handling of the principle of emergence. I quite agree with him that it is an ontological principle as well as a scientific one. But he makes it too easy for his argument by assuming that order and organization are not intrinsic to even inorganic systems and that out of simpler forms of order more complex forms cannot emerge through integrative causality. I fear that his scientists are too tempting because of their careless use of categories like chance and mechanism. It is a good dialectical display but hardly convincing to the naturalistic philosopher. And, of course, we are brought here to the sharp opposition between finalistic hylomorphism and evolutionary materialism to whose matter activity, relations, and intrinsic order are not alien. A materialism which finds a place for organization reverses Aristotelianism, for it moves in an exploratory way from the lower to the higher and not in a finalistic and hierarchical fashion from the higher to the lower.[10]

V

And so we find ourselves overlooking the perennial problems of becoming with intrinsic endurance, of quantity with quality, of eternity with time. How are composite, individual substances generated, maintained, and corrupted within an ocean of intrinsic endurance? How can there be qualitative gain or loss along with conservation of the amount of stuff or being? How can eternity include time? The logic of reformed materialism points to answers. In this concluding section I can only make suggestions.

As I see it, generation applies to the composite and integrated and presupposes the intrinsic endurance of the stuff which is integrated. Were any part of this to lose its intrinsic endurance that would mean that being had collapsed into not-being, which is unthinkable, meaningless.[11] Generation and becoming, therefore, belong to another ontological dimension than intrinsic endurance. To assert that A is generated and continues to exist for a while and then is corrupted is a statement about the tides of organization within being with its intrinsic endurance. In neither generation nor corruption does one move outside the context of being. All of which means that activity and organization reside in the very substance of being. Here we turn our back on any Eleatic motif in the most drastic manner. Matter implies process and process implies matter. It is a materialistic *devenir,* not, as with Bergson, a vitalistic and mystical one.

Generable qualities and capacities accompany becoming[12] and it is for this reason that the conservation of the amount of being does not conflict with qualitative gain and loss. We humans are born, live some three score and ten, and then vanish from existence. Is there not quality to our lives, often unique quality? Values are realized, and *lost* because no longer sustained by the persons and groups who found them desirable. Such is the more or less tragic texture of human life.

Now I take it that the whole concept of quality in ontology has been mishandled because stupidly put in the context of projected sensuous qualities, for the naive realist plastered on the surface of denoted things. Critical realism has turned its back upon such pictorial and external conceptions of quality. No; quality must be internal and intrinsic to being itself and a variable congenital with organization, changing capacities, and abilities. Quality is the changing context of being as causal integration proceeds and recedes. But, alas! our own intuition of it is limited to that "natural isolate," the private stream of our experiencing. But how could it be otherwise? It is important to note the presence of meanings based on operations of denotation and comparison. Consciousness reflects intellection as well as sensing. Empiricism has not always done justice to intellection.

I may remark incidentally that I do not see that, as the Marxists maintain following a clue in Hegel, quantity changes into quality. It is true, however, that the allocation of quantity does affect quality in that it affects wholes and relations. But I intend to examine this question more thoroughly in a paper on dialectical materialism.[13]

It would follow from this ontological analysis that quality, like generation and corruption, is an existential variable in no wise in conflict with the intrinsic endurance of material being. When philosophers, following Leibniz, speak of possible worlds, it seems to me that they should refer to existence rather than to being. Being is the context of existence. As I see it, being is beyond fact, for it is the source and foundation of fact. We discover being in its processes and manifestations, of which consciousness is the unique case of qualitative participation.

And here I shall allow myself some cosmological speculations which seem to me reasonable but have no connection with any high *a priori* road. The outlook is existential and pluralistic. Thus it is my feeling that cyclical and linear cosmologies are essentially monistic. By linear cosmologies I mean those that picture the cosmos as moving abreast down a supposed stream of time. Creationalistic analogies are, I think, apt to be operative in such cosmologies. There is a beginning and an end, a cosmic direction and a path; even God has an antecedent and a consequent nature. But, for reformed materialism, ontological time is but the fact of activity and existential process. It is local and covers both emergence and recession. It is tightly tied up with space. Chronology with its past, present, and future stretched out easily leads to ontological illusions. Only, as Eddington saw, if the second law of thermodynamics has cosmic validity is there an ontological arrow intrinsic to being.[14] The process, or existential, capacities of being would thereby be limited. Needless to say, I am skeptical. It seems to me that cyclical notions are really monistic and assume some kind of unified and recurrent cosmic pattern, after the analogy of the great year of the ancients. But pluralism—and I take it that relativity is causally pluralistic—must seek another pattern.

Being a believer in the eternity of the universe and skeptical of linear and cyclical notions, I am naturally led to suppose that the universe has always been much as it is now, a variegated existential domain with a floor, much the same everywhere, above which rise here and there mountain peaks of emergent becoming followed in time by recession. The picture is that of a qualitative rising and subsiding in quite plural and local ways with a cosmic floor woven of particles in their dynamic relations. Biological existents and qualities occur but rarely; and it may well be that mental abilities and symbolic processes are seldom generated. To the traditional religionist this is not a congenial picture and he would like a celestial ceiling or another story. But the naturalistic humanist is ready to accept an austere ontology, austere even though this earth harbors no secret hostility to man. The human drama is local but not without its engrossing qualities of life and death. Cosmic spies must be left to the theist and to all those who, denying the intrinsic endurance of nature, speculate on a metaphysics.

It seems to me logical to hold that the stuff of being neither increases nor decreases. The first possibility suggests minimum beginnings and maximum endings; it is a linear way of approach. The second would be just the reverse of the first. And would not both be based on naive biological analogies? If the stuff of being is intrinsically active and relational I should expect all generation and corruption to be an affair of integration and disintegration, neither violating the principle of conservation which expresses the intrinsic endurance of being. It is in this fashion that eternity includes existential time or process.

How far the fountain of qualitative, existential life will rise on this planet we do not know. The imagination still has free range. . . . There is relative, cumulative directionism guided by structure but no finalism. It is only in the behavior of individuals—and not in their genesis—that ends-in-view are set up, evaluated, and chosen. I have not the Platonic daring of Whitehead which assigns affective lure to eternal objects. Here, I suppose, is where the materialist has more of an agnostic streak than the panpsychist. What guides integrative causality at levels below the cortex? We have as yet little but words. Least action, equilibrium, dynamic tension? The genius of Whitehead shows in his philosophical daring. . . .

VI

I offer, in conclusion, some summarizing theses:

1. Ontology expresses a horizon entailed by realism.

2. Materialism postulates the intrinsic endurance of material being and is the logical correlate of naturalism.

3. Intrinsic endurance is not Eleatic and is opposed to creation, emanation, and all forms of contributed endurance.

4. The opposite of materialism is meta-physics in its various forms.

5. Reformed materialism rejects the caricatures of reductive materialism associated with Cartesian dualism and classical physics.

6. External, or nonparticipative, knowledge must be supplemented by the fact of the participative knowledge we have of our own organic selves.

7. The intrinsic endurance, or self-conserving, characteristic of being suggests the eternity of the material universe.

8. Linear cosmologies should be replaced by the postulate of a floor from which emergent levels arise quite locally and exceptionally.

9. Existence is best kept as a term for the factual recognition of describable denotables.

10. There may be a denotable corresponding to the symbol A; and there may not be. "A exists" and "A does not exist" are contradictories which bring out the epistemic side of existence.

11. Existents are qualitative and their existence precarious and historical.

12. In contrast to existence, being is a purely ontological term. It is describable only in terms of categorical distinctions.

13. The nonexistence of A has meaning and so has the Leibnizian principle of existential possibility, but I doubt that not-being or nothing is significant. At the most it would signify the denial of intrinsic endurance.

14. Aristotelian hylomorphism must be stood on its head, as the Marxists say of Hegel, by so changing the conception of matter that it includes form and activity. Directionism and emergence would then take the place of finalism and its theistic ceiling.

15. By distinguishing between being and existence and by giving up essences, except as descriptions, existence ceases to be something mysterious added to essences or quiddities.

Notes

1. It may be of some slight historical interest to note the fact that I proposed the term "new materialism" in the preface to *Critical Realism* (Chicago: Rand-McNally & Co., 1916). Santayana became the only living materialist somewhat later.

2. For this distinction see my article, "Causality and Substance," *Philosophical Review* 52 (January 1943): 1–27.

3. I refer to E. W. Hall's contribution to the book *Twentieth Century Philosophy*, ed. Dagobert D. Runes (New York: Philosophical Library, 1947). I hope the positivists will reply to his critique of their position. Also see L. S.

Stebbing's criticism of C. E. M. Joad's astonishingly naive epistemology in the recent Aristotelian Society symposium (cf. *Proceedings of the Aristotelian Society* 9 [1929]: 126–61). He is almost as artless as most positivists for whom epistemology is *sinnlos*.

4. Garnett follows Stout in this tradition and so establishes an immaterial self and God. Not being able to read everything, he limited himself to British theories of emergence. Colonially minded Americans do the same.

5. Hume's discussion of personal identity is illuminating. Memory does not produce the identity but discloses it. But he cannot explain it on his assumptions.

6. See Roy Wood Sellars, *The Philosophy of Physical Realism* (New York: Macmillan & Co., 1932), ch. 12.

7. I have reconstructed this traditional theory into a correspondence-theory of the *conditions* of knowledge and truth. I define *true* as a case of knowledge or as expressing a fact. Criteria are empirical and illogical. Correspondence is a justified inference.

8. In my opinion perception has a marked symbolic side. That is why it can be expressed in public terms and has its semantic content.

9. I refer, of course, to Etienne Gilson's argument in *God and Philosophy* (New Haven, Conn.: Yale University Press, 1941).

10. Cf. my article, "Causality and Substance."

11. Perhaps this is too strong. See Parker's comment. I mean that being, unlike an existent, has no contrast term. At most, it would signify the snuffing out of reality by itself, an internal collapse into nothingness. I can see no *why* to this. But the theists assume it; why can't the poor materialist do the same?

12. These must rest upon *primordial* qualities and capacities.

13. This paper appears in the July issue of *Philosophy and Phenomenological Research* 5 (1944–45): 157–79

14. Entropy seems to be statistical and macroscopic and not to apply to the Alpha or "floor" level.

2

Are Naturalists Materialists?*

John Dewey, Sidney Hook, and Ernest Nagel

Professor Sheldon's critique[1] of contemporary naturalism as professed in the volume *Naturalism and the Human Spirit* consists of one central "accusation": naturalism is materialism pure and simple. This charge is supported by his further claim that since the scientific method naturalists espouse for acquiring reliable knowledge of nature is incapable of yielding knowledge of the mental or spiritual, "nature" for the naturalists is definitionally limited to "physical nature." He therefore concludes that instead of being a philosophy which can settle age-old conflicts between materialism and idealism, naturalism is no more than a partisan standpoint, and contributes no new philosophical synthesis. Whether or not contemporary naturalists have broken new ground in philosophy is too large a theme for a brief discussion, and is in any case a historical question. But the other issues raised by Mr. Sheldon serve as a challenge to naturalists to make their views clearer on a number of points and to remove some obvious misunderstandings concerning the positions they hold. It is to these tasks that the present discussion is devoted.

*Originally published in *Journal of Philosophy* 42 (Sept. 13, 1945): 515-30. Subsequently published in *The Later Works of John Dewey, Vol. 15: 1942-1948*, ed. J. A. Boydston (Carbondale, Ill.: Southern Illinois University Press, 1989). Reprinted by permission of the Board of Trustees, Southern Illinois University.

I

According to Mr. Sheldon, the "real issue" between materialism and other philosophies is the following: "Can the states or processes we call mental or spiritual exercise a control over those we call physical, to some degree independent of any spatio-temporal redistributions; or, if we really understood what is going on when minds seem to control bodies, should we see that the spatio-temporal redistributions are the sole factors?" (pp. 225–56). The issue so conceived is held to be an intensely practical one. For if one answers the second question in the affirmative, "You are going to order your life in a very different way from the way you would order it if they are not. . . . When I accuse the naturalists of materialism, I mean a working materialism, a philosophy that goes beyond pure theory to set up a way of life." As Mr. Sheldon sees the issue, the program and method of the naturalists

> leads to or implies that in the last analysis all processes in the known universe, mental, spiritual, vital, or what not, are wholly at the beck and call of the processes we have agreed to call physical, and therefore the only reliable way of control over nature—and over other men— is secured by knowledge of spatio-temporal distributions. That is the only materialism that counts, that has bearing on human life and the prospects of man's future.
>
> You may, as a materialist, believe in graded levels—inorganic, animal, man, none of which can be wholly described in terms of the levels below it. . . . On the other hand, you may believe each level can be fully defined in terms of a lower level. In either case you may remain a materialist. The crucial point is whether the *behavior* of the higher (mental) level can be *predicted* and therefore *controlled* surely and accurately from a knowledge of the lower. It is power that counts, it is power that the naturalist hopes by his scientific method to gain: power to ensure the arrival of things on the higher level by proper "redistribution" of things on the lower. The question of logical reducibility is beside the point. . . . (p. 256)

It appears at first blush that the issue thus raised is a genuinely factual one which can be settled by appeal to empirical evidence. For the issue seems to be concerned simply with the most effective way in which things and their qualities can be brought into, maintained in, and ushered out of existence. One is materialist, on Mr. Sheldon's showing, if one believes that power is acquired by learning how to manipulate embodied things, if one attempts to guide the destinies of men and their affairs by redistributing spatio-temporal objects. Everyone who pursues a vocation in this world whether as engineer or physician, sociologist or educator, statesman or farmer, is perforce a materialist. One is a materialist even when one tries to influence one's fellows by communicating ideas to them, for, as Mr. Sheldon notes, such a method of influencing them employs physical means: verbal and written speech, the arts, and other symbolic structures. Apparently, therefore, only those can call themselves nonmaterialists who maintain that causal efficacy resides in some disembodied consciousness, unexpressed wishes, silent prayers, angelic or magical powers, and the like. A nonmaterialist, on this conception, is one who regards minds as substances, capable of existing independently of spatio-temporal things, but logically incapable of being adjectival or adverbial of such things. A materialist, on the other hand, is one who believes there is no evidence for the existence of minds so described, and who in addition finds insuperable difficulties in supposing that a mind so conceived can enter into causal relations with anything else. If this is indeed the difference between a materialist and one who is not, then the naturalists whom Mr. Sheldon accuses of materialism are glad to find themselves in his company—for in his *practical* commitments (the only ones that really count, according to himself) if not his theoretical ones, he is certainly a materialist. In any event, the evidence from materialism so construed is overwhelming; and naturalists will cheerfully admit his accusation of themselves as materialist not as a criticism but as an acknowledgment of their sanity.

Nevertheless, it is unlikely that so innocuous an interpretation of Mr. Sheldon's critique can be faithful to his intent. For though he insists that the issue he is raising is a highly practical one, and though he dismisses as so much irrelevant subtlety various types of materialism which naturalists and others have carefully distinguished, his intent is presumably to tax naturalists with a view in which they themselves "sense bad odor" (p. 257).

What is this view? Unfortunately, Mr. Sheldon nowhere makes it explicit. He accuses naturalists of excluding from nature everything but the physical, and of adopting a method of inquiry which deprives them of any knowledge of the mental. Indeed, he formulates the issue between materialism and idealism in terms of a sharp contrast between the physical and the mental. But he is not very helpful in making clear what are the marks which set off one of these kinds from the other. He does, to be sure, suggest that the physical is simply that which is capable of spatio-temporal distribution and redistribution; and since the mental is for him an exclusive disjunct to the physical, he also suggests by implication that the mental is that which is not capable of such distribution. However, these suggestions are hardly sufficient for the purpose at hand. Are such properties and processes as temperature, potential energy, solubility, electrical resistance, viscosity, osmosis, digestion, reproduction, physical in Mr. Sheldon's system of categories? Since they are all properties or powers or activities of things having spatio-temporal dimensions, the answer is presumably in the affirmative. Nevertheless, though they characterize things having spatial dimensions, none of the items mentioned has itself a spatial dimension; thus, temperature has no volume, solubility no shape, digestion no area, and so on. And if a property is to be regarded as physical provided that it qualifies something having a spatio-temporal dimension, why are not pains, emotions, feelings, apprehensions of meanings, all subsumable under the physical? For to the best of our knowledge such "mental" states and events occur only as characteristics of spatio-temporal bodies—even though, like potential energy or viscosity, they do not themselves possess a spatial dimension. Accordingly, Mr. Sheldon formulates no clear criterion in terms of which the physical can be sharply demarcated from the mental; and he has therefore not provided sufficient hints as to what the doctrine is which he finds naturalists holding. A distinction between two types of materialist doctrine therefore appears to be in order.

According to one type of materialism, the mental is simply identical with, or is "nothing but," the physical. It is of this type that Mr. Sheldon is thinking when he declares that a genuine materialist "will insist that an idea is but a potential or tentative muscular response" (p. 256). This view can be stated with some precision in approximately the following manner. Let us call those terms "physical terms" which are commonly employed in the various physical sciences of nature; this class of expressions will then include such words and phrases as "weight," "length," "molecule," "electric charge," "osmotic pressure," and so on. And let us call those terms "psychological terms" of which no use is made in the physical sciences, but which are customarily employed in describing "mental" states; this class of expressions will contain such phrases as "pain," "fear," "feeling of beauty," "sense of guilt," and the like. Materialism of the type now under consideration may then be taken to maintain that every psychological term is *synonymous with,* or has *the same meaning* as, some expression or combination of expressions belonging to the class of physical terms. Proponents of this view, if any, can be imagined to argue somewhat as follows: Modern science has shown that the color *red* appears only when a complicated electromagnetic process also occurs; accordingly, the word "red" has the same *meaning* as the phrase "electromagnetic vibration having a wavelength of approximately 7100 angstroms." (This latter phrase is unduly simple. It requires to be complicated by including into it other terms denoting physical, chemical, and physiological states of organic bodies. But the point of the illustration is not affected by the oversimplification.) And those professing this view must be taken to claim that analogous synonyms can be specified for the distinctive psychological terms such as "pain" and "feeling of beauty."

When the consequences of this view (frequently given the label "reductive materialism") are strictly drawn, statements such as "I am in pain" must be regarded as *logically entailing* statements of the form "My body is in such and such a physico-chemico-physiological state." Whether any competent thinker has ever held such a view in the specific form here outlined is doubtful, though Democritus, Hobbes, and some contemporary behaviorists are often interpreted to assert something not very dissimilar to it. Those who do hold it maintain often that the obvious differences between a color and an electromagnetic vibration, or between a felt pain and a physiological condition of an organism, are "illusory" and not "real," since only physical processes and events (i.e., those describable exclusively with the help of physical terms) have the dignity of reality. But whatever may be said for reductive materialism—and very little can be said in its favor—it can be categorically asserted that it is *not* a view which is professed, either tacitly or explicitly, by the naturalists whom Mr. Sheldon is criticizing. If "materialism" means reductive materialism, then those naturalists are not materialists.

But there is a second and different type of materialism, though it is sometimes confused with the preceding one. It maintains that the occurrence of a mental event is contingent upon the occurrence of certain complex physico-chemico-physiological events and structures—so that no pains, no emotions, no experiences of beauty or holiness would exist unless bodies appropriately organized were also present. On the other hand, it does not maintain that the specific quality called "pain," for example, is "nothing but" a concourse of physical particles ordered in specified ways. It does not assert that "an idea is but a potential or tentative muscular response." It does not declare that the word "pain," to use the technique of exposition of the preceding paragraphs, is synonymous with some such phrase as "passage of an electric current in a nerve fiber." It does assert that the relation between the occurrence of pains and the occurrence of physiological processes is a contingent or "causal" one, not an analytical or logical one. Many proponents of this view entertain the hope that it will be possible some day to specify the necessary and sufficient *conditions* for the occurrence of mental states and events in terms of the distributions, behaviors, and relations of a special class of factors currently regarded as fundamental in physical science—for example, in terms of the subatomic particles and structures of contemporary physics. Sharing such a hope is not a *sine qua non* for this type of materialism, and in any case whether the hope is realizable cannot be settled dialectically but only by the future development of the sciences. However, whether a materialist of this type entertains such a hope or not, he does not claim but denies that propositions dealing with mental events (i.e., those employing psychological terms) are *logically deducible* from propositions dealing exclusively with physical ones (i.e., those containing only physical terms).

The question of the truth of materialism of this type can be decided only on the basis of empirical evidence alone. Many of the details of the dependence of mental upon physical processes are far from being known. Nevertheless, that there is such a dependence cannot reasonably be doubted in the light of the evidence already accumulated. A system of philosophy built on a conception of mind incompatible with this evidence is therefore nothing if not willful and undisciplined speculation. Accordingly, if "materialism" signifies a view something like the one just outlined, Mr. Sheldon is not mistaken in his accusation of naturalists as materialists. And if the issue between materialists and idealists can be settled only by adopting a notion of mind which denies that minds are adjectival and adverbial of bodies, then he is also right in declaring that naturalists have done nothing to settle it. Nor would they wish to resolve an age-old conflict on those terms.

It is relevant to ask now whether naturalists believe the mental to be "wholly at the beck and call" of the physical, and how they would reply to Mr. Sheldon's query whether "the states or processes we call mental or spiritual exercise a control over those we call physical, to some degree independent of any spatio-temporal redistributions." Two things should be noted. First, there is a certain sting in Mr. Sheldon's metaphors which must be removed in order not to prejudice discussion. To speak of the mental as being "wholly at the beck and call" of the physical suggests a degrading status for the mental, a slavish helplessness, which outrages our sense of fact. Physical processes, in any but a magical view of things, do not beckon or call—only human beings do. If there is a suggestion here that the properties of organized matter on any level *must* be read back into matter organized on any other level, then as already indicated naturalists do not subscribe to such notions of the *physical.* Second, if the point of these questions rests on a conception of minds as substantial but ethereal entities, capable nevertheless of controlling or being controlled by physical substances, naturalists will dismiss the questions as not addressed to themselves; they simply do not subscribe to such notions of the *mental.* On the other hand, if these views of the physical and mental are not assumed by the questions, there remains very little for the naturalists to say in reply—as will immediately appear.

For suppose a chemist were asked whether he believed that the properties of water are at "the beck and call" of hydrogen and oxygen atoms, or whether he thought that water "controlled" the behaviors and properties of its constituents. Would he not reply that the questions are meaningful only on the assumption that the properties of water are not only *distinguishable* from those of its constituents taken singly or in isolation from each other, but are also *substantially distinct* from the properties of hydrogen and oxygen atoms when these are related in the way in which water molecules are organized? On the other hand, the chemist would certainly maintain that the existence of water and its properties is contingent upon the combined presence of certain elements interrelated in definite ways. But he would call attention to the fact that when these elements are so related, a distinctive mode of behavior is exhibited by the structured unity into which they enter. Nevertheless, this structured object is not an *additional* thing which, in manifesting its properties, controls from some external vantage point the behavior of its organized parts. The structured object in behaving the way it does behave under given circumstances is simply manifesting the behavior of its constituents *as* related in that structure under those circumstances. To be sure, the occurrence of those properties we associate with water may be controlled by "redistributing" spatio-temporal things—provided always that the combination of the atomic constituents of water can be effected practically. But in undergoing such redistributions the constituents themselves come to behave in precisely the manner in which their relations to one another within a structured molecule of water requires them to behave: their behavior is not *imposed* upon them from without.

The naturalist proceeds in an essentially no different manner in giving his account of the status of minds. Like the chemist in reference to the properties of water, he maintains that the states and events called mental exist only when certain organizations of physical things also occur. And also like the chemist, he holds that the qualities and behaviors displayed by physical things when they are properly recognized—the qualities and behaviors called mental or spiritual—are not exhibited by those things unless they are so organized. But these qualities and behaviors of organized wholes are not additional things which are *substantially* distinct from the properties and behaviors of spatio-temporal objects in their organized unity. Accordingly, naturalists most emphatically acknowledge that men are capable of thought, feeling, and emotion, and that in consequence of these powers (whose existence is contingent upon the organization of human bodies) men can engage in actions that bodies not so organized are unable to perform. In particular, human beings are capable of rational inquiry, and in the light of their findings they are able to "redistribute" spatio-temporal things so as to ensure the arrival and departure of many events both physical and mental. They achieve these things, however, not as disembodied minds, but as distinctively organized bodies. To the naturalist, at any rate, there is no more mystery in the fact that certain kinds of bodies are able to think and act rationally than in the fact that cogs and springs arranged in definite ways can record the passage of time or that hydrogen and oxygen atoms ordered in other ways display the properties of water. "Things are what they are, and their consequences will be what they will be; why then should we desire to be deceived?"

II

Mr. Sheldon claims that in adopting scientific method as the way for securing reliable knowledge, naturalists seriously restrict the class of things concerning which they can acquire knowledge. As naturalism envisages the nature of this method, according to him, the method is applicable only to things which are physical or "public," and not to states and events which are mental or "private." How valid is this claim? Are naturalists precluded by their choice of method from ever discovering anything about things divine or angelic if the universe contains them? And, in particular, must a naturalist if he is serious in his adoption of scientific method rule out of court the "private" data of introspective observation?

A preliminary distinction between two meanings of "scientific method" will help clear the way for the naturalist's reply. For the name is often used interchangeably both for a set of general canons with the help of which evidence is to be gathered and evaluated, and for a set of specialized techniques associated with various instruments each of which is appropriate only for a limited subject matter. Mr. Sheldon draws part of his support for his conclusions concerning the scope of scientific method from this double sense of the name. He contends that methods are not produced *in vacuo,* and are not independent of subject matter. "No mere methodology," he declares; "a method envisages, however tentatively, a metaphysic" (p. 258). And he cites in illustration the telescope, which is an excellent instrument for studying the stars, but is hardly suited for dissecting the seeds of plants. No one, surely, will think of denying the truth of this last observation. However, it does not therefore follow that the logical canons involved in testing the validity of propositions in astronomy are different from the logical canons employed in biology; for the fact that a telescope is the suitable technical means for exploring stars but not seeds is not incompatible with the claim that a common set of principles are adequate for appraising evidence in all the physical domains which encompass these subject matters. Nor does it follow that because principles of evidence are competent to guide inquiries into physical subject matter, they are not so competent for inquiries into psychological subject matter. In any event, however, it is scientific method as the use of a set of general canons of inquiry, not as a class of special techniques, which is professed by naturalists as the reasonable way for securing reliable knowledge. And although Mr. Sheldon complains that naturalists have supplied no standard analysis of scientific method (p. 258), it surely can be no secret to him that the writings of many naturalists are in fact preoccupied with just such general principles of evidence.

But Mr. Sheldon's chief complaint is addressed to the naturalists' account of the nature of the verificatory process. The naturalists maintain that "reliable knowledge is publicly verifiable." Do they not therefore exclude the very possibility of knowledge concerning matters that are not "public" but are "private"? "Does the mystic verify the Divine being by direct observation?" asks Mr. Sheldon. "Can the introspective psychologist experiment with private minds?" (p. 258). If, however, what is thus private is excluded from the domain of application of scientific method, is not the naturalist forever compelled to remain in the domain of the physical?

The following remarks may serve to clarify the naturalist's position on this matter.

a. In maintaining that scientific method is the most reliable method for achieving knowledge, the naturalist means what he says. He recommends that method for acquiring *knowledge,* for achieving *warranted assertions,* but not for acquiring aesthetic or emotional experiences. He does not wish to deny that men have mystic experiences of what they call the Divine, that they enjoy pleasures and suffer pains, or that they have visions of beauty. He *does* deny that *having* such experiences constitutes knowledge, though he also affirms that such "mental states" can become *objects* of knowledge. Accordingly, while he insists that the world may be encountered in other ways than through knowledge and admits that scientific method possesses no valid claim to be the sole avenue for such encounters, he also insists that not every encounter with the world is a case of knowledge. Indeed, for many naturalists, the experience of scientific method is instrumental to the enrichment of other modes of experience. This point is elementary but fundamental. It completely destroys the vicious circle in which Mr. Sheldon has attempted to trap the naturalist—the circle according to which nature for the naturalist is what is open to scientific method, while scientific method is simply the method recommended for approaching nature (p. 263). What is viciously circular in maintaining that if anything is to be *known* (in whatever other manner it may be *experienced*), reliable knowledge of it is acquired through the use of scientific method? For things can be encountered without first having to be known, and scientific method can be described and employed without everything in nature having first to be experienced. It no more follows from this that everything in nature is known or can be experienced only as a mode of knowledge, than it follows that since every assertion about anything whatsoever is *statable,* everything has already been stated or exists only as a possible statement.

b. Though Mr. Sheldon sometimes appears to suggest that the observable alone is confirmable or verifiable, the naturalist maintains that the meanings of these terms do not coincide. Mr. Sheldon declares:

> Scientific method demands experiment and observation confirmable by fellow men. Mental states or processes, just insofar as they are not physical, not "behavior," are not open to such observation. He says they are "inaccessible." Scientific method thus means, to the naturalist, that observation of the nonpublic has no sense or mean-

ing. Publicity is the test; the private and hidden is ruled out of court. (p. 262).

The crux of this argument resides in the transition from the statement that mental states are not open to observation by one's fellow men, to the conclusion that therefore the private and the hidden are ruled out of court by the naturalist. But this is a non sequitur. For let us grant, at least for the sake of the argument, that A's mental states cannot be observed by his fellow men. Let us even accept the much stronger claim that statements like "B cannot experience A's feelings" are *analytically* true, so that it is *logically impossible* for B to experience A's feelings. Does it follow that B cannot publicly verify that A does experience some feeling, of pain, for example? That it does not follow will be evident from applying Mr. Sheldon's argument to the supposition that a subatomic interchange of energies is taking place in accordance with the specifications of modern physical theory. No one will claim that such subatomic events are literally observable, at least by human investigators. Nevertheless, though those events are not observable, propositions about them are certainly confirmable or verifiable—and in fact publicly verifiable by observations on the behaviors of macroscopic objects. Evidently, therefore, there may be states and events which are not observable, even though propositions about them are publicly verifiable.

c. Nevertheless, so Mr. Sheldon urges, if the naturalist is consistent he cannot rely on scientific method to yield reliable knowledge of the mental *qua* mental or "private." He cannot use this method to assure himself that he has an abdominal pain, for example, unless a surgeon first exhibits and publicly verifies the existence of an inflamed appendix.

But the imputation of such views to the naturalist is a caricature of the latter's position. The latter does maintain, to be sure, that A's feelings of pain have their physical and physiological causes. Since, however, the naturalist is not a reductive materialist, he does not maintain that the painful quality experienced by A is "nothing but" the physical and physiological *conditions* upon which its occurrence depends. He will therefore not assert that the dentist who notes a cavity in A's tooth experiences A's pain; on the contrary, he will insist that A's body is uniquely favored with respect to the pains A suffers—a circumstance which he attributes to the distinctive physiological events that are transpiring in A. Accordingly, the naturalist will recognize that the proposition that A is experiencing a pain is verifiable in two ways: directly by A, in virtue of the privileged position in which A's body occurs; and indirectly by everyone (including A) who is in a position to observe processes causally connected with the felt pain.

However, and this is the essential point, the fact that A can directly verify the proposition that he is in pain, without having to consult a surgeon or dentist, does not make the proposition any the less *publicly verifiable.* For the surgeon or dentist can also verify it, not, to be sure, by sharing A's qualitative experience, but in other ways: by asking A, for example, or by noting the condition of A's body. In brief, therefore, to maintain that propositions about the occurrence of pains and other mental states are publicly verif*iable,* does not mean that they must always be verif*ied* indirectly; and, conversely, to acknowledge that propositions about mental states have not been directly verif*ied* is not incompatible with the thesis that they are publicly verif*iable.*

d. The point involved is important enough to deserve some amplification. It is well known that the temperature of a body can be determined in several alternative ways: for example, with the aid of an ordinary mercury thermometer or of a thermocouple. In the one case, changes in temperature are registered by variations in the volume of the mercury, or in the other by variations in the electric current flowing through a galvanometer. The instruments thus exhibit two quite disparate qualitative alterations: for the thermometer is not equipped to register the effects of thermoelectric forces, while the thermocouple lacks the necessary structure to record thermal expansions. It is evident, therefore, that the qualities and behaviors displayed by each instrument are a consequence of its specific mode of construction and of the special position it occupies in a system of physical transactions. Nevertheless, in spite of the qualitative differences between them, each instrument can be satisfactorily employed for ascertaining temperature variations— at any rate within specifiable limits of such variations. It is well to note, incidentally, that in recording the temperature of some other body, an instrument is at the same time indicating its own temperature. Moreover, if the instruments are both in working connection with some other body so that they serve to measure the latter's temperature, it is possible to use the behavior of either instrument in order to predict certain aspects of the behavior of the other, and thus to determine the temperature of the other. Were the instruments blessed with the powers of consciousness (let us permit ourselves this fancy), the thermometer would experience a unique quality when it was recording the temperature of some body—a quality or state which would be "private" to the thermometer and incommunicable to the thermocouple. Nevertheless, even though the thermocouple would be unable, because of its own distinctive mode of organization and unique physical position, to experience the qualities exhibited by the thermometer, it would not be precluded from recording (and thus "verifying") the temperature both of the third body and of the thermometer itself.

Consider now the bearing of this physical illustration upon the issue raised by Mr. Sheldon. A cannot *experience* B's mental states, any more than the thermometer can exhibit (or experience) the distinctive qualitative behaviors of the thermocouple, and for the same reasons. But A can *know* that B is undergoing some specified experience, just as the thermometer can be employed to measure the temperature of the thermocouple. The distinction between the public and the private, upon which Mr. Sheldon builds his case against the naturalist, thus consists—so far as questions of *knowledge* are involved—in the differences between the causal relations of two distinct or differently organized bodies.

e. In thus admitting as publicly verifiable all the facts designated by Mr. Sheldon as "mental," naturalists do not, of course, thereby commit themselves to the various propositions for which such data are often cited as evidence. Thus, naturalists do not as a matter of principle, deny that mystics have had ecstatic visions of what they call the Divine, any more than they deny that men experience pains; for they believe that the occurrence of such visions and experiences has been publicly verified. On the other hand, recognizing as warranted the proposition that such *events* do not occur does not, by itself, decide what further propositions are confirmed by those occurrences. Indeed, this question cannot be decided in general, and requires detailed investigation for each proposition considered. The point is that there is surely a difference between admitting as true the proposition that someone has undergone the experience he calls "experience of the Divine," and admitting as therefore true the proposition which affirms the existence of a Deity— just as there is a difference between acknowledging a pain and attributing it to a heart lesion. In either case, the proposition mentioned last requires the confirmation of independent evidence if it is to be counted as a validly established one. The testimony of a mystic is *testimony,* but is not necessarily *evidence* for the proposition the mystic asserts—though it may be evidence for some *other* proposition—no more than a patient's report about his pains is necessarily evidence for the truth of his belief that he is suffering from a fatal disease. If naturalists disagree with those who assert the existence of gods and angels, they do not do so because they rule out of court the testimony of all witnesses, but because the testimony does not stand up under critical scrutiny. The *horror supernaturae* with which Mr. Sheldon not unjustly charges the naturalists is therefore not a capricious rejection on their part of well-established beliefs: it is a consequence of their refusal to accept propositions, like the belief in ghosts, for which the available evidence is overwhelmingly negative.

f. One final point requires some attention, for it is briefly hinted at by Mr. Sheldon and is often given central prominence in discussions such as the present one. The point concerns the alleged greater certainty of some propositions than others, and in particular the greater certainty of propositions about introspective observations than of propositions about other matters.

Mr. Sheldon raises the issue in connection with a behaviorist attempt to establish the fact that someone is undergoing an experience of the beautiful. He believes that if a naturalist, faithful to scientific method, wishes to be sure that someone is having such an experience, he must apply physical apparatus to the glandular and muscular responses of the person in question. For the naturalist, according to Mr. Sheldon, cannot take the person's word for it: "that is a report about something private, outside the realm of verifiable truth" (p. 267). But it should be clear at this stage of the present discussion that Mr. Sheldon would have a point only if the naturalist were a reductive materialist: that is, if the naturalist were to maintain that a feeling of beauty is "nothing but" a glandular and muscular response. However, since the imputation of such a view to the naturalist is a mistaken one, why should the latter proceed in the fashion suggested by Mr. Sheldon? For a man's glandular and muscular responses are no more identical with his feelings of beauty than are his oral reports that he is having them. An oral report may be more reliable evidence for the occurrence of such feelings than is the reaction of some brass instrument—especially since, as in the present instance, we possess little accurate knowledge concerning the glandular and muscular conditions for the occurrence of such feelings. To be sure, the naturalist will not deny himself the use of physical apparatus if such instruments do provide decisive evidence on disputed matters and if people are suspected of prevarication concerning their feelings—witness, for example, the occasional reliance on "lie detectors." But such instruments do not supply *inherently* more reliable evidence simply because they are physical; whether they do in fact supply such evidence is something that must be settled by detailed inquiry.

But does a naturalist, it is sometimes asked, believe himself justified in accepting a proposition about his "private" experiences, if that proposition is not confirmable by others? Does not a naturalist have to maintain, if he holds reliable knowledge to be publicly verifiable knowledge, that such a proposition as "I now have a bad headache" which he might utter is not made certain simply by the pain he is feeling, but must be confirmed by others before it can be regarded as well-established? In brief, must not a naturalist declare *all* propositions to be unwarranted, unless they are verifiable by other than introspective evidence? In answering these questions in the affirmative, so one criticism runs, the naturalist is adopting a dogmatic and arbitrary criterion for warranted knowledge, a criterion in conflict with common sense as well as with the practice of many competent psychologists.

However, a distinction previously introduced must be repeated here. The naturalist takes seriously his characterization of reliable knowledge as publicly verifi*able* knowledge. Accordingly, the proposition "I now have a bad headache," if it constitutes a piece of knowledge, must be confirm*able* by others as well as by the person making it. But it by no means follows from this that the proposition must actually be confirm*ed* by others if the person making it is to be justified in accepting it as true. Just how much confirmatory evidence must be available for a given proposition before it can be accepted as warranted cannot be specified once for all. But undoubtedly there are cases (as in the instance of the proposition about the headache) in which a minimum of evidence (i.e., the felt pain) suffices to warrant its acceptance by the person asserting the proposition—so that any additional evidence will be, for him, supererogatory. But the possibility here considered is not unique to propositions about matters of introspective observation. A chemist who observes that a piece of blue litmus paper turns red when immersed in a liquid, will assert that the paper is indeed red and conclude that the liquid is acid. He will normally regard it a waste of time to search for further evidence to support either of the propositions he is asserting, even though other evidence could be found for them.

On the other hand, the naturalist—like disciplined common sense and the experienced introspective psychologist—is sensitive to the dangers and limitations of "pure" introspection. He knows, for example, that introspection alone cannot discover the causes (nor, for that matter, the precise locations) of the pains he feels; for statements asserting the mere *existence* of qualities do not provide theoretical knowledge of the *relations* in which those qualities stand to other things. Even the fact that the felt quality of a pain is "private" is not established by introspective methods alone; this fact, like the fact that certain pains are associated with contemporaneous physico-chemical changes in teeth and nerve fibers and can therefore be controlled by "redistributing" spatio-temporal things, can be ascertained only by overt experiment involving manipulation of "public" things. Theoretical knowledge of pains thus opens up fresh directions for human activity and new types of experience—possibilities which remain unrealized as long as attention is directed simply to the sheer *occurrence* of painful qualities. Assured knowledge of the nature of pains, however, is not the product of mere introspective study. In any event, the annals of physics as well as of medicine and psychology have made clear to the naturalist the serious errors into which men fall when they accept introspective observations without further experimental controls. It is needless to belabor this point—even the textbooks are full of illustrations for it. As eminent psychologists have themselves noted, introspective observation is not radically different from any other kind of observation. Whether one employs one's body or some recording instrument for making qualitative discriminations, one must in either case take great care in interpreting its reports and drawing conclusions from them. Moreover, the psychological and social sciences would be denuded of nearly everything of interest if the propositions they asserted were exclusively confined to matters that are capable of direct observation or acquaintance, and if those sciences did not attempt systematically to *relate* the qualities and events immediately apprehended with things and events not so experienced. The dichotomy so insistently and frequently introduced between the "inner" and "outer," between the "private" and "public," therefore seems to many naturalists as little more than a relic from a conception of the mind as a substantial, autonomous agent, operating mysteriously in a body which is not its natural home. Neither this concept nor the dichotomy serve to further the progress of either philosophy or science.

Indeed, this conception of mind has tragic consequences for the human values which Mr. Sheldon wishes to defend against what he believes is the threat of scientific method. For it flies in the face of mountains of evidence concerning the place of man in nature, and leaves human values unanchored to any solid ground in experience. It is not the philosophy of naturalism which imperils human values but Mr. Sheldon's dualism. By ruling out as irrelevant investigation into the natural causes and consequences of the value commitments men make, it deprives human choice of effective status, opens the door wide to irresponsible intuitions, and dehumanzies the control of nature and society which scientific understanding makes possible. In spite of Mr. Sheldon's deprecating remarks about the uncertain conclusions which anthropology, social psychology, psychiatry, and the other social sciences have been able to reach concerning the "mental aspect" of human activities (pp. 257–58), no one familiar with the history of these disciplines will question the claim that our assured knowledge and our control of these matters has increased as a consequence of introducing into those domains the method of modern science. Is there any competent evidence for believing that the continued use of this method will retard the advance of such knowledge and control rather than promote it? What viable alternative to this method does Mr. Sheldon propose that has not already been tried and discredited? What good reason can he offer for entrusting the maintenance and the realization of human goods to a historically provincial dualism between the mental and the physical—a dualism which the progress of science has made increasingly dubious? It is this doctrine from which Mr. Sheldon's critique of naturalism derives, and not the philosophy attacked by him, which requires a responsible defense.

Note

1. W. H. Sheldon, "Critique of Naturalism," *Journal of Philosophy* 42 (1945): 253–70. All page references are to this article.

3

Empirical Pluralism
and Unifications of Nature*

John Herman Randall, Jr.

I

I am here proposing to approach Nature directly, and with none of that preliminary methodological discussion which is so much in the current mode. For I share the distaste of many for those desert sands that stretch on endlessly toward the mirage of confirmability; though I also believe that sand is an important ingredient in the hard roads that can take us places. But I am here inviting neither to excursions, nor to tours to distant scenes. I am proposing rather to explore the old homestead, the familiar Nature with whose accustomed features we have long lived in harmony and compatibility.

The Nature we encounter exhibits a thoroughgoing diversity or plurality. It is a fundamental metaphysical fact that Nature is radically and ineradicably manifold. Since William James's insistence on the "pluriverse" we live in, metaphysical inquiry has rejected all idealistic

*Originally published in John Herman Randall, Jr., *Nature and Historical Experience* (New York: Columbia University Press, 1958). Reprinted by permission.

monism. Some form of ontological pluralism has come to be accepted again by most responsible metaphysicians, just as they have once more come to take time "seriously."

But it is likewise a fundamental metaphysical fact that Nature can *become* unified in human vision. Again and again the world has provoked man to many a different scheme of unification. From the beginning men have seen the world whole, through the vision that is myth and symbol, through the great creation myths of primitive cultures. More recently, some have tried to see it entirely through the vision that is knowledge and science, through the working out of progressively more unified general ideas and theories, that seem to point to an eventual unification in a single unified formula—a unified field theory, perhaps.

Whether in the end "knowledge" and "science" operate to unify Nature in a way that is fundamentally different from the way of myth and symbol— whether science is, as we say, less "symbolic" and more "literal"—has been a vexed philosophical issue, especially in modern times. I have tried to frame the question—and I might indeed claim that this is one fruit of the metaphysical leading principles here set forth—in such a way as to transform what has been an "issue" to be interminably debated, into a problem that can be inquired into, with some hope that inquiry can bring to light pertinent facts. Knowledge and science are certainly no less—and no more—"human" than are myths and symbols; and no less— and no more—"natural." Both ways of seeing the world whole employ characteristic instruments of unification. In their unifying function, sci- entific hypotheses, theories, and systems, together with myths and symbols, "regulative ideas" and human ideals, and such complex elaborations of symbols as mathematics, logic, and theology, and the greatest of all, discourse and language itself—all these varied instruments of unification seem to possess much in common. They all seem to enjoy the same happy ontological status: they all fall, in my metaphysical classification of "predicables," or ways of functioning,[1] into the group called "Con- nectives" or "Conjunctions." They are all "functionally real," they are all "real" as functioning to institute objective relations. They are all human ways of cooperating with other natural processes. Their distinctive ways of functioning, their characteristic behavior, at times their misbehavior, is a matter for detailed inquiry into facts.

The position here being developed may hence be called a "functional realism." So important are Connectives in any unification of Nature that their status demands an initial clarification. In general, the structures and characters grasped and formulated in knowledge and "warranted discourse" have a determinate status in the world encountered. They are "there," in Substance—in the language of medieval realism, they are "in re." They are discoverable "there" in Substance experienced, in its complex cooperation of powers—they are there in the universe of action or the situation. Now, certain structures and factors can be said to be "there," and to be discoverable, even when the factor of which they are the structure is not functioning in a process. Examples of such structures would be the physico-chemical structure of the seed, the mechanical structure of the sewing machine, the psychological structure of human nature, or the musical structure of the symphony. Such structures we have called "formal" or "constitutive" structures, and have found them as the frames of mechanisms and materials that can, on occasion, function as means or powers in processes. Other structures and characters are not "there," are not discoverable, unless these factors are functioning as means in a process—unless the seed is growing, the sewing machine sewing, the men acting, the symphony being performed and heard. Such characters and structures we have called "functional structures."

But such functional structures enjoy an equally determinate status in the world encountered, in Substance. They are equally discoverable in its process, they are equally "real," equally "in re." Their locus is *not* in things apart from their functioning, but in that functioning of powers; they are "there," they are "real," in their functioning in a specific cooperation of powers. They are "real" as belonging to and as discoverable in that cooperation. Their "reality" can be said to be precisely their functioning. They can be said to be "functionally real," and to enjoy a "functional" status. In general, that is "real" which functions determinately and discoverably in the complex of processes that is Substance.

Now, much that is in this sense "functionally real," that has its locus and status and is discoverable in a cooperation of powers, is not operative or "actual" if because of the absence of certain necessary conditions the cooperation does not take place—if the seed does not grow, but remains a mere set of powers, or if the symphony remains a mere score. And likewise, there is much that is "functionally real" and discoverable in Substance encountered that is not operative or "actual" in the absence of the participation of *human* activities in Substance. It is here that Connectives belong. Thus the so-called "values" that function in human experience of the world, in action, art, and science, are not operative in the absence of that human participation—when they are not functioning as means to human ends. But when, with man as one factor in the situation, they are so operative, they are then "functionally real" and "objective"; they are not "subjective," but are objectively determinable—they are "good for" in the perfectly objective sense of being "good for men." The same holds true for all Connectives. Thus, in the chief Connective, language, the structures of discourse are not functioning factors unless men are talking and communicating. But they have their locus and status, they are "functionally real," in the process of communication—in Substance expressed and communicated, in Substance reflectively experienced, in Substance participated in through discourse. Just how these various factors function in Substance—i.e., how they act—how precisely they are "real"—is in each case an objective for inquiry. And the answer is always relative to the process or situation in which they are functioning as cooperating factors.

It is in this sense that the Connectives that operate in unifications of Nature can be said to be "functionally real."

II

I want to push a little further what is implied in each of the two aspects of Nature emphasized: the fact that the world is encountered as *plural,* and the fact that it lends itself to *unifications* through the functioning of Connectives.

I start with the fact that Substance is radically plural. Substance, it will be recalled, is defined as "the encountered context, or situation," within which reflective experience can distinguish a variety of processes and structures. Substance is always encountered as specific and determinable, and this means as "relative"—relative to the direction or end the encountering itself generates. The field or situation can be extended indefinitely, as that end makes more and more of Nature relevant to itself. But we never reach or encounter "the ultimate field, context, or situation." We encounter only the field, situation, or context that is "ultimate for" that particular substance or situation.

This suggests certain further implications of the metaphysical pluralism here being explored—the Aristotelian pluralism of "determinate substances," expressed in the language of the philosophies of being, and the Deweyan pluralism of "specific situations," expressed in the language of the philosophies of experience. Every substance, every situation, every universe of action and experience—whatever name we choose to give the complex of cooperating processes that is encountered—is always encountered as something specific and determinable—as *a* substance, *a* situation, *a* universe of interaction. We never encounter "*the* Universe"; we never act toward, experience, or feel being or existence as "a whole." Despite Santayana and others of like habit of speech, "pure being" seems to be pure bunk. Our encountered and experienced world is always selective and determinate. We can indeed *talk* significantly about "the Universe." But when we do, we are talking distributively, about *every* universe of action and experience, about *every* situation, substance, or field. We are not talking about some unified, all-embracing Substance or Field.

There is hence no discoverable "ultimate context," no "ultimate substance." There is only the widest context that is relevant to any particular activity, process, or specific cooperation of processes, and is hence "ultimate for" that cooperation. "Ultimate," that is, is always relative, never "absolute"; it is always "ultimate for." Talking, discourse, has the widest context of all: we can talk significantly of any or all universes of discourse, and these universes of discourse tend to become more and more unified in the talking. The only sense in which we can speak meaningfully of "the Universe" is as the widest "Universe of discourse." But there is no discoverable "ultimate context" of discourse, save all the *other* contexts: there is no discoverable "context of contexts." In other words, Spinoza was wrong, and Kant was right: we can say nothing valid about "the Universe as a whole," or as a "totality," because we can never encounter or experience it as a whole or a totality, even in reflective experience. We possess no "adequate knowledge of the infinite and eternal essence of Nature." This may be called the "empirical principle": its fundamental character justifies calling this metaphysical pluralism an "empirical pluralism."

Hence "the Universe," or "Nature," is not "a process"—a single process—though any "Universe of action and experience" is a complex of processes. Nor has "the universe," or "nature," any "meaning"—any single meaning—as a whole, save as the sheer *locus* of all processes, contexts, and meanings. Every process has a context or field of other cooperating processes, in terms of which it has a discoverable meaning— a "meaning *for*" that context. The "meaning" of any process is the way it functions in its context. What has no context can have no function, and hence no "meaning."

Now of course it is quite possible to take "the Universe" as a single process, with a single "meaning." Most of the greatest philosophies have done just this, to say nothing of a multitude of religious schemes. But when this is done, we find that we must then invent a further "context" for "the Universe," or Nature. We must go beyond metaphysics to *philosophical theology*. We can indeed thus generalize and unify our analysis of determinate processes, as many a philosopher and philosophic theologian has done. Finding, for instance, that every particular process is always directed toward a correlative objective or "stimulus" *external* to that process—χωριστός—in the context of other cooperating processes, we may then, with Aristotle, generalize that external objective or stimulus to be found in every determinate process, into an objective or stimulus—a unified "Unmoved Mover"—external to all determinate processes. Or, finding that every process is always conditioned by its context, we may then, with Spinoza, generalize that conditioning context of every determinate process into an "Unconditioned Conditioner" of all processes. Again, finding that every process has a "source" or "origin" in antecedent processes, we may then generalize that circumstance into a Source or Origin of all processes—into a "First Cause" antecedent to all "secondary causes."

But in terms of the empirical principle, apart from their function as unifying devices, there *is* no discoverable or implied Unmoved Mover, there *is* no Unconditioned Conditioner, there *is* no Source or Origin of "the Universe." Such generalizations of factors revealed by analysis in particular processes are "metaphysical myths."[2] They are logical constructions or extrapolations, like physical theories, and they possess similar functions. In their ontological status, they are what I have called unifying Connectives or "Conjunctions." Metaphysics can say nothing about "the Universe"; it can speak only of *any* "universe of interaction." It can say nothing about "the ultimate context" or "the ultimate field"; it can speak only of *any* context or field. This our philosophies of experience, from Kant down, have taught us. The attempt so to speak leads to the invention and deployment of myths or Connectives.

Now, such myths are very far from being "meaningless." Like all Connectives, they have a perfectly definite function which can be objectively inquired into. They may well be basic in the living of human life, which often enough gets *its* "meaning" from their use—or rather, which uses them to find and express its "meaning." It may even be true that though "the Universe" has no meaning in terms of a context external to itself, human life derives its meaning by making use of just such a "mythical" context—just such a metaphysical myth, or Connective. It may be true, as Woodbridge puts it, that though Nature has no "justification," man is "justified" by "the Supernatural"—that is, by the Ideal. The pursuit of knowledge, he maintains, does not and cannot take us beyond Nature; but the pursuit of happiness does. This may indeed be true: as Woodbridge puts it, the "judgment of the race" has maintained it. But nevertheless, Woodbridge insists, "it is faith, and not knowledge, that 'justifies.' " And no very intelligible meaning seems to be involved in saying that "the Supernatural" or "the Ideal" lies "outside Nature," or "outside history," as is often said by theologians nowadays. To be sure, "the Supernatural" certainly can be said to lie "outside" this or that particular human life, until it "comes into" it—in theological terms, until it "breaks through"—and it may well "extend beyond" all human life, and thus be "transcendent." All these ways of speaking seem to refer to facts that are familiar to those who have some sense of the religious dimension of experience.

But if this be indeed so, then "Nature" must find some secure place in her domain for "the Ideal," "the Transcendent," and even for "the Supernatural." Indeed, it is clear that any adequate philosophical "naturalism" must have room for all the genuine and obvious facts that such Connectives as "the Supernatural" have referred to; and in that sense, must find some place for "the Supernatural" itself.

Such myths or Connectives—of "the meaning" of "the Universe" in the mythical context of the Unmoved Mover, of the Unconditioned, of the Supernatural, of the Ideal, of God—are not, so long as metaphysics maintains the empirical principle, parts of metaphysical knowledge. Metaphysics can only inquire, What is implied in the fact that human life can employ them to give "meaning" to itself? How do they function to organize the values of existence? How is the actual unified in the light of the Ideal?

I am by no means suggesting that a wise philosophy will of necessity confine itself to what metaphysics can exhibit and denote, and will refuse to go on to "philosophical theology" and its myths. I have myself a great respect for philosophical theology—far more than most theologians today, who seem to have rejected it for an exclusive emphasis on kerygmatic theology. I find men today do not *know* nearly enough about God—not even those who talk to Him with the greatest familiarity. But philosophical theology is a different discipline from metaphysics. Metaphysics has nothing to say about "God" or "the Universe" as the "ultimate context" of existence. But it has much to say about the way such myths or Connectives function in the particular contexts of human living—about any "God," or any "Universe as a whole." For such metaphysical myths or Connectives are factors encountered in Substance. They are "objective facts"; and what they do, how they work, what values they achieve, are likewise objective "facts." Myths and Connectives have a natural and objective function to perform in Nature's complex cooperation of processes. To function as a Connective, or a myth, is one of the fundamental ways in which natural processes can function.

III

This empirical pluralism, implied in the fact that what is encountered as Substance, as a situation or universe of action, is always encountered or experienced as specific and determinate—or determinable—even in reflective experience or discourse, does not deny the possibility or the value of the search for unification, so intimately bound up with the search for control, for the power of manipulation. I now wish to turn to the other aspect of Nature, to examine those unifications she brings about, and some of the ways in which they are achieved.

The demand for unification is impressive. It is persistent, and doubtless ineradicable. We have only to reflect on the tremendous kick the most unlikely men manage to get out of "Oneness" and "Unity." What do our hard-boiled and skeptical positivists today cherish above all other concerns? Nothing other than "Unity"—the unity of science. I am sure any good *Existenzphilosoph* could find this craving for "unity" and "integrity" rooted in "the human situation," springing from the disunities and "dialectical tensions" to which the contemporary German "soul" at least has fallen prey. Gilbert Murray has sought to explain it by another myth: he calls it "the groping of a lonely-souled gregarious animal to find its herd or its herd-leader." But however we attempt to account for the craving for unity, it seems to be a deeply rooted human demand. Like James's "sentiment of rationality," which is indeed but a particular variant of it, it is a sentiment and a demand long before it is justified by any discovered facts.

Logically, of course, the demand for unification and unity is a colossal assumption. Consider the insistence that existence, what is encountered, be found somehow to be a system and order, despite the inexhaustible and ineradicable variety and individuality it exhibits. Man requires that existence exhibit a common set of principles and laws, as the very condition of being found "intelligible" to the human mind. When imposing philosophies, like those of Thomas or Kant, in the process of working out an adjustment between two different sets of beliefs which for historical reasons have come into conflict, arrive at a division between different sets of principles for different "realms" of experience, this neat partition always seems unsatisfactory, and inevitably proves unstable. In the next generation these two sets of principles are unified in a common system, in the thought of a Duns Scotus or a Hegel. When a Descartes—or a Kant—divides the world between the two realms of what his intellectual method can deal with, and what it cannot, that soon appears as a methodological inadequacy, and men like Spinoza and Leibniz—or the whole generation of post-Kantians—set to work to develop a more adequate method that will not clash with the required unity of knowledge. The great historic dualisms, based on the distinction between what a given method can handle and what it cannot—Platonic, Cartesian, or Kantian—always tend toward unification—even if only by making the latter the "appearance" or the "expression" of the former.

Or consider those unifications accomplished not through a logical system of principles, but through a temporal scheme of history. There are the great creation myths, which achieve unification through deriving existence from a common source and origin. There is that most imaginative of all temporal myths, the idea of "evolution." When we ask why it is that men have so often turned to history in their craving for unification, the answer seems clear. Time itself is indeed the great unifier. For historical understanding is always unified in the focus of the present or the future. Consider the power of the "Christian epic" and its unification of the world in the eschatological myth of the Last Judgment—or of its Marxian variant, the revolution that will produce the "classless society."

Then too there is the practical motive for unification, embodied in the demand for a unity of Nature that will sustain a continuity of method: the conviction so strong in our own Augustinian and Baconian tradition, that power and control will come from the universal application of the method that has proved successful within some particular field. There must be a universal method—the Platonic dialectic, the Cartesian mathematical interpretation of Nature, the Baconian induction—that will render men the masters and possessors of Nature. And so men pass lightly over the specific conditions of different subject matters. Consider the many earnest attempts to carry over into human affairs the different methods developed in the successive stages of the enterprise of natural science, from the "geometrical method" of Spinoza in the seventeenth century to the statistical methods of our sociologists today, or the hypothetico-experimental method of Dewey. Or take the drive to make politics into a human engineering, to be treated by technological methods—despite the inadequacy of what has so far been achieved, in comparison with the continued power of the age-old political and religious methods for enlisting for what has to be done the cooperative support and action of men.

But though these various demands for unification rest upon faith rather than proof, it is a faith that has flowered in good works. That both understanding and power do come with increasing unification is scarcely to be denied. To be sure, it never turns out to be quite so simple a matter as we assume, whether in our logical schemes of laws and principles, in our historical unifications through myths, or in our universalized methods. In the variety of Nature's riches, all these schemes inevitably leave out of account those traits and characters they are unable to handle. That is why they require constant and unremitting criticism, an ever-renewed confrontation with Substance encountered, with Nature in the raw, before she has been washed and brushed and tidied up, her hair done in the latest fashion and her nose carefully powdered. Ceaseless vigilance is the price of metaphysical adequacy.

And inevitably these schemes of unification demand the use of unifying Connectives of one sort or another—of myths and symbols, of logical constructions like physical theories, of philosophies of history, of social and political ideals. All these varied types of Connectives function to unify different substances and situations that are in fact encountered as plural and disparate. The "unity" of experience, or of the world, is not a simple discovery. It is rather a process—a *process of unification,* whose achievement demands a heavy reliance on Connectives—on myths, symbols, hypotheses, theories, ideals.

These unifications that Nature achieves in cooperation with man are clearly not "merely human"; above all, they are not "subjective," in that sense that divorces man from Nature and leaves him in splendid isolation in an alien world. To be sure, those unifications attained in vision and in knowledge all involve human cooperations with other natural operations. But it is not man alone—above all, it is not man descending from another realm and trailing clouds of glory—who connects and unifies and brings Nature to a focus in his transcendent lens. It is Nature herself, existence cooperating with men. These unifying Connectives, like the greatest of all, Discourse herself, and her noble daughter Mathematics, are factors in Substance, and function in interaction with other factors in its complex transactions. They are, as we have insisted, functionally real and objective. They may be conventional, but they are not arbitrary.

IV

In preliminary summary, then:

1. Nature is not a "unity"—of substances.

2. Nature is a *continuity*—of natural process, making possible a continuity of analysis, of knowledge, and of scientific methods.

3. But Nature is not a continuity of ends or outcomes, in any sense that would obliterate encountered distinctions of value. Uniqueness and individuality are characteristic of Nature's productions. Nature exhibits a variety of "dimensions" in her achievements: she is not "one-dimensional"—though this is often said by those whose primary interest lies in realms of being that lie "beyond" Nature, and are thus in the literal sense "supernatural." Nature is rather "multi-dimensional": she possesses, and exhibits in her products and outcomes, all those varied "dimensions" she is found to display.

This fact is sometimes expressed: Nature exhibits many different "levels." But this doctrine of "levels" has for the most part been captured by the supernaturalists, alas!, who are concerned to deny the continuity of the mechanisms by means of which Nature effects her ends, and the consequent continuity of analysis, which has led to the triumphs of scientific inquiry. Here it is insisted that Nature exhibits different "levels" of ends and outcomes, and at the same time a continuity of means and mechanisms: the former is in no wise incompatible with the latter circumstance. The greatest conceivable difference in value between the ends of Nature's productivity sets no limits to the discovery of as much continuity as we can find between the mechanisms on which that production depends. There are no antecedent limits set to the experimental exploration of the structure of means.

This would seem not to be controversial. Yet in the same mail there were received two papers, controverting it from opposed positions. One was a defense, naive and revealing, of "materialism," by a college instructor. It ran, "Only matter exists"—that is, only means and mechanisms exist. "Love" and "beauty" do not "exist": they are "words only, for material states and situations." What is effected by mechanisms—activities, processes, outcomes, eventuations—these do not "exist." In the rendition of a violin sonata, all that can be said to "exist" is "the dragging of the tail of a dead horse across the entrails of a dead cat." Of course, the music is "delightful," it is "important," it may even be called "real"; and the author goes on to distinguish between "what exists in a simple location"—his criterion of "existence"—and "what is merely 'real.' "

Insofar as this is not a mere quibble about the meaning of the term "exist," and an undue restriction of that meaning, this illustrates where one gets when one does not take activities and processes as primary and irreducible subject matter. A sound metaphysics would say, activities, operations, and processes "exist," and are effected by means of mechanisms distinguished as facts involved in those processes. "Materialism" locates the means and mechanisms involved, then, by reductive analysis, holds that *only* these mechanisms can be said to "exist"—what they *do* does not "exist," but is merely something else.

The other paper was a defense, likewise naive and revealing, of "dualism." It happened to be by another instructor at the same college: there has never been any unity of knowledge at this seat of learning. This paper ran: Because man acts in certain distinctive ways, not encountered as the ways of acting of any other being, and therefore distinctively human ways (the paper was defending the "Humanism" of Irving Babbitt) he must perform these acts by means of a mechanism specifically different from the continuity of mechanisms by which all other natural processes are effected. The argument runs: Man perceives universals, therefore man must "have" a "simple unextended immaterial spiritual principle," by means of which to do it. This argument starts with an activity, which *is* distinctive and of "unique" value, and then assumes a mechanism not only distinctive, like all specific mechanisms, but also unanalyzable ("simple") and discontinuous with all other natural mechanisms. Where can such an argument stop? with a unique and discontinuous mechanism for each distinctive way of acting encountered in the world? The author, being a Catholic, goes on from what he calls "Dualistic Integral Humanism" to "Trialistic Supernaturalized Humanism": certain human activities demand a third unique mechanism, the "grace of God." And so on, *ad infinitum.*

Does Nature, in addition to this continuity of mechanisms, display also a continuity of genesis, as the early evolutionists believed? The last generation was much concerned to set forth how human experience, in all its manifold variety and complexity, might have "arisen" out of a prehuman and subhuman "experience" in the evolutionary process. Much indeed of the evolutionary emphasis is left over in the thought of those who, like Dewey, in their own lifetime fought through these intellectual battles of the Darwinian age.

Today, the question of the "genesis" of human experience out of lower forms has pretty much ceased to be a debatable issue. It is accepted on every hand as an undoubted fact; the details have become a problem for factual inquiry. But at the same time we have come to have grave doubts about the validity of the speculative anthropology in which our fathers so easily engaged—Dewey among the best of them! We realize we were not there when it all happened, and have doubts as to whether that prehistory can be recovered. And we have come to have even graver doubts of the explanatory value of such an account of the way in which our familiar experience "arose," even if we had accurate details. Our human problem, we have come to feel, is to understand things in terms of the way they function and operate now; that is at least something that is experimentally observable. The genetic problem of how things came to be as they are, is, after all, Nature's problem of Creation—or God's. Man's primary problem, our generation holds, is rather to understand the ways in which what is, however it may have been created, continues to operate and function.

When we approach this human problem, in sober truth, the structures distinguished in Substance by reflective experience, and formulated in discourse and knowledge, are found to be bound up with and involved in structures of other substances and situations. These relatednesses, this continuity of structure, can be explored and followed on indefinitely; and in such inquiry and discourse they tend to become more and more unified. In this process of exploration, we find structures that are not functions of any particular universe of action or any particular encountered complex of processes, but seem to be involved in all processes, in all actions and cooperations. These structures are found to be "invariant" throughout a great variety of contexts. They can hence be "isolated" from any particular context: they "transcend" the limitations of any determinate situation or substance. This fact makes them of fundamental importance for human knowledge and action. A knowledge of such structures proves to be of the widest instrumental value in all contexts. These "invariant" structures can be used, and must be conformed to, in *any* "universe of interaction," in *any* situation.

Expressing this fact as an experimental discovery, we may say, the exploration of the continuity of mechanisms by which Nature operates has led us to formulate these ways of operating in terms of physical and chemical laws. It would perhaps be more accurate to say, that those structures that are invariant through the widest diversity of contexts constitute a delimitation of the subject matter of physico-chemical inquiry. We find also, of course, structures that obtain in more limited types of context, that possess a more limited range of invariance. And these structures are formulated as the "laws" of more restricted "fields," more limited ways of acting, in other sciences.

This encountered unification of structures of a certain type has suggested to many not only a factually verifiable continuity of processes in Nature, but also an eventual "unity" of discovered structure. Such a thoroughgoing unity of the objective of knowledge, making possible the eventual unification of knowledge into a single system, possesses great value as an ideal of knowledge and of formulated discourse—as what Kant calls a "regulative idea." It also unquestionably possesses great dangers, and conceals many pitfalls. Witness the "Unity" of the Neoplatonic dialectic, which came to be elevated above the subject matter of which it was originally taken to be the "Unity," and set over against it, making of what it was at first intended to organize a "mere appearance." Witness also the "Absolute" of the post-Kantians, like F. H. Bradley, and the many purely dialectical and hence completely unreal problems in which it involves its adherents.

We may, then, with due caution, envisage an eventual unification of structure. But the process of the encountered continual unification of structure does not suggest any "unity of substance"—even "eventually." This is not even a "regulative idea." Spinoza's use of the term "Substance" to designate the unified structure of the universe—the "Order of Nature"— is perverse and misleading—even when repeated in so good a pluralistic Aristotelian as Woodbridge.[3] To avoid obliterating a fundamental distinction, it is well to follow Aristotle on this basic point. "Substance," the subject matter encountered in any universe of action, is *never* a comprehensive, all-embracing Unity, Whole, or Totality. It remains a particular and τόδε τι.[4]

V

In conclusion, I should like to raise certain questions about one of the most characteristic ways in which Nature achieves unification—through cumulative temporal development, in the many *histories* she brings to pass. These unifications I find of peculiar interest. For when man cooperates with other natural processes to push further Nature's temporal unifications in the unifying focus of his own history, he and Nature find themselves compelled to employ that particular variety of Connective we call in the more precise sense "myths." The way in which Nature achieves unification through the operation of "myths" has been far less explored than the way she gains it through logical constructions and mathematical theories.

Now the "history" of anything—the history that a thing possesses as the outcome of its fortunes among the other impinging processes of Nature, the "history" that historical knowledge attempts to understand, not the "history" that is that understanding itself—is the significant or relevant past of that thing, the past that is relevant for what it now is. A thing's history is those processes and events that have contributed to its being, gathered into a focus in the present.[5]

Nature is full of such temporal "gatherings into a focus," such "historical unifications," such cumulative outcomes and achievements. Galaxies and stars, mountain ranges and forests, as well as human societies, institutions, and ideas, are all what they are because of their respective pasts. They are "concretions" and "cumulative conservations" of the cooperations of processes into which they have previously entered. If Nature were in truth mere "flux," if she did not exhibit countless patterns of historical unification, and hosts of teleological structures of means and eventuations with a temporal spread, then human histories would indeed be wholly anomalous. Men's unification of their own history, their discovery of the significance of their own past, through knowledge or vision, would be quite impossible. So likewise would be any discovery of "the meaning" of the world, or of human life.

But Nature being what she inescapably is, such human unifications in knowledge or vision are but a pushing further of nature's own unifying powers. So important is this ability of men to extend further the cumulative unifications of Nature that, in order to be emphatic about it, some have said that this power of man to understand his own history "transcends Nature"—forgetting that it is a fundamental character of Nature to be forever "transcending" herself, to be productive, and creative of new outcomes—nowhere more clearly than in her human parts.

When men bring Nature to a focus in the discovered "meaning" of human history, the past becomes unified in the perspective of the present, and is understood as leading up to our own goings on, to our own ideas and problems. Such a temporal unification of the life of man in Nature we usually call a "philosophy of history." These attempts to find an interpretation of "history as a whole" involve an appraisal of the present in the light of the future it suggests. They interpret the past, whose deposit constitutes our resources, in terms of the envisaged future. The nature of the world and of human societies is such as to generate philosophies of history.

A philosophy of history attempting to construe history "as a whole" thus involves two kinds of unification. History can be unified in terms of its materials and resources, of the significant past; and it can also be unified in terms of its envisaged future. Thus philosophies of history normally employ two somewhat different kinds of unifying Connectives or myths: myths of origin and myths of outcome, creation myths and eschatological myths. The origin myths serve primarily to reveal the character of the materials of history: the nature of men and their behavior, or the nature of those groups that play the role of dramatic protagonists in history—races, nations, or classes. Thus we are led to see history whole in terms of the fall of man, or of the state of nature, or of primitive communism. For centuries we could not understand our history except as beginning in a "state of nature." Today we are more apt to call it "primitive society," and to go to anthropology to find the significance of the history of our own institutions. When the Germans used to do it, and discoursed passionately of blonde beasts, we smiled—or swore—according to the degree of our philosophical resignation. When we do it ourselves, and dwell upon the Kwakiutls, the bushmen, the Andaman Islanders, and coming of age in Samoa, we are sometimes convinced that in drawing upon the anthropologists for an understanding of our own history, we are being very "scientific" indeed.

In their purest form these origin myths describe the emergence of human nature from nonhuman nature. When we used to consider man a fallen angel, the meaning of human history depended on the history and fall of the angels. Now that we are inclined to look on him rather as a great ape that has almost made good, the meaning of human history clearly depends on the history of the success story of the great apes—on the history of the "evolution of mankind." These prehuman histories are wonderfully illuminating—in both cases, that of the angels and that of the apes. The only problem is how this "pre-history" can be so illuminating, since we know hardly anything about it: our actual knowledge of the history of the apes is about as sketchy as that of the angels. Human history as a whole, clearly, seems to take on a meaning only when we view it as springing full-blown out of an antecedent myth.

On the other hand, a philosophy of history can also achieve its unification by considering the present in terms of the possible future, of the ends implicit in it, and the means to their attainment. It is selective in its focus: it involves a choice among the determinate possibilities of the present of that "tendency," or predicted future, which we judge to be "dynamic" or "controlling." This choice of focus involves a choice of allegiance, a faith—the faith that the future will display a certain character. Normally again this faith in one kind of outcome is expressed in terms of a myth—the millennium, the kingdom of God, the classless society, or the triumph of social intelligence.

Both origin myths and outcome myths are instruments for unifying our history, for bringing it to a focus from which it can be understood as a whole, and can reveal its significance and meaning. The actual way these myths function is very complex, and demands careful exploration. The two kinds seem to operate rather differently, yet both are clearly involved in historical unifications. There seems to be no discoverable "meaning of history as a whole" without some outcome myth—without some "ideal," which is another name we give to such Connectives. We can no more find the significance of "history as a whole" without an ideal than we can find the significance of life—or of the world—without one. History would then indeed be as meaningless and futile as would life, a meaningless "flux."

But history, life, or Nature herself is a "flux" only to ignorance.

Each is full of implicit ends or ideals, full of values, because each alike is an affair of processes, of mechanisms producing outcomes, of causes and necessary conditions of results, of means and ends. They are all alike full, that is, of things that are "better" and "worse" for other things. Nature is in truth teeming with "entelechies"; and it takes but a single flower to refute the absurd contention that there are no "values" in Nature, no achievement of ends through valuable means. We can even say that it is obviously "good for" the planet to go round and round.

Of course, neither the flower nor the planet can be said to "find" it good: in our experience, only men "find" anything. But surely it does not follow that because only men find anything, what they find is not found. The finding is a genuine cooperation of men with Nature. Ideal Connectives are not "fictions," not "imaginary" or "arbitrary." They are as "natural," as "objective," as any other way in which existence functions in Substance. They all, to be sure, involve human cooperations with other natural operations. Without man's activities, they would remain as powers of Substance. But it is not man alone who connects and unifies: it is existence cooperating with men. And the powers of existence to connect and be connected, to unify and become unified in vision, are essential to the character of existence.

Of course, it is the significance of *our* history *for us* that we discover through the unifying foci of myths or ideals—just as it is the meaning of the world for us that any Connective can generate. A star might well find a different meaning—or a being from Mars. However, there is no evidence that stars find anything significant; and if there be Martians, their philosophies remain unknown. But the fact that we must understand Nature from a human focus is not only a fact about human understanding—and, since human understanding is the only one we know of, a fact about all understanding; it is also a fact about Nature. Nature is brought to a selective unification only in a focus, an ideal, that Nature has herself generated in revealing her possibilities to men. Likewise, the fact that we must understand our history in the light of a selective unification, an outcome myth, that history has itself generated, does not mean that we cannot understand it.

We can understand it best, in the degree to which the suggested focus or outcome is based on knowledge—in which it unifies what we are, what we are doing, and what we still can and must do. It is sometimes said that the ideal which reveals the significance of our history must itself stand "outside history." What this means seems clear: it must be a genuine ideal. But unless that ideal stands at the same time "inside history"—unless it is *our* ideal, rooted in what we are and in what we can become, and relevant to our problems—it will not give us a genuine understanding, or reveal the significance and pattern of our history. Nature, and history, can achieve genuine unification only through Connectives and myths which, though they be conventional, are nevertheless not arbitrary, but are rooted in the very nature of things.

If we start with the world as a *unity*, it is impossible to get from that unity to the encountered plurality of things, which remains therefore a mystery. Only God has been able to turn that trick, and he has not revealed how he has done it: human theologians have never been able to explain the process, not even the evolutionists. But if we start with the encountered plurality, there is nothing to prevent us from tracing as much of *unification* as we may. Such unity as has been achieved, in our vision or in our knowledge, is the outcome of our processes of unification.

Notes

1. See chapter 6, "Substance as a Cooperation of Processes," pp. 176, 194, in John Herman Randall, Jr., *Nature and Historical Experience* (New York: Columbia University Press, 1958).

2. See the classification of myths in ibid., p. 262.

3. See F. J. E. Woodbridge, *Nature and Mind* (New York, 1937), "Structure," pp. 148–59.

4. For a fuller treatment of unities in knowledge, see Epilogue, "Unifications of Knowledge," in J. H. Randall, Jr., *Nature and Historical Experience*, pp. 296–309.

5. See ibid., pp. 35–36.

4

Probing the Idea of Nature*

Justus Buchler

I

Both in colloquial and in methodic discourse the idea of nature has functioned in a large number of ways, and the variety of these ways makes it seem impossible to find significant relatedness among them. Nature has been distinguished from man, from art, from mind, from chance, from purpose, from history, from eternity, from irregularity, from society, from civilization, from God, from evil, from good—to name some of the best known historical contrasts. Yet with respect to every one of these same ideas, nature also has been made inclusive of it or synonymous with it or continuous with it. I have no intention of trying to explain how all this has come about. But it will not be irrelevant to remark that the very fact of the concept "nature" lending itself to so many and conflicting uses can be seen as a cue, a hint to metaphysical thinking rather than as a ground for despair. My subject

*Originally published in *Process Studies* 8, no. 3 (Fall 1978): 157–68. Subsequently published in Justus Buchler, *Metaphysics of Natural Complexes,* 2nd ed., ed. K. Wallace, A. Marsoobian, and R. Corrington (Albany, N.Y.: SUNY Press, 1990), pp. 260–81. Reprinted by permission

will take the form of considering two broad philosophic tendencies which have determined specific conceptions of nature. One of the tendencies is to regard nature as limited, and the other is to regard nature as unlimited. After asking what the difference comes to, and after persuading you to think exactly as I do, I shall propose a possible way of defining nature. But first, some observations that are more or less historical.

According to Collingwood's book *The Idea of Nature,* the two most frequently used broad senses that have been given to the word "nature" are: first, the collective sense of a "sum total or aggregate," and second, the sense of a "principle" or *arché,* a source which defines or informs whatever is called "natural" and which justifies our speaking also in the plural, of "natures" or "essences." This second sense is held to be the original and so-called proper sense of *physis.* I think it would be better to identify these two ways of conceiving nature as "orientations" rather than senses or direct meanings. The first of them I would call the domain orientation; the second, the trait orientation. Thus reframed, each can be seen in a way that permits certain distinctions to emerge. For example, with regard to the first orientation, nature conceived as a domain may be, but *need* not be, conceived as a collection or sum or aggregate; instead, it may be conceived as a certain *kind* of domain. And with regard to the second orientation, nature as the principle or source of traits that are called "natural" can be thought of as just that— a principle of traits—and not a principle only of those traits that are called "essential." Thus it is at least possible to omit the notion of inherent essences without violating this second orientation. We may observe, in general, that it is a trait orientation which has given rise to concern about the natural vs. the *un*natural, or the natural vs. the artificial, and that it is a domain orientation which has given rise to concern about the natural vs. the *super*natural. In the present discussion such concerns are reduced to the general issue of the natural vs. the nonnatural, which is one way of rendering our question of nature unlimited vs. nature limited.

It is within what we are calling the domain orientation that Collingwood believes the difference is to be found between nature conceived as unlimited and nature conceived as a limited or restricted domain. A restricted domain in Collingwood's version is one that is not independent but dependent on some other. He believes that in the basic tradition of European thought the dominant view by far is this view of nature as limited: it implies that nature has "a derivative or dependent status in the general scheme of things," that "the world of nature forms only one part or aspect of all being." It is dependent "on something prior to itself." Historically, the reasons underlying the restricted view, the one called dominant, are extremely diverse. But the view as such is held or presupposed by scientists as well as philosophers, and it goes back to the time when the entire general issue of the scope of nature was debated in early Greek thought.

It is very hard to assess a contention about what is the dominant view. My interest here is mainly theoretical rather than historical. But even historically, we cannot gauge the issue solely by trying to figure out a numerical majority of opinions. For among them there are implicit emphases which have been as influential as those which are visible on the surface. We could also cite powerful counter-examples like Erigena, Aquinas, and Spinoza, who in their different ways conceive of a divine nature and in effect make nature the inclusive, or an equivalent of the inclusive, category. Probably many others were likewise convinced that, since whatever is has a nature, the notion of a nonnature is absurd. Collingwood, as we might suspect, pays small attention to that particular medieval tendency which dwells on *natura naturans* and *natura naturata*. When, however, he alters his angle and calls the dominant view the "modern" view, he is on securer ground. Then we recognize the so-called world of nature as the spatio-temporal world, and we begin to understand why science, for so long called "natural philosophy," still wishes to be called "natural" science.

I still have a bone to pick on the historical level. It is surprising for a historical account (especially a serious account like Collingwood's) to interpret a restrictive conception of nature as one in which nature has "a derivative or dependent status." In the modern restrictive tendency what is called the world of nature, far from being considered necessarily dependent, is as often assigned the reverse status, namely that upon which any other "world" is "dependent" (e.g., the "world of number" or the "moral world") or that of which any other world is an appearance or that which is "more real" than any other world.

II

The notion of "the world of nature" usually involves the cognate notion of "the order of nature" or "the natural order." It is interesting to reflect that philosophers like Peirce and Whitehead, esteemed for their intensive concern with science as well as for their independent spirit, tend to think of nature in the limiting or restrictive way. They deal at considerable length with "the order of nature," a phrase the components of which seem to receive from them a certain type of explicit consideration, but which as a phrase remains dim in both of them. I suppose that the order-of-nature habit of thought is an oblique commitment to the idea of "laws of nature," which would be a much more difficult idea to defend if the domain orientation were of the unlimited kind. Whitehead says in *The Concept of Nature*, "Nature is that which we observe in perception through the senses." In *Process and Reality* he says that when "we speak of the 'order of nature' " we mean "the order reigning in that limited portion of the universe . . . which has come under our observation." And as late as *Modes of Thought* he says, "Nature, in these chapters, means the world as interpreted by reliance on clear and distinct sensory experiences, visual, auditory, and tactile." Whether these statements of the same theme are perfectly harmonious in themselves or with one another, I am not sure. But they surely accentuate the restrictive position. In *The Concept of Nature* Whitehead had said also, "Natural science is the science of nature." And again, "[N]ature can be thought of as a closed system whose mutual relations do not require the expression of the fact that they are thought about." In *Process and Reality* the term "nature" serves the purpose of defining subject matter basic to science. Treating philosophically of nature thus apparently boils down to focusing the more general metaphysical categories on such concepts as space and time. In contrast to what is sought by science, there is said by Whitehead to be "an essence to the universe" which is sought by metaphysics or speculative philosophy. Metaphysics, he believes, seeks to understand "the system of the universe." I refrain from comment for the time being, except to note that Whitehead also occasionally uses phrases like "the womb of nature" and "the divine nature," which may or may not suggest a tacit alternative usage of nature in a wider sense.

Let us return to the idea of "the order of nature," which often seems to function less as an idea than as a name or slogan conventionally identifying a roughly associated group of problems. In contexts where it is presumably under discussion, specifically those of Peirce and Whitehead, it is hard to find out whether the phrase presupposes order *in* nature or nature as *an* order. If there is any difficulty in taking "the order of nature" to mean "that order which is called nature," then the difficulty should attach to the expression "the world of nature," which has the same type of import. But leaving aside the question of what sense we should accept, the distinction between order as belonging to nature and the order called nature is of utmost importance. It reflects the difference between "order" as a definite familiar kind of trait and "an order" as a complex of traits, a location of traits, regardless of what kind. Order in the former sense is contrasted with "disorder," whereas *an* order, construed as a complex of traits, can be contrasted only with other orders: as we will find, there is no meaning to a nonorder. "Order" contrasted with "disorder" is not a distinction at the most general ontological level. But "an order" in the sense I am suggesting has little to do with order in the sense of arrangement or pattern, such as a pattern of regularity or of chance. It is to be understood as a complex with an integrity. In other words, the concept of an order or complex is universally applicable.

We pursue this now in more detail. Let us suspend temporarily the entire issue of the scope of nature, of whether we can maintain a distinction between natural and nonnatural. And in our metaphysical stance, let us think of anything at all, whether it be classified as an individual, a sensation, an event, a relation, a structure, a grouping, a change, a process, an eternal form, an hallucination, or whatnot. It has traits. It is a complex of traits. It is a plurality of traits. The plurality will follow if only from each trait's being itself ramified, from each trait's standing in relations; from each trait's, in other words, being itself a complex. No trait is at some point cut off relationally from *every* other. If there is such a point of absolute disconnectedness, we have yet to identify it or certify it in the history of man. The traits of a given complex will differ in some respect from those constituting any other and will resemble them in some respect. This is another way of saying that each complex limits and relates its traits in the way that it does. By "the way that it does" or "the respect in which it does" we imply an order. We have already posed the reciprocal idea of an order as a complex of traits. And we have just now been speaking in ordinal terms.

To improve the cohesiveness of this truncated account, we must lay fuller emphasis on two concepts which are interwoven with the others in the reciprocal way just employed. These are the concepts of integrity and ordinal location. Insofar as each complex both differs from and resembles others, it has a trait makeup. Yet if our description went no farther than this, we could not say that a complex has an integrity but only certain constituents thereof, including plurality. The other and indispensable factor is the location of the complex in an order, that is, in an order other than itself, a more inclusive order. By its location the complex is delimited and hence distinguished in a given way from other complexes. As ordinally located it may be thought of as playing a role in a setting—a spatial setting or a moral setting or an occupational setting or any environing complex—even if the role at bottom is that of excluding other traits and being in a specific relation. But a complex may be located in many orders and may therefore have many integrities. If not located in a given order, it does not have an integrity relevant to that order. It is not defined or delimited in that respect. But ordinally located it must be. To omit this consideration is to inject contradiction into the concept of a complex. It follows directly that every complex of traits is not only located or included in various orders, but locates and includes other complexes, subcomplexes, and is an indispensable determinant of *their* integrity. Orders, being complexes of traits, thus derive their integrities from their status in more inclusive orders, and no order is an order if it is not inclusive and included, locative and located. But the "no order if" phrase is, of course, a merely rhetorical addition, for on the approach I am describing, what is not an order *is* not.

Returning to the problem of nature and the natural: the issue as formally stated was put in terms of the domain orientation, i.e., is nature a limited or an all-inclusive domain? But the issue also can be put (as we have implied) in terms of the trait orientation, i.e., is nature a source or principle of traits limited to the so-called essential trait of any being, or is it a principle universally applicable to any trait whatever? We stated a miniature argument for the unrestricted conception, attaching it to the outlook of such as Erigena, Aquinas, and Spinoza. It went: since whatever is has a nature, we cannot give meaning to the notion of a nonnature. To this it might be objected, first, that the use of the expression "a nature" to apply to whatever is, decides the issue by definition and settles it in advance; and second, that the use of the expression "a nature" confounds the domain orientation with the trait orientation, for we are talking about the scope of nature and not about this or that nature.

But in fact, as we now can see, we do not need the expression "a nature" at all. We are able to say that whatever is has an integrity; it is the integrity of a complex. We are able to say that a complex, necessarily being located in *some* order, cannot have a nonintegrity. And in general we are now able to see that a trait orientation and a domain orientation are merely two sides of one and the same effort of interpretation. For a domain is an order, and there is no order without traits, just as there are no traits, no complexes, unlocated in any order.

The view of nature as restricted amounts to the view that there is a widespread order of complexes called nature, which is either located in another or other orders or includes other orders but not every other. In the now popular but actually more customary language of "worlds," nature restricted is a world that is seen as somehow related to other worlds. Of course, once we see each of these worlds as an order, the pressure to specify the order and to clarify its relatedness, to get rid of the "somehow," becomes greater.

As for the unrestricted view, it too now can be stated without interference by old associations of the term "nature." We seem required to say that nature unrestricted must include all worlds, indeed all orders whether they are to be called worlds or not. But a careful statement of the unrestricted view cannot be achieved all at once. There are problems that have to be solved.

III

I introduced the common term "domain" to help clarify a historical distinction and to help launch the present discussion. At this point we are in a position to see that although we can speak of a domain as an order, and perhaps vice versa, we cannot speak of a domain or order of nature in the unrestricted sense. The reason is emphatically not the Kantian view that nature or the world as a whole cannot be "given in experience," cannot be "objects of possible experience." To begin with, on the basis of such a reason we could argue that *nothing* as a whole can be an object of possible experience or be given, since we must take into account the indefinite spread of its relations and its potentialities. Actually we are aiming at an affirmative metaphysical conception instead of a conception based on a supposedly necessary structure of knowing and experiencing. Yet even if we approach the matter in epistemological terms, we certainly need not accept Kant's sense-appearance paradigm of the content of "experience," or what is meant by "given in experience" or "object of experience." And we certainly need not accept Kant's view of nature as "an aggregate of appearances." We shall have to say, instead, that though nothing at all is present as a "whole" in experience, yet nature is present in every instance of experience and every process of experiencing.

The reason that nature unlimited is not a domain may be put in the following way. A domain is an order, an order of traits. There is no order without delimitation, trait delimitation. If nature were an order, it would be an order of all orders. But if it is unlimited, not delimited, it cannot be an order at all. For it would have to include every order without being included in any. It would have to locate every order without being located. If it is not ordinally located, it has no integrity. If it has no integrity, it cannot itself be the location of any other order and determine *that* order's integrity. An order cannot be defined by another which has no constitution of its own traits. And an order which does not locate and is not located does not constitute and is not constituted. The conclusion, then, must be that if nature is an order it is limited in scope and that if it is unlimited it is not an order. In familiar terms we would say that nature is not analogous to *a* nature. But of course it is the metaphysical explanation for the unsoundness of the analogy that is important.

A consequence of all this is that a conception merely of nature unrestricted is not enough. It needs to be augmented and clarified. If, as we have seen, it is so formulated that it can both utilize and abandon the concepts of a complex and an order, the idea of unrestrictedness is jeopardized. The way Kant, for instance, identifies the meaning of the terms "world" and "nature" jeopardizes the idea, by our standard. "World," he says, "signifies the mathematical sum total of all appearances and the totality of their synthesis"; and "[t]his same world is entitled nature when it is viewed as a dynamical whole." Actually Kant cannot be speaking of nature in an unrestricted sense as that is here understood, if only because he associates nature intrinsically with a principle of causality, which is itself a restrictive condition. But what is relevant to our problem is the kind of formulation that we find in Kant. "Syntheses" and "wholes" are complexes of traits. They are integrities determined by ordinal location. Thus World and nature as identified by Kant would have to be ordinally located. But their location would mean inclusion in another order. And this contradicts the requirement in terms of which they are identified, namely, being inclusive and not being included.

The position that nature unlimited cannot be an order of all orders will remain puzzling to those for whom the latter idea has an emotional no less than an analytical aspect. They are inclined to think that nature unembraced is nevertheless all-embracing in *some* sense. The sentiment as such is not only understandable but acceptable—when we say *what* sense and say it more satisfactorily. But if it entails bald commitment to a superorder, then the burden falls on its exponents to develop another conception of what an order is or to discriminate two conceptions, one of which is uniquely applicable to nature. Pending that development, there is no good reason to exempt the idea of nature from the criteria of the ordinal conception we have found basic. After all, we are not faced with an impasse or a hopeless paradox. I shall define nature unlimited otherwise than as an order, even if the result is not conveyed in the form of a conventional package. I think that behind the insistence on an order that is to be uniquely distinguished from all others there are no doubt various convictions mirroring conscious or unconscious models. But whatever models are adopted, the issue of integrity and demarcation must be explained or explained away. An order differentiated only by the all-inclusiveness ascribed to it, and itself without a principle of integrity, is as self-contradictory as an infinitely extended enclosure, a territory without boundaries, a habitation without environment, a definition without limits.

From the viewpoint at which we have arrived thus far, two general observations are pertinent. The first is that there is no longer any need to speak nor any meaning in speaking of "the unity of nature." This idea, which is another of the venerated metaphysical slogans, seems most at home in a restricted view of nature and in particular the historical view defending the universal applicability of scientific law and explanation to all that is measurable in the world. Another and even older version of the unity of nature is the idea of the inherent purpose or purposes of nature, "what nature intended." It too is familiar, morally and metaphysically—and remarkably obscure in meaning.

The second general observation is that no reason can be assigned for speaking of what Whitehead (among many others) calls "the system of the universe." "The universe" seems to be Whitehead's term for the most comprehensive order, and "nature," as we saw, is called by him a "portion" of the universe. We will recall also that intimately related to this assumption of a system is his view of "an essence to the universe," an essence allegedly sought by metaphysics. But, once again, the universe, deemed all-inclusive, cannot be itself an order and, therefore, cannot be called a system. A system is differentiable not only from its own subaltern systems but from alternative systems. If it is inclusive of all others, it is left without an integrity and is therefore not a system at all. Hence there is also no meaning in saying that it has an essence.

On the basis of the unrestricted view as stated thus far, science would be said to be concerned not with nature in an unqualified sense but with a given world or worlds—the physical world, the social world, the psychological world. These worlds are pervasive orders of nature, for we no longer can make sense of "the" order of nature. The diverse problems of science emerge in suborders or levels and, when resolved, provide integrities expressed in formulae. Included among the complexes of these orders are the methods and processes of scientific activity itself.

And just as we no longer need struggle to make intelligible "the" order of nature, we no longer need to dignify the so-called rationality of nature. Aside from the metaphysical ineptitude of this particular attribution, the notion as such was framed to fit applied mathematical thinking. A tenable conception of nature recognizes many orders occupied by man among the innumerable orders not occupied by man and many orders devised by man. Among the latter are the orders of query, of which science or inquiry is one and art or contrivance is another, both, of course, indefinitely subdivisible. It is orders of query which yield different possible forms and manifestations of rationality.

We are obliged now to translate the foregoing considerations into terms which convey an idea of nature more directly. If nature is undelimited and therefore to be identified as coextensive with whatever is, we can say that by nature we mean "orders, of whatever variety and number." This is safe from the difficulties mentioned, if not altogether congenial psychologically. Nothing is implied about a totality or whole or collectivity, no embarrassing commitment made to an ultimate integration which lacks an integrity. But needless to say, it is a somewhat clumsy way of expressing an equivalent meaning. In calling it clumsy I do not want to be saying that every adequate metaphysical conception must be rendered in a grammatically facile way. If I had the time, I would argue that philosophic and in particular metaphysical judgment is not always best articulated or even best understood in the form of assertions. Not less fundamental is the force of mutually enhancing ideas which recur in different contexts. These form a conceptual array. The array is what communicates metaphysical query in the firmest sense and preserves a structure over and above specific weaknesses. A structure of metaphysical query has an assertive dimension, but it also is one type of exhibitive judgment. In the exhibitive mode of metaphysical judgment we discriminate traits that are not only comprehensible (at the level chosen) but meant to be satisfying in virtue of that comprehensiveness as *portrayed.* The degree of satisfactoriness (and I do not mean acceptance) will reflect itself in continuing query compelled by the original portrayal, by the conceptual array. But let us resume the effort to define nature.

Now the term "the World" is what we may well think of as the most highly generalized notion that can serve to express the human sense of encompassment. In a parallel and correlative way, the term "nature" may be thought of as the most highly generalized notion that can serve to express the human sense of characterization and traithood. Elsewhere I have defined the term "the World" partly through the following statements: "By 'the World' we must mean: Innumerable natural complexes (each located, each locating) which distributively include any given complex and which have no collective integrity . . . 'Innumerable' is intended both in the sense of being indefinitely numerous and in the sense of being not in all respects numerable." In accord with this, and complementary to it, "nature" may be defined as the ordinality of any complex—any of the innumerable complexes. We define more fully by adding that nature is the complexity of any order—any of the innumerable orders. And more fully yet by adding that nature is indeed the complexity of any complex, the ordinality of any order; it is the ordinality that limits each complex, the complexity that pluralizes each order.

I can imagine someone questioning whether ordinality is not itself an order, whether complexity is not itself a complex, and whether therefore we do not lapse back into the idea of nature as the superorder. But I have already said that nature can be defined as "orders, of whatever variety and number" and that we are introducing only a more fluent, equivalent version. This leaves no implication of a superorder. In speaking of nature as the ordinality of any order we are affirming distributively that complexes named at random (say, a political community or the order of traits known as an apple) are first and last ordinal, whatever their specific traits may be. But it is not ordinality that includes and locates, it is one or another order. It is not ordinality as such that will provide an integrity. It is not nature that locates but an order of nature. It is not the World that locates but one or more of the innumerable complexes. The integrity of a complex is determined at a given level. A carpenter is defined by the order of activity to which he belongs. The integrity of an hereditary trait is determined by the genetic order in which it is located.

When nature is defined baldly as "orders, of whatever variety and number," too little is suggested of a difference in emphasis between the concepts of nature and the World. The focus is on *natura naturata*: we are given the crop, but not the seeding, not the productive principle. The definition in terms of ordinality corrects this. Some years ago I defined nature as providingness, the provision of traits. The intent was to abstract from the partly eulogistic common suggestion of purposive or planned accumulation, as well as of energy, and to amplify the suggestion of sheer putting forth or bringing forth, sheer geniture, for better and for worse. The conceptions of nature as providingness and as ordinality are continuous with one another and with the conception of nature as "orders." This continuity can be conveyed by utilizing both members of the twin *natura naturans* and *natura naturata.* Nature as ordinality is *natura naturans;* it is the providing, the engendering condition. Nature as "orders" is *natura naturata;* it is the provided, the ordinal manifestation, the World's complexes.

The foregoing conception of nature means that no complex can be regarded as, so to speak, transcendently free-floating, as nonordinal, as superseding all orders. It means, for example, that what are labelled as fictions, illusions, and contradictions also have an ordinal environment and an integrity or integrities, whether these be verbal or logical or emotional. It means that nothing is "contrary to nature," nothing distinctively "in accordance with nature." But one important way to see what the proposed conception implies is to understand its impact on the concepts of possibility and actuality. In denying "free-floating" status to any natural complex, we are, first, identifying any possibility as a complex and hence a subcomplex; and second, denying that any is a so-called pure possibility, one undetermined, unaffected by conditions both of actuality and related possibility. If ordinality is ubiquitous, then possibilities must be ordinally located. What is possible is possible only under given conditions. The conditions may be broad or narrow, constant and perpetual, or fleeting. They may be temporal or nontemporal, contingent or mathematical. When allegedly pure possibilities are thought of, they are in fact thought of ordinally, but the relevant conditions which are latently implied are unwittingly suppressed or overlooked. If a possibility were wholly independent of all other complexes, we surely could not conceive or envisage it, nor could we describe or formulate it. For whatever we could be talking about would relate to some complex that we bring to bear. It would relate to what we know or envision or can think of. We certainly can think of new possibilities, but not in complete discontinuity and isolation from all else. The complexes which we choose to talk and think about are partly but necessarily determining factors of the way we talk about them. A nonlocated possibility could not be identified. An integrity could not be framed for it. By contrast, to acknowledge that possibilities are traits and have subaltern traits is to acknowledge that each is bounded, limited. Perforce we ask: possibility of what, possibility in what respect, what direction?

The case is precisely the same with actuality. Every actuality is native to an order or orders. A complex is determined ordinally to have the actuality and kind of actuality it has. Some philosophers who would not wish to speak of pure actuality in the way they speak of pure possibility nevertheless think that way and presuppose a notion of what is inherently and distinctively actual. Their model is the spatio-temporal, publicly measurable world, and even then, most often only the individuals of that world. Shakespeare they would consider actual—actual at one time, at least—but not the man Hamlet. If they became aware of the ordinal levels and locations that are relevant to the validation of all our judgments and modes of judgment, they might come to say (with the appropriate qualifications) that Shakespeare no longer is actual and that Hamlet still is or that since Shakespeare is indeed actual in an order of history his present efficacy is the efficacy of all the persons and relations he has actualized. It is not unusual to hear that art poses possibilities. It is less readily perceived that art produces actualities and that such actualities can be and have been more influential in the life of man than many actualities of the familiar public historical world. A genuinely ordinal conception of nature recognizes products of art to be orders in the same sense as other products, like technological orders and legal orders. Orders may, of course, interpenetrate one another. Having identified the relevant order, the order we are interested in, we accept what we find. We accept the actualities and possibilities of that order. Gertrude actually is the mother of Hamlet. Ophelia cannot possibly be that. Hamlet actually sees the ghost of his father. Those who would deny that Shakespeare's persons actually have eyes would hesitate to deny that Donatello's angels actually have wings. It must be that a bias toward certain kinds of art goes along with a bias toward certain kinds of actuality.

But we do not have to depart from everyday situations to grasp the ordinality that is nature. The first note of ordinal metaphysics was struck in 1951, when I suggested that a house may fluctuate in its actual size, just as it may fluctuate in its monetary worth. Many philosophers who would agree that when we stand before a house it is the house that we see, not an image or sense-datum or appearance of the house, would balk at the ordinal consequences. As we move away from the house, it becomes smaller. I am not saying, in the manner of certain epistemologies earlier in this century, that the house appears smaller, each appearance being just as much a reality as the house itself. I am saying that if what is called the "house itself" appears smaller, it is because it *gets* smaller. It is in the order of vision that it gets smaller. That is one of its ordinal locations, as much an ordinal location as its geometrical or financial location. As we move away from the house, it actually occupies a progressively smaller space in the visual order. This can be predicted and measured. The house is the same house, but in a different order. The different order yields a different integrity, another integrity of the same complex. What we should call the "nature" of the house is its network of integrities, its contour of ordinal locations.

There is, finally, a broad danger of ambiguity and confusion that needs to be guarded against. A persistent view of actuality is that it *is* an order, the order called "the world of actuality" or "the actual world." And there is a corresponding description of possibility as well, often associated with the idea of pure possibility, namely, that there is indeed an order called the realm of possibility. Now, we know that it has been chronically difficult to give a plausible account of how a realm of possibility and a realm of actuality are related or get related. But my main concern here is that this pseudo-ordinal stance not be confounded with an ordinal conception of nature. For all actualities to be massed together in one realm and all possibilities in another is to remove them all from the various orders in which they belong or in which they arise. It is to remove them from their spheres of relevance and thereby to reject if not to destroy the conception of ordinality. Orders may not only prevail but eventuate or cease to prevail. The reason that a special realm of possibility or of actuality must be denied is that *every order* is a realm of possibility and of actuality. *Every* order or complex of traits has its traits of possibility and its traits of actuality. Even what we might abstractly call an order of possibilities arising in reflection or confronting social action has its aspects of actuality; for example, there is an actual succession of one possibility by another in the course of thinking or in the course of social occurrences.

In these remarks I have said nothing at all about how possibility may be defined or how actuality may be defined. I have tried only to argue the status of possibilities and actualities as natural complexes. The further explicit definition of these concepts adds support to the ordinal approach in general. But it requires further theoretical apparatus that cannot be adequately introduced here. The same must be said of other concepts I have scarcely mentioned, specifically those which I name prevalence and alescence. These are required for the fullest conception of nature along the lines indicated. They are designed, as a team, to do work which other philosophers may prefer to assign to the concept of Being.

Yet, notwithstanding these omissions, should it be hard to see that every natural complex has its mode of actuality and has possibilities that represent its limits? Or that whatever we produce, whatever we discriminate, whether a technological trend or a unicorn, a teapot or the bush that was not consumed, cannot be dismissed, ruled out, or declared null, but calls for ordinal definition? Should it be hard to see that an order of poetry, like an order of poets, is an order of nature?

Part II

Nature, Experience, and Method

Section 3

Experience

Experience is a central topic in naturalist philosophy for several reasons. One of them is that naturalism has tended to accept the philosophic significance of any and all forms of experience, not only or even primarily the cognitive. A second reason experience is a central topic is that naturalists would agree that good philosophy is in some ways and in some degree empirical. While they might disagree about just what that means, they will agree that it points to the need for a careful study of experience. Finally, for some naturalists, the nature of experience is the key to an understanding of nature in general. All three of these points appear in the essay by Dewey in this section. In this piece, which is an excerpt from the first chapter of *Experience and Nature,* his major work on metaphysics, Dewey says that he is trying to develop a theory of the relation between experience and nature on the model of the role of experience in science. Philosophy has yet to adapt to the empirical method, a method which on Dewey's view implied a neutralist, Jamesian conception of nature, wherein such categories as matter or mind are products of reflective experience, not objects of primary experience. There is an instrumentalist conception of experience and knowledge in Dewey's arguments, and we have an example here of a distinctly pragmatist strain of naturalist thought.

It is precisely the pragmatist flavor of Dewey's naturalism with which Cohen is most displeased. Morris R. Cohen was born in Minsk in 1880, and moved with his family to New York City in 1892. He entered City College in 1895, and later pursued graduate studies at Columbia and Harvard, receiving his doctorate from Harvard in 1906. He returned to New York and in 1912 became an assistant professor of philosophy at City College, from which he retired in 1938. Though he taught briefly at Harvard and the University of Chicago, Cohen spent most of his time until his death in 1947 developing his philosophic ideas. The short piece included in this section is the epilogue to *Reason and Nature,* which first appeared in 1931. The intriguing title of this short essay, "In Dispraise of Life, Experience, and Reality," is Cohen's way of expressing his distaste for several prominent strains of contemporary philosophy, including Dewey's instrumentalist version of naturalism. Cohen criticizes the influential "philosophies of life," stemming largely from Nietzsche or Bergson, as well as the tendency to extend the scope of the concept of experience so far that it becomes virtually synonymous with nature. The problem with these philosophic positions, Cohen argues, is that they obscure certain distinctions which have traditionally been and continue to be crucial for philosophic inquiry: between the experience of truth and the experience of illusion; between life and the good life; and between reality in general and a reality free of ugliness.

Cohen's objections to prominent strains of European philosophy notwithstanding, one of the more original and intriguing naturalist treatments of experience is Marvin Farber's attempt to appropriate phenomenology. Farber was born in Buffalo, New York, in 1901, and received his Ph.D. in philosophy from Harvard in 1925. He also studied in Germany, where he developed a relationship with Edmund Husserl, the influential phenomenologist. Farber became the first proponent of Husserlian phenomenology in the United States, and he was the founder and editor of the influential journal *Philosophy and Phenomenological Research.* Farber taught at the State University of New York at Buffalo, where he was emeritus professor of philosophy at the time of his death in 1980. The piece reproduced in this volume is a chapter from Farber's *Naturalism and Subjectivism,* and in the essay he explores the nature of reflection as an aspect of experience. It is in the study of reflection that Husserl's phenomenology is important, Farber argues, but he gives it a naturalist rendering. Since experience always occurs in a broader natural context such as the physical environment, culture and society, the study of reflection must take the natural context of experience into account. In this way Farber attempts to reconcile what he regards as the insightful aspects of Husserlian phenomenology with naturalism, in fact with materialism.

Not surprisingly, Buchler would not be content with either Husserl's more subjectivist treatment of reflection or Farber's materialist appropriation of it. In addition to his interest in general ontology, an example of which is his discussion of nature in section 2, Buchler was also interested in exploring what it is to be a *human* being. His answer to this question took the form of what he called a theory of judgment or a theory of utterance, the details of which can be found in his first two books of original philosophy, *Towards a General Theory of Human Judgment* and *Nature and Judgment.* Buchler's view is that there are three modes of judgment, which is to say three ways in which human beings interact with and place an imprint on our environing conditions. The three modes of judgment are the active, the assertive, and the exhibitive, and no one is more important or more fundamental than the other two. Buchler's theory of judgment encompasses the concerns with which other philosophers deal in their discussions of experience, and in the essay here taken from *Nature and Judgment* he says that indeed a general theory of judgment needs an adequate theory of experience. Too many philosophers, he thinks, misread the nature of experience. Dewey was too restrictive in that he was inclined to see experience primarily in terms of assertive judgment, while Whitehead had the opposite problem of being too expansive, reading experience and mind into nature such that all relations became relations of experience. Buchler develops what is on his view a more satisfying conception of experience through what he calls a theory of proception.

1

Experience and Philosophic Method*

John Dewey

The title . . . *Experience and Nature* [editor's note—the volume in which this essay originally appeared—see introduction to section 3] is intended to signify that the philosophy here presented may be termed either empirical naturalism or naturalistic empiricism, or, taking "experience" in its usual signification, naturalistic humanism.

To many the associating of the two words will seem like talking of a round square, so engrained is the notion of the separation of man and experience from nature. Experience, they say, is important for those beings who have it, but is too casual and sporadic in its occurrence to carry with it any important implications regarding the nature of Nature. Nature, on the other hand, is said to be complete apart from experience. Indeed, according to some thinkers the case is even in worse plight: Experience to them is not only something extraneous which is occasionally superimposed upon nature, but it forms a veil or screen which shuts us off from nature, unless in some way it can be "transcended." So

*Now published in *The Later Works of John Dewey, Vol. 1 (1925): Collected Articles and "Experience and Nature,"* ed. J. A. Boydston (Carbondale, Ill.: Southern Illinois University Press, 1981). Reprinted by permission of the Board of Trustees, Southern Illinois University.

something nonnatural by way of reason or intuition is introduced, something supra-empirical. According to an opposite school experience fares as badly, nature being thought to signify something wholly material and mechanistic; to frame a theory of experience in naturalistic terms is, accordingly, to degrade and deny the noble and ideal values that characterize experience.

I know of no route by which dialectical argument can answer such objections. They arise from associations with words and cannot be dealt with argumentatively. One can only hope in the course of the whole discussion to disclose the meanings which are attached to "experience" and "nature," and thus insensibly produce, if one is fortunate, a change in the significations previously attached to them. This process of change may be hastened by calling attention to another context in which nature and experience get on harmoniously together—wherein experience presents itself as the method, and the only method, for getting at nature, penetrating its secrets, and wherein nature empirically disclosed (by the use of empirical method in natural science) deepens, enriches, and directs the further development of experience.

In the natural sciences there is a union of experience and nature which is not greeted as a monstrosity; on the contrary, the inquirer must use empirical method if his findings are to be treated as genuinely scientific. The investigator assumes as a matter of course that experience, controlled in specifiable ways, is the avenue that leads to the acts and laws of nature. He uses reason and calculation freely; he could not get along without them. But he sees to it that ventures of this theoretical sort start from and terminate in directly experienced subject matter. Theory may intervene in a long course of reasoning, many portions of which are remote from what is directly experienced. But the vine of pendant theory is attached at both ends of the pillars of observed subject matter. And this experienced material is the same for the scientific man and the man in the street. The latter cannot follow the intervening reasoning without special preparation. But stars, rocks, trees, and creeping things are the same material of experience for both.

These commonplaces take on significance when the relation of experience to the formation of a philosophic theory of nature is in question. They indicate that experience, if scientific inquiry is justified, is no infinitesimally thin layer or foreground of nature, but that it penetrates into it, reaching down into its depths, and in such a way that its grasp is capable of expansion; it tunnels in all directions and in so doing brings to the surface things at first hidden—as miners pile high on the surface of the earth treasures brought from below. Unless we are prepared to deny all validity to scientific inquiry, these acts have a value that cannot be ignored for the general theory of the relation of nature and experience.

It is sometimes contended, for example, that since experience is a late comer in the history of our solar system and planet, and since these occupy a trivial place in the wide areas of celestial space, experience is at most a slight and insignificant incident in nature. No one with an honest respect for scientific conclusions can deny that experience as an existence is something that occurs only under highly specialized conditions, such as are found in a highly organized creature which in turn requires a specialized environment. There is no evidence that experience occurs everywhere and everywhen. But candid regard for scientific inquiry also compels the recognition that when experience does occur, no matter at what limited portion of time and space, it enters into possession of some portion of nature and in such a manner as to render other of its precincts accessible.

A geologist living in 1928 tells us about events that happened not only before he was born but millions of years before any human being came into existence on this earth. He does so by starting from things that are now the material of experience. Lyell revolutionized geology by perceiving that the sort of thing that can be experienced now in the operations of fire, water, pressure, is the sort of thing by which the earth took on its present structural forms. Visiting a natural history museum, one beholds a mass of rock and, reading a label, finds that it comes from a tree that grew, so it is affirmed, five million years ago. The geologist did not leap from the thing he can see and touch to some event in bygone ages; he collated this observed thing with many others, of different kinds, found all over the globe; the results of his comparisons he then compared with data of other experiences, say, the astronomer's. He translates, that is, observed coexistences into non-observed inferred sequences. Finally he dates his object, placing it in an order of events. By the same sort of method he predicts that at certain places some things not yet experienced will be observed, and then he takes pains to bring them within the scope of experience. The scientific conscience is, moreover, so sensitive with respect to the necessity of experience that when it reconstructs the past it is not fully satisfied with inferences drawn from even a large and cumulative mass of un-contradicted evidence; it sets to work to institute conditions of heat and pressure and moisture, etc., so as actually to reproduce in experiment that which he has inferred.

These commonplaces prove that experience is *of* as well as *in* nature. It is not experience which is experienced, but nature—stones, plants, animals, diseases, health, temperature, electricity, and so on. Things interacting in certain ways *are* experience; they are what is experienced. Linked in certain other ways with another natural object—the human organism—they are *how* things are experienced as well. Experience thus reaches down into nature; it has depth. It also has breadth and to an indefinitely elastic extent. It stretches. That stretch constitutes inference.

Dialectical difficulties, perplexities due to definitions given to the concepts that enter into the discussion, may be raised. It is said to be absurd that what is only a tiny part of nature should be competent to incorporate vast reaches of nature within itself. But even were it logically absurd one would be bound to cleave to it as a fact. Logic, however, is not put under a strain. The fact that something is an occurrence does not decide what kind of an occurrence it is; that can be found out only by examination. To argue from an experience "being an experience" to what it is of and about is warranted by no logic, even though modern thought has attempted it a thousand times. A bare event is no event at all; *something* happens. What that something is, is found out by actual study. This applies to seeing a flash of lightning and holds of the longer event called experience. The very existence of science is evidence that experience is such an occurrence that it penetrates into nature and expands without limit through it.

These remarks are not supposed to prove anything about experience and nature for philosophical doctrine; they are not supposed to settle anything about the worth of empirical naturalism. But they do show that in the case of natural science we habitually treat experience as starting point, and as method for dealing with nature, and as the goal in which nature is disclosed for what it is. To realize this fact is at least to weaken those verbal associations which stand in the way of apprehending the force of empirical method in philosophy.

The same considerations apply to the other objection that was suggested: namely, that to view experience naturalistically is to reduce it to something materialistic, depriving it of all ideal significance. If experience actually presents esthetic and moral traits, then these traits may also be supposed to reach down into nature, and to testify to something that belongs to nature as truly as does the mechanical structure attributed to it in physical science. To rule out that possibility by some general reasoning is to forget that the very meaning and purport of empirical method is that these things are to be studied on their own account, so as to find out what is revealed when they are experienced. The traits possessed by the subject matter of experience are as genuine as the characteristics of sun and electron. They are *found,* experienced, and are not to be shoved out of being by some trick of logic. When found, their ideal qualities are as relevant to the philosophic theory of nature as are the traits found by physical inquiry.

To discover some of these general features of experienced things and to interpret their significance for a philosophic theory of the universe in which we live is the aim of this volume. From the point of view adopted, the theory of empirical method in philosophy does for experienced subject matter on a liberal scale what it does for special sciences on a technical scale. It is this aspect of method with which we are especially concerned in the present chapter.

If the empirical method were universally or even generally adopted in philosophizing, there would be no need of referring to experience. The scientific inquirer talks and writes about particular observed events and qualities, about specific calculations and reasonings. He makes no allusion to experience; one would probably have to search a long time through reports of special researches in order to find the word. The reason is that everything designated by the word "experience" is so adequately incorporated into scientific procedures and subject matter that to mention experience would be only to duplicate in a general term what is already covered in definite terms.

Yet this was not always so. Before the technique of empirical method was developed and generally adopted, it was necessary to dwell explicitly upon the importance of "experience" as a starting point and terminal point, as setting problems and as testing proposed solutions. We need not be content with the conventional allusion to Roger Bacon and Francis Bacon. The followers of Newton and the followers of the Cartesian school carried on a definite controversy as to the place occupied by experience and experiment in science as compared with intuitive concepts and with reasoning from them. The Cartesian school relegated experience to a secondary and a most accidental place, and only when the Galilean-Newtonian method had wholly triumphed did it cease to be necessary to mention the importance of experience. We may, if sufficiently hopeful, anticipate a similar outcome in philosophy. But the date does not appear to be close at hand; we are nearer in philosophic theory to the time of Roger Bacon than to that of Newton.

In short, it is the contrast of empirical method with other methods employed in philosophizing, together with the striking dissimilarity of results yielded by an empirical method and professed nonempirical methods that make the discussion of the methodological import of "experience" for philosophy pertinent and indeed indispensable.

This consideration of method may suitably begin with the contrast between gross, macroscopic, crude subject matters in primary experience and the refined, derived objects of reflection. The distinction is one between what is experienced as the result of a minimum of incidental reflection and what is experienced in consequence of continued and regulated reflective inquiry. For derived and refined products are experienced only because of the intervention of systematic thinking. The objects of both science and philosophy obviously belong chiefly to the secondary and refined system. But at this point we come to a marked divergence between science and philosophy. For the natural sciences not only draw their material from primary experience, but they refer it back again for test. Darwin began with the pigeons, cattle, and plants of breeders and gardeners. Some of the conclusions he reached were so contrary to accepted beliefs that they were condemned as absurd, contrary to common sense, etc. But scientific men, whether they accepted his theories or not, employed his hypotheses as directive ideas for making new observations and experiments among the things of raw experience—just as the metallurgist who extracts refined metal from crude ore makes tools that are then set to work to control and use other crude materials. An Einstein working by highly elaborate methods of reflection, calculates theoretically certain results in the deflection of light by the presence of the sun. A technically equipped expedition is sent to South Africa so that by means of experiencing a thing—an eclipse—in crude, primary, experience, observations can be secured to compare with, and test the theory implied in, the calculated result.

The facts are familiar enough. They are cited in order to invite attention to the relationship between the objects of primary and of secondary or reflective experience. That the subject matter of primary experience sets the problems and furnishes the first data of the reflection which constructs the secondary objects is evident; it is also obvious that test and verification of the latter is secured only by return to things of crude or macroscopic experience—the sun, earth, plants, and animals of common, everyday life. But just what role do the objects attained in reflection play? Where do they come in? They *explain* the primary objects, they enable us to grasp them with *understanding,* instead of just having sense-contact with them. But how?

Well, they define or lay out a path by which return to experienced things is of such a sort that the meaning, the significant content, of what is experienced gains an enriched and expanded force because of the path or method by which it was reached. Directly, in immediate contact it may be just what it was before—hard, colored, odorous, etc. But when the secondary objects, the refined objects, are employed as a method or road for coming at them, these qualities cease to be isolated details; they get the meaning contained in a whole system of related objects; they are rendered continuous with the rest of nature and take on the import of the things they are now seen to be continuous with. The phenomena observed in the eclipse tested and, as far as they went, confirmed Einstein's theory of deflection of flight by mass. But that is far from being the whole story. The phenomena themselves get a far-reaching significance they did not previously have. Perhaps they would not even have been noticed if the theory had not been employed as a guide or road to observation of them. But even if they had been noticed, they would have been dismissed as of no importance, just as we daily drop from attention hundreds of perceived details for which we have no intellectual use. But approached by means of theory these lines of slight deflection take on a significance as large as that of the revolutionary theory that led to their being experienced.

This empirical method I shall call the *denotative* method. That philosophy is a mode of reflection, often of a subtle and penetrating sort, goes without saying. The charge that is brought against the nonempirical method of philosophizing is not that it depends on theorizing, but that it fails to use refined, secondary products as a path pointing and leading back to something in primary experience. The resulting failure is threefold.

First, there is no verification, no effort even to test and check. What is even worse, secondly, is that the things of ordinary experience do not get enlargement and enrichment of meaning as they do when approached through the medium of scientific principles and reasonings. This lack of function reacts, in the third place, back upon the philosophic subject matter in itself. Not tested by being employed to see what it leads to in ordinary experience and what new meanings it contributes, this subject matter becomes arbitrary, aloof—what is called "abstract" when that word is used in a bad sense to designate something which exclusively occupies a realm of its own without contact with the things of ordinary experience.

As the net outcome of these three evils, we find that extraordinary phenomenon which accounts for the revulsion of many cultivated persons from any form of philosophy. The objects of reflection in philosophy, being reached by methods that seem to those who employ them rationally mandatory, are taken to be "real" in and of themselves—and supremely real. Then it becomes an insoluble problem why the things of gross, primary experience, should be what they are, or indeed why they should be at all. The refined objects of reflection in the natural sciences, however, never end by rendering the subject matter from which they are derived a problem; rather, when used to describe a path by which some goal in primary experience is designated or denoted, they solve perplexities to which that crude material gives rise but which it cannot resolve of itself. They become means of control, of enlarged use and enjoyment of ordinary things. They may generate new problems, but these are problems of the same sort, to be dealt with by further use of the same methods of inquiry and experimentation. The problems to which empirical method gives rise afford, in a word, opportunities for more investigations yielding fruit in new and enriched experiences. But the problems to which nonempirical method gives rise in philosophy are blocks to inquiry, blind alleys; they are puzzles rather than problems, solved only by calling the original material of primary experience, "phenomenal," mere appearance, mere impressions, or by some other disparaging name.

Thus there is here supplied, I think, a first-rate test of the value of any philosophy which is offered us: Does it end in conclusions which, when they are referred back to ordinary life experiences and their predicaments, render them more significant, more luminous to us, and make our dealings with them more fruitful? Or does it terminate in rendering the things of ordinary experience more opaque than they were before, and in depriving them of having in "reality" even the significance they had previously seemed to have? Does it yield the enrichment and increase of power of ordinary things which the results of physical science afford when applied in everyday affairs? Or does it become a mystery that these ordinary things should be what they are; and are philosophic concepts left to dwell in separation in some technical realm of their own? It is the fact, I repeat, that so many philosophies terminate in conclusions that make it necessary to disparage and condemn primary experience, leading those who hold them to measure the sublimity of their "realities" as philosophically defined by remoteness from the concerns of daily life, which leads cultivated common sense to look askance at philosophy.

These general statements must be made more definite. We must illustrate the meaning of empirical method by seeing some of its results in contrast with those to which nonempirical philosophies conduct us. We begin by noting that "experience" is what James called a double-barrelled word.[1] Like its congeners, life and history, it includes *what* men do and suffer, *what* they strive for, love, believe and endure, and also *how* men act and are acted upon, the ways in which they do and suffer, desire and enjoy, see, believe, imagine—in short, processes of *experiencing*. "Experience" denotes the planted field, the sowed seeds, the reaped harvests, the changes of night and day, spring and autumn, wet and dry, heat and cold, that are observed, feared, longed for; it also denotes the one who plants and reaps, who works and rejoices, hopes, fears, plans, invokes magic or chemistry to aid him, who is downcast or triumphant. It is "double-barrelled" in that it recognizes in its primary integrity no division between act and material, subject and object, but contains them both in an unanalyzed totality. "Thing" and "thought," as James says in the same connection, are single-barrelled; they refer to products discriminated by reflection out of primary experience.[2]

It is significant that "life" and "history" have the same fullness of undivided meaning. Life denotes a function, a comprehensive activity, in which organism and environment are included. Only upon reflective analysis does it break up into external conditions—air breathed, food taken, ground walked upon—and internal structures—lungs respiring, stomach digesting, legs walking. The scope of "history" is notorious: it is the deeds enacted, the tragedies undergone; and it is the human comment, record, and interpretation that inevitably follow. Objectively, history takes in rivers, mountains, fields and forests, laws and institutions; subjectively it includes the purposes and plans, the desires and emotions, through which these things are administered and transformed.

Now empirical method is the only method which can do justice to this inclusive integrity of "experience." It alone takes this integrated unity as the starting point for philosophic thought. Other methods begin with results of a reflection that has already torn in two the subject matter experienced and the operations and states of experiencing. The problem is then to get together again what has been sundered—which is as if the king's men started with the fragments of the egg and tried to construct the whole egg out of them. For empirical method the problem is nothing so impossible of solution. Its problem is to note how and why the whole is distinguished into subject and object, nature and mental operations. Having done this, it is in a position to see *to what effect* the distinction is made: how the distinguished factors function in the further control and enrichment of the subject matters of crude but total experience. Nonempirical method starts with a reflective product as if it were primary, as if it were the originally "given." To nonempirical method, therefore, object and subject, mind and matter (or whatever words and ideas are used) are separate and independent. Therefore it has upon its hands the problem of how it is possible to know at all how an outer world can affect an inner mind; how the acts of mind can reach out and lay hold of objects defined in antithesis to them. Naturally it is at a loss for an answer, since its premises make the fact of knowledge both unnatural and unempirical. One thinker turns metaphysical materialist and denies reality to the mental; another turns psychological idealist, and holds that matter and force are merely disguised psychical events. Solutions are given up as a hopeless task, or else different schools pile one intellectual complication on another only to arrive by a long and tortuous course at that which naive experience already has in its own possession.

The first and perhaps the greatest difference made in philosophy by adoption respectively of empirical or nonempirical method is, thus, the difference made in what is selected as original material. To a truly naturalistic empiricism, the moot problem of the relation of subject and object is the problem of what consequences follow in and for primary experience from the distinction of the physical and the psychological or mental from each other. The answer is not far to seek. To distinguish in reflection the physical and to hold it in temporary detachment is to be set upon the road that conducts to tools and technologies, to reconstruction of mechanisms, to the arts that ensue in the wake of the sciences. That these constructions make possible a better regulation of the affairs of primary experience is evident. Engineering and medicine, all the utilities that make for expansion of life, are the answer. There is better administration of old familiar things, and there is invention of new objects and satisfactions. Along with this added ability in regulation goes enriched meaning and value in things, clarification, increased depth and continuity—a result even more precious than is the added power of control.

The history of the development of the physical sciences is the story of the enlarging possession by mankind of more efficacious instrumentalities for dealing with the conditions of life and action. But when one neglects the connection of these scientific objects with the affairs of primary experience, the result is a picture of a world of things indifferent to human interests because it is wholly apart from experience. It is more than merely isolated, for it is set in opposition. Hence when it is viewed as fixed and final in itself it is a source of oppression to the heart and paralysis to imagination. Since this picture of the physical universe and philosophy of the character of physical objects is contradicted by every engineering project and every intelligent measure of public hygiene, it would seem to be time to examine the foundations upon which it rests, and find out how and why such conclusions are come to.

When objects are isolated from the experience through which they are reached and in which they function, experience itself becomes reduced to the mere process of experiencing, and experiencing is therefore treated as if it were also complete in itself. We get the absurdity of an experiencing which experiences only itself, states and processes of consciousness, instead of the things of nature. Since the seventeenth century this conception of experience as the equivalent of subjective private consciousness set over against nature, which consists wholly of physical objects, has wrought havoc in philosophy. It is responsible for the feeling mentioned at the outset that "nature" and "experience" are names for things which have nothing to do with each other.

Let us inquire how the matter stands when these mental and psychical objects are looked at in their connection with experience in its primary and vital modes. As has been suggested, these objects are not original, isolated, and self-sufficient. They represent the discriminated analysis of the process of experiencing from subject matter experienced. Although breathing is in fact a function that includes both air and the operations of the lungs, we may detach the latter for study, even though we cannot separate it in fact. So while we always know, love, act for and against *things,* instead of experiencing ideas, emotions and mental intents, the attitudes themselves may be made a special object of attention, and thus come to form a distinctive subject matter of reflective, although not of primary, experience.

We primarily observe things, not observations. But the *act* of observation may be inquired into and form a subject of study and become thereby a refined object; so may the acts of thinking, desire, purposing, the state of affection, reverie, etc. Now just as long as these attitudes are not distinguished and abstracted, they are incorporated into subject matter. It is a notorious fact that the one who hates finds the one hated an obnoxious and despicable character; to the lover his adored one is full of intrinsically delightful and wonderful qualities. The connection between such facts and the fact of animism is direct.

The natural and original bias of man is all toward the objective; whatever is experienced is taken to be there independent of the attitude and act of the self. Its "thereness," its independence of emotion and volition, render the properties of things, whatever they are, cosmic. Only when vanity, prestige, rights of possession are involved does an individual tend to separate off from the environment and the group in which he, quite literally, lives, some things as being peculiarly himself. It is obvious that a total, unanalyzed world does not lend itself to control; that, on the contrary, it is equivalent to the subjection of man to whatever occurs, as if to fate. Until some acts and their consequences are discriminatingly referred to the human organism and other energies and effects are referred to other bodies, there is no leverage, no purchase, with which to regulate the course of experience. The abstraction of certain qualities of things as due to human acts and states is the *pou sto* of ability in control. There can be no doubt that the long period of human arrest at a low level of culture was largely the result of failure to select the human being and his acts as a special kind of object, having his own characteristic activities that condition specifiable consequences.

In this sense, the recognition of "subjects" as centers of experience together with the development of "subjectivism" marks a great advance. It is equivalent to the emergence of agencies equipped with special powers of observation and experiment, and with emotions and desires that are efficacious for production of chosen modifications of nature. For otherwise the agencies are submerged in nature and produce qualities of things which must be accepted and submitted to. It is no mere play on words to say that recognition of subjective minds having a special equipment of psychological abilities is a necessary factor in subjecting the energies of nature to use as instrumentalities for ends.

Out of the indefinite number of possible illustrations of the consequences of reflective analysis yielding personal or "subjective" minds we cite one case. It concerns the influence of habitual beliefs and expectations in their social generation upon *what* is experienced. The things of primary experience are so arresting and engrossing that we tend to accept them just as they are—the flat earth, the march of the sun from east to west and its sinking under the earth. Current beliefs in morals, religion, and politics similarly reflect the social conditions which present themselves. Only analysis shows that the *ways* in which we believe and expect have a tremendous effect upon *what* we believe and expect. We have discovered at last that these ways are set, almost abjectly so, by social factors, by tradition, and the influence of education. Thus we discover that we believe many things not because the things are so, but because we have become habituated through the weight of authority, by imitation, prestige, instruction, the unconscious effect of language, etc. We learn, in short, that qualities which we attribute to objects ought to be imputed to our own ways of experiencing them, and that these in turn are due to the force of intercourse and custom. This discovery marks an emancipation; it purifies and remakes the objects of our direct or primary experience. The power of custom and tradition in scientific as well as in moral beliefs never suffered a serious check until analysis revealed the effect of personal ways of believing upon things believed, and the extent to which these ways are unwittingly fixed by social custom and tradition. In spite of the acute and penetrating powers of observation among the Greeks, their "science" is a monument of the extent to which the effects of acquired social habits as well as of organic constitution were attributed directly to natural events. The depersonalizing and desocializing of some objects, to be henceforth the objects of physical science, was a necessary precondition of ability to regulate experience by directing the attitudes and objects that enter into it.

This great emancipation was coincident with the rise of "individualism," which was in effect identical with the reflective discovery of the part played in experience by concrete selves, with their ways of acting, thinking, and desiring. The results would have been all to the good if they had been interpreted by empirical method. For this would have kept the eye of thinkers constantly on the origin of the "subjective" out of primary experience, and then directed it to the function of discriminating what is usable in the management of experienced objects. But for lack of such a method, because of isolation from empirical origin and instrumental use, the results of psychological inquiry were conceived; to form a separate and isolated mental world in and of itself, self-sufficient and self-enclosed. Since the psychological movement necessarily coincided with that which set up physical objects as correspondingly complete and self-enclosed, there resulted that dualism of mind and matter, of a physical and a psychical world, which from the day of Descartes to the present dominates the formulation of philosophical problems.

With the dualism we are not here concerned, beyond pointing out that it is the inevitable result, logically, of the abandoning of acknowledgment of the primacy and ultimacy of gross experience—primary as it is given in an uncontrolled form, ultimate as it is given in a more regulated and significant form—a form made possible by the methods and result of reflective experience. But what we are directly concerned with at this stage of discussion is the result of the discovery of subjective objects upon philosophy in creation of wholesale subjectivism. The outcome was, that while in actual life the discovery of personal attitudes and their consequences was a great liberating instrument, psychology became for philosophy, as Santayana has well put it, "malicious." That is, mental attitudes, *ways* of experiencing, were treated as self-sufficient and complete in themselves, as that which is primarily *given,* the sole original and therefore indubitable data. Thus the traits of genuine primary experience, in which natural things are the determining factors in production of all change, were regarded either as not-given dubious things that could be reached only by endowing the only certain thing, the mental, with some miraculous power, or else were denied all existence save as complexes of mental states, of impressions, sensations, feelings.[3]

One illustration out of the multitude available follows. It is taken almost at random, because it is both simple and typical. To illustrate the nature of experience, what experience really is, an author writes: "When I look at a chair, I say I experience it. But what I actually experience is only a very few of the elements that go to make up a chair, namely the color that belongs to the chair under these particular conditions of light, the shape which the chair displays when viewed from this angle, etc." Two points are involved in any such statement. One is that "experience" is reduced to the traits connected with the *act of experiencing,* in this case the act of seeing. Certain patches of color, for example, assume a certain shape or form in connection with qualities connected with the muscular strains and adjustments of seeing. These qualities, which define the act of seeing when it is made an object of reflective inquiry, *over against what is seen,* thus become the chair itself for immediate or direct experience. Logically, the chair disappears and is replaced by certain qualities of sense attending the act of vision. There is no longer any other object, much less the chair which was bought, that is placed in a room and that is used to sit in, etc. If we ever get back to this total chair, it will not be the chair of direct experience, of use and enjoyment, a thing with its own independent origin, history, and career; it will be only a complex of directly "given" sense qualities as a core, plus a surrounding cluster of other qualities revived imaginatively as "ideas."

The other point is that, even in such a brief statement as that just quoted, there is compelled recognition of an *object* of experience which is infinitely other and more than what is asserted to be alone experienced. There is the *chair* which is looked at; the *chair displaying* certain colors, the *light* in which they are displayed; the angle of vision implying reference to an organism that possesses an optical apparatus. Reference to these *things* is compulsory, because otherwise there would be no meaning assignable to the sense qualities—which are, nevertheless, affirmed to be the sole data experienced. It would be hard to find a more complete recognition, although an unavowed one, of the fact that in reality the account given concerns only a selected portion of the actual experience, namely that part which defines the act of experiencing, to the deliberate omission, *for the purpose of the inquiry in hand,* of *what* is experienced.

The instance cited is typical of all "subjectivism" as a philosophic position. Reflective analysis of one element in actual experience is undertaken; its result is then taken to be primary; as a consequence the subject matter of actual experience for which the analytic result was derived is rendered dubious and problematic, although it is assumed at every step of the analysis. Genuine empirical method sets out from the actual subject matter of primary experience, recognizes that reflection discriminates a new factor in it, the *act* of seeing, makes an object of that, and then uses that new object, the organic response to light, to regulate, when needed, further experiences of the subject matter already contained in primary experience.

The topics just dealt with, segregation of physical and mental objects, will receive extended attention in the body of this volume.[4] As respects *method,* however, it is pertinent at this point to summarize our results. Reference to the primacy and ultimacy of the material of ordinary experience protects us, in the first place, from creating artificial problems which deflect the energy and attention of philosophers from the real problems that arise out of actual subject matter. In the second place, it provides a check or test for the conclusions of philosophic inquiry; it is a constant reminder that we must replace them, as secondary reflective products, in the experience out of which they arose, so that they may be confirmed or modified by the new order and clarity they introduce into it, and the new significantly experienced object for which they furnish a method. In the third place, in seeing how they thus function in further experiences, the philosophical results themselves acquire empirical value; they are what they contribute to the common experience of man, instead of being curiosities to be deposited, with appropriate labels, in a metaphysical museum.

There is another important result for philosophy of the use of empirical method which, when it is developed, introduces our next topic. Philosophy, like all forms of reflective analysis, takes us away, for the time being, from the things had in primary experience as they directly act and are acted upon, used and enjoyed. Now the standing temptation of philosophy, as its course abundantly demonstrates, is to regard the results of reflection as having, in and of themselves, a reality superior to that of the material of any other mode of experience. The commonest assumption of philosophies, common even to philosophies very different from one another, is the assumption of the identity of objects of knowledge and ultimately real objects. The assumption is so deep that it is usually not expressed; it is taken for granted as something so fundamental that it does not need to be stated. A technical example of the view is found in the contention of the Cartesian school—including Spinoza—that emotion as well as sense is but confused thought which when it becomes clear and definite or reaches its goal is *cognition*. That esthetic and moral experience reveal traits of real things as truly as does intellectual experience, that poetry may have a metaphysical import as well as science, is rarely affirmed, and when it is asserted, the statement is likely to be meant in some mystical or esoteric sense rather than in a straightforward everyday sense.

Suppose however that we start with no presuppositions save that what is experienced, since it is a manifestation of nature, may, and indeed, must be used as testimony of the characteristics of natural events. Upon this basis, reverie and desire are pertinent for a philosophic theory of the true nature of things; the possibilities present in imagination that are not found in observation, are something to be taken into account. The features of objects reached by scientific or reflective experiencing are important, but so are all the phenomena of magic, myth, politics, painting, and penitentiaries. The phenomena of social life are as relevant to the problem of the relation of the individual and universal as are those of logic; the existence in political organizations of boundaries and barriers, of centralization, of interaction across boundaries, of expansion and absorption, will be quite as important for metaphysical theories to the discrete and the continuous as is anything derived from chemical analysis. The existence of ignorance as well as of wisdom, of error and even insanity as well as of truth will be taken into account.

That is to say, nature is construed in such a way that all these things, since they are actual, are naturally possible; they are not explained away into mere "appearance" in contrast with reality. Illusions are illusions, but the occurrence of illusions is not an illusion, but a genuine reality. What is really "in" experience extends much further than that which at any time is *known*. From the standpoint of knowledge, objects must be distinct; their traits must be explicit; the vague and unrevealed is a limitation. Hence whenever the habit of identifying reality with the object of knowledge as such prevails, the obscure and vague are explained away. It is important for philosophic theory to be aware that the distinct and evident are prized and why they are. But it is equally important to note that the dark and twilight abound. For in any object of primary experience there are always potentialities which are not explicit; any object that is overt is charged with possible consequences that are hidden; the most overt act has factors which are not explicit. Strain thought as far as we may and not all consequences can be foreseen or made an express or known part of reflection and decision. In the face of such empirical facts, the assumption that nature in itself is all of the same kind, all distinct, explicit and evident, having no hidden possibilities, no novelties or obscurities, is possible only on the basis of a philosophy which at some point draws an arbitrary line between nature and experience.

In the assertion (implied here) that the great vice of philosophy is an arbitrary "intellectualism," there is no slight cast upon intelligence and reason. By "intellectualism" as an indictment is meant the theory that all experience is a mode of knowing, and that all subject matter, all nature, is, in principle, to be reduced and transformed till it is defined in terms identical with the characteristics presented by refined objects of science as such. The assumption of "intellectualism" goes contrary to the facts of what is primarily experienced. For things are objects to be treated, used, acted upon and with, enjoyed and endured, even more than things to be known. They are things *had* before they are things cognized.

The isolation of traits characteristic of objects known, and then defined as the sole ultimate realities, accounts for the denial to nature of the characters which make things lovable and contemptible, beautiful and ugly, adorable and awful. It accounts for the belief that nature is an indifferent, dead mechanism; it explains why characteristics that are the valuable and valued traits of objects in actual experience are thought to create a fundamentally troublesome philosophical problem. Recognition of their genuine and primary reality does not signify that no thought and knowledge enter in when things are loved, desired, and striven for; it signifies that the former are subordinate, so that the genuine problem is how and why, to what effect, things thus experienced are transformed into objects in which cognized traits are supreme and affectional and volitional traits incidental and subsidiary.

"Intellectualism" as a sovereign method of philosophy is so foreign to the facts of primary experience that it not only compels recourse to nonempirical method, but it ends in making knowledge, conceived as ubiquitous, itself inexplicable. If we start from primary experience, occurring as it does chiefly in modes of action and undergoing, it is easy to see what knowledge contributes—namely, the possibility of intelligent administration of the elements of doing and suffering. We are about something, and it is well to know what we are about, as the common phrase has it. To be intelligent in action and in suffering (enjoyment too) yields satisfaction even when conditions cannot be controlled. But when there is possibility of control, knowledge is the sole agency of its realization. Given this element of knowledge in primary experience, it is not difficult to understand how it may develop from a subdued and subsidiary factor into a dominant character. Doing and suffering, experimenting and putting ourselves in the way of having our sense and nervous system acted upon in ways that yield material for reflection, may reverse the original situation in which knowing and thinking were subservient to action-undergoing. And when we trace the genesis of knowing along this line, we also see that knowledge has a function and office in bettering and enriching the subject matters of crude experience. We are prepared to understand what we are about on a grander scale, and to understand what happens even when we seem to be the hapless puppets of uncontrollable fate. But knowledge that is ubiquitous, all-inclusive and all-monopolizing, ceases to have meaning in losing all context; that it does not appear to do so when made supreme and self-sufficient is because it is literally impossible to exclude that context of noncognitive but experienced subject matter which gives what is *known* its import.

While this matter is dealt with at some length in further chapters of this volume, there is one point worth mentioning here. When intellectual experience and its material are taken to be primary, the cord that binds experience and nature is cut. That the physiological organism with its structures, whether in man or in the lower animals, is concerned with making adaptations and uses of material in the interest of maintenance of the life process, cannot be denied. The brain and nervous system are primarily organs of action-undergoing; biologically, it can be asserted without contravention that primary experience is of a corresponding type. Hence, unless there is breach of historic and natural continuity, cognitive experience must originate within that of a noncognitive sort. And unless we start from knowing as a factor in action and undergoing we are inevitably committed to the intrusion of an extranatural, if not a supernatural, agency and principle. That professed nonsupernaturalists so readily endow the organism with powers that have no basis in natural events is a fact so peculiar that it would be inexplicable were it not for the inertia of the traditional schools. Otherwise it would be evident that the only way to maintain the doctrine of natural continuity is to recognize the secondary and derived character aspects of experience of the intellectual or cognitive. But so deeply grounded is the opposite position in the entire philosophic tradition, that it is probably not surprising that philosophers are loath to admit a fact which when admitted compels an extensive reconstruction in form and content.

We have spoken of the difference which acceptance of empirical method in philosophy makes in the problem of subject-object and in that of the alleged all-inclusiveness of cognitive experience.[5] There is an intimate connection between these two problems. When real objects are identified, point for point, with knowledge-objects, all affectional and volitional objects are inevitably excluded from the "real" world, and are compelled to find refuge in the privacy of an experiencing subject or mind. Thus the notion of the ubiquity of all comprehensive cognitive experience results by a necessary logic in setting up a hard and fast wall between the experiencing subject and that nature which is experienced. The self becomes not merely a pilgrim but an unnaturalized and unnaturalizable alien in the world. The only way to avoid a sharp separation between the mind which is the center of the processes of experiencing and the natural world which is experienced is to acknowledge that all modes of experiencing are ways in which some genuine traits of nature come to manifest realization.

The favoring of cognitive objects and their characteristics at the expense of traits that excite desire, command action, and produce passion, is a special instance of a principle of selective emphasis which introduces partiality and partisanship into philosophy. Selective emphasis, with accompanying omission and rejection, is the heartbeat of mental life. To object to the operation is to discard all thinking. But in ordinary matters and in scientific inquiries, we always retain the sense that the material chosen is selected for a purpose; there is no idea of denying what is left out, for what is omitted is merely that which is not relevant to the particular problem and purpose in hand.

But in philosophies, this limiting condition is often wholly ignored. It is not noted and remembered that the favored subject matter is chosen for a purpose and that what is left out is just as real and important in its own characteristic context. It tends to be assumed that because qualities that figure in poetical discourse and those that are central in friendship do not figure in scientific inquiry, they have no reality, at least not the kind of unquestionable reality attributed to the mathematical, mechanical or magneto-electric properties that constitute matter. It is natural to men to take that which is of chief value to them at the time as *the* real. Reality and superior value are equated. In ordinary experience this fact does no particular harm; it is at once compensated for by turning to other things which since they also present value are equally real. But philosophy often exhibits a cataleptic rigidity in attachment to that phase of the total objects of experience which has become especially dear to a philosopher. *It* is real at all hazards and only it; other things are real only in some secondary and Pickwickian sense.

For example, certainty, assurance, is immensely available in a world as full of uncertainty and peril as that in which we live. As a result whatever is capable of certainty is assumed to constitute ultimate Being, and everything else is said to be merely phenomenal, or, in extreme cases, illusory. The arbitrary character of the "reality" that emerges is seen in the fact that very different objects are selected by different philosophers. These may be mathematical entities, states of consciousness, or sense data. That is, whatever strikes a philosopher from the angle of the particular problem that presses on him as being self-evident and hence completely assured, is selected by him to constitute reality. The honorable and dignified have ranked with the mundanely certain in determining philosophic definitions of the real. Scholasticism considered that the True and the Good, along with Unity, were the marks of being as such. In the face of a problem, thought always seeks to unify things otherwise fragmentary and discrepant. Deliberately action strives to attain the good; knowledge is reached when truth is grasped. Then the goals of our efforts, the things that afford satisfaction and peace under conditions of tension and unrest, are converted into that which alone is ultimate real Being. Ulterior functions are treated as original properties.

Another aspect of the same erection of objects of selective preference into exclusive realities is seen in the addiction of philosophers to what is simple, their love for "elements." Gross experience is loaded with the tangled and complex; hence philosophy hurries away from it to search out something so simple that the mind can rest trustfully in it, knowing that it has no surprise in store, that it will not spring anything to make trouble, that it will stay put, having no potentialities in reserve. There is again the predilection for mathematical objects; there is Spinoza with his assurance that a true idea carries truth intrinsic in its bosom; Locke with his "simple idea"; Hume with his "impression"; the English neorealist with his ultimate atomic data; the American neorealist with his readymade essences.

Another striking example of the fallacy of selective emphasis is found in the hypnotic influence exercised by the conception of the eternal. The permanent enables us to rest, it gives peace; the variable, the changing, is a constant challenge. Where things change something is hanging over us. It is a threat of trouble. Even when change is marked by hope of better things to come, that hope tends to project its object as something to stay once for all when it arrives. Moreover we can deal with the variable and precarious only by means of the stable and constant; "invariants"—for the time being—are as much a necessity in practice for bringing something to pass as they are in mathematical functions. The permanent answers genuine emotional, practical, and intellectual requirements. But the demand and the response which meets it are empirically always found in a special context; they arise because of a particular need and in order to effect specifiable consequences. Philosophy, thinking at large, allows itself to be diverted into absurd search for an intellectual philosopher's stone of absolutely wholesale generalizations, thus isolating that which is permanent in a function and for a purpose, and converting it into the intrinsically eternal, conceived either (as Aristotle conceived it) as that which is the same at all times, or as that which is indifferent to time, out of time.

This bias toward treating objects selected because of their value in some special context as the "real," in a superior and invidious sense, testifies to an empirical fact of importance. Philosophical simplifications are due to choice, and choice marks an interest *moral* in the broad sense of concern for what is good. Our constant and unescapable concern is with prosperity and adversity, success and failure, achievement and frustration, good and bad. Since we are creatures with lives to live, and find ourselves within an uncertain environment, we are constructed to note and judge in terms of bearing upon weal and woe—upon value. Acknowledgment of this fact is a very different thing, however, from the transformation effected by philosophers of the traits they find good (simplicity, certainty, nobility, permanence, etc.) into fixed traits of real

Being. The former presents something *to be accomplished,* to be brought about by the *actions* in which choice is manifested and made genuine. The latter ignores the need of action to effect the better and to prove the honesty of choice; it converts what is desired into antecedent and final features of a reality which is supposed to need only logical warrant in order to be contemplatively enjoyed as true Being. . . .

Notes

1. *Essays in Radical Empiricism,* p. 10.

2. It is not intended, however, to attribute to James precisely the interpretation given in the text.

3. Because of this identification of the mental as the sole "given" in a primary, original way, appeal to experience by a philosopher is treated by many as necessarily committing one to subjectivism. It accounts for the alleged antithesis between nature and experience mentioned in the opening paragraph. It has become so deeply engrained that the empirical method employed in this volume has been taken by critics to be simply a restatement of a purely subjective philosophy, although in fact it is wholly contrary to such a philosophy.

4. *Experience and Nature,* chapters 4 and 6.

5. To avoid misapprehension, it may be well to add a statement on the latter point. It is not denied that any experienced subject matter whatever may *become* an object of reflection and cognitive inspection. But the emphasis is upon "become"; the cognitive never *is* all-inclusive; that is, when the material of a prior noncognitive experience is the object of knowledge, it and the act of knowing are themselves included within a new and wider noncognitive experience—and *this* situation can never be transcended. It is only when the temporal character of experienced things is forgotten that the idea of the total "transcendence" of knowledge is asserted.

2

In Dispraise of Life, Experience, and Reality*

Morris R. Cohen

In speaking of the new philosophic movement which began with the present century, William James remarked: "It lacks logical rigor, but it has the tang of life." It is strikingly significant of the temper of our age that this was intended and has generally been taken as praise of the new philosophy. To any of the classical philosophers, to whom not life, but the good life was the object of rational effort, James's dictum would have sounded as a condemnation. For life devoid of logic is confused, unenlightened, and often brutish. Indeed the new philosophy itself maintains that it is precisely because unreflective life is so unsatisfactory that it gives rise to logic. Why then should the word *life* itself be a term of praise except to those who prefer the primitive and dislike intellectual effort?

I can imagine that a classical philosopher living long enough amongst us to penetrate some of our bewildering ways might conclude that our

*Originally published in Morris R. Cohen, *Reason and Nature* (New York: Harcourt, Brace, and Co., 1931), Epilogue. Reprinted in a second edition by The Free Press (Glencoe, Ill., 1953) and by Dover Publications (New York, 1978). Reprinted by permission.

worship of mere life, rather than the good or rational life, reflects the temper of an acquisitive society, feverishly intent on mere accumulation, and mortally afraid to stop to discriminate between what is worthwhile and what is not. The same preference for terms of promiscuous all-inclusiveness, rather than for those that involve the discrimination essential to philosophic clarity, shows itself also in the use of the terms *experience* and *reality*. It is of course true that surface clarity can readily be obtained by ignoring fundamental difficulties, and that we cannot dispense with terms indicating the unlimited immensities of which our little formulated systems are but infinitesimal selections. But if the world contains many things and therefore distinctions between them, ignoring these distinctions is not the same as profundity. The honorific use of nondiscriminating terms can only serve to darken counsel. That this has actually been the case in ethics and in theories of knowledge, in religion and in art, is the burden of this brief epilogue.

That the continuance of mere physical life is an absolute moral good seems to be axiomatic in current ethics. It serves as a basis for the unqualified moral condemnation of all forms of suicide and euthanasia. Now I do not wish to question the biologic proposition that there are forces which make the organism continue to function after we have lost all specifically human goods, such as honor and reason. What I do wish to point out is that this setting up of mere life as an absolute moral good, apart from all its social conditions, is inconsistent with the moral approval of the hero or the martyr who throws away life for the sake of honor or conscience. It would be pathetically absurd to praise the abandoning of life by John Huss or Giordano Bruno on the ground that it increased or prolonged the total amount of life. Indiscriminate increase of population beyond any definite limit is of very doubtful moral value—despite the arguments of those who oppose all forms of birth control. We must not lose sight of the fact that life always carries with it not only the seeds of disease and inevitable death, but also the roots of all that is vicious and hideous in human conduct. We cannot, therefore, dispense with the classical problem of defining the good and discriminating it from the evil of life—a difficult and baffling problem, to be sure; but those who find it profitless are under no obligation to pursue moral philosophy.

The confusion of moral theory by the eulogistic use of the word *life* can be readily seen in the Nietzschean ethics—all the more instructive because Nietzsche himself starts from the classical perception of the inadequacy of ordinary utilitarianism in face of the moral values of heroism. The good life involves the sacrifice of ease and comfort, the receiving as well as the giving of hard blows. But just because Nietzsche is impatient of definition he falls into the easy error of sharply opposing the pursuit of life to the pursuit of knowledge—witness his essay on history. But the pursuit of knowledge is itself a form of life. This fact cannot be obscured by rhetorical contrasts between the life of the closet philosopher and the open-air or what is euphemistically called *real* life. To the eye of philosophic reflection the scholar or persistent thinker shows as much life or vitality as those who have to cover their naked restlessness by a gospel of strenuous but aimless perpetual motion— in no particular direction. This is not the occasion to sing the praises of the intellect and what it has done to humanize life. We may grant that the distaste for arduous intellectual tasks is natural, blameless, and in some cases even providential. But when such distaste sets itself up as a philosophy of life it is only ridiculous.

This brings us to our second point, the vitalistic theory of knowledge—or perhaps we should refer to it as the theory of a vitalistic intuition superior to knowledge—I mean the widespread notion that by mere living we get an insight superior to that of the intellect operative in mathematical and natural science. To prevent misunderstanding, let me say that I am not referring here to genuine mysticism which asserts that all intellection and language move in the mist of appearances and cannot reach the ineffable reality. Genuine mysticism always holds fast to the idea that the substance of reality is altogether beyond the power of language, and hence it does not use language to describe this reality. It holds that language can at best only indicate its own shortcomings and thus point the way beyond itself. When, however, as in the Bergsonian theory, the claim of the scientific intellect is set aside for an instinctive intuition, and when this is held to provide a superior explanation of empirical phenomena like the formation of the eye of the scallop, it seems to me that philosophy is then not far removed from glorified quackery where the philosopher's stone is expected to remove the effects of the evil eye or cure toothaches and other empirical ailments. We may grant that biology as a natural science does not carry us very far into the mystery of life. But it does not follow that our ignorance can be cured in any other way. The fallibility of scientific reasoning is best corrected only by definite experiments and the critical reasoning of science itself. When men despair of solving theoretic problems and appeal to undefined words like *life* they show themselves devoid of intellectual stamina. It is doubtless true that in the process of living our ideas develop, mature, and receive a solid amplitude through an enriched content. Time tests our judgments and eliminates clever, plausible sophistries. But it is also true that the older a lamb grows the more sheepish he gets. Nothing seems so solidly established by anthropology and history as that men will not learn from what has actually happened to them unless they have developed the power of reflection. The idea that experience alone will teach everybody is a thin optimistic illusion.

The use of the word *experience* without any ascertainable meaning is perhaps the outstanding scandal of recent philosophy. In its original sense, which it still retains in ordinary, intelligible discourse, and from which we cannot altogether liberate ourselves in philosophy, experience denotes conscious feeling or something which happens to us personally. Thus I make my meaning clear when I say, "I did not experience any pain during an operation," or "I have never experienced what it is to be struck by lightning." I may also speak of not having experienced the panic of 1872 or the other side of the moon. The absence of such experience need not, however, prevent me from knowing a good deal about the operation, the lightning, the panic of 1872, and the other side of the moon—more indeed than about many of my own experiences. For experience in this personal and ordinary sense is but an infinitesimal portion of what is going on in the world of time and space, and even a small part of the world of ordinary human affairs. To identify the substance of the world with the fact of our experience of some part of it is to set up an anthropocentric universe, compared to which the medieval one is sane and respectable. For the medieval one rebuked the silly and arrogant pretensions of humanity by setting against it the great glory of God.

The absurdity of identifying the whole realm of nature with our little human experience of it is obscured in two ways—to wit, (1) by confusing the nature of possible experience, and (2) by stretching the word *experience* until it *excludes* nothing and therefore includes no definite meaning.

That things known are all objects of a conceivable possible experience to some possible being more or less like us need not be denied. But the object of a possible experience is a matter of intellectual consideration, not the object of actual personal experience. If, on the other hand, we stretch the meaning of the word *experience* and make it include everything that we can think about, e.g., the state of the earth before the advent of life, then there remains no difference between an object considered and an object experienced, and the proposition that knowledge rests on experience ceases to have significance. It is vain to define words so as to deny the fact that we know many things to be beyond our experience. In general, the term *experience* either means something personal and therefore limited, or it becomes so promiscuously all-inclusive that it ceases to have any intelligible negative. Without an alternative term to denote what is not experience it cannot have any pragmatic meaning. With characteristic sensitiveness to the difficulties of his own account, Professor Dewey has realized something of this dilemma in which the use of the term *experience* involves him. He has tried to defend it by the analogy of the use of the terms *zero* and *infinity*. But zero and infinity indicate at least definite directions. They indicate which of two definite terms is to the left or right of the other in a series. The term *experience,* however, in Professor Dewey's thought is equally applicable to everything that is an object of consideration. I cannot therefore see that it serves any definite intellectual function beyond carrying the faint aroma of praise.

In general, when familiar words are stretched and put to new uses, confusion is bound to result. For the meaning we attach to words is based on habits which arbitrary resolutions cannot readily change, and we invariably drag the old meaning into the new context.

An instructive instance of the confusing use of the term *experience* is the current phrase *religious experience,* used by those who regard it as a substitute for rational theology. Here again, I have no quarrel with anyone who claims to have had the beatific vision of God or a special revelation of the truths of religion. One who makes such a claim puts himself beyond argument except when he asks others to believe what he believes. Then the doubt which Tennyson applied to his own vision certainly becomes relevant. Nor is my quarrel with those who assume the truths of their religion on the authority of an historic church or revelation fortified by the necessary truths of reason. The current fashion which talks about religious experience distrusts the great streams of historic tradition as it does the claims of systematic theology—witness James's *Varieties of Religious Experience,* in which none of the great historic religions receives any attention. He thinks he can establish "piecemeal supernaturalism" by the methods of natural science and the rules of empirical evidence. An elementary consideration, however, of the logic of induction shows the impossibility of proving the existence of miraculous or supernatural interventions on the basis of the postulate of the uniformity of nature involved in induction. Indeed, the naturalist can well maintain that as instances of mystic experiences have their parallel in the effects of drugs, starvation, etc., the naturalistic explanation of them is the only one that is scientifically worth investigating. In any case, the spiritualistic hypothesis does not lend itself to the crucial test of affording us verifiable predictions. Not only a scientist but even a court of law would be derelict if it accepted as proved anything which rests on no better evidence than that offered by abnormal psychology for a finite, personal God and the immortality of the individual soul.

It is of course true that most people do not hold these beliefs as scientific hypotheses at all. Indeed, most people regard the cold, logical analysis of their religion with a horror like that which would be evoked by a funeral orator who proceeded to give a scientific examination of the character of the deceased. We come to mourn and praise our friend, not to hear him psychoanalyzed. But all this is irrelevant in moments of reflection or when our beliefs are challenged by the contrary beliefs of others. One may say: I hold these truths and the faith in them strengthens my life. But such assertions cannot keep out the lurking doubt that it is the psychologic attitude rather than the truth of what is assumed that produces the practical effects. The pragmatic glorification of belief contains the deep poison of skepticism as to what really exists, and this like a Nessus shirt will destroy any religious belief that puts it on. Religion may begin in ritual and conduct, but it inevitably goes on to reflective belief that must submit to the canons of logic. The popular and superficial contrast between religion and theology ignores the fact that where a diversity of religion exists it is impossible to stop a process of reflection as to which of two conflicting claims is true. In such a society, religious creed or theology (including the possibility of a negative or atheistic theory) becomes inescapable. Hazy talk about religious experience will not adequately meet the difficulties.

If terms that have no genuine negatives are to be condemned as devoid of significance, the word *reality* should head the list. I am not unmindful of the many attempts to define the unreal. But the question is: What corresponds to these definitions? The Hindu mystic is deeply irritated when the wise Chinese suggests that the realm of Maya or illusion does not really exist, or that it is not worthwhile worrying about it. The reality of illusion is the emphatic center of the Hindu's philosophy, and, similarly, of all those who sharply contrast reality and appearance. The difficulty here is classic. What I am more especially concerned about, however, is to call attention to the fact that the word *reality* maintains itself as a term of praise rather than of description. To be "in touch with reality" is our way of expressing what our less sophisticated brothers and sisters do by the phrase "in tune with the infinite." It is an expression which carries an agreeable afflatus without dependence on any definite meaning. Such edification is pleasing and would be harmless if it did not also cause intellectual confusion. This the eulogistic use of the word *reality* certainly does in the theory of art, especially in its realistic and expressionistic form.

Professor Neilson defined the realistic motive, in poetry and art generally, as the sense of fact. But whatever else art may involve, the process of selection is certainly essential to it in all its forms, useful as well as ornamental. Hence, the honorific use of a nondiscriminating term like *reality* undoubtedly tends to justify the introduction of the inept and the ugly, which certainly cannot be denied to have real existence. But it is not only realism that is thus encouraged to escape or confuse the fundamental problem of what is relevant, fitting, or beautiful in representation and ornament. Expressionistic theories glorify the same lack of discrimination between the beautiful and the ugly. For expressionism is but a subjective realism. This becomes clear when we reflect that the real denotes, first, human affairs, then physical things, and now vivid impressions or emotions, so that abstractions are not real to us. The praise of reality, therefore, now has as its core the glorification of vivid impressions or violent expressions, regardless of fitness or coherence. This shows itself in an indiscriminate admiration for the breaking of all hitherto accepted rules of art—as if all rules were necessarily hindrances. But rules of art like the so-called rules of nature are at bottom only statements of what is relevant and what irrelevant to any given case. Hence it is doubtless true that new situations in art cannot always be profitably decided by old rules. But this again is a question of specific fitness, not to be disposed of by the violent assertion that the expression of inner reality is inconsistent with all rules.

It is doubtful, for instance, whether such a convention as the rules of the sonnet ever hindered a great poet from expressing himself, though it doubtless has aided many minor ones, perhaps unduly so.

To conclude, we cannot praise life without including in our praise moral and physical evil, corruption and death. As experience certainly includes error and illusion, we cannot praise it indiscriminately as a support of truth. Finally, as reality undoubtedly includes the useless and the ugly, its praise cannot but confuse the arts.

Instead of life we want the good life. Instead of accepting experience science discriminates between the experience of truth and the experience of illusion. Not all reality, but only a reality free from ugliness and confusing incoherence is the aim of art. Conduct, science, and art thus depend on rational discrimination. Rational philosophy tries to meet this need by defining the good, the true, and the beautiful. The essence of the romantic use of the terms *life, experience,* and *reality* is that it avoids this necessary task, and is therefore flattering to those to whom the use of reason is irksome. But the way to serenity and happiness through wisdom is more arduous and requires a purified vision into our hearts as well as courage to face the abysmal mystery of existence.

3

Naturalistic and Pure Reflection*

Marvin Farber

On Subjectivism and the Meaning of Reflection

Every philosophy that is concerned with experience is reflective. But there are different kinds and degrees of reflection. A thoroughly reflective philosophy is an ideal, in the sense of inspecting all aspects of experience. That would mean the complete examination of the contents, grounds, motives, and aims of experience.

The term reflection is often used more narrowly, with the emphasis upon "inner" experience, or the "subjective conditions" of experience. According to Locke, reflection is the knowledge which the mind has of its own activity, whereby these activities rise in the understanding. For Kant, reflection is concerned with the determination of the subjective conditions under which we are able to attain concepts.

In recent philosophy Shadworth Hodgson was among those who attempted to elaborate a pure philosophy of reflection. In his *Philosophy of Reflection,*[1] philosophy is distinguished from science by the "inner and indelible characteristic" of reflective perception or self-consciousness, which

---

*Originally published in Marvin Farber, *Naturalism and Subjectivism* (New York: Charles C. Thomas, 1959), chapter 2. Reprinted by permission.

he holds to be the central and cardinal feature in philosophy.[2] The method of reflection "consists in a repeated analysis of phenomena as they are *in* consciousness . . . and not in their character as objects outside consciousness" (99f.). The latter may be treated *also* as objects *in* consciousness, so that this method is more general, being applicable to *all* phenomena. Hodgson's procedure is to trace consciousness back to its "sources," and to come to primary states which are "undistinguished into objective and subjective." Psychology assumes a world of "things," and "supposes them to impress another 'thing,' the sensitive organism, with primary feelings" (16f.). Hodgson asks how the world of "things," as we know it by science, has grown up out of the world of primary feelings as we know it at the beginning of our knowledge. The subjective method which he proposes is characterized in the following passage: "It is a reexamination of the phenomena of primary and direct consciousness, under the guidance of the principle of examining their objective and subjective aspects in conjunction with each other, which is a method only possible in reflection. Reflection first makes the discovery of the double aspect and then applies it and the continued and methodological application of it is metaphysic" (133). There are no "new or transcendent discoveries."

The program proposed by Hodgson has important features of similarity to Husserl's early formulation of phenomenology. Husserl did not know of Hodgson's work until after the appearance of his *Logical Investigations* (1900–1901), when W. E. Hocking, who studied with Husserl early in the latter's Göttingen period, brought it to his attention. In a general way, Hodgson anticipated the idealistic leaning of the later Husserl. Maintaining that only philosophy can answer the question as to the nature of existence, if an answer can be given at all, he defines existence as "presence in consciousness" (49). For all the modes of existence, such as actual existence, imaginary existence, and necessary existence, "there are corresponding modes of presence in consciousness, and without a corresponding mode of presence in consciousness we should have no knowledge whatever of any mode of existence. In short, consciousness itself is the subjective aspect of existence. . . . We know existence as consciousness, and to know that we do so is self-consciousness" (50). The argument that we should have no knowledge of any mode of existence without a "corresponding mode of presence in consciousness" is really tautologous: one cannot *know* without experiencing, or knowing. But this line of thought had a widespread appeal. Thus Josiah Royce, America's foremost idealist, offered a reward to anyone who could produce an object that was not known. It is difficult to understand how able thinkers could be convinced by such an argument, even in the 1870s; and still more difficult to understand how that could happen in the present generation, as is the case. Only an antecedent will to believe that warms the heart and dulls the mind can explain such a curious circumstance.

Hodgson would be right in regarding philosophy as being reflective in character if he construed reflection broadly enough. His view that philosophy has a distinct method and a distinct and positive content (30) ought to be extended to comprise all devices that may be required for philosophical purposes. There is oversimplification if one speaks of "a distinct method," construed in subjective terms. A subjective procedure, while useful for special philosophical and psychological purposes, must be aligned with the other procedures used in philosophy as well as in the special sciences.

The Function and Aims of Reflection

Just as there is no one meaning of the term "reflection"—indeed, some of the crucial issues of philosophy turn upon the different meanings and conditions assigned to "reflection"—there is no general agreement on the function and aims of reflection. The reasons are only in part due to the difficulty of getting others to understand one's point of view.

But there is a real problem of philosophical intelligibility, which has received serious attention. The use of one of the major philosophies of the past, the philosophy of Kant, for example, as the means of communication among philosophers would hardly be a solution. That would only add one more difficulty to an already admittedly bad situation, for an initial agreement on the interpretation of the chosen philosophy might well detain scholars indefinitely. No doubt that could be a way of disposing of the problems of philosophy, pending progress beyond the point of clarifying the Kantian terminology. The difficulty would be even greater if Hegel, Husserl, or Whitehead were selected. But there is a point here anyway. Philosophy cannot be a monologue; it is social in its conditions and reference, and must be communicated. Complete and exact understanding is an ideal which need not be realized, even for philosophical purposes. An approximation is sufficient here, just as it is in the special sciences. On the other hand, should general agreement be set up as an aim of reflection? Demonstration, validity, and correctness should be the aim. General agreement is hoped for, to be sure. But a minority of one may be right, which is the important thing.

Dewey speaks of reflection as follows: "Empirically, all reflection sets out from the problematic and confused. Its aim is to clarify and ascertain. When thinking is successful, its career closes in transforming the disorderly into the orderly . . . the unclear and ambiguous into the defined and unequivocal."[3] The need for reflection is a general one in experience. It is prompted by the occurrence of problems which require reflection for their solution. Philosophy shares that with the sciences, and with thinking in all regions of experience.

Reflection need not be "autobiographical" in the sense of reviewing the events of one's own history. Its aim need not be to give an account of one's own conscious processes. On the other hand, the subjective process of reflection must use the conscious experience of one subject as the medium for the analysis. How could it be otherwise? It is an individual subject who reflects and describes what is observed. He may check his results—either factual descriptions or "essential findings"—with the experience of other persons, and thus seek to avoid mistaking invention and wishful thinking for observations. The phenomenologist proposes to reflect with the greatest possible thoroughness, and to question his experience about the evidence for other persons, so that he feels compelled to begin as an individual. Unless he is careful to acknowledge clearly the factual and *real* priority of nature and society to the individual, he is apt to become involved in archaic nonsense, no different from the speculative excesses so prominent in the tradition of philosophy.

One describes in reflection. It may be supposed that one can "see" correctly, at least most of the time. But does one see with Humean eyes, or Kantian eyes, or a Gestaltist's eyes? It is clearly important to attempt to "get back of" the interpretations and theories in terms of which we view the world of experience. Thus reflection itself must be examined, in the hope that an interpretation which appears to be a datum will be revealed as such. The "given" in experience comes to us as already interpreted, unless one uses the term "given" in a special sense, as the ideal limit to be determined by an exacting process of analysis. But the latter is an ideal which may well never be realized completely. This should not be construed as being in any sense a concession to the anti-intellectualistic view of experience, or of the mind. That experience occurs as interpreted will always be the case for us. The point is, that a deep-seated problem is engendered therewith.

The guiding precept for a thoroughgoing philosophy of reflection must be: *Question everything.* The alleged "self-evident" is not exempt therefrom, but, on the contrary, must be scrutinized all the more carefully for its evidence. The universal process of "questioning" challenges the very problems of philosophy, and all traditional philosophy. Thus one endeavors to probe to the "ultimate grounds and elements" of all knowledge and experience; and these are naturalistic and social-historical as well as logical and epistemological in character. To illustrate the latter, Husserl is interested in determining "what is presupposed in all presupposing." "Radical" and complete understanding constitute the ideal goal. That involves an analysis of experience, which must be undertaken periodically because of changing objective and subjective conditions. If it is granted that the mind contributes interpretations to experience, then it clearly follows that finality cannot be expected in the case of any one analysis of experience. The reflective analyses themselves must be dated.

In addition to the theoretical aims that have been indicated, there is also the goal of constructing a logical theory of values. Whether a philosopher must also consider the means of realizing his ideals has been debated. Professor Ralph Perry restricted the *philosopher* of values to the formulation of criteria, leaving it to others to find ways and means for the realization of values. That he did not shrink from the arena of practical affairs is well known, however. In taking a stand on this question one should bear in mind the fact that when a man becomes a philosopher he does not therewith cease to be a man, or a citizen. The disciplines making up the philosophical enterprise, including phenomenology (meaning the descriptive analysis of experience as viewed in all its modes and structures), logic, and value theory, by no means forbid the inspiring spectacle of a philosopher in action, rare though that happens to be. They require practical activity for the realization in experience.

Types of Reflection

The style as well as the aims of reflection have their history. Thus Locke was determined by the science of his period, by the concept of atomism, and also by the prevailing social and political motivation. The promotion of the welfare of mankind was an aim of his *Essay,* in which he expressed the hope that his analysis might be of some use to man. Consider his questions and what he tried to achieve, and did achieve in his way. By means of his critique of innate ideas and principles and his positive empirical program he helped to undermine the authoritarian tradition. Disclaiming the ideal of knowing all things, he was interested in the truths which concern our conduct.[4] Although his program was empirical in its intent, it was not realized correctly, the data for reflection being in part the products of theoretical thinking. The dogma of the simple idea as a unit of experience, and the ill-fated definition of knowledge as the discernment of the agreement or disagreement among our ideas, were responsible for much confusion, and soon bore fruit in the subjective idealism of Berkeley. Locke may be criticized for his errors, which were serious and important; but there is also a basis for the tribute James pays him (in his *Principles of Psychology*), as "the immortal Locke."

We, too, have our style of reflection, an improved if not a completely satisfactory psychological theory, and our historical motivation. Do we, like Locke, want to contribute to the good of man? If so, then a "pure" philosophy cannot be adequate, i.e., one for which the actual empirical world is irrelevant. One cannot then retire to a detached realm of essences or "Ideas." We also have the task of sweeping away and combating traditional errors. The development of the special sciences, as compared with Locke's period, reacts upon philosophy, changing its form as well as content. When the great diversity of social-historical motives is considered, in connection with the question whether there is one unitary aim for philosophy, the historical character of reflection is clearly seen.

A few illustrations will be pertinent. (1) There are new types of error, as well as familiar old ones, already prominent in Locke's time. Authoritarianism persists, and adds to its forms and types. Relativism appears in new forms, more formidable than the earlier types advanced by skeptics. A narrow pragmatic relativism in the philosophy of logic and the confusion of truth with validity are examples. (2) The fact that the special sciences now cover so much more territory than in the seventeenth century has important consequences for philosophy. The progress of the sciences renders obsolete the dualism of qualities and the dogma of the simple idea as the unit of experience. That the task of philosophy is not lightened, but is, on the contrary, still more exacting, is due to the necessity of acquiring an understanding of the most important findings and principles of the sciences, an achievement which ought to be made a professional requirement. (3) Philosophy in the abstract cannot be considered apart from its concrete embodiments in the various systems of thought. Such systems are incomprehensible unless their historical progenitors and contemporary social and scientific influences are known. That being the case, how can one speak of a unitary aim of philosophy? One philosopher defends religion, and regards philosophy as the handmaid of theology. He has his passing historical function, especially in the medieval period. Another philosopher champions the rights of the individual by way of an attack upon the dominant realism of the Church, defending the thesis that only individuals are real. Philosophy was conspicuous in the eighteenth-century preparation for the great French Revolution, from Voltaire to Holbach, in recognizing the interests and extolling the virtues of the bourgeoisie. Responding to conditions developing after the revolution, Comte tempered his program of scientific philosophy by calling for the perpetuation of the "natural" hierarchy of classes in society (he speaks of the employers as the "natural leaders" of the workers). The social function of utilitarianism, and of materialism and idealism in various historical periods, are further examples of instructive themes deserving more attention than they have received by professional philosophers.

The classification, already mentioned, of philosophies into philosophies of renunciation and of participation, is suggestive. Otherwordly, ascetic, and mystical philosophies practice or eventuate in renunciation. The Cynics' contempt for worldly goods and cultural pursuits; the mystics' ecstatic experience as a means of salvation; the scourging of the flesh and the devaluation of this life in view of the belief in a better life to come, in the Christian tradition; and the restriction of philosophy to a purely descriptive program, or to purely logical processes—these are some of the ways of practicing renunciation of social issues. Vastly different though they may be among themselves, they all agree in one respect: they do not attempt to change the status quo of society. Philosophies of participation, on the other hand, comprise conservative and reactionary as well as melioristic and revolutionary types. The utilitarians were interested in social reforms, within cautious limits, and in extending the suffrage. Early English materialism, as illustrated by Hobbes, was a means of combating the Church in its struggle for supremacy over civil society. Similarly, French materialism in the eighteenth century was directed against the feudal-ecclesiastical tradition. At other times, however, materialists may be seen to be socially conservative, defending the existing economic system while rejecting supernaturalism. Because they aim to transform the existing social system, the dialectical materialists may be regarded as broadly similar to the French materialists, although, to be sure, their historical derivation is not accounted for thereby. As for idealism, it may be noted that German idealism from Kant to Hegel had its progressive as well as conservative features, whereas their idealistic followers illustrate ways in which philosophy has been reconciled with prevalent social conditions.

Historically, it is true that most philosophers have assumed the task of defending and justifying values. If that task is made subject to logical standards and viewed systematically, it may be used to unify all the activities of the philosopher. The concept of value, broadly conceived in terms of human interests and their fulfillment, embraces the descriptive program that is peculiar to philosophy, a program which is universal in its possible scope and comprises all "phenomenological" or "purely reflective" descriptions. Logical activities are similarly embraced by the concept of value.

Philosophical reflection must be distinguished from ordinary common-sense reflection, and from psychological reflection with a "natural attitude," or a "natural view of the world." If the natural view of the world is simply taken for granted, with all its theoretical elements, one's point of view is uncritical to that extent—uncritical philosophically, that is to say. It does not matter if the principles involved are not given up following a reflective inquiry. The term "uncritical" simply means that they are taken over without question. Because it is the concern of philosophy to examine the supposedly self-evident all the more carefully, the natural view of the world must come in for a searching analysis. It turns out to be permeated with interpretations, and with "deposits" of meaning going back to bygone cultural periods. Since naturalistic psychology assumes whole groups of sciences as well as the prevailing view of the world, it does not provide reflective analyses that could satisfy the philosophical requirements, in the form in which they are carried through. It was a great weakness of the psychologistic type of philosophy to have failed to recognize that fact.

Philosophical reflection must furthermore be distinguished from scientific reflection in general. Every science is critical to a certain extent; it "questions" a certain set of beliefs, and is reflective in a field of inquiry which is marked off. The philosopher undertakes to carry the process of analysis as far back as possible. Everything must be placed in question, including the procedure itself. That is what is meant by the term "radical" in this context. It must be "all-sided," in the sense that the natural view of the world is examined from the point of view of critical (or "radical") reflection, and the latter is viewed in terms of its status and function for the interests of the naturalistic view. Philosophical reflection thus requires a distinctive "attitude" and a well-defined procedure. Neither Hodgson nor Dewey provide the latter adequately. Hodgson's choice of subjectivism doomed his procedure to one-sidedness and falsification. Dewey does indeed contribute significantly by his emphasis upon the cultural conditions and aims of reflection, and also by some notable examples of reflective analysis. Husserl's program for a reflective philosophy, while defined in great detail, is advanced in an idealistic setting, like that of Hodgson. As a result, he fails to remember the indebtedness of pure reflection to the naturalistic view, in the course of his later development. But his elaborate formulation of a procedure for philosophy is an important contribution to philosophical method, despite the critical reservations that must be made in appraising it.

Described very briefly at this point, it begins by submitting the natural attitude toward the world, as well as the theoretical, valuational, and other types of attitude, to an examination *in toto,* from a carefully defined subjective point of view. All other views concerning the world and knowledge may be "suspended" for the purpose of questioning them. No "denial" is involved. Perhaps the term "suspension" is an unfortunate one. All the activities of experience and their objects as meant must be capable of being brought to view. Just as an official can be "investigated" while he still holds office and is actively engaged in his duties, so may the natural modes of experience be viewed in reflection. The ideal of examining every belief and construction is brought to emphatic expression in the procedure of "suspension." There are dangers and excesses to be avoided in the presentation of this procedure. Thus, there is the misleading use of metaphorical language, and modes of expression such as "only by *leaving* the natural point of view or attitude can you become aware of it." The Germanism "in the reflective attitude" or "in the natural attitude" (*in der natürlichen Einstellung*) may suggest that one has gotten into a special kind of container.[5]

The first stage of this reflective procedure, the suspension of belief (the *epoché*) appears to be negative in character. But there is a positive descriptive program which develops in phenomenology, since the critical ground has been prepared. The means to the end, the procedure itself, must be inspected, in accordance with the requirement, emphasized by Husserl, that everything be questioned for its justification. Everything must be "seen," must be brought to view. General objects, conceptual constructions, and relationships can be "seen," just as particular objects in sensory experience can be observed. The logical and conceptual structures which are of interest in philosophy can thus be described and analyzed. In addition to examining every step of the reflective procedure in its own terms and in the light of its own precepts, it is necessary to consider its social-historical significance and its relationships to the sciences.

Conditions Bearing on Reflection

How important this initial stage of reflection, the suspension of beliefs, is as a condition for philosophy may be seen in the case of such a writer as Urban, whose curious distrust of "modernism" is expressed in his book *The Intelligible World.* But the full list of those conspicuously in need of an *epoché* would make an impressive volume—whereby it is not implied that any philosopher may feel free to ignore the *epoché.*

The philosophical process of reflection upon experience and knowledge is a never-ending task, and must be undertaken again and again. The changing cultural conditions forbid finality, so that the efforts of the most gifted thinkers are unavoidably incomplete and historically conditioned. It is not enough to point out, as Schopenhauer did, that experience is the object of philosophy. It is necessary to recognize the *conditions* of experience. As Schopenhauer expressed it, "The object of philosophy is experience, not like the other sciences, this or that definite experience, but just experience itself, in general and as such, with respect to its possibility, its domain, its essential content, its inner and outer elements, its form and matter."[6] As the history of philosophy shows, there is a danger of subjectivism in making experience to be the theme of philosophy, the danger of restricting the interpretation of reality to a specified set of reforms of experience. To speak of the "possibility" of experience is not necessarily to say much, unless *real* conditions of possibility are understood. Such conditions are neglected by the representatives of the idealistic tradition. The "essential content" of experience is of course structural in character, so far as philosophical analysis is concerned. To settle upon the general nature of experience is a major problem in itself, as shown by the varied views in the tradition. How the treatment of experience differs from that of the special sciences, as well as "common sense," must be indicated clearly.

The basic conditions for reflection are twofold, and two important types of problem are determined thereby. There are philosophical conditions, such as a well-defined language, and an understanding of the ways in which the mind contributes to experience. Furthermore, there are the conditions under which the philosopher lives, which act upon him. He must understand his social system and the factors of temperament and personal bias, so that he may critically examine the traditional categories and theories. The analysis of the contributions of the mind to experience and the consideration of historical conditions are of the greatest importance for the achievement of objectively valid knowledge in philosophy, although personal factors may at times be decisive.

To begin with preconceived ideas and beliefs, or with prejudices, is to violate the very first precept of a sound procedure. Should "the whole man, with heart and head," come into action, as Schopenhauer advocates? Or should the "heart's desires" be consulted, as was the case with Lotze, and so many others? The intrusion of the heart can act in either direction, as an aid for the realization of a great purpose, or as a deterrent from objective inquiry.

A. E. Taylor is more frank than most philosophical writers in admitting his motivation. "The one thing I have had it long on my conscience to say, is that I have always wished my book to be understood in a definitely theistic, indeed, in a definitely Christian sense. I have never disguised to myself that when I speak of the 'Absolute' I mean by the word precisely that simple, absolutely transcendent source of all things which the great Christian scholastics call God."[7] Philosophy therewith becomes a matter of faith, and of loyal adherence to one particular fideistic tradition. Taylor's helpful statement may be compared with Feuerbach's declaration in his *The Philosophy of the Future,* to the effect that Hegel, in his philosophy of spirit, made the last grand attempt to restore Christianity through philosophy. For a rational inquiry, statements expressing articles of faith should be treated as conclusions that are judged logically, rather than as premises or unclarified preliminary motives.

Prejudgments are by no means restricted to those who belong to the prominent historical traditions. They are illustrated readily enough in the schools, the sects, and even by those who disclaim prejudgments and seek to chain themselves down to the "given" in experience. The term "naturalism" meets with hostility, or as is also the case, with emotional warmth, depending upon the conditioning of its hearers.

The ideal of "freedom from presuppositions" includes the elimination of prejudices and the programmatic suspension of all assumptions. The universal abstention from belief would guarantee negatively the desired "beginning." It is clear that a strict logical procedure with strong safeguards is necessary to prevent the old prejudices from returning.

Such a procedure must at the same time provide for the examination of all hitherto accepted principles, and must make clear by detailed descriptive analyses how the mind contributes concepts and interpretations to experience. Only then can one hope to have a sound basis for achieving objective truth. Just as reality is temporal, so all items of experience are historical and belong to a definite cultural period. The passing, historical factor belongs to the content of the descriptive inquiry which is concerned with it; and a correct description of something historical is not therefore a passing description. It may be said: Once true, always true, if only in the modus "having been" (to use one of Husserl's expressions). There are no fateful or insuperable difficulties in the way of achieving historical objectivity.

In designating a procedure as "subjective" one must recognize its limitations in addition to crediting it with the merit of helping to make complete reflection possible. It might be well, however, to avoid the use of the tradition-laden and highly ambiguous term "subjective" and to speak of "pure reflective analysis," in which full justice is done to the activities of the knower. The "subjective realm" has been so much misused that logical abuses appear to many to be self-evidences.

A treatise might well be written on the theme "The Reasons for Differences among Philosophers." Such a factual study would provide many pertinent illustrations for the present discussion. "What should be" may not be considered apart from "what is the case." The problem of the achievement of objective truth in reflection is raised when one considers the motives that actually impel philosophers and the social-historical significance of philosophy in general. The frequently disdainful treatment of dialectical philosophy by representatives of opposing movements illustrates the force of extraphilosophical factors.

Dewey has made much of the influence of social-historical conditions on the thought systems of the philosophers, although mainly in a general manner rather than with specific references to economic and social conditions.[8] The "social-historical" study of philosophy brings many revealing facts to light. In ancient Greece the philosophers enjoyed the necessary leisure for their way of life because of the existence of slavery. Their status in social life clearly molded their thought, and predetermined their point of view in important respects. The attitude of Plato and Aristotle toward slavery is a case in point. Aquinas in relationship to the medieval church, and Hobbes as a defender of monarchy, are pertinent illustrations. The words of Shakespeare in *Timon of Athens* will also be recalled: "The learned pate ducks to the golden fool." Such considerations indicate obstacles in the way of the attainment of objective truth. How can one know whether he is, or is not, prejudiced, or how can one know the extent to which he is led by motives issuing from his status in society? The question at issue here goes beyond the psychological process of rationalization, for one may act and think in accordance with his own interests and still speak the truth. The problem is simply the establishment of truth.

This question may be subsumed under the larger theme of the interpreting activity of the mind in general, which has already been considered in connection with the error of irrationalism. Just as there is no general cognitive predicament, in the sense that the mind, despite all its virtues and powers, shuts us off from the "ultimate" truth, there is also no special predicament which deprives us of objective knowledge for social and individual reasons. The assumptions underlying the alleged general predicament are responsible for an artificial problem. An untenable view of the mind, and of experience, is at the basis of the difficulty, and that view predetermines the conclusion. But the mind is not outside nature; and there is no evidence for a "general" or "absolute" mind. Hence the conception of the ordering of nature by the mind is at best a sterile hypothesis. The nature of the mind, its practical function for living beings, guarantees that it is capable of achieving objective truth. Experience shows that in innumerable ways, and it is a condition of survival. There is no need to doubt it as a matter of principle, even for the most exacting philosophical purpose. In special cases, methods of proof must be devised, but there need be no proof for the capacity of the mind for truth.

Can the more specialized question regarding private and socially induced motives also be answered, as a matter of principle? Motives that operate include fear, religious hopes, class interests and private advantage, and temperament. There is no available method which would enable us to guarantee the achievement of "objectivity" in every single case. There are however safeguards to be observed. The process of reflection must be extended to include a view of the thinker in his historical conditions. There must not only be an *epoché* with regard to concepts and principles; the thinker must be viewed in his position in society and in cultural history. What are his interests? How do they bear upon the questions at issue? He may indeed, and with right, be led by his interests. So long as he does so explicitly and announces that fact, he is not guilty of the usually covert error of being influenced by his interests while claiming personal detachment and social "neutrality." It is necessary to reduce all normative statements, all preferences, to theoretical and factual propositions, so that they can be tested. The philosopher who has no preference, no interests of any kind, is a fiction.

The problem of the attainment of objective truth requires all-sided consideration of the individual, social, historical, and existential facts involved. The naturalistic reflection which is "radicalized" and added to in pure reflection must in turn be supplemented by the inspection of social-historical significance. The alternative would be to rest in the "pure immanence" of a subjective realm with the aid of an absolute consciousness that is removed from all problems of matters of fact. The procedure of pure reflection is a stage in the complete process of reflection. It is sufficient for one dimension of problems—the clarification of basic concepts and structures in terms of direct experience—and is thus an important auxiliary method. But it should not be used exclusively, beyond its proper range of application.

According to a naturalistic metaphysics, reflection is itself "a natural event occurring *within* nature because of traits of the latter."[9] One underlying condition for reflection is correctly described in that way; but it is also essential to point out the social-historical conditions of reflection. It is certainly true that all types of reflection are "natural events," just as it is true that they cannot occur without the human organism. But that is not to say that one has to accept the basic assumptions and concepts of the current sciences as unquestionable in reflection. Their philosophical examination is a supplement to their scientific criticism. Those philosophers who think that they are rising "above" nature, however, exhibit incredible naiveté, surprising even if that is maintained as a mode of response to religious or vested academic interests. That reflection is itself an event in existence is a statement of simple fact. All "purely reflective" procedures and analyses of abstractions, etc., are natural events. In a very real sense, one cannot get himself, or his thinking, outside the natural order. The "questioning" of all our knowledge of the natural order as such is still a "natural" process of questioning. That fact should not be lost sight of when one introduces a special terminology to name the new attitude that is systematically adopted for "questioning" not only the natural order but all the provinces of experience, "ideal" as well as real. . . .

The Subjective Procedure of Phenomenology

The phenomenological method is designed to apply to all phases of experience. That its limitation to a subjective context prevents it from realizing this aim, and that it was an irresistible temptation to Husserl to adopt a general idealistic philosophy, is made clear by a study of its development. Husserl is preeminent in the phenomenological movement, for his type of analysis has yielded results which command the respect of other investigators most widely. Like some of his predecessors in the idealistic tradition (Hegel, for example), he was able to achieve valuable results despite the restricted and ultimately repressive setting of his philosophy.

As a continuator of the empirical tradition, Husserl aimed to analyze experience. The method of philosophy was declared to be descriptive, direct "seeing" being the ideal. The field for description proved to be in need of extension, even on that level, and Husserl in his early period emphatically argued for the direct observation of "general objects," discussing them in his first published work, *Philosophy of Arithmetic* (1891). He was careful in this period to accord full importance and value to the various scientific methods, in keeping with his own excellent scientific training.

The original aim of phenomenology was quite different from that of Dewey, or from that of any of the philosophers deriving from the natural and social sciences. It led Husserl into the ranks of the opponents of the scientific philosophy developed at the close of the nineteenth century. As for his own conscious motivation, his primary aim was to overcome logical psychologism, or the view that logical validity can be construed in psychological terms and derived from psychological principles. In other words, an admittedly erroneous position taken by logicians who were reacting to naturalistic and empiricist influences became the target of Husserl's initial criticism, and led him first of all to a "neutral" position on the issue of idealism and realism. The phenomenology which was first formulated in his *Logical Investigations* (1900–1901) was concerned with direct description, and was even called descriptive psychology. Some years later the "phenomenological reduction" (i.e., to "pure consciousness"—the restriction to conscious experiences and their correlates) was formulated, and it was advanced as the first prerequisite for philosophical analysis. It was intended to define the field for philosophy to begin with, and it defined the setting for a transcendental philosophy. In Husserl's exposition, there was a strong feeling of opposition to naturalistic procedures.

It is possible to construe the "reduction" in nonidealistic terms, as an auxiliary method in philosophy, and to align it with other methods, under the general heading of methodology. It should be regarded as one type of reflection among others, with its own peculiar value for philosophical understanding. Representatives of the last stage of Husserl's development have objected to that, however, maintaining that the subjectivistic procedure of phenomenology is something *sui generis,* absolutely unique, different in principle from all other ("mundane") methods. Such claims could hardly promote sympathetic understanding, or even an attempt at sympathetic understanding; and they are as unnecessary as they are unwarranted. It is hardly helpful to portray Husserl after the fashion of Porphyry's treatment of Plotinus. To make phenomenology ineffable and indescribable (in "natural" terms) would be to deprive it of all scientific interest. The analysis of "intentional" experience in all its types constitutes a self-contained study. The phenomenological datum for analysis is my-experiencing-the-object, whether the latter be real or fictive in character. That there should be a temptation to constitute *reality* out of the experiences is understandable, but nonetheless inexcusable. That has had the unfortunate result of tending to discredit phenomenology as a whole. The subtle arguments in question[10] are no better basically than Berkeley's well-worn argument for subjective idealism.

The descriptive analyses of phenomenology are intended to be independent of the question of the demonstration of reality or unreality, and independent also of all causal-genetic considerations involving "natural" time. Thus the description of the content and structure of experience shows how an experience of reality is incompatible with one of illusion, for example. It portrays the structure of each type of experience. But it does not give us a test of reality. There is no "pure phenomenological" way to reality in the sense of a being independent of the knowing of it. The analysis is concerned with the context of the knower and his objects, everything being viewed from the perspective of its being known or experienced, so that there can be no talk of being apart from knowing, from that point of view. The analysis is confined to the determination of general structures, and it does not deal with factual situations except as exemplifying such structures. They are described as they are manifested in experience, where they are found. So are all the constitutive activities of thought seen in operation, through reflection. They are studied in their "essential" types by means of reenacting and reactivating experiences such as remembrances, conceptual abstractions, and recognitions.[11] The experiencing of evidence, of truth, of adequacy, can be contrasted with the experiencing of error, of inadequacy, etc. They are seen to rule one another out "essentially." One may be quite wrong, however, in his descriptive analysis of an "essential" structure. On this level one is no more secure against error than he is on the "naturalistic" level of scientific description, say in the description of an ant colony. Thus the vaunted superiority of "inner" over "outer" experience is seen to be unfounded. But both types are necessary.

If, as the present writer maintains, Husserl's idealism is untenable, and violates his own explicitly formulated precepts, the really challenging question that must be faced concerns the fruitfulness of the entire procedure. That every sound descriptive proposition in phenomenology can be asserted in objective terms within the framework of a naturalistic (realistic, or materialistic) philosophy has been indicated. One does not leave nature when holding its concepts in question for the sake of analysis. It is appropriate to point out its contribution to the understanding of the structure of knowledge and experience, and to the clarification of basic concepts.

Generally speaking, it is safest to welcome any and all descriptive findings, just as it is best to allow "pure" scientists complete freedom of investigation, without continually raising the possibly myopic demand for direct results. This is well illustrated in modern pure mathematics. The fundamental studies of the philosopher, *qua* descriptive investigator, affect the entire structure of knowledge. They represent a necessary dimension of inquiry which may well be endless. They can never be the whole story for philosophy, but they are an important part of it. It remains a function of philosophy to call attention to neglected facts, and if necessary, to include them in its field of inquiry. That applies to the analysis of experience by means of "inner description," from which psychology has turned away, leaving it to philosophers and novelists.

No descriptive work in that area should be ignored. The phenomenological method is not the only way of clarifying the basic ideas. It is one way, and it adds to the understanding of their meaning and structure. The social-historical interpretation or explanation of an idea also "clarifies"; and so does a simple historical account. All who contribute parts of truth should realize that they can coexist. Standpoint commitments and conflicting interests should not be allowed to obscure that fact.

Notes

1. (London: Longmans, Green, and Co., 1878), two volumes.

2. Vol. 1, p. 49.

3. John Dewey, *Experience and Nature,* pp. 65f., vol. 1 of *The Later Works of John Dewey,* ed. J. A. Boydston (Carbondale, Ill.: Southern Illinois University Press, 1981).

4. Cf. John Locke, *Philosophical Works* (London: George Bell & Sons, 1894), vol. 1, p. 133.

5. Cf. M. Farber, *The Foundation of Phenomenology* (Albany, N.Y.: SUNY Press, 1967), last chapter, for a criticism of such errors.

6. *Sämmtliche Werke* (Leipzig: F. A. Brockhaus, 1922), vol. 6, p. 18.

7. *Elements of Metaphysics* (London: Methuen & Co., 1924), p. xiii.

8. Cf. his *Experience and Nature, The Quest for Certainty, The Influence of Darwin on Philosophy, Reconstruction in Philosophy,* and *Logic, The Theory of Inquiry.*

9. John Dewey, *Experience and Nature,* p. 68.

10. Cf. E. Husserl's *Formale und Transzendentale Logik* (Halle: M. Niemeyer, 1929), e.g., especially the argument for idealism, pp. 205ff. Husserl's exploitation of his method for idealistic purposes is shown by his conclusion: "There is no conceivable place where the life of consciousness could be pierced and we could come to a transcendence, which could have another meaning than that of an intentional unity appearing in the subjectivity of consciousness."

11. Dewey's distinction between "having" and "knowing" is therewith taken account of. Certainly the phenomena must be experienced in order to be described. How the description can be carried through without introducing a classificatory scheme presents a difficulty for *any* method or point of view. In the case of phenomenology, however, the unusually thorough effort to suspend assumptions for the sake of a complete inquiry, the systematic effort to distinguish between interpretations and the "primitive" elements of experience, brings us closer to the ideal of sheer description, an ideal which may perhaps never be realized completely. It will be recognized, of course, that phenomenological description is by no means the only kind of description.

4

Experience*

Justus Buchler

I

Among the circumstances that have impeded a general theory of utterance, one in particular continues to flourish among philosophers. This is the tendency to interpret the principal terms that relate to human processes as naming "operations" of some organ or "acts" stemming from some power, or as reflecting one of two spheres, psychical and physical, supposedly defining the scope of human life. Thus—taking the more defensible instances first—breathing is an activity associated directly with the lungs, somewhat less directly with a respiratory "system," and still less directly but no less unmistakably with body. Remembering is an activity associated directly with a power of imagery and a power of possessing past events, and indirectly but surely with mind. By and large there is nothing wrong with these attributions. Nor is there anything wrong with the mind-body classification simply as a classification. The distinction of mind and body, wholly apart from its various philosophic

---

*Now published in J. Buchler, *Nature and Judgment* (Lanham, Md.: University Press of America, 1985). Copyright 1985 by University Press of America. Reprinted by permission.

elaborations, expresses age-old discernment of major factors in individual life. It facilitates the identification of one or another human merit or ill or limitation. It recognizes conflict and separation among human functions. It recognizes qualitative differences of function. The resistance of the psychical and the physical to integral philosophic explanation is at the same time a resistance to mere ingenuity and reductionism.

But like all conceptions equitably based, that which first posits and then in each instance looks for "operations of the mind" and "operations of the body," by its inertia has become overly inflexible and therefore consistently deceiving. One reason for the narrowness of the traditional version of judgment is that it is depicted as an operation of mind— plausible enough, perhaps, when the only other conceived alternative is to make it an operation of body. The notions of thought and inquiry seem harmlessly associated with "the life of the mind," but such an association is woefully inadequate to the notion of query. And the same is true for the notion of "experience." Although in many phases of actual usage this term is not treated exclusively as an operation, since the context of expressions like "human experience" and "the experience of mankind" suggests other factors, there is an almost universal conviction that experience is somehow connected, if not necessarily with "the present testimony of our senses, or the records of our memory" (Hume), at least in some sense primarily with mind or consciousness or thought or reflection. Even Dewey, who contributed so greatly and lastingly to the correction of exclusively psychologistic conceptions of human life, and who climaxed a fifty-year movement that aimed to introduce biological and social dimensions into the interpretation both of experience and of mind itself, persisted in regarding "thought" or "reflection" as the fullest and most genuine manifestation of "experience." Partly because of a limited conception of judgment and of query, and partly because of difficulties inherent in his version of the relation between experience and nature, Dewey wavered in his approach to the role of mind in the experiencing process. The typical activities of mind appeared in his view to be the condition for experiencing in a more authentic or more complete sense of the term. Ontologically, however, the process of experiencing, simply as process, can be neither more nor less complete. It either obtains in a natural individual or it does not. What thought or intelligence does bring to completion is a certain moral power in experience. But intelligence as a condition of maximum good in experience is to be distinguished from intelligence as somehow a condition of maximum being in the process. The reason this distinction is blurred in Dewey is that the moral flavor which he assigned to the meaning of "*an* experience" (see section III of this chapter) also crept into his notion of "experiencing."

Fundamental, to Dewey, is "the contrast between gross, macroscopic, crude subject matters in primary experience and the refined, derived objects of reflection. The distinction is one between what is experienced as the result of a minimum of incidental reflection and what is experienced in consequence of continued and regulated reflective inquiry. For derived and refined products are experienced only because of the intervention of systematic thinking."[1] Again, experience "reaches down into nature; it has depth. It also has breadth, and to an indefinitely elastic extent. It stretches. That stretch constitutes inference."[2] Now if the culmination of crude or gross experience lay in the process of assertive judgment alone, and if inquiry were the only way of ordering judgment, it would be true that "derived and refined products are experienced only because of the intervention of systematic thinking." If, however, active and exhibitive judgment are taken into account, and if inquiry is seen as only one mode of query, Dewey's position leaves much to be desired. The breadth and elasticity of experience, its "stretch," is much vaster than is indicated by "inference." Inference is the stretch of assertion. It is a phase of articulation and intervention, but not a necessary phase. The stretch of experience is multifarious. Moreover, it cannot be limited to production, even when the conception of production, in terms of the modes of judgment, is greatly expanded. What happens to the individual, either in consequence of his judging or over and above it or in spite of it, belongs to the stretch. Those who, like Whitehead in his later work, have wished to broaden the conception of experience without restriction to the traditional purview of mind, have suffered mainly from inability to define their limits. Experience in Whitehead's version overflows the bounds of human life and becomes virtually synonymous with relatedness of any kind among things of any kind. And even then, the ironic consequence is that, though experience is construed as escaping the confines of mind, it does so in a dubious sense, because the categories of mind themselves, as it turns out, have been extended to the whole of nature.

A just conception of experience is essential in the analysis of utterance; for whatever the interpretation given, it seems necessary to say that the products of the individual occur in his experience and come through experiencing, and that these products, which judge in different ways, can only judge what is in some way experienced, though the judging is itself partly constitutive of the experiencing. If a satisfactory concept of experience is needed for the theory of knowledge, it is doubly needed for the more general or underlying theory of judgment. Yet the facts of judgment must very largely influence the framing of this concept. The process of human experience must fit the facts of human utterance, even though it is not limited to these facts.

The human individual is only one kind of individual, but the kind of which it is meaningful to say that it experiences. Philosophers have written much on the nature of "personal identity." For us it will be sufficient to say that *a* human individual is whatever is identified or denominated as such. The fact that man is characterized by a state of natural debt, by a perpetual incompletion, does not cast doubt on the existence of individuals but emphasizes only the extended nature of individuality, its communicative essence, and the indefinite burdens of its relatedness. At the same time, philosophic restraint and a sense of evidence cautions against the position of Whitehead that "every actual entity [or individual] is present in every other actual entity."[3] Repugnance to the doctrine of disconnected substances need imply not the opposite extreme but the more conservative likelihood that an individual *can* be "present in" other individuals. We require, then, to avoid two positions: that of anthropomorphism, by limiting "experience" to human individuals; and that of the doctrine of internal relations, by not merely admitting degrees of relevance (which Whitehead actually professes to do) but so couching the conception of experience as to recognize a meaning for irrelevance.

In order the better to understand the group of complex properties that philosophers aim to encompass when they speak of "experience" and "experiencing," we shall in what follows often subordinate these terms or lay them aside, however peculiar such a procedure may seem. For the terms are so laden with a burden of contrary and confused differentia, so encumbered by the hoary banalities which cognate terms like "empiricism" and "empirical" suggest, that a fresh start with superior conceptual equipment is necessary. After reformulation and the delineation of essential traits we may presumably return to the older language with great control of its usage. In a sense, of course, this older language can be superseded only in a limited way, and cannot be totally abandoned. It remains the language of common sense—even if, as we are too likely to forget, the language of common sense, influenced by standards of literate expression, inevitably reflects some ideational bias. Common sense needs to abstain from qualification, and needs to make its discriminations rough and sure, if it is to make possible elementary human intercourse and the business of simple existence. The identifications it makes in nature are not like sharpshooting, which risks failure in behalf of higher stakes, but like the broadside, more secure if less exact. . . .

II

We start necessarily with the discernment of an all-embracing movement characteristic of the individual life. This movement is at the very least in time and in space. Temporal movement is continuous, uninterrupted, and pervasive—beyond the individual's control. Spatial movement, which is partly within the individual's control, is subject to suspension, sometimes because of and sometimes in spite of the control. One portion of this individual process, the portion known as growth, itself has temporal and spatial characteristics, and is actually divisible into many kinds of growth. The entire process is determined and predetermined: physical, social, genetic, morphological, physiological, intellective, and affective forces, all feeding impulses, habits, and dispositions, ensure the outcome of the process as human. The unique pattern, on the other hand, of those concerted forces, ensures the individuality and contingency of the process. It will not do to describe the process simply as the "living process," for living processes are perfectly conceivable without the presence of anything called "experiencing." So far as most philosophers are concerned, the addition of experiencing to living amounts to the addition of conscious awareness—an attribute which is only part of the process, and not a necessary part of all its manifestations. Dewey, observing that philosophers have spoken mainly of experience at large, and wishing to stress the importance of particular experiences, of "an" experience, holds that "life is no uniform uninterrupted march or flow. It is a thing of histories, each with its own plot."[4] But the living individual as such has a history, and *this* history *is* certainly an uninterrupted flow. And it is the nature of this history or process that is most in need of investigation. Here, then, we may augment our nomenclature, lest important traits be obscured by tenacious associations. We must expect the meanings of the terms to emerge as we proceed and not to be completed instantaneously. For it is not possible instantaneously to detail all of the applications that contribute to a meaning.

We shall name the process in question *proception* or the *proceptive* process, and describe the human individual as a *proceiving* individual or *proceiver*. The individual "proceives" or is said to "proceive," and these terms will be used grammatically much in the way that terms like "functions" and "to function" are. "Proceives" (like "functions") is not the present tense of an operation, not something done *to* something else or visited *upon* something else. So that if we speak, as it sometimes will be convenient to speak, of "the world insofar as it is proceived" or of "existence proceived," this will be only an elliptical way of designating an ontologic situation, an entire relation together with its relata, and will not imply that something has become the object of an act. We shall have to speak of *procepts* and of the *proceptive domain*. The suitability of the term "proception" stems in part from the fact that it permits these derivatives. If a term must suggest certain properties at the outset or be useless, then at the risk of initial imprecision let "proception" suggest the inseparable union of process with receptivity, of movement in nature with impact by nature, of things shaped with events accepted. The emphasis is on historicity and natural involvement. Most simply, we shall subsequently be in a position to say, proception is the actualization of procepts. As the term "proception" is needed to identify and to preserve conceptually the precise character of individual historicity, individuated process, so the term "procept" is needed to identify and to fix the status of a natural complex that enters into this process.

But what can be made clear from the outset is that "proception" and "proceiving," though corresponding in usage very roughly to "experience" and "experiencing," are free from certain questionable metaphysical assumptions permitted by the ambiguities of the latter terms. Thus, philosophers often speak of "the realm of experience." Some of them mean to distinguish it from a realm of "existence," implying that what is to be found "in experience" may not, insofar, be said to "exist." Others, distinguishing experience from nature, intend a contrast between two existential orders, the precise interrelation of which they conceive to be a principal problem of philosophy. Still others regard the "realm" of experience as a part of the "realm" of nature. Proception eliminates these equivocations. It is a natural process, distinguishable in specific terms from other natural processes.

The first trait to be distinguished in the proceptive process is its directed and propulsive character. "The inmost texture of [man's] being is propulsive," says Santayana; in all of human existence "there is a self-reproductive, flying essence."[5] Birth and growth, the primary propulsive forces, place the natural commitments of the individual directly before him. To some extent propulsion is as it were ornamented or qualitatively augmented by the individual, as in the process of query, or in the pursuance of affective drives. To some extent it is constantly modified by the larger natural complexes of which he is part; events push him in one path rather than another. Even when he is said to be thwarted in his purposes or impulses, he is being pushed on, in a complex that works itself out with the component of disapproval. The propulsions of the individual together with the specific directions in which they lead constitute his *proceptive direction*. This is the resultant direction, or directed outcome, of all that comprises his life. It is variable, or malleable by events. Among other factors, it entails what, in a now common but not altogether felicitous phrase, is called "funded experience." "Funded experience," to be sure, is much more compatible with the notion of proceptive direction than is the classical "stock of ideas" or "store of impressions." But it is not easily reconciled with the factor of movement, and its use seems to suggest that a fund, once established, is there forever; that it can be affected only by quantitative increase and not equally by the content of an addition to it. Actually there is no fund the significance of which, or the total character of which, cannot be altered and even revolutionized by the character of subsequent situations. It can be rendered paltry and inconsequential or enhanced in its relative power. The concept of the proceptive direction avoids making the funded past a bundle separate from present involvement, a store to which items are occasionally added and from which judgment can borrow, making it instead integral with the individual and with the world presently pertinent to the individual. The individual's past persists as a proceptive complex—that is, as a natural complex which is essential to the uniqueness of the total individual-in-movement. This description conveys what will be meant by saying that anything is or becomes a part of the individual's experience, namely, that it is predicable of the individual as individual, of his makeup; not *merely* of his mind, his foot, his heart, or his estate.

The notion of a proceptive direction in no way excludes from the content of individual life the common facts of conflict and indetermination. On the contrary, the proceptive direction is the outcome, partly actual and partly potential, representative of any configuration of facts. That any number of diverse facts and traits fit into some identifiable structure is a truism; if they did not, it would not be possible to speak of "an individual" at all. Nor is the proceiver anything separable from the plurality of traits and circumstances distinguishable in his history: it is quite enough to say that they make history and are not just a plurality. Proceptive direction, moreover, has nothing to do with what a man envisions for himself, or with his having a "purpose in life." It is a name for the discriminable effect and prospect of a history. If there are human individuals there must be proceptive directions. But this fact stated, another may be added without delay. With the notion of proceptive direction it may be possible to help define "human"; proceeding the other way round is not very promising.

A stone, dislodged from a mountainside, must roll in some direction, however fortuitously. Whether it rolls eastward or westward depends solely upon the conjunction of circumstances. The proceptive direction, likewise, is the direction effected by the conjunction of the circumstances relevant to the individual. Though it entails spatial and temporal facts about the individual, it is itself no more of a spatial or temporal term than the terms "development" and "growth" are. And like the term "individual" it is devoid of any eulogistic significance. Were there no proceptive direction, there could be no characterization of the course of an individual life, and hence no individual life except in a purely biological sense. Although in practice such a characterization is always a challenge, it is also always possible. To say that an individual necessarily has a proceptive direction means, then, that certain potentialities of doing, making, and saying, and certain potential relations to other things, are excluded from his future while others are included in it, all by virtue of the cumulative power of his past in total relation to his world.

Proception, the natural historicity of the individual, thus cannot be propulsive and directed without being cumulative. The importance of understanding this often recognized trait emerges when we consider that it embraces other traits which philosophers have found to be distinctive of "experience." For instance, Aristotle and various others have called attention to the duplicative and repetitive element in what is properly called experience, as distinguished from specific functions (or "operations") like sensation or perception. We are said to perceive a quality or an occurrence. But only insofar as the occurrence is identified, classified, or recognized as relating to other repeatable occurrences is it said to be experienced or to be part of our experience. This property is also implied in the phrase "human experience" and in the context "human experience shows that. . . ." That is, repeated instances of the same kind reveal certain conclusions; numerous individuals confirm one another's repetitions. Hegel, rebelling against the tendency to regard experience as a kind of faculty, and against the conception of experience at large as a mere collection of experiences, portrayed individual history as embattlement. The movement of experience, like the movement of social history, lay in the harmonization of ideas (or as Dewey freshly but analogously formulated it, in the resolution of indeterminate situations). Though Hegel continued the chronic association of experience with the life of consciousness, he came closer to the realization that a cumulative process underlies and gives meaning to the repetitive factor. For there may be any number of repetitions or recurrences without significance and without effect in individual life. Whether, as in the intellectualistic view, the instances of fact that men encounter are connected with one another experientially by a bond of reflection, or whether, more generally, they are each germane to a pervasive interest within the individual's life, their character as experience is their role in a history.

The cumulative factor in perception embraces other factors that have received independent emphasis but that are alike indigenous. It explains the emphasis on repetition and the emphasis on novelty, which at first notice are incompatible. One strain in both common and philosophic usage suggests that without replenishment and spontaneous newness "experience" is dormant or even nonexistent. A current writer discerns that adequate recognition of this trait is one of Locke's merits. "Locke is that very rare thing, a *genuine* empiricist who has turned philosopher instead of writing novels. His world amazes him; a pineapple, a dreamless sleep, a dual personality, a ground almond, a rational parrot constantly pop up to be explained and to destroy the continuity of his thought. It is the temper of the Royal Society, shrewd, sensational, omnivorous of physical detail. . . . [implying that] life is infinitely various: do not try to bottle her in scholastic jars."[6] In a related and not dissimilar vein, Peirce sets as the essence of experience shock, resistance, and constraint. The confrontation and absorption of oddity by the individual, or the encounter with brute newness, is by no means a matter of resolving something that is incongruous with what has gone before. It belongs to the primitive texture of human existence, as does the sheer recurrence of events. It is in part (when taken on the level of awareness) a *sense* of oddity; and more broadly, a natural *acceptance* and a natural *utilization* of oddity by a perceiver (by an individual insofar as he is said to "experience"). When one is said to "reveal his experience" to another, or to "share his experience" with another, the assumption involved is that what has become integral to one individual's life may be communicated as a trait relatively novel to that of another. Both repetition and novelty, then, turn out to be factors in the cumulative process of proception. Repetition fixes and solidifes the events of this process, while novelty increases its breadth and helps, by sharpening the qualitative difference between past and present, to define the proceptive direction. The traditional phrase "to learn from experience" is extraordinarily complex. Its verbal equivalent, transitional to interpretation, is "to profit from the past." It presupposes all three of the factors just enumerated: many repeated instances of occurrence, a cumulative efficacy in these repetitions, and an integration of new instances with the old.

III

Proception, like every other process, may be said to transpire "in" nature, and the relations of an individual as proceiver (as "experiencer") may be said to be "to" or "with" other natural complexes. The "in" here may be understood partly in the familiar sense. The individual is simply contained within a framework that is larger and older. No sentiment about the ultimate eternality or the potential infinitude of the self can conceal its littleness in the natural order. But although the natural order, transcending the being and the reach of the individual, may be said literally to envelop him, it does not follow that every natural situation of which the individual is part is an envelopment relation. To be "in" a situation— in thought, in love, in danger—is to be specifically related, a sense not comparable with being "in" the natural order. There is a third "in" that links the other two together. Basically, experience or the proceptive process is "in" nature in the sense that it is continuous with other forms of order and existence, possessing, as each form does, traits peculiar to itself and traits common to other forms; and this applies equally to being "in a situation." Where the relation of an individual is said to be "to" or "with" things natural, a more direct and pressing problem is posed. This problem is not to recite as many different instances of the relation as possible, but to define the common character of these instances as constituting the individual a proceiver. Proception being a process, in terms of what substantive elements does this process go on? Or: how are the complexes of nature related to an individual history? Or, in more conventional terms: what is meant by the "content" of experience? Here we shall need to utilize the notions of procept and proceptive domain.

    An individual is a natural complex contingently associated with, affecting, and affected by other natural complexes. The complexes, including every part or phase of his own individuality, that are related to him within the span of his history comprise an aggregate. This aggregate, possessing within itself an indefinite number of patterns analytically discoverable, is his world. And this world is a part of the world at large; or, it is the world at large insofar as it can be said to be modified by his presence in it. It is the world that ultimately sustains his being; that comprises what he reacts to, thinks of, and theorizes about; that comprises his situations, happenings, and products. The world not included in "his" world is the world that cannot be said to be related to him, except in the remote sense that his and all other spheres of existence alike exemplify processes of nature. On the other hand, "his" world is no insular box. It is continuous with the world of all other individuals, identical with theirs insofar as neither he nor they as individuals make it any different, but uniquely determined insofar as it is an aggregate of complexes which are not in *all* respects the same as those of the other aggregates.

Now it is essential to observe that an individual's world is not co-extensive with his "experience." Everything in his experience is necessarily part of his world, but not everything in his world is necessarily part of his experience. For the further distinction must be made between what is related to him insofar as he is a natural complex not different from other natural complexes, and what is related to him insofar as he is an individual, or natural complex that is unique. For example, sunlight, and the air pressure in his environment on earth, would ordinarily, simply as such, be related to him in the former way, indifferently with other men and other things; whereas the house he lives in would be related to him uniquely. And on the other hand, a brick built into his house, like a star in the heavens, is a complex that might fall into the former category: it might be in his world and not in his experience. The aggregate of such complexes as are related to him uniquely constitute the "content of his experience." This is a subaggregate of the aggregate that constitutes his world. And this subaggregate is his proceptive domain. Any natural complex (any fact, thing, relation, event, situation, state) within a proceptive domain is a procept; so that any complex within *his* proceptive domain is a procept for *him*.

It is the need for this distinction between the "larger" and "smaller" worlds of an individual—between "his world" and "his experienced world"—that makes it ambiguous to speak simply of the world that is "available" to him. For this might mean the world that sustains his existence along with other existences, or the world that has formed his existence and no other; the former a world that is proceivable, that could possibly be proceived by him, the latter a world that he has proceived and is proceiving. More strictly, there are *three* "worlds": the world that includes both complexes related to and complexes unrelated to a given individual; the world that includes only the complexes related to him; and the world that includes only the complexes related to him uniquely. Theoretically, the first world might have been identical with the second. And the first, therefore, as well as the second, is proceiv*able*—that is, it is logically possible for anything at all that exists or has existed, to become relevant to the uniqueness of some individual, whether through some type of existential effect or through its seizure by query, as in discovery by astronomy or by historical inference. The first world (the indefinite "whole of nature") is the entire actual and possible world, past, present, and future; the second ("his world") is the world without which a given individual would not be; the third (the proceptive domain, or "content of an individual's experience") is the world without which he would not be what he is. The three worlds are of respectively diminishing inclusiveness, concentrically related to one another.

A procept, we said in an earlier but unelaborated context, is a natural complex that relates to or affects the individuals as an individual. To "affect," or to "relate" to, the individual in *this* sense means either to help perpetuate what he uniquely is or to alter the character of this uniqueness. As in other words, any existence becomes a procept for an individual when it serves either to stabilize or to modify his proceptive direction. Thus the natural complex known in a particular instance as growing thin is a procept, a happening that has affected a given individual, an event relating to him in a particular way. The natural complex which consists in the seeing of a blue hat at a certain time is a procept for a given individual: being an instance of similar previous vision and similar previous identification, it strengthens by repetition a habit of that individual (though it may modify his direction in another respect). The natural complex which is called the death of an individual, if it happens to modify the life of another, is a procept for the latter. Each of these complexes is an existing something which affects someone. A "thing" is what may affect any individual. A procept is that thing insofar as it does not affect a given individual. Thus a hill, a war, a cloud, a hat, an election, a heat wave is one and the same fact or thing potentially related to any or all individuals. Insofar as it enters into the history and commitment of each, it is a procept for each, and therefore in some respect different for each. It may enter the history by being endured or by being perceived or by an indefinite number of possible relations. We often speak of the "events in our experience." And we should continue to do so. Events are events whether they are experienced or not. But neither the experience nor the events in question have the same status as before. Both we and the events are now part of the relational situations. An effect has taken place in our proceptive direction; the events have become procepts. The factors strengthening us in what we now are or altering us from what we now are may not be such factors for others. Procepts for me are events effectively relevant to me. The events that are procepts for me may be either different or utterly nonexistent in the world that constitutes another's proceptive domain.

A procept, therefore, is a natural complex relevant to a proceptive domain (or natural complex that has become "part" of a proceptive domain). A proceptive domain is an ordered aggregate of procepts. Proception is the process whereby a proceptive domain acquires its order. A proceptive direction is the character of the potentialities in proception. A proceiver is an individual that possesses the properties of proception (or, less formalistically, an individual considered not merely insofar as he exists or even lives but insofar as he proceives, or relates continuously and uniquely to a world).

A procept is not "in the mind" or in the body (except insofar as the complex in question happens to be a bodily event) or "in" the individual; nor is it "external" to the mind (whatever that may mean) or to the individual; nor is it some proxy ("essence," "idea," "datum") between the individual and another existence. A procept is the *existence itself,* the existing act, state, situation, or other natural complex *insofar* as it is relevant to an individual as individual. Likewise, proception *is* the continuing interrelation of the individual with other existences of whatever kind; and the proceptive domain *is* the existential order in which an individual's life and history and self consists. The complexes of nature are not "presented" to experience. They occur, and when their occurrence involves an individual they *constitute* experience. The reason for these asseverations emerges when we try to reproduce the foregoing distinctions wholly in the locution of "experience."

For instance, are we to say that "a procept" is the equivalent of "an experience"? Instead, we should ask whether by "an experience" we mean simply and essentially "a procept." If we adopt the reverse order of questioning, the question is begged. For what *do* we mean by "experience" in the phrase "an experience"? Do we mean a "sense-datum"? an "act of consciousness"? a happening in someone's life? Thus Dewey, for example, speaks of "an experience" very differently from the way he speaks of "experience." "An" experience transpires only when "the material experienced runs its course of fulfillment"; experience which is "anesthestic," which lacks "completeness" and "unity," which has no "consummation in consciousness," no aesthetic or felt "quality," is not "an" experience.[7] Plainly, these qualifications apply not to all but only to some procepts, and to a relatively small class at that. From a purely technical point of view, there is nothing to prevent a decision that "an experience" shall be stripped of its rhetorical associations and be made equivalent to "a procept." But if this is not done, the expression "a procept" finds no concise equivalent in existing terminology.

Are we to say that "proceptive domain" is the equivalent of "fund of experience"? Once more the question is begged if we try to determine equivalence by taking the older form of expression as the standard. For what kind of thing *is* it that is funded—habits? ideas? acts? objects? And does "funded" mean the same in all these cases? Again, is the phrase "to proceive" the equivalent of "to experience"? We may say that the former expresses for the latter a more generalized and more precise meaning than the latter ordinarily has. We may not say that the two phrases are always substitutable for one another. "Proceive," when it appears to be used transitively, is only an ellipsis for a more complex relational account; "nature proceived" means, not the object of an operation, psychic or otherwise, but nature insofar as it is related to a given individual history. "Experience" is used both transitively and intransitively, transitively when it is said, for instance, "He experienced a storm." "To proceive" means "to function as an individual, directively and cumulatively"; "to experience" has many and incompatible meanings.

Every one of an individual's judgments is necessarily one of his procepts. For what stems from him is part of that which makes him what he is. The individual as producer is organically part of the individual as proceiver. Feelings, thoughts, or judgments are natural complexes which *must* be procepts for some individual: they are existences that occur only in relations of an individual and are necessarily relevant to some proceptive direction. Considered in their particularity as occurrences, feelings or thoughts belonging to one individual may or may not become procepts for another, depending on whether they acquire relevance to the latter's life: they may become stimuli to his own feelings and thoughts, or influences on his action. There are numerous complexes literally related to individuals and yet not ordinarily related to them as procepts, such as the microorganisms in their shoes; for such facts in their triviality, no less than the laws of electromagnetism or astronomy in their universality, are as a rule indifferent to the uniqueness of the individual. Whether certain facts like the standards of living in Asia are or are not procepts for given individuals is a specific problem of discovery and analysis. Such specific problems are of direct concern to the historian, psychiatrist, biographer, or ethnologist. There is, however, no particle or configuration in nature which may not conceivably enter into relation to some individual-as-proceiver (rather than as-sheer-natural-complex) and thereby acquire the status of procept. If the air pressure or the light of day, which ordinarily are related to all individuals indifferently, do become procepts or uniquely relevant existences in the lives of some individuals, it is as subjects of query or of simple judgment, as causes of unique individual effects, or as neurotically pertinent objects.

Awareness is one possible factor among others in proception. The enlargement and continual repatterning of the proceptive domain of an individual is dependent only in part and only at times on awareness. This truth, neglected by contemporary philosophers, is a commonplace to the older philosophers of the passions, to poets and storytellers since antiquity, and to almost all of the differing schools of modern psychology. Most "empiricist" philosophers think that the world becomes experientially available through "data." And there would be nothing wrong with this if the "data" were construed not primarily as noises and patches, or even as tables and chairs, but as the circumstances of rearing and growth, as pervasive and imperceptible moral influences, as the structures of human togetherness, as the contingent stimuli to curiosity and emotion, as the forms of health and disease, as the boundaries imposed by the facts of society, heredity, and mortality. "Data" in the significant sense are materials, constituents, subject matters, not sensory "surfaces." When awareness does become prominent as a factor in what men call the highest phases of experiencing, particularly moral relations and in the processes of query, it is truly *awareness* that is prominent, and not simply the activity of "thought." For reflective or inferential awareness alone will not fit the patterns of active and exhibitive judgment, or indeed of assertive judgment, nor the diversity of invention and communication.

The "data of experience" cannot be other than the complexes of the world as proceived. The general distinction between appearance and reality, customarily invoked by philosophers to support a more special distinction between "datum" and "object," is legitimate only in the realm of common sense practice and the realm of "explanation." For in these realms it is a functional distinction between a standard, universally identified thing or configuration and something else deemed an irregular, unexpected, private, or adventitious version of it; for instance, between a waking journey and a dreamt-of journey, or between a round, engraved penny and a flat, unfamiliar copper rectangle that proves to be its edge. Philosophically, the intrinsic, fixed distinction between appearance and reality or shadow and substance is inexcusable, reflecting an indulgent bias for one form of reality as against every other form. If, as has sometimes been suggested, this bias is the symptom of one kind of valuational preference in opposition to another, there is still no reason for conceptually ordering the cosmos in accordance with such a preference. Among those philosophers for whom the real means the permanent or eternal and the apparent the transitory, a valuational and an ontological distinction clearly (and understandably) coincide. In the light of a more comprehensive conception of experience than that which prevailed anciently, the one realm is as experienceable as the other, and each is a factor in any proceptive domain. Those philosophers, however, for whom in monstrous but unwitting irony the real is the inaccessible, have succeeded not in sundering nature from experience but in providing perennial fodder for the philistines. They have, as Whitehead suggests, actually tried to make two natures, nature meant and nature dreamt. But what is intrinsically inaccessible cannot be meant; and a dream which has uninterrupted order and continuity, a dream to which there can be no alternative condition, is no dream at all.

It follows from the foregoing considerations, first, that in every instance where a natural complex becomes a procept, a change takes place in the status both of the individual and the other existence involved. Two natural complexes each become modified in their total relations, and a full description of each would have to record the role of each in a larger or newer complex of which it is an element. Thus "naive realism," "representationalism," and similar approaches grounded in a dubious metaphysics have no meaning here. On the other hand, the general approach sometimes called "objective relativism" is given support. Secondly, since not all natural complexes are procepts, that is, not all are necessarily pertinent to the unique being of any given individual, a doctrine of "internal relations" is avoided. And thirdly, since all natural complexes can conceivably become procepts, a doctrine of intrinsically unavailable realities is avoided.

It is not difficult, in terms of the concept of proception, to account for usages of "experience" ostensibly not about individuals. Commonly we speak of "social experience," and of what men learn from it; of "the French experience of parliamentary government" or "the American experience of competition." There are "lessons of human experience," and when men are urged to "appeal to experience" or to "consult experience," it is oftener than not something different from their individual environment or their sensory powers to which reference is made. Social forces, social products, and social histories do not have to be explained away. Neither does "social experience." What simply has to be acknowledged is that there are real similarities between one individual and other individuals. The similarities obtain between spans of one individual history and spans of other individual histories. Similarity of this kind is proceptive parallelism. Proceptive parallelism makes a social history and social experience possible. For without it, the "history" of a group is a history of unrelated masses rather than of representative traits. Proceptive parallelism, instead of implying the reduction of social existence to individual experience, on the contrary prevents the atomization of the social. What we generically call "human experience" is not the mere multiplicity of all human happenings: that is not what we could be urged to "consult." It is rather the tissue of likeness in individual human histories. We are urged to "appeal" to what can be appropriated in some mode of judgment by one individual and another and still another. It would make no sense to appeal to what is available in one way to this individual, in another to that, and in no way to all. There is no social experience, and actually no social being, without community, and there is no comunity without proceptive parallelism.

IV

It should be evident why the individual does not "experience" with his mind or with his body or "with" anything at all. "Experience" is primarily predicable of an individual history: as an attribute expressed by a verb, it is the distinctive movement of this history; as an attribute expressed by a noun, it is the structure of this history. Or in the terms that fix these meanings and define the nature of this history, the relation between an individual and the world affecting him as such is the relation between two natural complexes of very different magnitudes, each of constantly varying determinateness with respect to the other. This relation, the essential natural status of the individual, works itself out as the proceptive process. In the proceptive process we can distinguish a structure of complexes (the proceptive domain) constitutive of the complex called the individual, and a resultant definitive inclination (the proceptive direction). It is not to be feared that in such an account the "subject of change," the existence of "personal identity," has been lost. Body, mind, person, organism are all in residence. The fact that these are identified collectively as phases of a natural complex does not dissolve any of the permanencies in man. His blood still moves, "as it were, in a circle"; his viscera are still there to serve and to trouble him. It is an old story that philosophy respects and adopts but may not worship the entities of common belief, and above all may not be intimidated by them. If common traitors are occasionally ruled out of court, it is for the greater glory of good citizenship.

In what way can recognition be given to the distinction between the individual as an initiator of experience and the individual as, so to speak, a collector of experience? Philosophers have debated the relative weight of activity and passivity in experience, and the scale of emphases has been a major criterion for the classification of their opinions. "Sensationalism," "intellectualism," "rationalism," and "empiricism" are often regarded primarily as answers to this question. Is the portrait to be that of a train rider looking out on the countryside? Or an organism struggling uphill on foot? Or a framer of categories for mute data? Or a solver of problems? Each of these analogies presupposes its own metaphysics of the individual. The first and third centralize the role of mind in experience, one making it a recipient of impressions, the other making it a power that bestows intelligibility. The second makes the individual a sentient body that moves "as on a darkling plain." The fourth emphasizes the role of mind not in a central but still in an unmistakable way, making it not a sufficient but a necessary condition of experience, and conceiving of the individual as an organism oscillating repeatedly between the fringe of intelligence or reflection and the heights of inquiry.

Now in describing the further properties of proception there is no great harm in using the terms "active" and "passive." But as in previous instances of nomenclature, these terms suffer from the twin liability of being laden with unhappy associations and being insufficiently fertile for a generalized account. We shall do better to ascribe to proception two generic dimensions, manipulation and assimilation, which are inseparable, as dimensions of a process must be. The proceiver does not alternately manipulate and assimilate. As a bidimensional being, he may be studied with major emphasis now on the one dimension and now on the other, just as the length of an object may be examined in disregard of its breadth, or vice versa, without denying either the inseparability or the equal status of the dimension functionally disregarded. In the language of activity and passivity, the individual is not merely both an agent and patient but an active patient and a patient agent, occasionally considered for purposes of abstraction in one or the other of these capacities. Manipulation and assimilation are inclusive dimensions. Memory, attention, imaging are dimensions of the individual's awareness; digestion, circulation, respiration are dimensions of the individual's physiology; but manipulation and assimilation in the sense here intended are dimensions of the individual as proceiver. It is important to understand what this characterization means. It does not mean that manipulation and assimilation apply to the individual in general in the sense that they apply to none of his functions in particular. On the contrary, it means that each of his special functions, contributing to the nature of a whole, contributes to the manipulative and assimilative character of that whole. . . .

The distinction that invites comparison with the present one is Dewey's distinction between "doing" on the one hand and "undergoing" or "receptivity" on the other, the latter in some contexts called "having" and in some contexts "enjoyment." It is important, both for the development of the present distinction and for the notion of proception in general, to observe the differences.

First of all, "doing" in Dewey's sense is an emphasis on instrumental experience, on an ordering of means to ends. But manipulation is not necessarily instrumental in character. The man who inadvertently inhales more deeply and quickly on approaching another is ordering his environment but not acting instrumentally—unless we insist on locating a naive teleology in the situation. The man who juxtaposes two facial images in memory, though experiencing manipulatively, need not, in the juxtaposition as such, be acting instrumentally. And the man who rises and runs unaccountably, in panic for unknown causes, can be said to be adjusting means to ends only by the most intellectualistic and reductive construction of this idea. Yet the situation is part of his proceptive economy. It is part of an underlying organization the pattern of which is unintelligible by common behavioral standards and in which means and ends are nonexistent or indistinguishable.

Secondly, "receptivity," "undergoing," "suffering," "having," "enjoying" are almost invariables associated by Dewey with "immediacy" of experience, with "qualitative experience" or "the experience of quality," with experience insofar as it is "final" or "terminal," and hence with what, in virtue of these properties, is ineffable. But assimilation is a process to which "immediacy" does not apply very meaningfully. Omnipresent in the individual's life, it consists in the elemental acceptance of existences that is one condition of their being procepts for him. The facts and the qualities, the structures and the limits of his world, insofar as they have occurred, are irreversible. Whether or not the individual is aware of these occurrences and existences, whether he approves or repudiates them, he is bearing them as data for his life. Assimilation consists in "receptivity" not merely to "quality" but to the very addition of procepts to the proceptive domain. Dewey describes "having" as "sensible, affectional, or appreciatorial." He says of "immediate events" (or "qualitative events") that their *occurrence* is one with their being sensible, affectionally, and appreciatively *had*."[8] But an event which enters into an individual history, which becomes a procept, has, merely in such a capacity, nothing to do with any "experience of quality" in the sense suggested. Assimilation may or may not be, and preponderantly is not, characterized by sensible, affective, or appreciative states. What an individual assimilates is what he sustains, not what he feels; though he may sustain an event primarily through the medium of feeling, as when he is struck in the face or when he is frightened by the prospect of death. But when, for example, he is slandered by his neighbors, in the total absence of awareness on his part, great changes may take place in his possibilities and relationships, and the course of his subsequent experience altered; yet these occurrences are assimilated into his proceptive direction, sustained by his involved and related self, in utter independence of any "immediate or qualitative experience." So contrary is this notion of assimilation to Dewey's "undergoing," and to his conception of experience in general, that he often writes as if he were concerned to reject it. Thus: "Suppose fire encroaches upon a man when he is asleep. Part of his body is burned away. The burn does not perceptibly result from what he has done. There is nothing which in any constructive way can be named experience."[9]

Thirdly, "doing" and "undergoing," according to Dewey, can vary inversely with each other, or suppress each other. An "excess of doing" may reduce "receptivity" to almost nothing, and an "excess of receptivity," a "mere undergoing," may crowd out action or "contact with the realities of the world."[10] Or in a different context, but analogously, the immediacy of "having" excludes "knowing," and the concern of knowing with sequences, relations, and coexistences is an alternate experience to having. Ideally, says Dewey, doing (or knowing) and undergoing (or having) should each enhance the growth and extension of the other. We have seen that manipulation and assimilation are related in an entirely different way. To speak of one as suppressing or inhibiting the other is nonsense. Being codimensional, they are also each continuous. It is possible to speak of an individual as ceasing to "know" (in the sense of ceasing to reflect), but an individual who has ceased to manipulate or to assimilate has ceased to be. The individual cannot be said to assimilate, or to manipulate, in greater degree at one time than at another, any more than he can be said to proceive in greater or lesser degree. When we say, in ordinary speech, that one individual has a greater power of assimilation than another, or that he can assimilate "more," we are speaking of the comparative character of their experiencing, not of its degree or quantity as experiencing. The "more" describes the kind of traits and facts assimilated, not the function of assimilating; it applies to the kind of elements in the proceptive domain, not to the proceptive process. When we limit a comparison to a particular form of experience— we say, for example, that one man assimilated certain ideas more fully than another did—a quantitative aspect seems more plausibly to be present; but this is actually a colloquial version of the fact that the assimilative experience of two men is differently allocated. The world that any man assimilates, though subject to comparison by one standard and in one respect with that of another, is never more or less truly a world.

When, similarly, we say that one individual has "more experience" than another, we are elliptically describing or evaluating their differences in a given respect, for instance, the extent of their travel or the duration of their professional career; for one is not more of an experiencing animal than another. The comparison is like the rhetorical statement that one man is "more alive" than another, which refers to the character of the two lives and is a dramatic appraisal, not a quantitative measurement. Nor can one man "judge" more or less than another; the makings, doings, and statings of one can be compared with those of another only in relative value. What each man assimilates, he assimilates. He is not less or more of an assimilative or manipulative being than any other, but a being that in part assimilates different things; and this is indeed what, by definition, makes him a different being. One man cannot absorb the world that another can. But it is precisely because men have different powers that their worlds are in some respect different. That which a man is powerless to assimilate is simply that which is no part of his perceptive domain. As assimilative power is an acceptance, assimilative impotence is an exclusion. The manifestations of manipulation and assimilation are endless in number. It makes sense to say not that the degree but that the way in which we manipulate and assimilate alters, for changes in the affairs of life relate us differently to the world. Likewise, the process of query makes it meaningful to speak of methodical manipulation and methodical assimilation, for the ways in which a man's environment is ordered by him and borne by him are to some extent determinable by his choice. Choice is itself at once a shaping and an acceptance: a subject-of-query is manipulated because it can be sustained or endured as a procept, and endured or assimilated because it can be shaped to be the procept that it is.

It is plain, then, that the distinction between doing and undergoing, between the instrumental and the final or immediate in experience, is a less generalized one as well as a differently oriented one than that between the two proceptive dimensions, and is not easily adaptable to the concept of proception.[11] And yet, how much less faithful to the complexity of experience is the tradition which Dewey attacked and which held him in its grip more than he suspected. In this tradition, the sole manifestation of "activity" in what is called "experience" is "thinking," and the sole manifestation of "passivity" is "sensing." Rationalists and empiricists alike have made a travesty of experience, and have argued in a dark corner rather than in the full light of day. That they have been concerned with experience mainly insofar as it bears upon "knowledge" does not condone the narrowness of their common framework, since the conception of knowledge has itself been, in consequence, correspondingly narrowed and dogmatized. They have inadvertently left it to art to deal with experience in its proper breadth and to render exhibitively what they should equally have recognized and encompassed assertively. "Thinking," as activity, is only one instance of manipulation, and "sensing," as passivity, is only one instance of assimilation. But the true measure of the traditional narrowing of experience reveals itself when we realize, as a moment's consideration can enable us to do, that the assimilative dimension is present in thinking, and the manipulative in sensing.

Proception or experience is the diversified interrelatedness of manipulation and assimilation, a process comprising an order of things manipulated as well as a manipulating, an order of things assimilated as well as an assimilating. As assimilator, the individual is a witness, a gatherer, a patient, a recipient of the complexes of nature. As a manipulator, he is a shaper, a transformer, an initiator, an agent of these complexes. Implicit throughout the course of the permutations in proception is the role of the individual as commentator on nature, including his own nature. This commentary is utterance or judgment. Utterance is the succession of "positions" or "postures" in proception. Each of these takes the form of a product, an instance of making, saying, or acting. And it is because every product is inherently a position in nature—inherently a pronouncement and appraisal—that it is a judgment. The judgments of man appear on first consideration to be instances solely of manipulation. To produce, to comment explicitly or implicitly on things, is to help actualize new properties, to bring about for oneself (and indirectly or directly for others) new procepts, or (what is the same) to modify present procepts. But it is only this particular way of describing judgment that conceals its assimilative aspect. For in doing, making, or saying, we are inviting what we have not yet possessed. We are accumulating situations and traits as well as initiating them. We sustain whatever it is that we modify. Metaphysically speaking, there is no such thing as "touch and go." In "touching" we accept and in "going" we bring. This follows directly from the natural status of proceiving. For as we have seen, every change in a procept (or, every advent of a procept) entails some change of status both in the existence involved and in the individual to whom this existence is relevant.

We noted earlier that the present conception of experiencing emphasizes historicity and natural involvement. Recently a philosopher has said, of other philosophers, that whenever they are at a loss for a precise word to denote some relation under study they resort to the vague panacea "involve." This witty falsehood does not conceal the fact that in many cases, and particularly in the case of experiencing, probably no other word than "involve" could so precisely satisfy the character of the process. In experience there is a proceiver and there are other natural complexes. The proceiver is in a state of natural involvement in consequence of his natural historicity. What are the alternatives to this formulation? Is experiencing a relation of "subject and object"? Without rehearsing the difficulties and ambiguities of these terms, which of the relata is the subject and which is the object—and why? Is the subject the relatum endowed with mind? And is experience therefore "mental activity"? What is the effect on the distinction of subject and object when both relata are said to be minds? It does not take long to see that by making such terms basic we are committed to the metaphysics of egocentrism that plagues modern epistemology with arbitrary assumptions and dead ends. Most of the current terms roughly synonymous with "experiencing" are not only terms signifying "mental operations" but are derivatives of the supposed subject-object relation—perceiving, feeling, knowing, and the like. The term "involvement," perhaps more familiarly applicable to the proceiver's history than to the natural complexes which are his procepts, but in all strictness equally applicable to the latter as related to a given proceiver, expresses first, the common presence and common relevance of all the relata or determinants of proception, and second, the modification imposed by proception on all its relata. To be involved is to be affected or uniquely modified by a relation. To perceive an object is one form of involvement. To inherit a fortune, to be a child, to become ill, to feel momentary pleasure, are other forms. The term "involve" not only leaves room for the discoverable presence and specification of various forms of itself—social, mental, historical, physical, and whatever other forms are not yet satisfactorily characterized—but effectively reminds us that elements of experience glibly selected out by discourse may be continuous with one another and integrally related in fact.

The experiential relation is an "object-object" rather than a "subject-object" relation. Only if the latter pair of terms is appropriated for specific occasions and interpreted functionally, that is, used in order to name or discriminate the situational differences between related complexes, is it sometimes a desirable way of speaking. We discriminate one of the involved complexes, possibly either, as proceiver, and the other as procept. The difference between the complexes is not a difference of incorrigible status (for instance, between "mind and the external world" or between "percipient and datum") but of natural or existential traits. Proceivers are human complexes; their procepts may or may not be human. The experiential relation is a natural fact, like any other relation in nature, with describable differences between the complexes related. The proceiver does not "construct the world out of data" or "infer existence from experience" or "recover the world from appearances" or "posit the reality of a non-ego beyond consciousness" or "transcend immediacy"; nor is he immersed in a "sentient whole." We must guard against other false implications and equivalences. Proception or natural involvement, unlike Dewey's "experience," does not "reach down into nature": however deep down or high up it is alleged to go, it remains in the center. It is not to be identified simply with togetherness. In the broadest sense, "togetherness" belongs to coexistence of any kind, and hence to the "coexistence" of proceiver and procept; in which sense, though it is presupposed by, it does not explain or imply, proception. Nor, finally, can natural involvement be equated with "transaction" or "interaction," which suggest one dimension of involvement but fail without aid to suggest the other, or assimilative, dimension. . . .

Notes

1. John Dewey, *Experience and Nature,* vol. 1 of *The Later Works of John Dewey,* ed. J. A. Boydston (Carbondale, Ill.: Southern Illinois University Press, 1981), pp. 3–4.

2. Ibid., pp. 4a–1.

3. Alfred North Whitehead, *Process and Reality* (New York, 1929), p. 79.

4. John Dewey, *Art as Experience,* vol. 10 of *The Later Works of John Dewey,* ed. J. A. Boydston (Carbondale, Ill: Southern Illinois University Press, 1987), p. 35.

5. George Santayana, *Reason in Society* (New York, 1905), pp. 1–2.

6. Mary Scrutton, review of various books, *New Statesman and Nation,* February 14, 1953, p. 184.

7. Dewey, *Art as Experience,* chapter 3.

8. Dewey, *Experience and Nature,* p. 140.

9. John Dewey, *Reconstruction in Philosophy* (New York, 1920), p. 86. Likewise, in *Art as Experience,* Dewey says: "To put one's hand in the fire that consumes it is not necessarily to have an experience. The action and its consequence must be joined in *perception*" (p. 44; italics added).

10. Dewey, *Art as Experience,* pp. 44–45.

11. Toward the end of his essay "Qualitative Thought" (in *Philosophy and Civilization* [New York: Minton, Balch, & Co., 1931]), Dewey uses the term "assimilation" in the following sense: "*Sheer* assimilation results in the presence of a single object of apprehension. To identify a seen thing as a promontory is a case of assimilation" (p. 115).

Section 4

Science, Logic, and Knowledge

In section 3 we received a taste of what in the contemporary philosophic world Morris Cohen did not like. In this chapter we have the opportunity to look at a sustained account of his positive conceptions. Like many American naturalists in the first several decades of this century, Cohen was impressed by the ability of the natural sciences to resolve theoretical questions and to solve practical problems. And as Dewey in his own way appropriated the method of science in his reconstruction of the concept of experience, Cohen also argued that philosophy needs to make use of the scientific method. In Dewey's hands the method of science meant primarily an intellectual flexibility, an inclination to treat one's ideas as hypotheses, and a willingness to accept the results of experience and experiment in judging the worth of one's ideas. Cohen, however, emphasizes what he takes to be some of the ontological implications of the method. In the essay here reproduced from his book *Reason and Nature,* Cohen argues that the scientific method implies the rejection of an Absolute, a rejection of both nominalism and atomism, and that it is inconsistent with organicism. Again he criticizes what he calls the "antirational" philosophies of vitalism, organism, and action on the grounds that they deny the constancies of nature and thereby cannot help us acquire knowledge. A "rational" philosophy, that is, one that employs the method of science, is on the contrary able to achieve knowledge. Cohen also argues here that the scientific method implies

243

materialism in the sense, as he puts it, that "all phenomena depend on material conditions." And interestingly enough he supports what he calls a principle of polarity, which is the view that all things consist of opposites. Cohen makes it clear, however, that he does not interpret this overtly Hegelian point of view as implying logical contradiction, nor does it imply Hegel's idealism. In endorsing the contradictory character of natural entities within a materialist framework, Cohen's ideas are reminiscent of Marx and Engels.

Ernest Nagel was a close colleague of Cohen, and the two collaborated on studies of logic and the scientific method. Nagel, however, was more inclined than Cohen to employ an instrumentalist approach to these issues, and he does so here in his essay "Logic Without Ontology," which originally appeared in *Naturalism and the Human Spirit.* He points out that over the centuries different forms of naturalism have had different approaches to the nature of logical and mathematical principles. There is, for example, an Aristotelian tradition which holds that the principles of logic are necessarily true of all reality. There is by contrast an empiricist approach in which logical and mathematical principles are treated as more or less reliable empirical generalizations. And then there are those who might interpret logic and mathematics as arbitrary symbol systems. Nagel argues that each of these treatments is inadequate, and that we are better served to take an operational approach to both logic and mathematics, though only his discussion of logic has been included here.

Perhaps the most influential American philosopher of science, logic, and mathematics in this century has been W. V. O. Quine. Quine was born in Akron, Ohio, in 1908, and received a B.A. degree in 1930 from Oberlin College. Having already developed an interest in mathematical logic, the fact that Whitehead, one of the authors of *Principia Mathematica,* was then at Harvard attracted Quine to Cambridge for graduate study. At Harvard he worked with Whitehead, though more with C. I. Lewis and other Harvard logicians, and he received his Ph.D. after only two years, in June 1932. After studying and traveling in Europe, and after a junior fellowship from Harvard, Quine accepted an appointment as faculty instructor at Harvard in 1936. He retained his position there, along the way working and lecturing at many of the major universities around the world, until his retirement in 1978. In his article in this section, first published in 1969, Quine explores the traditional project of empiricist epistemology, and he likens it to developments in mathematics in the early twentieth century. The attempt had been made, notably by Russell and Whitehead, to reduce mathematics to logic, eventually to logic and set theory. This is analogous, Quine suggests, to the attempt to interpret knowledge in terms of sensory experience. Epistemologists have used various methods in trying to reduce knowledge claims to propositions about sense data. There have been new methods of definition, for example Russell's theory of descriptions, and there has been the attempt, by Rudolph Carnap for example, to translate knowledge claims in terms of observations. The motivation for these attempted reductions, in mathematics and in natural knowledge, is the same, namely to discover in one case the foundations of mathematics and in the other the foundations of knowledge, the purpose of which is to help achieve certainty in science. This is an enterprise of dubious value, but Quine holds that even though there is reason to despair of the Cartesian quest for certainty, there remains the central epistemological question of the relation between observation and science, or knowledge. Quine argues here that the best way to approach this question is to turn to psychology, the study of the natural process of the acquisition of knowledge.

1

The Metaphysics of Reason and Scientific Method*

Morris R. Cohen

The Relation Between Philosophy and Science

Those who rank the truth value of natural science very high and wish to utilize its results in their philosophy have followed one of three ways. They have tried to build a world-view either (a) on the results, (b) on the presuppositions, or (c) on the method of science.

PHILOSOPHY AS A SYNTHESIS OF THE SCIENCES

To take the generally accepted results of the various sciences and to weave them together into a picture of reality seems to many the readiest and safest way of philosophizing. The difficulties in the way of this are much more serious, however, than is commonly recognized. In the first place, it is difficult for anyone but a specialist to know what *are*

---

*Originally published in Morris R. Cohen, *Reason and Nature* (New York: Harcourt, Brace, and Co., 1931), chapter 4. Reprinted in a second edition by The Free Press (Glencoe, Ill., 1953), and by Dover Publications (New York, 1978). Reprinted by permission.

the results of any one special science. He who relies on popular expositions is apt to get more of the picturesque than of the true. For popular accounts necessarily simplify; and in the interest of such simplification the "results" of science are purified of the detailed qualifications essential to their truth, and separated from the technical methods by which they are obtained and which are essential to their scientific meaning.

An even more important consideration is the fact that a synthesis of the results of science is not necessarily scientific. Such synthesis may be and generally has been dominated more by practical, dramatic, and aesthetic than by scientific motives. Indeed, since it is the absence of evidence that generally compels the sciences to stop short in their synthesis and remain in the fragmentary state, it seems that attempts to carry our synthesis beyond what the various sciences have been able to effect cannot be strictly scientific. This does not deny the practical and aesthetic value of an imaginative synthesis beyond the necessarily fragmentary results that can be scientifically established. But the interests of truth demand a clear distinction between an imaginative synthesis and a strictly scientific one.

We are thus seemingly faced with a dilemma. Either scientific philosophy makes no attempt to fill the gaps in our scientific knowledge or else it must do so by methods which the sciences themselves will not use, so that our result cannot claim to be scientific even though elements of our picture may be borrowed from the sciences.

PHILOSOPHY AS A CRITIQUE OF THE PRESUPPOSITIONS OF SCIENCE

One of the ways of avoiding the horns of this dilemma is to view philosophy not as a synthesis of the results of science but as a dialectic argument concerning its presuppositions. This is the road made classic by Kant, who called it the transcendental method. Kant assumes that science results in synthetic propositions a priori, and asks what must be the nature of mind (and ultimately of the world) to render such knowledge possible. Without passing judgment on the gains which have accrued to philosophy from this method, we must note two insuperable logical objections to it.

In the first place, we cannot possibly in the light of modern mathematics and physics accept Kant's assumption that in Euclidean mathematics and Newtonian physics we have a priori knowledge of nature; and in the second place, as has already been pointed out, it is a downright logical fallacy, the familiar one of affirming the consequence, to argue that any theory (like the Kantian one) that explains how knowledge is possible, is thereby demonstrated to be true. Of course the fact that a theory explains something renders it to that extent more probable, but the Kantian view will not grant any room for probabilities in metaphysics precisely because it fails to discriminate clearly between the existential propositions of physics and the dialectic or purely logical ones of pure mathematics. The latter, of course, must be demonstrably true or false. Even in the computation or determination of probabilities we cannot proceed without the demonstrable truths of pure mathematics. But the latter are truths concerning the connection between possible hypotheses and their consequences. They can never prove our initial physical hypotheses or assumptions to be free from all elements of contingency or possible error.

PHILOSOPHY AS AN EXTENSION OF SCIENTIFIC METHOD

A view which is both old and widely accepted today claims that philosophy can be scientific only by applying scientific methods to its own subject matter which is distinct from the subject matter of the other sciences. This subject matter may be *being* as such, *reality* as distinguished from appearance, the nature of the *mind,* or the nature of *knowledge,* etc.

No one can well deny that in this way great pains have been made for philosophy, especially in the careful analysis of specific concepts. But a philosophy that excludes the subject matter of the special sciences, natural and social, cannot satisfy that interest in the cosmos which has at all times been the heart of philosophic endeavor. This is shown by the work of Locke, Hume, and the psychologic school of philosophy to whom scientific method means the method of natural history applied to mental and moral issues. In this way a great deal has been done for psychology, but the philosophy of nature has certainly been impoverished. Nor can the use of the older deductive method *more geometrico* be fruitful in natural philosophy unless illumined by the factual knowledge of the sciences. Without such knowledge we are apt to accept propositions as self-evident when they are in fact questionable or vague or even meaningless.

These difficulties in the paths of scientific philosophy are not readily surmountable. Yet difficulties are not vetoes to courageous effort at the "supreme good of the intellect." Philosophy, seeking the most comprehensive vision, cannot ignore the insight gained by the sciences, but must go forward to envisage their possible synthesis. Though such synthesis is necessarily speculative it may be well to note: (1) that a certain speculative element is necessary for the substantial growth of science, and that the various sciences have in fact thus been nurtured by philosophy, and (2) that a scientific philosophy corrects the dangers of speculation by a rigorously logical analysis of fundamental concepts and assumptions, so that it should be aware of how much certainty can be attached to its wider speculative reaches. In recent years the work of the mathematical or neo-Leibnizian philosophers has remarkably clarified such traditional concepts as infinity and continuity, and the logical nature of inference and proof. We know better, thanks to the labors of Peirce, Frege, Whitehead, and Russell, what is requisite for rigorous proof, and we can be more honest in estimating the degree of probability that may attach to our various answers to the questions which science is not yet in a position to attack directly. In this respect philosophy is continuous with science in method. For, contrary to popular impression, science does not eschew speculative ventures into the unknown, though it is very cautious not to confuse anticipation with verification. The nature of number, matter, and life does not cease to be a concern of philosophy because definite light has been thrown upon these problems by modern logic, physics, and biology. But as the sciences grow by constantly correcting their content, it is the inescapable lack of the philosopher to use the invariant principles of scientific method to go back to ever more rigorous analysis of the elements of rudiments of our knowledge, to examine the ideals which guide scientific effort, and to anticipate where possible what science *may* conquer in the future.

The Principle of Sufficient Reason

Scientific method, it is generally recognized, depends on the principle of causality. This, however, is only a special instance or application to temporal events of the wider principle of sufficient reason. The latter, as applied in mathematics, as well as in natural science, may be formulated as follows: *Everything is connected in definite ways with definite other things, so that its full nature is not revealed except by its position and relations within a system.* This is a familiar commonplace. Yet I venture to assert that its precise meaning is seldom justly appreciated in metaphysical discussion.

Let me illustrate some of the most widespread and influential of its misapprehensions.

REASON AND CONTINGENCY

Contrary to the usual views of it, the principle of sufficient reason as actually relied on in scientific procedure is not only compatible with a domain of chance, contingency, or indetermination, but positively demands it as the correlative of the universality of law. We may see this in the application of any law of mechanics or physics. For the most thoroughgoing mechanism necessarily involves: (1) contingent data, e.g., the actual position of the elements, (2) abstraction from other aspects or elements which are thus regarded as irrelevant and independent, and (3) rules of connection which themselves have a contingent aspect.

1. *Contingency of scientific data.* That the data in any physical inquiry are in fact contingent, that they are discovered by observation and measurement and cannot possibly be rationally deduced except by reliance on other data, no one can possibly doubt. We cannot derive facts or existential properties from pure formulae without any data. But, you may insist, these data are undetermined only for us. In themselves they are subject to laws. Granted! But note that we do not thereby really eliminate all contingency. We merely push it back one step. Thus the present arrangement of particles in the universe may be the result of mechanical forces operating on a previous distribution. But as mechanical forces cannot be supposed to operate except on some given

distribution of material particles the contingency of the latter is as ultimate as the existence of the laws.

2. *Contingency of irrelevant facts.* Every mechanical or physical law asserts that a certain phenomenon or characteristic depends on one or a few factors and on nothing else. The acceleration of gravitation depends upon mass and distance. Everything else is indifferent to it. The freezing of water depends on temperature and pressure, and nothing else is relevant. To hold seriously to the popular dictum that everything is connected with everything else would make the scientific search for determinate connection meaningless. There would be no use seeking for *the* cause of cancer, or *the* reason why sugar disintegrates the enamel of the teeth, if all things were causal factors. We put this in the accurate language of mathematics by saying that the laws of nature must be expressed in functions containing a limited number of variables.

3. *Contingency of scientific laws.* Why the particular laws of nature which we have observed to prevail do so, rather than others, is a question which can never be answered without assuming certain contingent characteristics of the universe. For we cannot prove all propositions without assuming certain undemonstrated premises. It is always desirable to reduce the number of physical laws to a minimum. But the assumption that in this way we can eliminate all contingency is inadmissible. Even if all the laws of the universe could be derived from one—an assumption which the study of deduction shows to be impossible—that one would still be itself contingent. This uneliminable character of contingency is but the legal expression of the metaphysical fact of individuality. There is no universe without a plurality of elements, of atoms, of moments of time, etc. It is a blind hostility to pluralism, a preference for lazy monism wherein all distinctions and differences are swallowed up, that leads to blatant panlogism from which all contingency is banished. But the latter attempt defeats itself. In the end the universe of existence has the particular character which it has and not some other; and contingency is not removed by being funded in the conception of the whole universe or made into the essential characteristic of reason itself.

REASON AND THE ABSOLUTE

This brings us to an obvious but important observation: the principle of sufficient reason as actually employed in science is incompatible with the view that regards the total universe as the cause of any of its constituent facts. For the scientifically adequate cause of anything must be something determinate and the universe as a whole is not determinate in the sense in which any given fact in it can be made determinate. The total universe is by definition never actually complete in any moment of time and the principle of causality means that something occupying a given position in time and space can be determined only by something else also occupying a definite position in space and enduring over a definite time interval. This is not to deny the determinateness of the physical universe in its distributive sense, i.e., in the sense that each thing in it is determinate. But the absolute collective whole is—at least from the point of view of scientific method—undetermined by anything outside of it; nor can the absolutely total universe be said to have any definite character such that from it we can infer that some particular entity has one rather than another determinate trait. Attempts to characterize the universe as a whole, as one (not many), continuous (not discontinuous), conscious or purposive, and the like, all involve a stretching of the ordinary use of words to include their opposites, and from this only confusion rather than determination can result.

We may put this in a different form by saying that scientific determinism is concerned with the definite character of things rather than with their brute existence. Rational scientific investigation is not concerned with the mystery of creation whereby existence may have come into being out of the void. It is concerned rather with the transformations whereby things or events require a determinate character within a given system. Even if the various parts of the universe influence each other and their relations can be rationally formulated, their brute existence cannot be thus derived.

REASON AND THE REALITY OF UNIVERSALS

If the foregoing observations have stressed the incompatibility between organicism and the principle of sufficient reason it is because the incompatibility between the latter and the various forms of atomism or individualism is more obvious. Thus it ought to be obvious that the application of laws to phenomena presupposes the existence of real classes, that many things and processes are really alike. If there were no real likeness, no examples of identity in different instances, the formulation of scientific laws would be without any possible application. The great convenience of classification and the fact that the same things can be classified in different ways for different purposes, do not justify the conclusion that there is nothing in the things classified corresponding to the properties which serve as *principia divisionis*. There is no evidence for the nominalistic or phenomenalistic view that the universe *really* consists of atomic sensations and that scientific laws are fictions or nothing but convenient shorthand symbols for groups of separate facts that have nothing real in common. The scientific pursuit of rational connection presupposes that things do have certain common natures and relations. The economic efficiency of scientific knowledge is based on something in the facts.

REASON AND DISCONTINUITY

While the application of the principle of causality thus implies the genuine existence of constant class properties it is well to note that in order that these classes be recognizable there must be discontinuities in nature. Thus we could never recognize any biologic species if there were not gaps between certain classes of animals (or plants) and others. The same is notably true in chemistry where the laws of multiple proportion and the properties of the different elements all involve discontinuity. If there had been other elements indistinguishable from hydrogen except in atomic weight, we should have called them all hydrogen and could not have suspected the constancy of the atomic weight of what we now isolate as hydrogen.

Our insistence that the interdependence assumed in the principle of sufficient reason is limited and involves independence as well as dependence, thus warns us against vicious forms of atomism, organicism, and mysticism. Atomism is vicious if it makes every entity a complete and independent universe and thus annihilates real relations between them. Such vicious atomism may be seen in the various forms of individualistic anarchy or pleas for irresponsible self-expression of every momentary impulse. Vicious organicism, the denial of all relative independence or externality of relation between the constituent elements of a system, may be seen in the various forms of social fanaticism, of which indiscriminate worship of the social or group "mind" is a characteristic example. Mysticism is vicious or obscurantist if it denies the definite or determinate character of things in the interest of beliefs which cannot stand the light of reason.

Science in thus emphasizing interdependence exercises a function analogous to that of social sense or sanity aware of the demands of a situation, while in refusing to eliminate independence, its function is analogous to that of the sense of beauty in which the individuality of things is intensified (though the atmosphere wherein they exist is not destroyed). In its opposition to obscurantism science operates very much like a keen sense of humor which is quick to note the absurdity of claims or the delicate lines which separate the sublime from the ridiculous.

REASON AND PROBABILITY

The recognition that the material truths of physical science are more or less probable both corrects and enriches our conception of a metaphysic based on the requirements of rational or scientific method. It makes us less pretentious or arrogant in our claims and leads us to recognize the necessity of supporting our inferences by a multitude of diverse considerations rather than by a single dialectic chain. But more positively it calls our attention to the capital fact that in constantly increasing the relative probabilities of its results science is essentially a self-corrective system. The apodictic certainty of science is not the absolute certainty of any specific result or material proposition, but the dialectic demonstration that any inaccuracy or false step can be corrected only by relying on principles inherent in the system of science itself. This is a position unassailable by any argument that can pretend to have any evidence in its favor. We can discuss the rational alternative to any single proposition, but we cannot claim to have drawn any valid and significant inference without recognizing rules of implication or evidence. On purely historical grounds also, we have ample reason for the view that the methods of science which make it self-corrective form a more permanent feature of its continued existence than any specific results.

A metaphysic of scientific method is, then, concerned with the nature of a world in which the result of scientific investigation is always subject to contingency and error, but also to the possibility of self-correction according to an invariable ideal. This ideal is the direction from which correction must come if more adequate truth is to be attained. The analogy of remediable organic and social ills suggests a universe of parts closely interconnected in certain ways and yet in some degree independent of each other. Neither sensations (or other forms of immediacy) nor mediating relations by themselves can exhaust the full nature of existence; but every true existent has a domain of uniqueness and a domain in which its true existence is beyond itself: to wit, the larger system of which it is a part.

Complete nature cannot reveal or exhibit itself in any moment or interval of time as far as that moment excludes other moments. But insofar as the meaning and content of each *here* and *now* necessarily involves some essence or character that is more than merely here and now, we have a point of view in which the whole of time is included. The point of view to which the whole of time and space has a meaning may be called the eternal (as distinct from the everlasting, which applies to what endures in time and space). It is true that in no moment or interval of time can we grasp or see as actually present to us the whole content of time and space which we call *the* universe. But in knowing the meaning of any fragment as a fragment we know the direction of completion. In this sense there can be no valid objection to the assertion that a knowledge of the absolute is involved in any true knowledge of phenomena.

Eternity may thus also be viewed as the limit or ordering principle of a series of expanding vistas. Such a limit may be called ideal. But the objective validity of such an ideal is not to be dismissed as merely mental. It is a genuine condition of the series of stages in the self-corrective system of natural science.

The Nature of Things

If we thus take the principle of sufficient reason seriously we are justified in examining the nature of things without worrying about the egocentric predicament of how we know that such knowledge is possible. The assumption of the critical philosophy that we can know only our own ideas is itself a dogmatism which involves an infinite regress. If the fact that I know a given entity does not determine any of its specific characteristics—and it is hard to see how it can determine any one known trait more than any other—then the fact of knowledge can be eliminated from the most general formula for the nature of things, though the existence of knowledge is itself a most important fact in our universe.

The fundamental metaphysical issue between rationalism and the various forms of antirationalism may be stated thus: Is the nature of things revealed most fully in developed rational science, or is it so well known in nonrational ways that we are justified in saying that science is a falsification or a merely practical device for dealing with dead things? Actually the various forms of antirationalism dogmatically assert the nature of things to be "really" individuality or continuous experience, spontaneity, or practical experience, etc. But an attempt to justify any one of these formulae by evidence commits the antirationalist to the canons of scientific method.

The main metaphysical contention of antirationalism with its banal shibboleth about life, the organic, the dynamic, etc., is that things have no constant nature, that everything is pure change and nothing else. Historically we can understand the motive for this when we reflect how many of the old constancies have had to be abandoned in the progress of physics and biology. But though the principle of identity has undoubtedly been abused, the effort of the reaction to draw an account of the world without any element of identity in it is clearly self-defeating. Changes cannot have any definite character without repetition of identical patterns in different material. If the growth of science dissolves the eternity of the hills or the fixity of species, it is also discovering constant relations and ordering changes which previously seemed chaotic and arbitrary. In daily life we find no difficulty in asserting that an individual or object maintains its character in the stream of change. Scientifically this constancy is expressed in the accurate language of mathematics by the concept of the *invariant,* not the isolated constant but that which remains identical amidst variation. We may say then that the nature of anything is the group of invariant characters.

From this point of view we are justified in making the ordinary distinction between the nature of anything and its manifestations. The fact that science seeks the invariant properties amidst the flux makes clear why science is never satisfied with empirical fact, and always seeks for explanation why things are constituted or behave in their particular way. The answer to the question *why,* is always a reason which puts the fact to be explained into a system, so that knowing the nature of the system and certain data (or given existences), we can deduce or form a rational account of the events to be explained. The fact that the abstract law makes the concrete particular intelligible does not, of course, prove that this law is less real or is more the product of our arbitrary fiat than the fact explained.

This view as to what is meant by the nature of things necessarily assigns a large and necessary role to the realm of possibility. If the actual is identified with the immediate, and the immediate with the sensuous, then the actual is certainly an infinitesimal portion of the wider world which it is found to presuppose. The sensuous vividness of the immediate may often be precisely what is meant by reality. But scientific reflection must and always does assume a larger world than that which is immediately before us or actual. Most of the sensuous material of the past, and of remote space, is beyond us and yet conditions the actuality before us. To be sure, the realm of possibility may be partly anticipated in actual imagination. But this is at best necessarily fragmentary. We may also denote by the word *actual* the historical order—all the things that have happened or will happen in all time and space, including one's dreams as themselves events. But shall we include in actuality the relations or implications of things which no one has perceived and which no one will, because of human limitations? Clearly we must distinguish here between knowledge by reference and knowledge by realized acquaintance. The totality of nature through all time and space is a limit which we can never attain and yet the idea of it is a necessity of scientific method. For the explanation of any part of the world always presupposes still other parts necessary to its complete determination. A completed rational system having nothing outside of it nor any impossible alternative to it, is both presupposed and beyond the actual attainment of any one moment. It coincides in part with the Bradleyan Absolute, but it is an ideal limit rather than an actual experience. Unrealized possibilities are within it precisely to the extent that it contains endless time.

Rationalism, Naturalism, and Supernaturalism

It is frequently asserted that the principle of scientific method cannot rule out in advance the possibility of any fact, no matter how strange or miraculous. This is true to the extent that science as a method of extending our knowledge must not let accepted views prevent us from discovering new facts that may seem to contradict our previous views. Actually, however, certain types of explanation cannot be admitted within the body of scientific knowledge. Any attempt, for instance, to explain a physical phenomenon as directly due to Providence or disembodied spirits, is incompatible with the principle of rational determinism. For the nature of these entities is not sufficiently determinate to enable us to deduce definite experimental consequences from them. The Will of Providence, for instance, will explain everything whether it happens one way or another. Hence, no experiment can possibly overthrow it. A hypothesis, however, which we cannot possibly refute cannot possibly be experimentally verified.

In thus ruling out ghostly, magical, and other supernatural influences, it would seem that scientific method impoverishes our view of the world. It is well, however, to remember that a world where no possibility is excluded is a world of chaos, about which no definite assertion can be made. Any world containing some order necessarily involves the emanation of certain abstract or ungrounded possibilities such as fill the minds of the insane.

From this point of view, what may be called the postulate of scientific materialism, viz. that all natural phenomena depend on material conditions, is not merely a well-supported generalization but the requirement of an orderly world, of a cosmos that is not a chaotic phantasmagoria.

As materialism has served as a sort of "bogeyman" to scare immature metaphysicians, it is well to make more explicit its relation to rational scientific method. If materialism means the denial of emotions, imaginings, thoughts, and other mental happenings, it is clearly not something worthy of serious consideration. It is contrary to facts of experience and clearly self-refuting. But this in no way disposes of the materialism of men like Democritus, Lucretius, Hobbes, or Spinoza, or of the assumption that every natural event must have a bodily or material basis.

The truth of the latter proposition is obscured by the popular confused concept of mental efficiency. Even technical discussion of the relation of mind and body is often vitiated by an inadequate analysis of the principle of rational determinism and a consequent misapprehension of the force of principles such as the conservation of energy. If, as it was contended before, scientific causality applies only to certain abstract aspects of entities, there is no reason why entities that determine each other in one way in a certain system may not be found together in another way in another system. The presence of causal relation does not involve the denial of teleologic relations, while the assertion of the latter presupposes the former.

The principle of conservation of energy, for instance, leaves a wide realm of indetermination that other relations can make determinate. For the assertion that amidst all the transformations of a system the total amount of energy remains constant, is an assertion that clearly does not determine the character of the transformations other than in the one trait explicitly mentioned. The second law of thermodynamics does endeavor to indicate a general direction of phenomena, viz. toward a maximum of entropy. But this is largely unproblematic in certain regions, and in any case it often leaves room for all sorts of indetermination. Whether energy shall remain potential or be transformed into energy of motion is not completely determined by either principle, since either principle remains fulfilled whether the transformation takes place or not. Teleologic determinations are therefore not ruled out by the laws of energy.

Now the ordinary conception of mental efficiency combines elements of teleologic with strictly causal determination. We achieve certain purposes by taking advantage of natural mechanism. But this is in no way inconsistent with the proposition that every material change is correlated with a previous material condition in accordance with certain laws. What is inconsistent with scientific procedure is the argument that the existence of a mental motive makes the coexistence of a physical cause unnecessary.

Besides the objection from the existence of mental efficiency there is another line of arguments against materialism, viz. that matter is purely passive and cannot explain the activity of the world. Now it is doubtless true that the close connection between the notion of matter and that of mass or inertia, leads to the view that matter by itself cannot explain the active processes of nature, and this leads to the introduction of forces which are the ghosts of spirits or of the volitions often connected with our own bodily movements. This argument, however, is based on a logical fallacy, taking the nature of matter to consist solely in its exclusive and passive aspect. But there is no valid reason against supposing that a purely material system without external influence can contain motion within it; and there is no conclusive argument against the view that under certain conditions material systems such as those which constitute the human body are capable of organic processes, feeling, etc.

The one serious objection to materialism from the point of view of the requisites of scientific method comes into play when materialism allies itself with sensationalistic empiricism and belittles the importance of relations and logical connection between things. The identification of empiricism with the scientific attitude is just a bit of natural complacency. The excessive worship of facts too often hides a disinclination to enter into a genuine inquiry as to whether they are so. A rationalism that is naturalistic must, of course, agree with empiricism in maintaining the factual or immediate aspect of existence. But scientific rationalism is incompatible with the complacent assumption that in sensations or in self-sufficient "facts" we have the only primary existences.

We do not have pure particulars any more than pure universals, to begin with. We begin with vague complexes which raise difficulties when we wish to give a rational or coherent account of them. It is scientific procedure itself which enables us to pass from vague impressions to definite propositions. Definite individuals are, therefore, the goals or limits rather than the data of scientific method. When we attain knowledge of particulars we see that their nature depends upon the universal connections which make them what they are.

To realize that the substance or nature of the individual consists of universals we must get rid of the Lockian confusion between matter and substance, and return to the Aristotelian distinction of ὕλη and ὀυσία. Ὕλη or matter is a relative concept. Bricks are ὕλη for a building but are formed substances for one who makes them out of clay. Absolute primary ὕλη or matter is a limiting concept, not a starting point. The intelligible substance of things, however, is not pure formlessness or empty possibility, but the actual universals which, though arrived at as a result of inquiry, are conditions of what exists. Indeed, inquiry like all other forms of human effort must begin with the partial and can attain the whole or universal—if at all—only by seeing how the parts are conditioned.

The view that identifies the genuine substance of things with those relations or structures which are the objects of rational science is so opposed to the nominalistic tendency of our time, that a host of objections to it is naturally to be expected.

The most serious objection is one that cannot be answered—it is the habit which associates substance with reality and reality with the sensuously or psychologically vivid. But, however decisive the appeal to the subjectively vivid may be in practice, it is after all no evidence as to the objective constitution of the natural world.[1] More specific objections to our identification of the order of scientific ideas with the intrinsic order of things are the following: (a) Rational scientific method is devised for practical purposes only. Its fictional devices cannot give us truth. (b) The abstractions which science employs have correspondence with or real existence in the natural world. (c) Reasoning supplies us only ground for belief not ground for existence.

FICTIONALISM

Philosophers as diverse as Bradley, Mach, and Bergson rely heavily on the so-called fictions of science, e.g., corpuscles of light, the ether, etc., which have proved useful, though not literally true. With regard to this we may observe that many of these so-called fictions, e.g., atoms, have turned out to be very much like other empirical entities. We count them, we weigh them and study their behavior—philosophers to the contrary notwithstanding. I have elsewhere tried to show that contrary to the contention of Vaihinger, none of the so-called fictions of science involve any contradiction.[2] If they did so, they could not be useful, since no consistent inferences could be drawn from them. Even when not completely true, they are analogies which offer useful suggestions just to the extent that they are true. To the extent that they fail they are subject to the process of correction.

CONCEPTUALISM

The form of reasoning to which science always seeks to attain is mathematics. But do the steps of a mathematical process correspond to anything in the objective world—even when the initial premises and final conclusions do? Mathematical physicists like Duhem and Mach categorically deny this. What have our equations, differentiations, and integrations to do with natural objects? If the result of a mathematical calculation gives us a true account of objective nature, may not the mathematical process correspond to the sharpening of tools or to the mixing of colors, processes which surely do not correspond to the features which the artist wishes to represent? We must not however allow analogies to lead us away from the facts. Mathematical propositions do relate to the properties of all possible objects. Valid mathematical reasoning therefore deals with processes to which the objects before us are as subject as any others. It is often difficult to recognize these universal aspects in the particular, just as it may be difficult to recognize that an enemy is also a human being, yet truth requires the recognition of just such obvious general or universal aspects. Mathematical reasoning may indeed be too general for a specific situation (if we lack the proper data) but if true it always has objective meaning.

IRRATIONALISM

Bradley has argued that while reasoning determines the ground of our belief, it does not even pretend to determine the ground of existence. In our reasoning, he claims, some datum suffers alteration. Why assume that reality transforms itself in unison? This objection is largely based on the false suggestion of the word *transformation*. Logical reasoning does not produce any temporal change in the object reasoned about. The latter remains the same when we make progress in the recognition of its nature. But the ground of a true belief differs after all from the ground of a false belief precisely in this—that the former *is* connected (though not directly identical) with the ground of existence. For this purpose the most favorable example, for Bradley's objection, would be the case where I conclude that my idea of a given object is false. But even here the ground of existence and the ground of true belief are not independent. I begin in fact with an hypothesis as to the nature of the object. I consider what consequences it (with other things) has if it is true. I find the consequences are impossible because in conflict with actual existence, and I conclude that my original hypothesis is false. If my reasoning is valid it is because it has come into contact with actual facts and the transformations of the entities reasoned about do correspond to reality.

We conclude, then, that if the abstract is unreal, reality is of little moment. For what that is humanly interesting is not abstract? Mr. Bradley has gone through the whole gamut from qualities, relations, and things to our precious selves, and shown with a logic that is more readily ignored than refuted, that all these things are but abstract or detached parts of the absolute totality. But the conclusion that everything short of the absolute totality is appearance and not reality is a logical consequence of an arbitrary view of reality, which identifies it with purely immediate feeling or experience. But though the craving of the flesh for strong sensations and feelings is an important element of life, it is certainly not conclusive even as to the guidance of life. Even the hedonistic ideal cannot be realized except by organizing life on the basis of an intellectual recognition of our possibilities and the rational evaluation of the different factors which determine our happiness.

The contention that abstractions or logical relations form the very substance of things does not, according to the foregoing account, involve panlogism. Rationality does not exhaust existence. The relational form or pattern points to a nonrational or a logical element without which the former has no genuine meaning. For to deny the existence of any irrational elements is to make rationality itself a brute, contingent, alogical fact. The fact that we can rationally use terms like *irrational, alogical, inexpressible,* and the like has given rise to interesting paradoxes. These paradoxes, however, disappear if we recognize that a word may point to something which is not a word at all, and though the pointing is rationalized fact the thing pointed to may not be. Rational distinctions and relations and all expression hold in the field of being which is thus presupposed but never fully described—just as the various lines on a blackboard may indicate the various objects represented on it but do not fully represent the blackboard itself which conditions them. If this doctrine that our universe thus contains something fundamental to which we may point but which we cannot fully describe be called mysticism, then mysticism is essential to all intellectual sanity. Language ceases to be significant if it cannot indicate something beyond language. But if we use the word *mysticism* to denote this faith in a universe that has ineffable and alogical elements, we cannot too sharply distinguish it from obscurantism. For the former denies our power to know the whole of reality, while the latter holds reality to be definitely revealed to us by nonrational processes. Rationalism does not deny that clear thoughts may begin as vague or obscure premonitions. But the essential difference between rationalism and obscurantism depends upon whether our guesses or obscure visions do or do not submit to the processes of critical examination and logical clarification. Our reason may be a pitiful candle light in the dark and boundless seas of being. But we have nothing better and woe to those who willfully try to put it out.

The Principle of Polarity

The foregoing considerations are all applications of a wider principle, viz. the principle of polarity. By this I mean that opposites such as immediacy and mediation, unity and plurality, the fixed and the flux, substance and function, ideal and real, actual and possible, etc., like the north (positive) and south (negative) poles of a magnet, all involve each other when applied to any significant entity. Familiar illustrations of this are: that physical action is not possible without resistance or reaction and that protoplasm, in the language of Huxley, cannot live except by continually dying. The idea is as old as philosophy. Anaximander expressed it in saying that determinate form arises out of the indefinite (το ἄπειρον) with the emergence of opposites like hot and cold, dry and moist, etc. And Heraclitus insisted that strife was the father of all things and that the balancing of opposite forces, as in the string of the bow or lyre, gave form to things. The essential Hellenic wisdom of Socrates and Plato which viewed justice and the other virtues as conduct according to measure (Aristotle's mean) involves the idea of adjustment of opposite considerations. The relativity of form and matter, according to Aristotle, is determinative of all existence (save the divine essence).[3]

This principle of polarity seems to me to represent what is sound in the Hegelian dialectic without the indecent confusion at which we arrive if we violate the principle of contradiction and try to wipe out the distinctions of the understanding. The being and nonbeing of anything are always opposed and never identical, though all determination involves both affirmation and negation. Far from overriding the distinctions of the understanding the principle of polarity shows their necessity and proper use. Thus physical science employs this principle when it eliminates the vagueness and indetermination of popular categories like *high* and *low, hot* and *cold, large* and *small, far* and *near*, etc. It does so by substituting a definite determination such as a determinate number of years or degrees of temperature. The indetermination and consequent inconclusiveness of metaphysical and of a good deal of sociologic discussion results from uncritically adhering to simple alternatives instead of resorting to the laborious process of integrating opposite assertions by finding the proper distinctions and qualifications.

Under the head of polarities we may distinguish between contradictions, antimonies, and aporias or difficulties. Strictly speaking, contradictions are always dialectical, i.e., they hold only in a logical universe. Thus if I say a house is thirty years old, and someone else says it is thirty-one years old, the two statements are contradictory in the sense that both cannot possibly be true at the same time and in the same respect. Both statements, however, can certainly be true if we draw a distinction, e.g., thirty-one years since the beginning and thirty years since the completio of its building.

Thus two statements which, taken abstractly, are contradictory may both be true of concrete existence provided they can be assigned to separate domains or aspects. A plurality of aspects is an essential trait of things in existence. Determinate existence thus continues free from self-contradiction because there is a distinction between the domains in which these opposing statements are each separately true. When opposing statements are completed by reference to the domains wherein they are true, there is no logical difficulty in combining them. In the purely logical or mathematical field, however, we deal not with complexes of existence, but with abstract determinations as such. Here two contradictory assertions always produce a resultant which is zero, i.e., the entity of which they are asserted is absolutely impossible.

Of incompletely determined existence—as in the case of the total universe—contradictory propositions do not annihilate each other (since they refer to a complex of existence); and yet they cannot always (because of the indefiniteness of the subject) be reconciled with each other. This gives rise to the antinomies of metaphysics.

In general, the opposite statements that are true in regard to existing things give rise to difficulties when we cannot see how to draw the proper distinction which will enable us to reconcile and combine these seeming contradictions. Thus we frequently find certain facts in a scientific realm calling for one theory, e.g., the corpuscular theory of light, and other facts calling for a diametrically opposite one, viz. the wave theory. Such difficulties are solved either by discovering new facts which give one of these theories a preponderance or else by discovering a way of combining the two theories. Sometimes an intellectual dilemma is avoided by re-jecting both alternatives. This is illustrated by the old difficulty as to whether language was a human invention or a special revelation. The difficulty was avoided by introducing the concept of natural growth.

Nature also presents us with seeming impossibilities in the form of practical difficulties, e.g., how to live long without getting old, how to eat our cake and yet have it too, etc. Such contingent or physical impossibilities may baffle us forever. Yet some of them may be solved by finding the proper distinction. Thus the invention of boats enabled us to eliminate a former impossibility—namely, how to cross a river without getting wet.

This analysis puts us on guard against two opposite evil intellectual habits: on the one hand to regard real difficulties as absolute impossibilities, and on the other to belittle such difficulties by calling them false alternatives. Thus it is not sufficient to say that the old controversy between the claims of the active and those of the contemplative life represents a false alternative, and that we need both. It is in fact most frequently impossible to follow both and the actual problem of how much of one we need to sacrifice to the other often requires more knowledge than is at our disposal.

If it be urged that this after all is the essence of the Hegelian logic I should not object—provided it does not include Hegel's explicit identification of the historical and the logical, the real and the rational. The heart of Hegel's philosophy is, after all, the attempt at a synthesis calculated to do justice both to the classic rationalism of the Enlightenment and to the inspiring sweep of the romanticism of Fichte, Schelling, and their associates. Such a synthesis seems to me to be the great desideratum of our age. We cannot today accept Hegel's methods and results precisely because they are not—despite all their pretensions—sufficiently rational or logically rigorous. But Hegel's tremendous influence in law, art, and religion, as in the development of all the social sciences, shows that he grappled with a vital problem. If, as I think we should all admit, he was guilty of indecent haste due to intellectual ὕβρις, it is for us to face a similar task with greater patience and honest resoluteness not to minimize the obstacles to rational inquiry.

These suggestions of a possible metaphysics may be objected to either as commonplace, as unimportant, or as unjustified. Against the first objection we must note that sound metaphysic like science itself should begin—though it should not end—with the commonplace. As against the second and third objections we may urge that the full meaning, importance, and justification of a metaphysical doctrine can be seen only in its development. Toward this development the present chapter can offer only the barest hints.

PART II: NATURE, EXPERIENCE, AND METHOD

Notes

1. "If reality," argues Bradley, "consists in actual sequence of sensuous phenomena, then our reasonings are all false because none of them are sensuous." To which we reply that if reality consists of sensuous material arranged in certain form or order then all the reasoning which is faithful to that form or order is true.

2. See "The Logic of Fictions," *Journal of Philosophy* 20 (1923): 477.

3. The reading of Plato's *Parmenides* first impressed upon me the lesson taught to the young Socrates, viz. that it is impossible to arrive at sound philosophy without experience in tracing the diverse and opposed dialectic implications of such propositions as "unity exists" and thus learning to guard oneself against their pitfalls. Propositions are not bare tautologies but significant predications because nonbeing has being of a sort and *the one* is inseparable from, though not identical with, *the other*.

I am indebted to Professor Felix Adler for the figure of the scissors to denote the fact that the mind never operates effectively by using both unity and plurality like the two blades which move in opposite directions. Professor Marshall, in his *Principles of Economics,* has used the same figure to express the mutual dependence of the two factors of supply and demand. We may, if we like, also use the figure of the pestle and mortar, of our jaws in mastication, or of applying brakes when going down a hill.

2

Logic Without Ontology*

Ernest Nagel

The fact that the world we inhabit exhibits periodicities and regularities has been frequently celebrated by poets, philosophers, and men of affairs. That frost will destroy a fruit crop, that a convex lens will concentrate the heat of the sun, or that populations tend to increase toward a fixed maximum, are typical of the uniformities discoverable in innumerable sectors of the physical and social environment; and however we may formulate such uniformities, no philosophy which construes them as anything else than discoveries will conform with the long experience of mankind. Every form of naturalism, to whatever extent it may emphasize the impermanence of many of these regularities or note the selective human activities involved in discovering them, will recognize them as basic features of the world; and even when it attempts to account for them, it will do so only by exhibiting a more pervasive, if more subtle, pattern in the behavior of bodies.

Nevertheless, no demonstrable ground has yet been found which can guarantee that such regularities will continue indefinitely or that the

---

*Originally published in *Naturalism and the Human Spirit,* ed. by Yervant H. Krikorian (New York: Columbia University Press, 1944), chapter 10. Reprinted by permission.

propositions asserting them are necessary. If, as many philosophers have maintained, the proper objects of scientific knowledge are principles capable of a priori validation, both the history of science and the analysis of its methods supply ample evidence to show that no science of nature has ever achieved what is thus proclaimed as its true objective. There are, indeed, relatively few practicing scientists today who place any credence in arguments claiming to prove that any principle about an identifiable subject matter is at once logically necessary and empirical in content.

No such general agreement can be found, even among lifelong students of the subject, concerning the status of various logical and mathematical principles constantly employed in responsible inquiries. Indeed, it is difficult to ascertain which natural structures, if any, such propositions express; and it is often no less difficult to exhibit clearly and without self-deception the grounds upon which they are acknowledged. In any event, many of the sharp divisions between professsed naturalists are centered around the different interpretations which they assign to principles as familiar as the so-called "laws of thought," the basic assumptions of arithmetic or the axioms of geometry. Thus, one classical form of naturalism maintains, for example, that the principle of noncontradiction is a necessary truth which is descriptive of the limiting structure of everything both actual and possible; another form of naturalism holds this principle to be a contingent, but highly reliable, conclusion based on an empirical study of nature; and a third type of naturalism takes this principle to be void of factual content and an arbitrary specification for the construction of symbolic systems. Analogous differences among naturalists occur in their interpretation of more complicated and recondite mathematical notions.

Such disagreements among those professing naturalism is not a source of embarrassment to them, since naturalism is not a tightly integrated system of philosophy; perhaps the sole bond uniting all varieties of naturalists is that temper of mind which seeks to understand the flux of events in terms of the behaviors of identifiable bodies. Nevertheless, a naturalistic philosophy must be consistent with its own assumptions. If it professes to accept the methods employed by the various empirical sciences for obtaining knowledge about the world, it cannot with consistency claim to have a priori insight into the most pervasive structure of things. If it aims to give a coherent and adequate account of the various principles employed in acquiring scientific knowledge, it cannot maintain that all of them are empirical generalizations when some are not subject to experimental refutation. And if it admits that logical principles have a recognizable function in certain contexts (namely, in inquiry), it cannot consistently hold those principles to be completely arbitrary simply on the ground that they are void of actual content when considered apart from those contexts.

No one seriously doubts that logic and mathematics are used in specific contexts in identifiable ways, however difficult it may be to ascertain those ways in any detail. Does it not therefore seem reasonable to attempt to understand the significance of logico-mathematical concepts and principles in terms of the operations associated with them in those contexts and to reject interpretations of their "ultimate meaning" which appear gratuitous and irrelevant in the light of such an analysis? Such, at any rate, is the point of view of the present essay. In what follows, the difficulties and futilities of some nonoperational interpretations of logical principles will first be noted; the limitations of certain naturalistic but narrowly empirical approaches to logic will then be discussed; and finally, an operational interpetation of a small number of logical and mathematical notions will be sketched. However, and this is perhaps the common fate of essays such as the present one, no more than the outline of an argument will be found in the sequel. The present essay contributes no unfamiliar analyses. Its sole objective is to make plausible the view that the role of the logico-mathematical disciplines in inquiry can be clarified without requiring the invention of a hypostatic subject matter for them; and to suggest that a naturalism free from speculative vagaries and committed to a thoroughgoing operational standpoint expresses the temper of modern mathematico-experimental science.

I

1. Among the principles which Aristotle believed "hold good for everything that is" and therefore belong to the science of being qua being, he counted certain axioms of logic. These principles, according to him,

were to be asserted as necessary truths and were not to be maintained as hypotheses, since "a principle which everyone must have who knows anything about being is not a hypothesis." One such principle is that "the same attribute cannot at the same time belong and not belong to the same subject in the same respect."

Aristotle's formulation of the principle contains the qualification "in the same respect." This qualification is important, for it makes possible the defense of the principle against all objections. For suppose one were to deny the principle on the ground that an object, a penny for example, is both sensibly circular in shape and sensibly noncircular. The standard reply to this alleged counterexample is that the penny is circular when viewed from a direction perpendicular to its face and noncircular when viewed from a direction inclined to the face, and that since the different shapes do not occur "in the same respect" the principle has not been invalidated. But if one were now to ask for an unequivocal specification, antecedent to applying the principle, of a definite "same respect" with regard to the penny, so that the principle might then be subjected to a clear-cut test, a skillful defender of the principle as an ontological truth would refuse to supply the desired stipulation. For he would recognize that if a "respect" is first specified, it is always possible to find within that respect a way of apparently violating the principle.

For example, suppose a "same respect" is specified as viewing the penny from a direction perpendicular to its face. The penny will, nevertheless, subtend an angle of thirty degrees and also an angle of sixty degrees. To this, the obvious and proper retort is: "But not at the same distance from the face of the penny." Nevertheless, the principle is saved only by a new restriction upon what is to be understood by "the same respect"; the defender of the principle has altered his *initial* specification of what is the *same* respect. It is, of course, possible, when an attribute is suitably specified, to discover a set of conditions under which a thing does not both have and not have that attribute. The crucial point is that in specifying both the attribute and the conditions, *the principle is employed as a criterion* for deciding whether the specification of the attribute is suitable and whether those conditions are in fact sufficiently determinate. Because of the manner in which the qualification "the same respect" is used, the principle cannot be put to a genuine test, since no proposed case for testing the principle will be judged as admissible which violates the principle to be tested. In brief, conformity to the principle is the condition for a respect being "the same respect."[1]

Analogous comments are relevant for the phrases "same attribute," "belong," and "not belong," which are contained in Aristotle's formulation of the principle. For example, how is one to tell in a disputed instance of the principle whether an attribute is "the same" or not? If someone were to maintain that a penny has a diameter of 11/16 of an inch and also a diameter of 12/16 of an inch, he would be told that the assertion is impossible, because even though the attributes are not "the same," in predicating the former one implicitly excludes the latter; and he would, perhaps, be asked whether the measurements were carefully made, whether the same system of units was really employed, and so forth. In short, since the assertion in effect maintains "the same attribute" to belong and also not to belong to the same subject, it is absurd. But let us press the question why, if the penny has the first of these attributes, it cannot have the other. The impossibility is not simply an empirical one, which rests on inductive arguments; for if it were, the supposition would not be absurd, contrary to the hypothesis, that an unexpected observation may one day discover the penny's diameter to have both dimensions. The impossibility arises from the fact that we use the expressions "length of 11/16 inches" and "length of 12/16 inches" in such a way—in part because of the manner in which they may have been defined in relation to one another—that each formulates a different outcome of measurement. We may be sure that no penny will ever turn up with a diameter having both dimensions, because what it means for the diameter to have one of the attributes of dimension is specified in terms of the absence of the other attribute. The principle of contradiction is impregnable against attack, because the "sameness" and the "difference" of attributes are specified in terms of the conformity of attributes to the principle.

Accordingly, the interpretation of the principle as an ontological truth neglects its function as a norm or regulative principle for introducing distinctions and for instituting appropriate linguistic usage. To maintain that the principle is descriptive of the structure of antecedently determinate "facts" or "attributes" is to convert the outcome of employing the principle into a condition of its employment. The Aristotelian view is thus a gratuitous and irrelevant interpretation of one function of this logical law.

2. More recent advocates of an ontological interpretation of logical principle argue their claim in terms of the conception of logical relations as in variants of all possible worlds—a conception also sponsored by Leibniz. "Pure logic and pure mathematics," according to an influential proponent of this view, "aims at being true in all possible worlds, not only in this higgledy-piggledy job-lot of a world in which chance has imprisoned us." Reason, according to this interpretation, is an investigation into the very heart and immutable essence of all things actual and possible: "Mathematics takes us into the region of absolute necessity, to which not only the actual world but every possible world must conform." As another version puts it, logic is the most general of all the sciences: "Rules of logic are the rules of operation or transformation according to which all possible objects, physical, psychological, neutral, or complexes can be combined. Thus, logic is an exploration of the field of most general abstract possibility." According to this view, then, logical principles are "principles of being," as well as "principles of inference"; they formulate the most general nature of things, they are universally applicable, and they express the limiting and necessary structure of all existence.

Two issues raised by these brief citations from contemporary literature require comment.

a. When logical principles are asserted to hold for "all possible worlds," what is to be understood by the adjective "possible"? The crux of the matter lies in ascertaining whether "possible worlds" can be specified without using the principles of logic as the *exclusive* means of specification. For if a "possible world" is one whose sole identifiable trait is its conformity to the principles of logic, the view under consideration asserts no more than this: the subject matter of logical principles is whatever conforms to them. In that case no "possible world" could fail to satisfy the principles of logic, since anything which failed to do so would not, by hypothesis, be a possible world.

The point involved is so fundamental that it is desirable to illustrate it in another way. Consider any abstract set of postulates *E*, for example,

Hilbert's postulates for Euclidean geometry, contained the *uninterpreted* terms *P*, *L*, and *N*. It is clearly not significant to ask whether *E* is true as long as these terms have this character. But physical experiments become relevant for deciding the truth or falsity of *E* if, for example, *L* is used to denote the paths of light rays, *P* the intersections of such two paths, and *N* the surfaces determined in another way by any two intersecting paths. Nevertheless, an experimental inquiry can be undertaken only if the paths of light rays can be identified in some manner *other* than by the sole requirement that light rays are things satisfying the formal demands contained in *E*. For if a different method for identifying light rays did not exist, it would not be possible to ascertain whether a particular physical configuration is such a path without first establishing that the configuration conforms to the implicit specifications of *E*—that is, without first ascertaining the truth of *E* for that configuration. Accordingly, since by definition nothing could be a path of a light ray which did not satisfy *E*, the question whether *E* is true of all paths of light rays would not be a matter to be settled by experiment.[2] It is evident, therefore, that if the question of the truth of a set of principles is to be a factual or experimental issue, their subject matter must be identifiable in terms of some other characteristic than that it satisfies those principles.

Let us apply these considerations to the formula: "Not both *P* and non-*P*." If it is simply a formula in some uninterpreted symbolic system, the question whether the formula is true in "all possible worlds" cannot arise. On the other hand, if its constituent symbols are interpreted in some manner, great care must be used in deriving further conclusions from the fact that on one such interpetation the formula expresses a "necessary truth." Thus, suppose that the letter "*p*" is taken to denote any "proposition" and that the other expressions in the formula are assigned their usual meanings; the formula will then express the principle of noncontradiction. But either there is some way of identifying propositions other than by the criterion that anything is a proposition which satisfies the formula, or there is not. On the first alternative, the assertion that the formula holds for all propositions will be a statement strictly analogous to general hypotheses in the empirical sciences; the evidence for the assertion, considerable though it may be, will be only partially complete, and in any case there will be no reason to regard the formula as expressing a necessary truth. On the second alternative, the assertion will be an implicit definition of what a proposition is; the principle of noncontradiction will be a necessary truth, since nothing could be a proposition which does not conform to it.[3]

The view that logic is the science of all possible worlds thus suffers from a fundamental ambiguity. If the only way of identifying a "possible world" is on the basis of its conformity to the canons of logic, logic is indeed the science of all possible worlds. But the view is then no more than a misleading formulation of the fact that logical principles are employed as stipulations or postulates, which define what we understand by the consistency of discourse.

b. The second point requiring comment bears on the view that logical principles express the limiting and necessary structures of all things. If the domain of application of logical principles is identified on the basis of the actual use to which those principles are put, this view cannot be construed literally. For it is not things and their actual relations which are said to be logically consistent or inconsistent with one another, but propositions or statements about them; and it is to the latter that principles such as the principle of noncontradiction are relevant. No one will hesitate to acknowledge that "the table on which I am now writing is brown" and "the table on which I am now writing is white" are mutually inconsistent statements. But this inconsistency cannot, according to the view under discussion, be predicated of two "facts," "states of affairs," or "objects"; for if there were such facts the view would be self-refuting. Accordingly, inconsistency is something which can be located only in discourse, among statements, not among things in general. And if so much is admitted, an obvious dialectic requires that consistency be localized in a similar domain, in discourse and among statements.

But dialectic aside and bearing in mind only the identifiable functions of logical principles, there is no obvious warrant for the claim that the latter are the rules in accordance with which all possible objects can be transformed or combined. Certainly they are not rules of operation upon things in any familiar or literal sense of "transformation of things"— unless, indeed, the things said to be transformed and combined are elements of discourse, constellations of signs of varying degrees of complexity. The "pervasive traits" and "limiting structures" of all "possible worlds" which logic is alleged to formulate thus appear to be traits of discourse when it has been ordered in a certain way. The interpretation of logical principles as ontological invariants seems therefore, on closer view, to be an extraneous ornamentation upon the functions they actually exercise. But the regulative role of logical principles, suggested by the foregoing discussion, will be exhibited more clearly in the sequel.

II

Empirically minded naturalists, convinced that propositions concerning matters of fact must be supported by sensory observation, but convinced also that logical principles have factual content, have not had an easy time in accounting for the apparent universality and necessity of these principles. The interpretation of logical principles widely accepted by both traditional and contemporary empiricists is that they are hypotheses about traits of minds and things, based on inductive arguments from experience. Mill declared:

> I readily admit that these three general propositions [the Laws of Thought] are universally true of all phenomena. I also admit that if there are any inherent necessities of thought, these are such. . . . Whether the three so-called Fundamental Laws are laws of our thoughts by the native structure of the mind, or merely because we perceive them to be universally true of observed phenomena, I will not positively decide; but they are laws of our thoughts now, and invincibly so.

More recent writers concerned with defending an empirical philosophy, though they may reject Mill's psychological atomism and sensationalism, frequently do not differ from him on the view that logical principles are inductive truths. The following is a sufficiently forthright contemporary statement of this conception.

> *Logical* validity is grounded on *natural* fact. . . . When we are in doubt as to the logical validity of an argument, there is only one test. If

the class of such arguments gives us materially true conclusions from materially true premises, it is vaild, if not, it is invalid. . . . The crucial question which this frankly empirical approach to logic must face is whether it can explain the formal characters of logical inference. The experimental hypothesis attempts the explanation by showing that those inferential procedures which have brought knowledge in the past exhibit a certain invariant *order* whose metaphysical correlate is to be sought in the *serial* characters of existence. . . . The laws of logic . . . cannot be disproved, but they may become inapplicable and meaningless. We can say nothing about the *probability* of this being so, but we can just conceive of the possibility that the so-called *a priori* laws of logic may not enable us to organize our experience. That is why they are not formal or empty. That is why they tell us something about the *actual* world. That is why we can say that every additional application of logic to existence is an experimental verification of its invariance.

However attractive such an interpretation of logical principles may appear to a consistent empirical naturalism—to a philosophy which appreciates the limitations natural structures place upon our thought and action, but which nevertheless finds no warrant for the assertion that a priori knowledge of such structures is possible—there are insuperable difficulties involved in it. These difficulties are in the main because those who profess such an interpretation misconceive the character of empirical or scientific method.

1. Little need be said in refutation of the view that logical principles formulate the "inherent necessities of thought" and are generalized descriptions of the operations of minds. Surely the actual occurrence in the same person of beliefs in logically incompatible propositions makes nonsense of the claim that the principle of noncontradition expresses a universal fact of psychology. Moreover, if logical principles were true descriptions of anthropological behavior, they would be contingent truths, refutable on evidence drawn from the observation of human behavior; but in that case, the necessity which is so generally attributed to logical principles, however much this may be disguised by calling their contradictories "unbelievable," would be left unexplained.

2. The view under consideration maintains that the validity of a type of inference sanctioned by logic can be established only by presenting

empirical evidence to show that an inference of that form always leads from materially true premises to materially true conclusions. It must be admitted, of course, that a valid inference is often defined as one which invariably yields true conclusions from true premises. But it by no means follows that an inference ever is or can be established as valid in the manner proposed. Suppose, for example, "*A*" and "If *A* then *B*" are asserted as true statements (the expression "if . . . then" being used in some one of the customary ways), so that the conclusion that "*B*" is true may be drawn in accordance with the familiar rule of *ponendo ponens*. Let us now imagine that as a matter of fact "*B*" is false and that we are therefore urged by someone to abandon the rule as a universal logical principle. Would not such a suggestion be dismissed as grotesque and as resting upon some misunderstanding? Would we not retort that in the case supposed "*A*" or "If *A* then *B*" must have been asserted as true mistakenly or that if this is no mistake then the assertion of the falsity of "*B*" must be an error? Would we not, in any event, maintain that statements of the form: "If *A* and (if *A* then *B*) then *B*" are necessarily true, since not to acknowledge them as such is to run counter to the established usage of the expressions "and" and "if . . . then"?

Proponents of the view under discussion often declare that in interpreting logical principles as empirical hypotheses they are offering a justification for logic in terms of the procedures and standards of adequacy employed in the most advanced natural sciences. It is worth noting, therefore, that not a single instance can be cited from the history of science which would support the conception that the validity of logical principles is ever established by the suggested method. Is it not significant that whenever consequences derived from premises believed to be true are in disagreement with the facts of experimental observation, it is not the logical principles in accordance with which these consequences were drawn that are rejected as experimentally unwarranted? Indeed, it is not apparent how the suggested method for establishing the validity of logical principles could operate in any typical inquiry. For the truth of most premises employed in the sciences cannot be established except on the basis of an investigation of the consequences which are drawn from them—drawn in accordance with and with the help of logical principles. For example, the principles of Newtonian mechanics, which constitute part of the premises in many physical inquiries, cannot be established as adequate to their subject matter unless it is first discovered what these principles imply. This will be even more obvious if we note that these premises employ such complex notions as differential coefficients, real numbers, and point masses; the premises cannot be construed as "descriptions" of matters of fact accessible to a direct observation, that is, as statements whose truth or falsity may be settled prior to examining their logical consequences. The proposed method for establishing the validity of arguments is thus clearly not a feasible one since no experimental control can be instituted for determining the alleged material truth of logical principles.

It follows that no "metaphysical correlate" to logical principles need be sought in the "serial character of existence." And if logical principles do not function as contingent hypotheses about matters of fact, if they are not to be established inductively on the ground of their conformity to "certain structural and functional invariants of nature," there is no clear sense in which "every additional application of logic to existence is an experimental verification of its invariance." Logical principles are compatible with any order which the flux of events may exhibit; they could not be in disagreement with anything which inquiry may disclose, and if they should ever require revision, the grounds for such alterations must lie elsewhere than in the subject matter of the natural sciences. To be sure, should the cosmos become a chaos to the extent of making the continued existence of reflective thought impossible, the use of logical principles would thereby also become impossible. But as the above discussion indicates, the continued employment of those principles is not contingent upon the invariance of structures other than those which sustain the continuance of reflective inquiry.

3. In spite of its profession of allegiance to scientific methods as the canonical techniques of competent inquiry, the empiricistic interpertation of logic is based upon an inadequate conception of what is involved in those methods. Indeed, even when, as has already been noted, those subscribing to this interpretation explicitly reject Mill's psychological atomism, they do not always successfully free themselves from his oversimple views on the formation of scientific concepts. Two closely

related points require brief discussion in this connection: the narrow criterion of meaningful discourse which is explicitly or tacitly assumed by many empirical naturalists; and the inadequate conception which they hold of the role of symbolic constructions in the conduct of inquiry.

   a. It has often been maintained that the theoretical sciences deem to be ultimately meaningful only the statements which either formulate directly observable relations of qualities and things or can be translated without remainder into statements that do so. According to another version of this thesis, every meaningful statement must consist of terms which either denote simple, directly experienceable qualities and relations or are compounded out of terms denoting such simples. Even false hypotheses, so it has been urged on occasion, are meaningful only because they formulate the structure of some actual observable situation—a structure which happens to be wrongly attributed to a given situation. Since the familiar logical and mathematical principles seem so obviously significant, and since in their usual formulation they are ostensibly about the relations which properties of things bear to one another, the interpretation of these principles as empirical hypotheses is sometimes deduced as a corollary from this general view.

   Little need be said to show the inadequacy of the suggested criterion of meaning. If it were applied consistently, most of the theories employed in the various positive sciences would have to be dismissed as in fact meaningless; and indeed, those who have accepted the criterion have been consistent enough to exclude almost all general statements as not expressing "genuine propositions." For in the first place, to the extent that theoretical propositions have the form of unrestricted universals, they do not formulate the explicit outcome of any actual series of direct observations. And in the second place, many theoretical statements contain terms such as "point-particle," "light wave," "electron," "gene," and the like) which denote nothing that can be directly observed and cannot be construed as being explicitly definable with the help of only such terms as do so. Moreover, there is surely no evidence for the claim that for every false hypothesis there is a situation for which it is true.[4] It is clear that underlying the suggested criterion of meaningful discourse is an ill-concealed reproductive psychology of abstraction and that in any case those who employ it cannot do justice to the actual procedures of the sciences.

A naturalism which is based on modern scientific methods cannot afford to propose liberal restrictions upon inquiry. It must recognize that no formula can be constructed which will express once for all "*the* meaning" of any portion of scientific discourse. Instead of attempting to construct such formulae, it must turn seriously to the analysis of specific uses and functions of specific systems of expressions in specific contexts. It will have to note that statements in scientific discourse always occur as elements in a system of symbols and operations, and it will therefore attempt to understand the significance of statements in terms of the complicated uses to which they are subject. It will, accordingly, not assume dogmatically that the directly observed qualities and relations of the explicit subject matter of a science must constitute the sole and ultimate reference of every significant complex of its symbols. It will surely recognize that according to standard scientific procedure evidence taken from sensory observation must be relevant to propositions alleged to be about matters of fact: such propositions must entail consequences, obtained by logical operations in determinate ways, which can be experimentally tested when the appropriate circumstances occur. It will thus accept the pragmatic maxim that there is no difference between the objects of beliefs and conceptions where there is no possible difference in observable behavior. But it will not, therefore, insist that all significant statements must be descriptive of what can be directly observed. And it will remain sensitive to the possibility that even statements about the explicit subject matter of a science may involve a reference to the operations (overt and symbolic) performed in inquiries into that subject matter.

b. Nowhere is the systematic undervaluation of the constructive function of thought in inquiry more glaring than in the widespread neglect of the role played by symbolic manipulations in scientific procedure. The more comprehensive and integrated a theoretical system, the more obvious does the need for such manipulations appear. For especially in the theories of modern science symbols usually occur which refer to nothing that can be directly experienced; and the significance for matters of direct experience of the conceptual constructions which enter into those theories cannot be made explicit except with the help of extensive symbolic transformations. Accordingly, no statement detached from the symbolic system to which it is integral can be evaluated for its empirical validity; and no isolated concept can be judged as warranted on the basis of the essentially irrelevant criterion of pictorial suggestiveness. But since calculation or symbolic manipulation thus acquires an indispensable though intermediary role in inquiry, the need for reliable techniques of constructing and expanding symbolic systems becomes progressively more pressing; the institution of an entire department of investigation devoted to the formal study of symbolic systems is the practically inevitable consequence.

It is a common and tempting assumption that in performing a chain of calculations one is at the same time acting out the existential connections between things, so that the formal pattern of symbolic transformations reproduces in some manner the structure of the subject matter under investigation. However, the specific mode in which theories are constructed and bodies of knowledge are integrated is only partially determined by experimental findings. Various norms or ideals—such as the desire for a certain degree of precision, for intellectual economy and notational convenience, or for a certain type of comprehensiveness—also control the direction of inquiry and the articulation of theories. Many symbolic constructions and operations are therefore indices of the standards regulating the course of systematic investigations, and are not merely indications of the expected conclusions of experiment or of the intrinsic relations between phases of subject matter. A myopic concern with the sensory warrants for scientific findings—such as often characterizes traditional empiricism—easily leads to neglect of this aspect of systematic scientific formulations; the traits of discourse are then identified as traits of subject matter,[5] and principles whose function it is to institute a desired order into inquiry are not distinguished from statements about the explicit subject matter of inquiry. When the identification is made, the construction of symbolic systems (including the use of hypotheses) is in effect viewed as an inessential scaffolding for attaining some form of intuitive knowledge. When the distinction is not made, logical principles are in effect deprived of their identifiable functions.

III

The preceding discussion has, in the main, been negative. There remains the task of making explicit the suggestions it contains concerning an alternative interpretation of some logical and mathematical notions. Nothing like a systematic account of logic and mathematics can be attempted, and only a small number of logical principles and mathematical terms will be briefly examined. But even such an examination may exhibit the fruitfulness of an operational analysis of formal concepts and may make plausible the view that the content of the formal disciplines has a regulative function in inquiry.

1. Although logic is one of the oldest intellectual disciplines, considerable difference of opinion exists as to the scope of logical theory and as to which concepts and principles properly belong to logic. The present discussion will be confined to such admittedly formal principles as the so-called laws of thought and other "necessary truths" and to principles of inference such as the principle of *ponendo ponens*. The discussion will be facilitated if at the outset two senses are distinguished in which logical principles are commonly asserted: as principles which are explicitly about symbolism or language; and as necessary truths whose ostensible subject matter is usually some nonlinguistic realm.[6]

a. The three laws of thought are employed in the first sense in cases something like the following. Suppose that in a bit of reasoned discourse the term "animal" occurs several times. The argument will clearly be a cogent one only if in each of its occurrences the word retains a fixed "meaning"—that is, only if it is used as a name for the same kind of object. The requirement that in a given context a term must continue to be used in essentially the same manner, is expressed as the principle of identity. Analogously, the principle of noncontradiction requires that in a given context a term must not be applied to a given thing and also denied to it; and the principle of excluded middle is formulated in a corresponding way.

When stated in this manner, these principles are obviously *prescriptive* for the use of language, and as such are not *descriptive* of actual usage. They specify minimal conditions for discourse without confusion, for they state at least some of the requirements for a precise language. Everyday language, and to some extent even the specialized languages of the sciences, are vague in some measure, so that they do not entirely conform to the requirement set by these principles.[7] Although fairly effective communication is nevertheless possible in connection with many pursuits, situations do arise in which a greater precision in the use of language is required. The laws of thought thus formulate an ideal to be achieved—an ideal which is capable of being attained at least approximately—and they indicate the direction in which the maximum of desired precision may be obtained.

Few will deny that the laws of thought as here formulated have a regulative function. Nevertheless, the admission is often qualified by the claim that if the ideal these laws formulate is a reasonable one, not an arbitrary norm, there must be an objective ground—a "structural invariant"—which lends them authority. Moreover, it is sometimes urged that this ideal must be a necessary and inescapable one, since otherwise a genuine alternative to it would be possible; however, communication would be impossible if language were so employed as to conform, for example, to the denial of the principle of identity. But this latter argument for the intrinsic necessity of these principles is surely circular. For if by "communication" is understood processes similar to those in which we are familiarly engaged when talking, writing, or carrying on research—processes which illustrate the use of symbols in at least partial conformity to the laws of thought—communication would indeed be impossible were the requirements set by these laws satisfied in no degree; but communication would not be possible simply because these laws are analytic of what is understood by the word "communication." Whatever might be the human needs which communication satisfies, the desire to communicate and the desire to enforce the ideal specified by the laws are directed toward the same end. It must, nevertheless, be acknowledged that the ideal of precision in using language is not an arbitrary one. It is not arbitrary because communication and inquiry are directed to the achievement of certain objectives, and these objectives are best attained when language is employed in a manner approximating as closely as possible the norms expressed by the laws of thought. The assertion that this is so requires support by empirical evidence—evidence which it is possible to produce. But the available evidence is drawn from the study of the behavior of men engaged in inquiry; it does not come from a consideration of structural invariants found in other domains.

The three laws of thought are, however, not the only principles of logic explicitly dealing with symbolism, and some consideration must now be given to that important class of principles known as rules of inference—of which the rule of *ponendo ponens* is, perhaps, the most familiar. The first point to note in connection with such principles is that it is possible to specify accurately what rules govern the valid inferences in a language only when the "meanings" of certain terms in that language are precise—that is, when terms like "and," "or," and "if—then" are used in determinate ways. In fact, however, the ordinary usage of such terms is vague and unclear. Everyday language, in the main, is employed according to routine habits which are fixed and stable over a narrow range, but which are indeterminate in many crucial cases; accordingly, inferences are drawn and sanctioned on the basis of crude intuitive considerations as to what is "really meant" by the terms involved.[8] The explicit formulation of canons of inference serves to clarify vague intent; and what is, perhaps, less commonly recognized, such formulations help to fix usages when they have previously been unsettled; they serve as proposals for modifying old usages and instituting new ones.

The various modern systems of formal logic must, accordingly, be viewed, not as accounts of the "true nature" of an antecedently identifiable relation of "implication," but as alternative proposals for specifying usages and for performing inferences. The adoption of a system such as is found in Whitehead and Russell's *Principia Mathematica* is in effect the adoption of a set of regulative principles for developing more inclusive and determinate habits for using language than are illustrated in everyday discourse. No known recent system of formal logic is or can be just a faithful transcription of those inferential canons which are embodied in common discourse, though in the construction of these systems this may be taken from current usage; for the entire *raison d'être* for such systems is the need for precision and inclusiveness where common discourse is vague and incomplete, even if as a consequence their adoption as regulative principles involves a modification of our inferential habits.

The question naturally arises whether the conventions which explicitly formulated rules of inference institute are entirely arbitrary—whether, in other words, the adoption of one set of regulative principles for reconstructing linguistic behaviors is as "justifiable" as the adoption of a different set. The issue raised does not refer to the construction of various abstract "uninterpreted" symbolic calculi, for which diverging rules of "inference" or "transformation" may be developed; for it is usually admitted that the arbitrariness of such abstract systems can be limited only by the formal requirements of symbolic construction. The issue refers to the ground upon which one system of regulative principles is to be preferred to another system, when such principles are to be employed in the conduct of scientific inquiry. But this manner of putting the question suggests its own answer. If everyday language requires completion and reorganization for the sake of attaining the ends of inquiry, the "justification" for a proposed set of regulative principles will not be arbitrary and can be given only in terms of the adequacy of the proposed changes as means or instruments for attaining the envisaged ends. Thus, if inquiry is directed toward achieving a system of physics which will be coherent, comprehensive, and economical in its use of certain types of assumption and operation, one set of canons for inference will be preferable to another if the former leads to a closer approximation to this goal than does the latter. The choice between alternative systems of regulative principles will then not be arbitrary and will have an objective basis; the choice will not, however, be grounded on the allegedly greater inherent necessity of one system of logic over another, but on the relatively greater adequacy of one of them as an instrument for achieving a certain systematization of knowledge.[9]

It is needless to dwell further on the function of rules of inference: their primary role is to guide the development of discourse in a certain direction, namely, in the deduction of the consequences of sets of statements; they thereby contribute to making the use of language more determinate and precise and to attaining the goals of specific inquiries. It must be admitted, however, that it is frequently difficult to exhibit adequate evidence for the superior efficacy of one type of inferential system over another, especially when the specific goals of inquiry are themselves vague and are conceived, in part or at least, in aesthetic terms.[10] The point to be stressed is that however great this difficulty may be, it can be resolved only by considering the specific functions of such logical principles in determinate contexts of inquiry; it cannot be resolved by investigating the causal factors which lead men to adopt those principles or by a genetic account of inferential habits.

For example, the view has been advanced that certain simple forms of inference are generated by physiological mechanisms sharing a common character with mechanisms present in the subject matter of inquiry in which those inferences are used; and it is sometimes said that a theory of logic is "naturalistic" only if it holds that rational operations "grow out of" the more pervasive biological and physical ones. It may be safely assumed that there are causes and physical conditions for habits of inference, even when we happen to be ignorant of them. It is not evident, however, especially since habits of inference may change though the subject matter in connection with which they are employed does not, that the mechanism underlying a specific habit of inference is identical with the mechanism involved in that subject matter. And it is even less evident how, even if this were the case, the causal account would enable us to evaluate inferential principles, since the cogency of such an account is established only with the help of those principles. Suggestions for inferential canons may indeed be obtained from observations of natural processes; but the fact that a principle may have been suggested in this way does not explain its normative function. Again, the known facts about the earth's history make it most reasonable to assume that the higher and more complex activities of men did not always exist and that they have been developed out of more primitive ones; and it would certainly be a matter of great interest to learn just how this has come about. However, in the present state of our knowledge a genetic account of logical operations is at best a highly speculative and dubious one; and what is more to the point, even if a well-supported genetic account were available, it would contribute little or nothing to an understanding of the present functioning of logical principles or to the explanation of the grounds of their authority. In the absence of a detailed knowledge of the past, the reaffirmation of the historical and structural continuity of our rational behavior with the activities of other organisms is an act of piety; it does not increase the clarifying force of an experimentally oriented naturalism.[11]

b. Logical principles are also asserted as necessary truths which do not refer to linguistic subject matter. Thus, "Everything is identical with itself" and "If *A* then *A*" (where "*A*" is any statement) are formulations of the principle of identity; "Nothing has and also lacks a given property" and "It is not the case that *A* and not-*A*" (where "*A*" is any statement) are formulations of the principle of noncontradiction; while "If *A* and (if *A* then *B*), then *B*," and "If (if *A* then *B*) then (if not-*B* then not-*A*)" (where "*A*" and "*B*" are any statements) are examples of other principles usually regarded as necessary. These principles are ostensibly about things, their attributes and their relations, not about symbols for them; they are held to be necessary truths, because their denials are self-contradictory.

The first point to note about these logical laws is that if they are asserted as necessary truths, they are asserted to be such in some more or less precisely formulated language, whether in the crudely precise language of everyday use or in some more exact artificial symbolic system. And it is not difficult to show that although their subject matter is not the language of which they are parts, they occur in that language because of the habits of usage or the tacit or explicit rules which govern that language. For example, if the characterizations "true" and "false" are employed in the customary manner, no statement can properly (that is, without contravening that usage) be characterized as both true and false; and if the word "not" is so used in connection with acts of affirming and denying statements that a false statement is rejected as not true, the principle of noncontradiction is instituted as a necessary truth. More generally, if a precise usage is fixed for a number of expressions in a symbolic system, statements constructed out of some of these expressions will usually occur such that to deny them is to misuse those expressions. Accordingly, the laws which are regarded as necessary in a given language may be viewed as implicit definitions of the ways in which certain recurrent expressions are to be used or as consequences of other postulates for such usages. No language is so utterly flexible in its formal structure that no limits exist as to the way expressions in it can be combined and used. The necessary statements of a language help to specify what these limits are. But to the extent to which ordinary language is not precise, which statements in it are necessary cannot be determined exactly. The so-called systems of "pure logic" do not suffer from this fault; they can therefore be used as norms for instituting a more precise employment of language in situations in which such precision is essential for the task at hand. Indeed, as is well known, one result of such instituted precision is to facilitate the process of deriving consequences from premises and to supply dependable means for checking inferences.

This function of logical laws—to serve as instruments for establishing connections between statements which are usually not themselves logically necessary—is too familiar to require more than passing mention. A point worth observing, however, is that the necessary laws of logic can be reformulated so as to become principles of inference, having as their explicit subject matter the relations of expressions in a symbolic system. For it can be shown that a given language may be so reconstructed that it no longer will contain necessary truths—without thereby affecting the original possibilities for deducing statements which are not necessary—provided that corresponding to the necessary truths initially in the language appropriate rules of inference are introduced. The cost of such a reconstruction may be prohibitive in terms of the inconveniences and complexities which arise from it.[12] Nevertheless, the theoretical possibility of making it helps to show that the function of necessary truth is to regulate and control the process of deduction. It follows that the previous comments on rules of inference apply with equal force to laws expressing necessary connections.

A few final remarks concerning the grounds for accepting logical laws must be made. The main stress which is to be made in this connection is that any "justification" of such laws can be given only in terms of the adequacy of the language in which they are part to the specific tasks for which that language is employed. This point can be enforced by recalling that in the empirical sciences it is not possible to perform experiments which would subject isolated statements to a crucial test, since every experiment actually tests a vaguely delimited system of theoretical and factual assumptions involved in the experiment and the statement. Analogously, it is not feasible to "justify" a law of logic by confronting it with specific observational data; the belief that it is possible to do so is part of the heritage of traditional empiricism. On the other hand, since logical laws are implicit laws for specifying the structure of a language, and since their explicit function is to link systematically statements to which data of observation are relevant, logical laws may be evaluated on the basis of their effectiveness in yielding systems of a desired kind. Thus, it has recently been suggested that in order to develop the theory of subatomic phenomena in a manner conforming both to experimental evidence and to certain ideals of economy and elegance, a "logic" different from those normally employed may have to be instituted.[13] The suggestion is still in a speculative stage, and it is interesting only as a possibility. Nevertheless, it calls attention to the fact in a striking way that under the pressure of factual observation and norms of convenience familiar language habit may come to be revised; and it indicates that the acceptance of logical principles as canonical need be neither on arbitrary grounds or on grounds of their allegedly inherent authority, but on the ground that they effectively achieve certain postulated ends.

It must be emphasized, however, that this way of justifying logical principles has nothing in common with the view which construes them as descriptive of an intrinsic and pervasive structure of things. It has been argued that just as in geometry there are intrinsically different kinds of surface and each kind imposes "certain limits on the range of alternative coordinate systems which can be used to map it out," so "the objective structure of the system of fact imposes some limitation on the alternative systems of language or symbolism which are capable of representing it." The conclusion drawn from this argument by analogy is that propositions which would describe this structure "would almost inevitably take the form of propositions which formulate certain very abstract and general and widespread linguistic usages"; and since logical principles do "formulate" these usages, there can be only one genuinely valid logic, only one absolute system of necessary truths. But even if one accepts the questionable analogy which underlies the argument, elementary considerations of scientific procedure must lead one to reject the conception of "*the* objective structure of *the* system of fact" capable of being known without the mediation of any selective symbolic system. The study of scientific inquiry requires us to admit that structures cannot be known independently of activities of symbolization; that structures considered for investigation are selected on the basis of special problems; that the various structures discovered are not, according to the best evidence, all parts of one coherent pattern; and that the precise manner in which our theories are formulated is controlled by specifically human postulates no less than by experimental findings. The attempt to justify logical principles in terms of their supposed conformity to an absolute structure of facts thus completely overlooks their actual function of formulating and regulating the pursuit of human ideals. If the preceding discussion has any merit, however, the reasonable view is that the relative success of a system of logic in doing these things is the sole identifiable and objective basis for measuring its worth. . . .

Notes

1. The point at issue involves noting the difference between the following two statements: "However an attribute is selected, it is possible to find a respect such that a given attribute does not at the same time belong and not belong to a given subject in that respect," and "It is possible to find a respect such that, however an attribute is selected, the given attribute does not at the same time belong and not belong to a given subject in that respect." The hypothetical defender of the principle can successfully maintain the first, though not the second, because he undertakes to specify the "sameness" of respects only after he has selected an attribute—that is, after the principle is used to determine a respect, which will thus automatically satisfy the principle.

2. Of course, the question whether *a particular physical configuration* is the path of a light ray (that is, whether it satisfies E) would remain an experimental issue.

3. This discussion is obviously oversimplified. Thus, if the formula is a logical consequence of some set of axioms which are used as implicit definitions for propositions, then the principle of noncontradiction will be a necessary truth even though it now falls under the first of the above two alternatives. However, the point of the discussion is not affected by the neglect of such complications. In the present essay the word "proposition" is used loosely, and is frequently employed interchangeably with the word "statement." It is, of course, important in many contexts to distinguish between a proposition and a statement, since the former is often taken to be the "meaning" of the latter.

However, the issues under discussion are fairly neutral with respect to the different views which are current concerning what propositions are so that no serious confusions need arise from the loose use of the word.

4. For example, within the framework of the Newtonian analysis of motion, an indefinite number of false hypotheses for gravitational attraction can be constructed, since a false theory of gravitation is obtained if the exponent "2" in Newton's formula is replaced by a different numeral. Are these different theories to be dismissed as meaningless because there do not happen to exist an infinity of situations for which these theories are true?

5. An example of such a transference is found in the claim that, because the consistency of a set of formal postulates is established by exhibiting a group of related objects—a so-called "concrete model"—satisfying those postulates, logical traits (such as consistency) must represent pervasive ontological or empirical invariants. In point of fact, however, not only can some postulate sets be established without recourse to empirical facts in the indicated manner; most postulate systems cannot be shown to be consistent by genuinely empirical methods. But what is perhaps more to the point, this argument for identifying logical with existential properties fails to observe that consistency is demanded of symbolic systems as part of an ideal for the organization of statements and is not a trait subsisting in nature independently of symbolic formulations.

6. This distinction roughly corresponds to the difference noted in much current literature between "metalogical" statements and statements in the "object-language" of a science.

7. Thus if the term "red" is vague, there is a class of colors concerning which it is indeterminate whether the term applies to them or not, so that the principle of excluded middle fails in this case.

8. For example, everyone who has an elementary knowledge of English would agree that the rule of *ponendo ponens* is a correct canon of inference. On the other hand, a person unsophisticated by training in formal logic and not committed to one of the modern logical systems, may hesitate to accept the rule that a statement of the form "Either A or B" is a consequence of "A," where "A" and "B" are any statements; and he will probably seriously doubt the correctness of the rule that "If A then (if B then C)" follows from "If A and B, then C," where "A," "B," and "C" are any statements. The hesitation and the doubt must be attributed to the fact that "or," "and," and "if— then" are frequently used ambiguously and have fairly clear and determinate meanings only in relatively few contexts.

9. Something more will be said on this point below. These remarks should

not, however, be taken to mean that all habits of inference, and in particular language itself, have been instituted on the basis of a deliberate convention. How language first arose and how some of our common modes of inference actually came into being, are questions of fact about which there is in general little reliable information and concerning which everyone seems to be equally in the dark.

10. For example, when a theory is required to be "simple" and "elegant."

11. These comments should not be construed as a rejection of some form of "the principle of continuity" as a fruitful guide and norm in inquiry. Nor should they be taken as denying that the study of simpler and more basic biological behavior may provide an illuminating context and essential clues for the understanding of the "higher" functions. These remarks are included simply as a protest against frequent abuses of a useful postulate of procedure.

12. For example, the necessary truth "if (if A then B), then (if not-B then not-A)" could be eliminated from our language, provided that we introduce the rule that a statement of the form "if not-B then not-A" is deducible from a statement of the form "if A then B." On the other hand, it is usually assumed that when "A," "B," "C," "D" are any statements, they may be combined to form the new statements "if A then B," "if C then D," and "if (if A then B), then (if C then D)"; accordingly, since "not-A" and "not-B" are statements, "if (if A then B), then (if not-B then not-A)" must be accepted as a statement on the basis of the stipulation just mentioned. Hence, if the occurrence of such necessary truths is to be prevented, more complicated rules must be introduced for combining statements to form new ones.

13. See Garrett Birkhoff and John von Neumann, "The Logic of Quantum Mechanics," in *Annals of Mathematics* 37 (1936): 823–43. The proposed logical system involves abandoning certain rules of inference which seem truistic both to "common sense" and to those accustomed to the system of *Principia Mathematica.*

3

Epistemology Naturalized*

W. V. O. Quine

Epistemology is concerned with the foundations of science. Conceived thus broadly, epistemology includes the study of the foundations of mathematics as one of its departments. Specialists at the turn of the century thought that their efforts in this particular department were achieving notable success: mathematics seemed to reduce altogether to logic. In a more recent perspective this reduction is seen to be better describable as a reduction to logic and set theory. This correction is a disappointment epistemologically, since the firmness and obviousness that we associate with logic cannot be claimed for set theory. But still the success achieved in the foundations of mathematics remains exemplary by comparative standards, and we can illuminate the rest of epistemology somewhat by drawing parallels to this department.

Studies in the foundations of mathematics divide symmetrically into two sorts, conceptual and doctrinal. The conceptual studies are concerned with meaning, the doctrinal with truth. The conceptual studies are concerned with clarifying concepts by defining them, some in terms of others. The doctrinal studies are concerned with establishing laws by

*Originally published in W. V. O. Quine, *Ontological Relativity and Other Essays* (New York: Columbia University Press, 1969). Reprinted by permission.

proving them, some on the basis of others. Ideally the obscurer concepts would be defined in terms of the clearer ones so as to maximize clarity, and the less obvious laws would be proved from the more obvious ones so as to maximize certainty. Ideally the definitions would generate all the concepts from clear and distinct ideas, and the proofs would generate all the theorems from self-evident truths.

The two ideals are linked. For, if you define all the concepts by use of some favored subset of them, you thereby show how to translate all theorems into these favored terms. The clearer these terms are, the likelier it is that the truths couched in them will be obviously true, or derivable from obvious truths. If in particular the concepts of mathematics were all reducible to the clear terms of logic, then all the truths of mathematics would go over into truths of logic; and surely the truths of logic are all obvious or at least potentially obvious, i.e., derivable from obvious truths by individually obvious steps.

This particular outcome is in fact denied us, however, since mathematics reduces only to set theory and not to logic proper. Such reduction still enhances clarity, but only because of the interrelations that emerge and not because the end terms of the analysis are clearer than others. As for the end truths, the axioms of set theory, these have less obviousness and certainty to recommend them than do most of the mathematical theorems that we would derive from them. Moreover, we know from Gödel's work that no consistent axiom system can cover mathematics even when we renounce self-evidence. Reduction in the foundations of mathematics remains mathematically and philosophically fascinating, but it does not do what the epistemologist would like of it: it does not reveal the ground of mathematical knowledge, it does not show how mathematical certainty is possible.

Still there remains a helpful thought, regarding epistemology generally, in that duality of structure which was especially conspicuous in the foundations of mathematics. I refer to the bifurcation into a theory of concepts, or meaning, and a theory of doctrine, or truth; for this applies to the epistemology of natural knowledge no less than to the foundations of mathematics. The parallel is as follows. Just as mathematics is to be reduced to logic, or logic and set theory, so natural knowledge is to be based somehow on sense experience. This means explaining the notion of body in sensory terms; here is the conceptual side. And it means justifying our knowledge of truths of nature in sensory terms; here is the doctrinal side of the bifurcation.

Hume pondered the epistemology of natural knowledge on both sides of the bifurcation, the conceptual and the doctrinal. His handling of the conceptual side of the problem, the explanation of body in sensory terms, was bold and simple: he identified bodies outright with the sense impressions. If common sense distinguishes between the material apple and our sense impressions of it on the ground that the apple is one and enduring while the impressions are many and fleeting, then, Hume held, so much the worse for common sense; the notion of its being the same apple on one occasion and another is a vulgar confusion.

Nearly a century after Hume's *Treatise,* the same view of bodies was espoused by the early American philosopher Alexander Bryan Johnson.[1] "The word iron names an associated sight and feel," Johnson wrote.

What then of the doctrinal side, the justification of our knowledge of truths about nature? Here, Hume despaired. By his identification of bodies with impressions he did succeed in construing some singular statements about bodies as indubitable truths, yes; as truths about impressions, directly known. But general statements, also singular statements about the future, gained no increment of certainty by being construed as about impressions.

On the doctrinal side, I do not see that we are farther along today than where Hume left us. The Humean predicament is the human predicament. But on the conceptual side there has been progress. There the crucial step forward was made already before Alexander Bryan Johnson's day, although Johnson did not emulate it. It was made by Bentham in his theory of fictions. Bentham's step was the recognition of contextual definition, or what he called paraphrasis. He recognized that to explain a term we do not need to specify an object for it to refer to, nor even specify a synonymous word or phrase; we need only show, by whatever means, how to translate all the whole sentences in which the term is to be used. Hume's and Johnson's desperate measure of identifying bodies with impressions ceased to be the only conceivable way of making sense of talk of bodies, even granted that impressions were the only reality. One could undertake to explain talk of bodies in terms of talk of impressions by translating one's whole sentences about bodies into whole sentences about impressions, without equating the bodies themselves to anything at all.

This idea of contextual definition, or recognition of the sentence as the primary vehicle of meaning, was indispensable to the ensuing developments in the foundations of mathematics. It was explicit in Frege, and it attained its full flower in Russell's doctrine of singular descriptions as incomplete symbols.

Contextual definition was one of two resorts that could be expected to have a liberating effect upon the conceptual side of the epistemology of natural knowledge. The other is resort to the resources of set theory as auxiliary concepts. The epistemologist who is willing to eke out his austere ontology of sense impressions with these set-theoretic auxiliaries is suddenly rich: he has not just his impressions to play with, but sets of them, and sets of sets, and so on up. Constructions in the foundations of mathematics have shown that such set-theoretic aids are a powerful addition; after all, the entire glossary of concepts of classical mathematics is constructible from them. Thus equipped, our epistemologist may not need either to identify bodies with impressions or to settle for contextual definition; he may hope to find in some subtle construction of sets upon sets of sense impressions a category of objects enjoying just the formula properties that he wants for bodies.

The two resorts are very unequal in epistemological status. Contextual definition is unassailable. Sentences that have been given meaning as wholes are undeniably meaningful, and the use they make of their component terms is therefore meaningful, regardless of whether any translations are offered for those terms in isolation. Surely Hume and A. B. Johnson would have used contextual definition with pleasure if they had thought of it. Recourse to sets, on the other hand, is a drastic ontological move, a retreat from the austere ontology of impressions. There are philosophers who would rather settle for bodies outright than accept all these sets, which amount, after all, to the whole abstract ontology of mathematics.

This issue has not always been clear, however, owing to deceptive hints of continuity between elementary logic and set theory. This is why mathematics was once believed to reduce to logic, that is, to an innocent and unquestionable logic, and to inherit these qualities. And this is probably why Russell was content to resort to sets as well as to contextual definition when in *Our Knowledge of the External World* and elsewhere he addressed himself to the epistemology of natural knowledge, on its conceptual side.

To account for the external world as a logical construct of sense data—such, in Russell's terms, was the program. It was Carnap, in his *Der logische Aufbau der Welt* of 1928, who came nearest to executing it.

This was the conceptual side of epistemology; what of the doctrinal? There the Humean predicament remained unaltered. Carnap's constructions, if carried successfully to completion, would have enabled us to translate all sentences about the world into terms of sense data, or observation, plus logic and set theory. But the mere fact that a sentence is *couched* in terms of observation, logic, and set theory does not mean that it can be *proved* from observation sentences by logic and set theory. The most modest of generalizations about observable traits will cover more cases than its utterer can have had occasion actually to observe. The hopelessness of grounding natural science upon immediate experience in a firmly logical way was acknowledged. The Cartesian quest for certainty had been the remote motivation of epistemology, both on its conceptual and its doctrinal side; but that quest was seen as a lost cause. To endow the truths of nature with the full authority of immediate experience was as forlorn a hope as hoping to endow the truths of mathematics with the potential obviousness of elementary logic.

What then could have motivated Carnap's heroic efforts on the conceptual side of epistemology, when hope of certainty on the doctrinal side was abandoned? There were two good reasons still. One was that such constructions could be expected to elicit and clarify the sensory evidence for science, even if the inferential steps between sensory evidence and scientific doctrine must fall short of certainty. The other reason was that such constructions would deepen our understanding of our discourse about the world, even apart from questions of evidence; it would make all cognitive discourse as clear as observation terms and logic and, I must regretfully add, set theory.

It was sad for epistemologists, Hume and others, to have to acquiesce in the impossibility of strictly deriving the science of the external world from sensory evidence. Two cardinal tenets of empiricism remained unassailable, however, and so remain to this day. One is that whatever evidence there *is* for science *is* sensory evidence. The other, to which I shall recur, is that all inculcation of meanings of words must rest ultimately on sensory evidence. Hence the continuing attractiveness of the idea of a *logischer Aufbau* in which the sensory content of discourse would stand forth explicitly.

If Carnap had successfully carried such a construction through, how could he have told whether it was the right one? The question would have had no point. He was seeking what he called a *rational reconstruction*. Any construction of physicalistic discourse in terms of sense experience, logic, and set theory would have been seen as satisfactory if it made the physicalistic discourse come out right. If there is one way there are many, but any would be a great achievement.

But why all this creative reconstruction, all this make-believe? The stimulation of his sensory receptors is all the evidence anybody has had to go on, ultimately, in arriving at his picture of the world. Why not just see how this construction really proceeds? Why not settle for psychology? Such a surrender of the epistemological burden to psychology is a move that was disallowed in earlier times as circular reasoning. If the epistemologist's goal is validation of the grounds of empirical science, he defeats his purpose by using psychology or other empirical science in the validation. However, such scruples against circularity have little point since we have stopped dreaming of deducing science from observations. If we are out simply to understand the link between observation and science, we are well advised to use any available information, including that provided by the very science whose link with observation we are seeking to understand.

But there remains a different reason, unconnected with fears of circularity, for still favoring creative reconstruction. We should like to be able to *translate* science into logic and observation terms and set theory. This would be a great epistemological achievement, for it would show all the rest of the concepts of science to be theoretically superfluous. It would legitimize them—to whatever degree the concepts of set theory, logic, and observation are themselves legitimate—by showing that everything done with the one apparatus could in principle be done with the other. If psychology itself could deliver a truly translational reduction of this kind, we should welcome it; but certainly it cannot, for certainly we did not grow up learning definitions of physicalistic language in terms of a prior language of set theory, logic, and observation. Here, then, would be good reason for persisting in a rational reconstruction: we want to establish the essential innocence of physical concepts, by showing them to be theoretically dispensable.

The fact is, though, that the construction which Carnap outlined in *Der logische Aufbau der Welt* does not give translational reduction either. It would not even if the outline were filled in. The crucial point comes where Carnap is explaining how to assign sense qualities to positions in physical space and time. These assignments are to be made in such a way as to fulfill, as well as possible, certain desiderata which he states, and with growth of experience the assigments are to be revised to suit. This plan, however illuminating, does not offer any key to *translating* the sentences of science into terms of observation, logic, and set theory.

We must despair of any such reduction. Carnap had despaired of it by 1936, when, in "Testability and meaning,"[2] he introduced so-called *reduction forms* of a type weaker than definition. Definitions had shown always how to translate sentences into equivalent sentences. Contextual definition of a term showed how to translate sentences containing the term into equivalent sentences lacking the term. Reduction forms of Carnap's liberalized kind, on the other hand, do not in general give equivalences; they give implications. They explain a new term, if only partially, by specifying some sentences which are implied by sentences containing the term, and the other sentences which imply sentences containing the term.

It is tempting to suppose that the countenancing of reduction forms in this liberal sense is just one further step of liberalization comparable to the earlier one, taken by Bentham, of countenancing contextual definition. The former and sterner kind of rational reconstruction might have been represented as a fictitious history in which we imagined our ancestors introducing the terms of physicalistic discourse on a phenomenalistic and set-theoretic basis by a succession of contextual definitions. The new and more liberal kind of rational reconstruction is a fictitious history in which we imagine our ancestors introducing those terms by a succession rather of reduction forms of the weaker sort.

This, however, is a wrong comparison. The fact is rather that the former and sterner kind of rational reconstruction, where definition reigned, embodied no fictitious history at all. It was nothing more nor less than a set of directions—or would have been, if successful—for accomplishng everything in terms of phenomena and set theory that we now accomplish in terms of bodies. It would have been a true reduction by translation, a legitimation by elimination. *Definire est eliminare.* Rational reconstruction by Carnap's later and looser reduction forms does none of this.

To relax the demand for definition, and settle for a kind of reduction that does not eliminate, is to renounce the last remaining advantage that we supposed rational reconstruction to have over straight psychology; namely, the advantage of translational reduction. If all we hope for is a reconstruction that links science to experience in explicit ways short of translation, then it would seem more sensible to settle for psychology. Better to discover how science is in fact developed and learned than to fabricate a fictitious structure to a similar effect.

The empiricist made one major concession when he despaired of deducing the truths of nature from sensory evidence. In despairing now even of translating those truths into terms of observation and logico-mathematical auxiliaries, he makes another major concession. For suppose we hold, with the old empiricist Peirce, that the very meaning of a statement consists in the difference its truth would make to possible experience. Might we not formulate, in a chapter-length sentence in observational language, all the difference that the truth of a given statement might make to experience, and might we not then take all this as the translation? Even if the difference that the truth of the statement would make to experience ramifies indefinitely, we might still hope to embrace it all in the logical implications of our chapter-length formulation, just as we can axiomatize an infinity of theorems. In giving up hope of such translation, then, the empiricist is conceding that the empirical meanings of typical statements about the external world are inaccessible and ineffable.

How is this inaccessibility to be explained? Simply on the ground that the experiential implications of a typical statement about bodies are too complex for finite axiomatization, however lengthy? No; I have a different explanation. It is that the typical statement about bodies has no fund of experiential implications it can call its own. A substantial mass of theory, taken together, will commonly have experiential implications; this is how we make verifiable predictions. We may not be able to explain why we arrive at theories which make successful predictions, but we do arrive at such theories.

Sometimes also an experience implied by a theory fails to come off; and then, ideally, we declare the theory false. But the failure falsifies only a block of theory as a whole, a conjunction of many statements. The failure shows that one or more of those statements is false, but it does not show which. The predicted experiences, true and false, are not implied by any one of the component statements of the theory rather than another. The component statements simply do not have empirical meanings, by Peirce's standard; but a sufficiently inclusive portion of theory does. If we can aspire to a sort of *logischer Aufbau der Welt* at all, it must be to one in which the texts slated for translation into observational and logico-mathematical terms are mostly broad theories taken as wholes, rather than just terms or short sentences. The translation of a theory would be a ponderous axiomatization of all the experiential difference that the truth of the theory would make. It would be a queer translation, for it would translate the whole but none of the parts. We might better speak in such a case not of translation but simply of observational evidence for theories; and we may, following Peirce, still fairly call this the empirical meaning of the theories.

These considerations raise a philosophical question even about ordinary unphilosophical translation, such as from English into Arunta or Chinese. For, if the English sentences of a theory have their meaning only together as a body, then we can justify their translation into Arunta only together as a body. There will be no justification for pairing off the component English sentences with component Arunta sentences, except as these correlations make the translation of the theory as a whole come out right. Any translations of the English sentences into Arunta sentences will be as correct as any other, so long as the net empirical implications of the theory as a whole are preserved in translation. But it is to be expected that many different ways of translating the component sentences, essentially different individually, would deliver the same empirical implications for the theory as a whole; deviations in the translation of one component sentence could be compensated for in the translation of another component sentence. Insofar, there can be no ground for saying which of two glaringly unlike translations of individual sentences is right.[3]

For an uncritical mentalist, no such indeterminacy threatens. Every term and every sentence is a label attached to an idea, simple or complex, which is stored in the mind. When on the other hand we take a verification theory of meaning seriously, the indeterminacy would appear to be inescapable. The Vienna Circle espoused a verification theory of meaning but did not take it seriously enough. If we recognize with Peirce that the meaning of a sentence turns purely on what would count as evidence for its truth, and if we recognize with Duhem that theoretical sentences have their evidence not as single sentences but only as larger blocks of theory, then the indeterminacy of translation of theoretical sentences is the natural conclusion. And most sentences, apart from observation sentences, are theoretical. This conclusion, conversely, once it is embraced, seals the fate of any general notion of propositional meaning or, for that matter, state of affairs.

Should the unwelcomeness of the conclusion persuade us to abandon the verification theory of meaning? Certainly not. The sort of meaning that is basic to translation, and to the learning of one's own language, is necessarily empirical meaning and nothing more. A child learns his first words and sentences by hearing and using them in the presence of appropriate stimuli. These must be external stimuli, for they must act both on the child and on the speaker from whom he is learning.[4] Language is socially inculcated and controlled; the inculcation and control turn strictly on the keying of sentences to shared stimulation. Internal factors may vary *ad libitum* without prejudice to communication as long as the keying of language to external stimuli is undisturbed. Surely one has no choice but to be an empiricist so far as one's theory of linguistic meaning is concerned.

What I have said of infant learning applies equally to the linguist's learning of a new language in the field. If the linguist does not lean on related languages for which there are previously accepted translation practices, then obviously he has no data but the concomitances of native utterances and observable stimulus situation. Granted, the linguist will end up with unequivocal translations of everything; but only by making many arbitrary choices—arbitrary even though unconscious—along the way. Arbitrary? By this I mean that different choices could still have made everything come out right that is susceptible in principle to any kind of check.

Let me link up, in a different order, some of the points I have made. The crucial consideration behind my argument for the indeterminacy of translation was that a statement about the world does not always or usually have a separable fund of empirical consequence that it can call its own. That consideration served also to account for the impossibility of an epistemological reduction of the sort where every sentence is equated to a sentence in observational and logico-mathematical terms. And the impossibility of that sort of epistemological reduction dissipated the last advantage that rational reconstruction seemed to have over psychology.

Philosophers have rightly despaired of translating everything into observational and logico-mathematical terms. They have despaired of this even when they have not recognized, as the reason for this irreducibility, that the statements largely do not have their private bundles of empirical consequences. And some philosophers have seen in this irreducibility the bankruptcy of epistemology. Carnap and the other logical positivists of the Vienna Circle had already pressed the term "metaphysics" into pejorative use, as connoting meaninglessness; and the term "epistemology" was next. Wittgenstein and his followers, mainly at Oxford, found a residual philosophical vocation in therapy: in curing philosophers of the delusion that there were epistemological problems.

But I think that at this point it may be more useful to say rather that epistemology still goes on, though in a new setting and a clarified status. Epistemology, or something like it, simply falls into place as a chapter of psychology and hence of natural science. It studies a natural phenomenon, viz. a physical human subject. This human subject is accorded a certain experimentally controlled input—certain patterns of irradiation in assorted frequencies, for instance—and in the fullness of time the subject delivers as output a description of the three-dimensional external world and its history. The relation between the meager input and the torrential output is a relation that we are prompted to study for somewhat the same reasons that always prompted epistemology; namely, in order to see how evidence relates to theory, and in what ways one's theory of nature transcends any available evidence.

Such a study could still include, even, something like the old rational reconstruction, to whatever degree such reconstruction is practicable; for imaginative constructions can afford hints of actual psychological processes, in much the way that mechanical stimulations can. But a conspicuous difference between old epistemology and the epistemological enterprise in this new psychological setting is that we can now make free use of empirical psychology.

The old epistemology aspired to contain, in a sense, natural science; it would construct it somehow from sense data. Epistemology in its new setting, conversely, is contained in natural science, as a chapter of psychology. But the old containment remains valid too, in its way. We are studying how the human subject of our study posits bodies and projects his physics from his data, and we appreciate that our position in the world is just like his. Our very epistemological enterprise, therefore, and the psychology wherein it is a component chapter, and the whole of natural science wherein psychology is a component book—all this is our own construction or projection from stimulations like those we were meting out to our epistemological subjects. There is thus reciprocal containment, though containment in different senses: epistemology in natural science and natural science in epistemology.

This interplay is reminiscent again of the old threat of circularity, but it is all right now that we have stopped dreaming of deducing science from sense data. We were after an understanding of science as an institution or process in the world, and we do not intend that understanding to be any better than the science which is its object. This attitude is indeed one that Neurath was already urging in Vienna Circle days, with his parable of the mariner who has to rebuild his boat while staying afloat in it.

One effect of seeing epistemology in a psychological setting is that it resolves a stubborn old enigma of epistemological priority. Our retinas are irradiated in two dimensions, yet we see things as three-dimensional without conscious inference. Which is to count as observation—the unconscious two-dimensional reception or the conscious three-dimensional apprehension? In the old epistemological context the conscious form had priority, for we were out to justify our knowledge of the external world by rational reconstruction, and that demands awareness. Awareness ceased to be demanded when we gave up trying to justify our knowledge of the external world by rational reconstruction. What to count as observation now can be settled in terms of the stimulation of sensory receptors, let consciousness fall where it may.

The Gestalt psychologists' challenge to sensory atomism, which seemed so relevant to epistemology forty years ago, is likewise deactivated. Regardless of whether sensory atoms or Gestalten are what favor the forefront of our consciousness, it is simply the stimulations of our sensory receptors that are best looked upon as the input to our cognitive mechanism. Old paradoxes about unconscious data and inference, old problems about chains of inference that would have to be completed too quickly—these no longer matter.

In the old antipsychologistic days the question of epistemological priority was moot. What is epistemologically prior to what? Are Gestalten prior to sensory atoms because they are noticed, or should we favor sensory atoms on some more subtle ground? Now that we are permitted to appeal to physical stimulation, the problem dissolves; A is epistemologically prior to B if A is causally nearer than B to the sensory receptors. Or, what is in some ways better, just talk explicitly in terms of causal proximity to sensory receptors and drop the talk of epistemological priority.

Around 1932 there was debate in the Vienna Circle over what to count as observation sentences, or *Protokollsätze*.[5] One position was that they had the form of reports of sense impressions. Another was that they were statements of an elementary sort about the external world, e.g., "A red cube is standing on the table." Another, Neurath's, was that they had the form of reports of relations between percipients and external things: "Otto now sees a red cube on the table." The worst of it was that there seemed to be no objective way of settling the matter: no way of making real sense of the question.

Let us now try to view the matter unreservedly in the context of the external world. Vaguely speaking, what we want of observation sentences is that they be the ones in closest causal proximity to the sensory receptors. But how is such proximity to be gauged? The idea may be rephrased this way: observation sentences are sentences which, as we learn language, are most strongly conditioned to concurrent sensory stimulation rather than to stored collateral information. Thus let us imagine a sentence queried for our verdict as to whether it is true or false; queried for our assent or dissent. Then the sentence is an observation sentence if our verdict depends only on the sensory stimulation present at the time.

But a verdict cannot depend on present stimulation to the exclusion of stored information. The very fact of our having learned the language evinces much storing of information, and of information without which we should be in no position to give verdicts on sentences however observational. Evidently then we must relax our definition of observation sentence to read thus: a sentence is an observation sentence if all verdicts on it depend on present sensory stimulation and on no stored information beyond what goes into understanding the sentence.

This formulation raises another problem: how are we to distinguish between information that goes into understanding a sentence and information that goes beyond? This is the problem of distinguishing between analytic truth, which issues from the mere meanings of words, and synthetic truth, which depends on more than meanings. Now I have long maintained that this distinction is illusory. There is one step toward such a distinction, however, which does make sense: a sentence that is true by mere meanings of words should be expected, at least if it is simple, to be subscribed to by all fluent speakers in the community. Perhaps the controversial notion of analyticity can be dispensed with, in our definition of observation sentence, in favor of this straightforward attribute of community-wide acceptance.

This attribute is of course no explication of analyticity. The community would agree that there have been black dogs, yet none who talk of analyticity would call this analytic. My rejection of the analyticity notion just means drawing no line between what goes into the mere understanding of the sentences of a language and what else the community sees eye to eye on. I doubt that an objective distinction can be made between meaning and such collateral information as is community-wide.

Turning back then to our task of defining observation sentences, we get this: an observation sentence is one on which all speakers of the language give the same verdict when given the same concurrent stimulation. To put the point negatively, an observation sentence is one that is not sensitive to differences in past experience with the speech community.

This formulation accords perfectly with the traditional role of the observation sentence as the court of appeal of scientific theories. For by our definition the observation sentences are the sentences on which all members of the community will agree under uniform stimulation. And what is the criterion of membership in the same community? Simply general fluency of dialogue. This criterion admits of degrees, and indeed we may usefully take the community more narrowly for some studies than for others. What count as observation sentences for a community of specialists would not always so count for a larger community.

There is generally no subjectivity in the phrasing of observation sentences, as we are now conceiving them; they will usually be about bodies. Since the distinguishing trait of an observation sentence is intersubjective agreement under agreeing stimulation, a corporeal subject matter is likelier than not.

The old tendency to associate observation sentences with a subjective sensory subject matter is rather an irony when we reflect that observation sentences are also meant to be the intersubjective tribunal of scientific hypotheses. The old tendency was due to the drive to base science on something firmer and prior in the subject's experience; but we dropped that project.

The dislodging of epistemology from its old status of first philosophy loosed a wave, we saw, of epistemological nihilism. This mood is reflected somewhat in the tendency of Polányi, Kuhn, and the late Russell Hanson to belittle the role of evidence and to accentuate cultural relativism. Hanson ventured even to discredit the idea of observation, arguing that so-called observations vary from observer to observer with the amount of knowledge that the observers bring with them. The veteran physicist looks at some apparatus and sees an x-ray tube. The neophyte, looking at the same place, observes rather "a glass and metal instrument replete with wires, reflectors, screws, lamps, and pushbuttons."[6] One man's observation is another man's closed book or flight of fancy. The notion of observation as the impartial and objective source of evidence for science is bankrupt. Now my answer to the x-ray example was already hinted a little while back: what counts as an observation sentence varies with the width of community considered. But we can also always get an absolute standard by taking in all speakers of the language, or most.[7] It is ironical that philosophers, finding the old epistemology untenable as a whole, should react by repudiating a part which has only now moved into clear focus.

Clarification of the notion of observation sentence is a good thing, for the notion is fundamental in two connections. These two correspond to the duality that I remarked upon early in this lecture: the duality between concept and doctrine, between knowing what a sentence means and knowing whether it is true. The observation sentence is basic to both enterprises. Its relation to doctrine, to our knowledge of what is true, is very much the traditional one: observation sentences are the repository of evidence for scientific hypotheses. Its relation to meaning is fundamental too, since observation sentences are the ones we are in a position to learn to understand first, both as children and as field linguists. For observation sentences are precisely the ones that we can correlate with observable circumstances of the occasion of utterance or assent, independently of variations in the past histories of individual informants. They afford the only entry to a language.

The observation sentence is the cornerstone of semantics. For it is, as we just saw, fundamental to the learning of meaning. Also, it is where meaning is firmest. Sentences higher up in theories have no empirical consequences they can call their own; they confront the tribunal of sensory evidence only in more or less inclusive aggregates. The observation sentence, situated at the sensory periphery of the body scientific, is the minimal verifiable aggregate; it has an empirical content all its own and wears it on its sleeve.

The predicament of the indeterminacy of translation has little bearing on observation sentences. The equating of an observation sentence of our language to an observation sentence of another language is mostly a matter of empirical generalization; it is a matter of identity between the range of stimulations that would prompt assent to the one sentence and the range of stimulations that would prompt assent to the other.[8]

It is no shock to the preconceptions of old Vienna to say that epistemology now becomes semantics. For epistemology remains centered as always on evidence, and meaning remains centered as always on verification; and evidence is verification. What is likelier to shock preconceptions is that meaning, once we get beyond observation sentences, ceases in general to have any clear applicability to single sentences; also that epistemology merges with psychology, as well as with linguistics.

This rubbing out of boundaries could contribute to progress, it seems to me, in philosophically interesting inquiries of a scientific nature. One possible area is perceptual norms. Consider, to begin with, the linguistic phenomenon of phonemes. We form the habit, in hearing the myriad variations of spoken sounds, of treating each as an approximation to one or another of a limited number of norms—around thirty altogether—constituting so to speak a spoken alphabet. All speech in our language can be treated in practice as sequences of just those thirty elements, thus rectifying small deviations. Now outside the realm of language also there is probably only a rather limited alphabet of perceptual norms altogether, toward which we tend unconsciously to rectify all perceptions. These, if experimentally identified, could be taken as epistemological building blocks, the working elements of experience. They might prove in part to be culturally variable, as phonemes are, and in part universal.

Again there is the area that psychologist Donald T. Campbell calls evolutionary epistemology.[9] In this area there is work by Hüseyin Yilmaz, who shows how some structural traits of color perception could have been predicted from survival value.[10] And a more emphatically epistemological topic that evolution helps to clarify is induction, now that we are allowing epistemology the resources of natural science.[11]

Notes

1. A. B. Johnson, *A Treatise on Language* (New York, 1836; Berkeley, 1947).

2. *Philosophy of Science* 3 (1936): 419–71; 4 (1937): 1–40.

3. See W. V. O. Quine, "Speaking of Objects," in *Ontological Relativity and Other Essays* (New York: Columbia University Press, 1969), pp. 1–25.

4. See Quine, "Ontological Relativity, in *Ontological Relativity and Other Essays*, pp. 26–28, especially p. 28.

5. Carnap and Neurath in *Erkenntnis* 3 (1932): 204–228.

6. N. R. Hanson, "Observation and Interpretation," in *Philosophy of Science Today*, ed. S. Morgenbesser (New York: Basic Books, 1966).

7. This qualification allows for occasional deviants such as the insane or the blind. Alternatively, such cases might be excluded by adjusting the level of fluency of dialogue whereby we define sameness of language. (For promoting this note and influencing the development of this paper also in more substantial ways I am indebted to Burton Dreben.)

8. Cf. Quine, *Word and Object* (Cambridge, Mass.: MIT Press, 1960), pp. 31–46, 68.

9. D. T. Campbell, "Methodological Suggestions from a Comparative Psychology of Knowledge Processes," *Inquiry* 2 (1959): 152–82.

10. Hüseyin Yilmaz, "On Color Vision and a New Approach to General Perception," in *Biological Prototypes and Synthetic Systems*, ed. E. E. Bernard and M. R. Kare (New York: Plenum, 1962); "Perceptual Invariance and the Psychophysical Law," *Perception and Psychophysics* 2 (1967): 533–38.

11. See Quine, "Natural Kinds," in *Ontological Relativity and Other Essays*, pp. 114–38.

Part III

Values Ethical and Social

Section 5

Ethical Theory

However the relations among logic, science, and knowledge may be worked out, many naturalists have been convinced that science is crucial to all areas of philosophy, including ethical theory. Abraham Edel, perhaps the most prominent naturalist ethical philosopher over the past four or five decades, suggests here that the scientific method, along with an endorsement of the primacy of matter and the pervasiveness of change, are the most essential traits of naturalism. Edel was born in 1908, received his degree from Columbia University, and has spent his career at the City College of New York and University of Pennsylvania. He is currently research professor of philosophy at the University of Pennsylvania. The article reprinted in this chapter was originally published in 1944 in *Naturalism and the Human Spirit*. Between that time and this, one of the dominant themes in much of Edel's writings on ethics has been the relation between ethical theory and other disciplines, primarily biology and the social sciences. As Edel points out in his article, the nonnaturalist traditions in ethical theory have tended to exclude empirical concerns in favor of more formal analysis. Whether they pursued an abstract, ideal "good" or tried to sort out individuals' ethical intuitions, these traditions have not been terribly interested in what the sciences have to offer. By contrast, since it is likely to take seriously the contexts of individuals, their decision making and their actions, naturalism must also take seriously the study of those contexts, especially the biological aspects of human nature and the knowledge of human relations which can be gained from sociological and anthropological studies. The importance of empirical science, however, does not mean that naturalist ethics can forego formal analysis, as Edel makes abundantly clear here. As he puts the point, it remains necessary to determine what is the raw material of ethical theory. Unlike much other empirically minded ethical theory, for which "pleasure" or the "object of desire" is the basic meaning of "good," Edel argues that the subject matter of ethical theory is in fact choice, or the very act of choosing itself.

The piece by Evelyn Shirk included here was originally published in 1965 as a chapter in her book *The Ethical Dimension*. Shirk is a native of the Long Island suburbs of New York City, and she received her A.B. degree from Wilson College and her Ph.D. from Columbia University. Shirk spent her career teaching philosophy at Hofstra University, where she is currently professor emeritus. In *The Ethical Dimension* Shirk is concerned both with issues in ethical theory in general and with the application of the results of ethical inquiry to contemporary life. In the essay "My Good, Your Good, and Our Good" she treats specifically the relation between egoism and altruism, which is the expression in ethics of the more general problem of the relation of the individual and the community. Shirk suggests that in many of the cultural and intellectual traditions in Western civilization, from Christianity to Hobbes, Freud, and Nietzsche, one finds the individual and the community treated as if they were in conflict. But on this point the same sensitivity to contextuality which influenced Edel's ethical theory reappears in Shirk. The alleged conflict between the individual and the community is in her view artificial. Not the opposition but the interrelation between self and other is the condition in which ethical judgments must be made, so that my good, your good, and our good may intersect rather than contradict one another.

1

Naturalism and Ethical Theory*

Abraham Edel

In our Western tradition ethical analysis has been far from naturalistic. The investigation of ethical values has not been considered an empirical project. The dominant stress has been on insight, introspection, and the immediate apprehension of essences. Results have been framed in the absolutes of conviction rather than the probabilities of science, for scientific method has been held to be inapplicable to the world of the spirit.

For these reasons present-day naturalism is bound to emphasize the need for extending empirical or scientific method to the treatment of values. A naturalistic approach involves reanalysis of ethical ideas in terms of our present logical equipment, designation of the empirical material with which ethics is concerned, and continual testing of the utility of ethical formulations in terms of this material. Insistence on such testing is part of the naturalistic stress on the primacy of matter; recognition that ethical formulations may require alteration is a consequence of noting the pervasiveness of change. Reliance on scientific method, together with an appreciation of the primacy of matter and the pervasiveness of change, I take to be the central points of naturalism as a philosophic outlook.

---

*Originally published in *Naturalism and the Human Spirit,* ed. by Yervant H. Krikorian (New York: Columbia University Press, 1944). Reprinted by permission.

In constructing its ethical theory naturalism today may draw upon two major sources. One is the results of the sciences, especially the biological, psychological, and social studies. The other is the history of ethical theory in which a broad naturalistic current may be traced through portions of many theoretical writings. Thus we may draw upon the formal analysis of Aristotle, who built a structure upon the "nature" of man, which he filled in with biologic material and everyday observations and prejudices. The history of materialism from Democritus through Hobbes and the French materialists to the Marxian school provides a long tradition in which the naturalistic approach achieved maturity. In addition, there is the temporal stress of evolutionary ethical theory and the stubborn empiricism of much of the utilitarian structure. In American philosophy of our own time Dewey in his various writings and Santayana in his *Life of Reason* have to some extent gathered the strands and produced substantially naturalistic ethical systems.

This essay aims both to characterize the approach of naturalism in ethical theory and at the same time to analyze more intensively a few of the problems that are crucial in the internal development of naturalistic ethics itself.

Interpretation of Ethical Terms

The need for empirical interpretation of ethical terms has been strongly denied in nonnaturalistic ethics. For example, Hartmann has written: "The settlement of the matter depends upon demonstrating that there is a self-existent ideal sphere in which values are native, and that, as the contents of this sphere, values, self-subsistent and dependent upon no prior experience, are discerned a priori."[1] In the intuitionist tradition ethical concepts become clear, certain types of action are seen self-evidently to be right or good, to have some moral or value character. As W. D. Ross puts it:

We have no more direct way of access to the facts about rightness and goodness and about what things are right or good than by thinking about them; the moral convictions of thoughtful and well-educated

people are the data of ethics just as sense-perceptions are the data
of a natural science. . . . The verdicts of the moral consciousness of
the best people are the foundation on which he must build; though
he must first compare them with one another and eliminate any
contradictions they may contain.[2]

Of course, as Aristotle says, "this is not evident except to the good
man; for wickedness perverts us and causes us to be deceived about
the starting points of action."[3] Or, to quote Hartmann again,

But it is here just as it is with mathematical insight. Not everyone
is capable of it; not everyone has the eye, the ethical maturity, the
spiritual elevation, for seeing the situation as it is. Nevertheless the
universality, necessity and objectivity of the valuational judgment hold
good in idea. For this universality does not at all mean that everyone
is capable of the insight in question. It only means that whoever is
capable of it—that is, whoever has attained the adequate mentality—
must necessarily feel and judge thus and not otherwise.[4]

In a naturalistic ethics, since ethical statements that are not analytic
or conventional are to be empirically verifiable, there must be among
ethical terms those capable of empirical interpretation. Thus Hobbes
says, "Whatsoever is the object of any man's appetite or desire; that
is it, which he for his part calleth *good*." Similarly, "good" has at various
times been interpreted as productive of pleasure, an object of striving,
of approval, of interest, of enjoyment, of active tension, and so forth.
In all those cases the *ethical* term is being translated into *psychological*
terms, and it is assumed that psychological science or common usage
provides the empirical procedures by which statements containing the
psychological terms may be tested. Or the ethical term may be translated
into "what enables the group to survive"; here the empirical identifications
of the constituent terms are left to sociology and biology, and so forth.

Where in a system or a statement such terms are used and no
empirical interpretation given—even where empirical interpretation is
ruled out—a naturalistic ethics will examine the specific ways in which
the term is applied and from these contexts discover what is in fact

being employed as an interpretation. Thus Aristotle constantly defines the virtues as ways of organizing the raw materials of character according to the mean, and the mean as an ability to act in the right fashion toward the right persons to the right extent, and so forth, and right is defined as what a man of practical wisdom would do in a particular context. We have thus a system worked out for possible application, but it can be applied only if men of practical wisdom are pointed out to us, so that we can learn empirically what right conduct is, or if the empirical procedures by which conduct may be judged right are given us so that we may identify empirically the men of practical wisdom. Ross takes "the moral convictions of thoughtful and well-educated people" as the data of ethics, so that ultimately his system finds its empirical interpretations in what such persons will say. However, precision would require specification of how "well-educated" is to be interpreted. Is it limited to graduation from Oxford or Cambridge, or does it include as well those who have gone to the special higher school reserved for first-born sons of the chiefs among the Maori? Similarly, when we examine Hartmann's *Ethics* we find we need to know the empirical marks of "ethical maturity" and "spiritual elevation." Again, when it is argued that things taken to be good have no common character, so that one may merely list them[5] (for example, pleasure, friendship), the interpretation of good is really reduced to "what is either pleasure or friendship, etc." Usually, however, there is implicit some vague mode of identification, such as "that towards which I have a certain feeling, a feeling grossly recognizable but not yet analyzed" or "that towards which I prefer to guide my conduct," or "that which I am ready to use as grounds for approving of conduct," or even "that which I have been taught to call good." On the other hand, it may be that "good" is being equivocally applied. A term of such wide usage frequently turns out to be equivocal. What is important is that eventually there be some empirical interpretation, whether one or several conjointly. If there is none whatsoever, then the statements containing the term belong to a system having no application.[6]

In the light of the variety of interpretations offered for "good" in the naturalistic tradition, must it be said that *any* interpretation is bound to be arbitrary? Logically, of course, the interpretation has the status of a convention. It is a kind of "coordinating definition," where it is not purely a "nominal definition." But to stress the conventional side overmuch is to lose sight of the mass of material (broadly speaking, man's evaluations) that is to be systematized. As in establishing the meaning for any term by the examination of usage, the result is a convention, but it is one which preserves a wide range of common usage and *thereafter* helps determine what usage will become common. Thus, the initial material does not remain completely fixed, but may at some points be altered in the process. The problem is the same as that faced in attempts to demarcate the subject matter of a science. Physics has been called the science of motion, or of bodies in motion. A more advanced physics may choose, however, to define its subject matter as what its most general formulas apply to and may shift the boundary lines as it finds application beyond for its laws. Thus, in time large portions of physics and chemistry have coalesced because laws have been discovered having consequences exemplified in both.

Similarly, ethics need have no finally delimited subject matter. We may start with any of the traditional interpretations of good—in terms of pleasure, desire, striving, interest, and so forth—and reject one in favor of another on a basis such as that it is too wide or too narrow for the domain we have implicitly or, if possible, explicitly accepted as a starting point. Shall we, for example, start with men's pleasures or men's desires as the material of ethics? That is, shall we decide on "pleasure" or "object of desire" as the interpretation of "good"? Since desire involves a state of deprivation and some pleasures may occur without antecedent deprivation or even anticipation, the two interpretations delimit different though overlapping fields for study. Shall we therefore say that "pleasure" as an interpretation of "good" gives us too wide a field, or that "object of desire" narrows too much the field of ethics? Clearly it does not matter too much which we do. If "pleasure" is taken as the interpretation of "good," we shall have to say that not all of ethics refers to conduct aiming at the satisfaction of desire; if "object of desire" is decided upon, we shall have to say that not all values in conduct are embraced in ethics. The results on any one set of conventions could be translated into the results on any other, if the whole field to which both refer is ordered, whether in one system or several conjointly. The choice between interpretations is therefore to be made in the hope of achieving the most systematic account of the field.

In contrast to a great part of the modern naturalistic tradition[7] I should like to present the view that the act of choosing is the existential material to which ethics most systematically refers, that choosing is not the secondary application of rules, but the primary material whose tendency ethical rules describe and delimit, in short, that ethical terms can best be interpreted as referring to phases and elements of choice.

Our attention is directed toward choice as soon as we begin to examine carefully the actual interpretation of the psychological and social terms into which traditional naturalistic ethics has translated "good." In most cases there is a direct or indirect reference to the initiation of conduct, that is, to choice or a series of choices. Frequently the test of man's being pleased by x is taken to be the fact that he prefers it or keeps on choosing it. The fundamental error of many critics of Bentham and Mill was to take them literally and to assume that the psychological properties of pleasure were crucial to utilitarianism. In terms of their actual procedure in concrete ethical discussion, "to be pleased" meant simply to choose or be ready to choose certain courses of action or sets of results.[8] Similarly, striving, active tension, desire, and enjoyment would be made manifest by actions and sets of choices. Approval and interest might more likely issue in discourse on a person's part, and in the case of pleasure, too, he might report on his feelings. We have, therefore, to decide between a material of ethics that is discovered merely by introspection, or one in which introspective materials will be a part correlated with and checked up by more readily observable conduct. The decision need not be forced upon us. We may try both and see which produces a more systematic science.

Our preference for an interpretation in terms of choice is based on several factors. There is the fact, just noted, that many traditional interpretations are themselves indirect appeals to sets of choices. Again, choice is the beginning of conduct, and ethics, interested in guiding conduct, should pay attention to starting points where control is rendered possible. It is also more objectively discoverable. The reliability of direct inspection of the self and its attitudes may be seriously questioned. The traditional emphasis upon it is a consequence of the dualist's dichotomy of the realm of mind and the realm of nature. Of course, if one of the traditional notions can be rendered more precise and capable of refined distinctions and manipulation, especially if it permit of quantitative measurement, it might be used as the material of ethics even if it be correlated only roughly with choice. But in spite of the hopes of the hedonistic calculus, it cannot be said that present-day studies in the psychology of feeling have achieved results comparable, for example, to the substitution of thermometer readings for sensations of hot and cold in determining therapy.

The task of giving ethical terms an interpretation with reference to choice is an elaborate one. We may illustrate it with the fundamental notion of *good* or *ethical value,* turning our attention in "*x* is good" to the typical case in which *x* is a general term. The problem is tremendously clarified when we compare it to many similar issues in the field of legal theory, where the ethical statement is writ large in the legal statement.

If we take rules of law to be the rules manifest or discoverable as general trends in judicial decisions (a position of growing importance since Gray's classic work *The Nature and Sources of the Law*), we get an interpretation that has the following advantages:

1. It provides a *descriptive* meaning to "a law." Whether such-and-such is law becomes a question for empirical investigation in a clearly designated material.

2. It preserves a *normative* character for a rule of law in two senses, first with reference to the judge who may feel obligated to consider seriously an established rule, and second with reference to the public, who may investigate what they must or must not do, at what cost to themselves.

3. It guarantees no theoretical certainty which does not exist in fact, since it indicates the creative role of judges, in whose decisions even established rules may be weakened or sharply broken.

4. It preserves a fundamental point in permitting the *criticism* of decisions on legal grounds, not merely on moral ones. Thus any one decision may be declared legally wrong in the light of a trend of decisions,

while a whole trend may be estimated in the light of its consistency with prevailing rules in the body of law.

5. It distinguishes between law and the sources of law. Sources may have two senses—what judges in fact look to in rendering decision (statute, precedent, custom, and so forth) and what the causes of decision may be insofar as they lie in the judge and in circumstances.

There is no reason why the analysis of an ethical rule such as "*x* is good" should be simpler than the analysis of the legal rule. An ethical rule thus interpreted states the general trends discoverable in acts of choice, both in the initiation of conduct and in reflection thereon. This interpretation presents the same advantages as its analogue in legal philosophy:

1. It makes the statement that such-and-such is good an empirical proposition referring to the forms of choice in the conduct and reflection of some implicitly specified individual or group.

2. It preserves a normative character, because it is a fact that men often guide themselves in present choice by the character of their previous acts of choice and the results of their reflection upon them. Similarly, in many relationships (child-parent, pupil-teacher, and so forth) people guide their conduct by the choices that others make.

3. It does not guarantee a theoretical certainty even concerning one's own values or judgments of goodness. In spite of the old notion that a man can read off his values from within himself, it is pretty clear that we are frequently mistaken. The interpretation likewise makes manifest the creative role of present choice. It is not simply a point at which a man struggles with himself to follow some preexistent moral rule, but is a genuine pivot for weakening, breaking, continuing or strengthening value, beginning new paths, offering new suggestions, and so forth.

4. It meets the superficial objection that men choose something because it is good, and it is not good because they choose it. For the interpretation allows for the *criticism* of choices, which it could not do if it identified "good" simply with "object of choice" and made ethics identical with psychology. Thus a man's or group's particular choice can be estimated in the light of his or their accepted trend of choice,

and any trend of choice can be criticized in the light of the consistency with the whole body of trends of choice of that individual or group. Finally, corresponding to moral criticism of rules of law is the possibility of extraneous criticism in the light of the trends of choice of some other individual or group than the one concerned.

5. It can distinguish between good and the "sources" of good. Again sources may have two senses—what the person judging looks to (whether it pleases or attracts, whether it is what he has always done, or what venerable people have done, and so forth) and what the causes of choice may be (psychological, social and cultural, physiological, and so forth).

The interpretation offered enables us to resolve two traditional disputes about ethical statements, whether they are "normative" or "descriptive" and whether there are any distinctively ethical statements. In both cases the difficulties are seen to be due to the demand for an absolute answer.

As was pointed out above, ethical statements are descriptive in one context and normative in another. They are descriptive in that they tell about someone's or some group's trend of choice. They are normative to the person or group adopting them as rules of choice. This adoption may be implicit in conduct, or it may be explicit in reflection on conduct. Such adoption in reflection is itself really a choice—*a choice of a class of choices to be made in subsequent conduct on relevant occasions.* Such reflection on conduct, frequently a process of justification for action performed or of analysis of implicit adoption of a rule, may thus be viewed as a second-order choice.[9]

The ethical statement which is normative in respect to each of the first-order choices is descriptive when seen as a second-order choice. Similarly, another second-order choice may function normatively in respect to this one. For example, I may choose in a particular case to persist in a course of action in spite of difficulties and justify myself by saying that strength of character is good. This rule reflectively adopted functions normatively for my particular choice. Descriptively it is, according to our analysis, a second-order choice, to issue in a whole class of kindred actions if I do not falter or retract it. Now, if I justify strength of character by saying that it is an integral element in the achievement of "success" and that success is a good, this latter second-order choice functions normatively in respect to my evaluation of strength of character, and may itself in turn be descriptively considered. There need be no other theoretical end to this process, although for any person or group at any one time there probably is.

The second question—whether there are any distinctively ethical statements—is settled in a similar fashion. Absolutely, there are not, since the implied reference to a particular individual or group enables us to investigate whether these are in fact his or its values (trends of choice). But clearly in each context there are distinctly ethical statements, since any statement such as "I desire this" can be intelligibly countered with "But is it good?" and even "I find this good" can be met with "But is it good?" Aristotle described this part of the ethical process in a fashion which corresponds closely to everyday ethical exhortation. The good in a particular act of choice he called the apparent good. When he did not approve of the choice, it could be called mistaken. Now while this tended to neglect the genuinely pivotal character of the particular act of choice, we may readily rewrite the Aristotelian description in the light of a fuller naturalism. The distinction between my apparent good and my real good becomes that between the object of choice in any single act of choice or reflection of conduct and the object of choice when reflection is ideally complete. Expanding reflection frequently shows the relation of the present particular good to wider goods. It does not necessarily reduce them to a subsidiary role, but examines whether they are permitted by, compatible with, and part of a complex pattern of organized pervasive good which constitutes my "general good." I may thus come to see that what appeared to me to be my good really is my good, or in other cases, really is not my good. First-order choices thus become strengthened or rejected in second-order choices, just as conversely second-order choices are tested and completed or discarded in first-order choices. If a man's analysis of his aims, activities, and role could be furnished with entire certainty, he would be able to follow the advice of Socrates to its conclusion; he would know himself and his real good.[10] The notion of a man's real good is therefore to be understood as the organized system of his choices in an ideally completed process of reflection on choice, anything short of which is his apparent good. Now, since this ideal represents and allows of indefinite perfection, what a man has in mind when he offers principles of what men should do, is the widest system on which he operates at present.

So far we have dealt with "good" as a single term. To complete its interpretation, even for illustrative purposes, we should recognize such differences as are intended by "good" and "a good" on the one hand, and "good for" on the other. This emerges in ethical discourse as the contrast of "end" and "means" or "valuable" and "instrumental." Because so much controversy has centered and still centers in such questions as whether ends and means can be divorced, whether the end justifies the means, and so forth, it is useful to examine the interpretation of these distinctions. This is aided by a closer inspection of choice as an act.

Choice implies that an individual in a definite situation is adopting one of alternative courses of action. He need not be standing still about to embark on one or another path; he may be in the midst of action, choosing whether to continue on one path or turn toward another.[11] A choice is not the occurrence of an action, but its beginning. Hence a choice determines conduct only as part of an act determines the act— that is, by limiting the variety of possible completions. But for the most part that is important enough to determine the direction of the act. Now, since the act of choice is a beginning, it is also capable of analysis with reference to its projected middle and end. This is the source of the categories of means and ends.

It follows on such an approach that "means" and "ends" should not be taken out of the context of a process and made to characterize things or events or actions in themselves. To say that something is an end is to say that it occupies the position of projected terminus in a process involving a means. To say that something is a means is to say that there is a process for which a terminus is projected beyond the means. Whenever ambiguity arises it is always salutary to go back to this point and find the process which those employing the terms have in mind.

It likewise follows that propositions such as "ends and means cannot be divorced" are in one sense analytic.[12] Without reference to possible choice as a beginning of conduct, neither ends nor means can be identified. Given that reference, both are necessarily involved. Something may, of course, be independently "prized" or "wished for," but it cannot be "willed" or "chosen" without the initiating of conduct, hence a reference to means. Nor, again, can there be pursuit of a means without an end, since by definition if the means is pursued as "ultimate" it is itself the end and the distinction of means and end will be made afresh in its own analysis.

Means and ends in choice tend to be or to become systematized separately. Means are judged by their efficacy in achieving projected ends. With the development of the sciences the means in some first-order choices achieve a high degree of separateness. They become "purely technical" questions, and choice tends to pass over them as colorless, to deal with the ends. This refers, of course, to the means in first-order choice. For the process of first-order choice consists in initiating one course of means-end action where the projected terminus is the end to be achieved. We do not know too much about the means required in second-order choice. Here the alternatives are sets of first-order choices (or in traditional language, ethical principles), and the projected terminus is the actual selection or act of will which constitutes first-order choices. The means are our available resources—psychological, physical, and social—for "sticking to our principles" and finding out where they are applicable. The problem is complicated by the role of second-order choice, explored especially by the Freudians, as "rationalizations" rather than embedded principles for future action.

Ends tend to be systematized as a catalogue of "goods" or "values," intended to function as suggestions for first-order choices. The systematization of ends is therefore the very process of second-order choice. In any particular situation in which we wish to apply them we must know some means before choice can take place. The first-order choice occurs when motion toward the end is initiated, regardless of whether it will in fact achieve it.

It is a commonplace that this systematization of ends separately from means has often led to their undue divorce from means and to the view that ethics is concerned solely with ends. This tendency was considerably strengthened by the way in which essence-philosophies ascribed fixed natures to coexistents, issuing in the doctrine of fixed ends or goals in nature. Current naturalistic discussions of the means-end relationship (for example, by John Dewey) have as a constant background the rejection of this doctrine. Such attacks upon the separation of means and ends are not merely pointing out their analytic or conceptual relationship described above. They intend to make empirical assertions about what goes on in men's lives. The factual implications of the naturalistic denial that means and end can be divorced, may be set forth as follows:

1. There is a tremendous variety of men's ends; theoretically, no activity or object would seem incapable of being an end; hence there are no fixed ends.

2. The ends of one group (or person) turn out on empirical investigation to be the means of another, and vice versa.

3. The ends of one group (or person) at one time are found sometimes to be the means of the same group (or person) at another time.

4. Any particular act that is a means in one respect may be an end in another respect.

5. An end in action (or reflection) may come to be regarded as a means in further action (or reflection), and vice versa. Similarly, an end in action (or reflection) may become regarded as a means in reflection (or action), and vice versa.

6. In the process of action and reflection new ends may arise (as well as new means), which may replace the previous ones even before they are achieved.

7. Ends have consequences themselves, and so point beyond, just as means have other consequences besides the end at which they are directed. Hence, reflective appraisal looks beyond both ends and means.

8. To hold to fixed values produces an inability to adapt oneself. The same is true of holding to fixed means without regard to increasing knowledge.

This naturalistic critique is intended to be a clarification, not a destruction, of the means-end relationship. It should not appear, as it sometimes does, that ends are not really ends because they are themselves evaluated by the worth of their consequences. The consequences may be examined simply in order to see whether they detract sufficiently to withhold that particular choice, just as the means may be examined to see whether they are too costly for that particular choice. The status as an end is not affected unless the *usual* consequences or *regularly available* means detract *sufficiently frequently and to such an extent* that this *type of choice* is retracted, or they become so attractive that a new goal emerges in an altered type of choice, so that the former end becomes subsidiary or may even thereafter be treated as a means. Thus, the test of an end is its functioning as an end, and when it ceases so to function in some person or group it has ceased to be an end.

Similarly, the naturalistic critique need not militate against the separate systematization of means and ends. It is one thing to ground the distinction by reference to individuals or groups in spatio-temporal contexts; it is another to destroy the scientific direction which the systematization of means and ends embodies. The procedure of starting with the ends and then adding or subtracting values affected in the means or in the consequences of the ends is an eminently reasonable one. That the starting points may be changed in the process does not challenge the need for starting points in a given context. In this fashion we are able to isolate phases of the events for separate study, although in prediction and planning action we must bring them together again. A statement of *my* ends is a hypothesis which you may test (or I myself may test if I can watch myself with sufficient objectivity) with regard to the set of choices I make in specified types of situation. Normatively, viewed by me (for whom the ends are the objects of second-order choice), the statement of my ends is a set of suggested termini in first-order choices. But both in your predictions about my reaction in particular cases, and in my planning any action in particular cases, attention must be paid to means and consequences before it will be settled whether the end is here and now to be actualized.

There is one objection to the above analysis of the means-end relationship in terms of the middles and projected ends of choices and their systematization. This is the fact that the means-end category is sometimes employed where the temporal reference disappears. For example, it is said that pleasure is the end of some actions, even though pleasure is concomitant with, not consequent to, these actions. This objection is, however, only apparent. The fundamental notion in the means-end relation emerges as causal rather than temporal. It is, however, concerned with practice, and so instead of implying merely "invariant relationship" it never loses the idea of control which is also predominant in the practical use of cause. Thus, actions which pleasure invariably accompanies may be regarded as causally productive of it, hence as means to it.

There is another sense in which pleasure in this example might be regarded as an end. It may be the terminus in the process of reflection on or justification of first-order choice and therefore be an end in a second-order choice. For example, you say that your justification for eating this food is that it has a chocolate flavor, and you want a chocolate flavor because it gives you pleasure. The process of justification thus terminates here in pleasure which you have taken to be good, a stable end in many first-order choices. Nevertheless, we should hardly feel free to use the notion of "means" for whatever enters into the reckoning which culminates in the reflective choice of pleasure as the end, for the result might be that the "means" would turn out to be subsequent to the end, for example, where future pains are accepted in anticipation in the process of validating present pleasures.

It is probably better, therefore, to take the means-end relationship to be limited to the domain in which causality is applicable and the means to retain the idea of "instrumentality." Beyond that, different categories must be developed. These should be terms in which we can express the cost or price of embodying an end choice—whether it be the cost of the means or of the consequences of choosing to act in that particular way. Terms serving such a purpose are: positive value, negative value, better, worse, and so forth. The categories suggested are not identical with the means-end relationship, but are categories in which both means and ends may be evaluated in broadened or altered contexts.[13]

We have thus seen that there is an interpretation of "a good" and "good for" in terms of the end-and-means phases of choice. This strengthens the initial interpretation of "good" by reference to choice. Its utility will become clearer if the remainder of the present terminology of ethics—better, best, bad and its degrees, right, wrong, ought, duty and so forth—is given comparable interpretation by reference to phases of the act of choice or series of acts. The same should be done for the psychological notions of intention, motive, and purpose and for any other term that may be introduced. As suggested above, this need not be a terminology fixed for all time, but is to be judged by its efficacy in enabling us to systematize the realm of ethics. The ideal of such efforts would, of course, be the kind of strictly related terms which some philosophers have elaborated as pure systems.[14] At present such precise formulations seem to me to be premature in that they will not enable us to deal with the complex materials of ethics. It may, for example, even be advisable to give "bad" the independent interpretation of a rule of avoidance in choice rather than regard it as some purely mathematical function of "good."

Verification in Ethics

In theory the problem of verification in ethics should be no different from the same problem in any other field. Historically it has, however, been complicated by the belief that since the material of ethics consists of men's values it is somehow more accessible to men. We ought, accordingly, to be able to peer within ourselves and to read off our values. This assertion that we can discover our values by direct internal inspection rests upon the traditional dualism according to which matter is external and can be only indirectly known, whereas mind is our very being and so can be experienced. The view has had serious consequences upon social science. On the assumption that any man understands them, terms designating attitudes and values have been left without precise empirical analysis. Hence verification has been difficult and ambiguity rampant. For the naturalist, on the other hand, knowledge of the self, its values and activities, is on the same theoretical plane as knowledge of objects. The apparent difference arises only if we confuse experience as an event with ascribing some predicate to that event. Thus, the assertion "I want to help him" does not merely say that I am having some feeling but also attributes a definite character to the feeling. In such matters contemporary psychological theory, with its talk of unconscious desires, has made well known the fallibility of self-knowledge and the pervasiveness of "rationalization." Hence verification is required.

In this part of our discussion we shall touch on problems of verification with respect to the following: assertions about instrumentalities, general and singular ethical statements, ethical statements involving logical relations.

Instrumentality assertions have, of course, been conceded to be empirical by all ethical theories. No special points are involved in their verification. The statement that a certain means will in fact achieve a specified end is tested in ordinary experience or in one or another of the sciences. When complex instrumentalities are to be estimated in the social sciences (for example, whether a system of private ownership of land and industries or a system of public ownership will best provide general security) difficulties arise for two reasons—the complexity of the material and the introduction of questions of value. The latter refers not only to the values of the investigator but also to the fact that the estimation of instrumentalities involves at the same time an assessment of collateral values or disvalues to which the means will give rise. Hence, consideration of means and ends becomes intertwined. Careful analysis, the distinction of problems, and the elaboration of a standard of values alone provide a way of solving the problem.

The verification of ethical statements about "general values" or ends has taken a number of different forms in the naturalistic tradition. The utilitarians, for example, reduced them to instrumentality assertions: "x is good" meant "x on the whole achieves a maximum of pleasure for men." The fundamental value statement "pleasure is the good" was not taken by them to be merely a coordinating definition of "the good." Sidgwick held to the statement on grounds of intuition, whereas J. S. Mill tried to treat it as an empirical. Implicitly, he was aiming at the type of interpretation here offered and arguing that pleasure is the constant object of choice.[15] Once we take a value to be a choice of choices, as was suggested above, the mode of verification sought must lie in the types of choice that would ensue. A general statement that something is good means, therefore, that it is the rule of choice for a specified individual, a group, or all men or groups.

This is what is referred to both in ordinary life and in social psychology when we speak of "holding a value." We judge a man's values by his acts, by the way he chooses between possible alternatives, in part by what he says, and especially by the way he reacts in unexpected situations. We may estimate our own values in the same fashion, reflecting on our reactions and feelings in diverse situations, the directions in which we readily choose or feel impelled to choose, the feelings of satisfaction or regret, joy or remorse, approval or guilt. In the more careful attitude-testing of social psychologists we find a procedure essentially no different, except that it is more calculated to take us off our guard, to reveal inconsistencies in value, and to give a more precise empirical meaning to general values. Thus has arisen, for example, the question whether there really are very general values at all. A student may approve of honesty in general and may manifest it in any matter in which money is concerned, but think nothing of taking assistance during an examination. Is this inconsistency on his part, or is the scope of a general value indeterminate? Which it is for a specified individual or group is a thoroughly empirical problem. Thus, in the extreme case, that of Kant, there seems to be no doubt that he was ready to identify truth-telling by very explicit and unambiguous marks and to follow it in any and every possible subsumption under it.[16] Any deviation on his part would have been an inconsistency. Most people would not devote themselves so completely to a single value, and a more complex hierarchy of values within more or less specified domains is the more common occurrence.

A statement about a group's values is, of course, really about the frequency and distribution of these values among its members and about its use of methods for inculcating a specified pattern. This can be tested in a simple statistical fashion, as we would test "Americans like ham and eggs for breakfast," or in a more complicated way when an interplay of such investigations is required. Thus the assertion "Americans take divorce to be an evil" would require to be tested not only in a study of attitudes on the subject but also by investigations such as: the way in which typical individuals behave in stress situations in the family; the statistical frequency of divorce; the lack of provision in our society for typical family life for children of divorced parents; the behavior of various types of groups toward divorced persons; the state laws governing freedom of divorce and the extent to which they are relaxed;

attitudes—expressed in language and behavior—toward the remarriage of divorced persons; publicity and notoriety attaching to divorce cases and to the lives of the much-remarried.

If we wish to study more minutely the process of verification in ethics, we ought to look not merely at the way in which we contest the holding of a general value by a group or individual—which implies a constancy in the trend of choices—but also at the process by which we verify the fact that a particular act of choice exemplifies or fails to exemplify the trend. For at such points the rule becomes confirmed or rejected.

Broadly speaking, we can observe the particular choice as it takes place, starting from a selective want emerging as a present preference and issuing in the direction of energies toward a particular end. Nevertheless, difficulties of interpretation sometimes occur. Suppose I want wine now and choose port; but suppose that upon sipping it I feel a strong aversion to drinking it and in fact do not. Does this mean that I was mistaken in thinking I wanted it then, or that my mood has changed? Does such a happening confirm or disconfirm the statement I might have made that port is good? Or is the most that we can do merely to discover that given the state of self $s1$ at time $t1$, I assert value $v1$: given $s2$ at $t2$, I assert $v2$, and so forth. Verification in ethics may be analogous to the appeal from Philip drunk to Philip sober, but there must be some constant Philip underlying the two states, or we shall simply say: given the imbibing of so many quarts, the judge condemns to death; given abstention for so many hours, he renders a verdict of acquittal.

The role of the constancy of self must, however, be exaggerated. There is a constancy required in every experiment of any sort, which consists in those assumed facts about which there is agreement in the context of the experiment; for example, statements about perceived qualities. These statements may, however, be made the subject of experiment in a context in which something else is assumed. So it is with the constancy of self in ethical verification. It need never be a general constancy, a "metaphysical" self, an existent behind all bodily phenomena. Rather it is always some specific pattern of tendencies or values, assumed to remain constant throughout the period during which the verification concerning a single value is taking place. If questioned, it suffers the same fate as any hypothesis when it is scrutinzed—it is independently tested in a context of fresh experiment with other assumptions, in this case of some other constancy of self. Thus, in the example given above, my aversion to port at time $t2$ renders it probable that I did not really want wine at time $t1$ if the set of my relevant desires is assumed constant from $t1$ to $t2$ and if other factors may be assumed to have been equal; for example, that this port is a fair sample of the port I drink, or that I have not eaten or drunk in the interval, or that I am not sick. If circumstances did change, then of course it is left undetermined whether I did or did not want wine at $t1$, and may be that I did. Now the task of establishing the constancy of change of relevant desires and circumstances consists in specifying them and gathering all available evidence: for example, whether I am usually fickle in my tastes, whether there was anything unusual taking place at the time (such as cumulative effect of past drinking), the relative frequency with which in the past a desire for wine issued in drinking, and so forth.

This pattern of interpreting the single event becomes clearer if we take a more extended process of choice manifesting the same difficulties. Mr. A. buys a philosophy book as the first step toward reading it, but does not get down to reading it, although he starts several times. Did this act of choice embody the fact that he holds philosophy as a value, that is, does it confirm or disconfirm the view that he values philosophy? Clearly there will be no adequate interpretation of the particular choice until we know how difficult the book was or how representative, whether Mr. A. is overworked at other tasks, whether he constantly buys philosophy books without reading them, whether he engages in philosophical discussion or turns aside every opportunity with an epigram, and so forth. Thus we shall determine objectively whether his value is buying philosophy books (and the rest pious sentiment), in which case the particular act of choice was completed, or really philosophizing, in which case the analysis of the particular will yield the factors which thwarted successful completion of what was then chosen.

The process is usually complex, and most results are tentative; but reflection will show that it is precisely such a process and no other that we employ in testing most of our judgments about our own characters or the characters of others. It is especially clear in reflection upon extreme changes in attitude. The confirmed bachelor, after being happily married, may decide that he had always really liked the opposite sex and point to actions he had hitherto incorrectly interpreted. The religious convert may desire to demonstrate an altered self and therefore point to factors which produced a rapid change. The ivory-tower poet who becomes socially conscious may have altered his values, which he would show by his attitude to his previous work, or he may have retained the values, but have come to realize that they were socially grounded and required a special type of attained social stability.

The cases most difficult of analysis are those in which a man confesses that a value $v1$ previously held has given away to some contrary value $v2$ and yet still insists on calling $v1$ a mistake. His assertion would seem upon analysis to imply that there is some constant value (V), which seemed to him to yield or require $v1$, which he came over a course of time to hold for its own sake and later discovered to be incompatible with V, which really required $v2$ as an accompanying element. Thus, a man may abandon a profit system ($v1$) for a socialist system ($v2$), having genuinely hitherto approved of the first, whereas public security may be the constant value (V) with which he formerly associated $v1$ and now associates $v2$. The relation is not a simple one of means and ends. It is to be noted that the change of value, although it may on rare occasions take the form of a whirlwind substitution, would regularly seem to involve some constant value which acts as a pivot for the transformation. But the pivot of one change may itself be shifted when some fresh value has become stable enough to act as a pivot.

We have now seen roughly the way in which verification occurs when a man has been asserted correctly or mistakenly to hold a certain value, when there has been a change of value, and when a value formerly held was said to be mistaken. In all these the conception of the self implied is thoroughly empirical, that of a core of dominant, relatively stable values or a pattern of choice. The breadth and continuity of the self is likewise to be empirically determined and may vary considerably from person to person. Thus the traditional attempt to build up a whole good for a whole man by which he may check his present desires[17] is merely formal, referring to the fact of a stable core of values at any one time by which others are tested. If it attempts to be material and invariably to cover all fields of a man's possible interest and the whole duration of his life, it runs the risk of being unwarranted generalization. If it threatens us with the bogey of a completely disintegrated self as the only alternative to its description of the unity of life, its picture is palpably false. We may readily grant (being farsighted philosophers) that we value a kind of self which lays its plans and guides its choice on a full-life basis, a self for whom "the same thing is always painful, and the same thing always pleasant, and not one thing at one time and another at another; he has, so to speak, nothing to repent of."[18] But this represents a definite preference, and quite other preferences do in fact occur. The period of life may be shortened in calculated comparison to a brief span of glory, as Achilles chose; or some may live for life's first half without in fact, as the moralist would like it, regretting their choice thereafter. Or again, some may in fact approach the type of a series of discrete states with a minimum of connection, and choose relatively for the moment. Differences of type are sometimes made manifest by the general attitude, after a large-scale change of values, toward the values abandoned. Some may repent of the past, others, treating it as a discrete and now detached portion of their lives, may think serenely, even benignly, upon their earlier folly. Still others may reckon the past to have been appropriate to its time of life and inexperience. We are obviously in a field in which insufficient empirical classification and study of forms has been carried on. From the naturalist's point of view the important thing is that in such a study we are dealing with ultimate values, that is, values functioning in those who hold them for the determination of other more special kinds of choice and frequently operating without being clearly recognized in spite of their pervasiveness, or perhaps just because of it and because they are less likely to alter. But in recognizing that they function as ultimate in the lives of specific individuals or groups, naturalist ethics does not give them an intuitive or transcendental status. Ultimate values can be explained by showing historically how they arose, replaced predecessors if any, and what were the determinants of this process. Ultimate values are simply intense or pervasive attitudes of men in a natural and social world functioning in a special way with relation to their other values. In the light of varying values—arising out of individual and social change—they may be accepted or rejected; in the light of growing understanding they may occasionally be susceptible of increasing control.

Our final problem in the analysis of verification is the interpretation to be given to apparently logical relations in ethical statements. Although frequently these are designated by logical terms, such as "contradiction" or "consistency"—as well as by metaphorical terms, such as "coherence" or "harmony," "conflict" or "clash," and by more neutral terms, such as "compatibility"—the reference turns out to be for the most part to material relations the establishment of whose presence involves actual verification, not merely logical certification. This emerges most clearly in an analysis of the various conditions under which the term "contradiction" is employed in dealing with ethical material. It may, of course, be used in its logical sense, as when I say, "I value this x," and you reply, "It is not the case that you value this x." But apart from the logical relation of propositions, we find the word applied to the act of valuing and to the relations of objects of value (object including activity), or briefly speaking, values.

With respect to the act of valuing, it must be noted that to value and to disvalue—that is, to think good or choose as good and to think evil or reject as evil—are not contradictories. "I value this x" and "I disvalue this x," even if they refer to the same x at the same time in the same respect, are not contradictories; for x may be indifferent, that is, an object neither of value nor of disvalue. In fact, it may be questioned whether they need even be contraries. Although a man may not both do and not do x (when x is in action) and though he cannot, perhaps, wholeheartedly choose both to do and not to do x—for this would be akin to moving in two opposite directions at the same time—he may not merely waver in the sense of being undecided, but actually feel both drawn and repelled. It is the traditional predicament of Hamlet and of Catullus when he poured out his "Odi et amo." Modern psychology of the unconscious makes much of this phenomenon of ambivalence. Plato used it to prove that there are different parts of the soul which may aim in different directions, finding a difference in the self when there was none in the object of desire and aversion.[19]

If this is the case, valuing and disvaluing cannot simply be spoken of as contradictory acts.[20] Three sets of conditions, however, may be suggested which might lead to the employment of the term or analogous ones.

1. It might be known that a specified individual is of such a character that his inclinations are generally transformed into decisive choice, either for the most part or with reference to a special class of values. On the basis of this *knowledge of character* it might be said in his case, or in those domains, that valuing and disvaluing were opposed, contrary, or (a better term) incompatible. Likewise, for a group, either in general or in a specific domain, the same assertion could be given a rough statistical meaning.

2. It might be known, from the nature of a certain type of activity and the circumstances generally surrounding it or conditions required to bring it about, that there is little likelihood of ambivalence about it. On the basis of such *knowledge of the activity and its conditions* one might speak of valuing and disvaluing it as incompatible.

3. There might be an additional value presupposed or used implicitly as a standard of reference, whose realization will be hindered by both valuing and disvaluing. Thus, if I value wholehearted choice and ambivalence yields either no completed choice, or a deflection into fancy, or the suppression of one alternative which retards the decisiveness of the other choice, I may call the constituent act of valuing and disvaluing contrary or incompatible. This is obviously a derived incompatibility, since what they are incompatible with is the achievement of wholehearted choice. On the other hand, if the regulative value were the creation of intense feelings, provoking self-searching, the simultaneous valuing and disvaluing of the same object would no doubt be reckoned simply as a cooperation of causes. On the basis of their *effect upon some implicit value's achievement,* acts of valuing and disvaluing may be deemed incompatible.

These three sets of conditions have been discussed with reference to the valuation and disvaluation of the same object by the same person. The analysis will likewise apply whether the subject of the acts be the same or different, whether the acts be all of valuing or all of disvaluing or some of the one and some of the other and whether the object be one in number, the same in form, or different in form. Likewise, the analysis should apply to groups, whether in a rough statistical sense or with reference to the organized activities of groups.[21] Thus, we may examine the general forms of "A values x" and "B values y," remembering that many substitutions can be made of A, B, x, y, and that "disvalue" in either statement can be substituted for "value." When it is known from the existent character of A and B, or from the nature and conditions of x and y, or simply as a probability from examination of a series of cases of the same form that if either statement is true the other must be false, then, assuming that both may be false, the statements are of course contrary, and the acts of valuing concerned are incompatible. The third condition specified above would refer to the case in which both acts are not incompatible in this sense, but there is some implicit value z on the basis of which it is known that the existence of the acts of valuing of x by A and of y by B would prevent the actualization of z.

The third condition, it will be noted, goes beyond the others in being concerned, not with the possible coexistence of two or more acts of valuing, or holding of values, but with the effect upon the actualization of the value held. By actualization of a value is here meant, not the fact that something of that form is actually chosen or valued, but that the end chosen is actually attained or produced. It is, perhaps, attainment that most people have in mind when they speak of incompatible values. For, as we saw, choice involves reference to a beginning and an end of some determinate activity, and the end or outcome is what becomes systematized as a general value. "Value x is incompatible with value y" therefore would yield on analysis: "A values x," and "B values y" and "in specified circumstances the achievement of x by A and y by B cannot both occur." It must be remembered again that A and B may be the same or different, individual or group, and that some revisions in the precise mode of verification have to be made in the various cases. In general the analysis given for acts of holding a value will apply here. There is, of course, no correlation between the incompatibility of the acts of valuing and the incompatibility of the values, except when the former has been assigned on the third type of condition examined above. In the other cases, the compatibility of the acts of valuing is a necessary precondition for the incompatibility of the values, though the latter may be stated abstractly without the existence of the former. For if the two acts of valuing cannot occur together, there is no problem concerning the compatibility of two objects of value. In short, to judge values to be incompatible we must know, from the character of the actors or the nature of the objects or the circumstances in which the values would have to be achieved, that the values cannot be achieved together; or there must be reference to some implicit or recognized value whose achievement would be prevented by the joint achievement or attempt to achieve the values at issue which are derivatively called incompatible.

It follows that the incompatibility of specific values is relative to a system of natures, conditions, and sometimes other values. Hence only on the assumed constancy of such a system can the specific values be reckoned as stably incompatible. Close attention is therefore required when we are dealing with the values or aims of large opposing groups, to their conditions and to predictions concerning the duration of these conditions, the way in which these conditions will change, and whether and how the values involved will be altered. For value apparently compatible may turn out to be incompatible once we discover hitherto unrecognized consequences of their attempted actualization; and these very consequences may differ from age to age. A judgment of large-scale opposition of values, such as the Marxian theory of the irreconcilability of the aims of capital and labor, therefore involves a whole social science and complex historical analysis.

We have so far used predominantly the terms "compatible" and "incompatible," implicitly defining the former as the contadictory of the latter with reference to values and acts of valuing. "Consistent," taken in the literal sense of "standing together," would be a good synonym for "compatible" if it had not so definitely a logical usage. "Contrary" seems not unsuitable for some purposes we examined, and "contradictory" might even be used in those special cases in which the scene has been so carefully set that only two values monopolize the field, neither capable of realization without impeding the other. On the whole, however, it would be conducive to clarity to limit the terms which have a distinct logical flavor to the relations of propositions describing the values and system of conditions and to employ the remainder of the terms at present available for acts of valuing and values. Thus, acts of valuing might best be called "compatible" if they are "mutually tolerant," whereas values which we have referred to the actualization and coexistence of conduct might be called "coherent" if they "stick together" or "conflicting" if they "strike at one another" or "clash." A fuller analysis than that here begun will no doubt find more fruitful distinctions and, if necessary, enlarge the vocabulary sufficiently.

Relation of Ethical to Nonethical Systems

The logical pattern of the possible relationship between an ethical and a nonethical system is, of course, the same as for any two systems. That is, terms of one and terms of the other system, each independently interpreted, are empirically correlated. If ethical terms are thus correlated with terms in another system, ethical statements might thereafter turn out to be deducible from statements in the nonethical system. We may illustrate by the complete connections which exist in the following somewhat Hobbesian theory. In this, the ethical expression "x is good" is taken to be correlated with the psychological expression "A desires x." And since feeling is declared to be a kind of interior movement, "A desires x" is eventually translated (with the aid of correlation statements into the language of physics as "the complex of particles, A1, A2, A3 is moving in a certain fashion with regard to x." This is therefore correlated with "x is good." The remaining terms of ethics being likewise translated, it would then be hoped that the generalizations of ethics could be deduced from physical laws. Thus "self-preservation is good" might be deducible from a physical law that certain movements (into which desire was ultimately translatable) would occur whenever certain other movements (into which self-preservation was resolved) occurred. This complete translation of terms and the complete deducibility of ethical from physical generalizations would constitute an ideally necessary connection—what has traditionally been called the complete "reduction" of ethics to physics.

The direction of such "reduction" is not limited a priori. Thus, even when ethical terms are translated into psychological ones, it is impossible for the psychological to be translated into something other than physical terms. This sort of thing has actually happened in some evolutionary theories, where "x is good" is equated with the "biological" assertion "x has survival value for the group," and the latter is accompanied by the belief that evolution is the deity's special plan to make the universe culminate in man. Hence the ultimate translation of "x is good" would be "x fulfills the divine plan." But it could equally well have ended in a physical rather than a theological translation.

The traditional problem of "free will" versus "determinism" may itself be translated into the empirical question of the relation of ethics to nonethical systems. On this analysis, free will is equivalent to insistence on the "autonomy" of choice and the ethical system; determinism is equivalent to the belief in (or hope for) discoverable interrelations of ethical and nonethical systems. Complete or universal determinism postulates a complete "reduction"—usually to physical terms and laws.

The fact that ethics has not so been "reduced" is sometimes taken by nonnaturalistic philosophies to be evidence for "emergent qualities," "autonomous domains," or a dualism between the mental field, where ethics belongs, and the physical, where the physical sciences fall. A naturalistic approach is committed neither to such inferences or to a complete determinism. The failure to discover the interrelations of ethics and nonethical domains has no more significance than the inability to "reduce" psychology to physiology or physiology to physics. For the relation of the sciences is an empirical matter, and there is no a priori reason to believe that complete "reduction" of any domain to another must be either impossible or inevitable. Natural events are rich enough and complex enough so that relatively irreducible phases are possible. Any assertion of ultimate result remains program, not metaphysical fact.

Nevertheless, the development of common experience and scientific knowledge has been sufficient to indicate that the act of choice is not utterly unrelated to other natural events occurring around it. A choice itself is an event in nature, complex indeed, but clearly grounded in the influences of physical, psychological, and social factors. There is no reason why the preconceptions of an idealist or a dualist philosophy should linger to bar the most intensive exploration of its relations. The field of ethics not only may be but is being constantly developed by the progress of all other sciences, especially the psychological and social studies.

Since any attempt to describe the interrelations of ethical and nonethical phenomena is bound to be sketchy or progammatic, I shall limit the discussion to brief comments on the empirical studies from which it seems to me ethics can most profit at present.

The first of these is the careful scrutiny (psychological and phenomenological) of the act of choosing or valuing. Ordinary language bears witness to possible differences within the act itself. There is wholehearted choice and halfhearted choice, and a whole possible scale of intensity. To study it one would have to focus attention on the way in which alternative rules and developed habits function in the act of choice. This might be done both introspectively and by observing the relative frequency of specific types of choice in regulated situations, or by any other device the scientific imagination may formulate. In fact, Aristotle began this study at some length in his ethics, when he distinguished the virtuous man from the continent man and the vicious from the incontinent. The continent and the incontinent have internal struggles in their choice, the former checking evil desires, the latter yielding to them against his better judgment; the virtuous man has no evil desires to fight against, whereas the vicious man takes pleasure in carrying out his evil desires and so has no pain, remorse, or struggle concerning them. In terms of such an investigation ordinary phrases like "strength of character" will find more precise empirical significance.

Again, within the evaluating act, on its reflective level, ordinary language reveals a differentiated series of degrees of approval and disapproval which certainly can be rendered more precise and may or may not be correlated with the previous differentiations in choice. Hartmann, for example, works such a rising scale out of the predicates employed by Aristotle in the *Nicomachean Ethics*. The predicates are: worthy of praise (ἐπαινετόν); beautiful (καλόν); worthy of honor (τιμητόν); lovable (φιλητόν); admirable (θαυμαστόν); superb (μακαριστόν).[22] It may well be the case that in scales of this sort different shades of emotion are attached to each predicate. Or perhaps in some instances there is also a differentiation in fields of subject matter. Such analysis will aid in the discovery of any consistent scales which may be implicitly employed and in the development of such scales as may be deemed desirable.

The second study is the discovery (historical and anthropological) of the varieties of values that have actually existed. This involves both description and conceptual refinement. It examines, for instance, the content of jealousy among present-day Eskimos, French, and Americans; and the persons to whom reverence is obligatory in various societies; and how the notion of honor differs in a knight quick to resent insult and a businessman scrupulous in paying his debts. Inevitably the problem will arise why in each case differing manifestations are grouped together as exemplifying the same value and whether in fact they should be so grouped. Solutions to this problem will also provide empirical meaning to broad values. Sometimes the varying content will be found to have a psychological unity in the fact that there are different ways in which the same deep-seated impulse is expressed, as in the sexual drive. Sometimes the unity will lie in the fact that there are different ways of meeting a common social need, as in avoiding in-group conflict. Often the unity lies in the production of a similar effect; for example, the common ideal of justice may express merely the widespread desire for the removal of suffering at the hands of others. Often the common element will turn out to be merely analogy, as when desire for prestige is treated as a form of acquisitiveness. In such cases the result may be the substitution of several motives for a single notion. This general study may also provide empirical criteria for the affirmation of identical elements in cultural diversity. For the student of ethics it will likewise suggest tentative patterns which may be applied with alterations to meet problems within another culture. In short, the task is not merely fact-gathering, to be performed by handmaiden sciences, but it entails philosophical analysis throughout.

The third study (involving all the sciences, from biology and physiology to economics, social psychology and history) is the search for causal elements or necessary conditions of men's choice. The holding of a particular value or pattern of values by an individual or group is not simply a brute fact; it calls for causal explanation. Several factors point toward the possibility of success in such a study. There is the common core of conscious education of taste or preference in ourselves and others. There is a growing recognition that values are not innate traits or elements of character stamped in men by nature, but products in the growing child and still malleable adult of tremendous cultural and social pressures. Our insight into the force of tradition, the pervasive influence of economic factors, and the critical role of existent attitudes has grown tremendously. We thus realize that the fashioning of values is a task carried on in a society whether knowingly or in ignorance of what we are in effect doing. The observation around us of mass transformations in fundamental values has directed attention to the study of change. The large-scale investigation of causality in choice may perhaps be best carried out by examining historically what changes in values go along with other social changes and tracing more minutely their relations.

The naturalistic tradition in philosophy has constantly pointed to the need for causal examination of values and the relation of ethical to nonethical phenomena. It has sought the aid of the prevailing sciences and in turn mapped programs for them. As the sciences grew, naturalism had concomitant phases. It interpreted values on a physical analogy as special movements of the particles or internal movements. Nineteenth-century naturalism was to a great extent biological, under Darwin's influence. Marxian materialism was an exception, and it marked the beginning of a fuller naturalism, which recognized the causal role of social factors.

The study of conditioning elements of men's values and the broad discovery that they lie to a great extent somewhere in the domain of human activity have revealed the possibility of the redirection of values. In spite of the shuddering of some poets and some philosophers, mankind at large would probably welcome a discovery that the milk of human kindness could be injected into the bloodstream by means of a gland extract or even, as some novelistic psychology would have it, that men could shift their character values with their climate. Although the problem is tremendously more complicated than these simple dreams, there is no reason to oppose the causal study of values on the ground of a special human spontaneity called "freedom of the will." There is plenty of room for spontaneity in human affairs, but it is an empirical phenomenon that falls within the context of men who are striving to achieve their values, to redirect some, and preserve others. It is not an explanation of their doings. The mere assumption of freedom tends to make men leave the direction of change of values to chance. Freedom, in a naturalistic ethics, is to be found in the widest understanding that may be attained of the conditions and causes of choice, so that choice may be a function of knowledge.

What we have spoken of as the redirection of values is not, however, an appeal from the ethical to the nonethical. It is carried on within a set of values and involves altering some to preserve or enhance or achieve others. It occurs in social groups, as in our personal lives, when a conflict of values drives us to seek consistency by shifting some goals to make room for others, when we discover fresh goals emerging and estimate the interplay of means and ends. Redirection of values is not the mere occurrence of this process, but its conscious occurrence.

The stress of a naturalistic ethics emerges most clearly in the analysis of the redirection of social values. A naturalistic ethics does not consider the problem to be purely a matter of the individual's purification of his heart, whether on the principles of a specific theology or in some moral rearmament. It does not appeal to an unknown good to justify the evil that exists or to men's patience and resignation to enable them to endure. It does not urge that men's wickedness is a ground for their misfortunes. It does not turn ends into autonomous internal values restricted to consciousness and disregard means as mere technicalities. It does not commit itself to eternal values irrespective of their specific content and social consequences. On the contrary, it insists on the continuous testing of goals in the light of their social functioning, on the deep roots of values in the practices and institutions of a society, on the necessity of altering institutions and social forms as part of the process of achieving and redirecting values, on the need for a comprehensive view of the way in which values fit together, what causal props they have, what are to be the consequences of various means. In short, the naturalistic moral philosopher, estimating the values of his group or society, cannot stop short of fashioning a whole conception of good men functioning well in a good society.

Notes

1. Nikolai Hartmann, *Ethics,* trans. Stanton Coit (New York: Macmillan, 1932), pp. 1, 165.

2. W. D. Ross, *The Right and the Good* (Oxford: Clarendon Press, 1930), pp. 40–41.

3. *Nicomachean Ethics,* 1144a, 34–36.

4. Hartmann, *Ethics,* pp. 1, 225.

5. G. E. Moore's view in *Principia Ethica* is an illustration of this position.

6. The use of a metaphysical interpretation merely postpones the demand for an empirical one. "Good" may be translated into theological terms as "according to the nature God has implanted in man." The nonnaturalistic elements arise in the question of empirical procedures for identifying the translation. On the other hand, where "right" is equated with "what God wills" it has sometimes been argued that God wills it because it is right, and not that it is right because God wills it. This is, in effect, denying the correctness of "what God wills" as the primary interpretation of "right."

7. Choice does occupy a central position in the ethics of Plato and Aristotle.

8. Cf. the standard Latin form *placuit senatui* for "the senate decided."

9. A first-order choice is thus a direct initiation of conduct, a second-order choice an indirect one. That first-order choices do not thereafter always manifest the second-order choice shows simply that a good intention of firm conviction may falter on a specific occasion. Neither does a first-order choice always get carried through with its initial ardor.

10. This enables us also to understand why Socrates stubbornly adhered to the view that no one voluntarily chooses evil; for to choose is to evaluate. Of course his assertion could not be proved, since its logical status was that of a proposed interpretation.

11. Hence, frequently "to avoid a choice" is itself to make a choice.

12. In what sense such statements are intended to be empirically verifiable will be discussed below.

13. In terms of such categories we can analyze questions like "Does the end justify the means?" This one is obviously in need of considerable analysis. Clearly some ends justify some means and not others. In general form, it is like asking, "Is the object purchased worth the cost?"

14. For example, A. P. Brogan, "The Fundamental Value Universal," *Journal of Philosophy* 16 (1919): 96–104; Felix Cohen, *Ethical Ideals and Legal Systems* (New York: Falcon Press, 1933), chapter 3; Albert Hofstadter and

J. C. C. McKinsey, "On the Logic of Imperatives," *Philosophy of Science* 6 (October 1939): 446–57.

15. In his argument that pleasure is good because all men aim at it, Mill implied that good meant object of preference. He then proposed to show that pleasure is in fact the constant object of preference. But in preparing for the test, he defined pleasure in such a way that being pleased was indistinguishable from preferring (*Utilitarianism,* chapter 4).

16. See his essay, "On a Supposed Right to Tell Lies from Benevolent Motives," in *Critique of Pure Reason and Other Writings in Moral Philosophy,* ed. L. W. Beck (Chicago: University of Chicago Press, 1949).

17. For example, Henry Sidgwick, *The Methods of Ethics* (Charlottesville, Va.: Ibis Pub., 1986), 7th ed., book 3, chapter 13, especially, pp. 381–83.

18. Aristotle, *Nicomachean Ethics,* 1166a, 27ff.

19. Plato, *Republic* 4, 439–40.

20. For the social counterpart of such ambivalence see Robert S. Lynd, *Knowledge for What?* (Princeton, N.J.: Princeton University Press, 1940), pp. 60–62, where antithetical assumptions in American life are brought together.

21. The discussion may readily be extended to cover general acts of valuing if it be remembered that a general value judgment states a preference covering most or all occasions of relevant choice, with varying standards for the strictness of "most." Whether two such statements are contraries is readily apparent.

22. Hartmann, *Ethics,* 2, pp. 58–60.

2

My Good, Your Good, and Our Good*

Evelyn Shirk

My Worth and the Worth of Others

The Christian tradition has had considerable influence in developing and spreading the notion that altruism is a good and egoism an evil. What essentially have these terms meant? In a very basic sense, "egoism" means placing one's own claims above those of another, while "altruism" means placing another's claims above one's own. In Christianity these ideas have some subtle overtones of meaning. Particular emphasis is placed upon the conviction that man is born in sin, that the very fact of individuality and selfhood is the source of evil. Impressed by the consideration that organic life necessitates mortality, that birth sentences man to death, Christianity stresses the original isolation of each man both from God and his fellow men. Biological uniqueness sharpens and intensifies experience and makes it personally urgent. Each man is a physiological isolate. No one can feel pain, or breathe or digest for anyone else. The two greatest virtues outlined by Christianity are the emotional postures of charity and humility, attitudes which serve to

*Originally published in Evelyn Shirk, *The Ethical Dimension* (New York: Meredith Publishing Co., 1965). Reprinted by permission.

351

minimize a sense of self and heighten a sense of others. It is only through loss of self in service to God that the isolate which is man becomes reunited with powers outside of himself and gains for himself the quality of eternity. The self for Christianity is spirit, imprisoned by the body. When spirit is freed from its physiological and worldly necessities, it can be one with God. Even in those strains of Christianity in which self, apart from body, remains individuated and is judged, its isolation has been overcome; its self-centeredness has been conquered.

Self-interest, in short, is man's most besetting sin. And Christianity sees man as having great difficulty extending his horizon beyond his itching nose. It takes for granted that human nature apart from the experiences of grief and from the awareness of sin, has, as its most fundamental propensity, the tendency to overvalue the self, to be unaffected by the presence of others and unconcerned with their interests. The formulation of the Golden Rule indirectly embodies this conviction. To do unto others what you would have done unto you is to imply that self-regard is natural and regard for others derivative, that concern for others must be shaped by utilizing the only available model, namely, that of self-concern, that treatment of self will be indulgent while treatment of others will be niggardly. The Golden Rule presupposes that the experiences selfhood entails are so central that conduct toward others can be guided by no more reliable model. The greatest of all commandments for human conduct, as stated originally in the Old Testament, is to love thy neighbor as thyself. Self-love is taken as the given, the inevitable, and the preliminary datum of ethical life. Love for others is learned. So difficult is it to achieve this that lessons in suffering are sometimes required to teach it. The self, as the source of evil, the instigator of sin, the delimiter of perspective, is a burden. The major task of ethics is to learn to neglect it, to despise it as an end, to debase it and to be deaf to its bodily needs. Christian martyrdom consists in the triumph over self and its demands. The monastery and its rule of poverty, chastity, and obedience offer the means of accomplishing this most difficult task of vanquishing the natural man. Salvation consists of losing self to others and submerging it in God.

Not only does the Christian tradition take self-interest for granted as the primary fact of existence, but it has further been taken to imply that your good and mine are inevitably opposed and in conflict. It has been understood to mean that service to one's own needs necessitates neglect of those of others, that love of self excludes love of others, that true love of others precludes love of self and that such an either/or alternative faces every valuer. Either he loves God or mammon, either he is dominated by self-interest or he must, with great difficulty, substitute love of others for it.

The Theory of Native Egoism: Hobbes and Freud

Hobbes agrees with the Christian tradition that individual life pursued solely as an end in itself is "solitary, poor, nasty, brutish, and short."[1] Hobbes understands the political state as a body, like man himself. He concurs with the Christian view that both man and the state are committed to the so-called first law of life—to the sustaining and preserving of self and to its corollary, the necessity of self-interest. Men are centers of militant, aggressive self-regard. They exist in a state of perpetually incipient warfare each against every other. To each man every other is his natural competitor, his born enemy. Each wants everything for himself and all are embattled by the struggle to get anything. Mankind, apart from the confining bounds and limitations put on its innate expression of desire by the civil state, is in a state of war of all against all.

So primary does Hobbes see the demands of self-love to be that even so-called charitable or sympathetic acts—acts which in some way express concern for others—have an ultimate basis in self-interest. We give charity because we ourselves do not wish impoverishment, our gifts serving as a sort of magical agreement with fate to protect us. We give love because we want the service we can then inveigle from others. We give of ourselves in order to manipulate others into giving us what we want. Regardless of how overtly altruistic his acts seem to be, man is hedged in by uncontrollable self-interest; he carries forever the heavy burden of insatiable self-love.

Being interested in the political rather than the religious implications of self-love, being more concerned with the relation of human life to the civil state rather than to God, Hobbes draws his picture of the state as the alleviator of this human ill. When wisdom is incorporated into the state, it can bring succor to the human plight of insatiability. In and through rationality, men see the necessity of compromise with their needs and agree on a civil authority to adjudicate conflict as fairly as possible. Hence the state exists to provide legal regulation of the self-interest of each in order to permit limited but secure expression of the insistent desires of all. The state serves to control man's natural bent, curbing his hunger for freedom but rewarding him with guarantees of safety and order.

Freud expresses the same type of pessimistic sentiments as Hobbes and the same disillusioned temperament in contemplating human affairs. Being concerned with the psychological welfare of the individual rather than his political destiny, Freud focuses his attention on the person. For Freud, the human animal driven by the insatiable desire to be, to have, to hold, to consume, and to destroy, is primarily a bundle of primordial energy which is undirected and undifferentiated. He seethes with needs and acts in a blind struggle to fulfill them. A drive for life controls him; a fierce push to possess and to incorporate the world into the self drives him. This aspect of the psyche Freud calls the "id." Its activities are not immoral but nonmoral. They are impervious to considerations of time, place, and condition of existence. The drives of the id just *are;* they are inescapable.

Civilization, however, soon sets limits to blind primordial egocentrism. Enculturation puts restrictions in the form of social rule and sanction on the gasping infant. The young child, being totally dependent on his parents for love and care, soon learns to restrict his own self-centeredness through the painful prospect of loss of the love which is necessary to his existence. "The process of socialization" means a capitulation to the demands of others. Through this process the young human psyche incorporates or internalizes the commands and prohibitions of those about him into himself, and a new psychic entity, the conscience of "superego," is generated. Desires then become redirected or channeled into socially useful acts. But the originally unbridled pleasure principle or "id drives" continue to meet the reality principle or the demands of society in incessant combat. Civilization, in short, has reaped its discontents.

Freud, however, cannot resist attacking the Christian concept of love for the universalized other or one's "neighbor." "Love" for Freud is a sexual merger of two excluding all others. Hence love for all others is meaningless. The very notion of brotherly love is a myth and a deception, and an attempt to realize it is but a disguised and attenuated form of repressed sexual desire.

The Justification of Egoism: Nietzsche

For Nietzsche, egoism and self-love are not only necessary, they are also infinitely desirable. Their unlimited pursuit is the condition of human excellence. Also an opponent of the Christian doctrine of brotherly love, Nietzsche turns Christian values upside down or "transvalues" them, and repudiates them as entirely inappropriate to this world. Impressed with the facts of life as Darwin had presented them, impressed with the conviction that genus homo battled its way to the benefits of civilization by cunning and violence, Nietzsche asserts that to change this order of events is to sacrifice precious gains. Christian virtue is for weaklings unable to face the facts of the world Darwin described. It is inadequate to preserve life. Only a superman or strong man— one who has the physical and moral stamina and courage to recognize and become reconciled to these facts—is the rightful inheritor of the earth. The morally strong can face a world of problematic situations where such pleasantries as love of one's neighbor is inept if not impossible. Only the weak need the reward of heaven as a compensation for self-denial. The strong renounce rewards and assert their defiance as men. Only the strong can be the model for action, and the superman rightfully scorns his weaker brother in the interest of the improvement of the human species and its conditions of life.

According to Nietzsche, the weak deserve their fate. They are of little asset either to themselves or to the species. The Christian virtues of love and charity are subtle countermoves on the part of the weak to protect themselves from the strong. By means of the doctrine of brotherly love and through threat of punishment for its infringement, the weak hope to seduce the strong and clip their Samsonian locks. To many, Nietzsche is an anti-Christ who reveals the ethical horrors implicit in a translation of the facts of the Darwinian world into ethics. Very probably his interpretation of the ethical meaning of those facts contributed to the feeling that the teaching of evolution was a special kind of attack on Christianity.

Unlike Freud and Hobbes, who are troubled by the conflict between self and society, Nietzsche finds this conflict to be ethically desirable. The natural self-interest of the individual is the basis of human daring and innovation and the enemy of herd morality or slavishness.

Competition and Cooperation in Nature

The inevitability of self-interest as a pervasive part of human nature is indicated by the very facts of organic life. Part of what we mean by living is precisely the activities subsumed under the notion of self-preservation. So vividly do all species exhibit a propensity to persist that it has excited both the contempt and the awe of many thinkers. Built into the fact of biological existence lies the need to protect that existence.

Psychologically, as well as biologically, the organism is a center of sensations and feelings which have been spoken of as private, unsharable, and incommunicable. It is so axiomatic that our emotions seem appropriate, and so difficult to imagine that anyone could feel differently, that one of the major psychotherapeutic problems is to break into a locked emotional house. Psychiatrists attest to the fact that some houses are so well fortified against truth-bearing intruders that it is practically impossible to devise ways of entering. William James puts the matter of psychological isolation and self-centeredness in still another way, commenting on the fact that the world we know is made a part of ourselves in the knowing. We appropriate whatever we experience. Gordon Allport suggests that such appropriation and incorporation is part of the specific genius and excellence of the human psyche.

Let us grant that the biological and psychological facts of organism require a self-centeredness in the human species. But must we or even can we use these facts in the way Hobbes, Freud, or Nietzsche do? Men may be self-centered, but this is not identical with their being aggressive or with their being wicked. They may be moved by drives of the id, but this does not necessarily mean that they are governed exclusively by a pursuit of pleasure. Self-interest may be fundamental to the human species, but this need not be taken to mean that each desires power over others. Men can be concerned for their own welfare without having to resort to either cunning or violence to further that welfare. The fact that men may be egoistic, self-centered and self-concerned need not involve the further ethical contentions which Hobbes, Freud, and Nietzsche build on that fact.

The assumed facts of self-interest have some significant challengers. J. S. Mill, for example, comments on the benefits of selfishness for ethics and civil government. Were men not self-concerned and self-dependent they could not achieve moral independence. In Mill, the very condition for ethics is self-trust and self-reliance—to be able to rely on what one can do for oneself rather than on what others can do for one. In turn, the basis for democracy is moral autonomy and independent selfhood. The contemporary psychiatrist Ian Suttie maintains that the ability to love is as much a human potentiality as the ability to hate. He finds evidence from psychiatric practice that love is actually the primary experience while hate is a derivative of being denied love. The human individual can be as interested in the world around him and in others as he is in himself. Only threat to the well-being of the self destroys the outgoing, cooperative, and social part of the self; only deprivation of his psyche turns his native sociality into withdrawal and his native cooperativeness into self-centered competition. According to Suttie, neither enculturation nor the restriction of desire need destroy man's native ability to love but only enculturation accomplished irrationally and restriction of desire imposed brutally.

Erich Fromm, as well, challenges the so-called facts of self-interest by distinguishing between two types of self which persons may develop and which come to form the "I." The "real" self is the self of spontaneously generated activity, the source of uniqueness and the center of creative activity. The "pseudo-self" is the self of stylized action imposed by society, the self which does what others expect it to do and plays a role determined by others.[2] It is the self composed of false, derivative acts of thinking, feeling, and willing which are adopted to satisfy others. It is the "I" of "I am as you desire me," the self as made by what others think, want, and expect.[3] The "real" or "total" self is the self experiencing all of its feelings, as against the "partial" self or the self acknowledging only the sensations and feelings it believes it ought to have. For Fromm, the human being could be said to be naturally egoistic and self-centered only if the self is the pseudo or partial self. If the self which has developed is the real self, then love for oneself, self-regard, and self-respect are the conditions for loving anyone else. Far from being vices in the Christian sense, self-love is the necessary condition for loving one's brother. Only when the self which loves is the pseudo and opportunistically derived self, is self-love antithetical to the love of others and the self incapable of loving anyone—including itself. Fromm takes the Christian tradition to task, as well, for the assumption that natural love of self necessarily precludes natural love of another. He insists that we can only do unto others what we do unto ourselves. Love and respect for self is the prototype of any other kind, for if we are harsh with ourselves, we are harsh with others; if we are impatient and unreasonable with others, we are so with ourselves. Self and other are not dichotomized but become partners in a total psychic unity.

The fact of self-interest, sometimes called "psychological egoism," was generalized by Darwin into a basic principle extending throughout the natural world. This conviction, in turn, was translated by many thinkers into ethical terms. The self-interest and competition of a dog-eat-dog universe was seen not only as sanctioned by nature but commanded by her. Nature required of all species the aggressive violence embodied in the idea that only the fittest should survive. In this way the natural fact of self-interest justified the pursuit of self-interest. This view, known as "ethical egoism," existed historically prior to Darwin, but his work gave it sustenance.

But such a literal transcription of the facts of the natural world into an ethical norm was challenged, for example, by Kropotkin and by the contemporary writer Ashley Montagu, on the grounds that there is as much evidence in the natural world for cooperation as for competition. Nature, they find, cooperates with man to support and sustain life. There are as many natural defenses against disease as there are forces of biological invasion. Some creatures live an entirely symbiotic existence with the life and welfare of each depending on the life and welfare of the other. What has sometimes been interpreted as nature's wastefulness with life can be interpreted as well to prove that nature deals with many kinds equitably. It might even be contended that every cell of a particular organic unit serves every other. Built into each intercooperating cell is the necessity of coming to the aid of its fellows to protect the entire organism from danger.

Darwin taught that the survival of the biologically fittest takes place by means of natural selection and the inheritance of biological traits capable of withstanding the hostilities of nature. Malthus's famous work on population, a half century earlier, had suggested a way in which nature periodically eliminated the weak. The reproductive abundance which nature has provided for plant and animal life results in more creatures than there is food to supply. Mankind tends to increase its numbers out of all proportion to the resources of nature. As a result, misery and premature death appear to be the unavoidable lot of the generations.

For ethics, perhaps the most telling response to the insights of both Darwin and Malthus comes from Thomas Huxley. Huxley points out that "nature" includes man, that human nature is part of nature. Now if we understand nature as exclusive of man, we take our lessons in ethics too much from the lichen and the lion. We draw our conclusions regarding nature only from the humble beginnings of life and generalize from its least developed state. To view the issue adequately, we must include man in our generalizations; we must see all of nature and not just part. Man is capable of evaluating the situation of blind, irrational competition in nature and of deploring it; he is able to organize himself and other living things in ways which preserve rather than destroy them. He is able to lessen the blow of irrational forces on both himself and other creatures. Nature, in and through that part of her which is human, can evaluate herself and correct her more crude deficiencies. It is the responsibility of man, then, to develop the possibilities making for cooperation in himself, his species, and nature at large. As assessor, as reasoner, and as planner, man is able to further the better forces and restrict the worse. In all of nature only man is capable of this service. Man alone can determine the better from the worse; he alone can set standards the lesser species are incapable of. Man alone is able to use the world around him in infinitely complex ways and can learn to use it well.

Sometimes the issue regarding inevitable human selfishness and competitiveness is stated not so much in terms of competition and cooperation in nature at large but in terms of whether human nature is intrinsically good or evil. To trust at least some part of human nature is almost a psychological necessity. Most thinkers have taken the view that at least *some* aspect of human nature is "good," and some have taken a totally optimistic position regarding its inherent goodness. They have felt that the human self contains a divine spark which makes the total person in some sense akin to God. Some, impressed by man's ability to shape ideals, have felt that, in virtue of that ability, human nature is sacred. Some have shaped their God in the image of a person and have seen in each person an image of God. Certain contemporary existentialists affirm the innate potentiality of the human even when it is understood to be expressed by a self-destructive act. On the other hand, the Christian tradition, as we have seen, has been a powerful exponent of the more somber view that at least one part of the human self is inherently imperfect and corrupt.

But some recent American thinkers have interpreted the facts of the case otherwise. They have suggested that the fact of the self's independent existence is neither to be heralded nor deplored. Man is as capable of constructive acts as he is of wasteful and destructive ones. Granting that the human being is possessed of an animal self, the mere facts of animal life are neither good nor evil. While animality is part of the human psyche, man can use its limitations to advantage. As Santayana puts it, "Spirit cannot fly . . . without material wings."[4] Love, even love of God, requires glands; energetic pursuit of good requires natural sustenance; the most elevated thought requires a nervous system and the sticky grey matter of a brain.

Human nature, in short, is laden with the most varied possibilities. There are factors within it which serve as the basis for the human rather than the merely animal. Men are possessed of intelligence and a desire to learn, they aspire toward ends and goals, and they have the ability to foresee outcomes of action. They have a capacity for reflection and for seeing things whole, and they have a native desire for consistency in thought and action. With all of these assets, human nature can be grand, but it can also be pathetic. Capable of both charity and brutality, cooperation and hostility, knowledge and ignorance, human nature is plastic and expansible in all directions. Just which of many potentialities become actualized, which traits are activated, depends on the conditions in which man finds himself. Human nature apart from an environment which supports some of its possibilities and suppresses others is non-existent—a fatal abstraction.

Agreement: The Sharing of a Context

The view that altruism is to be commended and egoism despised suggests the corollary that my good and yours are natively in opposition and only infrequently and accidentally conjunctive. It suggests that for the most part our values will conflict. Is this so? Can we ever expect agreement regarding ethical choice? Considering the variety of ethical situations, can values ever see eye to eye? Ethical relationism makes it possible to observe that your interests and mine need not conflict and indeed can be harmonious and even identical. A and B *may* agree if they share the same context and face the same circumstances. Yet do men ever actually face the same circumstances? Do they ever have genuinely common interests? While it is surely true that our situations are never completely identical, they may nonetheless overlap and provide communities of interest. For example, all men share pretty much the same biological environment; all men with ulcers more or less share a still narrower environment. All Americans share the situation of being Americans, as a trip abroad seems to testify; all Americans who live in big cities share another which, to some extent, overlaps with the larger one of Americans in general. All Americans who live in New York City share still another context. Women as women, people who live in suburbs, college students, all share contexts. Each context has innumerable subcontexts; each class of context-sharers has innumerable subclasses. We inhabit some of these more or less stably and permanently; we move in and out of others with alacrity. Each context or community of interest has its own special character, its own particular problems, and its particular alternatives for which better or worse choices may be made. There are divergencies in each of these situations, but within each there are common goods, sharable better and worse choices, mutually desirable alternatives.

Furthermore, within each context, the questions to be asked, the problems to be faced, and the alternatives from which to choose are determined by the situation. Hence if a particular valuer finds something desirable because of the properties it possesses, any other valuer may also find it desirable just insofar as the contexts of each overlap. If both A and B share a context the better answer among a number of possible answers is frequently better for them both. The interests of Americans coalesce in a situation of widespread unemployment and economic depression. The interests of New Yorkers become very similar in a subway strike. Even those who do not use the subway cannot escape involvement insofar as other means of transportation become inconveniently overburdened. Mutuality can become greatest when opposition is ostensibly at its peak. The interests of Russians and Americans, as peoples bent on survival, merge under conditions of atomic war. Insofar as both peoples share the same biological world, the pollution of air, soil, and water is a prospective disaster to both.

But there are complicating conditions; for instance, while A and B may share a particular context, they may also inhabit many communities of interest they do not share. The total interests of A therefore diverge from those of B and alter his evaluation of the facts in the context they have in common. Thus contextual community sets the conditions for A and B to agree, but it is only a sufficient and not a necessary condition for them to agree. They may do so but they need not. To believe that A and B *must* agree just because they share some community is to deny that experience may and sometimes does have irresolvable problems and ethical surds. It is to deny the impact of individual uniqueness on the general principles of ethics and to indulge in blind optimism. Nothing prevents ethical viewpoints from being irreconcilable. This is not to say that such is the usual case or that what is actually the case can be decided in advance.

Not only may A and B disagree within the same context, but one or the other may be wrong. Both may be wrong. They may weigh the facts of one and of the same situation differently. Reason may not prevail. To expect that at least one or the other of two opposed viewpoints will be right and that every situation will contain some key to eventual agreement, is not to ask for objectivity but for preordained simplicity. The issues may be extremely complicated and difficult to assess. The practical knowledge that men have of their own situations is hardly ever abundant, and there are psychological impediments to understanding. The fact that men can reason hardly guarantees that they will reason well any more than it guarantees that they will reason poorly. The fact that A and B do not agree does not prove that they cannot possibly agree or would not agree were their vision clearer and were they in command of all their powers. Nor does it necessarily prove that failure to agree is caused by ignorance or whim. It may merely underline the fact that we each belong to innumerable communities of interest; it suggests one very significant way in which men might be said to be unique.

In the same context, regardless of profound disagreement concerning the most effective means to the common end, the end may be and very frequently is the same for all, and whatever accomplishes it is good for all. In the same community of interest, the interests of self and other are frequently mutual and even identical whatever intervening irrationalities may prevent the perception of that fact. Perhaps social life has no more important function than to propose and develop new contexts of interests to which men can willingly give communal allegiance and new ways in which they can discover mutual goods.

Egoism and Altruism as Criteria for Evaluation

How reliable are the notions of self-interest and other-interest for ethical assessment? Are they adequate tools of ethical inquiry? Is the egoistic act always worse and the altruistic act always better? Does the motive of self-interest always taint or indict an act? Let us consider. First of all, the biological nature of man requires a large draught of self-interest, self-centeredness, and self-concern to permit the persistence and survival of the organism. An altruism which fails to take account of this fact and to grant that one's own interests are inherently part of any situation in which one is involved is misled and shortsighted. An egoism which fails to grant that the interests of others are also part of one's own situation reaps the consequences of faulty perspective. You and I are both part of the world we share; both our interests must be met. The self that we find ourselves necessarily interested in, is never alone; it never exists apart from association, interaction, and intersecting choice of goods. Men live in groups and subgroups of nation, local community, family, or club. If an altruistic perspective can be said to be better than an egoistic one, it is not because the values of others are more sacred than our own but because such a perspective is wide enough to encompass the whole of a situation and not just part of it, because the more inclusive conception of a situation allows greater recognition of the diversity of claims.

How then shall we interpret egoism and altruism as criteria for assessing conduct? As John Dewey analyzes the matter, to assume that self-interest is necessarily bad has strange implications. Is an interest bad or inferior just because it happens to be ours? Is there anything intrinsically good about the interest of others just because it is theirs and not ours? Everyone acts sometimes as "self" and sometimes as "other." Is there anything particularly wrong when one acts in the former capacity? What causes a claim from one direction to pollute an issue and that from another to purify it? Should we not say rather that the question of whose interest it happens to be is irrelevant? Is not the more pertinent question one concerning the nature of that interest—the method used to gain it, the outcome for self, for others, and for the situation? The important question ethically is not who holds the interest but what consequences will accrue with its accomplishment. Consider some interests which serve self, for instance, those of getting an education or paying attention to one's health. Such claims have beneficial results for all concerned, while failure to enter these claims may be communally undesirable. On the other hand, interests which serve others, such as those of compassion and charity, can sometimes be detrimental to their objects. Insistence on one's own political rights has fostered laws making an entire group free, while insistence on what constitutes the political rights of others has often produced second-class citizens.

Dewey maintains that the basic issue is one of evaluating the nature and quality of the interests sought. It does not center on whose interest it happens to be but on what kind of an interest it is. It revolves about whether the interest is short-term, narrow and shallow or whether it is sufficiently long-term, wide and deep; whether it is trivial or important, fleeting or enduring, perspectivally distorted or clear.

Interests presuppose goals or ends which in turn shape and form the self, which give a direction to character and which give substance and meaning to the kind of person we are. We are, in part, the kinds of things we choose. The quality of our interests reflects itself in us. Therefore we may ask not only the worth of the goal we seek but also what kind of persons we are to become in choosing it. Part of our estimation of the value of any goal is to be found in its effects on us, in the way it will alter our character, and in the kind of habits formed by wanting it.

While exclusive self-regard tends to narrow the ethical horizon and altruism tends to widen it, neither egoism nor altruism is, in itself, an adequate or trustworthy yardstick for the measurement of good conduct. Both evade the central issue of weighing without distortion the ends pursued. Perhaps the real ethical problem is not that of learning how to put the interests of others first but learning how to weigh all interests, including one's own, on an impartial scale. It is not to become schooled in underestimation of self or in self-abasement but to become adept in weighing all claims critically—those of ourselves as well as those of others.

Altruism: Responsiveness to Others

Self-regard and other-regard are not only motives for action but forms of sensitivity as well. They are measuring rods of emotional propensities, accounts of the things which impinge on our awareness and alert us. In one sense, what we mean by declaring someone egocentric rather than altruistic is that he is more alert to that which immediately affects his own senses than he is to the needs and condition of others.

The power to identify with others and to be sympathetically responsive to them is one of the primary marks of a developed ethical awareness. That men tend to be short on this virtue is perhaps the only reason for considering altruism as ethically superior to egoism. Some writers have claimed that life in the vast network of an internationally related society puts an especially severe tax on the ability of persons to relate sensitively to others. The sheer multiplicity of events throughout the world, which modern communication makes available, tends to dull our sensitivities and blunt our awareness. Fire, flood, earthquake, war, violence—disasters of all sorts to humankind—can become so commonplace as to arouse little or no response. But if the contemporary world is more destructive of sensitivity to others than was life in a frontier town, the need to recognize this state of man is of corresponding ethical importance.

Notes

1. Thomas Hobbes, *Leviathan,* in *Hobbes: Selections,* ed. by F. Woodbridge (New York: Scribner, 1930), part 1, chapter 13.

2. Erich Fromm, *Escape from Freedom* (New York: Holt, Rinehart and Winston, 1941), p. 205.

3. Erich Fromm, *Man for Himself* (New York: Holt, Rinehart and Winston, 1947), pp. 67ff. and chapter 4.

4. George Santayana, *Soliloquies in England and Later Soliloquies* (New York: Scribner, 1922), prologue.

Section 6

Humanism and Social Relations

By explicitly abandoning a supernatural reality, naturalism places itself at odds with much of Western culture's tradition, in questions of metaphysics to be sure, but even more importantly in social theory. It has been commonplace for millennia to regard the principles of human interaction to have their foundations in the supernatural, usually in the form of a divine will. However, during the past century Western culture has become increasingly secular, and at the same time it has developed new sets of individual and social problems. Those whose ethical and social ideas are rooted in more traditional perspectives sometimes charge that contemporary social problems are the result of abandoning traditional Western theology, and that human happiness and meaning require a supernatural foundation. In this section Sidney Hook responds to this charge, and to several other common criticisms of a secular, scientifically oriented humanism: that scientific explanation cannot account for what is distinctively human, that it is necessarily reductionist, and that it is especially inadequate to account for moral experience. In addressing these criticisms Hook defends a cornerstone of naturalism and humanism, which is that reason, what Hook following Dewey calls the "method of intelligence," rather than dogmatism and tenacity can be the only defensible and in the long run successful response to social problems.

While naturalistic humanists will have little trouble agreeing with Hook on the general point that rational inquiry is the appropriate way to address social problems, they will disagree over the results of that inquiry, which is to say they will disagree over social theory. One of the most explicit and outspoken supporters of naturalistic humanism has been Paul Kurtz. Kurtz as an undergraduate was a student of Hook, and he went on to a career in philosophy at the State University of New York at Buffalo, where he is now professor emeritus. He is also chairman emeritus of Prometheus Books. Kurtz argues that the humanist is committed to individual liberty, which in his interpretation means above all freedom from social control, whether governmental, economic, religious, or otherwise. As a result of this emphasis, Kurtz defends a traditional libertarianism, which opposes state incursions into the economy and into social relations of any kind. He is careful to point out, however, that individual liberty as he understands it is not equivalent to license and relativism. Genuine freedom may imply moral autonomy, but it also requires moral maturity.

In his social theory Kurtz leans toward a traditional reliance on the independent individual and in this respect his humanism differs from that of Corliss Lamont. While Kurtz has been a leading spokesman for a libertarian strain of naturalistic humanism, Lamont has been one of the more influential representatives of naturalism's more socialist possibilities. Lamont was a lecturer in philosophy at Columbia University, and from the 1940s to the 1960s he was an active and influential participant in New York City's intellectual life. Like Kurtz, Lamont thinks that humanism implies the importance of individual freedom. But if Kurtz reads freedom as independence *from* social controls, Lamont interprets it as freedom *for*; in other words, Lamont is interested in the social conditions which enable individuals to act and to develop, and freedom in this view is the set of the most enabling social conditions. He regards democracy as an appropriate form of social organization to enhance free conditions, and he argues here that there are various types of democracy, and they are interrelated in such a way that they are all required for a fully democratic society and life. While we need political democracy, Lamont argues, freedom also requires economic democracy, democratic social relations with respect to race, ethnicity, and gender, and international democracy as well. It is toward these ends that Lamont defends a socialist humanism.

1

Nature and the Human Spirit*

Sidney Hook

The present situation in human history is a challenge to philosophers to vindicate their traditional claim to the possession of a vision of man that can help integrate and enrich human experience. What is required of such vision is that it avoid arbitrariness and pretentiousness, and hold out some promise—however modest—of fruitful cooperation among those different peoples and cultures of the world which have a will to cooperate.

Viewed in the light of the history of philosophy, the great danger of all philosophical thought which goes beyond logical analysis of categories is not an excess of speculation—which has at least an imaginative appeal—but an excess of salvationary zeal. The great systems have made promises that they cannot possibly fulfill. For they have ignored the fact that the concrete issues which divide men and inspire conflict have their primary locus in economic, political, and national life. No philosophical vision or synthesis can provide viable answers to them in their own terms. It is well to admit openly that there is no royal philosophical road to social salvation, however it may be with

*Originally published in Sidney Hook, *The Quest for Being and Other Essays* (New York: St. Martins Press, 1934; now published in Buffalo, N.Y.: Prometheus Books, 1991), pp. 196–208.

the quest for personal salvation. And if by personal salvation we mean the achievement of a sane and dignifed order in the life of individuals, recent history furnishes a grim but conclusive reminder that for the overwhelming majority of men this is impossible until a stable and more equitable social order has been introduced.

Nonetheless it is undeniable that philosophical attitudes have a broad even if indirect bearing upon the problem of human experience. To the extent that they symbolize human attention and effort along some lines and divert them from others, they have practical consequences even when they preach detachment and withdrawal. I am not here maintaining that any *specific* philosophical doctrines have logical consequences for specific problems—in fact I shall be concerned to deny this—but only that certain basic points of view which express value judgments have a selective impact upon the variety of problems given at any moment, and on the possible approaches to these problems.

The position of this chapter is that the philosophy of *naturalistic humanism*, which regards man as an integral but distinctive part of nature, as wholly a creature of natural origin and natural end, offers an adequate and fruitful basis for the social reconstruction which is essential for the emergence of patterns of human dignity on a world-wide scale. This view in recent years has been the object of sustained criticisms from various quarters which have called into question the self-sufficiency of man. Some years ago, adopting a phrase from Gilbert Murray's account of the stages of Greek religion, I referred to this antinaturalistic movement as "the new failure of nerve." Since then it has taken on the proportions of a tidal wave in philosophy, theology, literature, and the philosophy of history. Characteristic of its views are two beliefs: (1) that our time of troubles is primarily a historical and logical consequence of the abandonment of the religious and metaphysical foundations of Western civilization and of a shift to secular life; and (2) that what gives genuine happiness to man, and relief from the multiple alienations which fragmentize both personality and society, in the words of St. Augustine "is something which does not proceed from human nature but which is above human nature." And from these beliefs the criticism follows that naturalism in any form is incapable of doing justice to the actually experienced qualities of human life, particularly the nature of man's moral experience.

Before proceeding to logical analysis of these criticisms a few historical remarks are in order. The notion that the decline of medieval supernaturalism gave rise to a secular naturalistic humanism which enjoyed the same position of authority and prestige as the philosophy it replaced is a legend that will no more bear examination than its countermyth which holds that the rise of Christian supernaturalism resulted not from the bankruptcy of pagan supernaturalism but from the alleged failure of Greco-Roman secularism. The life of a culture is expressed primarily in its institutions, and the *institutional* history of Europe nowhere reveals the presence of a unifying humanistic secular philosophy to integrate with the heritage of the past the radical changes precipitated by war, scientific technology, and the expansion of the capitalist economy. On the contrary, the new tendencies of industrialization, urbanization, and nationalism were neither predicted nor prepared for by any philosophy, either supernaturalist or naturalist. They made their way in the teeth of the old traditions, which were helpless to cope with them and which ultimately were compelled by the logic of events to make uneasy compromises with the historical situations they could not exorcise. The defenders of traditional supernaturalism systematically engaged themselves not so much with the social *problems* resulting from the uncontrolled expansion of the new productive forces in Europe as in a furious polemic against the humanistic striving to find the new social forms and institutions which, without aborting the burst of creative energy unleashed by the industrial revolution, would sustain through the operating institutions of a reconstructed society, the dignity of all human beings.

One could make a far better historical case for the contrary view. To the extent that the dilemmas and tragedies of modern culture are attributable to ideological factors, a greater responsibility rests with a supernaturalist philosophy which was powerless to prevent the emergence of the tendencies it deplored or to give them a moral direction once they appeared, than to the chaotic multitude of doctrines—among which naturalistic humanism was the weakest—that sought, often by transparent rationalizations of sectional and class interests, to give some moral meaning and direction to the new social developments.

Nor in face of the assertion that the wars, revolutions, and beastial atrocities of our century are a consequence of the abandonment of the transcendent religious and metaphysical beliefs of the past, must we overlook the significance of the fact that those centuries when European culture rested on religious foundations were marked, once allowance is made for scale, by practices of persecution and extermination almost as inhuman as those committed by modern totalitarianisms.

1. But historical considerations aside, it is demonstrable that no set of metaphysical or theological statements by themselves entail any specific empirical consequences about the life of man or the structure of human society. Without raising the questions here of the criteria of meaningfulness and verification of such statements, it is apparent that they are compatible with mutually inconsistent social beliefs and the most diverse social institutions. For example, the same set of premises about divine existence, immortality, the nature of substance and the self have been held by believers in feudalism, capitalism, and socialism, by democrats as well as by totalitarians. This indicates that belief in the first set of propositions is not a sufficient condition of belief in the second set of propositions. And we are all acquainted with principled advocates of democracy or dictatorship, capitalism or socialism, who regard the metaphysical and theological propositions often offered in alleged justification of these institutions as either meaningless or false, which establishes that belief in them is certainly not a necessary condition of social doctrine and action. Indeed, *logically,* with sufficient technical ingenuity, allegiance to any social system can be squared with belief in any metaphysical systems whatsoever.

This has sometimes been denied by those for whom metaphysical and theological statements are value judgments in disguise. When challenged they retreat to the position that the validity of moral judgments rests upon transcendental truths of a metaphysical or theological nature. Not only does such a position destroy the autonomy of moral experience, it is exposed to the same logical and historical difficulties that we have noted above. To the extent that transcendental beliefs are disguised value judgments, the actual relation between theology and morals is obscured. For, as we have seen in earlier chapters, it is indisputable that far from morals being historically derived from theological beliefs, men have always created their gods in their own moral image.

2. Any attempt to find a basis to improve the human estate by resort to a principle "above human nature" is doomed to failure because it cannot supply definite criteria to guide the construction of the programs of action required to meet the concrete needs, wants, and aspirations of men which are very much part of human nature and in which the most pressing problems of a domestic and international character are rooted. Ideals and ends that are out of time and so lack a natural basis can never be brought into logical and causal continuity with the means recommended to achieve them, for all such means are temporal acts with temporal consequences. The result of postulating ends that are outside of time and of postulating principles above human nature is that the *choice* of means, without which ends cannot be realized or tested, is lamed at the outset. Freed from critical direction, human choice *professedly* oriented to principles above human nature, oscillates between the extremes of dogmatism and opportunism.

The proposal of naturalistic humanism is to approach the problems of men in their natural and social contexts and to test the validity of all theoretical claims, not by examining their presuppositions but by investigating their empirical consequences. In refusing to allow this concern with antecedent presuppositions to dominate intellectual activity, in pointing out that conflicting varieties of presuppositions are equally compatible with verifiable fact, the naturalistic humanists seek to give the criterion of fruitfulness the same standing in all inquiry as it has in inquiry in the natural sciences. There is no guarantee, of course, that human beings, endowed with variant as well as common needs, will agree upon consequences, but a great deal of human experience testifies that in some areas and in some periods this is possible, sometimes even normal. One of the most impressive expressions of that human experience is the existence of democratic communities in which to a large part a consensus of belief and action in respect to political institutions and processes has been established among individuals holding the most varied metaphysical and theological presuppositions. What is being suggested by this proposal to take consequences not presuppositions as a point of departure is that those processes of inquiry by which in some parts of the world idealists and materialists, atheists and theists, Catholics, Protestants, Jews, and Mohammedans have been able to reach a community of working agreement be employed to explore all the empirical problems and difficulties that beset men today.

Where needs are common, there are as a rule much less differences among human beings as to what constitutes endurable or unendurable, satisfactory or unsatisfactory resolutions of problems than there are over metaphysical or theological suppositions. To wait upon agreement on first or last principles as a precondition for a solution of what may be called "the intermediate" problems of human experience is hardly a counsel of wisdom in view of the fact that there is no accepted method by which the conflict of first or last principles of this type can be settled, whereas objective methods of settling "intermediate problems" exist that can extend the area of *uncoerced* agreement among men. To be sure, the results won in the latter case are tentative and piecemeal but they make up in impressive number for what they lack in pretentious promise. It would hardly be an exaggeration to say that any attempt to make agreement on philosophical presuppositions a condition precedent for cooperative action would hopelessly divide the world and destroy the working unity established in many existing human communities.

The obvious retort to this is that naturalistic humanism has its own presuppositions. Certainly, but what I am urging here is not the acceptance of its presuppositions but of its program of orientation and work, a program which would find justification by its fruitful consequences, and not by its alleged presuppositions. The argument avoids vicious circularity because at the outset it makes no other appeal than to the reasonable procedures recognized not only by philosophers but by all other men in their successful working practice in solving the problems that confront them in daily life.

It is in the light of those reasonable procedures that naturalistic humanism sees no warrant in experience for belief either in two separate worlds or two truths or two generic methods of reaching truths although it recognizes plural modes or levels of association and existence within nature, and a multiplicity of special methods and techniques which reflect the characteristic differences between the living and the nonliving, the purposeful and the nonpurposeful, the historical and the nonhistorical. Just as it refuses to separate man from society and society from nature, so, for reasons already given in previous essays, it refuses to draw a sharp line of separation or opposition between scientific method on the one hand, and the reasonable procedures in the primary knowledge-getting activities of men struggling to control their environment, on the other.

It is in its allegiance to the continuity of scientific analysis from field to field that naturalistic humanism differentiates itself from all other varieties of humanism, and in its insistence on the plurality and qualitative specificity of the different fields of experience that it differentiates itself from all other varieties of naturalism. It is not in virtue of any of its alleged presuppositions but because it follows the lead of scientific method from its primal to advanced stage that it holds that the occurrence of all qualities and events depends on the organization of a material system in space-time, and that their emergence, development, and disappearance are determined by change in such organization.

3. At first blush it would seem that the philosophy of naturalistic humanism would be regarded as not inadequate—in its intention, at least—to encompass the whole life of man. For it recognizes the complex natural interrelations of man—interrelations made even more complex by his behavior as an historical creature in time, with a developing society and consciousness which, within certain limits, can influence the natural conditions of his existence. But for historical reasons which I shall not here examine, such a philosophy has been criticized for impoverishing human experience, denigrating the human status in the cosmos, and closing the avenues to new truths and insights.

The grounds on which such criticisms have been based are many. But I limit myself only to three: (a) that scientific explanation is inadequate to what is distinctly human, (b) that it necessarily entails "reductionism," and (c) that even if everything else distinctively human could be shown to be accessible to scientific analysis, it is, and will remain, helpless before the facts and problems of moral experience.

a. Scientific explanation is of various kinds but even if we identify it with its ideal type—the legitimacy of which has been sharply disputed—the first objection cannot be sustained. Let us assume that the ideal type of explanation consists in the subsumption under general laws of particular phenomena which have fulfilled certain initial defining conditions, thus enabling us to predict and sometimes to control events. To say, therefore, that scientific explanation cannot account for what is *uniquely* human is in one sense a truism, in another sense false. It is a truism in the sense that we cannot explain any completely unique event, not only in history but in physics. It is false, however, in suggesting that despite its uniqueness, a phenomenon cannot share common traits of relations with other unique phenomena. It is false further in suggesting that any trait which differentiates a class of phenomena from other classes, whether it be the mammary glands of mammals or man's rationality or sense of humor, cannot be correlated with material conditions of determination, physical or social. It is false in suggesting that scientific explanation is concerned with the totality of any event or even with one total event or that it pretends to finality or exhaustiveness in its account of any event or any aspect of any event.

The main question about human motives, for example, which are cited by Professor William Hocking and others as beyond scientific explanation, is not whether their existence can be accounted for in terms of law about neural impulses or electronic movements. Although highly unlikely, this is not inconceivable. The question is whether determinate relations can be established between the occurrence, variation, and intensity of motives and any changes in the historical, material space-time systems in which all individuals develop. A social or historical explanation of the operation of motives is entirely legitimate even if we do not understand very well its physical or biological basis. In biology, for example, the laws of genetics are accepted as explanations of the facts of heredity although we cannot derive them from physical laws governing molecular phenomena. Yet it would be admitted that despite its lack of comparable exactness, biology is no less scientific than physics.

b. This first criticism of naturalistic humanism is usually a preface to a more comprehensive indictment of scientific explanation as guilty of reductionism, of explaining away the very phenomena, particularly the consciousness of qualities, given in human experience. That some formulations of materialism in the past have given a superficial justification for this charge hardly extenuates this interpretation of modern naturalism. It is true that the language in which the *causes* of changes in qualitative experience is expressed contains terms which differ from those employed in the *descriptions* of human experience. But it is a complete non sequitur to infer that therefore the existence of the qualities of human experience are rendered precarious in any way. The experience of qualities, whether it be the taste of sugar or the sense of awe, is irreducible as an experience. But it is not therefore inexplicable. Whether any particular naturalist is faithful in his descriptions is an empirical matter to be decided by controlled observation. And since the adequacy of his causal explanations depends in part on whether the experience in question can be reduplicated or transformed under certain conditions, it is literally absurd, if we take note of his procedure, to charge him with reductionism.

It is noteworthy that the charge of reductionism is rarely made against the physicist who explains variations in the distinctive properties of physical things, for example, their sound or color, by variations in the quantities or qualities of another order. It is only when the distinctive qualities of human experience are explained that we hear the charge that according to naturalists man is "nothing but" this or that, "merely" a handful of salts in a solution of water, etc., despite the fact that he is proceeding no differently from the physicist who explains a snowflake in terms of certain laws of temperature and liquids without "reducing" the geometrical or aesthetic patterns of snowflakes to such laws. It is appropriate to retort here that in virtue of its commitments to the logic of scientific method, naturalism proclaims that "Nothing is *nothing—but*" and "Nothing is *merely* one thing and not anything else."

It is hard to see how any scientific explanation of the qualities of the human spirit can in any way endanger those qualities, no matter how frail and exquisite they are. On the contrary, by revealing the structure of the material patterns in which they are enmeshed, they can, if we wish, be made more secure. Because it refuses to hypostasize these qualities and insists upon exploring their causes and consequences in the same spirit that it explores the qualities of the physical world, naturalistic humanism has from time to time provoked the hostility of those who feared that increasing knowledge might transform the world. Although such opposition asserts in argument that naturalism ignores the qualities of the human spirit, its secret hope is that materialism will ignore these qualities lest the power to control them be exercised in unacceptable ways.

In this connection two other points must be briefly touched on. Insofar as mechanism is the belief that all human phenomena can be explained or predicted on the basis of the most general laws of physics, naturalistic humanism is not mechanistic. For it, variation, novelty, and diversity are not only undeniable facts of experience, it seeks to bring them about in different areas. And in virtue of its efforts, its failures as well as successes, it recognizes that many more things will occur than we can predict or control. It knows that human ideals and human volition, as well as knowledge of what transpired in the past, may enter as contributing conditions in redetermining the movement of events. The *same* antecedent conditions which determine objective alternatives do not determine the human perception and action which alter the probabilities that one or the other alternative will in fact be realized.

Nor is it true that according to naturalistic humanism only what can be observed exists. Both in science and common life many things may be reasonably inferred to exist from what is observed, and then confirmed by further observations. It does hold that where there is no evidence drawn from observed or *observable* effects, existence cannot be responsibly attributed. Otherwise the distinction between fact and fantasy disappears.

c. As far as the facts of moral experience are concerned, it is clear that we must distinguish between the causal explanation of moral qualities, and the proper analysis of those qualities. Naturalistic humanists differ among themselves as to the proper analysis of moral statements— some maintaining that they are commands without cognitive significance and others that they make a genuine knowledge claim. But it is certainly illegitimate to infer from the fact that one or another school contests the validity of a particular analysis of moral experience that it denies the existence of moral experience. That we experience moral obligation is a fact to be explained. What is denied by all naturalistic schools is that the explanation requires any transcendent ideal or power. The alleged requirement cannot be made part of the datum of the experience of obligation.

The most common objection to naturalistic humanism is not that it has no place for moral experience but that it has no place for an *authoritative* moral experience except one which rests merely on arbitrary preference, habit, or force. In consequence, it is accused of lapsing into the morass of relativism despite its desire to discover inclusive and enduring ends which will enable human beings to live harmoniously together. The impression that relativism is entailed by every form of naturalism is reinforced by the refusal of current humanists to content themselves with the affirmation of general ends certified to immediate intuition and by their insistence that ends must be related to means and both to determinate conditions of trouble and difficulty in specific historical situations. This makes value judgments in the only form in which they count, "relative"— but "relative" not in the sense of subjective but rather relational. The opposite of "relative" is not "objective" but "absolute" or "unconditioned." This emphasis upon relational character reflects the dependence of value qualities, like *all* other qualities in nature, upon activities in process of objective interaction with each other. It should then be clear that the assertion "a value is *related* to a situation of concrete historical interests"— and the further assertion that "a judgment of value is warranted when reflection indicates that what is declared valuable promises to satisfy these interests," does *not* add up to the view that anyone can legitimately believe that *anything* is valuable in *any* situation. On the contrary. Inquiry into the relational character of values, their historical, cultural, and psychological reference, aims to find reliable values to guide action, reliable because they have objective grounds.

The impression that because values are relational they are therefore subjective is the consequence of confusing two different problems. The first is whether values have objective status and validity; the second is whether in case of conflict, objective values and the interests to which they are related, can be shared, i.e., whether a new value situation can be constructed which will transform the conflicting values into a satisfying integrated whole.

One can hold to the belief in the objectivity of values without *guaranteeing* that agreement among conflicting values, all of which are objective from their own point of view, can be won. How far such agreement can be won cannot be foretold until actual investigation into the conditions and consequences of value claims in definite situations is undertaken—and this is precisely what naturalistic humanists propose to do instead of taking moral intuitions as absolute fiats subject to no control. The assumption that in any particular case agreement can be won, that an objective moral resolution of value conflicts is possible, entails the belief that men are sufficiently alike to work out ways of becoming *more* alike, or sufficiently alike to agree about the permissible limits of *being different.*

Rationality or reasonableness in conduct is the ability—which men possess—to envisage alternatives of action, to apply the test of observable consequences to conflicting proposals, and to accept or reconstruct these proposals in the light of consequences. The institutional expression of this rationality is the communal process of deliberation and critical assessment of evidence which alone make possible a *freely* given consent. The willingness to sit down in the face of differences and reason together is the only categorical imperative a naturalistic humanist recognizes. And reliance upon the rules of the game by which grounded conclusions concerning concrete value judgments are reached is the only methodological absolute to which he is committed. This places authority solely in the untrammeled processes of inquiry and any alleged humanism, whether Thomistic humanism or so-called Soviet humanism, which places primary authority in institutions or dogmas, is guilty of the most transparent kind of semantic corruption.

Insofar as our age requires a unifying faith, it is clear that it cannot be found in any official doctrine or creed but rather in the commitment to the processes and methods of critical intelligence. Just as science made its way without an official metaphysics or theology, so it *may* be possible to build up a body of social science as a guide to action independently of the plural *overbeliefs* which its practitioners entertain provided only that those beliefs do not encourage the erection of non-trespass signs to inquiry about man and all his works.

In the nature of the case the philosophy of naturalistic humanism cannot promise what the facts of human involvement with nature rules out as unlikely. But within the range of possibilities it promises so much that it is willful romanticism to demand more. It does not deprive human beings of their responsibility but rather brings home to them their own responsibility, within the constraining conditions of nature and social traditions. By nature man is a creature who can make his own history. But he did not make the world in which that history is open to him. Because he did not make the world is not a valid ground for the belief that any other species did—natural or supernatural. Nor does it follow that, because he refuses to worship any supernatural power, he must worship himself or any natural power whether person, force, or thing. Man can live with a natural piety for the sources of his being. He can rely upon nature and himself without worshipping them. Man in fact relies only on his own natural and human resources even when he claims to rely on other resources.

Once men realize this then the chances become better—not certain—that these resources will be sufficient to develop a dignified human existence in a just social order. We need not repine that we are not gods or the children of gods. The politics of despair, the philosophy of magical idealism, and the theology of consolation forget that although we are not gods, we can still act like men.

2

Libertarianism:
The Philosophy of Moral Freedom*

Paul Kurtz

What is the relationship between liberty and morality? Can one coherently espouse libertarianism, yet deny that it presupposes a moral philosophy? To attempt to so argue, in my judgment, is contradictory; for the defense of liberty assumes a set of underlying values. A problem of definition emerges when we attempt to ascertain the meaning of *libertarianism*. It has been taken as an economic doctrine concerned primarily with preserving economic liberty and the free market against the encroachments of government. It has also been used in political philosophy to defend human or natural rights, civil liberties, and the open democratic society. Economic and political liberties are indeed central to the libertarian philosophy, but they are, I submit, derivative from an even more fundamental libertarian ideal: the high moral value placed upon individual freedom of choice.

The classical liberal is concerned with expanding the autonomy of persons over their own lives. This means that social restraints placed upon individual choices should be reduced. These are many, for large-

---

*Originally published in *Modern Age* (Spring 1982) and *In Defense of Secular Humanism* by Paul Kurtz (Buffalo, N.Y.: Prometheus Books, 1983).

scale governmental power is a primary threat to individual freedom. Twentieth-century "liberals" under the influence of Marx have abandoned the classic libertarian emphasis on individual freedom in favor of a concern for social welfare. They have sought to extend the paternalistic role of the state in regulating the private sector and fulfilling functions that they believe are not being adequately performed by other institutions. The welfare liberal believes that it is the duty of society to ameliorate the lot of poor persons and to redistribute wealth—all in the name of a theory of "justice," "fairness," or "equity." Welfare-statist mentality has unleashed a self-righteous egalitarianism that has undermined the incentives of productive citizens in favor of the disadvantaged. The principle of equality in its extreme form has led reformists beyond "equality before the law" and "equality of opportunity" to guaranteeing equality of results. They argue that since not everyone has the same access, social policies must equalize the conditions of opportunity. They would force people to be equal against their will. Libertarians thus have rightly pointed out that doctrines of social equality have been counterproductive, smothering individual initiative and in Marxist cultures leading to the infamous Gulags of the spirit.

The libertarian agenda is incomplete, however, if it is only concerned with the evils of government. For government is not the only social institution that can unduly restrain human freedom. They can limit an individual's freedom by defining the conditions of employment, fixing prices, driving out competition, and setting the whole tone of social life. I am not taking the Marxists' side here, for I believe that a capitalist society is the best guarantee of human freedom. Wherever the state has a monopoly of power, both economic and political freedom soon disappear. A free market and a strong private sector are thus necessary conditions for political freedom. One needs vigorous competition and a pluralistic economy, in which there are diverse centers of economic decision making.

Libertarians abhor governmental control of the media of communication. The libertarian seeks a free market of ideas. Yet he must likewise be apprehensive of the de facto domination of the media by powerful corporate interests. Much of the mass media—television, movies, magazines, and newspapers—have been dominated by one point of view—

ritualistic liberalism. If conglomerate control of the publishing industry continues to grow, it may tend to push out small publishers and debase the quality of publishing. Still, Western capitalist societies still allow more freedom than others. Thus I do not agree with Marcuse's pessimistic diagnosis outlined in *One-Dimensional Society*. Nevertheless, not all capitalists are libertarians; nor are they necessarily concerned with preserving and extending individual freedom.

The erosion of freedom can also be seen accompanying the enormous growth in size and power of labor unions. The right to work does not exist in industries where the closed shop operates. Of course, there are sound reasons for collective bargaining; the lone individual working for General Motors is no match for the corporation. By entering into a voluntary association with his fellow workers, his ability to bargain collectively more nearly equalizes his economic position. But where unions seek to deny the right to work to those who are not members, they limit choice. No doubt this has been caused by the big hand of government. But government has been able to legislate the closed shop because of the power of the unions and their members.

What I have been saying seems also to be the case in respect to religious institutions. Powerful churches have often suppressed unbelievers. In this regard, religious institutions may function as oppressively as the state, dictating thought and practice, regulating morality and sexuality, on a de facto if not a de jure basis. I am always surprised to discover that some conservatives will defend economic liberty yet readily condone the suppression of religious dissent. Fortunately, American society has had a proliferation of religious denominations and as a result has developed a truce based on the principles of ecumenism. Given the fact of opposing sects, all should have a place in the sun. In some areas—fundamentalism in the South or Roman Catholicism in the North—freedom of conscience in religion and morality are still suspect. There is hardly room left for the secular humanist, free-thinker, or village atheist in a society dominated by religious tradition. The religious liberal thus defends the separation of church and state and liberty of conscience. Yet conformist pressures seek to impose sanctions on those who violate prevailing religious conventions.

Perhaps the most encouraging development in the past two decades on the freedom agenda has been the growth of moral libertarianism. The moral premise is familiar: individuals should have the right to satisfy their tastes, cultivate their values, develop their lifestyles as they see fit so long as they do not impose their values on others or prevent them from exercising theirs.

Moral libertarianism, as is apparent, has made considerable progress in democratic societies. There has been a noticeable lessening of censorship in the arts, television, movies, the theater, magazine and book publishing. Liberty of expression has been extended far beyond what was imagined only a generation ago—but it has led to the growth of a pornography industry. In sexual morality, there has been a loosening of traditional restrictions; divorce has been made easier and is now widespread. Laws regulating sexual practices have been replaced, as well as those concerned with adultery, anal-oral sexuality, etc. The belief that two or more consenting adults should have the right to pursue in private their sexual proclivities without social or legal interference is now widely accepted by a significant sector of the community. This has led in part to the "gay liberation" movement. Similar changes have occurred in regard to women, who demand that they be treated as persons capable of choosing their own destinies. Permissive attitudes have also developed concerning drugs. If the state permits alcohol and cigarettes, why not marijuana? Today marijuana is as common in some circles as soft drinks and beer, and, regretfully, so are cocaine and heroin.

In one sense these new freedoms—though they liberate people from stultifying customs—have gone too far. Although one may in principle agree that individuals ought to be allowed to do their own thing, in practice this may lead to a breakdown of civilized conduct, indiscriminate promiscuity, violence, drugs, and lack of moral virtue and excellence. This is particularly the case with many young people. Many college graduates have betrayed the hope and promise placed in them. They are the products of broken homes and a narcissistic morality gone astray. The rejection of the work ethic is widespread. Living off the generosity of relatives, friends, or social welfare, many have abandoned self-reliance and have become self-indulgent. How can one simply defend moral liberty and ignore the loss of virtue? This question is not simply theoretical, but has high practical import for our society. In mass consumer-oriented society, products are manufactured and sold and tastes conditioned without any regard for their moral worth. The immediacies of enjoyment are taken as ends in themselves, divorced from the hard work and effort necessary to achieve them. The quality of life has given way to banality.

This is the indictment of the libertarian society that one hears today. It is no doubt overstated. Nonetheless it has an element of truth. If a choice were to be made between a free society and a repressive one, libertarians would opt for the former over the latter, even though they recognize unfortunate byproducts as the price of freedom. Moreover, perhaps the only way for some to learn to appreciate responsible freedom is to experience the consequences of their mistakes. Nevertheless, at times liberty may surely lead to license when it should be accompanied by virtue. Is the breakdown of the moral order due to the excessive moral freedom we have enjoyed? May it be attributed to the decline in religious faith and the growth of secular humanism and libertarianism? Can morality prevail only if it is guided by religion?

I do not think it is evident that religious societies are any more moral than nonreligious ones. It may be true that outward displays of sexual conduct and other "immoral" practices are often prohibited in repressive religious communities. Yet they may be masking a hypocritical double standard. Religious societies may be insensitive to other forms of injustice. They may seek to impose order, hierarchy, and the status quo on those who resist it. But more decisively, a libertarian conception of the moral life which has a secular foundation is different from a religious-theistic one. It is not obedience to a prescribed moral code that is the mark of the moral person but the flowering of the free personality.

The libertarian in ethics maintains as his first principle the autonomy of moral choice. And this means the independence of the ethical judgment: that is, values and principles are not to be deduced a priori from absolute rules, but grow out of moral inquiry. Ethical choice requires a sensitivity to moral dilemmas, a willingness to grapple with conflicts in values and principles, rights and duties, as they are confronted in actual life. Authoritarian and legalist systems of ethics are not based on final or fixed standards. Many traditional religious systems may seek to indoctrinate a set of norms by fiat. This is supposed to guarantee stability and regularity of conduct and inhibit sinful behavior. A religious code such as is found in the Ten Commandments, the Koran, or the Sermon on the Mount may be supported by the authority of clergy and tradition. It may act as a regulative force, guarding against "deviant," "anomic," or "amoral" behavior. But in what sense are these systems moral? There are traditionalist libertarians in the economic sphere who insist that liberty needs to be supported by religious strictures. And they justify religious-moral repression for channeling conduct along approved lines.

A moral libertarian by way of contrast rejects authoritarianism in the moral domain as much as he does political statism or economic regulation. Yet he is faced with a profound dilemma. For if individuals were suddenly released from all restrictions—political, social, moral, and traditional—what would ensue? Would they be, as the romantic anarchist hopes, noble, beneficent, sympathetic in their relations to other individuals? Would they be temperate and rational in their inner personal lives? Would their choices be truly autonomous and issue from reflective deliberation?

Regretfully, to emancipate individuals who are unprepared for it from all social restraints may indeed result in license. Autonomous choice is not genuine unless individuals are first nurtured to appreciate and handle it. Perhaps the familiar distinction between two kinds of freedom needs to be restated: freedom from restraint is not the same as the developed freedom of a person to realize his potentialities. But there is still another dimension: the full autonomy of choice can only occur in a developed personality.

Some theists attempt to impose authoritarian structures from without by establishing rules of conduct and instilling them in the young, offering no rhyme or reason other than God's commandments. These homilies often do not take hold, for they do not issue from within a person's felt life. Although they may erect defenses against temptation and immorality, they can often be weakened and may collapse. Basically irrational, they do not serve the individual in a changing social world in which new challenges are constantly being presented to him. If they are overthrown, what can the libertarian offer in their place?

The solution to the problem seems to me to be clear: libertarianism in its full sense—that is, the development of autonomous individuals capable of free choice—is not possible unless certain antecedent conditions are fulfilled: a program of moral education and growth is necessary to instill virtue in the young, not blind obedience to rules but the ability for conscious reflective choice. The Thrasymachian man, the absolute tyrant, as Plato long ago observed, is prey to every lust and passion, every temptation of power and ambition. He is buffeted by random irrational drives within, unable to resist or control them, and amoral power conflicts from without. The truly free individual is one whose choices in some sense emanate from a harmonious personality, one with some developed character, a set of dispositional traits, capable of a deliberate process of reasoned decision making.

This seems to me to be the message of the great philosophic tradition from Socrates and Aristotle to Spinoza, Mill, and Dewey: that rationality and virtue are the source of freedom. If this is the case, to grant freedom without preparation to a child or adolescent, a savage or despot, incapable of reflective choice or mature judgment, unrestrained by a seasoned disposition, is hardly a test of his freedom, for he may be at the mercy of impulses.

Accordingly, freedom makes no sense and is literally wasted unless it is first nourished in the soul of moral growth, where it can be watered and fed. It is as if democracy were suddenly imposed on a people unready for it, or for which it was alien. It can only function effectively where there are values of tolerance, respect for the views of others, a willingness to negotiate and compromise differences; and a sense of civic virtues and responsibilities. Similarly, true freedom for the individual presupposes the concomitant emergence of moral development. It presumes moral education.

What kind of education and by whom and for what ends? These are important questions. Education is a social process. It goes on constantly—in the family, the churches, the schools, business organizations, the media, in the greater society. It is not the sole responsibility of the state, for that may convert it into a form of mere indoctrination. By education, I mean the Greek form: self-actualization. We need to educate individuals so that they can realize their intellectual, aesthetic, and physical talents. And part of moral education is the developing capacity for self-mastery and control. It also involves the maturation of the ability to appreciate the needs of other human beings. In other words, moral education is training in responsibility: first, toward one's self, one's long-range self-interest in the world, learning how to cope with and solve problems that emerge in the environment; and second, toward others, developing altruistic concern for other human beings, an ability to share life's experiences, to help and be helped, to cooperate with others.

Kohlberg and Piaget have written at length about what they consider to be the stages of moral growth. One need not accept the precise theory as presented: from anticipation of reward and punishment, or conformity to social expectations, as motives of moral behavior, to considerations of utility, or the development of a sense of justice, as higher stages of moral growth. Nevertheless, one should surely recognize that there is a process of moral development. For there is a clear difference between the narcissistically self-centered individual (although some self-interest is an important component of a realistic ethics) and the person able to relate to others under conditions of mutual respect and cooperation. One should be more willing to entrust freedom to the latter person, and may be apprehensive about entrusting it to the former. Mill himself recognized that there is an important distinction between the "lower" and "higher" pleasures; the biological pleasures differ in kind from the aesthetic, intellectual, and moral pleasures of a developing human being. As a libertarian he was disturbed by the possible abuse of the hedonic criterion and insisted that pleasures differ on a qualitative scale.

To argue, as I have, that a philosophy of liberty most appropriately should involve a theory of virtue, does not imply that we should deny freedom to those who are incapable of using it in the fully developed sense. Nor should the government or any self-appointed group set itself up as the arbiter of human freedom. One may consistently believe in a free society, yet also recognize that we have a double obligation: to grant freedom to individuals and also to encourage them to acquire a taste and capacity for growth and autonomy. The best way of doing the latter is not by dictate but by means of education and persuasion. Because we tolerate diversity does not mean that we necessarily approve of every style of life, however bizarre or offensive, that has been adopted. We need constantly to keep alive the art of criticism and moral suasion.

Liberty does not imply permissiveness. It needs to be accompanied by an ethic that highlights the virtues of the mature personality. This includes *wisdom* (some capacity for intelligent reflective choice), *prudence and moderation* (some concern for one's long-range good) and *responsibility* (a genuine interest in the needs of others). Without virtue, the person freed from restraint may indeed be transformed into a moral monster.

Philosophers of ethics have consistently maintained that in the last analysis intelligence in an ordered personality is the most reliable guide for moral choice. What we ought to do is a function of a deliberate process wherein we examine alternatives, means and consequences and after a comparative analysis make a choice that we consider to be the most suitable in the situation. One of the tasks of moral education is to develop persons who are capable of engaging in moral inquiry.

This will not do, we are reminded by critics of moral libertarianism, particularly those of a nonsecularist bent. Merely to have an autonomous individual is no guarantee that he will behave morally toward himself or others. We cannot educate men to be virtuous, we are told, without the authority of divine sanction. If the only guide is utilitarian ends, whether for the individual or the social good, then anything is possible and all things may be permissible. The critics of secular humanism and libertarianism also attack the effort now under way to develop moral education and values clarification in the schools. They believe this is a "secular religion" that will only further undermine the moral standards of society.

Now it is true that many or most libertarians have emphasized utilitarian considerations in the decision-making process. Moral principles are held to be largely instrumental in the fulfillment of ends or values. The hedonic calculus judges actions by whether they maximize pleasure or happiness in the individual and society. Most libertarians have been relativists, situationalists, and naturalists. Such ethical theories have lacked a well-grounded theory of moral duty and obligation. In my view, however, this need not be the case. Libertarianism is incomplete as a moral philosophy and remains seriously in need of repair unless it is willing to modify its ethical system so that it can introduce deontological considerations.

What I have in mind here is the recognition that there are general ethical principles that ought to prevail in human relationships. These are grounded in human experience, and have been tested in the crucible of history. Moral principles, in my judgment, are not simply an expression of subjective taste or caprice, but may have some empirical foundation. They are amenable to objective criticism. The human decencies are readily recognized by most human societies. We ought to tell the truth, be sincere, honest, and deal fairly with others; we ought to be cooperative, kind, considerate, thoughtful, helpful; we ought not to waste our patrimony needlessly; we ought not to misuse others, be arrogant and unforgiving; we ought not to inflict pain needlessly or cruelly, not be excessively vindictive; we ought to have friends not simply acquaintances; we ought to seek justice and be beneficent.

This list of ethical principles is embodied in the proverbial truths discovered in human affairs. Many or most—but perhaps not all—are transcultural. They are general guides to conduct, not universal or absolute, since exceptions can be made to them on occasion. Nor are they intuitive or self-evident; if they are tested, it is by their observable consequences in conduct. They have some foundation in our sense of reason; and they may be given some strength in our motivation, and be enhanced by emotion and feeling. They involve both our attitudes and beliefs. They are prima facie, for they would seem to express general rules of conduct, which people come to recognize and respect as binding. How they apply and to what extent depends on the context. Sometimes one or more ethical principles may conflict. They may conflict with our cherished values. Moral deliberation is usually difficult, and often we must choose between the lesser of two evils. Or there may be a clash between two goods or two rights, both of which we cannot have.

These ethical principles embody moral truths. We may learn from practical experience that they cannot be easily violated without unfortunate consequences. They may be certified on their own merits without being derived or deduced from questionable theological or metaphysical assumptions. Human experience lends them authenticity.

Thus one may respond to the critics of moral libertarianism in the following manner:

1. Moral conduct is possible without belief in God, or benefit of religion or clergy. (Believers are not more moral than unbelievers.)

2. Reasonable moral choices can be made and moral knowledge discovered in the process of human living and experience.

3. Accordingly, there can be an intelligent basis for moral obligations and responsibility.

One can be a moral libertarian and a secularist without being a libertine or a degenerate, and one may display the marks of nobility and excellence as part of the good life (as exemplified in the philosophies of Aristotle and Spinoza). In this post-Freudian age one may also live a significant moral life, which contains passion and reason, enjoyment and happiness, creativity and responsibility.

Freedom is not simply a claim to be made against society or a demand to be left alone. Freedom is not to be experienced indiscriminately nor squandered stupidly. It is an art to be cultivated and nourished intelligently. The intemperate person is neither autonomous nor civilized in respect to himself or his relations with others. Liberty and moral development go hand in hand; one can enhance the other. There is no complete freedom until there is the developed capacity for maturity in judgment and action. There can be no fully autonomous person unless there is realized growth.

Various forms of libertarianism can be defended independently of a secular focus. One can be an economic or civil libertarian and at the same time a born-again Christian, Buddhist monk, practicing Jew, devout Hindu, or Roman Catholic. We should not insist that secular libertarianism is the only basis for the moral life. I happen to believe that it is the one most in accord with the realities of nature and the promise of individual attainment. In a pluralistic society, those who wish to believe in God or to base their morality on religious faith should be perfectly free to do so. For many moderns, however, God is dead. But to be committed to the secular city does not mean that morality is dead or without moorings. Ethics is a vital dimension of the human condition, and a recognition of the ethical life has deep roots within Western philosophy, antecedent even to the Judeo-Christian tradition. The current attack on secular morality is a display of ignorance about the origins of Western civilization in Hellenic culture and its historic philosophic development. It is an attack on the philosophical life itself.

The charges against moral libertarianism are thus unfounded. Those who now oppose it cannot tolerate moral freedom nor can they stand to see other individuals suffer or enjoy life as they choose. But who are they to seek to impose their values on others? The fact that they assume a mantle of divine sanction for their views does not make them authoritative. Moreover, they fail to appreciate the fact that a moral person is not one who obeys a moral code out of fear or faith but who is motivated to behave morally out of a sense of moral awareness and conviction. The exemplar for the moral libertarian is the free person, capable of choice, yet one who has achieved some measure of moral growth. He is the master of his own fate, responsible for his own career and destiny.

The free person is unlike the obedient servant or slave, who follows a moral code simply because it is commanded by authority or tradition. The free individual is independent, resourceful, and has confidence in his power to lead the good life. Moreover, he can enter into dignified relationships of trust and sincerity with his fellow human beings. He can live a constructive, productive, and responsible life. The moral philosophy of libertarian humanism is thus worthy of admiration. It need not apologize to those who seek to demean or denigrate its excellence or virtue. In a sense it is the highest expression of moral virtue: a tribute to the indomitable creative spirit of human achievement and personality.

3

Humanism and Democracy*

Corliss Lamont

Humanist principles demand the widest possible extension of democracy to all relevant aspects of human living. The humanist conception of democracy naturally incorporates earlier contributions to the democratic ideal such as the guarantees embodied in the American Bill of Rights, and the stirring battle cry of the French Revolution, "Liberty, Equality, Fraternity." Also humanists the world over subscribe to the internationally valid tenets of the Universal Declaration of Human Rights adopted by the United Nations General Assembly in 1948.

Democracy is of course a method as well as a goal. It is the most intelligent method of conduct in political life, of carrying through social changes and of settling disagreements in the realm of public affairs. The life of reason, the appeal to the supreme court of the mind, for which philosophy stands, implies in its very essence peaceful persuasion through the free exchange and competition of ideas in the wide arena of social discussion. The philosophic ideal is the transformation of our

*Originally published in Corliss Lamont, *Humanism as a Philosophy* (1949). Subsequently published as *The Philosophy of Humanism* (New York: Continuum, 1990). Copyright © 1990 by Corliss Lamont. Reprinted by permission of The Continuum Publishing Company.

bitter social and economic disputes into great Platonic dialogues carried on in legislative bodies and the organs of public opinion—dialogues, however, that in due course have a definite outcome and therefore do not end as inconclusively as most of those in which Socrates took part.

Humanism's support of the democratic way is a matter of both idealism and realism. To quote Professor Reinhold Niebuhr's epigram, "Man's capacity for justice makes democracy possible; but man's inclination to injustice makes democracy necessary."[1] Democracy is a comparatively new thing in the world; and a very radical thing. Violence, bloodshed, coercion, and war—both civil and international—are the old, traditional methods of resolving deep-going conflicts of opinion and interest. Such methods have been wasteful, in terms of human life and economic dislocation, beyond all computation. Often they have succeeded in curing one evil only by substituting another.

Since humanism as a functioning credo is so closely bound up with the methods of reason and science, plainly free speech and democracy are of its very lifeblood. For reason and scientific method can fully flourish only in an atmosphere of civil liberties. Humanism envisions a republican society where humanists and everyone else can express unorthodox ideas on any subject without risking persecution, prosecution, execution, exile, obloquy, or loss of employment. As a minority position at present humanism must defend democracy on the grounds of both the social good and sheer self-interest. Only if the channels of opinion are kept open can the humanist viewpoint hope to win a majority in the nation and the world.

A true democracy welcomes differences and disagreements and cherishes, as a creative force in society, minority criticisms of existing institutions and prevailing patterns of thought. The democratic spirit is not dogmatic, for it recognizes the value of constant challenges to basic assumptions. The crackpot may turn out to be the trailblazer; the genius usually starts his career as a dissident minority of one; and many a leading statesman spent much of his earlier life in a jail or prison camp.

Humanism, then, urges complete democracy as both an end and a means; and insists that the idea of democracy has developed in history mainly in a humanistic way, needing no support or sanction in supernatural revelations or metaphysical guarantees. The humanist requires no cosmic spokesman to inform or remind him of the dignity of man and the ideal of human brotherhood. The most democratic countries certainly are not and have not been those most steeped in supernatural religion. Humanist belief in democracy as the goal and in democratic processes as the method is not derivative from extrahuman sources; it stands on its own feet.

In the past Americans have been prone to think of democracy mainly in terms of political democracy and civil liberties. These basic forms of democracy are crucial because they provide the central mechanisms for orderly change and progress. But from the humanist standpoint they are not in themselves sufficient, even when fully actualized, for a completely democratic society. Needless to say, such actualization has never taken place in the United States or any other country that professes to be democratic.

Humanists advocate the broadest possible application of democracy to the functioning of nongovernmental agencies and organizations and in extrapolitical fields such as those of economics, cultural activity, and race relations. Humanism recommends, too, affirmative federal and state legislation in America to strengthen the enforcement of democratic rights throughout the country, with recognition of the principle that modern democracy in a complex industrial society demands not only safeguards against governmental tyranny, but also positive action by government to safeguard freedom.

Unfortunately, *democracy* has become one of those infinitely ambiguous terms that defy the dictionaries, confound the statesmen, and confuse the people. Yet it remains a good and useful word. An essential task of humanism as a philosophy is to clarify the meaning of an important idea such as that of democracy. One way of doing this is to break down this very general concept into various categories, to think of democracy in its specific applications. Thus I find that there are at least ten different types of democracy, all interrelated and to some extent overlapping, but all susceptible to differentiation.

First, there is *political democracy,* that is, government of, by, and for the people under republican or parliamentary institutions. Political democracy establishes and enforces suitable regulations for free elections, majority rule, major and minor political parties, and the functioning of government. In a democracy the state is the servant of the people and is controlled by the people. Though a democracy must proceed on the basis of majority decisions, it has the obligation of fully protecting the rights of minorities. The principle of majority rule is unacceptable unless fair opportunity is given for the evolution of minorities, new or old, into majorities.

Second, there are *civil liberties,* under which all individuals and groups have the right to free speech, due process of law, and equality before the law. In the United States our basic civil liberties are outlined in the federal Constitution, primarily under the first ten amendments, known as the Bill of Rights. These original guarantees have been greatly broadened and complicated by the development of new and potent media for the transmission of ideas, such as motion pictures, radio, television, and newspapers with a mass circulation; by the growth of monopolies in these same fields of communication; and by the increasing strength and scope of the labor movement. The movies and television underscore the point that the right to see is now one of the most important of civil liberties. The freedom of people to see, hear, and read—for acquiring knowledge or for enjoyment—is as essential as the individual's right to speak, write, or create as an artist.

In my judgment civil libertarians have stressed too much the undoubted fact that freedom of expression is the best way for men to arrive at the truth. The justification for free speech goes deeper than that. For the realm of significant meaning and cultural creativity is far wider than the realm of truth. Novels, poetry, and art do not need to be true in a factual or scientific sense; the human imagination cannot permit itself to be fettered by fact. Moreover, human thought at all levels is bound up with language and communication, which is necessary for men's intellectual development and training in the use of reason. Communication is also necessary to learning and mastering the processes of democratic self-government.

After World War II a dangerous and widespread movement developed in the United States to abrogate or abridge the ordinary civil liberties of individuals and groups who did not conform to prevailing patterns of opinion.* Reminiscent of the repressive years following World War I, this antidemocratic campaign made headway under the guise of fighting communism and Communists. True to form, government officials and government bodies have encouraged this campaign and in many ways have led it.

For example, various congressional committees have run wild over the past two decades. The House Un-American Activities Committee, the Senate Subcommittee on Internal Security, and the Senate Permanent Subcommittee on Investigations (at one time known as the McCarthy committee) have consistently flouted the Bill of Rights. Legislation repressing free speech and association has been passed, such as the Smith Act, the Internal Security Act, the Communist Control Act, and a spate of state laws—all ostensibly aimed at Communists, but also intended to silence criticism by frightening the nonconformist. Hand in hand with such legislation have gone harsh administrative strictures on the part of federal and state governments. Widespread loyalty programs, blacklists of organizations and individuals, and denials of passports have been the order of the day.

The drive against freedom has extended to every field of cultural activity. Education, book publishing, newspaper reporting, religion, the movies, radio and television, drama, painting, music, and the other arts have all been seriously affected. Pressure groups such as the Daughters of the American Revolution and the American Legion have joined enthusiastically in the attempt to suppress heterodoxy or even mild liberalism.

At the very height, however, of the repressive movement known as McCarthyism the judiciary of the United States began to reassert the rights of the individual. This return to constitutional principles in the realm of law became particularly marked in 1957 when the U.S. Supreme Court, under the leadership of Chief Justice Earl Warren, handed down a number of far-reaching decisions favorable to basic civil liberties. These decisions drastically curtailed the sweeping powers

---

*For a detailed survey of the civil liberties crisis in the United States from approximately 1946 to 1956, see my book *Freedom Is as Freedom Does* (Horizon Press, 1956). This study includes the story of my successful battle against the McCarthy committee in its attempt to have me jailed for alleged contempt of Congress.

which had been assumed by congressional investigating committees; insisted that government loyalty programs and criminal prosecutions of Communists, labor leaders, and dissenters in general must conform to the Constitution; and upheld the traditional principle of academic freedom. The Supreme Court continued, with some qualifications, to make rulings in support of the Bill of Rights; and by the early sixties there had become evident in America a definite turning of the tide toward freedom.

Third in the humanist inventory of democracy there is *racial* or *ethnic democracy,* commonly known as *civil rights,* wherein all racial or national groups and minorities stand on an equal basis with other ethnic groups and are not subject to discrimination in any sphere of life. In the international sphere racial democracy has made rapid strides since World War II through the winning of liberation and nationhood by many colored colonial peoples in Africa and Asia. In the United States race prejudice is concentrated against the Negroes, more than 22,000,000 in number. It also operates against other minorities such as Indians, Jews, Orientals, and Puerto Ricans.

The epoch-making report of President Truman's Committee on Civil Rights, *To Secure These Rights* (1947), devotes the major portion of its space to recounting the extent and seriousness of racial inequality and injustice in America, from the brutal and violent lynchings of Negroes to the quiet ostracism of Jews through the "gentleman's agreement" and the pervasive rule of "restricted clientele" or "Christians only." The legal and extralegal discrimination, segregation, and general humiliation which America's minorities are compelled to suffer relegates them in effect to second-class citizenship.

The close relationship between ethnic and political democracy is seen in the barriers against Negroes' voting in the South during the more than one hundred years since President Lincoln's Emancipation Proclamation. This situation has recently improved somewhat. Complete racial democracy is impossible without economic and cultural democracy, a fact demonstrated, again, in the eleven Southern states of the Old Confederacy, where the acknowledged aim has been to keep the Negro "in his place" at a low economic and cultural level. The 1954 decision of the U.S. Supreme Court outlawing racial segregation in the public schools of America constituted a portentous step in the direction of educational and ethnic democracy for the Negro.

The nationwide disregard and defiant flouting of that decision, however, demonstrate up to the hilt that the enforcement of Supreme Court rulings in the United States does not take place automatically. It is dependent on both the posture of public opinion in a state or locality and the vigor of law enforcement officials. The Civil Rights Act, passed by Congress in 1964, was another step forward, but we may be sure that its actualization will take many, many years.

Humanism declares categorically that no country is truly democratic when racial minorities of whatever stock are denied the constitutional and other rights of citizens in general. The notion of inherent white superiority in a world of peoples predominantly black, brown, or yellow in color has no standing from a democratic, ethical, or scientific viewpoint. It is utterly contrary to the humanist outlook.

Fourth, there is *economic democracy,* the right of every adult to a useful job at a decent wage or salary, to general economic security and opportunity, to an equitable share in the material goods of this life, and to a proportionate voice in the conduct of economic affairs. Economic democracy, as I define it, goes far beyond freedom from want, since it does not mean merely material security. Such security can be established on a rather restricted minimum basis. Full economic democracy, however, implies a higher and higher standard of living for the whole population as the overall wealth of a nation increases. While not entailing equality of income, it does imply some surplus above minimum security, so that individuals and families can enjoy the cultural amenities and have an adequate chance for rest, recreation, and travel. Of course discrimination in employment or wage scale against any particular group, on grounds of race, religion, sex, or politics, constitutes a violation of economic democracy.

In his message to Congress of January 11, 1944, President Franklin D. Roosevelt outlined an extensive program of economic democracy. After referring to the inalienable constitutional liberties of the American republic, he stated:

As our nation has grown in size and stature, however—as our industrial economy expanded—these political rights proved inadequate to assure us equality in the pursuit of happiness. We have come to a clear realization of the fact that true individual freedom cannot exist without economic security and independence. . . . In our day these economic truths have become accepted as self-evident. We have accepted, so to speak, a second Bill of Rights under which a new basis of security and prosperity can be established for all—regardless of station, race or creed.

The president then enumerated the economic rights that he considered essential to freedom.

Fifth, there is *organizational democracy,* the carrying out of democratic principles in and by the manifold nongovernmental organizations, societies, associations, councils, and committees that operate in a nation like the United States. This covers the management and activities of churches, professional associations, fraternal bodies, clubs, trade unions, political parties, veterans' associations, and pressure groups of every complexion. Such organizations are so numerous in this country and wield such public influence that their democratic functioning, both internally and externally, is of great importance for American democracy. Since World War II there has been a serious recrudescence of private censorship and "vigilante" groups, such as the Ku Klux Klan and the recently organized John Birch Society, that are a constant menace to American liberties. On the other hand, labor unions have also been guilty of undemocratic practices, especially in that some of them still maintain a color bar to membership.

Sixth, there is *social democracy,* in which every person recognizes the inherent worth and dignity of every other person as a member of the human family, and in which social stratification, snobbery, and classes based on varying economic, intellectual, or other functions no longer exist. This form of democracy includes complete functional democracy, the realization that every productive job makes its particular contribution to the total community life and that therefore everyone who does useful work stands on a plane of ethical equality with everyone else so far as the nature of his work is concerned. Humanist democracy in this sense does not ask us to forget that differences in ability and intelligence will always prevail among men; it does insist that castes and snobberies stemming from such differencs be eliminated. And it is always mindful of Kant's classic statement: *"So act as to treat humanity, whether in thine own person or in that of any other, in every case as an end withal, never as a means only."*[2]

Very important in social democracy is a feeling of inner warmth and friendliness toward our fellow men, a sympathetic desire to see them prosper, a determination to be fair and honest in our dealings with them. This attitude includes the ability to argue firmly and un-compromisingly in private or public, yet to disagree with others in a tolerant manner; to experience victory or defeat in public affairs, yet not give way to anger, malice, or hatred. As Walter Lippmann has so well put it, democracy "is a fraternity which holds men together against anything that could divide them. It cools their fevers, subdues their appetites and restrains them from believing and saying and doing those irreconcilable, irreparable, inexpiable things which burst asunder the bonds of affection and trust."[3]

Seventh, there is *cultural and educational democracy,* the right of all to a full and equal opportunity to share in the cultural and educational, the artistic and intellectual life of the nation. True cultural democracy demands, in the first instance, the possession of enough leisure and money on the part of the masses of the people so that they can fully participate in the enjoyment of literature, music, painting, the theater, and the like; and so that those of really professional ability may enter the cultural field as a vocation and work upward to the summits of creative achievement.

The concept of educational democracy implies the administration of schools, colleges, and other educational institutions, whether public or private, according to democratic principles, including nondiscrim-ination in admissions policy toward such minority groups as Jews and Negroes. It also covers academic freedom. This means that all teachers and employees in school, college, or university are entitled to full liberty of expression and association, as guaranteed under the Bill of Rights, without any interference or penalization on the part of the educational institution which employs them. The teacher has the right to speak his mind in the classroom, as long as he maintains the recognized standards of professional competence and scholarship. Students also have the right to voice their opinions and to join organizations of their choice.

Eighth, there is *democracy in religion and philosophy,* the right of all individuals and groups to profess, practice, and publicize their chosen religion or philosophy. By the very nature of their beliefs, humanists are very much concerned with this type of democracy, which implies the liberty to be nonreligious or antireligious, to be agnostic or atheist. In the United States this right includes, according to the First Amendment, separation of church and state, and thus rules out intervention by the government on behalf of any particular religion. Yet during recent years Congress has made repeated inroads on this principle. In 1954 it amended the Pledge of Allegiance by inserting the words "under God"; and a year later passed an act requiring that the motto "In God We Trust" be printed on all U.S. paper currency.

Meanwhile, ecclesiastical authorities have increased their efforts to weaken the wall between church and state. In 1963 the U.S. Supreme Court counteracted these attempts to some extent by deciding eight to one in the Schempp-Murray case that the reading of Bible verses of the Lord's Prayer in public schools was unconstitutional. Admittedly, religious pressure groups remain quite powerful in curtailing or preventing public criticism of supernaturalistic doctrines, especially in the press and over the air. We cannot pretend that fair and equal treatment is accorded the discussion of humanism at the present time.

One of the battles humanists have been waging for decades is to win exemption from military service for conscientious objectors who oppose participation in war on ethical grounds instead of conventionally religious ones. Daniel Andrew Seeger has challenged in the courts of the United States the U.S. Selective Service Act's limitation of draft exemptions to those who have faith in a supreme being. In 1964 a federal appeals court in New York City handed down a unanimous decision in favor of Mr. Seeger in which it asserted: "The stern and moral voice of conscience occupies that hallowed place in the hearts and minds of men which was traditionally reserved for the commandments of God." The U.S. Supreme Court consented to hear an appeal filed by the Department of Justice in this case.

Ninth, there is *democracy between the sexes,* that is, equality between men and women in all relevant ways. This covers the legal, political, economic, educational, and moral spheres. In the East, where the legal and social inequality of the sexes used to be particularly deep-seated, nations such as Communist China and the Soviet Union have recently made immense strides in releasing women from traditional restrictions and giving them new freedoms. In the more advanced democracies of the West, such as Great Britain and the United States, it was only during the first part of the twentieth century that the female sex attained the right of suffrage. This has not, however, brought full political equality; and relatively few women in these countries have been elected to public office. Furthermore, many barriers remain against the female sex in the nonpolitical sectors of life.

In America we spend on the education of women a tiny percentage of what we spend on that of men. Only a small proportion of university professional schools admit members of the female sex. In the economic sphere, even in the United States with all its mechanical gadgets and labor-saving devices, women in general are still preoccupied with the routine tasks of cooking, washing, cleaning, and taking care of the children. The important careers of motherhood and home management are not given their due under what I have called functional democracy. At the same time the male tends to remain dominant in the home, with the wife spiritually subservient and curtailed in her freedom of opinion when her views happen to run counter to her husband's. The vice of "male chauvinism" has by no means become a thing of the past.

Tenth and last, there is *international democracy,* in which all peoples organized as nations live on terms of equality, freedom, and friendship, and do not interfere with the legitimate and peaceful aspirations of one another. This variety of democracy coalesces with the humanist aim of enduring world peace. It functions in all forms of international co-operation and more especially today in the International Court of Justice and, with definite limitations, in the United Nations. International democracy and the other types of democracy closely interlock and give moral encouragement and practical stability to one another. The peace that comes with genuine international democracy creates a world atmosphere of calm and security favorable to the growth of the other forms of democracy. Conversely, a state of hostility or war between different countries creates an atmosphere of tension, fear, and crisis unfavorable to democratic institutions and likely to weaken whatever democracy does exist.

My discussion of democracy again underlines the point that the philosophy of humanism is far more than opposition to supernatural beliefs and a corresponding concentration upon the things of this world. The mind of man knows of no adequate substitute for the democratic concept. The humanist holds that the idea of democracy in the broad sense has permanent validity for human living. Democracy in the narrow sense of formal political democracy is not only inadequate for the needs of men, but tends to discredit the democratic way, because when democracy is so restricted in function it cannot possibly solve the economic, social, and racial problems of mankind. There can be no adequate and complete humanism unless it is a full-fledged *democratic* humanism.

Notes

1. Reinhold Niebuhr, *The Children of Light and the Children of Darkness* (New York: Scribners, 1944), p. xi.

2. *Kant's Critique of Practical Reason and Other Works on the Theory of Ethics,* trans. T. K. Abbott (London: Longmans, Green, 1923), p. 47.

3. Walter Lippmann, "Today and Tomorrow," *New York Herald Tribune,* February 1, 1944.

Part IV

Values Aesthetic and Religious

Section 7

Art and Aesthetics

A naturalist philosophy of art, whatever else it might say, will look to integrate the artistic process into the broad range of human activities, and the authors represented in this chapter, each in his own way, do just that. In "The Live Creature," which is the first chapter of his 1934 book, *Art as Experience,* John Dewey contends that to understand art and its significance it must be understood in its relations with the rest of experience, and in fact it should be regarded as a dimension or aspect of experience in general. Dewey realizes that this may sound odd to us, since we are inclined to accept a "compartmental" conception of art, or what he also calls a "museum" conception, which removes art from its place in ordinary experience. He suggests, however, that this conception is itself the effect of identifiable, historical causes. With the rise of capitalism, nationalism, and colonialism, Dewey says, new nations needed both to boast of their past cultural achievements and to display their recently acquired booty; and, furthermore, the individual beneficiaries of European colonialism needed a way to display their wealth and position, and art provided the means to do that. Whatever its causes, we need to overcome the compartmental, museum conception of art and realize, Dewey argues, that the aesthetic is not something separate, but a quality of life itself. Experience, which is the interaction of organism with its environment, has both harmony and discord, and the aesthetic quality of experience is its harmony.

While Dewey is here interested in the aesthetic dimension of all experience, Meyer Schapiro in his essay is primarily concerned with the social character of art. Schapiro was born in 1904 in Lithuania, and came to the United States with his family in 1907. He grew up in Brooklyn, New York, and like so many other contributors to this volume studied at Columbia University. In 1929 he received his Ph.D. from the Department of Art History at Columbia. In 1928 he had accepted a lectureship in that department, and he taught there until his retirement in the late 1970s. Though not a philosopher by profession, Schapiro moved in the naturalist circles of Columbia and New York City intellectual life, and he was also active in New York's socialist and Marxist movements. He was, for example, a founding editor of *Marxist Quarterly* in 1937, and the essay reprinted here was first given at the 1936 American Artists' Congress, which bore the subtitle "Artists Against War and Fascism." Schapiro begins with an antireductionism common among naturalists, in this case that it would be a mistake in our analysis of art to try to reduce it to social factors such as economics or politics. Art, he points out, has its own materials and its own psychological characteristics. Despite its unique traits, however, it is the case that social factors go a long way in accounting for the ways we understand art, for what we think it is, for artistic styles, for the reasons we think its styles should or should not change, and for many of the aspects of art's formal elements and of our expectations. This is as true today, Schapiro argues, as it was in earlier epochs, or might still be in other societies, in which art was more overtly determined by ideological, religious, or political purposes. Like Dewey, Schapiro finds one of the crucial social factors to be economic class, thus the emphasis here on the class basis of modern abstract art.

In his 1974 book *The Main of Light,* from which his piece here is excerpted, Justus Buchler brings to bear both his general ontology and his theory of judgment on aesthetic theory, in particular on a study of poetry. A judgment, as Buchler uses the term, is any human product, whether deliberately or consciously produced or not, and in his theory human beings judge or produce in three modes—assertive, active, and exhibitive. Art, he argues, is exhibitive judgment. We have a tendency to associate certain activities with certain modes of judgment. We might think, for example, that language is assertive judgment, that bodily movement is active judgment, and that pictures are exhibitive judgment. This, Buchler argues, is a mistake. Any kind of activity can function in any mode of judgment, depending on the related factors which make up the activity's environing conditions. Thus, for example, language can function in any of the three modes. It can assert—"There is snow on the ground"; it can act—"I now pronounce you husband and wife"; and it can exhibit—"To sleep, perchance to dream. Ay, there's the rub." Poetry, and literary art in general, is linguistic utterance which judges exhibitively. Buchler is also interested in understanding the fact that though it is not assertive, poetry nevertheless has a probing character. Indeed, all three modes of judgment can be "exploratory," each in its own way. For example, we capture the exploratory character of science, or of philosophy, by calling them forms of inquiry. But poetry, though it too may "seek," is not inquiry. To understand its difference from and similarity to science or philosophy we need, Buchler contends, a conception of Query, which is the genus of which scientific inquiry and artistic interrogation are both species.

1

The Live Creature*

John Dewey

By one of the ironic perversities that often attend the course of affairs, the existence of the works of art upon which formation of an aesthetic theory depends has become an obstruction to theory about them. For one reason, these works are products that exist externally and physically. In common conception, the work of art is often identified with the building, book, painting, or statue in its existence apart from human experience. Since the actual work of art is what the product does with and in experience, the result is not favorable to understanding. In addition, the very perfection of some of these products, the prestige they possess because of a long history of unquestioned admiration, creates conventions that get in the way of fresh insight. When an art product once attains classic status, it somehow becomes isolated from the human conditions under which it was brought into being and from the human consequences it engenders in actual life experience.

When artistic objects are separated from both conditions of origin

---

*Originally published in John Dewey, *Art as Experience* (1934). Subsequently published in vol. 10 of *The Later Works of John Dewey,* ed. by J. A. Boydston (Carbondale, Ill.: Southern Illinois University Press, 1987). Reprinted by permission of The Board of Trustees, Southern Illinois University.

and operation in experience, a wall is built around them that renders almost opaque their general significance, with which aesthetic theory deals. Art is remitted to a separate realm, where it is cut off from that association with the materials and aims of every other form of human effort, undergoing, and achievement. A primary task is thus imposed upon one who undertakes to write upon the philosophy of the fine arts. This task is to restore continuity between the refined and intensified forms of experience that are works of art and the everyday events, doings, and sufferings that are universally recognized to constitute experience. Mountain peaks do not float unsupported; they do not even just rest upon the earth. They *are* the earth in one of its manifest operations. It is the business of those who are concerned with the theory of the earth, geographers and geologists, to make this fact evident in its various implications. The theorist who would deal philosophically with fine art has a like task to accomplish.

If one is willing to grant this position, even if only by way of temporary experiment, he will see that there follows a conclusion at first sight surprising. In order to understand the meaning of artistic products, we have to forget them for a time, to turn aside from them and have recourse to the ordinary forces and conditions of experience that we do not usually regard as aesthetic. We must arrive at the theory of art by means of a detour. For theory is concerned with understanding, insight, not without exclamations of admiration, and stimulation of that emotional outburst often called appreciation. It is quite possible to enjoy flowers in their colored form and delicate fragrance without knowing anything about plants theoretically. But if one sets out to *understand* the flowering of plants, he is committed to finding out something about the interactions of soil, air, water, and sunlight that condition the growth of plants.

By common consent, the Parthenon is a great work of art. Yet it has aesthetic standing only as the work becomes an experience for a human being. And, if one is to go beyond personal enjoyment into the formation of a theory about that large republic of art of which the building is one member, one has to be willing at some point in his reflections to turn from it to the bustling, arguing, acutely sensitive Athenian citizens, with civic sense identified with a civic religion, of whose experience the temple was an expression, and who built it not as a work of art but as a civic commemoration. The turning to them is as human beings who had needs that were a demand for the building and that were carried to fulfillment in it; it is not an examination such as might be carried on by a sociologist in search for material relevant to his purpose. The one who sets out to theorize about the aesthetic experience embodied in the Parthenon must realize in thought what the people into whose lives it entered had in common, as creators and as those who were satisfied with it, with people in our own homes and on our own streets.

In order to *understand* the aesthetic in its ultimate and approved forms, one must begin with it in the raw; in the events and scenes that hold the attentive eye and ear of man, arousing his interest and affording him enjoyment as he looks and listens: the sights that hold the crowd—the fire engine rushing by; the machines excavating enormous holes in the earth; the human fly climbing the steeple-side; the men perched high in air on girders, throwing and catching red-hot bolts. The sources of art in human experience will be learned by him who sees how the tense grace of the ballplayer infects the onlooking crowd; who notes the delight of the housewife in tending her plants, and the intent interest of her good man in tending the patch of green in front of the house; the zest of the spectator in poking the wood burning on the hearth and in watching the darting flames and crumbling coals. These people, if questioned as to the reason for their actions, would doubtless return reasonable answers. The man who poked the sticks of burning wood would say he did it to make the fire burn better; but he is nonetheless fascinated by the colorful drama of change enacted before his eyes and imaginatively partakes in it. He does not remain a cold spectator. What Coleridge said to the reader of poetry is true in its way of all who are happily absorbed in their activities of mind and body: "The reader should be carried forward, not merely or chiefly by the mechanical impulse of curiosity, not by a restless desire to arrive at the final solution, but by the pleasurable activity of the journey itself."

The intelligent mechanic engaged in his job, interested in doing well and finding satisfaction in his handiwork, caring for his materials and tools with genuine affection, is artistically engaged. The difference between such a worker and the inept and careless bungler is as great in the shop as it is in the studio. Oftentimes the product may not appeal to the aesthetic sense of those who use the product. The fault, however, is oftentimes not so much with the worker as with the conditions of the market for which his product is designed. Were conditions and opportunities different, things as significant to the eye as those produced by earlier craftsmen would be made.

So extensive and subtly pervasive are the ideas that set art upon a remote pedestal, that many a person would be repelled rather than pleased if told that he enjoyed his casual recreations, in part at least, because of their aesthetic quality. The arts which today have most vitality for the average person are things he does not take to be arts: for instance, the movie, jazz music, the comic strip, and, too frequently, newspaper accounts of love nests, murders, and exploits of bandits. For, when what he knows as art is relegated to the museum and gallery, the unconquerable impulse toward experiences enjoyable in themselves finds such outlet as the daily environment provides. Many a person who protests against the museum conception of art still shares the fallacy from which that conception springs. For the popular notion comes from a separation of art from the objects and scenes of ordinary experience that many theorists and critics pride themselves on holding and even elaborating. The times when select and distinguished objects are closely connected with the products of usual vocations are the times when appreciation of the former is most rife and most keen. When, because of their remoteness, the objects acknowledged by the cultivated to be works of fine art seem anemic to the mass of people, aesthetic hunger is likely to seek the cheap and the vulgar.

The factors that have glorified fine art by setting it upon a far-off pedestal did not arise within the realm of art nor is their influence confined to the arts. For many persons an aura of mingled awe and unreality encompasses the "spiritual" and the "ideal" while "matter" has become by contrast a term of depreciation, something to be explained away or apologized for. The forces at work are those that have removed religion as well as fine art from the scope of the common or community life. These forces have historically produced so many of the dislocations and divisions of modern life and thought that art could not escape their influence. We do not have to travel to the ends of the earth nor return many millennia in time to find peoples for whom everything that intensifies the sense of immediate living is an object of intense admiration. Bodily scarification, waving feathers, gaudy robes, shining ornaments of gold and silver, of emerald and jade, formed the contents of aesthetic arts, and, presumably, without the vulgarity of class exhibitionism that attends their analogues today. Domestic utensils, furnishings of tent and house, rugs, mats, jars, pots, bows, spears, were wrought with such delighted care that today we hunt them out and give them places of honor in our art museums. Yet in their own time and place, such things were enhancements of the processes of everyday life. Instead of being elevated to a niche apart, they belonged to display of prowess, the manifestation of group and clan membership, worship of gods, feasting and fasting, fighting, hunting, and all the rhythmic crises that punctuate the stream of living.

Dancing and pantomime, the sources of the art of the theater, flourished as part of religious rites and celebrations. Musical art abounded in the fingering of the stretched string, the beating of the taut skin, the blowing with reeds. Even in the caves, human habitations were adorned with colored pictures that kept alive to the senses experiences with the animals that were so closely bound with the lives of humans. Structures that housed their gods and the instrumentalities that facilitate commerce with the higher powers were wrought with special fineness. But the arts of the drama, music, painting, and architecture thus exemplified had no peculiar connection with theaters, galleries, museums. They were part of the significant life of an organized community.

The collective life that was manifested in war, worship, the forum, knew no division between what was characteristic of these places and operations, and the arts that brought color, grace, and dignity, into them. Painting and sculpture were organically one with architecture, as that was one with the social purpose that buildings served. Music and song were intimate parts of the rites and ceremonies in which the meaning of group life was consummated. Drama was a vital reenactment of the legends and history of group life. Not even in Athens can such arts be torn loose from this setting in direct experience and yet retain their significant character. Athletic sports, as well as drama, celebrated and enforced traditions of race and group, instructing the people, commemorating glories, and strengthening their civic pride.

Under such conditions, it is not surprising that the Athenian Greeks, when they came to reflect upon art, formed the idea that it is an act of reproduction, or imitation. There are many objections to this conception. But the vogue of the theory is testimony to the close connection of the fine arts with daily life; the idea would not have occurred to anyone had art been remote from the interests of life. For the doctrine did not signify that art was a literal copying of objects, but that it reflected the emotions and ideas that are associated with the chief institutions of social life. Plato felt this connection so strongly that it led him to his idea of the necessity of censorship of poets, dramatists, and musicians. Perhaps he exaggerated when he said that a change from the Doric to the Lydian mode in music would be the sure precursor of civic degeneration. But no contemporary would have doubted that music was an integral part of the ethos and the institutions of the community. The idea of "art for art's sake" would not have been even understood.

There must then be historic reasons for the rise of the compartmental conception of fine art. Our present museums and galleries to which works of fine art are removed and stored illustrate some of the causes that have operated to segregate art instead of finding it an attendant of temple, forum, and other forms of associated life. An instructive history of modern art could be written in terms of the formation of the distinctively modern institutions of museum and exhibition gallery. I may point to a few outstanding facts. Most European museums are, among other things, memorials of the rise of nationalism and imperialism. Every capital must have its own museum of painting, sculpture, etc., devoted in part to exhibiting the greatness of its artistic past, and, in other part, to exhibiting the loot gathered by its monarchs in conquest of other nations; for instance, the accumulations of the spoils of Napoleon that are in the Louvre. They testify to the connection between the modern segregation of art and nationalism and militarism. Doubtless this connection has served at times a useful purpose, as in the case of Japan, who, when she was in the process of westernization, saved much of her art treasures by nationalizing the temples that contained them.

The growth of capitalism has been a powerful influence in the development of the museum as the proper home for works of art, and in the promotion of the idea that they are apart from the common life. The *nouveaux riches,* who are an important byproduct of the capitalist system, have felt especially bound to surround themselves with works of fine art which, being rare, are also costly. Generally speaking, the typical collector is the typical capitalist. For evidence of good standing in the realm of higher culture, he amasses paintings, statuary, and artistic *bijoux,* as his stocks and bonds certify to his standing in the economic world.

Not merely individuals, but communities and nations, put their cultural good taste in evidence by building opera houses, galleries, and museums. These show that a community is not wholly absorbed in material wealth, because it is willing to spend its gains in patronage of art. It erects these buildings and collects their contents as it now builds a cathedral. The settings reflect and establish superior cultural status, while their segregation from the common life reflects the fact that they are not part of a native and spontaneous culture. They are a kind of counterpart of a holier-than-thou attitude, exhibited not toward persons as such but toward the interests and occupations that absorb most of the community's time and energy.

Modern industry and commerce have an international scope. The contents of galleries and museums testify to the growth of economic cosmopolitanism. The mobility of trade and of populations, due to the economic system, has weakened or destroyed the connection between works of art and the *genius loci* of which they were once the natural expression. As works of art have lost their indigenous status, they have acquired a new one—that of being specimens of fine art and nothing else. Moreover, works of art are now produced, like other articles, for sale in the market. Economic patronage by wealthy and powerful individuals has at many times played a part in the encouragement of artistic production. Probably many a savage tribe had its Maecenas. But now even that much of intimate social connection is lost in the impersonality of a world market. Objects that were in the past valid and significant because of their place in the life of a community now function in isolation from the conditions of their origin. By that fact they are also set apart from common experience, and serve as insignia of taste and certificates of special culture.

Because of changes in industrial conditions the artist has been pushed to one side from the main streams of active interest. Industry has been mechanized and an artist cannot work mechanically for mass production. He is less integrated than formerly in the normal flow of social services. A peculiar aesthetic "individualism" results. Artists find it incumbent upon them to betake themselves to their work as an isolated means of "self-expression." In order not to cater to the trend of economic forces, they often feel obliged to exaggerate their separateness to the point of eccentricity. Consequently artistic products take on to a still greater degree the air of something independent and esoteric.

Put the action of all such forces together, and the conditions that create the gulf which exists generally between producer and consumer in modern society operate to create also a chasm between ordinary and aesthestic experience. Finally we have, as the record of this chasm, accepted as if it were normal the philosophies of art that locate it in a region inhabited by no other creature, and that emphasize beyond all reason the merely contemplative character of the aesthetic. Confusion of values enters in to accentuate the separation. Adventitious matters, like the pleasure of collecting, of exhibiting, of ownership and display, simulate aesthestic values. Criticism is affected. There is much applause for the wonders of appreciation and the glories of the transcendent beauty of art indulged in without much regard to capacity for aesthetic perception in the concrete.

My purpose, however, is not to engage in an economic interpretation of the history of the arts, much less to argue that economic conditions are either invariably or directly relevant to perception and enjoyment, or even to interpretation of individual works of art. It is to indicate that *theories* which isolate art and its appreciation by placing them in a realm of their own, disconnected from other modes of experiencing, are not inherent in the subject matter but arise because of specifiable extraneous conditions. Embedded as they are in institutions and in habits of life, these conditions operate effectively because they work so unconsciously. Then the theorist assumes they are embedded in the nature of things. Nevertheless, the influence of these conditions is not confined to theory. As I have already indicated, it deeply affects the practice of living, driving away aesthetic perceptions that are necessary ingredients of happiness, or reducing them to the level of compensating transient pleasurable excitations.

Even to readers who are adversely inclined to what has been said, the implications of the statements that have been made may be useful in defining the nature of the problem: that of recovering the continuity of aesthetic experience with normal processes of living. The understanding of art and of its role in civilization is not furthered by setting out with eulogies of it or by occupying ourselves exclusively at the outset with great works of art recognized as such. The comprehension which theory essays will be arrived at by a detour; by going back to experience of the common or mill run of things to discover the aesthetic quality such experience possesses. Theory can start with and from acknowledged works of art only when the aesthetic is already compartmentalized, or only when works of art are set in a niche apart instead of being celebrations, recognized as such, of the things of ordinary experience. Even a crude experience, if authentically an experience, is more fit to give a clue to the intrinsic nature of aesthetic experience than is an object already set apart from any other mode of experience. Following this clue we can discover how the work of art develops and accentuates what is characteristically valuable in things of everyday enjoyment. The art product will then be seen to issue from the latter, when the full meaning of ordinary experience is expressed, as dyes come out of coal tar products when they receive special treatment.

Many theories about art already exist. If there is justification for proposing yet another philosophy of the aesthetic, it must be found in a new mode of approach. Combinations and permutations among existing theories can easily be brought forth by those so inclined. But, to my mind, the trouble with existing theories is that they start from a ready-made compartmentalization, or from a conception of art that "spiritualizes" it out of connection with the objects of concrete experience. The alternative, however, to such spiritualization is not a degrading and philistinish materialization of works of fine art, but a conception that discloses the way in which these works idealize qualities found in common experience. Were works of art placed in a directly human context in popular esteem, they would have a much wider appeal than they can have when pigeon-hole theories of art win general acceptance.

A conception of fine art that sets out from its connection with discovered qualities of ordinary experience will be able to indicate the factors and forces that favor the normal development of common human activities into matters of artistic value. It will also be able to point out those conditions that arrest its normal growth. Writers on aesthetic theory often raise the question of whether aesthetic philosophy can aid cultivation of aesthetic appreciation. The question is a branch of the general theory of criticism, which, it seems to me, fails to accomplish its full office if it does not indicate what to look for and what to find in concrete aesthetic objects. But, in any case, it is safe to say that a philosophy of art is sterilized unless it makes us aware of the function of art in relation to other modes of experience, and unless it indicates why this function is so inadequately realized, and unless it suggests the conditions under which the office would be succesfully performed.

The comparison of the emergence of works of art out of ordinary experiences to the refining of raw materials into valuable products may seem to some unworthy, if not an actual attempt to reduce works of art to the status of articles manufactured for commercial purposes. The point, however, is that no amount of ecstatic eulogy of finished works can of itself assist the understanding of the generation of such works. Flowers can be enjoyed without knowing about the interactions of soil, air, moisture, and seeds of which they are the result. But they cannot be *understood* without taking just these interactions into account—and theory is a matter of understanding. Theory is concerned with discovering the nature of the production of works of art and of their enjoyment in perception. How is it that the everyday making of things grows into that form of making which is genuinely artistic? How is it that our everyday enjoyment of scenes and situations develops into the peculiar satisfaction that attends the experience which is emphatically aesthetic? These are the questions theory must answer. The answers cannot be found unless we are willing to find the germs and roots in matters of experience that we do not currently regard as aesthetic. Having discovered these active seeds, we may follow the course of their growth into the highest forms of finished and refined art.

It is a commonplace that we cannot direct, save accidentally, the growth and flowering of plants, however lovely and enjoyed, without understanding their causal conditions. It should be just as common-place that aesthetic understanding—as distinct from sheer personal enjoyment—must start with the soil, air, and light out of which things aesthetically admirable arise. And these conditions are the conditions and factors that make an ordinary experience complete. The more we recognize this fact, the more we shall find ourselves faced with a problem rather than with a final solution. *If* artistic and aesthetic quality is implicit in every normal experience, how shall we explain how and why it so generally fails to become explicit? Why is it that to multitudes art seems to be an importation into experience from a foreign country and the aesthetic to be a synonym for something artificial?

We cannot answer these questions any more than we can trace the development of art out of everyday experience, unless we have a clear and coherent idea of what is meant when we say "normal experience." Fortunately, the road to arriving at such an idea is open and well marked. The nature of experience is determined by the essential conditions of life. While man is other than bird and beast, he shares basic vital functions with them and has to make the same basal adjustments if he is to continue the process of living. Having the same vital needs, man derives the means by which he breathes, moves, looks and listens, the very brain with which he coordinates his senses and his movements, from his animal forebears. The organs with which he maintains himself in being are not of himself alone, but by the grace of struggles and achievements of a long line of animal ancestry.

Fortunately a theory of the place of the aesthetic inexperience does not have to lose itself in minute details when it starts with experience in its elemental form. Broad outlines suffice. The first great consideration is that life goes on in an environment; not merely *in* it but because of it, through interaction with it. No creature lives merely under its skin; its subcutaneous organs are means of connection with what lies beyond its bodily frame, and to which, in order to live, it must adjust itself, by accommodation and defense but also by conquest. At every moment, the living creature is exposed to dangers from its surroundings, and at every moment, it must draw upon something in its surroundings to satisfy its needs. The career and destiny of a living being are bound up with its interchanges with its environment, not externally but in the most intimate way.

The growl of a dog crouching over his food, his howl in time of loss and loneliness, the wagging of his tail at the return of his human friend are expressions of the implication of a living in a natural medium which includes man along with the animal he has domesticated. Every need, say hunger for fresh air or food, is a lack that denotes at least a temporary absence of adequate adjustment with surroundings. But it is also a demand, a reaching out into the environment to make good the lack and to restore adjustment by building at least a temporary equilibrium. Life itself consists of phases in which the organism falls out of step with the march of surrounding things and then recovers unison with it—either through effort or by some happy chance. And, in a growing life, the recovery is never mere return to a prior state, for it is enriched by the state of disparity and resistance through which it has successfully passed. If the gap between organism and environment is too wide, the creature dies. If its activity is not enhanced by the temporary alienation, it merely subsists. Life grows when a temporary falling out is a transition to a more extensive balance of the energies of the organism with those of the conditions under which it lives.

These biological commonplaces are something more than that; they reach to the roots of the aesthetic in experience. The world is full of things that are indifferent and even hostile to life; the very processes by which life is maintained tend to throw it out of gear with its surroundings. Nevertheless, if life continues and if in continuing it expands, there is an overcoming of factors of opposition and conflict; there is a transformation of them into differentiated aspects of a higher power and more significant life. The marvel of organic, of vital, adaptation through expansion (instead of by contraction and passive accommodation) actually takes place. Here in germ are balance and harmony attained through rhythm. Equilibrium comes about not mechanically and inertly but out of, and because of, tension.

There is in nature, even below the level of life, something more than mere flux and change. Form is arrived at whenever a stable, even though moving, equilibrium is reached. Changes interlock and sustain one another. Wherever there is this coherence there is endurance. Order is not imposed from without but is made out of the relations of harmonious interactions that energies bear to one another. Because it is active (not anything static because foreign to what goes on) order itself develops. It comes to include within its balanced movement a greater variety of changes.

Order cannot but be admirable in a world constantly threatened with disorder—in a world where living creatures can go on living only by taking advantage of whatever order exists about them, incorporating it into themselves. In a world like ours, every living creature that attains sensibility welcomes order with a response of harmonious feeling whenever it finds a congruous order about it.

For only when an organism shares in the ordered relations of its environment does it secure the stability essential to living. And when the participation comes after a phase of disruption and conflict, it bears within itself the germs of a consummation akin to the aesthetic.

The rhythm of loss of integration with environment and recovery of union not only persists in man but becomes conscious with him; its conditions are material out of which he forms purposes. Emotion is the conscious sign of a break, actual or impending. The discord is the occasion that induces reflection. Desire for restoration of the union converts mere emotion into interest in objects as conditions of realization of harmony. With the realization, material of reflection is incorporated into objects as their meaning. Since the artist cares in a peculiar way for the phase of experience in which union is achieved, he does not shun moments of resistance and tension. He rather cultivates them, not for their own sake but because of their potentialities, bringing to living consciousness an experience that is unified and total. In contrast with the person whose purpose is aesthetic, the scientific man is interested in problems, in situations wherein tension between the matter of observation and of thought is marked. Of course he cares for their resolution. But he does not rest in it; he passes on to another problem using an attained solution only as a stepping stone from which to set on foot further inquiries.

The difference between the aesthetic and the intellectual is thus one of the place where emphasis falls in the constant rhythm that marks the interaction of the live creature with his surroundings. The ultimate matter of both emphases in experience is the same, as is also their general form. The odd notion that an artist does not think and a scientific inquirer does nothing else is the result of converting a difference of tempo and emphasis into a difference in kind. The thinker has his aesthetic moment when his ideas cease to be mere ideas and become the corporate meanings of objects. The artist has his problems and thinks as he works. But his thought is more immediately embodied in the object. Because of the comparative remoteness of his end, the scientific worker operates with symbols, words, and mathematical signs. The artist does his thinking in the very qualitative media he works in, and the terms lie so close to the object that he is producing that they merge directly into it.

The live animal does not have to project emotions into the objects experienced. Nature is kind and hateful, bland and morose, irritating and comforting, long before she is mathematically qualified or even a congeries of "secondary" qualities like color and their shapes. Even such words as long and short, solid and hollow, still carry to all but those who are intellectually specialized, a moral and emotional connotation. The dictionary will inform anyone who consults it that the early use of words like sweet and bitter was not to denote qualities of sense as such but to discriminate things as favorable and hostile. How could it be otherwise? Direct experience comes from nature and man interacting with each other. In this interaction, human energy gathers, is released, dammed up, frustrated, and victorious. There are rhythmic beats of want and fulfillment, pulses of doing and being withheld from doing.

All interactions that effect stability and order in the whirling flux of change are rhythms. There is ebb and flow, systole and diastole: ordered change. The latter moves within bounds. To overpass the limits that are set is destruction and death, out of which, however, new rhythms are built up. The proportionate interception of changes establishes an order that is spatially, not merely temporally patterned: like the waves of the sea, the ripples of sand where waves have flowed back and forth, the fleecy and the black-bottomed cloud. Contrast of lack and fullness, of struggle and achievement, of adjustment after consummated irregularity, form the drama in which action, feeling, and meaning are one. The outcome is balance and counterbalance. These are not static nor mechanical. They express power that is intense because measured through overcoming resistance. Environing objects avail and counteravail.

There are two sorts of possible worlds in which aesthetic experience would not occur. In a world of mere flux, change would not be cumulative; it would not move toward a close. Stability and rest would have no being. Equally is it true, however, that a world that is finished, ended, would have no traits of suspense and crisis, and would offer no opportunity for resolution. Where everything is already complete, there is no fulfillment. We envisage with pleasure Nirvana and a uniform heavenly bliss only because they are projected on the background of our present world of stress and conflict. Because the actual world, that in which we live, is a combination of movement and culmination, of breaks and reunions, the experience of a living creature is capable of aesthetic quality. The live being recurrently loses and reestablishes equilibrium with his surroundings. The moment of passage from disturbance into harmony is that of intensest life. In a finished world, sleep and waking could not be distinguished. In one wholly perturbed, conditions could not even be struggled with. In a world made after the pattern of ours, moments of fulfillment punctuate experience with rhythmically enjoyed intervals.

Inner harmony is attained only when, by some means, terms are made with the environment. When it occurs on any other than an "objective" basis, it is illusory—in extreme cases to the point of insanity. Fortunately for variety in experience, terms are made in many ways— ways ultimately decided by selective interest. Pleasures may come about through chance contact and stimulation; such pleasures are not to be despised in a world full of pain. But happiness and delight are a different sort of thing. They come to be through a fulfillment that reaches to the depths of our being—one that is an adjustment of our whole being with the conditions of existence. In the process of living, attainment of a period of equilibrium is at the same time the initiation of a new relation to the environment, one that brings with it potency of new adjustments to be made through struggle. The time of consummation is also one of beginning anew. Any attempt to perpetuate beyond its term the enjoyment attending the time of fulfillment and harmony constitutes withdrawal from the world. Hence it marks the lowering and loss of vitality. But, through the phases of perturbation and conflict, there abides the deep-seated memory of an underlying harmony, the sense of which haunts life like the sense of being founded on a rock.

Most mortals are conscious that a split often occurs between their present living and their past and future. Then the past hangs upon them as a burden; it invades the present with a sense of regret, of opportunities not used, and of consequences we wish undone. It rests upon the present as an oppression, instead of being a storehouse of resources by which to move confidently forward. But the live creature adopts its past; it can make friends with even its stupidities, using them as warnings that increase present wariness. Instead of trying to live upon whatever may have been achieved in the past, it uses past successes to inform the present. Every living experience owes its richness to what Santayana well calls "hushed reverberations."[1]

To the being fully alive, the future is not ominous but a promise; it surrounds the present as a halo. It consists of possibilities that are felt as a possession of what is now and here. In life that is truly life, everything overlaps and merges. But all too often we exist in apprehensions of what the future may bring, and are divided within ourselves. Even when not overanxious, we do not enjoy the present because we subordinate it to that which is absent. Because of the frequency of this abandonment of the present to the past and future, the happy periods of an experience that is now complete because it absorbs into itself memories of the past and anticipations of the future, come to constitute an aesthetic ideal. Only when the past ceases to trouble and anticipations of the future are not perturbing is a being wholly united with his environment and therefore fully alive. Art celebrates with peculiar intensity the moments in which the past reinforces the present and in which the future is a quickening of what now is.

To grasp the sources of aesthetic experience it is, therefore, necessary to have recourse to animal life below the human scale. The activities of the fox, the dog, and the thrush may at least stand as reminders and symbols of that unity of experience which we so fractionize when work is labor, and thought withdraws us from the world. The live animal is fully present, all there, in all of its actions: in its wary glances, its sharp sniffings, its abrupt cocking of ears. All senses are equally on the *qui vive*. As you watch, you see motion merging into sense and sense into motion—constituting that animal grace so hard for man to rival. What the live creature retains from the past and what it expects from the future operate as directions in the present. The dog is never pedantic nor academic; for these things rise only when the past is severed in consciousness from the present and is set up as a model to copy or a storehouse upon which to draw. The past absorbed into the present carries on; it presses forward.

There is much in the life of the savage that is sodden. But, when the savage is most alive, he is most observant of the world about him and most taut with energy. As he watches what stirs about him he, too, is stirred. His observation is both action in preparation and foresight of the future. He is as active through his whole being when he looks and listens as when he stalks his quarry or stealthily retreats from a foe. His senses are sentinels of immediate thought and outposts of action, and not, as they so often are with us, mere pathways along which material is gathered to be stored away for a delayed and remote possibility.

It is mere ignorance that leads then to the supposition that connection of art and aesthetic perception with experience signifies a lowering of their significance and dignity. Experience in the degree in which it *is* experience is heightened vitality. Instead of signifying being shut up within one's own private feelings and sensations, it signifies active and alert commerce with the world; at its height it signifies complete interpenetration of self and the world of objects and events. Instead of signifying surrender to caprice and disorder, it affords our sole demonstration of a stability that is not stagnation but is rhythmic and developing. Because experience is the fulfillment of an organism in its struggles and achievements in a world of things, it is art in germ. Even in its rudimentary forms, it contains the promise of that delightful perception which is aesthetic experience.

Note

1. "These familiar flowers, these well-remembered bird-notes, this sky with its fitful brightness, these furrowed and grassy fields, each with a sort of

personality given to it by the capricious hedge, such things as these are the mother-tongue of our imagination, the language that is laden with all the subtle inextricable associations the fleeting hours of our childhood left behind them. Our delight in the sunshine on the deep-bladed grass today might be no more than the faint perception of wearied souls, if it were not for the sunshine and grass of far-off years, which still live in us and transform our perception into love." George Eliot in *The Mill on the Floss.*

2

The Social Bases of Art[*]

Meyer Schapiro

When we speak in this paper of the social bases of art we do not mean to reduce art to economics or sociology or politics. Art has its own conditions which distinguish it from other activities. It operates with its own special materials and according to general psychological laws. But from these physical and psychological factors we could not understand the great diversity of art, why there is one style at one time, another style a generation later, why in certain cultures there is little change for hundreds of years, in other cultures not only a mobility from year to year but various styles of art at the same moment, although physical and psychological factors are the same. We observe further that if, in a given country, individuals differ from each other constantly, their works produced at the same time are more alike than the works of individuals separated by centuries.

This common character which unites the art of individuals at a given time and place is hardly due to a connivance of the artists. It is as members of a society with its special traditions, its common means

*Originally published in M. Baigell and J. Williams, ed., *Artists against War and Fascism* (New Brunswick, N.J.: Rutgers University Press, 1986). Copyright © 1986 by Rutgers, the State University. Reprinted by permission of Rutgers University Press.

and purposes, prior to themselves, that individuals learn to paint, speak, and act in the current manner. And it is in terms of changes in their immediate common world that individuals are impelled together to modify their no longer adequate conceptions.

We recognize the social character of art in the very language we use; we speak of Pharaonic art, Buddhist art, Christian art, monastic art, military art. We observe the accord of styles with historical periods; we speak of the style of Louis XV, of the Empire style and the Colonial style. Finally, the types of art object refer to definite social and institutional purposes—church, altarpiece, icon, monument, portrait, etc. And we know that each of these has special properties or possibilities bound up with its distinctive uses.

When we find two secular arts existing at the same time in the same society we explain the fact socially. We observe, this is a peasant art, this is a court or urban art. And within the urban art, when we see two different styles, it is sometimes evident without much investigation that they come from different groups within the community, as in the official academic art and the realistic art of France in 1850. A good instance of such a variety rooted in social differences are the contemporaries, Chardin and Boucher, an instance already grasped in its own time.

There is overwhelming evidence which binds art to the conditions of its own time and place. To grasp the force of this connection we have only to ask whether Gothic sculpture is conceivable in the eighteenth century, or whether Impressionist (or better, Cubist) painting could have been produced in African tribal society. But this connection of time and place does not by itself enable us to judge what conditions were decisive and by what necessities arts have been transformed.

But all this is past art. The modern artist will say: yes, this is true of Giotto who had to paint Madonnas because he worked for the Church. But I today take orders from no one; my art is free; what have my still life paintings and abstract designs to do with institutions or classes? He will go even further, if he has thought much about the matter, and say: yes, Giotto painted Virgins for the Church, but what has that to do with his art? The form of the work, its artistic qualities, were his personal invention; his real purpose was to make formal designs or to express his personality; and if we value Giotto today, if we distinguish him from the hundreds of others who made paintings of the same subject for the Church, it is because of his unique personality or design, which the Church certainly could not command or determine.

If—disregarding here the question of Giotto's intentions—we ask the artist why it is then that the forms of great artists today differ from the forms of Giotto, he will be compelled to admit that historical conditions caused him to design differently than one does today. And he will admit, upon a little reflection, that the qualities of his forms were closely bound up with the kind of objects he painted, with his experience of life and the means at his disposal. If Giotto was superior to other painters, his artistic superiority was realized in tasks, materials, conceptions, and goals, common to the artists of his immediate society, but different from our own.

If modern art seems to have no social necessity, it is because the social has been narrowly identified with the collective as the anti-individual, and with repressive institutions and beliefs, like the church or the state or morality, to which most individuals submit. But even those activities in which the individual seems to be unconstrained and purely egoistic depend upon socially organized relationships. Private property, individual competitive business enterprise or sexual freedom, far from constituting nonsocial relationships, presuppose specific, historically developed forms of society. Nearer to art there are many unregistered practices which seem to involve no official institutions, yet depend on recently acquired social interests and on definite states of material development. A promenade, for example (as distinguished from a religious procession or a parade), would be impossible without a particular growth of urban life and secular forms of recreation. The necessary means—the streets and the roads—are also social and economic in origin, beyond or prior to any individual; yet each man enjoys his walk by himself without any sense of constraint or institutional purpose.

In the same way, the apparent isolation of the modern artist from practical activities, the discrepancy between his archaic, individual handicraft and the collective, mechanical character of most modern production, does not necessarily mean that he is outside society or that his work is unaffected by social and economic changes. The social aspect of his art has been further obscured by two things, the insistently personal character of the modern painter's work and his preoccupation with formal problems alone. The first leads him to think of himself in opposition to society as an organized repressive power, hostile to individual freedom; the second seems to confirm this in stripping his work of any purpose other than a purely "aesthetic" [one].

But if we examine attentively the objects a modern artist paints and the psychological attitudes evident in the choice of these objects and their forms, we will see how intimately his art is tied to the life of modern society.

Although painters will say again and again that content doesn't matter, they are curiously selective in their subjects. They paint only certain themes and only in a certain aspect. The content of the great body of art today, which appears to be unconcerned with content, may be described as follows. First, there are natural spectacles, landscapes or city scenes, regarded from the viewpoint of a relaxed spectator, a vacationist or sportsman, who values the landscape chiefly as a source of agreeable sensations or mood; artificial spectacles and entertainments—the theater, the circus, the horse race, the athletic field, the music hall—or even works of painting, sculpture, architecture and technology, experienced as spectacles or objects of art; the artist himself and individuals associated with his studio and its intimate objects, his model posing, the fruit and flowers on his tables, his window and the view from it; symbols of the artist's activity, individuals practicing other arts, rehearsing, or in their privacy; instruments of art, especially of music, which suggest an abstract art and improvisation; isolated intimate fields, like a table covered with private instruments of idle sensation, drinking glasses, a pipe, playing cards, books, all objects of manipulation, referring to an exclusive, private world in which the individual is immobile, but free to enjoy his own moods and self stimulation. And finally, there are pictures in which the elements of professional artistic discrimination, present to some degree in all painting—the lines, spots of color, areas, textures, modeling—are disengaged from things and juxtaposed as "pure" aesthetic objects.

Thus elements drawn from the professional surroundings and activity of the artist; situations in which we are consumers and spectators; objects which we confront intimately, but passively or accidentally, or manipulate idly and in isolation—these are typical subjects of modern painting. They recur with surprising regularity in contemporary art.

Modern artists have not only eliminated the world of action from their pictures, but they have interpreted past art as if the element of experience in it, the represented objects, were incidental things, pretexts of design or imposed subjects, in spite of which, or in opposition to which, the artist realized his supposedly pure aesthetic impulse. They are therefore unaware of their own objects or regard them as merely incidental pretexts for form. But a little observation will show that each school of modern artists has its characteristic objects and that these derive from a context of experience which also operates in their formal fantasy. The picture is not a rendering of external objects—that is not even strictly true of realistic art—but the objects assembled in the picture come from an experience and interests which affect the formal character. An abstract art built up out of other objects, that is, out of other interests and experience, would have another formal character.

Certain of these contents are known in earlier art, but only under social conditions related to our own. The painting of an intimate and domestic world, of moments of nonpractical personal activity and artistic recreation (the toilette, the music lesson, the lacemaker, the artist, etc.), of the landscape as a pure spectacle with little reference to action, occurs, for example, in the patrician bourgeois art of Holland in the seventeenth century. In the sporadic, often eccentric, works of the last three centuries in which appear the playing cards, the detached personal paraphernalia, the objects of the table and the artistic implements, so characteristic of Cubism, there we find already a suggestion of Cubist aesthetic—intricate patterns of flat, overlapping objects, the conversion of the horizontal depth, the plane of our active traversal of the world, into an intimate vertical surface and field of random manipulation.

Abstract forms in primitive societies under different conditions have another content and formal character. In Hiberno-Saxon painting of the eighth century the abstract designs are not freshly improvised as in modern art, as a free, often grotesque, personal fantasy, but are conceived ornamentally as an intricate, uniformly controlled and minute, impersonal handicraft, subject to the conventional uses of precious religious objects. Hence in these older works, which are also, in a sense, highly subjective, there is usually a stabilizing emblematic form, a frequent symmetry and an arrangement of the larger units in simple, formalized schemes. In modern abstract art, on the contrary, we are fascinated by incommensurable shapes, unexpected breaks, capricious, unrecognizable elements, the appearance of a private, visionary world of emerging and disappearing objects. Whereas these objects are often the personal instruments of art and idle sensation described above—the guitars, drinking vessels, pipes, books, playing cards, bric-a-brac, bouquets, fruit and printed matter—in the older art such paraphernalia is completely absent. A more primitive and traditional content, drawn from religion, folklore, magic and handicraft—Christian symbols, wild beasts, monsters, knotted and entangled bands, plait-work and spirals—constitutes the matter of this art.

A modern work, considered formally, is no more artistic than an older work. The preponderance of objects drawn from a personal and artistic world does not mean that pictures are now more pure than in the past, more completely works of art. It means simply that the personal and aesthetic contexts of secular life now condition the formal character of art, just as religious beliefs and practices in the past conditioned the formal character of religious art. The conception of art as purely aesthetic and individual can exist only where culture has been detached from practical and collective interests and is supported by individuals alone. But the mode of life of these individuals, their place in society, determines in many ways this individual alert. In its most advanced form, this conception of art is typical of the rentier leisure class in modern capitalist society, and is most intensely developed in centers, like Paris, which have a larger rentier group and considerable luxury industries. Here the individual is no longer engaged in a struggle to attain wealth; he has no direct relation to work, machinery, competition; he is simply a consumer, not a producer. He belongs to a class which recognizes no higher group or authority. The old stable forms of family life and sexual morality have been destroyed; there is no royal court or church to impose a regulating pattern on his activity. For this individual the world is a spectacle, a source of novel pleasant sensations, or a field in which he may realize his "individuality," through art, through sexual intrigue, and the most varied, but nonproductive, mobility. A woman of this class is essentially an artist, like the painters whom she might patronize. Her daily life is filled with aesthetic choices; she buys clothes, ornaments, furniture, house decorations; she is constantly rearranging herself as an aesthetic object. Her judgments are aesthestically pure and "abstract," for she matches colors with colors, lines with lines. But she is also attentive to the effect of these choices upon her unique personality.

Of course, only a small part of this class is interested in painting, and only a tiny proportion cultivates the more advanced modern art. It would be out of place here to consider the reason for the specialized interests of particular individuals; but undoubtedly the common character of this class affects to some degree the tastes of its most cultivated members. We may observe that these consist mainly of young people with inherited incomes, who finally make art their chief interest, either as artists and decorators, or as collectors, dealers, museum officials, writers on art, and travelers. Active businessmen and wealthy professionals who occasionally support this art tend to value the collecting of art as a higher activity than their own daily work. Painting enters into little relation with their chief activities and everyday standards, except imaginatively, insofar as they are conscious of the individual aspect of their own careers and enjoy the work of willful and inventive personalities.

It is the situation of painting in such a society, and the resulting condition of the artist, which confer on the artist today certain common tendencies and attitudes. Even the artist of lower middle-class or working-class origin comes to create pictures congenial to the members of this upper class, without having to identify himself directly with it. He builds, to begin with, on the art of the last generation and is influenced by the success of recent painters. The general purpose of art being aesthetic, he is already predisposed to interests and attitudes imaginatively related to those of the leisure class, which values its pleasures as aesthetically refined, individual pursuits. He competes in an open market and therefore is conscious of the novelty or uniqueness of his work as a value. He creates out of his own head (having no subject matter imposed by a commission), works entirely by himself, and is therefore concerned with his powers of fantasy, his touch, his improvised forms. His sketches are sometimes more successful than his finished pictures, and the latter often acquire the qualities of a sketch.

Cut off from the middle class at the very beginning of his career by poverty and insecurity and by the nonpractical character of his work, the artist often repudiates its moral standards and responsibilities. He forms on the margin of this inferior philistine world a free community of artists in which art, personalities, and pleasure are the obsessing interests. The individual and the aesthetic are idealized as things completely justified in themselves and worth the highest sacrifices. The practical is despised except insofar as it produces attractive mechanical spectacles and new means of enjoyment, or insofar as it is referred abstractly to a process of inventive design, analogous to the painter's art. His frequently asserted antagonism to organized society does not bring him into conflict with his patrons, since they share his contempt for the "public" and are indifferent to practical social life. Besides, since he attributes his difficulties, not to particular historical conditions, but to society and human nature as such, he has only a vague idea that things might be different than they are; his antagonism suggests to him no effective action, and he shuns the common slogans of reform or revolution as possible halters on his personal freedom.

Yet helpless as he is to act on the world, he shows in his art an astonishing ingenuity and joy in transforming the shapes of familiar things. This plastic freedom should not be considered in itself an evidence of the artist's positive will to change society or a reflection of real transforming movements in the everyday world. For it is essential in this antinaturalistic art that just those relations of visual experience which are most important for action are destroyed by the modern artist. As in the fantasy of a passive spectator, colors and shapes are disengaged from objects and can no longer serve as a means in knowing them. The space within pictures becomes intraversable; its planes are shuffled and disarrayed, and the whole is reordered in a fantastically intricate manner. Where the human figure is preserved, it is a piece of picturesque still life, a richly pigmented, lumpy mass, individual, irritable, and sensitive; or an accidental plastic thing among others, subject to sunlight and the drastic distortions of a design. If the modern artist values the body, it is no longer in the Renaissance sense of a firm, clearly articulated, energetic structure, but as temperamental and vehement flesh.

The passivity of the modern artist with regard to the human world is evident in a peculiar relation of his form and content. In his effort to create a thoroughly animated, yet rigorous whole, he considers the interaction of color upon color, line upon line, mass upon mass. Such pervasive interaction is for most modern painters the very essence of artistic reality. Yet in his choice of subjects he rarely, if ever, seizes upon corresponding aspects in social life. He has no interest in, no awareness of, such interaction in the everyday world. On the contrary, he has a special fondness for those objects which exist side by side without affecting each other, and for situations in which the movements involve no real interactions. The red of an apple may oppose the green of another apple, but the apples do not oppose each other. The typical human situations are those in which figures look at each other or at a landscape or are plunged in a reverie or simulate some kind of absorption. And where numerous complicated things are brought together in apparent meaningful connection, this connection is cryptic, bizarre, something we must solve as a conceit of the artist's mind.

The social origins of such forms of modern art do not in themselves permit one to judge this art as good or bad; they simply throw light upon some aspects of their character and enable us to see more clearly that the ideas of modern artists, far from describing eternal and necessary conditions of art, are simply the results of recent history. In recognizing the dependence of his situation and attitudes on the character of modern society, the artist acquires the courage to change things, to act on his society and for himself in an effective manner.

He acquires at the same time new artistic conceptions. Artists who are concerned with the world around them, its action and conflict, who ask the same questions that are asked by the impoverished masses and oppressed minorities—these artists cannot permanently devote themselves to a painting committed to the aesthetic moments of life, to spectacles designed for passive, detached individuals, or to an art of the studio.

There are artists and writers for whom the apparent anarchy of modern culture—as an individual affair in which each person seeks his own pleasure—is historically progressive, since it makes possible for the first time the conception of the human individual with his own needs and goals. But it is a conception restricted to small groups who are able to achieve such freedom only because of the oppression and misery of the masses. The artists who create under these conditions are insecure and often wretched. Further, this freedom of a few individuals is identified largely with consumption and enjoyment; it detaches man from nature, history, and society, and although, in doing so, it discovers new qualities and possibilities of feeling and imagination, unknown to older culture, it cannot realize those possibilities of individual development which depend on common productive tasks, on responsibilities, on intelligence and cooperation in dealing with the urgent social isuses of the moment. The individual is identified with the private (that is, the privation of other beings and the world), with the passive rather than active, the fantastic rather than the intelligent. Such an art cannot really be called free, because it is so exclusive and private; there are too many things we value that it cannot embrace or even confront. An individual art in a society where human beings do not feel themselves to be most individual when they are inert, dreaming, passive, tormented, or un-controlled, would be very different from modern art. And in a society where all men can be free individuals, individuality must lose its exclu-siveness and its ruthless and perverse character.

3

Poetic Judgment and Poetic Query*

Justus Buchler

. . . II

A man's being acquires its essential character from two sources: the circumstances which befall him and the ways in which he judges the world. And the essential character of the world insofar as its relation to a man's being is concerned (insofar as it is "his" world) it acquires through the ways in which he judges it. These ways of judging inevitably derive from and are dependent upon more pervasive conditions than a man's own being provides. But they are the ways in which man grasps, delineates, bounds, and exposes his being and his world; they are the defining processes, the continuing definitions, of his being and his world.

The products of a man's life and history—described most generically as his acts or deeds, his assertions or declarations, and his contrivances— are his judgments. Such are the complexes that constitute utterance. To the extent that a man can be said to be the product of other natural complexes, he does not judge. To the extent that any complexes can be said to be his product, he judges. As in many fundamental distinctions,

---

*Excerpted from Justus Buchler, *The Main of Light: On the Concept of Poetry* (New York: Oxford University Press, 1974). © 1974 by Justus Buchler. Reprinted by permission of Oxford University Press, Inc.

the borderline is not easy to draw, and the specific determinations that depend upon its being drawn are numerous. This much can be said securely: certain conditions under which a man is product are themselves owing to his having produced in a way that he did. And certain conditions under which a man produces are owing to his having been product in a way that he was. No human product owes its being entirely to its producer or producers: the world of a producer must allow the production, that is, provide the conditions for it. On the other hand, products arising under conditions in which a man is entirely unconscious may yet be his products, for they may be attributed to what he has become and is, to what *his* cumulatively determined direction has made possible.

Human utterance or judgment is thus coextensive with all that is produced by the human process as such. A major historic misconception with respect to judgment is that it is necessarily deliberative. But human judging cannot be limited to occasions of intention or voluntary choice. It is the process wherein complexes which go to constitute the human creature perpetually impose upon him options. For the most part he cannot contemplate these; but owing to the duress of the world, he must selectively resolve the contrarieties they entail. Each instance of judging—though these instances are not to be regarded as neatly isolated—is at bottom an attitude or stance adopted. It is by his stances that a man, insofar as he can, determines and redetermines the complexes of his world. Each of his products is such a stance. It is a stand. He judges insofar as he exercises the selectiveness or discriminativeness inherent in his constitution; insofar as he actualizes the possibilities that lie in his accumulated traits. He judges continuously, through what he includes and excludes, preserves and destroys, is inclined to and averse to; through what he makes and fails to make, through the ways he acts and refrains from acting, through what he believes and disavows. His attitudes, and hence his commitments, are his whether he is aware of them or not.

To say that a man judges, for example, through what he makes, does not mean that he makes after he has discriminated and selected and become committed. It means that his making what he makes *is the way* he has discriminated and selected and become committed. The same applies to acting. When we ordinarily think of a stand or a commitment we tend to think of something dramatic: a heroic "stand," a "true" commitment. We overlook the minute stands, the small threads of utterance. These are the judgments that consist of the makings, sayings, and doings of everyday habit and impulse. In their collectivity and social efficacy, these threads of judgment are what determine the difference between a revolution and an abortive eruption, or between the firmness of a tradition and the weakness of a tradition.

An adequate conception of judgment must avoid two other, corollary misconceptions which have dominated virtually the entire history of philosophy. One is the view that judging is a specific operation, an operation like remembering, abstracting, or attending (to cite the standard examples). Judging has never been linked with walking, talking, hearing, breathing, or eating; for it has been construed not merely as an "operation" but as a "mental" operation. Such a view cannot be defended by moralizing that we are dealing here with a word that has always been used in a certain way and there is no reason for it to be used in any other way. As a matter of fact, the uses of the word "judgment" have varied, and varied with considerable range—suggesting, for example, "presumption," "evaluation," "estimation," "decision," "discernment"—despite their misconception in common. The possible thought that the way a man is judging the world around him, or his fellow men, may not be present to his awareness, and that it is as a man that a man judges rather than in virtue of a special judging faculty or power that he possesses, seems never to have taken hold. This failure can be explained in terms of a number of stiff philosophical bulwarks that will doubtless endure forever. Let it suffice here to say that it reflects a simple but disastrous equation of selection with conscious selection, of discrimination with deliberate discrimination, of attitudinal postures with voluntarily chosen outlooks.

The second corollary misconception, as ancient and persistent as the first, is that human judgment always takes the form of thinking something or saying something about something else. When we are said to judge, it is supposed that we venture a truth claim; that we affirm a room to be fourteen feet wide, one umbrella to be better than another, some reforms to be viable and others not. This propositional conception of judgment requires that all judgments be regarded as either true or false, as more likely or less likely to be verified, as either in accordance with "the facts" ("the case") or not. It is a bias of intellectualism, and it is held, ironically enough, by the philosophers who decry intellectualism. Probably the bias stems from the Greek conviction that theoretical knowledge is the "highest" form of human attainment, above the attainment of social practice or of art. This conviction is bolstered by others. The theoretical, quite understandably, is identified with linguistic rendition or deliverance, and linguistic rendition with propositional or declarative communication. Though the Greek view of what is "highest" has often been abandoned, mainly on the basis of moral consideration, its effect on the concept of judgment has not.

The propositional conception of judgment and conception of judgment as a mental operation sustain and perpetuate each other. The typical image of judging as requiring meditation, as requiring skill, as being something good to be able to do, as being something that we can suspend at will, and as culminating in the kind of expert authority exemplified by the judge on the bench, reflects the view of an intellective faculty that becomes developed professionally. And this image both fosters and is fed by the view of assertive language as the sharpest, the clearest, the most reliable, the most explicit, way of "expressing" ourselves, hence the only way of expertly judging. Thus the actual roots of judgment, which lie in the most basic dimensions of human functioning—in man's assimilation and manipulation of natural complexes—are obscured.

Human utterance is the net product of man and men. It is what emerges from the human order of judgment and particular orders within that order. It is not man's products reduced to propositions, a mistake which explains the widespread identification of utterance with linguistic utterance, even in the face of the fact that so much of language is not propositional at all. When the idea of utterance has been associated with man, and not merely this or that man, still another unfortunate transition has taken place: "utterance" has acquired a eulogistic import. But the tendency to think of human utterance as inherently good cannot be defended, any more than the tendency to think of man as inherently good. The products of men have been sometimes good and sometimes bad, and there is no way of separating utterance from its manifestations. Human utterance is manifested by concentration camps, bombs, and child beating along with agriculture, medicine, and poetry.

The bent of an individual's process of judging reflects the cumulative character of a human history. The varieties of judgment to be found in a perspective order will depend both upon what has happened to him who is defined by the order, including the impact of judgments not his own, and upon what previous judgments have been his. Every judgment arises in an order of judgment, and orders of judgment arise in a human order, as motions arise in a mechanical order and chromosomes in a biological order. The conditions which give rise to particular judgments that have some degree of human importance—say to a sociological hypothesis, a poem, and a vote cast in an election—are located (they function) in the common area as it were of several orders. Thus each of these judgments (which all happen to be of the purposive or intended kind) is located in a social order, a psychological order, a historical order, an order of products (other judgments) customarily linked to science, art, and citizenship, and an order (subaltern to the preceding order) of products customarily linked to sociology, poetry, and political action. The various traits of a judgment are rooted in one or more of these ordinal locations. Some orders may provide determinants of a judgment's occurrence. Others may provide determinants of its meaning, its communicative efficacy. The meaning of some judgments may be articulated partly by ascertaining the circumstances of their origin. The meaning of others may be articulated only by ascertaining the role(s) which they play in their continuing relations, and ulimately in the relational complexes of communication. As a product, a judgment, whether intended or unintended, has effect. Like any other natural complex, its relations may be far-reaching or may prevail in a highly restrictive domain.

Although there are many levels of judgment, and although judgment as such is inevitable and ubiquitous, it is imperative to understand the three principal modes into which it is divisible and in terms of which it is interpretable. Not that individual judgments always stand out clearly in practice. But the three modes of judgment are the essential ways in which human products *function*. A given complex produced by an individual without special foresight may, under appropriately different circumstances, function in all three ways. It is the differentiation, however, which is of greatest theoretical importance. (1) When we can be said to predicate, state, or affirm, by the use of words or by any other means; when the underlying direction is to achieve or support belief; when it is relevant to cite evidence in behalf of our product, we produce in the mode of assertive judgment, we judge assertively. (2) When we can be said to do or to act; when the underlying direction is toward effecting a result; when "bringing about" is the central trait attributable to our product, we produce in the mode of active judgment, we judge actively. (3) When we contrive or make, insofar as the contrivance rather than its role in action is what dominates and is of underlying concern; when the process of shaping and the product as shaped is central, we produce in the mode of exhibitive judgment, we judge exhibitively. On the methodic level, where (minimally) purposiveness and intention belong to judgments, assertive judgment is exemplified by science, or more generally, inquiry (including any discipline that makes a truth claim); active judgment, by deliberate conduct morally assessable; exhibitive judgment, by art.

Many everyday situations which are resignedly classified as perplexities and dilemmas are not without their possible explanation. But they cry out for theoretical clarification in a philosophic perspective. Often, for example, we cannot understand what it means for man to "say one thing" and "do another." We explain in terms of moral indecision, emotional confusion, and the like. But we fail to realize that when one phase of conduct does not square with another, we may be oversimplifying the process of judgment involved. A man who does not act in accordance with what he says is not "lapsing from" or "betraying" a judgment he has made. He is judging in another way, judging actively. In terms of his prevailing makeup and direction, or in terms of circumstances that gain influence, his judgment in one mode is superseded by his judgment in another, whether for better or worse. It works the other way too. Active judgment may be superseded by assertive. Or both active and assertive judgment may be superseded by exhibitive. An artist may make the most irresponsible assertions about art, or about his own art. But the actual pursuit and exemplification of his art, his process of exhibitive judgment, may be the best index to his fundamental direction, and may be the best order in which his meanings are conveyed.

It is worth repeating that the three modes of utterance are to be understood in terms of the way in which human products actually function. Although we associate certain types of products habitually with some one of these functions, and may be entirely justified in doing so, there is no fixed type of product required for any mode of judging, and it is possible for one and the same product to function in any mode or combination of the modes, depending on the order in which it is located and the conditions prevailing in that order. We tend to think, for instance, of declarative sentences as the medium of assertion, and of bodily movement as the vehicle of action; but sentences can acquire the function of judging actively, and bodily movements the function of judging assertively. Take the economic product which consists in a private purchase of swamp land that has been known to be detrimental to public health. Ordinarily, we should think of this as an active judgment, with economic and social consequences appraisable in moral terms. If however, the purchase occurs in the midst of controversy over the question whether private enterprise is more responsive to social need than government is, it may function as an assertive judgment which answers a standing question in the affirmative. But again, if the transaction functions as the beginning of a project to transform the swamp into landscaped terrain that is justified in terms of the transformation as such, it is an exhibitive judgment.

Treating the products of language as primarily assertive is a profound mistake. Language exemplifies an assertive function when it is propositional or intended as such. When language is poetic it is exhibitive in function. Language of whatever grammatical mood or emotional cast may actually function in any mode of judgment. The use of language to exhort, to arouse the performance of a deed, to bring about results—to function, actively—is known by everybody to be as common as language used to affirm belief.

Often a product is oriented toward a function in one mode but actually functions in another. Political discourse purporting to lay down verifiable contentions, to function assertively, may in intent or in effect or both, be a form of active judgment, determining a course of response. A medical technique practiced in a large number of cases may be a recurrent form of active judgment, but in the order of general medical awareness the same technique practiced may have an assertive function as bearing on the truth of a medical hypothesis.

All three of the modes of judgment may generate feeling, either in their products or in others to whom their products are related. All three may entail feeling on other levels. A feeling may function as an event, a concomitant of judgment among other concomitants, like glandular activity and the weather. It may function as an aspect of judgment, perhaps a beginning, an incipient phase of judgment; or as the guiding tone whose relative intensity and fluctuations help to determine force of judgment and change of judgment.

The present approach is to be distinguished from one which would merely lay stress upon man as sayer, doer, and maker. That stress can acquire force not by reiterating itself as a tripartite classification—for such a classification has always been more or less available—but by insisting on the relevance of all three functions in any adequate account of the human process and its products. Historically, saying, doing, and making have all been recognized at least tacitly as essential foci for man. Saying, because of its association with speech, has always been regarded as most distinctively human. It has been regarded as representing "mind" and therefore as most fundamental in the characterization of knowledge, experience, meaning, and judgment. The force of the tripartite recognition is thus defeated, though not solely because the three functions are accorded unequal importance. It is defeated because it is unaccompanied by the realization that a judicative character belongs to all three. To assume that stating is alone judicative is to assume that it is the sole means by which man discriminates and appropriates traits of his world. Yet, merely to recognize, for example, that a work of art exhibits and doesn't have to state, is not enough. The main consideration is that the work is an exhibitive judgment. Otherwise we have provided no basis for a function comparable to stating, and the false implication is allowed that the work of art always conforms to the model of a dumb-show pointing to one-knows-not-what, or to the model of total sensory-affective involvement—both wholly noncommittal.

None of the three modes of judgment is intrinsically more fundamental than any of the others. But any may become more deserving of emphasis than the others in the circumstances of living. None of the modes is reducible to either of the others in the sense that what it produces can be arrived at or be more satisfactorily produced by the other, or in the sense that one is a special case of the other. In thus assuming the irreducibility of each mode and the parity of importance that obtains among the three, the question of "translation" arises. The principle of irreducibility would seem to preclude any mode being translatable into another and the other not being translatable into it. Can the modes, then, be translated into one another? The concept of translation, as we saw in the preceding chapter, is ambiguous. For the purpose of answering the question, we may formulate in the briefest terms a distinction which is of utmost importance. None of the modes is translatable *into* any other. Any of the modes is translatable *by* any other. In other words, if "translation" means "achieving an interchangeable equivalent," mutual translation of the modes is not possible. If "translation" means "articulating in another order of utterance," mutual translation is possible. The modes of judgment, though not reducible, are relatable, and often related in practice. Translation in the second, broader sense, as articulation or continuing exposure of a product's traits, extending the being of a product into a perspectival order made newly available, is the foundation of criticism, literary or any other kind. Even in this sense, it may not be desirable in all situations. But ideally, it permits us to see how the various facets of human invention can accent and augment one another in the interest of human betterment.

III

Exhibitive judgment, exemplified on the methodic level by art, but in no way restricted to the commonly recognized arts, is the process whereby men shape natural complexes and communicate them for assimilation as thus shaped—as novel complexes distinguished from their bearing upon action and belief. To assimilate a novel complex exhibited *as* that complex does *not* imply immediate or unmediated response. Nor does it imply an all-or-none response, or a response concerned with a "surface." On the contrary, to a methodic exhibitive product, as to any other methodically wrought product of more than trivial significance, the only kind of response that can be called human is one that, potentially, continues and renews itself. The reason is that the meaning of a judgment, in any of the three modes, is grasped only through articulation of that judgment, and there is no foreseeable terminus to the process of articulation. It is even more accurate to say that the meaning of a judgment is *achieved* by articulation. The usual way of describing the matter suggests that a meaning already obtains and is already present in the product. Actually the meanings which already obtain have been transferred from similar perspectives ("contexts"); they are preliminary and obvious, and taken for granted as "there." Their obviousness makes us think of them as prior to articulation. But they are the result of articulations that have become standardized. The product "has" meaning. But being a judgment, it can have meaning only when it means, that is, when its communicative function takes effect, expands, and advances; when its role in a perspectival order is determined and increasingly well determined. As the response to artistic judgment must thus be considered to be the beginning of a process of response, so must the satisfaction attending that response. Being satisfied, like perceiving, and like understanding, is not an all-or-none result, is not attained all at once, and is not limited to single occasions of responding.

A poem, or work of poetry in whatever form, is an exhibitive judgment wrought in language. We may speak of exhibitive judgments within the poem. And we may speak of a sequence of poems, or an entire body of poetry, as an exhibitive judgment of greater sweep, multifariously constituted. As a linguistic contrivance, a poem must be distinguished from nonpoetic forms of literature. But initially we must think of it in the way we may think of all literature, as exemplifying a nonassertive mode of discriminating natural complexes, a mode which is itself diversified and continuingly defined by the range of literary products. . . .

We return to the general theme of poetry as a form of exhibitive judgment. Taken historically, in reaction to the misunderstanding of poetic utterance, Sidney's principle that the poet "nothing affirms, and therefore never lieth" is remarkably sound. To go on to say as he does that the poet "never affirmeth" is equivocal; the words should be read to mean "never affirmeth as poet." For actually there are poets, and perhaps many, who do seek to affirm without bothering about the interpretation of their procedure; and surely there is no reason for them to bother. There are even poets who seek to affirm that their art affirms.

> Why take the artistic way to prove so much?
> Because, it is the glory and good of Art
> That Art remains the one way possible
> Of speaking truth, to mouths like mine at least.

And then, as if by way of qualification,

> But Art,—wherein man nowise speaks to men,
> Only to mankind,—Art may tell a truth
> Obliquely, do the thing shall breed the thought,
> Nor wrong the thought, missing the mediate word.[1]

It is enough to say that assertive judgments may occur in poetry but are extrinsic to it, in the sense that they are not essential, not common, and not pursued with respect to assertive validation. The mere presence of what appear to be declarative statements in poetry is deceptive. We tend to think that the grammatical mood of the words is the key to their function—a carryover from the forms of everyday discourse, which are themselves no reliable index of function. But in any event, an assertive component of a poem does not make the poem assertive. In poetic drama assertions are definitely made by the characters. But the drama as such is exhibitive judgment, and so are the characters' assertions considered as poetic speech. The tissue of (assertive) argumentation, of consecutiveness and persuasivenes, that is often to be found in poetry (dramatic or other) is the strategic means (sometimes precisely because it is the most familiar means) by which a complex of traits is encompassed and bound together, integrated as an exhibitive structure. Nothing could be as irrelevant to such a structure, as incongruous with it, as the question of its inferential validity. Similarly misleading is that species of grammatical declarativeness to be found in the "descriptive" form or style of much poetry. Poetic description is not assertion. No one is significantly engaged by the issue of whether such a description is accurate, adequate, or appropriate; and no one is disposed to find out whether the inferential musings in which it is immersed are conclusive or inconclusive.

> The long triumphant nose attains—retains
> Just the perfection; and there's scarlet-skein
> My ancient enemy, her lip and lip
> Sense-free, sense-frighting lips clenched cold and bold
> Because of chin, that based resolve beneath!
> Then the columnar neck completes the whole
> Greek-sculpture-baffling body! Do I see?
> Can I observe? You wait next word to come?
> Well, wait and want! since no one blight I bid
> Consume one least perfection. Each and all,
> As they are rightly shocking now to me,
> So may they still continue! Value them?
> Ay, as the vendor knows the money-worth
> Of his Greek statue, fools aspire to buy,
> And he to see the back of! Let us laugh!
> You have absolved me from my sin at least!
> You stand stout, strong, in the rude health of hate,
> No touch of the tame timid nullity
> My cowardice, forsooth, has practiced on![2]

The poetic description cannot be appraised as right or wrong, or even as good or bad, for though it presupposes certain standards of verbal meaning, it presupposes no measure of credibility or propriety. The passage just quoted is a segment of a more comprehensive exhibitive judgment which frames a contour of traits, including visual appearances, sharp feelings, submerged attitudes, and links to antiquity. It is a process of definition, marking out an area of relatedness, plotting boundaries (in a human complex), as when we define a parcel of land or define the course of travel. In this sense all shaping, all contriving, all art, entails a process of defining. And in this sense removed to a deeper level, every actuality limits and bounds other actualities, partly defines their scope. The process of defining is thus not restricted to, and sometimes does not fit, the familiar procedure of arriving at formulae of usage designed to be recurrently applicable. It may aim at establishing an integrity for a complex not hitherto possessed (judged) by us, yet related to complexes in our ken. Poetic description is one of the forms of poetic definition, and poetic definition is one of the forms of exhibitive definition.

Poetically, the following lines (composed, in the original, about four thousand years ago) are a description in the very same sense as the lines just quoted.

> Death is in my eyes today
> As when a sick man becomes whole,
> As when one walketh abroad after sickness.
>
> Death is in my eyes today
> Like the scent of myrrh;
> As when one sitteth under the boat's sail on a windy day.
>
> Death is in my eyes today
> Like the smell of water-lilies;
> As when one sitteth on the bank of drunkenness.
>
> Death is in my eyes today
> Like a well-trodden road,
> As when one returneth from the war unto his home.
>
> Death is in my eyes today
> Like the unveiling of heaven
> As when one attaineth to that which he knew not.
>
> Death is in my eyes today
> As when one longeth to see his house again
> After he hath spent many years in captivity.[3]

These considerations may help us to see where Coleridge goes astray in thinking of certain types of poetry (like *The Ancient Mariner*) as requiring the reader to achieve "that willing suspension of disbelief for the moment, which constitutes poetic faith." For poetry of any kind, the suspension of disbelief is no more prerequisite than the suspension of belief. In general, belief and disbelief cannot be simply suspended; they cannot be provisionally undone by a personal resolution. Conviction is not dissolved and rebuilt gratuitously. The very idea is self-contradictory. Faith is not worth much if it can be set up and removed like an ornament on a mantelpiece. But in particular, the mode of poetic response is not a matter of belief at all. The traditional apologetic attitude in behalf of poetry, and the traditional condescension toward it, alike reflect the deficiency in the age-old version of judgment.

We have said that the three modes of judgment, though not reducible to any one of them, are mutually articulatable. Assertive judgments may be articulated actively or exhibitively, active judgments articulated assertively or exhibitively, exhibitive judgments articulated assertively or actively. For example, a social reform movement may, through its action, articulate a social theory. The articulation may proceed in the other direction: social thought about the nature of human institutions may articulate historical chains of action. In the same way poetry may exhibitively articulate a trend of ideation, such as a philosophic system or a general intellectual movement. In so doing it represents such a trend without becoming involved in evidential considerations. Like all articulative judgment, it extends the being of a product by a new perspectival determination of that product's traits. It defines the product's character in another order of human concern. Once again, the articulation may move in the opposite direction as well. A philosophic outlook may articulate propositionally what it finds in poetic utterance. How poetry can articulate products within its own order of judgment; how it can exhibitively probe a method, a life, a temperament, another poetic product, is profoundly conveyed by the lines of Shelley on Coleridge which Arthur Symons quotes to show the power of the poetic as critic.[4]

> You will see Coleridge—he who sits obscure
> In the exceeding lustre and the pure
> Intense irradiation of a mind,
> Which, with its own internal lightning blind,
> Flags wearily through darkness and despair—
> A cloud-encircled meteor of the air,
> A hooded eagle among blinking owls.[5]

Literary criticism may find that the character of a given poetic work reflects an ideational scheme or tradition by which it has been influenced. In articulating that scheme, the critic articulates the poetry. But not infrequently, his mistake is to think of the poetry itself as asserting the scheme. Whitehead, in his use of Milton, Pope, Wordsworth, Shelley, and Tennyson to express the historical position of mechanism and organicism helps to illustrate certain articulative aspects of their poetry. As he sees the matter, however, the broad scale on which their longer poems are projected "gives [the poems] a didactic character." This way of approaching poetry and the poetic articulation of philosophic thought runs into serious trouble. We soon find Whitehead condemning Tennyson's *In Memoriam* for avoiding the "problem" of "individual moral responsibility" while dealing with virtually every other "religious and scientific problem." He even concludes that "the enfeeblement of thought in the modern world is illustrated by the way in which this plain issue is avoided in Tennyson's poem."[6] However we may feel about a particular poem, or whatever function its author may have considered himself to be performing, it is a monstrous distortion to think of poetry in terms of philosophic completeness and adequacy, of argumentative cogency, or of problem-solving. Whitehead ultimately obscures the nature of poetic articulation for want of a distinction between assertive and exhibitive judgment.

IV

It should be increasingly clear that the theory of judgment needs to introduce a category that will help us understand the *exploratory* character which may belong to any type of judgments on the methodic level, and therefore to poetry. Traditionally, it is to science as inquiry, credible investigation of the world, and to philosophy construed as aspiring to scientific status, that the trait of "seriousness" is ascribed. The linguistic nature of poetry in virtue of which it has so often been thought pre-eminent among the arts, has also been the very basis of its disparagement in contrast to science: what can poetic language "say" if poetry is not inquiry? Hence, alternatively, the easy identification of poetry with play, frivolity, "fancy" or the unrestricted toleration of images, and linguistic self-indulgence. This identification cannot be combated by making poetry quasi-assertive. Poetry's exploratory character is of a different breed.

The first step in formulating this character is to determine the genus we need. Inquiry must be regarded as only one species of Query. Art is another. The art of poetry is another—a subspecies. All exemplify the interrogative temper. In poetry this does not entail asking a question and looking for an answer. In science it not only does, but further entails both the initial separation of questions and their structuring. For these questions do more than raise the hope of unequivocal answers; they guide the process of achieving them. When the ancient Greeks said that the pursuit of wisdom begins in wonder, they laid the foundation for the concept of query. But there are at least two kinds of wonder. There is the wonder that seeks to be appeased and the wonder to which appeasement is irrelevant. In the species of query exemplified by science, the former dominates; in that exemplified by poetry, the latter. Scientific wonder seeks to resolve the questions it provokes. Poetic wonder seeks no resolutions; its interrogativeness is not generated by vexations.[7] Each of these forms of query methodically discriminates traits in the world. Each combines, separates, juxtaposes, varies the configurations and frames of traits. Initially, science finds the traits to be problematical, potentially if not actually. Initially, poetry finds them to be just what it finds them to be. Terminally, a scientific *finding* excludes and opposes other findings previously thought to be possible. Terminally, a poetic *finding* opposes no others. Yet it is the finding that it is, and not another. Scientific wonder, despite its need for mitigation, extends itself systematically. Poetic wonder seeks its own extension, though each poetic product inevitably curbs itself as a contrivance, in order to be a contrivance at all. A scientific product eventually aims to relate to another as an explanatory whole of which the other is an evidential or implied part, or as a part of the other. A poetic product does not aim at such a relation. In saying that a poetic finding "opposes" no others, or that a poetic product does not "aim" at the kind of relation with another which obtains between scientific products, the reference is to the finding as finding, the product as product; to the nature of the product as a judgment. What a particular poet's motives are, what aims he may have to "oppose" or discredit some poetic trend that he deplores, is beside the point. No poem as such opposes any other poem, because all poems may coexist as independently justifiable manifestations of query, and none can be meaningfully "invalidated" by any other.

The interrogative temper of poetry, like that of science and other species of query, lies in its seeking. Its seeking and its finding are less easily distinguishable than those of science. Poetic wonder, accepted on its own account, adds to the store of wonder. This does not mean that the poetic stance as such is committed to admiration of the world's complexes. Even the formal poetic encomium exemplifies query insofar as it is poetry, and not necessarily insofar as it is an encomium. What poetry selects as its elements of contrivance attests its infinitely variable interest. What provides for these interests a poetic direction is not the kind of complex selected but the mode of judgment embodied.

The concept of exhibitive judgment makes it possible to avoid two untenable extremes of opinion. One is that poetry has its own kind of claim to truth, implicitly if not explicitly. The other is that poetry need not be construed as utterance at all—a view which, expectedly, or unexpectedly, is suggested by Archibald MacLeish's line "A poem should not mean but be," when this line is extracted (as it has been) to serve as a piece of criticism. The first of these extremes is much less confident of itself when confronted by the questions what constitutes poetic falsification, how poems can be said to oppose one another with conflicting claims, and whether and how such claims can be settled. A charitable interpretation of the second extreme is that it identifies the meaning of all products with assertive meaning, and hence understandably repudiates meaning so far as poetry is concerned. Insofar as it emphasizes a poem as something that simply "is," it obliterates the difference between (poetic) products and mere (unproduced) events. Yet events too can have meaning, when present in a perspective that becomes articulated through judgment. The repudiation of a narrow and unjust conception of meaning can easily fall into stultifying despair, with its own dogmatic conviction that no conception of meaning can possibly be adequate to poetry. The pessimism is exacerbated by other widely held assumptions about meaning—the assumption that if artistic meaning is incomplete, or gets expanded, as time goes on, it is necessarily cloudy or arbitrary to begin with; or the assumption that scientific meanings are complete and wholly determinate; or the assumption that a meaning must be unequivocal and determinate in order to be a meaning at all. That a scientific meaning cannot ever be deemed complete is clear from the simple logical consideration that there is no end to the number of consequences entailed by a proposition, and that therefore the burden of all the assertions latent in a proposition of science cannot be known at any given time. Different dimensions of scientific meaning lie in the relations which a scientific product can bear to previous and subsequent scientific products—such as logical and historical relations— not to mention other products generally, and other conditions of the physical or social world. To suppose a scientific meaning complete, fixed, and unequivocal in the midst of so many possible changes and perspectives is not merely to hold a dubious metaphysics but to ignore the history of science. About artistic meaning we puzzle ourselves no end, but less because of its kind of intricacy or because of our prior doubts about the artistic enterprise than because in our comparisons of art with everyday meaning we overestimate the constancy and availability of the latter. All meaning is achieved by the process of judicative articulation, and it is a serious error to regard this process as ever actually completed except in the sense that we have chosen to stop it. To think that an equivocal meaning is no meaning at all is very much like thinking that an undeveloped economy is no economy at all, or a perplexed person no person at all.

Seeing poetry in terms of the interrogative temper demands some caution, lest the seeing be too narrowly focused.

1. Poetry does not need to introduce the grammatical appearance, or the suggestion, of verbal questioning in order to be interrogative— in order to exemplify the process of query. Nor is it enough to say that the words shaped as a question in poetry need not and do not aim to be answered.

> My face in thine eye, thine in mine appeares,
> And true plain hearts doe in the faces rest,
> Where can we finde two better hemispheares
> Without sharpe North, without declining West?[8]

Grammatically shaped questions are not what is *relevant* to the exploratory genius of poetry.

2. The interrogative temper of poetry does not eliminate or transcend meaning. Meaning is not superseded by shaping but rather given its character as meaning in an order of exhibitive judgment.

The point of these two observations will be evident if we glance at a passage from Sartre's *What Is Literature?* Apart from the dubious emphasis we are using it to illustrate, it is a fine passage. It starts by quoting two lines from Rimbaud:

> Oh seasons! Oh castles!
> What soul is faultless?

> (*O saisons! O châteaux!*
> *Quelle âme est sans défaut?*)

And it goes on to say:

> Nobody is questioned; nobody is questioning; the poet is absent. And the question involves no answer, or rather is its own answer. Is it therefore a false question? But it would be absurd to believe that Rimbaud "meant" that everybody has his faults. As Breton said of Saint-Pol Roux, "If he had meant it, he would have said it." Nor did he *mean* to say something else. He asked an absolute question. He conferred upon the beautiful word "soul" an interrogative existence. The interrogation has become a thing as the anguish of Tintoretto became a yellow sky. It is no longer a signification, but a substance.[9]

1. Rimbaud certainly produced "an interrogative existence." But just as certainly, it is not upon the word "soul" alone that he conferred such an existence. All the poetry of Rimbaud, all poetry, is interrogative in its process of probing and in the radiation of wonder. All poets communicate the interrogative strain, even those whose manner is categorical, and those in whom we find a verbal order that seems to incarnate assertiveness.

> Thus God and Nature link'd the general frame,
> And bade self-love and social be the same.[10]

Pope is not a theologian, a moral theorist, a practical moralist, a historian of ideas, or a logician. We do not admire in him or in any other poet theoretical power or rigorous reasoning. Whether the grammatical garments he employs are those of satire, description, approbation, or demonstration, it is the complex of traits he has set before us as shaped that emerges, essential and indomitable, from query. The very same exhibitive process is going on when Pope employs the actual grammatical form of asking a question and of answering it.

> Who starves by nobles, or with nobles eats?
> The wretch that trusts them, and the rogue that cheats.[11]

What scientists, statesmen, philosophers, or revolutionists bring into the world is probed by the poet even as clouds, hopes, dreams, flowers, and love are; so that his subject as it appears poetically may appear in the shape of a doctrine, a conclusion, a social movement, a commentary. The issue of whether he is moralist or poet is settled not by what complexes he has chosen, or what titles he has given to his works; not by his decision, but by his mode of production. In poetry, as we have seen, even a body of assertions is not dealt with assertively. The exhibitive judgment of the poet, his mode of selection, control, and discrimination, molds a body of traits, and the molding may have been kindled by an assertion that he has encountered. The exhibitive discrimination of the assertive—of concepts, controversies, doctrines—is the rediscrimination of a complex. The concepts and doctrines are spirited into another order, relocated by the force of query.

> Mock on, mock on, Voltaire, Rousseau;
> Mock on, mock on; 'tis all in vain!
> You throw the sand against the wind,
> And the wind throws it back again.

> And every sand becomes a gem
> Reflected in the beams divine;
> Blown back they blind the mocking eye
> But still in Israel's paths they shine.
>
> The Atoms of Democritus
> And Newton's Particles of Light
> Are sands upon the Red Sea shore
> Where Israel's tents do shine so bright.[12]

2. The word become "substance" or "thing" does not cease to mean just because it is no longer exclusively verbal. Sartre thinks that, being a "substance," it is "no longer a signification." But a word or phrase never does signify or mean solely because it is verbal, or because it was once tied to a discriminandum. It signifies because it enters into a communicative function. Any natural complex can be appropriated for a communicative function. A word or other complex to which no independent "signification" can be attributed, yet has significance. The word that has become "more" than a word has meaning (it means) in virtue of the same process by which the word as such had meaning— insofar as its ordinal habitat and function have been articulated. And we must be clear that the interrogativeness of a poem or of its words is no special achievement of a particular poet. The poem as poem arouses further query—through its articulation in the form of critics, through its articulation (exhibitive and active) by other poems of the same tradition or movement, or through its cultivation of the desire for poetry. It arouses query through its contagion of seeking, in any mode, any medium, any degree. . . .

Notes

1. Robert Browning, *The Ring and the Book,* XII.
2. Browning, *The Inn Album,* IV.
3. An Egyptian poem of the 12th Dynasty. The translation is in *The Beginnings of Civilization* by Sir Leonard Woolley, which is volume 1, part

2 of *The History of Mankind* (part 1 is by Jacquetta Hawkes) (UNESCO, 1963). Reprinted by permission of Harper & Row and by permission of George Allen & Unwin.

4. Arthur Symons, introduction to Everyman's Library edition of *Biographia Literaria* (London: J. M. Dent and Sons, 1906, 1949).

5. P. B. Shelley, letter to Maria Gisborne, lines 202–208.

6. A. N. Whitehead, *Science and the Modern World* (New York: The Free Press, 1967), chapter 5.

7. Might it not be said that Greek tragic poetry, for example, seeks "resolutions"; that the resolutions express themselves in the cathartic process? There may indeed be resolutions of some kind in all tragic poetry. But it is not poetic *wonder* that is resolved or mitigated. On the contrary, after the resolution the poetic wonder is intensified. The tragedy resolves the perplexity, the rational obscurity, of a human situation. The wonder is achieved by the poetic judgment of what thus *prevails*. Catharsis, in the last analysis, is a species of clarification. Through exhibitive clarification, the tragic poet generates wonder anew.

8. John Donne, "The Good-morrow," lines 15–18.

9. J.-P. Sartre, *What Is Literature?*, trans. Bernard Frechtman (New York: Harper & Row, 1965), chapter 1.

10. Alexander Pope, *Essay on Man*, Epistle III.

11. Pope, *Moral Essays*, Epistle III.

12. William Blake, "Mock on, Mock on, Voltaire, Rosseau."

Section 8

Religion and the Religious

Santayana's well known essay "Ultimate Religion" was first published in 1933, after having been given at a conference in The Hague, the Netherlands, honoring the tercentenary of the birth of Spinoza. One assumes that it is not by accident that Santayana chose the occasion of a celebration of Spinoza to raise the issue of a religion suited to the naturalist temper. It was Spinoza, after all, who took what in the early seventeenth century was the courageous, and for him very costly, stand of equating nature and God. It was Spinoza who approached nature, with all its geometrical and mechanical beauty, with the reverence ordinarily reserved for the supernatural. It is the sense of the divine in nature that captures Santayana's imagination here. What, he asks, is the allegiance or faith which would be most appropriate for "a wholly free and disillusioned spirit?" If we face the world as directly as possible, as free as we can get of what we would like it to be, we encounter, Santayana says, fundamental "religious" perceptions. The first of them is the world's overwhelming power. We also encounter the many facets of nature, or existence, in which we may take spiritual and intellectual delight. In the spirit of Spinoza, we experience an intellectual love— of the order of nature and of knowledge of it. Still, Santayana says, an "ultimate religion" cannot simply be a love of knowledge, a love of what is, but rather it must be a love of good, a love of what *can* be. In other words, Santayana's faith resides not in the mechanical, finished nature of Spinoza, but in the nature "in the making" by now familiar in twentieth-century naturalism.

In his essay Santayana takes for granted the naturalist frame of reference and that there is a religious perspective suited to it. Dewey too takes naturalism for granted here, but he is far more interested than Santayana in defending the association of a religious dimension of experience with a naturalist point of view. His most developed discussion of this issue is in his 1934 book *A Common Faith,* excerpts from chapters 1 and 2 of which are reprinted here. Dewey raises the fundamental question bluntly: does the "religious" need to be associated with the supernatural? He answers that it does not, and claims further that what is genuinely religious in traditional religions will be emancipated when it is freed from its association with the supernatural. Dewey suggests that modern and immensely successful science, in its discoveries and in its methods, has thrown reliance on the supernatural into disrepute. That traditional religion continues to insist on the supernatural is one of the reasons for its decline, and in any case, he thinks, it is unnecessary. The genuinely religious function in experience, Dewey urges, is "the unification of the self through allegiance to inclusive ideal ends." In other words, many of the objects of traditional religious belief, including God, are in fact symbolic of the reality and power of the ideal values which inspire us and toward which we act. The mistake traditional religions make is to insist that these ideal values, for example love, goodness, wisdom and power, are real not only as ideal ends, but that they are already actual in some supernatural realm. Besides being unfounded intellectually, Dewey argues, this weakens the power they might have as ideals, so that it is in the interest of the religious dimension of experience that it be freed from the supernatural, and that its power in experience be recognized.

Both Dewey and Santayana are concerned to develop a religious sentiment which is consistent with the general traits of naturalist philosophy. However provocative or successful their attempts have been, there remains the fact that theists have criticized naturalism for being unable to provide satisfactory answers to many of the most persistent questions of human life. One of those questions concerns the fact of our inevitable deaths and the problem of meaning which that fact generates. In his 1986 essay "The Inevitability of Our Own Death," John McDermott contends that the meaning of both death and life, contrary to the theist's claims, is most vivid in natural terms. McDermott is a specialist in the history of American philosophy and in American culture. He is the editor of scholarly editions of the works of William James, Josiah Royce and John Dewey, and he is the author of several books of original essays, including *The Culture of Experience* and *Streams of Experience,* the volume from which the essay reprinted here is taken. McDermott has taught at Fordham University and at State University of New York at Stony Brook, and he is currently professor of philosophy at Texas A & M University. In this essay McDermott begins by pointing out that we all know that we face our own deaths, and that we respond in various ways. We fear it, often we forget about it, and occasionally we become active agents of our own death rather than its passive re-cipients. Another possible response is to deny it, and the form such denial commonly takes is a belief in immortality, a belief which though understandable is illegitimate. The question McDermott poses is whether it is possible to live an active, creative, meaningful life without immortality, without absolute meaning, without ultimate significance? His answer is that it is possible, in fact that it is just that kind of life under just those conditions which defines human being. Contrary to the view that only the supernatural and personal immortality, the absence of death, can provide meaning and value, McDermott contends that it is precisely our awareness of our own death which provides human life with its distinctive character, with its most profound meaning and significance. To be a "live creature" is to experience, is to grow, and growth is the process of making a life, of making a place. This is a most meaningful process, since it turns plain space into a human place, the world into a human world. There is no absolute place provided for us, so that without human growth we are, McDermott says, transients. Further-more, living provides meaning not only to place, but to time as well. It is living, not pretending not to die, that provides value and signifi-cance to human life, and living requires that we face death squarely.

1

Ultimate Religion*

George Santayana

Before this chosen audience, in this consecrated place, I may venture
to pass over all subsidiary matters and come at once to the last question
of all: What inmost allegiance, what ultimate religion, would be proper
to a wholly free and disillusioned spirit? The occasion invites us to consider
this question, and to consider it with entire frankness. Great as you
and I may feel our debt to be to Spinoza for his philosophy of nature,
there is, I think, something for which we owe him an even greater debt;
I mean, the magnificent example he offers us of philosophic liberty,
the courage, firmness, and sincerity with which he reconciled his heart
to the truth. Any clever man may sometimes see the truth in flashes;
any scientific man may put some aspect of the truth into technical words;
yet all this hardly deserves the name of philosophy so long as the heart
remains unabashed, and we continue to live like animals lost in the
stream of our impressions, not only in the public routine and necessary
cares of life, but even in our silent thoughts and affections. Many a
man before Spinoza and since has found the secret of peace: but the

---

*Paper read in the *Domus Spinoza* at The Hague during the commemoration
of the tercentenary of the birth of Spinoza. Originally published in *Septima Spinozana*
(The Hague: Martinus Nijoff, 1933), pp. 105–115.

singularity of Spinoza, at least in the modern world, was that he facilitated this moral victory by no dubious postulates. He did not ask God to meet him half way: he did not whitewash the facts, as the facts appear to clear reason, or as they appeared to the science of his day. He solved the problem of the spiritual life after stating it in the hardest, sharpest, most cruel terms. Let us nerve ourselves today to imitate his example, not by simply accepting his solution, which for some of us would be easy, but by exercising his courage in the face of a somewhat different world, in which it may be even more difficult for us than it was for him to find a sure foothold and a sublime companionship.

There is a brave and humorous saying of Luther's, which applies to Spinoza better, perhaps, than to Luther himself. When asked where, if driven out of the Church, he would stand, he replied: "Under the sky." The sky of Luther was terribly clouded: there was a vast deal of myth tumbling and thundering about in it: and even in the clear sky of Spinoza there was perhaps something specious, as there is in the blue vault itself. The sun, he tells us, seemed to be about two hundred feet away: and if his science at once corrected this optical illusion, it never undermined his conviction that all reality was within easy reach of his thought. Nature was dominated, he assumed, by unquestionable scientific and dialectical principles; so that while the forces of nature might often put our bodily existence in jeopardy, they always formed a decidedly friendly and faithful object for the mind. There was no essential mystery. The human soul from her humble station might salute the eternal and the finite with complete composure and with a certain vicarious pride. Every man had a true and adequate idea of God: and this saying, technically justified as it may be by Spinoza's definitions of terms, cannot help surpassing us; it reveals such a virgin sense of familiarity with the absolute. There could not but be joy in the sweep of an intelligence that seemed so completely victorious, and no misgivings could trouble a view of the world that explained everything.

Today, however, we can hardly feel such assurance: we should be taking shelter in a human edifice which the next earthquake might shake down. Nor is it a question really of times or temperaments: anyone anywhere, if he does not wish to construct a plausible system, but to challenge his own assumptions and come to spiritual self-knowledge, must begin by abstention from all easy faith, lest he should be madly filling the universe with images of his own reason and his own hopes. I will therefore ask you today, provisionally, for an hour, and without prejudice to your ulterior reasonable convictions, to imagine the truth to be as unfavorable as possible to your desires and as contrary as possible to your natural presumptions; so that the spirit in each of us may be drawn away from its accidental home and subjected to an utter denudation and supreme trial. Yes, although the dead cannot change their minds, I would respectfully beg the shade of Spinoza himself to suspend for a moment that strict rationalism, that jealous hard-reasoning, confident piety which he shared with the Calvinists and Jansenists of his day, and to imagine—I do not say to admit—that nature may be but imperfectly formed in the bosom of chaos, and that reason in us may be imperfectly adapted to the understanding of nature. Then, having hazarded no favorite postulates and invoked no cosmic forces pledged to support our aspirations, we may all quietly observe what we find; and whatever harmonies may then appear to subsist between our spirits and the nature of things will be free gifts to us and, so far as they go, unchallengeable possessions. We shall at last be standing unpledged and naked, under the open sky.

In what I am about to say, therefore, I do not mean to prejudge any cosmological questions, such as that of free will or necessity, theism, or pantheism. I am concerned only with the sincere confessions of a mind that has surrendered every doubtful claim and every questionable assurance. Of such assurances or claims there is one which is radical and comprehensive; I mean, the claim to existence and to directing the course of events. We say conventionally that the future is uncertain: but if we withdrew honestly into ourselves and examined our actual moral resources, we should feel that what is insecure is not merely the course of particular events but the vital presumption that there is a future coming at all, and a future pleasantly continuing our habitual experience. We rely in this, as we must, on the analogies of experience, or rather on the clockwork of instinct and presumption in our bodies; but existence is a miracle, and, morally considered, a free gift from moment to moment. That it will always be analogous to itself is the very question we are begging. Evidently all interconnections and sequences of events, and in particular any consequences which we may expect to flow from our actions, are really entirely beyond our spiritual control. When our will commands and seems, we know not how, to be obeyed by our bodies and by the world, we are like Joshua seeing the sun stand still at his bidding; when we command and nothing happens, we are like King Canute surprised that the rising tide should not obey him: and when we say we have executed a great work and redirected the course of history, we are like Chanticleer attributing sunrise to his crowing.

What is the result? That at once, by a mere act of self-examination and frankness, the spirit has come upon one of the most important and radical of religious perceptions. It has perceived that though it is living, it is powerless to live; that though it may die, it is powerless to die; and that altogether, at every instant and in every particular, it is in the hands of some alien and inscrutable power.

Of this felt power I profess to know nothing further. To me, as yet, it is merely the counterpart of my impotence. I should not venture, for instance, to call this power almighty, since I have no means of knowng how much it can do; but I should not hesitate, if I may coin a word, to call it *omnificent*: it is to me, by definition, the doer of everything that is done. I am not asserting the physical validity of this sense of agency or cause: I am merely feeling the force, the friendliness, the hostility, the unfathomableness of the world. I am expressing an impression; and it may be long before my sense of omnipresent power can be erected, with many qualifications, into a theological theory of the omnipotence of God. But the moral presence of power comes upon a man in the night, in the desert, when he finds himself, as the Arabs say, alone with Allah. It reappears in every acute predicament, in extremities, in the birth of a child, or in the face of death. And as for the unity of this power, that is not involved in its sundry manifestations, but rather in my own solitude; in the unity of this suffering spirit overtaken by all those accidents. My destiny is single, tragically single, no matter how multifarious may be the causes of my destiny. As I stand amazed, I am not called upon to say whether, if I could penetrate into the inner workings of things, I should discover omnificent power to be simple or compound, continuous or spasmodic, intentional or blind. I stand before it simply receptive, somewhat as, in Rome, I might stand before the great fountain of Trevi. There I see jets and cascades flowing in separate streams and in diverse directions. I am not sure that a single Pontifex Maximus designed it all, and led all those musical waters into just those channels. Some streams may have dried up or been diverted since the creation; some rills may have been added today by fresh rains from heaven; behind one of those artifical rocks some little demon, of his own free will, may even now be playing havoc with the conduits; and who knows how many details, in my image, may not have been misplaced or multiplied by optical tricks of my own? Yet here, for the spirit, is one total marvelous person, one thunderous force, confronting me with this theatrical but admirable spectacle.

Yet this is not all. Power comes down upon me clothed in a thousand phenomena; and these manifestations of power open to me a new spiritual resource. In submitting to power, I learn its ways; from being passive my spirit becomes active; it begins to enjoy one of its essential prerogatives. For like a child the spirit is attracted to all facts by the mere assault of their irrational presence and variety. It watches all that happens or is done with a certain happy excitement, even at the most fearful calamities. Although the essence of spirit may be merely to think, yet some intensity and progression are essential to this thinking; thinking is a way of living, and the most vital way. Therefore all the operations of universal power, when they afford themes for perception, afford also occasions for intellectual delight. Here will and intellect, as Spinoza tells us, coincide: for omnificent power flows in part through our persons; the spirit itself is a spark of that fire, or rather the light of that flame: it cannot have an opposite principle of motion. With health a certain euphoria, a certain alacrity and sense of mastery are induced in the spirit; and a natural effect of perspective, the pathos of nearness, turns our little spark for us into a central sun. The world moves round us, and we move gladly with the world. What if the march of things be destined to overwhelm us? It cannot destroy the joy we had in its greatness and in its victory. There may even be some relief in passing from the troubled thought of ourselves to the thought of something more rich in life, yet in its own sphere and progression, untroubled: and it may be easier for me to understand the motion of the heavens and to rejoice in it than to understand or rejoice in my own motions. My own eclipse, my own vices, my own sorrows, may become a subject to me for exact calculation and a pleasing wonder. The philosophical eye may compose a cosmic harmony out of these necessary conflicts, and an infinite life out of these desirable deaths.

Does it not begin to appear that the solitude of a naked spirit may be rather well peopled? In proportion as we renounce our animal claims and commitments, do we not breathe a fresher and more salubrious air? May not the renunciation of everything disinfect everything and return everything to us in its impartial reality, at the same time disinfecting our wills also, and rendering us capable of charity? This charity will extend, of course, to the lives and desires of others, which we recognize to be no less inevitable than our own; and it will extend also to their ideas, and by a curious and blessed consequence, to the relativity and misery of our own minds. Yet this intellectual charity, since it is inspired by respect for the infinite, will by no means accept all views passively and romantically, as if they were equal and not subject to correction; but doing better justice to the holy aspiration which animates them in common, it will rise from them all, and with them all, to the conception of eternal truth.

Here we touch the crown of Spinoza's philosophy, that intellectual love of God in which the spirit was to be ultimately reconciled with universal power and universal truth. This love brings to consciousness a harmony intrinsic to existence; not an alleged harmony such as may be posited in religions or philosophies resting on faith, but a harmony which, as far as it goes, is actual and patent. In the realm of matter, this harmony is measured by the degree of adjustment, conformity, and cooperation which the part may have attained in the whole; in a word, it is measured by *health*. In the realm of truth, the same natural harmony extends as far as do capacity and pleasure in understanding the truth; so that besides health we may possess *knowledge*. And this is no passive union, no dead peace; the spirit rejoices it; for the spirit, being, according to Spinoza, an essential concomitant of all existence, shares the movement, the *actuosa essentia* of the universe; so that we necessarily *love* health and knowledge, and *love* the things in which health and knowledge are found. Insofar as omnificent power endows us with health, we necessarily love that power whose total movement makes for our own perfection; and insofar as we are able to understand the truth, we necessarily love the themes of an intense and unclouded vision, in which our imaginative faculty reaches its perfect function.

Of this religion of health and understanding Spinoza is a sublime prophet. By overcoming all human weaknesses, even when they seem kindly or noble, and by honoring power and truth, even if they should slay him, he entered the sanctuary of an unruffled superhuman wisdom, and declared himself supremely happy, not because the world as he conceived it was flattering to his heart, but because the gravity of his heart disdained all flatteries, and with a sacrificial prophetic boldness uncovered and relished his destiny, however tragic his destiny might be. And presently peace descended; this keen scientific air seemed alone fit to breathe, and only this high tragedy worthy of a heroic and manly breast. Indeed the truth is a great cathartic and wonderfully relieves the vital distress of existence. We stand as on a mountaintop, and the spectacle, so out of scale with all our petty troubles, silences and overpowers the heart, expanding it for a moment into boundless sympathy with the universe.

Nevertheless, the moral problem is not solved. It is not solved for mankind at large, which remains no less distracted than it was before. Nor is it solved even for the single spirit. There is a radical and necessary recalcitrancy in the finite soul in the face of all this cosmic pomp and all this cosmic pressure: a recalcitrancy to which Spinoza was less sensitive than some other masters of the spiritual life, perhaps because he was more positivistic by temperament and less specifically religious. At any rate many a holy man has known more suffering than Spinoza found in the long work of salvation, more uncertainty, and also, in the end, a more lyrical and warmer happiness. For in the first place, as I said in the beginning, a really naked spirit cannot assume that the world is thoroughly intelligible. There may be surds, there may be hard facts, there may be dark abysses before which intelligence must be silent, for fear of going mad. And in the second place, even if to the intellect all things should prove perspicuous, the intellect is not the whole of human nature, nor even the whole of pure spirit in man. Reason may be the *differentia* of man; it is surely not his essence. His essence, at best, is animality qualified by reason. And from this animality the highest flights of reason are by no means separable. The very life of spirit springs from animal predicaments: it moves by imposing on events a perspective and a moral urgency proper to some particular creature or some particular interest.

Good, as Spinoza would tell us, is an epithet which we assign to whatsoever increases our perfection. Such a doctrine might seem egotistical, but is simply biological; and on its moral side, the maxim is a greater charter of liberty and justice than ever politician framed. For it follows that every good pursued is genuinely good, and the perfection of every creature equally perfection. Every good therefore is a good forever to a really clarified, just, and disinterested spirit; such a spirit cannot rest in the satisfaction of any special faculty, such as intelligence, nor of any special art, such as philosophy. That the intellect might be perfectly happy in contemplating the truth of the universe, does not render the universe good to every other faculty; good to the heart, good to the flesh, good to the eye, good to the conscience or the sense of justice. Of all systems an optimistic system is the most oppressive. Would it not be a bitter mockery if, in the words of Bradley, this were the best of possible worlds, and everything in it a necessary evil? The universal good by which the spirit, in its rapt moments, feels overwhelmed, if it is not to be a mystical illusion, cannot fall short of being the sum of all those perfections, infinitely various, to which all living things severally aspire. A glint or symbol of this universal good may be found in any moment of perfect happiness visiting any breast: but it is impossible unreservedly to love or worship anything, be it the universe or any part of it, unless we find in the end that this thing is completely good: I mean, unless it is perfect after its kind and a friend to itself, and unless at the same time it is beneficent universally, and a friend to everything else. Pure spirit would be lame, and evidently biased by some biological accident, if it did not love every good loved anywhere by anybody. These varied perfections are rivals and enemies in the press of the world, where there seems not to be matter or time enough for everything: but to impartial spirit no good can render another good odious. Physically, one good may exclude another: nature and natural morality must choose between them, or be dissolved into chaos:

but in eternity the most opposite goods are not enemies; rather little brothers and sisters, as all odd creatures were to Saint Francis. And that all these various perfections are not actually attainable is a material accident, painful but not confusing to a free spirit. Their contrariety increases sorrow, but does not diminish love; the very pain is a fresh homage to the beauty missed, and a proof of loyalty; so that the more the spirit suffers the more clearly, when it unravels its suffering, it understands what it loves. Every perfection then shines, washed and clear, separate and uncontaminated: yet all compatible, each in its place, and harmonious. To love things spiritually, that is to say, intelligently and disinterestedly, means to love the love in them, to worship the need which they pursue, and to see them all prophetically in their possible beauty. To love things as they are would be a mockery of things: a truer lover must love them as they would wish to be. For nothing is quite happy as it is, and the first act of true sympathy must be to move with the object of love towards its happiness.

Universal good, then, the whole of that to which all things aspire, is something merely potential; and if we wish to make a religion of love, after the manner of Socrates, we must take universal good, not universal power, for the object of our religion. This religion would need to be more imaginative, more poetical, than that of Spinoza, and the word God, if we still used it, would have to mean for us not the universe, but the good of the universe. There would not be a universe worshipped, but a universe praying; and the flame of the whole fire, the whole seminal and generative movement of nature, would be the love of God. This love would be erotic; it would be really love and not something wingless called by that name. It would bring celestial glimpses not to be retained, but culminating in moments of unspeakable rapture, in a union with all good, in which the soul would vanish as an object because, as an organ, it had found its perfect employment.

For there is a mystery here, the mystery of seeming to attain emotionally the logically unattainable. Universal good is something dispersed, various, contrary to itself in its opposite embodiments; nevertheless, to the mystic, it seems a single living object, the One Beloved, a good to be embraced all at once, finally and forever, leaving not the least shred of anything good outside. Yet I think this mystery may be easily solved. Spirit is essentially synthetic; and just as all the known and unknown forces of nature make, in relation to experience and destiny, one single omnificent power; and just as all facts and all the relations between facts compose for the historical and prophetic mind one unalterable realm of truth; so exactly, for the lover, all objects of love form a single ineffable good. He may say that he sees all beauties in a single face, that all beauties else are nothing to him; yet perhaps in this hyperbole he may be doing his secret heart an injustice. Beauty here may be silently teaching him to discern beauty everywhere, because in all instances of love only the sheer love counts in his eyes: and in the very absoluteness of his love he may feel an infinite promise. His ecstasy, which passes for a fulfillment, remains a sort of agony: and though itself visionary, it may, by its influence, free his heart from trivial or accidental attachments and lead it instead to a universal charity. Beggars in Catholic and Moslem countries used to beg an alms, sometimes, for the love of God. It was a potent appeal; because God, according to the Socratic tradition, was the good to which all creation moved; so that anyone who loved deeply, and loved God, could not fail, by a necessary inclusion, to love the good which all creatures lived by pursuing, no matter how repulsive these creatures might be to natural human feeling.

Thus the absolute love of anything involves the love of universal good; and the love of universal good involves the love of every creature.

Such, in brief, seems to me the prospect open to a mind that examines its moral condition without any preconceptions. Perhaps an empirical critic, strictly reducing all objects to the functions which they have in experience, might see in my meager inventory all the elements of religion. Mankind, he might say, in thinking of God or the gods have always meant the power in events: as when people say: *God willing.* Sometimes they have also meant the truth, as when people say: *God knows.* And perhaps a few mystics may have meant the good, or the supreme object of love, union with whom they felt would be perfect happiness. I should then have merely changed the language of traditional religion a little, translated its myths into their pragmatic equivalents, and reduced religion to its true essence. But no: I make no such professions: they would be plainly sophistical. The functions which objects have in experience no doubt open to us different avenues to those objects: but the objects themselves, if they exist, are not mere names for those functions. They are objects of faith; and the religion of mankind, like their science, has always been founded on faith. Now there is no faith invoked in the examination of conscience which I have made before you this evening: and therefore, properly speaking, what I come to is not religion. Nor is it exactly philosophy, since I offer no hypotheses about the nature of the universe or about the nature of knowledge. Yet to be quite sincere, I think that in this examination of conscience there is a sort of secret or private philosophy perhaps more philosophical than the other: and while I set up no gods, not even Spinoza's infinite *Deus sive Natura,* I do consider on what subject and to what end we might consult those gods, if we found that they existed: and surely the aspiration that would prompt us, in that case, to worship the gods, would be our truest heartbond and our ultimate religion.

If then any of us who are so minded should ever hear the summons of a liturgical religion calling to us: *Sursum corda, Lift up your hearts,* we might sincerely answer, *Habemus ad Dominum, Our hearts by nature are addressed to the Lord.* For we recognize universal power, and respect it, since on it we depend for our existence and fortunes. We look also with unfeigned and watchful allegiance toward universal truth, in which all the works of power are eternally defined and recorded; since insofar as we are able to discover it, the truth raises all things for us into the light, into the language of spirit. And finally, when power takes on the form of life, and begins to circle about and pursue some type of perfection, spirit in us necessarily loves these perfections, since spirit is aspiration become conscious, and they are the goals of life: and insofar as any of these goals of life can be defined or attained anywhere, even if only in prophetic fancy, they become glory, or become beauty, and spirit in us necessarily worships them: not the troubled glories and brief perfections of this world only, but rather that desired perfection, that eternal beauty, which lies sealed in the heart of each living thing.

2

A Common Faith*

John Dewey

Religion versus the Religious

Never before in history has mankind been so much of two minds, so divided into two camps, as it is today. Religions have traditionally been allied with ideas of the supernatural, and often have been based upon explicit beliefs about it. Today there are many who hold that nothing worthy of being called religious is possible apart from the supernatural. Those who hold this belief differ in many respects. They range from those who accept the dogmas and sacraments of the Greek and Roman Catholic church as the only sure means of access to the supernatural to the theist or mild deist. Between them are the many Protestant denominations who think the Scriptures, aided by a pure conscience, are adequate avenues to supernatural truth and power. But they agree in one point: the necessity for a Supernatural Being and for an immortality that is beyond the power of nature.

---

*Originally published in John Dewey, *A Common Faith* (New Haven, Conn.: Yale University Press, 1934). Subsequently published in vol. 9 of *The Later Works of John Dewey,* ed. by J. A. Boydston (Carbondale, Ill.: Southern Illinois University Press, 1986). Reprinted by permission of The Board of Trustees, Southern Illinois University.

The opposed group consists of those who think the advance of culture and science has completely discredited the supernatural and with it all religions that were allied with belief in it. But they go beyond this point. The extremists in this group believe that with elimination of the supernatural not only must historic religions be dismissed but with them everything of a religious nature. When historical knowledge has discredited the claims made for the supernatural character of the persons said to have founded historic religions; when the supernatural inspiration attributed to literatures held sacred has been riddled, and when anthropological and psychological knowledge has disclosed the all-too-human source from which religious beliefs and practices have sprung, everything religious must, they say, also go.

There is one idea held in common by these two opposite groups: identification of the religious with the supernatural. The question I shall raise in these chapters concerns the ground for and the consequences of this identification: its reasons and its value. In the discussion I shall develop another conception of the nature of the religious phase of experience, one that separates it from the supernatural and the things that have grown up about it. I shall try to show that these derivations are encumbrances and that what is genuinely religious will undergo an emancipation when it is relieved from them; that then, for the first time, the religious aspect of experience will be free to develop freely on its own account.

This view is exposed to attack from both the other camps. It goes contrary to traditional religions, including those that have the greatest hold upon the religiously minded today. The view announced will seem to them to cut the vital nerve of the religious element itself in taking away the basis upon which traditional religions and institutions have been founded. From the other side, the position I am taking seems like a timid halfway position, a concession and compromise unworthy of thought that is thoroughgoing. It is regarded as a view entertained from mere tendermindedness, as an emotional hangover from childhood indoctrination, or even as a manifestation of a desire to avoid disapproval and curry favor. . . .

Faith and Its Object

All religions, as I pointed out in the preceding chapter, involve specific intellectual beliefs, and they attach—some greater, some less—importance to assent to these doctrines as true, true in the intellectual sense. They have literatures held especially sacred, containing historical material with which the validity of the religions is connected. They have developed a doctrinal apparatus it is incumbent upon "believers" (with varying degrees of strictness in different religions) to accept. They also insist that there is some special and isolated channel of access to the truths they hold.

No one will deny, I suppose, that the present crisis in religion is intimately bound up with these claims. The skepticism and agnosticism that are rife and that from the standpoint of the religionist are fatal to the religious spirit are directly bound up with the intellectual contents, historical, cosmological, ethical, and theological, asserted to be indispensable in everything religious. There is no need for me here to go with any minuteness into the causes that have generated doubt and disbelief, uncertainty and rejection, as to these contents. It is enough to point out that all the beliefs and ideas in question, whether having to do with historical and literary matters, or with astronomy, geology and biology, or with the creation and structure of the world and man, are connected with the supernatural, and that this connection is the factor that has brought doubt upon them; the factor that from the standpoint of historic and institutional religions is sapping the religious life itself.

The obvious and simple facts of the case are that some views about the origin and constitution of the world and man, some views about the course of human history and personages and incidents in that history, have become so interwoven with religion as to be identified with it. On the other hand, the growth of knowledge and of its methods and tests have been such as to make acceptance of these beliefs increasingly onerous and even impossible for large numbers of cultivated men and women. With such persons, the result is that the more these ideas are used as the basis and justification of a religion, the more dubious that religion becomes.

Protestant denominations have largely abandoned the idea that particular ecclesiastic sources can authoritatively determine cosmic, historic, and theological beliefs. The more liberal among them have at least mitigated the older belief that individual hardness and corruption of heart are the causes of intellectual rejection of the intellectual apparatus of the Christian religion. But these denominations have also, with exceptions numerically insignificant, retained a certain indispensable minimum of intellectual content. They ascribe peculiar religious force to certain literary documents and certain historic personages. Even when they have greatly reduced the bulk of intellectual content to be accepted, they have insisted at least upon theism and the immortality of the individual.

It is not part of my intention to rehearse in any detail the weighty facts that collectively go by the name of the conflict of science and religion—a conflict that is not done away with by calling it a conflict of science with theology, as long as even a minimum of intellectual assent is prescribed as essential. The impact of astronomy not merely upon the older cosmogony of religion but upon elements of creeds dealing with historic events—witness the idea of ascent into heaven—is familiar. Geological discoveries have displaced creation myths which once bulked large. Biology has revolutionized conceptions of soul and mind which once occupied a central place in religious beliefs and ideas, and this science has made a profound impression upon ideas of sin, redemption, and immortality. Anthropology, history, and literary criticism have furnished a radically different version of the historic events and personages upon which Christian religions have built. Psychology is already opening to us natural explanations of phenomena so extraordinary that once their supernatural origin was, so to say, the natural explanation.

The significant bearing for my purpose of all this is that new methods of inquiry and reflection have become for the educated man today the final arbiter of all questions of fact, existence, and intellectual assent. Nothing less than a revolution in the "seat of intellectual authority" has taken place. This revolution, rather than any particular aspect of its impact upon this and that religious belief, is the central thing. In this revolution, every defeat is a stimulus to renewed inquiry; every victory won is the open door to more discoveries, and every discovery is a new seed planted in the soil of intelligence, from which grow fresh plants with new fruits. The mind of man is being habituated to a new method and ideal: there is but one sure road of access to truth—the road of patient, cooperative inquiry operating by means of observation, experiment, record, and controlled reflection.

The scope of the change is well illustrated by the fact that whenever a particular outpost is surrendered it is usually met by the remark from a liberal theologian that the particular doctrine of supposed historic or literary tenet surrendered was never, after all, an intrinsic part of religious belief, and that without it the true nature of religion stands out more clearly than before. Equally significant is the growing gulf between fundamentalists and liberals in the churches. What is not realized—although perhaps it is more definitely seen by fundamentalists than by liberals—is that the issue does not concern this and that piecemeal *item* of belief, but centers in the question of the method by which any and every item of intellectual belief is to be arrived at and justified.

The positive lesson is that religious qualities and values if they are real at all are not bound up with any single item of intellectual assent, not even that of the existence of the God of theism; and that, under existing conditions, the religious function in experience can be emancipated only through surrender of the whole notion of special truths that are religious by their own nature, together with the idea of peculiar avenues of access to such truths. For were we to admit that there is but one method for ascertaining fact and truth—that conveyed by the word "scientific" in its most general and generous sense—no discovery in any branch of knowledge and inquiry could then disturb the faith that is religious. I should describe this faith as the unification of the self through allegiance to inclusive ideal ends, which imagination presents to us and to which the human will responds as worthy of controlling our desires and choices. . . .

Were we to adopt the latter point of view, it would be evident not only that the intellectual articles of a creed must be understood to be symbolic of moral and other ideal values, but that the facts taken to be historic and used as concrete evidence of the intellectual articles are themselves symbolic. These articles of a creed present events and persons that have been made over by the idealizing imagination in the interest, at their best, of moral ideals. Historic personages in their divine attributes are materializations of the ends that enlist devotion and inspire endeavor. They are symbolic of the reality of ends moving us in many forms of experience. The ideal values that are thus symbolized also mark human experience in science and art and the various modes of human association: they mark almost everything in life that rises from the level of manipulation of conditions as they exist. It is admitted that the objects of religion are ideal in contrast with our present state. What would be lost if it were also admitted that they have authoritative claim upon conduct just because they are ideal? The assumption that these objects of religion exist already in some realm of being seems to add nothing to their force, while it weakens their claim over us as ideals, insofar as it bases that claim upon matters that are intellectually dubious. The question narrows itself to this: Are the ideals that move us genuinely ideal or are they ideal only in contrast with our present estate?

The import of the question extends far. It determines the meaning given to the word "God." On one score, the word can mean only a particular being. On the other score, it denotes the unity of all ideal ends arousing us to desires and actions. Does the unification have a claim upon our attitude and conduct because it is already, apart from us, in realized existence, or because of its own inherent meaning and value? Suppose for the moment that the word "God" means the ideal ends that at a given time and place one acknowledges as having authority over his volition and emotion, the values to which one is supremely devoted, as far as these ends, through imagination, take on unity. If we make this supposition, the issue will stand out clearly in contrast with the doctrine of religions that "God" designates some kind of Being having prior and therefore nonideal existence.

The word "nonideal" is to be taken literally in regard to some religions that have historically existed, to all of them as far as they are neglectful of moral qualities in their divine beings. It does not apply in the same *literal* way to Judaism and Christianity. For they have asserted that the Supreme Being has moral and spiritual attributes. But it applies to them nonetheless in that these moral and spiritual characters are thought of as properties of a particular existence and are thought to be of religious value for us because of this embodiment in such an existence. Here, as far as I can see, is the ultimate issue as to the difference between *a* religion and the religious as a function of experience.

The idea that "God" represents a unification of ideal values that is essentially imaginative in origin when the imagination supervenes in conduct is attended with verbal difficulties owing to our frequent use of the word "imagination" to denote fantasy and doubtful reality. But the reality of ideal ends as ideals is vouched for by their undeniable power in action. An ideal is not an illusion because imagination is the organ through which it is apprehended. For *all* possibilities reach us through the imagination. In a definite sense the only meaning that can be assigned the term "imagination" is that things unrealized in fact come home to us and have power to stir us. The unification effected through imagination is not fanciful, for it is the reflex of the unification of practical and emotional attitudes. The unity signifies not a single Being, but the unity of loyalty and effort evoked by the fact that many ends are one in the power of their ideal, or imaginative, quality to stir and hold us.

We may well ask whether the power and significance in life of the traditional conceptions of God are not due to the ideal qualities referred to by them, the hypostatization of them into an existence being due to a conflux of tendencies in human nature that converts the object of desire into an antecedent reality . . . with beliefs that have prevailed in the cultures of the past. For in the older cultures the idea of the supernatural was "natural," in the sense in which "natural" signifies something customary and familiar. It seems more credible that religious persons have been supported and consoled by the reality with which ideal values appeal to them than that they have been upborne by sheer matter-of-fact existence. That, when once men are inured to the idea of the union of the ideal and the physical, the two should be so bound together in emotion that it is difficult to institute a separation, agrees with all we know of human psychology.

The benefits that will accrue, however, from making the separation are evident. The dislocation frees the religious values of experience once and for all from matters that are continually becoming more dubious. With that release there comes emancipation from the necessity of resort to apologetics. The reality of ideal ends and values in their authority over us is an undoubted fact. The validity of justice, affection, and that intellectual correspondence of our ideas with realities that we call truth, is so assured in its hold on humanity that it is unnecessary for the religious attitude to encumber itself with the apparatus of dogma and doctrine.

Any other conception of the religious attitude, when it is adequately analyzed, means that those who hold it care more for force than for ideal values—since all that an existence can add is force to establish, to punish, and to reward. There are, indeed, some persons who frankly say that their own faith does not require any guarantee that moral values are backed up by physical force, but who hold that the masses are so backward that ideal values will not affect their conduct unless in the popular belief these values have the sanction of a power that can enforce them and can execute justice on those who fail to comply.

There are some persons, deserving of more respect, who say: "We agree that the beginning must be made with the primacy of the ideal. But why stop at this point? Why not search with the utmost eagerness and vigor for all the evidence we can find, such as is supplied by history, by presence of design in nature, which may lead on to the belief that the ideal is already extant in a Personality having objective existence?"

One answer to the question is that we are involved by this search in all the problems of the existence of evil that have haunted theology in the past and that the most ingenious apologetics have not faced, much less met. If these apologists had not identified the existence of ideal goods with that of a Person supposed to originate and support them—a Being, moreover, to whom omnipotent power is attributed—the problem of the occurrence of evil would be gratuitous. The significance of ideal ends and meanings is, indeed, closely connected with the fact that there are in life all sorts of things that are evil to us because we would have them otherwise. Were existing conditions wholly good, the notion of possibilities to be realized would never emerge.

But the more basic answer is that while if the search is conducted on a strictly empirical basis there is no reason why it should not take place, as a matter of fact it is always undertaken in the interest of the supernatural. Thus it diverts attention and energy from ideal values and from the exploration of actual conditions by means of which they may be promoted. History is testimony to this fact. Men have never fully used the powers they possess to advance the good in life, because they have waited upon some power external to themselves and to nature to do the work they are responsible for doing. Dependence upon an external power is the counterpart of surrender of human endeavor. Nor is emphasis on exercising our own powers for good an egoistical or a sentimentally optimistic recourse. It is not the first, for it does not isolate man, either individually or collectively, from nature. It is not the second, because it makes no assumption beyond that of the need and responsibility for human endeavor, and beyond the conviction that, if human desire and endeavor were enlisted in behalf of natural ends, conditions would be bettered. It involves one expectation of a millennium of good.

Belief in the supernatural as a necessary power for apprehension of the ideal and for practical attachment to it has for its counterpart a pessimistic belief in the corruption and impotency of natural means. That is axiomatic in Christian dogma. But this apparent pessimism has a way of suddenly changing into an exaggerated optimism. For according to the terms of the doctrine, if the faith in the supernatural is of the required order, regeneration at once takes place. Goodness, in all essentials, is thereby established; if not, there is proof that the established relation to the supernatural has been vitiated. This romantic optimism is one cause for the excessive attention to individual salvation characteristic of traditional Christianity. Belief in a sudden and complete transmutation through conversion and in the objective efficacy of prayer, is too easy a way out of difficulties. It leaves matters in general just about as they were before; that is, sufficiently bad so that there is additional support for the idea that only supernatural aid can better them. The position of natural intelligence is that there exists a *mixture* of good and evil, and that reconstruction in the direction of the good which is indicated by ideal ends, must take place, if at all, through continued cooperative effort. There is at least enough impulse toward justice, kindliness, and order so that if it were mobilized for action, not expecting abrupt and complete transformation to occur, the disorder, cruelty, and oppression that exist would be reduced.

The discussion has arrived at a point where a more fundamental objection to the position I am taking needs consideration. The misunderstanding upon which this objection rests should be pointed out. The view I have advanced is sometimes treated as if the identification of the divine with ideal ends left the ideal wholly without roots in existence and without support from existence. The objection implies that my view commits one to such a separation of the ideal and the existent that the ideal has no chance to find lodgment even as a seed that might grow and bear fruit. On the contrary, what I have been criticizing is the *identification* of the ideal with a particular Being, especially when that identification makes necessary the conclusion that this Being is outside of nature, and what I have tried to show is that the ideal itself has its roots in natural conditions; it emerges when the imagination idealizes existence by laying hold of the possibilities offered to thought and action. There are values, goods, actually realized upon a natural basis—the goods of human association, of art and knowledge. The idealizing imagination seizes upon the most precious things found in the climacteric moments of experience and projects them. We need no external criterion and guarantee for their goodness. They are had, they exist as good, and out of them we frame our ideal ends.

Moreover, the ends that result from our projection of experienced goods into objects of thought, desire, and effort exist, only they exist *as* ends. Ends, purposes, exercise determining power in human conduct. The aims of philanthropists, of Florence Nightingale, of Howard, of Wilberforce, of Peabody, have not been idle dreams. They have modified institutions. Aims, ideals, do not exist simply in "mind"; they exist in character, in personality and action. One might call the roll of artists, intellectual inquirers, parents, friends, citizens who are neighbors, to show that purposes exist in an *operative* way. What I have been objecting to, I repeat, is not the idea that ideals are linked with existence and that they themselves exist, through human embodiment, as forces, but the idea that their authority and value depend upon some prior complete embodiment—as if the efforts of human beings in behalf of justice, or knowledge or beauty, depended for their effectiveness and validity upon assurance that there already existed in some supernal region a place where criminals are humanely treated, where there is no serfdom or slavery, where all facts and truths are already discovered and possessed, and all beauty is eternally displayed in actualized form. . . .

For, I would remind readers in conclusion, it is the intellectual side of the religious attitude that I have been considering. I have suggested that the religious element in life has been hampered by conceptions of the supernatural that were embedded in those cultures wherein man had little control over outer nature and little in the way of sure method of inquiry and test. The crisis today as to the intellectual content of religious belief has been caused by the change in the intellectual climate due to the increase of our knowledge and our means of understanding. I have tried to show that this change is not fatal to the religious values in our common experience, however adverse its impact may be upon historic religions. Rather, provided that the methods and results of intelligence at work are frankly adopted, the change is liberating.

It clarifies our ideals, rendering them less subject to illusion and fantasy. It relieves us of the incubus of thinking of them as fixed, as without power of growth. It discloses that they develop in coherence and pertinency with increase of natural intelligence. The change gives aspiration for natural knowledge a definitely religious character, since growth in understanding of nature is seen to be organically related to the formation of ideal ends. The same change enables man to select those elements in natural conditions that may be organized to support and extend the sway of ideals. All purpose is selective, and all intelligent action includes deliberate choice. In the degree in which we cease to depend upon belief in the supernatural, selection is enlightened and choice can be made in behalf of ideals whose inherent relations to conditions and consequences are understood. Were the naturalistic foundations and bearings of religion grasped, the religious element in life would emerge from the throes of the crisis in religion. Religion would then be found to have its natural place in every aspect of human experience that is concerned with estimate of possibilities, with emotional stir by possibilities as yet unrealized, and with all action in behalf of their realization. All that is significant in human experience falls within this frame.

3

The Inevitability of Our Own Death: The Celebration of Time as a Prelude to Disaster*

John McDermott

> Their foot shall slide in due time.
> Deuteronomy 32:35

Untimely Meditations

How strange, how singular, how unusual, is our understanding of death. Each of us claims to know of death, yet our experience is necessarily indirect, vicarious, and at a distance. It is always someone else's death that we experience. Yet the power of that experience of the death of the other is such as to suffuse our very being with an intimacy of awareness, virtually equivalent to our own death.

---

*Originally published in *Texas Humanist* (April 1981). Subsequently published in *Streams of Experience: Reflections on the History and Philosophy of American Culture* (Amherst, Mass.: University of Massachusetts Press, 1986). Reprinted by permission of Texas Committee for the Humanities.

No reader of this chapter has died. Nonetheless, we speak of death as though we knew of which we speak. I do not contravene or even doubt such an assumption. Rather, I ask how it is possible that a vicarious experience can have such a direct hold on our deepest feelings and our most intense of personal anticipations? My response to this question is unpleasant and unsettling, but it is true. In the test of time, we are all terminal. And that fact, of which history, thus far, has allowed no exceptions, is the most repressed and denied of all facts in the human condition. In turn, it is this repression which makes the formal announcement that a person is terminally ill so devastating. Such an announcement is unnecessarily vulgar, for it acts to separate some of us from others of us in a drastic and absolute way. Yet it is only time which is in question here, for to be terminal is the foreordained future of each of us.

Why have we allowed this situation to develop? The major reason is not cheering to those of us who seek to attribute the best motivations to the activities of human life. It is as though we lived our lives in the context of a global roulette wheel, so that the announcement of someone else's impending death somehow lessened the possibility of ours. David Cole Gordon writes:

> The thought of our finitude and ephemerality is so frightening that we run away from this basic fact of existence, consciously and unconsciously, and proceed through life as though we shall endure forever. When we recognize the inevitability of death by the making out of our wills and buying life insurance, it is as though the wills and the insurance related to someone other than ourselves, and we live our actual life as though death is not likely to touch *us*. Insofar as we consider the possibility of our own death at all, it is as an event that is as remote as the end of time, and so we tend unconsciously to repress the fear and the fact of our ultimate doom, or consciously to forget it.[1]

This foolhardy version of our own demise is verified by the habituation of our obituary reading. What, for example, are we to make of a recent story from the *Times Record* newspaper of Troy, New York?

TROY, N.Y., Sept. 1 (AP) The switchboard at Times Record was flooded with calls this weekend, many of them from "really irate" citizens wondering what had become of the newspaper's obituaries.

Not a single paid death notice or local obituary appeared in the paper Saturday.

"Some people accused us of dropping the obituary page altogether," said Frank Dobisky, the managing editor.

"We haven't. Frankly, it never occurred to me that we should tell our readers that no one had died."

It *should* have occurred to the obituary editor to state publicly that no one had died. At a minimum, this would have brought reality to bear on the readers for whom only others die.

Irony aside, we have to face this peculiar masking of the inevitability of our own death. It is simply a matter of time passing before this inevitability emerges as personal, existential reality. In the opening lines of her brilliant essay *Illness as Metaphor,* Susan Sontag presents the irreducibility of our fundamental situation.

Illness is the night-side of life, a more onerous citizenship. Everyone who is born holds dual citizenship, in the kingdom of the well and in the kingdom of the sick. Although we all prefer to use only the good passport, sooner or later each of us is obliged, at least for a spell, to identify ourselves as citizens of that other place.[2]

Sontag proceeds to discuss the metaphoric versions of two diseases, tuberculosis and cancer, as ones which have acquired the status of separating them from us, or us from them. Both diseases have been associated with death and a sense of fatalism in those who were afflicted. Yet tuberculosis is now curable and cancer is under medical siege, with the cure rate, depending on the bodily location, ranging from 1 to 90 percent. Sontag's point, however, and mine as well, is that century by century we seem to need a scapegoat, that is, a disease which, ostensibly at least, bears terminality for the rest of us. The invidious comparison between the terminally ill and the rest of the population, which is a temporary distinction at best, serves no legitimate purpose except to foster alienation on the one hand and self-indulgence on the other.

Let us pursue this question of terminality somewhat further. In addition to the contemporary classic case of terminal cancer, we have a series of euphemistic versions of terminality. No matter what the illness, the physician may say to family and friends that the patient "has no chance." In itself, this is an interesting phrase from the point of view of scientific, allopathic medicine. Or the statement may be that all potential remedies have been exhausted, which in turn leads to the comment that it is now in the hands of whomever or whatever. These last categories embrace religious overbelief, the salvific arm of divine providence, a brace of homeopathic nostrums, or the utilization of banned "miracle" drugs. Each of these in turn are desperate efforts to reverse or forestall the inevitable. With the exception of the occasional instance in which such efforts release hidden energies in the body, they are for the most part futile, although pursuing them is profoundly understandable. Even the slightest time gained in these approaches constitutes an important personal victory, for it is not death which is the opponent in these situations. Rather, it is the intrusive finality of the announcement of terminality that constitutes the offense against the person. Time gained is a profoundly human advantage set over against the obstreperously public announcement, which summarily and objectively curtails our right to live.

Similarly, I offer that it is precisely this presumptuous seizure of the natural flow of events that is the offensive strand in capital punishment, rather than the asking for death as compensation. Terminality is no more dramatically announced than when a person is sentenced to death at an appointed time and place. The nomenclature of the waiting space is even more vivid: death row. Literature, journalism, and film are especially interested in the event of capital punishment, for they act as our stand-in, enabling us to vicariously grab the power of awarding death from its more traditional sources—nature or, for some, God. Nowhere were the macabre dimensions of the death announcement more pronounced than in the city of Ossining, New York. Formerly, at that city's Sing Sing prison, the activating of the electric chair caused many of the lights in the city to dim, as if much of the citizenry had a hand in bringing about the final moment of a human life.[3]

Still other instances of terminality abound, some of them potential, as in entering a war combat zone or participation in daredevil sports.

In such activities, the risk of death is an enlarged and even necessary specter which hovers over the event itself. The last days of the battles of Bataan and Stalingrad are grim reminders of the imminence of death. A German soldier, awaiting his fate at Stalingrad, writes as follows:

> Tomorrow I shall set foot on the last bridge. That is the literary way of saying "death," but as you know, I always liked to express things figuratively, because I took pleasure in words and sounds. Give me your hand, so that crossing it won't be so hard.[4]

In all of these instances of terminality, our death is due to forces outside of our control, even if we place ourselves in situations of jeopardy. One type of terminality, however, is of a decidedly different cast. I refer to that most prepossessing and intriguing of human acts, namely, the decision to commit suicide.[5] In so doing, it is we who announce to ourselves our own death. It is we who seize the time, the place, and the means. Modern Western civilization, especially in its Judeo-Christian version, has been largely unsympathetic with suicide and has placed negative religious and legal sanctions on it. We often work off the naive notion that the act of suicide entails some form of insanity, despite the fact that the certifiably insane rarely kill themselves.

One form of suicide that we tend to indulge somewhat is that of the person who responds to the announcement that he or she has a terminal disease. It is assumed that the reason for suicide in this case is due to the desire to avoid pain. To the contrary, I believe that this decision traces more to the refusal to have one's death announced by others, as though we were innocent bystanders to our own demise. More to the point of our present discussion are those suicides which are neither a response to impending death nor a result of temporary mental aberration. Consider those suicides which are self-conscious and self-possessed human acts designed to articulate a distinctive personal statement. Albert Camus once wrote, "There is but one truly serious philosophical problem, and that is suicide."[6] One can gainsay Camus's claim of singularity, but not of importance. Having played no role in our own coming into being, with all of its attendant cultural, familial, psychosocial, and genetic trappings, it should not strike us as perverse that we seek to preside over our own cessation from being. The most pessimistic version of the interval between our birth and our death is found in the writings of Sören Kierkegaard.

> What is reflection? Simply to reflect on these two questions: How did I get into this and how do I get out of it again, how does it end? What is thoughtlessness? To muster everything in order to drown out all this about entrance and exit in forgetfulness, to muster everything to re-explain and explain away entrance and exit, simply lost in the interval between the birth-cry and the repetition of this cry when the one who is born expires in the death struggle.[7]

This description of the bare bones of our situation is accurate, but it need not be indulged. After all, we can go against the grain. Camus writes, "I want to know whether I can live with what I know and with that alone."[8] And, I argue, it is precisely the integrity of living within the boundaries of such knowledge that can occasion our decision to withdraw from the fray, in our own time and on our own terms. By this reasoning, and I emphasize reasoning, suicide becomes a rejection of a dehumanizing determinism, while simultaneously signaling an existential choice, a true act of human freedom. William James, for one, saw such a decision in precisely those terms. In the midst of a personal crisis at the age of twenty-eight, he wrote in his diary:

> Hitherto, when I have felt like taking a free initiative, like daring to act originally, without carefully waiting for contemplation of the external world to determine all for me, suicide seemed the most manly form to put my daring into.[9]

Although many deeply reflective persons have committed suicide and are doing so at this moment, it is important to realize that neither Camus nor James did so. In fact, they developed imaginative and ameliorative strategies for coping with the stark reality of their own defense of the plausibility of suicide. I, too, have some suggestions for a human response to the avoidance of suicide and for dealing with the inevitability of our own death. Before turning to that discussion, however, we must consider a major way in which many persons shun the trauma of death—by belief in some form of salvation or immortality.

I do not refer here to a *hope* that somehow, somewhere, somewhen, all will go well for all of us who are, have been, or will be. Certainly, such a hope is a legitimate and understandable human aspiration. But to convert this hope into a commitment, a knowledge, a settled conviction, is to participate in an illegitimate move from possibility to actuality. It is understandable that we wish to escape from peril, but it is unacceptable to translate that desire into an assured belief that we have so escaped. The history of culture has presented many varieties of immortality. Perhaps the most ingenious, although the least plausible, is that of traditional Roman Catholicism, wherein each of us, *bodily,* is resurrected glorious and immortal or damned and immortal. The attraction here is that our eternal life will be affectively continuous with our mortal life. Other versions of the doctrine of immortality involve claims of reincarnation, metempsychosis, immersion, or absorption, each attempting to perpetuate the me which is me, in one form or another. Obviously, I have no final knowledge of these claims nor do I know of anyone who has. Evidence on their behalf is scanty, scattered, tentative, highly personal, and empirically dubious. Yet many of us cling to one or more of these solutions, as a redoubt, a trump card, or a last-minute reprieve from the overwhelming evidence that we are terminal.

Philosophical, political, and even religious thought of the last century and a half has been characterized by increasing dubiety about the possibility of immortality. Attention also has been given to the complex cultural reasons for the persistence in the belief in immortality, and the explanations are as varied as the doctrine in question. Marx, Freud, the existentialists, Dewey, and Norman O. Brown, among others, have all attempted to account for the persistence of this belief. Brown's version is especially fascinating, for in his judgment the quest for immortality is the *locus classicus* of *the* human disease. Following the Freud of *Civilization and its Discontents,*[10] Brown contends that our refusal to face our own death (Thanatos) has led us to repress the life force (Eros) in favor of comparatively permanent civilizational monuments. In short, our greatest neurosis is history through which we attempt to transcend the burdens of time and project ourselves as having meaning beyond our own lives. In this regard, the monument par excellence to our flight from temporality and from finitude is the "having" of children. By that means, we assert our transcendence from the sheerly local and death-bound character of our lives. In so doing, however, we abandon access to the nectar that comes to those who live the life of Eros, hear the call of immediacy, and, as such, for Brown, cease to be human organisms in any profound sense of that meaning. In his chapter "Death, Time, and Eternity," he writes:

> If death gives life individuality and if man is the organism which represses death, then man is the organism which represses his own individuality. Then our proud view of humanity as a species endowed with an individuality denied to lower animals turns out to be wrong. The lilies of the field have it because they take no thought of the morrow, and we do not. Lower organisms live the life proper to their species; their individuality consists in their being concrete embodiments of the essence of their species in a particular life which ends in death.[11]

Here we have the height of irony, for in our effort to transcend the life of the lower organisms, we fail to realize even that level of Eros, wallowing rather in a self-deceptive flight from the burden of time passing.[12] Brown's prescription for overcoming this false transcendence, this escape into self-deception, is complex and personally radical. At this point, I bypass the details of his resolution in order to say, quite directly, that in my judgment he asks us to marry our own death. He cautions against a preening narcissism, in which we take ourselves too literally, as well as against the fruitless flight from the temporal, the immediate, and transient Eros. At some point in our life, the sooner the better, we should confront the inevitability of our own death and absorb this awareness into the most active forefront of our consciousness. The message is clear and twofold: avoid the temptation to invest in meaning which transcends our own experience of the life-cycle; and affirm the imminence of death as the gateway to an unrepressed life in which the moment sings its own song, in its own way, once and once only.

Although I regard Brown's critique of immortality as devastating, his resolution in *Life Against Death,* and again in *Love's Body,*[13] is beyond the pale of possibility for all but the heroic figure, the person who lives perpetually on the horizon, on the furthest edge of each and every experience. The fundamental question is whether there is a median way between the self-deception of personal immortality, on the one hand, and the radical commitment to the moment, on the other. If we live within the bowels of the temporal process, can we not have also a sense of the future, a sense which does not delude us into thinking that we have transcended time? Put directly, can we experience ourselves as terminal and yet live creative, probing, building lives which, nonetheless, ask for no guarantees and for no ultimate significance to be attributed to our endeavor? I, for one, believe that we can live this way; nay, I believe that it is only in this way that we live a distinctively human life. In fact, I offer that a life lived consciously in the shadow of our own death is one which can prehend the scents of the most subtle of messages, namely, those intended only for creatures who risk living within the rhythm of time. With such an attitude, categories basic to human life and understanding undergo a change in our experience of them. As our fundamental expectation for human life changes, so too does our perception of time, growth, history, and experience undergo comparative changes. Let us now map these developments in some detail.

The Life of the Live Creature

I believe that we should experience our own lives in the context of being permanently afflicted, that is, of being terminal. This is not to propose a morbid personal style, but rather to ask that this attitude ride as an abiding presence in the active recesses of our conscious life. Surely the shift from ancient to contemporary cosmology has doomed the doctrine of the equivalence of cosmic space with human life. The unintelligible distances, activities, gestations, and denouements of contemporary cosmology have dwarfed us and rendered illusory any human effort at ultimate accountability by our appeal to our proper *place*. The place we claim in the infinite universe is precisely that, a claim, an assertion, a seizing, an activity unknown to and unfelt by infinite space. The cosmology of human life is scarcely more extensive than our sociology. We have domesticated one planet and one lunar satellite and have probed several other planets. Electronically and mathematically, we have extended ourselves somewhat further. Nonetheless, relative to galactic plurality, let alone infinite space, these extraordinary human efforts are scarcely more than explorations of one city block or of a fifty-acre farm. Further, we are told as one active possibility that cosmic reality itself is entropic, winding down on its inexorable way to nothing.[14] In short, whatever may be the long-range future of cosmology, I do not see any auspicious signs that it will provide a resolution of present personal plight.

Historically, a paradox emerges which is intriguing and instructive. When, in antique times, we held the universe to be finite, we also held that it was eternal. Human life had a fixed and natural place in this version of the world, and only *sub specie aeternitatis* could it play a permanently meaningful role in the cyclically repetitive flow of time. Modern cosmology, for the most part, holds reality[15] to be infinite and, on behalf of the doctrine of relativity, denies that we have a natural and fixed place. The paradox is that in the modern view time has no ultimate meaning, yet it does take on profound human meaning, for it is both unrepeatable and the distinctive way in which human life asserts its presence and significance in the context of infinite reality. Infinite space becomes increasingly domesticated by being subjected to human time.

Given this cosmological context, our fundamental situation is transiency. We are of the species *Homo viator,* persons on a journey, human travelers in a cosmic abyss. Actually, in my judgment, transients is a better word than travelers, for the latter often connote a definite goal, an end in view, or at least a return home. A transient, however, is one who is passing through. The meaning of a transient's journey is precisely that: the journey itself. In transiency, paraphrasing John Dewey,[16] it is the *quality* of the journeying which counts, not the end in view and certainly not the claim that we have journeyed. The quality of transiency is achieved by passing through rather than by passing by. We should make our journey ever alert to our surroundings and to every perceivable sensorial nuance. Our journey is a kaleidoscope of alternating experiences, mishap, setback, celebrations, and eye-openers, all undergone in the *qui vive.*

I repeat that space becomes meaningful for us to the extent that, through time, we build ourselves into it and convert space to place, to our place. It is necessary for us to make a place, for I do not believe that we have any inherited or natural place, as awarded. Just as the bottom line of death is that we are not around and about any more, so then does life mean to be in a place, from someplace, on the way to someplace. We cannot do this by ourselves, for to be in place is to be relative to some other place, someone else's place. Friendship, family, media all serve to context our place, as they set over against us another place. Our memories are thereby crucial to a human life, for they carry past places to a present place, enabling a single place to be laced with all of the places we have been. Memories save the loss of places and the loss of persons from total disappearance. Actually, our losses often become more intense aspects of our present experience than our present self. In the flow of the journey we hook ourselves to persons, places, things, and events, allowing us to reconnoiter, while passing through. A classic and profound hook is that of our junk drawer. Scraps and pieces of memorabilia tumble over one another, unworthy aside from their endowed meanings, given in a prior experience. An opera ticket, a ring, a watch, a baseball, a rejection slip, a cancelled check, defy their ejection from our junk drawer, for they are laden with meaning and they act as personal clots in the onrushing flow of our lives.

Nonetheless, despite the richness of our memoried past, we cannot allow ourselves to be trapped in nostalgia. Following William James, life is as much in the transitions, as it is in the events we experience directly.[17]

No doubt our past experiences should remain alive in our consciousness and should be stirred and restirred so that they envelop and enrich our present experiences. But it is to the future that we wend. We cannot stand still. If we do, atrophy awaits us. Our deepest personal need, then, is to grow, for personal growth is the only sure sign that we are not yet dead. And by growth we mean here the capacity to convert our environment into sources of personal nutrition, to eat experience, as it were. The deeper meaning of growth is not an increase of size, length, height, or any other quantitative measures. Rather, it has to do with fructification, enriching, enhancing, and the pregnant provision for still further growth. Dewey's much maligned comment—

"since in reality there is nothing to which growth is relative save more growth"—yields more than meets the eye.[18] In Dewey's understanding, growth is not characterized by a teleological movement to a final end. Rather, it is the quality of being humanly enriched by our experience, even if it be failure or loss. Further, growth is not simply an outcome or a result. It is the very nature of the live creature when participating in the flow of experience. In the following text, Dewey is referring to children, but he refers equally to all of us. "Where there is life, there are already eager and impassioned activities. Growth is not something done to them; it is something they do."[19] It is doing to the world and being done by the world which constitute the fundamental human transactions and allow for the possibility of growth. Hanging back while waiting to be rescued ultimately from the flow will not generate growth. Indulging and preening our ego, impervious to the messaging of the world, will not generate growth. In order to grow, that is, to live the life of a live creature rather than a life of second-handedness, we must forge a self-conscious relationship between our acceptance of our irreversible fragility and our creative energies. The most revealing focus of developing this relationship is our own version of the meaning of time and its attendant significance for the meaning of things, events, and history.

And now I come straight out and say where I stand on this issue. I believe that time is sacred. It is not sacred, however, because it has been so endowed by God, the gods, nature, or any other force. I believe that time is sacred because human history has endowed it with our meaning, our suffering, our commitments, and our anticipations. Can we sustain this position, if we place it over against our previous discussion of the inevitability of death? What can we say, for example, when faced with the following text from the ancient Roman philosopher, Marcus Aurelius: "And, to say all in a word, everything which belongs to the body is a stream, and what belongs to the soul is a dream and vapor, and life is a warfare and a stranger's sojourn, and after-fame is oblivion."[20]

The Aurelian text is candid and accurate. He resolves it by an appeal to the cycle of nature, which gives human explanation for the existence of the human organism. This resolution, however, does not remove the bite from the fact that we are born to live and destined to die. I contend that the utter frustration of this contradiction in our personal situation cannot be resolved. Rather, speaking for the living, I take my point of departure from a text by John Dewey.

> We always live at the time we live and not at some other time, and only by extracting at each present time the full meaning of each present experience are we prepared for doing the same thing in the future. This is the only preparation which in the long run amounts to anything.[21]

Here Dewey joins hands with the thought of Norman O. Brown and with the medieval tradition of the sacrament of the moment. Contrary to those positions, however, Dewey acknowledges no forces at work, neither Dionysian nor divine, other than the constitutive transactions of human life with the affairs of nature and the world. For better and for worse, we make the world and we endow nature with our presence, our values, our arrogance, and our fealty. You and I inherit thousands of years of human formulation, human judgment, human management, human violence, and human affection. Still, we come upon the world fresh, as if for the first time. The historically encrusted implications rush out at us as we seek to see, hear, touch anew. The novelty is not the world, for the world is tired, even jaded, with millennia of human hands and minds kneading it into a human image. No, the novelty, if it is to be at all, is found in us, in you, in me. It is not the monumental or the charismatic which provides the clue to the magnificence of being human. Rather, it is the celebration of the ordinary that enables us to make our way as truly human, avoiding the twin pitfalls of the humdrum, ennui, and boredom, and the equally dehumanizing attempt to escape from the rhythm of time on behalf of a sterile and probably self-deceptive eternal resolution. Most likely, we have no ultimate future. This should not keep us from participating in the explosive possibilities of our present, no matter what the situation. Setback enriches as well as breakthrough.

Our impending death is not the major obstacle to our becoming truly human. The obstacle is found in our running for cover on behalf of our escape from death. We sell ourselves short. We should listen to the poet Rainer Maria Rilke, who praises our very ephemerality.

But because being here amounts to so much, because all
this Here and Now, so fleeting, seems to require us and strangely
concerns us. Us the most fleeting of all. Just once,
everything, only for once. Once and no more. And we, too
once. And never again. But this
having been once, though only once,
having been once on earth—can it ever be cancelled?[22]

Indeed, can it, can we, ever be cancelled? I think not. Celebrate!

Notes

1. Cf. David Cole Gordon, *Overcoming the Fear of Death* (Baltimore: Penguin, 1972), p. 13.

2. Susan Sontag, *Illness as Metaphor* (New York: Vintage, 1979), p. 3.

3. For a profound analysis of capital punishment, see Albert Camus, "Reflections on the Guillotine," in *Resistance, Rebellion and Death* (New York: Alfred Knopf, 1961), pp. 175–234.

4. Anonymous, *Last Letters From Stalingrad* (New York: The New American Library, 1961), p. 125. Cf. Edith Wyschogrod, "Sport, Death and the Elemental," in *The Phenomenon of Death* (New York: Harper and Row, 1973), pp. 166–97. She writes, "To engage in sport as a mode of being in the elemental is not merely to *want* to die, but to be *willing* to do so" (p. 197).

5. Cf. A. Alvarez, *The Savage God: A Study of Suicide* (New York: Random House, 1972).

6. Albert Camus, *The Myth of Sisyphus* (New York: Random House, 1972), p. 3.

7. Søren Kierkegaard, cited in Alvarez, *Savage God,* p. 114.

8. Camus, *Myth of Sisyphus,* p. 40.

9. William James, "Diary," in *The Writings of William James,* ed. John J. McDermott (Chicago: University of Chicago Press, 1977), p. 8.

10. Sigmund Freud, *Civilization and Its Discontents* (London: Hogarth Press, 1953): "If the evolution of civilization has such a far-reaching similarity with the development of an individual, and if the same methods are employed in both, would not the diagnosis be justified that many systems of civilization—or epochs of it—possibly even the whole of humanity—have become 'neurotic' under the pressure of the civilizing trends?" (p. 141).

11. Norman O. Brown, *Life Against Death* (Middletown: Wesleyan University Press, 1970), p. 105.

12. Brown himself, subsequently, is to disappoint us in this regard, opting for a doctrine of the cycle, which effectively removes the novelty from time passing. Cf. Norman O. Brown, *Closing Time* (New York: Random House, 1973).

13. Cf. Norman O. Brown, *Love's Body* (New York: Vintage, 1968): "The world annihilated, the destruction of illusion. The world is the veil we spin to hide the void. The destruction of which never existed. The day breaks, and the shadows flee away" (p. 261).

14. Cf. Jacques Merleau-Ponty and Bruno Morando, *The Rebirth of Cosmology* (New York: Alfred Knopf, 1976), pp. 275–76.

15. Strictly speaking, we should no longer speak of "world," "cosmos," or "universe," all of which connote an order, a singularity, which is not verified by contemporary cosmology. Perhaps we should adopt the position of William James and speak of a pluralistic universe. Cf. William James, *A Pluralistic Universe* (Cambridge: Harvard University Press, 1977).

16. Cf. John Dewey, "The Need of a Theory of Experience," in *The Philosophy of John Dewey,* ed. John J. McDermott, vol. 2 (Chicago: University of Chicago Press, 1981):"Everything depends upon the *quality* of the experience which is had" (p. 508).

17. William James, *Essays in Radical Empiricism* (Cambridge: Harvard University Press, 1976), p. 42. Cf. John J. McDermott, "Life Is in the Transitions" in *The Culture of Experience: Philosophical Essays in the American Grain* (New York: New York University Press, 1976), pp. 99–117.

18. John Dewey, *Democracy and Education,* vol. 9 (1980) of *The Middle Works* (Carbondale, Ill.: Southern Illinois University Press, 1976–83), p. 56. See also John Dewey, "Education as Growth," in *Philosophy of John Dewey,* vol. 2, p. 492.

19. Dewey, *Democracy and Education,* p. 47.

20. Marcus Aurelius, *Meditations* (Chicago: Henry Regnery, 1956), pp. 18–19.

21. John Dewey, "Criteria of Experience," in *Philosophy of John Dewey,* vol. 2, p. 523.

22. Rainer Maria Rilke, "The Ninth Elegy," *Duino Elegies* (New York: W. W. Norton, 1939), p. 73.

Part V

Naturalism and
Contemporary Philosophy

Section 9

Nature Reconsidered

In the introduction to this volume it was pointed out that naturalism has not stood still during the course of the century, and indeed in recent years naturalist philosophers have addressed many of the issues central to contemporary philosophy. One of the most important of these has been the criticism of traditional conceptions of nature and knowledge which takes the form of a critique of modernity. The essays in this section take up the postmodernist challenge, and though there are disagreements among them, there is also a common thread. In each piece one encounters a sympathy with the critique of modernity coupled with a desire to retain aspects of the modernist philosophic program. In these essays, in other words, naturalism appears as a philosophic perspective within which it is possible to have the best of both modernity and its postmodernist critique.

It should also be pointed out that all three of these articles were originally presented as Patrick Romanell Lectures. Patrick Romanell has been an influential figure in the American philosophical tradition for many years, and in the mid-1980s he instituted a lecture series under the auspices of the American Philosophical Association which was intended to foster the development of naturalist philosophy. Each year there is an invited lecture presented at one of the annual conventions of the American Philosophical Association. The first Romanell Lecture was given by Abraham Edel in 1986, and as the articles reproduced

505

here indicate, the Romanell Lecture has quickly become an important forum for the advancement of American philosophic naturalism.

In her essay "Modernity and the Spirit of Naturalism," delivered initially in Chicago in April 1991, Thelma Z. Lavine addresses directly the relation between naturalism and "the philosophic discourse of modernity." Lavine is a prominent specialist in the history of philosophy and in social theory, both continental and American, and she is currently Clarence J. Robinson professor of philosophy and American culture at George Mason University. Lavine reads naturalism pragmatically, and in fact she uses the expression "American naturalistic pragmatism" to identify the philosophic tradition at issue. On her analysis it is the pragmatic character of naturalism which enables it to integrate elements of the Enlightenment and the counter-Enlightenment, the terms she uses to identify two major traditions within philosophic modernity. The "paradigm" of naturalistic pragmatism, Lavine argues, is a critique of modernity in that it provides a way to interpret both strands of modernity, to appropriate the more valuable aspects of each, and to respond to what she takes to be various inadequate contemporary criticisms of modernity.

John Lachs approaches all this somewhat differently. Lachs is one of the leading contemporary specialists on George Santayana, and an original philosopher in his own right. His work covers a range of fields from American philosophy to metaphysics to political philosophy, and includes his 1981 book *Intermediate Man*. Lachs is currently professor of philosophy at Vanderbilt University. His essay "Human Natures" was originally presented in Atlanta in 1989. In it Lachs does not so much discuss the relation of naturalism, modernity and postmodernism, as he uses insights derived from their convergence to illuminate a conception of human nature. One of the most fundamental criticisms of modernism has been directed at its presumption of an "objective," which is to say entirely "mind independent," world, and that such a world can be known "objectively," from a "God's eye view." If at least the world of our experience is not "objective" in the traditional sense, then it is constructed through social experience, personal perspective, or in some other way. Lachs too challenges the notion of a purely "objective" scientific method able to provide unmediated knowledge of the world. With respect to the question of an "objective" world, Lachs thinks that there is truth in both the modernist position and in its criticism. There are indeed objective facts, he suggests, and there are also facts which are conventional, which derive from our experience. The original and intriguing feature of his essay, however, is the suggestion that there is also a third class of facts which involve both objective and conventional elements. Lachs calls these "choice-inclusive facts," and he argues that in the end our conception of what counts as human nature is based on just such choice-inclusive facts.

Our final article, "Nature and Culture," is by Peter T. Manicas, and it is the Romanell Lecture delivered in Portland, Oregon, in March 1992. Manicas was a student of Marvin Farber at the State University of New York at Buffalo, from where he went on to teach philosophy at Queens College in New York City. He specializes in social and political philosophy and in the philosophy of the social sciences. He is the author of several books in these fields, the most recent being *War and Democracy*. Manicas retired from Queens College several years ago, and he is currently on the faculty of the Liberal Studies Program of the University of Hawaii at Manoa. In "Nature and Culture" Manicas considers the social sciences with an eye toward developing a naturalist conception of social science which takes account of recent criticisms of traditional conceptions of science without in the process losing those traits of the social sciences which make them as fruitful as they are. A naturalist conception of society, and of social science, must be able to take account of the fact that human societies are rooted in a nature which is in large measure not of our making, and of the fact that human societies are to no small degree human constructs.

1

Modernity and the Spirit of Naturalism*

Thelma Z. Lavine

I wish to express my gratitude to Professor Patrick Romanell, through whose philosophic vision the annual Romanell Lectures on Philosophical Naturalism were established. I present this Fifth Annual Romanell Lecture in memory of my friend, Yervant H. Krikorian, esteemed American philosophical naturalist and editor of the volume *Naturalism and the Human Spirit*.[1]

Naturalism and the Human Spirit Revisited

It was John Herman Randall who wrote the epilogue, "The Nature of Naturalism," to *Naturalism and the Human Spirit,* that collection of essays written by fourteen American philosophers, including John Dewey, as a joint public statement of the naturalistic viewpoint. Randall's legendary perceptiveness as intellectual historian and philosopher identified the formation of American philosophical naturalism as the uniting

*Originally published in *Proceedings and Addresses of the American Philosophical Association,* vol. 65 (Newark, Del.: American Philosophical Association, University of Delaware, 1991). Reprinted by permission.

of "two major strands"—idealism and the natural and social sciences. Randall develops the concept of the "two major strands" succinctly:

> Viewed in this extended perspective, and in the light of the great intellectual movements of the nineteenth century, contemporary naturalism thus represents at once the culmination of the idealistic criticism, and of the natural sciences of man and human culture. It carries on the idealistic emphasis that man is united to his world by a logical and social experience. But it rephrases the idealistic scheme of man's activities and environment in biological and anthropological categories. While like the idealists it makes them all amenable to a single intellectual method, it reformulates that method in experimental terms. At the same time, contemporary naturalism is rooted in the natural sciences, extending their content and scope, and expanding and rendering more flexible their methods to include a treatment of even those human activities formerly set apart as "spiritual."
>
> In the light of these two major strands that have united to form contemporary naturalism, its double opposition to supernaturalism and to reductionism should now be clearer.[2]

Randall notes that naturalism, as presented by the essays in this volume,

> is not so much a system or a body of doctrine as an attitude and temper: it is essentially a philosophic method and a program. It undertakes to bring scientific analysis and criticism to bear on all the human enterprises and values so zealously maintained by the traditional supernaturalists and by the more sophisticated idealists.

Naturalism has thus come to mean, he says, "not so much a continuity of genesis as a continuity of analysis."[3] And this contemporary naturalism, he continues, "may well claim to be a distinctively American philosophy."

And in a tone of unmistakable triumphalism, Randall issued these fateful words: "Today we are at last in possession of a science that insists on the importance and reality of all man's experience and enterprises . . . and [a philosophy] that can embrace in one natural world, amenable to a single intellectual method, all the realities to which human experience points."[4]

But at the time of writing his hopeful words of the promise of American naturalism, Randall did not see, and could not foretell, the impending philosophical avalanches which were about to descend upon American philosophical naturalism. His triumphal language is poignantly fateful in the light of the threatening advance of logical positivism, already underway as he wrote, followed by analytical philosophy which was soon to overpower American philosophical naturalism and to become the dominating philosophic viewpoint in American universities, in the organizational structure and functions of the American Philosophical Association, in funding agencies, and in publication.

Nor were Randall and his fellow naturalists able to foresee the influx into American philosophical and social scientific discourse after World War II of phenomenology, hermeneutics, Frankfurt School critical theory deconstruction or the challenge which these groups presented in turn to naturalism, logical positivism, and analytic philosophy. Nor could it then have been perceived that the new philosophic arrivals were not historical contingencies but were exemplars of the Enlightenment and the Counter-Enlightenment cognitive frameworks of Modernity which have provided the cognitive horizon of the West since the middle of the nineteeneth century. Nevertheless, in Randall's suggestion that contemporary naturalism "may well claim to be a distinctively American philosophy," and in his identification of its "two major strands"—idealism and the sciences, natural and social—he had discerned the formation of American naturalism and the structures of Modernity. American naturalism has indeed drawn upon those "two major strands" as a philosophical response to the social, economic, and political crisis in American life at the end of the nineteenth century.

With the development of American naturalistic pragmatism[5] American philosophy had taken the step of identifying the Enlightenment and the Counter-Enlightenment as the two great traditions of Modernity and also of attempting to integrate elements of both into a new type of philosophy for American culture and a new type of philosophic paradigm.

As Habermas has identified the uncompleted project of the Enlightenment, so it is also significant to identify the uncompleted project, after a long hiatus, of American naturalistic pragmatism. The reconstruction of the paradigm for philosophy which had remained implicit in American naturalistic pragmatism is its uncompleted project. It is the burden of this Romanell Lecture on philosophical naturalism to provide a preliminary sketch of the completed paradigm of naturalistic pragmatism and to suggest its significance for the philosophic discourse of Modernity.

The Frameworks of Modernity

It is only in the last decades of the twentieth century that the intellectual culture has gained sufficient reflective distance from its philosophic conflicts to begin to frame a conception of Modernity and of its contentious traditions and modes of interpretation.[6] It is only in the context of the conflicts of Modernity that the struggle of American philosophical naturalism and naturalistic pragmatism toward the formation of an integrative paradigm can be understood.

The conceptual structure of Modernity may be seen to be a framework which exists in the form of historically evolved counter-frameworks which are constitutive of it and which provide the horizon of our time. Modernity is the conflict and confluence of the Enlightenment and the Romantic Counter-Enlightenment cognitive views, each subverting and delegitimating the other's conception of human nature, truth, morality, politics, and the appropriate method for knowing them. The tradition of the Enlightenment arose in the seventeenth century as the first phase of the complex structure of Modernity.

Enlightenment Modernity as the first framework encompassed within Modernity may be briefly formulated as beginning with the scientific breakthrough of Newton, unifying the laws of terrestrial and celestial mechanics, and the political breakthrough of Locke, grounding politics upon the self-evident natural rights of human individuals and upon representative democracy. Both breakthroughs are founded on reason and share the claim to offer truths which are universal, absolute, realistic, and objective. Enlightenment Modernity claimed the primacy of reason in all significant domains, with substantive reason yielding true intuitions concerning human nature and society, and scientific instrumental reason yielding scientific laws of nature and technology. Together, they yield a natural law of rational progress.

But by the end of the eighteenth century only instrumental reason survived skeptical challengers to the intuitions of Enlightenment Modernity. A new phase of Modernity, Romantic Modernity, arose in cultural protest against the disenchanted, despiritualized, increasingly mechanized, technological world of Enlightenment scientific reason; and it arose in political protest against the Enlightenment, then waging the wars of liberation from Napoleon, the symbol of Enlightenment domination. Modernity arose as a cognitive framework linked to Enlightenment Modernity as its antithesis. The intuitions of Romanticism crystalized into a counter-framework of opposing conceptualizations: in opposition to Enlightenment primacy of reason, Romanticism affirms the primacy of spirit; in opposition to the scientific focus on fact and externality, Romanticism takes the inward path of subjectivity; in opposition to scientific reason in its pursuit of objective and valid knowledge, Romanticism holds to the truths of history, culture, the arts, the dialectic of personal and collective will; in opposition to the natural rights political autonomy of the Enlightenment individual, Romanticism asserts a politics of the group, of collectivism of the left or right; in opposition to Enlightenment-style rational liberation from the historical domination of church and state falsity, Romantic liberation is from the hegemony of the Enlightenment mentality in its abstract, a historical universalism, objectivism, and realism, and from the resulting bureaucratization of the social world. Here in Romantic Modernity we discover the counter-tradition to the Enlightenment.

Modernity is, then, cognitively pluralistic. The structure of Modernity may be seen to be a pluralistic framework, a framework which exists in the form of diametrically opposed counter-frameworks which are constitutive of it.

Thus the heritage of Modernity is the mutual destruction of its component mentalities. In response to this diremption, the great intellectual figures of Modernity have attempted to design integrating paradigms. Such integrating constructions provide a key to the work of Hegel, Marx, Weber, Mannheim, Durkheim, Freud, Dewey, and Habermas. I shall argue that the attempt to construct a paradigm integrative of Enlightenment and Romantic Modernity provides the key to the very rise of American philosophic naturalism and naturalistic pragmatism.

American Naturalistic Pragmatism and the Conflicts of Modernity

One may well view America as having been born into Modernity with the sailing of the *Arabella* in the spring of 1630, arriving in America in late June under the dissenting religious banner of the Protestant Reformation, in quest of religious freedom.

By the third quarter of the eighteenth century, American intellectuals such as Jefferson, Madison, and Hamilton inevitably shared the perspective on human nature and politics of the English Enlightenment. The same cluster of beliefs concerning human nature, knowledge, politics, and history which defined the intellectual style of seventeenth- and eighteenth-century England provided the form and content of the meaningful universe of the American Founders. But the British Enlightenment principles had been transferred by the errand into the wilderness to the New World of America, to the early experiment of the Puritan theocratic communities, to new experiences in American local self-government, and to physical and then political separation from British centers of commerce and culture, and to new exceptional economic conditions. Doubts with regard to the functionality of certain of the Enlightenment views to solve problems within the situation of the American reality led the Founders to reconstruct those doctrines, and so began the Americanization of the Enlightenment which came to a climax in the Constitutional Convention in 1787.

The reinterpreted and Americanized framework of Enlightenment Modernity into which the American nation was born is an instance of the interpretivism which characterizes American naturalistic pragmatism: the principle, stemming from Kant, which holds that whatever is known is in some measure constituted by the conferring of meaning or by the position of conceptual or linguistic structure. And under the necessity of problem-solving in situations in which Old World conceptions came into ineffectual conflict with new American conditions, there arose in practice what was to become, for Peirce and Dewey, the theory of inquiry as the analysis, interpretation, and resolution of a problematic situation. But following the Civil War, a problematic situation of crisis proportions was produced by Enlightenment Modernist forces of modernization: the rapid expansion of industrialization, corporate wealth and influence, urbanization, immigration, federal and state bureaucratization, and political collusion with corporate interests. One significant response took the form of the rise of classical American philosophy.

Classical American philosophy (naturalistic pragmatism) came into being as an intellectual and moral response to the post–Civil War national problematic situation brought on by the effects of Enlightenment modernization upon American life. The response of American philosophers was to assimilate the newly available philosophic views of European Romantic Modernity as an antithetical way of perceiving the problems of Modernity; and to integrate the two cultural styles, Enlightenment and Romantic Modernity into a philosophy for an America whose national, legal, and cultural identity was in Enlightenment truth. Each of the classical American philosophers worked through the conflict and the integration in his own way. Insofar as it is possible to speak of American philosophy, it is to perceive the characteristic form of American philosophy in the attempt to integrate the Enlightenment and Romantic modes of thought. What is characteristic of American naturalistic pragmatism is its incorporativeness, its attempt to hold together Enlightenment classical liberalism science and technology and Romantic communitarianism and the expressiveness of personal and group life.

After the long monologic hegemony of logical positivism, analytic philosophy, phenomenology, hermeneutics, structuralism, and deconstruction, the American naturalistic project of explaining, understanding, and working through the outcomes of the richly complex conflicts of Modernity is emerging as a blocked path that must now be reopened. Independently of the declining vitality of the monologic philosophies at the conflicting poles of Modernity, American naturalistic pragmatism is increasingly perceived as the only contemporary viewpoint[7] which has the philosophical resources to explain and interpret the great upheavals in the scientific and political culture of the present time: the advances in astronomy, physics, the biological sciences and their technologies; and the decline of the economic and political power of Marxist socialism in the Communist-bloc countries of Eastern Europe, in the Baltics, and in the Soviet Union; and the movement toward democracy.

The Naturalistic Paradigm

What is perhaps the key to discerning a paradigm for the unfulfilled project of naturalistic pragmatism is to be found in Dewey's early and persistent rejection of "apart thought" whether in the form of logic or modes of intuition which remain unconnected to "the causal category as a leading principle of existential inquiry."[8]

1. *The Continuity of Analysis Paradigm.* It is the rejection of "apart thought" which produces the convergence which Randall discovered among the contributors to *Naturalism and the Human Spirit* upon "the universal and unrestricted application of scientific method." "That continuity of analysis can thus mean only that all analysis must be scientific analysis . . . is the nerve of the naturalistic principle" and the spirit of naturalism which animates the Krikorian volume.

Continuity of analysis remains, however, an early and relatively undeveloped and narrow formulation of a paradigm for philosophical naturalism. Although it can claim the distinctiveness and recognizability of a paradigm, and thus a logic by which to contest opposing positions (as Dewey's own essay, "Antinaturalism in Extremis," contests current Roman Catholic theology), it is far from an exploration of the complexities and implications of its own paradigm. Equipped, however, with this narrow paradigm it is possible to practice what, borrowing from Thomas Kuhn, may be said to be "normal philosophy": "mopping up" a paradigm by problem-solving within it; contesting and critiquing problem-solving efforts within the paradigm and within other paradigms, taking a paradigm-dependent position on issues as they become the focus of philosophical discourse. (One thinks of the seven hundred pages of normal philosophy in *Dewey and His Critics* which Sidney Morgenbesser gathered from the *Journal of Philosophy* alone.) But a more adequate model was at hand.

2. *The Problematic Situation Paradigm.* Explicitly and precisely

developed in chapter 6 of Dewey's *Logic: The Theory of Inquiry* was his theory, or paradigm, of naturalistic pragmatism. It was the "Pattern of Inquiry," presented as the general formula of a single model of inquiry applicable to problem-solving in everyday life and in all areas of the natural and social sciences. Inquiry takes place within a concrete "pre-cognitive" situation, a unique "contextual whole"; inquiry is called into being by the indeterminate, disunified quality which the situation takes on, and the Hegelian function of inquiry is to effect a resolution, to convert, reconcile, transform. A successful resolution changes the elements of the original situation into a synthesized, unified whole. And this entire ideational and operational transformation is construed as the adaptive integration of an organism with its environment.

Dewey's pattern of inquiry, centered upon the problematic situation, may seen to be contextually interpretivist: the resolution of a problematic situation is a response to the empirical and ideational conditions within the problematic context. Generalized beyond its initial physicalistic presentation, in time Dewey's interpretivist paradigm of the problematic situation and its resolution pervaded American naturalistic pragmatism. The structure of the paradigm includes: an identifiable community, surviving in translation with its environment by means of reliable, grounded knowledge; the presence of an immediate or long-range "problem" which is generative of stress, conflict, or indecision; the explanatory analysis of the problem, causal, historical, ideational; the experimental, creative engendering of an interpretive structure which yields an understanding of the situation and attempts a resolution-reconstruction in action, the success of which is to be experientially tested.

The problematic situation paradigm of naturalistic pragmatism offers great advances over the earlier paradigm. It avoids the limitation to negativity of the continuity of analysis paradigm and the gratuitous issue of the genetic fallacy.[9]

Another advantage of the problematic situation paradigm is its comprehensive analysis of the structural components of the paradigm. And it has the further advantage of explicitly reflecting its integration of Enlightenment explanatory schemata and romantic counter-Enlightenment interpretive understanding. But the fateful weakness of the Hegelian problematic situation is that it is a model which permits no finalities, no fixities, no functional absolutes, but only the indiscriminate category of hypotheses which change as new situations present new disharmonies to be unified. It is a paradigm which relativizes all elements to the particular situation and thus permits no universals, no general principles, no scientific laws, no political or moral truths. Dewey's resolution of America's problematic situation was to utilize processes as a solvent for the obstructive fixities of American social life: the Constitution, the Bill of Rights, the Supreme Court, private property and the capitalist economic system. (Scientific method and democracy were themselves held to be processes which control process, but are not themselves dissolved by process.)

Thus the problematic situation paradigm leaves us only with a genetic pattern of inquiry, rooted in and flowing into the shifting processes of complex conditions, the pattern of all inquiry. But this instrument of inquiry is only procedural, a form for inquiry which dissolves substantive content.

3. *The Critique of Modernity Paradigm*. The vacuity of the problematic situation paradigm as Dewey leaves it, as process without content, as the solvent of all "fixities," has its significant counterpart in the outcome of the recent conflicts between the cognitive traditions of Modernity. On the one side of the conflict are the Enlightenment pursuers of rationally grounded objective, absolute, universal and realistic truth and the analytic philosophers who are their twentieth-century descendants, deploying Enlightenment-style empirical, epistemological, logical, and linguistic arguments to attack the Enlightenment intuitions of objective, absolute, universal, and realistic truth and a rational foundation for knowledge.

On the other side of the divide are the counter-intuitions of the Romantic displacers of reason by ontology, subjectivity, group consciousness and its projections, and by personal and collective will, as these are constitutive of history and culture. Their twentieth-century descendants among the phenomenologists, hermeneuticists, textualists, and deconstructionists are monologic interpretivists, asserting that historical conceptual structures and social webs of meaning mediate all areas of everyday life, science, and philosophy—thus undermining Enlightenment views old and new, the old Enlightenment ahistorical, unmediated rational foundations for knowledge and the new ahistorical unmediated analytic empiricism of forms of life and their language games, ordinary language philosophy, and speech acts.

In the conflict of frameworks mediators are currently attempting to discern developing lines of change and signs of convergence. Recent discernment of deficiencies on both the analytic and phenomenological sides have expressed their vulnerability—with the recognition of a two-fold deficiency on the analytic side in its ahistoricality and in its failure to acknowledge the mediation of conceptual structures; and on the phenomenological side, with the recognition of methodological deficiency and the failure of experiential testing. The more moderate mediators have been led by these vulnerabilities to agree on some or all of a set of convergences between the frameworks. The developing convergence[10] is toward opposition to foundationalism, essentialism, positivism, naturalism, universalism, traditionalism; opposition to all forms of cognitive transparency which claim an unmediated apprehension of truth, metaphysical, scientific, moral, and political; opposition to the sharp distinction between analytic and synthetic propositions and between realism and idealism; and opposition to all forms of historical or structural totalizing, including the historical cognitive structures of Modernity presented in this paper. Thus convergence is centered upon negativity, on rejection of legitimating grounds for previously or currently held intuitions and conceptualizations.

The cost of the convergence upon negations is that both sides of the conflict are emptied out of the intuitions and conceptual structures which historically, culturally, morally, and politically have defined them. Lost to the Enlightenment frame are its great achievements of substantive and instrumental reason: the self-evidence and inalienability of universal individual rights as the rational ground of political democracy; the comprehensive engagement of philosophy with the sciences, in methods, validations, and foundations; the sense of historical progress in democratization, in the sciences, and in the human betterment resulting from scientific technologies. All these have been philosophically delegitimated along with the possibility of their replacement. Lost on the Romantic side are the world-historical visions of Hegel, Marx, Weber, and Dewey, all with moral and religious subtextual significance. Lost are philosophic explorations of the dynamics of self and other, which mediate family, education, civil society, the arts, the nation, the world order, the sacred;

the interplay of personal and collective will, negative and positive liberty, bureaucracy and charisma; the development of self-consciousness on the part of slaves and masters and racial, economic, and gender-based social subgroups. All these philosophic achievements have been de-legitimated, as is the possibility of any replacement for them.

Implicit in *Naturalism and the Human Spirit*'s two-strand conception of philosophy, in the work of recent pragmatists[11] in Dewey's view of philosophy as culture criticism, and in the interpretivism, historically, and experiential testing of the problematic situation paradigm is the conception of Modernity itself as the complex, conflictual, richly historical conceptualization which is the problematic situation of our world. The cognitive structures of Modernity itself provide the models of what we define as problems and how they are to be resolved. Modernity is the problematic situation in which we find ourselves philosophically and find out how to work out philosophical problems. Modernity is thus the complex frame, the historical source, and the test of our philosophical structures; it is the historical, social, scientific web of meaning within which we function philosophically.

The paradigm of naturalistic pragmatism as critique of Modernity undertakes reflexively to explain and interpret the philosophic thought of Modernity by reference to its Enlightenment and Under-Enlightenment component structures. A sketch of this new paradigm redirects naturalistic pragmatism thus from a microlevel analysis of the problematic situation to a macrolevel in which Modernity itself is the problematic situation. In opposition to the ahistoricality and conceptual deficiency of monologic philosophies, this new paradigm entails the binding of all philosophic claims to the historical conceptual structures of Modernity. In opposition to the current philosophic convergence in negation, in which both sides of the conflicting structures of Modernity are emptied out of the historical conceptual meanings which have defined them, the new paradigm provides for the critical examination and re-appropriation of historical concepts. This critical reappropriation is made possible by the naturalistic requirement, entailed in the new paradigm, that all interpretive structures be subject to critique in terms of their contexts and consequences within the specific microlevel problematic situations of the macrolevel problematic situation of Modernity.

Entailed also in the new paradigm is the critical power which it makes possible: a criticism of "apart thought" represented by the isolation of the linguistic analysts and the phenomenologists; the concept of normal philosophy and the problem-solving with which it engaged in "mopping up" current paradigms; the detection of repetitions and revisions in philosophic problems and problem-solving, seen as functions of the limits of the framework imposed by Modernity; the identification of anomalies, philosophic stand-offs, in which contending arguments trail off without the possibility of resolution.

Empowered also by the new paradigm is the critical examination of characteristic philosophic responses to the major cognitive and cultural achievement within the time span of Modernity. The rise of natural science is perhaps the single most transformational development in modern history. How many Humes have risen to contest the validity of scientific laws and/or their realistic reference? How many Kants have discovered their transcendental conditions? How many contemporary scientific realists are being held at bay by empiricists, even under Hilary Putnam's challenge[12] that without some kind of realism, science becomes a miracle? And on the other side there is the "lordly indifference" to the philosophic significance of natural science on the part of the analysts and phenomenologists. A second major transformational event in the modern period is the rise of classical liberalism, which has suffered continuous criticism by antifoundationalists, empiricists, and analysts on the one side, and by collectivists and communitarians on the other. In a recent version of this perennial conflict of Modernity there is the retreat of Richard Rorty from Enlightenment liberal universalism into the particularism of "our own tradition"—but this retreat is ominously the path which Martin Heidegger followed into Nazism.[13]

And finally the new paradigm will incorporate the earlier paradigms of continuity of analysis and the problematic situation (on the microlevel). In encompassing these, the new model exhibits, within the restrictions of interpretivism, a qualified realism, causality, and fallibilism.

This, then, is a sketch of the long-delayed paradigm of naturalistic pragmatism. It is intended to reopen the blocked path of naturalistic pragmatism. It projects a paradigm of a fully self-conscious naturalistic pragmatism which proposes to explain, to interpret, and appropriate the conflicting frameworks of Modernity.

This sketch of an integrating, critical, and redemptive paradigm for naturalistic pragmatism is an immodest proposal. It is *integrating* in that it is in a position to command the scope of Modernity, the framework of its philosophy, the principal problems perceived and methods pursued, especially since the mid-nineteenth century when the conflict of the structures of Modernity sharpened. It is *critical* of "apart" thought and its separation from historicality and contextuality; its disengagement from continuity with the natural and social sciences; its monologic blindness; its practice of philosophy as symptom rather than as self-conscious interpreter and critic of Modernity; and its un-Deweyan silence on issues of public concern. It is *redemptive* of the cognitive and moral problems which, along with their resolutions, continually revise and reaffirm themselves; it sees these as the evolving truths available in the framework of Modernity, their causes and consequences made visible, their negative criticism evolving from oppositional structures which are themselves defined within the problematic situation of Modernity. Can it be that the spirit of naturalistic pragmatism as it appropriates the structures of Modernity is also the path to such wisdom as is possible for philosophy in our time?

Notes

1. Yervant H. Krikorian, ed., *Naturalism and the Human Spirit* (New York: Columbia University Press, 1944).

2. Ibid., pp. 373–74.

3. "This instance on the universal and unrestricted application of 'scientific method' . . . is well set forth by Miss Lavine: 'The naturalistic principle may be stated as the resolution to pursue inquiry into any set of phenomena by means of methods which administer the checks of intelligent experiential verification in accordance with the contemporary criteria of objectivity. . . . That scientific analysis must not be restricted in any quarter, that its extension to any field, to any special set of phenomena, must not be curtailed—this is the nerve of the naturalistic principle. "Continuity" of analysis can thus mean only that all analysis must be scientific analysis' " (pp. 358–59).

4. Ibid., p. 369.

5. It is as a principal component of American naturalistic pragmatism that American philosophical naturalism is currently recognized, and it is so understood in this lecture. The complex of themes characteristic of philosophic naturalism is distinctive of American naturalistic pragmatism and is present in no other major contemporary philosophic viewpoint. The question of derivation between the pragmatist and naturalist elements in Dewey's thought has often been raised. See H. S. Thayer, *Meaning and Action: A Critical History of Pragmatism* (New York: Bobbs-Merrill, 1968), p. 3: "Dewey's pragmatism was an evolving if central strand in a thoroughly elaborated philosophical naturalism." For a contrasting derivation, see Ernest Nagel's proposal of a contextualist naturalism which, although it "has historical roots in pragmatism, and although Dewey himself is an exponent of both, those professing the former do not in general feel committed to the technical pragmatic doctrines concerning the nature of truth or the function of knowledge (or) . . . the pragmatic or instrumentalist label. . . . Nevertheless, pragmatism is the matrix out of which, at least in America, contextualistic naturalism has emerged." Ernest Nagel, *Sovereign Reason and Other Studies in the Philosophy of Science* (New York: The Free Press, 1954).

6. See, e.g., Karl-Otto Apel, Daniel Bell, Isaiah Berlin, Richard Bernstein, Hans Blumenberg, Fred Dallmayr, Jacques Derrida, Michel Foucault, Francis Fukiyama, Ernest Gellner, Jurgen Habermas, Irving Howe, David Kolb, Joseph Margolis, Alisdair MacIntyre, Richard Rorty, Charles Taylor, Stephen Toulmin.

7. With the exception of Marxism, now compromised in theory and in practice.

8. *Logic: The Theory of Inquiry*, in John Dewey, *The Later Works, 1925–1953*, vol. 12 (Carbondale, Ill.: Southern Illinois University Press, 1938), p. 457. For a discussion of "apart thought" see R. N. Sleeper, *The Necessity of Pragmatism* (New Haven, Conn.: Yale University Press, 1986), pp. 19–20, 155, and 225, note 6.

9. For a discussion of the genetic fallacy see T. Z. Lavine, "Reflections on the Genetic Fallacy," *Social Research* (Autumn 1962): 321–26.

10. For a discussion of the current movement toward convergence see Joseph Margolis, *Pragmatism Without Foundations* (Oxford: Basil Blackwell, 1986), chapter 8, "A Sense of Rapprochement between Analytic and Continental European Philosophy."

11. Versions of the two strands, in varying degrees of explicitness, may be found in recent writings of American pragmatists. John McDermott provides

an explicit version. Interpreting Emerson ("[T]he whole of nature is a metaphor of the mind"), McDermott notes: "This text mirrors the binary strands found in subsequent American philosophy: the idealist-pragmatic epistemology of James, Royce, Dewey, and Peirce, each with an original emphasis of one strand over another." *Streams of Experience: Reflections on the History and Philosophy of American Culture* (Amherst: University of Massachusetts Press, 1986), p. 34.

12. Hilary Putnam, "What Is Realism?" in *Scientific Realism,* ed. Jarret Leplin (Berkeley: University of California Press, 1984).

13. See Victor Farias, *Heidegger and Nazism,* ed. Joseph Margolis and Tom Rockmore (Philadelphia: Temple University Press, 1989). See also T. Z. Lavine, "Thinking Like a Nazi," review essay of *Heidegger and Nazism* in *Washington Post Book World,* March 25, 1990; *International Journal of Group Tensions* 20, no. 3 (1990).

2

Human Natures*

John Lachs

If I drive south from Nashville, Tennessee, in less than ten hours I will run upon a large body of water. The existence of this sea is an objective fact: it was there before the first human being swam in it, it is there when no one beholds it, it will likely be there when we evacuate the earth and move on to pollute other planets. Even if, following some bizarre conception, a mad dictatorship denied its existence, its waves would continue to wash its shores, its fish would still frolic over oyster beds. I offer no comprehensive theory of the nature of objective facts. For my purposes it is enough to note that some things do not owe their existence to human thought or effort.

The body of water I run upon is called "the Gulf of Mexico." This is a conventional or choice-determined fact, a fact that depends on intersubjective agreements. We could refer to it by one of its old, Indian names, or call it "the Gulf of Contentment," or even, simply, "Sam." The water neither implies nor requires any particular name. Viewed from its perspective, therefore, what we decide to call it is not

---

*Originally published in *Proceedings and Addresses of the American Philosophical Association,* vol. 64 (Newark, Del.: American Philosophical Association, University of Delaware, 1990). Reprinted by permission.

only contingent but arbitrary: social, political, and geographic considerations conspired to establish it as the generally accepted one. Yet it continues to be a hostage to human decisions. The Florida Department of Tourism may well launch a campaign to rechristen it "the Gulf of Florida," and succeed in convincing everyone to use no other name.

It is not very difficult to identify objective and conventional facts. The distinction produces classes that are mutually exclusive and appear conjointly exhaustive. Many people, therefore, think that every fact is either objective or conventional and none is both. This unfortunately overlooks a third, intermediate class of facts, whose central significance has in any case been inadequately appreciated by philosophers. I have in mind facts whose constitution involves both objective elements and human decisions. Let us call these "choice-inclusive facts."

Since the days of Kant, the idea of realities constituted by human beings has been commonplace. The acts to which I wish to call attention, however, are not transcendental but quite ordinary and empirical. They are determined not by the nature of human cognitive faculties but by contingent and reversible choices. Everyone is familiar with such facts although, because they masquerade as objective, their proper nature tends to elude us.

How, for example, should we view the claim that the body of water I run upon is a gulf? Objective facts set our parameters. We are dealing with a certain volume of salt water located in a specific geographical area. Shall we call it a sea? This is clearly what its size suggests. It is, in fact, larger than most seas and much larger than many. Its geographical peculiarity, however, is that land bounds it on three sides, making it appropriate for us to call it an inlet or a bay. But, though Hudson Bay and the Bay of Bengal are large, bays on the whole tend to be relatively small bodies of water. This makes it acceptable for us to classify it as a gulf, which is a relatively large part of an ocean or sea extending into the land. Yet if it is a gulf, the Sea of Japan and the Baltic Sea, which are smaller and more bounded, should be gulfs also. The Gulf of Guinea, on the other hand, since it is much smaller and is bounded by land on two sides only, should not be a gulf.

The conclusion of this line of thought is obvious. It makes no sense to ask, "What is this body of water *really*? Is it *really* a bay, a gulf, or a sea?" Within limits, it is what we decide it is. The limits are imposed by its physical features: we cannot, without being silly, class it as a mountain range or as a coffee pot. But we have good reasons to classify it as a sea, as a bay, and as a gulf, and which of these carries the day is a matter of choice. The right question to ask, therefore, is "Which is the best way to classify this body of water?" And this is a question to which there is no unambiguous, or even meaningful, answer without a prior account of what we want the classification to do. In the case of the Baltic, with rival nations inhabiting its shores, it may well have been in everyone's interest to secure universal rights to navigation by declaring it a sea. Classification as a gulf, on the other hand, may have accomplished for the Gulf of Mexico the opposite desired effect, conveying to colonizing European powers the idea of a private American waterway.

There are several types and many instances of such choice-inclusive facts. All of them involve objective facts along with some decision, normally a social one, about classification. Some choices concerning how to categorize the objective facts are inappropriate or wrong: no large body of water is a flowering mimosa plant. But there is no single classification that is exclusively right. The facts allow flexibility in our concepts: depending on what we wish to accomplish, widely divergent ways of sorting and grouping the bounty of nature may be appropriate and useful.

In saying that someone is fat, for example, we do not disclose an objective fact about the person. There are, to be sure, objective facts involved: the body weight of the individual and its relation to the weight of other people in the population. But we can also detect a decision, such as that to be fat means to exceed by 20 percent or more the average weight of people of one's height. We could, of course, decide to draw the line elsewhere, say at exceeding the average by only 5 percent, or by 50. There may be good reasons to incline us in one direction or the other. But in no case do we accurately capture what it *is objectively* to be fat, for the simple and conclusive reason that there is no such thing.

Adulthood is another choice-inclusive fact, since it involves both the age of individuals and the decision, recently revised to the chagrin of young people, concerning where to draw the line (among other things) between those who can drink and those who cannot. Nothing is large, hot, or heavy and no one is poor, smart, weak, generous, tall, a failure, retarded or even dead[1] as a matter of objective fact. The reason is not that the application of these terms involves tacit comparisons between members of a class, but that the comparison does not by itself justify the application. We also need a decision to specify the point in the relationship of the compared items where we first wish to permit the term to apply.

Such decisions are, of course, not arbitrary. Normally, they are public, subserve some shared ends and involve a variety of formal and informal social mechanisms in their formulation. The decision about where to draw the line between the living and the dead, for example, is now being made through the political process. The traditional distinction, cast in terms of the cessation of cardiopulmonary function, had been rendered inadequate by the development of advanced techniques of resuscitation and life support. A presidential commission was appointed and made the novel suggestion that the irreversible cessation of whole-brain function be designated as the criterion of death. The new standard addresses some broad social concerns and is more clearly in line with technological realities than the now antiquated, traditional criterion. Accordingly, in the last dozen years or so, nearly thirty state legislatures have adopted the recommendation. With additional support, the new social decision about the point of death will be clearly in place, generating, as physicians declare people deceased, an indefinitely large number of choice-inclusive facts.

The continuing abortion controversy is also best seen as disagreement concerning the social decision about the beginning of life. There is no novel objective fact to be discovered in this sphere: no biological research or abstract philosophical reflection can tell us when human life begins. What we need is a generally acceptable decision about where, in the continuous process from fertilization to birth, it would be best to draw the line between merely biological and genuinely human existence. Too much is at stake for this determination to be groundless or arbitrary. The religious beliefs, personal values, and established lifestyles of people must all be taken into consideration, along with economic interests and the broad social implications of each proposed decision. The fact that consensus has eluded us for so many years is a result not of having failed to *discover* what we seek, but of the intensity of the feelings involved and the complexity of the balance among values that we must achieve.

The currently popular categories of biology are also choice-inclusive in character. The full continuum of plant and animal life serves as the objective foundation of the facts their application creates. In addition, however, there is also a tacit choice to cut up the continuum in a certain way and not in innumerable others. We could, for example, classify porpoises by their habitat and method of locomotion, in which case they would be a sort of fish, or by their weight, in which case they would be related to cattle, or by their intelligence, in which case they would belong in the same group as humans and the great apes. Viewed in this light, our current classification, based on method of respiration and reproduction, loses its apparent privilege. Each of these arrangements is legitimate and useful; each focuses on some interesting features of the animals and highlights some of their significant relations to others. To say that one and only one of them captures the way things really are amounts to a slanderous impoverishment of the world. All of them illuminate a bit of reality, though not necessarily the corner into which we wish to peer.

Biologists might respond, however, by contrasting our changing purposes with the enduring value of truth. Some classifications are simply better, they might argue, for learning the truth about animals. If we focus on the respiration and reproduction of porpoises, for example, we are more likely to discover their evolutionary origin than if we study the ways they use their tail. The right classification is like a key that opens the door to nature's secrets; when the key fits, we know that our idea is not only useful but also true. If this is so, our ordinary quests are not on a par with the search for the right classification, the pursuit of truth. Among other differences, their satisfactory termination presupposes that we get what we want. In the scientific search for truth, by contrast, there is no room for private whim or ulterior public purpose. When we operate under the constraint of objective facts, the only permissible desire is to ascertain the way things are.

This line of thought is impressive. It plays on our suspicions about our motives and appeals to our hunger for heroes. It depicts scientists as selfless devotees of truth and the rest of us as slaves to the shabby designs of daily life. I, for one, do not have the problem many philosophers experience today with acknowledging the independent reality of facts and truths; I even take pleasure, when summer approaches, that the Gulf of Mexico is there waiting for me. Nevertheless, it is worth remarking that not all truths are of the objective variety: choice-determined and choice-inclusive facts are also appropriate objects of the search for truth. And the rigors of this search have been much exaggerated. In fact, nothing is more plentiful and easier to get than truth. We are surrounded by truths on all sides; if we permit it, their sheer number will numb the mind. My car is made of roughly eighteen thousand parts. This gives eighteen thousand truths, if I care to enumerate them, along with millions more about how the parts are related. A colleague concerned about his record of speaking the truth told me that whenever he finds himself asserting too many dubious propositions, he quickly recites the multiplication tables to raise his daily truth average.

It is not truth we want, obviously, but relevant truths, general truths, novel truths, or interesting truths. Inquiry must be guided, therefore, by objectives and values beyond promiscuous curiosity or else it will drown in truth. These values express the multiplicity of our concerns and enterprises; they identify the corners of the world where we want to look, the sorts of things we want to find, the kinds of uses to which we wish to put our results. The scientific enterprise is not a detached, indiscriminate search for truth. It is an organized human activity, governed, like all others, by our needs and interests. The aim of at least portions of it may be purely epistemic: some scientists may want to identify those characteristics of objects that are central in the sense of connecting and concomitantly varying with the largest possible set of their other features. Such systemic objectives, however, express the long-term, deeply entrenched, need-based concerns of the vulnerable animals we are no less than do our more immediately practical interests. An omniscient God would pay no heed to central, unifying features; gods secure from injury would find their curiosity easily satisfied and consider the relentless search for knowledge an embarrassment. That porpoises breathe by means of lungs is no more of a truth than that they weigh about as much as cows. And the desire to determine their evolutionary origin is no less a contingent human purpose than the craving to study the engineering of their tails. However we relate and classify things, we will find some truths. Whatever choice-inclusive truths or facts we find, they will always have some purpose behind the decisions that give them structure or definition.

Now that I have angered those who believe in fixed and natural species with my comments about the choice-inclusive character of biological categories, I might as well proceed to infuriate the friends of human nature. The statements we like to make about what is and what is not a matter of human nature, about the identity of the human essence in everyone and about the endurance of human traits are also all based on choice-inclusive facts. Since the facts are choice-inclusive, they have an objective component that imposes constraints on what can be called a human characteristic and who can be classified as a human being. But the element that is independent of our choice establishes only the outer, and rather fuzzy, boundaries of appropriate categorization. Within these parameters, the facts that surround us do not mandate any particular classification; they are rich and flexible enough to permit a variety of organizational arrangements. How we order them, therefore, cannot be determined simply by what they are. Their features and relations provide a jungle of opportunities for the mind. Consciously or without awareness of what we do, we must resolve to focus on certain relationships and to disregard others.

Whom shall we classify as human beings? Primitive tribes tend to be notoriously exclusive, many of them reserving for themselves alone the distinction of being human. Even the civilized ancient Greeks were tempted to view only themselves as properly human and called outsiders uncouth and imperfectly human "barbarians." Although the story of Adam and Eve suggests a single origin and a single nature for us all, the Old Testament account of the struggles between the Israelites and surrounding tribes leaves no doubt about who were and who were not to be considered true sons of God. The history of humankind is at once the history of denying human status to selected groups: to women, children, blacks, Orientals, Jews, Indians, Slavs, infidels, Saracens, Christians, and Huns. The more civilized parts of the world have now reached consensus on the desirability of such exclusiveness. But this humane agreement has emerged not as a result of the general recognition of a single humane essence, but due to the decision to stress certain telling similarities among us and to dismiss our differences as irrelevant.

The twin facts that acknowledgment of the humanity of all promises significant benefits and that the campaign for this concession has been waged with such passion should have alerted us that this is an area not of objective but of choice-inclusive facts. Important values are at stake and these values give shape to our decisions about what similarities to stress and who to classify. The objective facts underlying the classification permit us to call everyone from Albanians to Zulus human no less than they allowed the exclusion of idiots and infidels. But they are not infinitely patient. Clouds and waves and slices of apple pie cannot reasonably be considered human beings, nor can home runs and the stars in the evening sky. So it is possible to be wrong about such matters, though not so easily and as often as philosophers suppose.

In certain other cases, it is not clear what the facts will allow. In such fuzzy borderline situations, the centrality of the decision presupposed by classification is plain to see. There used to be earnest philosophical discussions about whether humans could be but sophisticated robots and whether advanced machines could one day become human beings. Such questions masquerade as queries about objective facts. They cannot be resolved, however, on the basis of observation, of clever argument, or even of what a native speaker of our language could appropriately say. The fundamental flaw in the discussions is that the question generating the inquiry points in the wrong direction. It is unproductive to ask whether human beings might not, after all, *be* machines, and how complex a machine would have to be in order to it to *be* or *become* a human being. These are not matters of objective fact, of how things are. They are, instead, matters of conscious or unconscious human decision. The proper question to ask, accordingly, is concerning the circumstances that would have to obtain in order for us to decide that, for purposes of classification, the obvious differences between human beings and machines can be overlooked.

What might such circumstances be? We must note, first, significant similarities between humans and machines. The leprechauns that were supposed to have driven the gears of old clocks were sufficiently like us to enable us to call them small human beings. The gears were not, nor are internal combustion engines and hair clippers. Next, something about machines might engage our concern or sympathy. We might, for instance, be struck by the fact that they are very intelligent or that they act as if they could suffer pain. This would activate our value commitments and, as a result, certain of our general beliefs, such as that intelligence is worthy of respect and that gratuitously inflicted pain is evil, would gain extension to machines. We would then examine the consequences of classifying machines, or at least some machines, as humans. Such classification would have important social results: as human beings, computers and robots could no longer be sold and would have to be treated as employees or independent contractors rather than as inanimate tools. They would fall, moreover, under the protection of all labor laws, guaranteeing them lunch hours, overtime pay, periodic vacations, and workmen's compensation benefits. At some point, advanced robots may even launch a campaign for recognition as beings with rights. Faced with such a situation, we might well decide that it is better to classify them as humans, with all the costs that involves, than to endure the consequences of continued differentiation.

Might it not be, however, that such a decision is merely the political acknowledgment of a reality? Perhaps machines of a certain complexity just *are* human and have been all along while we were trying to decide how to classify them. We do, after all, tend to belive that blacks were fully human before they were accorded that status with the abolition of slavery. Why should the humanity of machines at a certain stage of their development be any different?

This view has some initial plausibility. For, should we ever decide that machines are human, some people are likely to say, "I've noticed for a long time now that they are *so much* like us." And others may well announce, "I have *always* thought of them as human beings dressed in metal." But shall we consider this intuitive plausibility adequate to convince us that when we classify machines as human we merely note an objective fact? This decision depends at least in part on the similarities between the circumstances surrounding the two situations. Does the process that is used in the announcement that machines are human resemble acquiescence in objective realities more than it resembles decision making?

On any careful and sensible examination, the answer to this must be no. Objective facts, such as the existence of the body of water we call "the Gulf of Mexico," are relatively easy to recognize. In such cases, we have little need for collecting evidence or for lengthy deliberation: the realities tend to impress themselves on us. Some earnest religious person might predict, for example, that the world will end on a specific date, say at nine o'clock in the morning. By one minute after nine, it will be blindingly clear to everyone that judgment day has not arrived: that the world continues on its merry way is an objective fact. Of course, there are some independent realities we cannot ascertain so easily. The presence of a planet beyond Neptune, the identity of Dwight Eisenhower's wartime lover, the whereabouts of Bonnie Prince Charlie were at one time or another all surrounded by uncertainty. But even in such cases, something other than a decision is required to settle the matter. Once we catch Pluto in our telescopes or the general in the boudoir, the controversy is resolved. Stubborn inquiry graced by luck suffices to get straight about these objective facts. Choosing the outcome here is not only inappropriate but also disastrous, because it obstructs the needed investigation and makes what we want a cheap substitute for what there is.

This is not at all the situation with the question concerning the humanity of machines. Humanity is not a feature that stares us in the face, but a designation we award on the basis of complex criteria and shrewd assessments. When the question is whether we should award it to machines, inquiry can reveal no additional facts adequate to develop an answer. To be sure, getting straight about the similarities of machines and humans is an indispensable element in moving toward a resolution, but the structure of the problem makes it impossible for this to suffice. For even if what machines do closely resembles our own activities, the issue of origin and ingredients remain. Machines, after all, are manufactured, while human beings are the results of more private and more pleasurable acts. And manufactured objects consist of nonliving components, instead of cells and organs that constitute our parts. The question of what level of resemblance in behavior, if any, is enough for us to overlook these obvious dissimilarities cannot be answered by reference to facts. It requires a decision and with it the assessment of purposes, desires, context, likely consequences, costs, and benefits. If someone declares, therefore, that machines cannot be human unless they are capable of falling in love or of liking strawberry shortcake, he is not stating objective fact but affording us an insight into how high a value he places on such things as caring in a sexual context and fresh fruit with whipped cream.

These considerations reveal that there is no compelling similarity between accepting or rejecting the humanity of machines, on the one hand, and recognizing, noting, or accepting objective facts, on the other. Might we not have compelling reasons, however, for deciding to treat questions concerning who is and who is not human as though they were queries about objective fact? We might, indeed, and we frequently do, though this can give no comfort to the objectivist. Making one's view appear to have a warrant in the very nature of things is an excellent strategy for convincing others and stilling one's own doubts. Declaring certain values natural rights, for example, puts us in a more powerful position than if we simply announced our intention to fight for them. Asserting that certain social structures, political arrangements or modes of behavior are direct outcomes of the nature of man makes them appear more weighty than if we merely said that we favor them. If we should ever decide that machines of an advanced design are really human things, we could therefore greatly facilitate public acceptance of this changed state of affairs by insisting that they have been humans all along and that we are only paying our belated respects to an objective fact. Obviously, however, neither our objectifying tendency nor the decision to treat certain choice-inclusive facts as if they were objective changes the nature of the facts. Although choice enters into the constitution of some classes of facts, to which class any given fact belongs is not a matter of choice.

The complex and variable criteria and the shrewd assessments involved in promoting certain groups of beings to the rank of humans were present throughout the long history of expanding the boundaries of our race. Little by little, we, or influential groups among us, made decisions to overlook the differences due to class, race, sex, religion, national origin, intelligence, drive, and physical endowment, and to treat a very broad selection of individuals as equally entitled to consideration and respect. The objective facts permitted these decisions without compelling them. Slaves, for example, resembled their masters as closely before emancipation as they did afterwards, but resemblance is sufficient for classification as human beings. Accordingly, to say that they had been human before they were set free is a misleading, ontological way of stating the moral truth that they should have been classified as humans long before.

It is precisely the moral context and the value consequences of such reclassifications that justified expanding membership in the human family. Clearly, we are all better off for having decided to treat blacks, women, members of different religions, the handicapped, even our enemies, as full-fledged human beings. The benefits of this increase in the range of the concept of humanity, however, have been mitigated by two powerful trends. One is the failure to recognize that the facts about human nature are choice-inclusive, rather than objective. This has left a simplistic ontology in possession of the field, in whose terms we continue to believe that all of us share a single essence and that granting people rights and respect is just a response to noting the presence of this independently occurring form. The second trend is supported by the first. Since we think of our concept of humanity as identifying a natural kind, we have failed to introduce into it the diversity needed to keep pace with the increase in its scope. We have admitted to membership in the human community a wide variety of individuals whose nature is at odds with established conceptions of what is properly human. Not having loosened these traditional standards, we now face a situation in which we fervently wish to continue calling such individuals subhuman and their practices unnatural, yet we cannot do so without revoking their newly gained status. This is the source of a fundamental ambiguity at the center of the modern world: we have come to accept the legitimacy of lives we cannot but condemn.

Important and valuable as it has been to embrace the idea of a single human nature uniting us all, we must therefore supplement it by the conception of human natures. The facts permit this manner of classification, and our needs and our purposes amply justify it. The human landscape is adorned by variety; vast differences frame our similarities. Philosophers interested in generalization tend to overlook the full range of this diversity and resist being reminded of it by shunning empirical observation. In fact, however, humans differ significantly in feelings, values, and activities. The commitments their lives express vary not only from society to society and from age to age, but frequently from individual to individual, as well. Moreover, some (such as the severely retarded) lack the capacity for higher mental functions, while others are virtually unable to experience emotions. Some alter their responses unpredictably and without cease, while others (such as catatonic schizophrenics) are unable to change much at all. Some probably perceive the world in ways the rest of us cannot appreciate, or lead internal lives rich in private images and meanings. Some are incapable of significant communication, and some that we unhesitatingly classify as human (such as hydrocephalics) share with us none of the activities supposedly differentiating of our species.

We must be careful not to suppose that every divergence among us is suitable as the basis of an irreducibly different human nature. The variations must be wide enough and central enough to enable us to avoid trivializing the notion. We certainly do not want to suppose that short and tall people, beer drinkers and teetotalers, individuals with 20/20 vision and with 20/40 vision are different by nature. The purposes that underlie our choice to distingish human nature revolve around appreciating our dissimilarities and tolerating those who live by divergent values. Accordingly, the differences we seek must be generic disparities in the commitments and in the lives that express the commitments of groups of human beings.

Such differences are not difficult to find if we focus on the desires, activities, and satisfactions of people. A desire is a wish gone active; it occurs when, as a result of prizing something, we develop a tendency to take steps to obtain it. These steps constitute the bulk of the activities of daily life: they are the seekings, the searchings, the habit-bound purposive routines, the dexterous moves and secret rituals that fill the everyday. It is a mistake to look for them only at the dramatic junctures of life. They constitute, first and foremost, the elements of our micro-behavior, such as the adjustments of eye and hand when we reach for a slice of pie and the movements of jaw and tongue as we chew it. Focusing on microbehavior makes the connection between action and satisfaction particularly easy to see. For even simple activities consist of action segments, each of which is carefully monitored to determine what change may be needed to move closer to the desired end. If the action segment is satisfactory, the activity proceeds apace, as when I continue to turn to respond to a voice behind my back. The unsatisfactoriness of the action segment, on the other hand, leads to rapid correction, as when I note that, in whirling around, I have managed to turn too far.

Desire, action, and satisfaction constitute, in this way, an unbroken and interactive chain. In our grand passions no less than in microbehavior, desires generate activities and unsatisfactions ratify the action. When our exertions yield no fruit, or produce it at too high a cost, we tend to question and eventually to revise both our desires and activities. The early hankering to fly by spreading one's arms, for example, is abandoned because of futility, while the hunger for throwing baseballs through large windowpanes (an easily performed and highly satisfying task) is surrendered only with the worldly wisdom painful consequences produce. In an ongoing process, therefore, desires, actions, and outcomes exert a determining influence on one another. Whatever we choose to believe about the nature and justification of values, this process is in fact their birthplace and their testing ground.

Human natures vary according to significant differences in the desires, activities, and satisfactions of people. That there are such differences is a matter of objective fact; that each defines a divergent human nature is a choice-inclusive fact. Stress on what is unlike about us must not, of course, be permitted to obscure our similarities. The differences, however, are so broad, so neglected, and so important to the growth of decency in the treatment of others that it is appropriate to dwell on them at length. Dissimilarities in desires, activities, and satisfactions make for different sorts of values that structure different sorts of lives. In honest moments, many of us quietly admit that it is unintelligible how others can act on the values and be satisfied with the lives they embrace. We know, however, that on reflection we must add that they surely feel the same way about us.

The desires, activities, and satisfactions, for example, that full-fledged membership in an acquisitive society requires render us human beings of an identifiable sort. The relentless drive to work, the incessant accumulation of new and old products, the savage haste make leisure as brief and rare as birdsong on a cloudy day. Even in universities, where life is supposed to afford reflective distance, people move in a swirl, or haze, of exertions, devoted to serving the needs of the moment, chasing name and visibility, not antique perfection. Such a life, viewed from the outside, might seem impoverished or wrapped in frustration or lit only by feeble pleasures. Yet many of us choose it eagerly and find happiness in nothing but its movement.

We can contrast such desires and activities in the flux with the lives of people who seek peace and rest in monasteries or under the bridge. A human nature passive in the face of contingency or resigned to the will of God operates by different values and seeks dissimilar satisfactions. The large houses, fancy trips, and car phones that measure meaning or the person on the make are, to this soul, ashes in the mouth. Acquiescence replaces drive and will; what desires remain aim at a simple and wholesome mode of life. Attempts to manipulate people and the world recede and the person, at one with nature, learns to move without motion, like a still bird carried by the wind. Some small percentage of the homeless, of welfare recipients, and of deeply religious people may well be such dropouts from acquisitive society. Spirituality and the simple life remain powerful ideals even in the worldly post-industrial age.

Adopting the view that there are multiple human natures removes one important line of support for dismissing unpopular values and alternative forms of life. It makes it impossible for people to claim that one and only one style of behavior is natural and right or that certain desires and activities and satisfactions are unnatural. To the extent that who we are determines what we value and how we ought to act, it constitutes the theoretical basis of a wholesome pluralism. In this way, we can at least secure the full legitimacy of our fellows: so long as they cause no harm, their differences from the majority in economic, religious, social, or even sexual values, or in the relative ranking of these values, will not justify their differential treatment. We will simply ascribe what appear to us as odd behavior and unfathomable bent to innocent differences in our human natures.

Modernity has taught us a double lesson. We have come to recognize that much in the world is contingent and that much of what is contingent can be improved. These discoveries were first made in relation to the physical world; only recently and gradually have we come to think of traditions and social and political arrangements as optional and open to intelligent control. It appears that we have not yet fully extended this recognition to our own thoughts and conceptual schemes. We continue to believe that there is one and only one correct or best way to think about things, and philosophers, unburdened by historical knowledge, tend to identify this with our current mode of thought. This is unfortunate. We must learn that our opinions, our distinctions, even the terms of our reflection, lead conditional lives and may need to be replaced. In many areas of thought, we enjoy vast flexibility and vast power to adapt our ideas to our broader purposes. Only intelligent and imaginative variations in how we think can help us achieve our epistemic goals and do justice to the astounding richness of the actual.

Note

1. Concerning the decisions involved in the definition of death, see my "The Element of Choice in Criteria of Death," in *Death: Beyond Whole-Brain Criteria,* ed. Richard M. Zaner (Dordrecht/Boston/London: Kluwer Academic Publishers, 1988), pp. 233–51.

3

Nature and Culture*

Peter Manicas

Introduction

My title intends to associate my effort with Dewey's *Experience and Nature,* better titled, he later thought, *Culture and Nature.* My main interest is to reconsider naturalism in the light of recent debates in the philosophy of the social sciences. I motivate this with a brief genealogy.

My teacher at Buffalo, Marvin Farber, often quoted the definition of naturalism given by his teacher, Ralph Barton Perry: It was, simply, the generalization of the sciences. The idea is sufficiently serviceable for some purposes, but of course, it leaves much out, including both how these sciences are to be conceived and how they are related. Farber, a student of Husserl, was founder of *Philosophy and Phenomenological Research,* and through this important journal he was also a close associate of Patrick Romanell. People are still surprised when I tell them that Farber's "uncautious" naturalism—which included deep sympathies with Marxism—were directed squarely at phenomenology.

*Originally published in *Proceedings and Addresses of the American Philosophical Association,* vol. 66, no. 3 (Newark, Del.: American Philosophical Association, University of Delaware, 1992). Reprinted by permission.

Another of my teachers at Buffalo, William T. Parry, was a founder of *Science and Society*. As I later discovered, my philosophical views owe much to him as well.

These naturalists all believed in science, but it must be admitted, I think, that up until very recently, empiricist philosophy of science, a subdiscipline which, we need to remember, emerged only in the 1950s, dominated *all* thinking about science. Presumably, everyone knew what science was. While there were problems which occupied philosophers of science, these, presumably, did not affect the general posture of naturalism. The physical sciences, of course, were the paradigm.

As regards these, antinaturalists had no qualms. But since at least Dilthey, the question of a human science had been very much contested. Could one hold, for example, that as there were physical laws, there were social laws? Could one argue that explanation proceeded in terms of these, just as, presumably, it does in the physical sciences? Could one hold that, even ideally speaking, the terms of the social sciences could be "reduced" to terms in the "physical language"?

Indeed, antinaturalism could be defined as the view that epistemological and ontological differences in the domains of nature and culture demand a wholly different methodology. Beginning with the Kantian cleavage between an empirical (phenomenal) realm subject to knowable law and an intelligible realm where agents are free, late-nineteenth-century thought dichotomized *Erklären* (causal explanation) and *Verstehen* (interpretative understanding), the nomothetic and the idiographic, the domain of nature and the domain of history. For antinaturalists, then, even if the methods of the natural sciences are apt for the investigation of nature, by virtue of the meaningful, linguistic or conceptual character of the human sciences, the methods of the human sciences need to be *toto coelo* different. They require a hermeneutic, phenomenological approach.

"Objective" vs. "Subjective" Weltanschauungen?

This bifurcation was the operative idea behind Maurice Natanson's much-used anthology of 1963, *The Philosophy of the Social Sciences*. In his foreword, Natanson wrote, "Two distinctly opposed philosophical attitudes are taken as polar positions underlying the social sciences: let us, for want of satisfying alternatives, call them 'objective' and 'subjective' Weltanschauungen."[1]

As the book unfolds, sociologist and naturalist George Lundberg is put against Georg Simmel's neo-Kantianism, essays by Ernest Nagel and C. G. Hempel on concept and theory formation in the social sciences are paired with one on the same topic by Alfred Schutz, an essay by A. J. Ayer is juxtaposed with one by Merleau-Ponty. But perhaps most striking was the exchange generated by Thelma Lavine's incisive essay, "Note to Naturalists on the Human Spirit."

Lavine sharply criticized any naturalism which was "content to be defined by a principle of continuity of analysis conceived of in terms of experiment and empirical verifiablity." This amounted, she insisted, "to forfeiting its status as a positive, i.e., constructive philosophy."[2] Naturalists not only exaggerated experimentalism but they confused the method of naturalism with methods stipulated by naturalism for inquiry into all types of subject matter. Finally, Lavine charged that naturalism had "thus far been able to satisfy its new-found concern with the human spirit by recommending the method of experimentation to the social sciences." By default, naturalists had failed to show that their naturalisms were not, finally, materialisms. In her view, these weaknesses could be overcome, but only if naturalists developed "a naturalistically recon-structed method of *Verstehen.*"[3]

Lavine's essay brought sharp rebuttals from both Nagel and Natan-son. Nagel found that the "difficulties she claims to find in current naturalism are only doubtfully genuine; and the specific recommenda-tion . . . of questionable worth."[4] Natanson much approved of Lavine's criticism but found that her recommendation was, finally, incoherent: "To reinvoke naturalistic criteria as correctives for a reconstructed naturalistic method is to take a step forward and follow with a step back."[5] For Natanson, since *Verstehen* was "foundational," the "way out" was "the transcension of naturalism in favor of a phenomenological standpoint."[6] Indeed, after saying that W. I. Thomas, Cooley, and Mead were "all representatives of the phenomenological standpoint," Natanson offered the opinion that this "transcension" could be achieved by adopting the phenomenological stance of Edmund Husserl.

In what follows, I argue that both Nagel and Natanson were wrong and that Lavine was correct. But to do this requires the rejection of mainstream, empiricist, neopositivist philosophy of science, including especially its characteristic philosophy of language and the (still dominating idea) that explanation proceeds by subsumption under law. Instead, I draw on recent work in realist philosophy of science.[7] In turn, I offer that in terms of this view of science, a human science may be secured with a robust naturalism of the sort defended by John Dewey and George Herbert Mead.[8] Antinaturalisms thrive because, beginning with the debates of the last decades of the nineteenth century, both sides of the argument have shared in assumptions about both nature and culture and about what natural science is. They still do.

Nature and Culture

Nature exists independently of human activities.[9] Society (and, significantly, *knowledge* of nature) does not.[10] Society is best construed as a relatively enduring ensemble of social relations, relatively enduring because social relations are incarnate in the activities of persons.[11] There would be no society without *human* activity. There would be no *human* activity without "culture," broadly, everything which has meaning, including then language and "the total range of material objects that are regularly used by people in mediating both their social and their environmental actions."[12] Although the activity-dependent character of society has implications for inquiry in the social sciences, this fact, emphatically, does not call for antinaturalism.

The philosophical basis for such a naturalistic (yet, nonreductive) view of society is hinted at by Marx (especially in *The German Ideology*), and was developed by G. H. Mead and Dewey. Alternative—and in the present view, badly mistaken—"naturalisms" are offered in the nineteenth-century positivist formulations of Spencer, Haeckel, and Engels and in more recent "eliminative materialism."[13]

For Dewey and Mead, life and mind are emergent evolutionary products; but as Tiles has argued, it is critical to see that most theories under this banner amount "to little more than dualism back from the laundry."[14] Characteristically, it is acknowledged that life and mind evolved, but then argued that mind is consciousness and that its contents are "ideas" (or intentions), qualities directly known only to "subjects." Within this Cartesian framework, meaning and communication require either reductionist strategies, for example, verificationism, behaviorism, or they remain miraculous, at the very least in need of some non-naturalistic solution.

A fully naturalistic posture will not merely allow mind (culture, meaning, and society) an evolution from the sentient, but will reject what Dewey called "intellectualism," the twofold error of operating "with an incomplete (abstracted) picture of what is to have [an] experience as seeing and recognizing, and on the other hand, [imposing] on all experience, specifically sentient experience, a structure which is present only in sophisticated (cognitive) developments of sentience."[15]

One cannot, I think, underestimate the hold of "intellectualism" on philosophers, psychologists, and social scientists who seek an under-standing of humans and society. Semantic theories of language, cur-rent "cognitive science," talk about "the cultural system" as in Parsonian-influenced theory or more radically, in the cultural work of Geertz or his opposite, Lévi-Strauss, who is antinaturalist, even Platonist. Simi-larly, the Parsonian conception of the affective as providing only a motivating, noncognitive role in action, recent rational-choice theory and the idea that all knowledge is discursive knowledge, each thrive on "intellectualism."

For Dewey, three general "plateaus" are easily—and empirically—discerned, "each of which incorporates the function and relations of those below it, and is such that it cannot be understood in isolation from the level (or levels) below it."[16] The first plateau is inanimate nature. In strongly realist terms, Dewey writes that "atoms and molecules show a selective bias in their indifferences, affinities and repulsions when exposed to other events."[17] For realist theory of science, "things," both the things of ordinary experience and the highly abstracted theoretical things of advanced science, are metaphysical "compounds." Ordinary table salt is a compound of different kinds of molecules even while it is mostly $NaCl$. $NaCl$, of course, is a theoretical entity, an item of the current ontology of science. Realist philosophy of science is strongly naturalistic in holding that "nature" exists independently of mind, even if the *nature* of nature is a scientific problem, to be settled by inquiry.[18]

In contrast to empiricisms, "laws" are not statements about empirical regularities but assertions about the dispositional powers of things— their "selective biases"—and these are understood as "natural necessities," in Dewey"s terms, "essences."[19] Theories are conceived as "representations" of enduring structures or mechanisms and have essential non-sentential dimensions, what Harré termed "imagined paramorphs," or models of causal mechanisms at work in the world.[20]

The second general plateau, life, is distinguished by "the *way* physico-chemical energies are interconnected and operate." Animate bodies seek "to maintain a temporal pattern of activity . . . to utilize conserved consequences of past activities so as to adapt subsequent changes to the needs of the integral system in which they belong." Thus, "iron as such exhibits characteristics of bias or selective reactions" but "iron as a genuine constituent of an *organized* body acts so as to tend to maintain the type of activity of the organism to which it belongs."[21] In an organism, it functions not to become iron oxide (as it would in a hinge), but to contribute to metabolism. As Dewey maintains, how some "element" of a concrete composite behaves depends upon its (theorized) dispositional properties, on how in the "integrated system" it is related to other "things," and on how the composite is related to "things" external to it. It is because iron—Fe—is what it is that it has properties which enable it to function differently in different relations. Compare here not only iron in hinges and in organisms but hinges in New Mexico and in Honolulu!

We experience patterns not invariances. Patterns are the result of relatively stable configurations of causal mechanisms. Salt (usually) dissolves in water; for human percipients, gold is—almost always appears—yellow; and to shift the example to the domain of society, there is a strong positive correlation between poverty and one-on-one crime. Indeed, in terms of Dewey's most basic metaphysical category, there is both precariousness and stability because "the world" is not, as empiricists have it, a determined concatenation of contingent events but a contingent concatenation of ensembles of complexly related natural necessities, a world of genuine change and novelty. The implications of this for a proper understanding of science are, without exaggeration, simply enormous.

Meaning, Mind, and Society

But if "vitalism" in biology is no longer persuasive, mind remains a problem, not only in the persistent mind/body dualism (and epistemological individualism) of most general psychology, but in the social sciences, in what is, effectively, a radical bifurcation of nature and culture.

As Dewey says, "Upon the whole, professed transcendentalists have been more aware than have professed empiricists of the fact that language makes the difference between brute and man." "The trouble is," he continues, "that they have lacked a naturalistic conception of its origin and status."[22] For Dewey (and Mead), society, meaning, and mind are tightly linked, and a genetic account is indispensible if we are not to fall into "the philosophic fallacy," the conversion of "eventual functions into antecedent existence."[23] Dewey's move, to shift the problem of mind to the problem of language, sounds remarkably *au courant*. But his naturalistic account of its origin and status has yet to be taken seriously. We can usefully supplement Dewey's account with G. H. Mead's.

Creatures which lack language nevertheless "gesture." Thus the perception by a dog that another "is ready to attack becomes a stimulus . . . to change his position or his own attitude. He has no sooner done this than the change of attitude . . . causes the first dog to change his attitude." "We have here," Mead notes, "a conversation of gestures."[24] But it would be an error to say these acts have *meaning* for the animals. Dewey and Mead insist that "meanings do not come into being without language" and these creatures lack language.[25] On the other hand, as Tiles writes, "Animals which do not already respond to each other's behavior cannot respond to each other's *intentions* to produce modifications in their behavior."[26] The plateau of coordinated animal response is not irrelevant to communication at the linguisitic plateau even if it is not reducible to it. Consider, then, a linguistically apt creature.[27]

Gestures can become "significant symbols." That is, "vocal gestures can arouse in an individual making them the response which they explicitly arouse, or are supposed to arouse, in other individuals." They can come to "stand for" a particular act or response. Significant symbols are meanings.

Mead wrote that the difference between a gesture and a significant symbol is that "the individual is conscious of the meaning of his own gesture." Indeed, Mead often refers to intentional acts which "entail an elaborate mental process."[28] David Rubenstein calls this an inconsistency in Mead, and says that it was the reintroduction of the "psychical entities" he tried to eliminate which invited interpretation of him as a phenomenologist. But this (not uncharacteristic) reading is a huge error, in Dewey's terms, a straightforward product of "the philosophic fallacy." Neither Dewey nor Mead deny that persons are conscious or that they have intentions. Rather, it is their claim that meaning cannot be *explained* in terms of "intentions" (or "intentional objects," psychic or otherwise). Thus, if someone is to be taken as, e.g., making a request, as Tiles writes:

> he has to be taken to have responded to the object not as a stimulus but from the standpoint of the [other]. And what establishes the possibility of *thus* adopting the standpoint of the other is the recognition of the regularity of the relationship holding between gesture and completed act.[29]

These perceived "regularities" are the foundation of socially constructed linguistic universals. In the absence of this plateau, meaning cannot be made intelligible. Thus, semantic theories which try to define meaning in terms of truth conditions without acknowledging that linguistic acts (or their vehicles) presuppose social activity fail to explain how a linguistic vehicle could get meaning. They must, finally, either beg the question or postulate meanings.

It follows, as well, that we need to reject nominalism, the dominating posture of Hume-inspired empiricist philosophies of language. As consequences of social interactions which depend upon regularities which can become habitualized and standardized, neither meaning nor essence are "adventitious and arbitrary." Yet, as important, linguistic universals are not Platonic entities or formulae which prescribe their application.

By explaining meaning, Dewey can also account for philosophy's enduring fallacies regarding it: Thus, "meanings that were discovered to be indispensible to communication were treated as final and ultimate in nature itself. Essences were hypostatized into original and constitutive forms of all existence"—the philosophic fallacy at work.[30] There is no objection to talk about either meanings or essences—as long as one fully appreciates them to be nothing more than relatively enduring social products.

On the other hand, exactly because meanings (and essences) are grounded in regularities of interaction and are the product of these, they are both objective and remain revisable. For Dewey, "meanings are rules for using and interpretating things; interpretation being always an imputation of potentiality for some consequence."[31] As before, gestures depend upon expected outcomes which presuppose the regularities of past experience. Accordingly, use is constrained, neither "adventitious nor arbitrary," but because in acting, agents decide, use is revisable. In noting that "the scope and limits of application are ascertained experimentally [practically] in the process of application,"[32] Dewey anticipates what has come to be called a "finitist" conception of rules; that is, the idea that since there is no universal or "natural" scale for weighing similarity against difference, the application of rules (including meaning-rules) are contingent, but constrained judgments by actors using materials at hand.[33] As I argue subsequently, the implications of seeing that meanings are both "objective" and reproduced and transformed by practice are critical for social science.

Epistemological Individualism

The failure to see that meaning is to be found in transactions is propelled by the failure to see that there is a radical difference between "individuals with minds" and "individual minds," the characteristic posture of epistemological individualism. To avoid a solipsism of the present moment, epistemological individualists need to hold that the experienced world is shared by individuals; but if it is not a social product, this world needs to be the world of the naive realist, a "naturalized" world where things are, pretty much, as they appear. Thus, in the mind-independent world, there are red apples, even if we must learn to call them "red apples." If, however, we take modern physical science and the evidence of history and anthropology seriously, we need to acknowledge a far more complicated story and that, accordingly, the capacity to identify the most mundane things of experience requires, in addition to a mind-independent natural world and our evolved "natural" capacities, a massive system of meaning which has been historically, regionally, and locally bequeathed. Indeed, the failure to acknowledge this would seem to be consequence of both "intellectualism" *and* the conversion of eventual functions into antecedent causes. But, as Dewey insists,

> the whole history of science, art and morals proves that the mind that appears *in* individuals is not as such individual mind. The former is in itself a system of belief, recognitions, and ignorances, of acceptances and rejections, of expectancies and appraisals of meanings which have been instituted under the influence of custom and tradition.[34]

A more esoteric example may make the point clearer and show also its relevance to the present essay. According to Bulmer, the terminal taxa of the Karam correspond very well with some 70 percent of the cases with species identified by a scientific zoologist. The cassowary is an instance of noncorrespondence. Karam have the taxon "yakt" for birds and bats, but the cassowary in not placed in this taxon. Instead, it appears is a special taxon, "kobity," making it a nonbird/nonbat. For Bulmer, this is an error explained by Karam willingness to allow "culture" to supersede "objective biological facts."[35] But in the present view, what counts as an objective scientific fact depends upon practices which may *differ* from culture to culture. If we think that Karam taxonomy is wrong, it is because we have reason to think that the practice of science generates better taxonomies.[36]

It should be clear enough that the text just quoted from Dewey does not betray a Hegelian, objective idealist prejudice. In such views, mind is severed from "natural existence" and individuals merely "participate" in mind. Here I refer you to the customary bifurcation of "cultural system" and "the social system," to the standard notion of "socialization" wherein selves are empty vessels into which meaning is poured, and to the "normative determinism" so characteristic of mainstream sociology. The foregoing account of meanings gives us the resources to hold that the idea of "individuals with minds" admits a fully naturalist interpretation. The difference between it and an idealist alternative, unfortunately, is easily missed.

The idea of a social supermind is a philosophical nightmare because it precludes agency. It makes agents merely "bearers" of cultural systems which, in the last analysis, determine action. By contrast, for Mead and Dewey, because meanings are "modes of natural interaction," culture is the continuous evolving product of recognitions and ignorances, acceptances and rejections, and expectancies and appraisals which are themselves the medium and product of conscious activity. Mind is social, not in the sense that meaning is intersubjective—between subjectivities—but in the sense that meanings are public, in the world, and not (only or merely) in our consciousness.[37]

Empiricism, Phenomenology, and Antinaturalism

Philosophical positions have never been irrelevant to the practice of social science—most often, I am afraid, for ill.[38] Attacks on empiricist philosophy of science beginning in the 1950s joined with phenomenological criticisms of empiricist social science. Both were unsettling to the mainstream, dominated, then and still, if less so, by the "objectivist" Parsonian synthesis. But these criticisms did not encourage a rethinking of naturalism in nonempiricist terms. Rather, they encouraged antinaturalism.

The work of Schutz was no doubt critical. On the one hand, his work contained many valuable insights, for example: that sociological constructs are constructs of social constructions, that the "stock of knowledge" is held in "typified form" and dispersed, and that commonsense knowledge is "a patchwork" in which "clear and distinct experiences are intermingled with vague conjectures; suppositions and prejudices cross well-proven evidences; motives, means and ends, as well as causes and effects, are strung together without clear understanding of their real connections."[39] This contributed heavily to undermining the

Parsonian theory of action, including the still standard theory of rationality.[40]

Similarly, Schutz's idea, derived and extended from Husserl, of a "life-world," which is the taken-for-granted beginning for inquiry (the *epoché* of "the natural attitude"), was a strong solvent for the naive realism of mainstream social science.[41] On the other hand, as Farber insisted, the life-world fell "like manna from heaven, as an unexpected answer to the prayer of persons seeking an alternative to the world view of a scientific philosophy, but for whom the existentialist bill of linguistic fare [was] unpalatable."[42] Even a "mundane phenomenology" could not (as Natanson agreed) consistently be grounded in naturalism. The trouble was not that Schutz remained committed to Husserl's transcendental project, but that he retained, as Giddens noted, "the umbilical tie to the subjectivity of the ego. For Schutz the social world is 'strictly speaking, my world.' "[43] Schutz did acknowledge that to study the social world, it was necessary to "abandon the strictly phenomenological method." But while he was comfortable to assume the existence of "the social world," not only did intersubjectivity remain, philosophically, a problem, but "the social world" seemed, at least, to be nothing more than a construction of consciousness. Put in other terms, it was difficult to see how to incorporate either the "natural" environment or the relatively enduring consequences of action into the account. Moreover, "interpretive social science" was restricted to describing and clarifying "what is thought about the social world by those living it." This thoroughly descriptivist, ethnographic orientation, even in the hands of sensitive inquirers, lost even the hint of causal explanation and in consequence, any capacity for critique. Finally, while Schutz often said that it was the aim of sociology to obtain organized knowledge about "the world of cultural objects and social institutions"—leaving unclear what exactly this meant—the discovery of "in order to" motives became the central task for sociological explanation. That is, phenomenology encouraged a highly psychologized notion of social science.[44]

Garfinkel, a student of Parsons, seems to have begun with Schutz, and before he was finished, offered a radical and powerful alternative to the Parsonian "action frame of reference." This included a strong emphasis on agency, and rejection of "motive analysis" in favor of inquiry into "situated actions." This was profoundly propelled by his generalized use of "indexicality" (indirectly owed to Peirce) and by finitism (derived from Wittgenstein).

Garfinkel, however, was but ambivalently naturalistic. In some readings, his principle of "ethnomethodological indifference" was not merely a recommendation to bracket temporarily aspects of the empirical world, but was converted into an ontological commitment wherein, as Giddens wrote, "social phenomena 'exist' only in so far as lay actors classify or identify them as 'existing' "[45]—an "intellectualist" dip into voluntarism and idealism. Moreover, Garfinkel was preoccupied with the conditions of action, ignoring almost utterly the consequences of action, intended and unintended. Thus, neither could he sustain an adequate notion of relatively enduring social relations. While he acknowledged that actors had resources which were the medium of their actions, his actors became so thoroughly disconnected from their bodies and the larger preexisting contexts in which they acted that these resources reduced to abstractly detached meaning-rules. In effect, his "intellectualism" led him to ignore the fact that his agents were fleshy, interested people acting in a geographical environment and embedded in socially sustained, but not always transparent social relations of power. Worse, betrayed by epistemologically generated worries, he often suggested that these meaning-rules were not "about" anything. As in current antirealisms, participants could cooperatively reconstitute them at will.

By the 1970s, phenomenologically inspired social science remained on the margin, but the unsatisfactory character of "objectivist" mainstream and Marxist approaches was more than noticed. The response was "cultural studies," inspired by the "structuralism" of Lévi-Strauss and Saussure and then, in response to this, "poststructuralism" and the hermeneuticial approach of Clifford Geertz, and, finally, by Marxist writers responding to Althusserian "structuralism."[46] Powerfully encouraged by the epistemological criticisms of empiricism, including here Kuhn's ambivalent *The Structure of Scientific Revolutions,* the work of Schutz, Garfinkel, and Erving Goffman, the hermeneutics of Ricoeur and Gadamer, and the more radical poststructuralism of Foucault and Derrida, "cultural studies" betrayed a decided shift toward idealism. As Alexander rightly pointed out,

Insofar as [sociological theory] seeks a purely hermeneutic analysis—not only is there always a cultural reference for every action but . . . there is only a cultural reference. Every change in action, every source of stability, everything that works for the good, everything that works for the bad—all must be explained in terms of the search for meaning itself. Every culturalist theory is . . . a form of sociological idealism.[47]

Nor did Marxists escape the drift toward idealism—especially those taken by strong readings of Gramsci (a student of Croce) and by "post-modernist" epistemology.[48] The response, in my view, is neither a return to "materialism," nor to some pseudo-solution which demands that we think "dialectically" about "culture" and "material life."[49] No such dialectic is possible because divorced of culture, material life is utterly empty. Here we are betrayed by systematic ambiguity as regards the very idea of "culture." At one time, "culture" was used inclusively to refer to "forms of life," to ensembles of meaningful patterns of activity which included work, play, marriage, worship. More recent cultural studies, however, have conceived culture far more narrowly, in terms of "mentalities," "values, "symbolic codes," "signs," "texts," and "discourses" that are effectively, if not so explicitly autonomous.[50] We need to return to the older idea; but we need to do this, as already suggested, with a strong, agent-centered, naturalistic conception of mind and society. That is, instead of supposing that meanings have independent existences, we need to see them in contexts of action.

A Naturalistic Alternative

Particularly, we move in the right direction by putting the insights of Schutz and Garfinkel onto the naturalistic footing provided by Dewey and Mead. As Rubenstein rightly said, it was a major motive of "phe-nomenological" and *Verstehen* approaches to social science to describe action in terms of mental components in order to combat the "naturalistic" inclination to treat action and social phenomena in the same way one treats the meaningless properties and events of nature. On the other hand, it was a major motive of empiricists to argue that "reliable knowledge cannot be established about what is essentially private to the actor."[51] But if the foregoing is sound, there is no reason to be suspicious of an approach that insists that the category of meaning is indispensable to the understanding of human behavior, and for the same reason, there is reason to be suspicious of those philosophies of language which inform empiricist philosophy of science. As work by Kuhn, Polanyi, and more recent sociology of scientific knowledge make clear enough, the meaning of scientific terms depends not on "operational definitions" and other semantic devices, but on taking account of science as a social activity in the sense of Dewey and Mead.

First, with Schutz, we can endorse *Verstehen* and the idea that sociological terms are constructions of what are already social constructions, what Giddens has called "the double hermeneutic." Social science (in contrast to the physical sciences) is involved in theorizing and communicating about an already meaningful social world. But because *Verstehen* is not some form of empathetic understanding—indeed, is a presupposition of *any* human activity, including, then, the practices of natural science—social science requires no special observational methods.

Second, *pace* Garfinkel, instead of a one-sided emphasis on action as meaning, we can shift to action as *praxis,* as Giddens writes: "the involvement of actors with the practical realization of interests, including the material transformation of nature through human activity."[52] So construed, "culture" is not bifurcated from "material activity," but is understood as inseparable, substantively and analytically, from it.[53]

Third, in consequence, "all social research has a necessarily cultural, ethnographic, or 'anthropological' aspect to it."[54] This will be largely descriptive, even though, inevitably, it will be theoretically informed. Thus, not only is literary style not irrelevant to the accuracy and communicability of such descriptions, but social scientists must draw on the same sources of "mutual knowledge" drawn on by novelists and journalists.[55]

But, fourth, because meaning is not "in the head," and "experience" is not reducible to conscious contents, we need to distinguish practical knowledge from discursive knowledge. That is, while the present view centers on agency and, unlike most mainstream and Marxist views, emphasizes that actors have complex skills and knowledge which they employ in acting and interacting, if we are to avoid the "intellectualist fallacy," much of this knowledge is not discursively available. As Bhaskar says, it is "tacit and implicit, spontaneous and not reflective, a matter of know-how rather than know-that."[56] Accordingly, even if what is discursively available (or made available) is true, acquiring knowledge of the *beliefs* of actors will not be sufficient to establish an understanding of their social world. That is, even a good ethnography must go well beyond "what people think about their world."

Of course, since social activity cannot be described at all unless the inquirer knows what actors know, accounts from actors are necessary and play a critical role in enabling us to assess accounts offered inquirers. But indeed, there is good reason to hold that beliefs discursively available are not always true! While practical activity is skillful and intended, it does not require true belief as regards either the conditions of action or consequences of action. Action always has an unintended consequence, viz., the reproduction and transformation of the very conditions of action. We do make history but, as Marx insisted, not with a plan and not with materials of our own choosing. Unacknowledged conditions, unknown and unintended consequences, self-deception and other obstacles limit our ability to cognize fully and accurately the social world which our own actions sustain. Were it otherwise, there would hardly be a point to human science.

This means, sixth, not only that social science can enlarge the understanding of members, but by so doing, it can have a critical and emancipatory dimension. That is, because the domain of the social sciences comprises social objects, institutions, social practices, and social relations, which are the product of social activity, and because this domain includes beliefs about these activities, when these beliefs can be shown to be false, distorted, or otherwise inadequate, agents have grounds to change these social forms. Consider the belief that males are superior. If this belief is constitutive of the relations which define the nuclear family, then if (as women increasingly appreciate!) this belief is false, people have good reasons for altering these relations—as indeed, they have been doing! That is, *Erklären,* the effort to explain how these forms have come to be and why people have the beliefs they have, is an essential part of the task of social science.

Seventh, such explanation is not via subsumption under law. For the realist, success in the theoretical sciences depends upon the capacity to abstract a stratum of the world and to identify, in theoretical terms, causal mechanisms within that stratum. Such theory gives us understanding, for example, an understanding of manifest differences in materials in terms of theoretical ideas which define tensile strength. But because the theoretical powers of "things" are never operating in a closed system—other "causes" are always operating on them—there are patterns, but no invariant empirical regularities. Everything that happens is caused, but it is complexly caused, a function of the causal powers of the "things" of the world and their continously changing relations and configurations. One explains the collapse of a landing gear by appeal to the tensile strength of the materials *and* a host of other pertinent causes, including, perhaps, the historical effects of the maintenance schedule and the decision to make an emergency landing on a field not heretofore used by such aircraft. Because causal conjunctures are contingent, we are often in a position to explain something which happened when we could not have predicted it. Stellar mechanics is the worst possible paradigm for a science exactly because, as regards the pertinent "variables," the solar system is relatively closed.

Explanation in social science has the same form, involving, on the one hand, the effort to identify the social mechanisms or structured processes being sustained by the activities of agents, and on the other, the effort to grasp, concretely, the capacities which agents have and the constraints to which they are subject, what they know and understand, and, finally, the uses to which they put their capacities and knowledge. Because all these are historically variable, social science, in contrast to the most successful of the physical sciences, is inevitably concrete and historical—and for the same reasons, it could never be finished.[57]

For example, one begins to understand a capitalist society by identifying the "logic" of capital. That is, given the (very different) resources made available to agents by capitalist social relations, as a consequence of their actions, intended and unintended, actors will promote a tendency toward overaccumulation. To be sure, because between Japan and the

United States, or between the United States in 1929 and the United States today, there will be immense differences in the concrete forms of these relations and their relation to other structured practices, there will be differences in the capacities, constraints, and forms of knowledgeability of actors in these different times and places.

On the other hand, the tendency to overaccumulation will surely figure in any account of the Great Depression, even if, as noted, any plausible account will need to integrate a host of other processes, contingent events, and decisions by persons, acting and interacting, as always, as cultural beings with beliefs and a range of meaningful material objects.

I conclude with what for me is the most important idea: The foregoing implies that the antinaturalistic Kantian bifurcation of "freedom" and "determinism" needs to be totally rejected. The problem of human freedom, naturalistically understood, is the problem of possessing the capacity to act in realizing one's genuine interests; and this involves understanding the sources of constraint and limitation, and then transforming these to "needed, wanted and empowering sources of determination."[58]

Notes

1. Maurice Natanson, ed., *Philosophy of the Social Sciences* (New York: Random House, 1963), p. viii.

2. Thelma Lavine, "Note to Naturalists on the Human Spirit," in ibid., p. 252.

3. Ibid., pp. 254, 258. In her Romanell lecture of last year, Professor Lavine argued that the "continuity of analysis paradigm" needed to replaced by a "problematic situation paradigm" which, if properly understood, was a viable alternative to the "critique of modernity paradigm," these days so fashionable. See her "Modernity and the Spirit of Naturalism," *Proceedings and Addresses of the American Philosophical Association,* vol. 65 (November 1991)—section 9, ch. 1, of the present volume. Professor Lavine writes that she would have preferred that I develop her more recent ideas.

4. Ernest Nagel, "On the Method of *Verstehen* as the Sole Method of Philosophy," in Natanson, *Philosophy of the Social Sciences,* p. 262.

5. Maurice Natanson, "A Study in Philosophy and the Social Sciences," in ibid., p. 282.

6. Ibid., p. 283.

7. To be clear, the realism assumed here is not of the variety associated with Hilary Putnam or Richard Boyd. It is, roughly, the "policy realism" of Rom Harré, an explicitly pragmatic version of realism, still too little appreciated in the United States. See Rom Harré, *The Principles of Scientific Thinking* (Chicago: University of Chicago Press, 1970); Rom Harré and Edward Madden, *Causal Powers* (Oxford: Basil Blackwell, 1975) and most recently, Harré, *Varieties of Realism* (Oxford: Basil Blackwell, 1987). See also Roy Bhaskar, *A Realist Theory of Science,* 2nd ed. (Brighton: Harvester, 1979) and *The Possibility of Naturalism* (Brighton: Harvester, 1979), and my *A History and Philosophy of the Social Sciences* (Oxford and New York: Basil Blackwell, 1987).

8. I say "of the sort" here since my interest is not to represent either Dewey or Mead. I use them to develop a position which is both naturalistic and realistic. Although influenced by R. W. Sleeper's defense of Dewey as a "transactional realist," I suspect that Dewey would not be entirely happy with the sort of realism defended here. See R. W. Sleeper, *The Necessity of · Pragmatism* (New Haven, Conn.: Yale University Press, 1986).

9. For discussion, see Marvin Farber, *Phenomenology and Existence: Towards a Philosophy within Nature* (New York: Harper Torchbooks, 1967).

10. It is thus that naturalisms need to be committed to strong versions of the sociology of knowledge. See P. T. Manicas and Alan Rosenberg, "Naturalism, Epistemological Individualism and 'The Strong Programme' in the Sociology of Knowledge," *Journal for the Theory of Social Behavior* 15 (March 1985), and Manicas, "Naturalizing Epistemology: Reconstructing Philosophy," in *Philosophy and the Reconstruction of Culture: Pragmatic Essays After Dewey,* ed. John J. Stuhr (Albany: State University Press of New York, 1992).

11. See, in addition to my *History* and Bhaskar's *The Possibility of Naturalism,* Anthony Giddens, *The Constitution of Society* (Berkeley: University of California Press, 1984).

12. See A. Martin Byers, "Structure, Meaning, Action and Things: The Duality of Material Cultural Mediation," *The Journal for the Theory of Social Behavior* 21 (March 1991): 3.

13. Thus Rorty asserts that "every speech, thought, theory, poem, composition, and philosophy will turn out to be completely predictable in purely naturalistic terms. Some atoms-and-the-void account of microprocesses within individual human beings will permit the prediction of every sound or inscription which will be uttered." (Richard Rorty, *Philosophy and the Mirror of Nature*

(Princeton, N.J.: Princeton University Press, 1979), p. 387.

14. See J. E. Tiles, *Dewey* (London and New York: Routledge and Kegan Paul, 1988), p. 49. I follow Tiles's excellent account.

15. Tiles, *Dewey*, p. 55.

16. Ibid., p. 56.

17. John Dewey, *Experience and Nature, The Later Works, 1925–1953*, vol. 1 (Southern Illinois Press, 1981), p. 162.

18. We need to distinguish philosophical ontology, what is presumed by inquiry, from scientific ontology, the result of (ongoing) inquiry. See Roy Bhaskar, *A Realist Theory of Science.*

19. Following James in his *Principles*, Dewey argues that "things are defined by means of symbols that convey only their consequences with respect to one another. 'Water' in ordinary experience designates an essence of something which has familiar bearings and uses in human life. . . . But H_2O gets away from these connections, and embodies in its essence only instrumental efficacy in respect to things independent of human affairs" (*Experience and Nature*, p. 151). In the foregoing terms, H_2O represents a theoretical entity, real but not "empirical." On "natural necessities," see Harré and Madden, *Causal Powers.*

20. See Harré, *Varieties of Realism*. It is an error of considerable importance to think of theories as "interpreted" deductive systems.

21. Dewey, *Experience and Nature*, p. 195.

22. Ibid., p. 134.

23. "The fallacy converts consequences of interactions of events into causes of the occurrence of these consequences" (*Experience and Nature*, p. 200). As Dewey recognized, this fallacy is widespread, but nowhere more vivid than in accounts of mind and of society. Such accounts of mind are epistemologically individualist in positing as given, an available language, beliefs expressed in this language and a rationality independently of the social relations which generate these. Accounts of society are methodologically individualist in believing that social relations are not presupposed in action. See below.

24. George Herbert Mead, *Mind, Self and Society*, edited with an introduction by Charles W. Morris (Chicago: University of Chicago Press, 1967), p. 43.

25. See Dewey, *Experience and Nature*, p. 226, and Mead, *Mind, Self and Society*, pp. 47ff.

26. Tiles, *Dewey*, p. 89.

27. See Derek Bickerton, *Language and Species* (Chicago: University of Chicago Press, 1990) for a superb evolutionary account of the genesis of linguistic

560   PART V: NATURALISM AND CONTEMPORARY PHILOSOPHY

capacity and of true language.

28. David Rubenstein, "The Concept of Action in the Social Sciences," *Journal for the Theory of Social Behavior* 7 (October 1977): 212.

29. Tiles, *Dewey*, p. 93.

30. Dewey, *Experience and Nature*, p. 145.

31. Ibid., p. 147. Meaning is not "a peculiar kind of thing," a Platonic Idea, a "subsisting concept" or "logical in a style which separates logic from nature."

32. Ibid., p. 148.

33. The idea is also critical to Wittgenstein in the *Philosophical Investigations*, although it may well be that Wittgenstein's version is not entirely free of nominalist fantasy. As we note below, finitism is a central part of Garfinkel's theory of action. My criticism of his use of the idea is that he ignores the powerful constraints of enduring social relations, well recognized by Dewey and Mead.

34. Dewey, *Experience and Nature*, p. 170.

35. I take this example from Barry Barnes, "On the Conventional Character of Knowledge and Cognition," *Philosophy of the Social Sciences*, vol. 11 (1981). Barnes puts it to the same purpose. See R. Bulmer, "Why the Cassowary is not a Bird?" *Man* (1967).

36. Exploiting Harré's policy realism, I develop this idea in my "Naturalizing Epistemology: Reconstructing Philosophy," in *Philosophy and the Reconstruction of Culture: Pragmatic Essays After Dewey*, ed. John J. Stuhr.

37. On the other hand, to say that mind is social is not to deny the individuality of individuals with minds. "Personality, selfhood, subjectivity are eventual functions that emerge with complexly organized interactions, organic and social" (p. 162). As Dewey wrote:

> Mind denotes the whole system of meanings as they are embodied in the workings of organic life; consciousness in a being with language denotes awareness or perception of meanings. . . . The greater part of mind is only implicit in any conscious act or state; the field of mind—of operative meanings—is enormously wider than that of consciousness. . . . Mind is, so to speak, structural, substantial, a constant background and foreground; perceptive consciousness is process, a series of heres and nows (p. 230).

38. See my *History and Philosophy of the Social Sciences*.

39. See John Heritage, "Ethnomethodology," in *Social Theory Today*, ed. A. Giddens and J. H. Turner (Cambridge: Polity Press, 1987), p. 230, quoting Schutz.

40. Roughly, actors distinguish means and ends, articulate governing norms, and assess "evidence" based on application of "scientific knowledge." For some discussion, see John Heritage.

41. More recently, of course, "deconstruction" has been an even more powerful solvent.

42. Marvin Farber, *Phenomenology and Existence,* p. 122. It is of some interest to note that Farber and Schutz were very close colleagues during the early years of *Philosophy and Phenomenological Research.* Schutz's biographer writes: "It was the close connection and collaboration with Farber, more than anything else, that was responsible for the early realization of Schutz's intention to establish contacts with American philosophers and find an opportunity to address American philosophical audiences" (Helmut R. Wagner, *Alfred Schutz: Intellectual Biograghy,* Chicago: University of Chicago Press, 1986).

Peter Hare reports that the archives of *PPR* show that Farber struggled hard to keep the pages of the journal open.

43. A. Giddens, *New Rules of Sociological Method* (Hutchinson of London, 1976), p. 31.

44. Avowed followers of Weber also express often what is at least a tension here, between a psychologistic explanation of some act and a sociological explanation of acts of that sort. Thus, one may need an "in order to" motive to explain why some particular person commits a crime, but understanding what structures criminal behavior will require more and other than this. See my "Intelligibility and Idealization: Marx and Weber," in *Intelligibility in Science,* ed. Craig Dilworth (Amsterdam: Editions Rodopi), forthcoming.

45. Giddens, *New Rules of Sociological Method,* p. 42.

46. For a useful critical overview, see Anthony Giddens, "Structuralism, Post-structuralism and the Production of Culture," in *Social Theory Today,* ed. A. Giddens and J. H. Turner (Cambridge: Polity Press, 1987). For Geertz, see *The Interpretation of Culture* (New York: Basic Books, 1973) and criticism by Jeffrey Alexander, *Twenty Lectures* (New York: Columbia University Press, 1987), lectures 16 and 17. As regards Marxism, see Perry Anderson, *Arguments within English Marxism* (London: Verso, 1980); Stuart Hall, "Cultural Studies: Two Paradigms," in *Culture, Ideology and Social Process,* ed. T. Bennett et al. (The Open University Press, 1981).

47. Alexander, *Twenty Lectures,* pp. 311–12.

48. For Gramsci, see Paul Piccone, *Italian Marxism* (Berkeley: University of California Press, 1983). A useful compendium is Cary Nelson and Lawrence Grossberg, eds., *Marxism and the Interpretation of Culture* (Urbana and

Chicago: University of Illinois Press, 1988). As the editors note, "As little as twenty years ago, it would have been impossible to imagine such a project and such a volume" (p. 2). See especially the essays by Gayatri Chakrovorty Spivak, Chantal Mouffe, and Ernesto Laclau.

49. The most powerful nonreductionist Marxisms come from Raymond Williams and E. P. Thompson. In my view, Williams's Marxism is far and away to be preferred. Hall ("Cultural Studies") quotes Thompson that, "The dialectical intercourse between social being and social consciousness—or between 'culture' and 'not culture'—is at the heart of any comprehension of the historical process within the Marxist tradition. . . . The tradition inherits a dialectic that is right but the particular mechanical metaphor through which it is expressed is wrong." Yet, it is hard to see how the "dialectic" is right in the absence of clarity about what could be the "right" metaphor? On the other hand, Thompson is quite correct to bring together the two elements—consciousness and conditions—around the concept of "experience."

For Williams, in this context, there is *no* interesting sense of "dialectic." Indeed, it nowhere appears in his important book, *Marxism and Literature* (1977). Instead, Williams insists that talk about "base/superstructure," "economy," "culture," and then, problems of "determination" and "mediation" are predicated on reifying abstractions. This is, he insists, particularly ironic since Marx's central emphasis was on a conception of productive activity in which "labour and language, as practices, can be seen as evolutionary and historically constitutive" (p. 33). As Hall says disapprovingly, "Williams so totally absorbs 'definitions of experience' into our 'ways of living,' and both into an indissoluble real material practice-in-general, as to obviate any distinction between 'culture' and 'not-culture' " (p. 26). This is, of course, very reminiscent of Dewey.

50. As Roy D'Andrade has remarked: "When I was a graduate student, one imagined people in a culture; ten years later culture was all in their heads" (Andrade, "A Colloquy of Cultural Theorists," in *Culture Theory*, ed. Richard A. Schweder and Robert A. LeVine [Cambridge: Cambridge University Press, 1987], p. 7).

For a representative sample of work which puts culture "all in their heads," see Jeffrey C. Alexander and Steven Seidman, eds., *Culture and Society* (Cambridge: Cambridge University Press, 1990). The conjunctive "and" in the title betrays the problem of much recent work.

51. Rubenstein, "The Concept of Action in the Social Sciences," p. 232.

52. Giddens, *New Rules,* p. 53.

53. As Paul Willis has insisted, "There is no question . . . of counterposing the 'cultural' with the 'productive' or the 'real,' as if the former had no actual constitutive role in the basic social relations which govern the form of . . . society" (in Alexander and Seidman, eds., *Culture and Society,* p. 184). Thus, the class relations of British proletariat toward the end of the century and of jute workers in British India were fundamentally different. See Dipesh Chahkrabarty, *Rethinking Working-Class History: Bengal, 1890–1940* (Princeton, N.J.: Princeton University Press, 1989).

54. Anthony Giddens, *The Constitution of Society* (Berkeley: University of California Press, 1984), p. 284. See also Michael Buroway's introduction to *Ethnography Unbound,* Michael Buroway et al. (Berkeley: University of California Press, 1991).

55. Indeed, as regards communicating an understanding of cultural milieu, novelists and journalists often do a better job than do academic social scientists!

56. Roy Bhaskar, *Scientific Realism and Human Emancipation* (London: Verso, 1986), p. 163.

57. See Giddens, *Constitution of Society,* p. 219.

58. Roy Bhaskar, *Philosophy and the Idea of Freedom* (Oxford: Basil Blackwell, 1991), p. 76. Bhaskar's book is a systematic naturalistic critique of the work of Richard Rorty.

Acknowledgments

I would like to express my gratitude to the many people whose encouragement and assistance have made this book possible. My friends and colleagues in the Society for the Advancement of American Philosophy have helped me to understand and appreciate the richness of the American philosophical traditions. Their influences both individual and collective on my own ideas are probably more extensive than even I realize. I also want to thank directly Paul Kurtz and Prometheus Books for their interest in this project and for their general interest in promoting naturalist and humanist philosophy.

I am grateful too to my students, whose interest in American philosophy has continued to motivate my own. I would like to thank in particular Susan Cochran and Shannon Kincaid for reading a draft of the introduction and for assuring me that it really does make sense.

Of the people who have in one way or another contributed to realizing this book, I want especially to express my gratitude to Peter H. Hare. Not only was the book his idea in the first place, but more generally Peter has for years encouraged and supported my work on this and other projects. He was one of the first philosophers other than my own teachers to take my work seriously, and for all those who have emerged from graduate school full of self-doubt, you will be able to appreciate how much that means. Peter is a good friend and colleague, and his support has meant far more to me than he can realize.

And I want finally to thank my wife, Colleen. Her support through all the moments of chaos and turmoil is in the end more responsible than any other single factor for the success of a project like this.